POWER, POLITICS, AND THE WORLD

Series editors: Christopher Dietrich, Jennifer Mittelstadt, and Russell Rickford

A complete list of books in the series is available from the publisher.

No Globalization Without Representation

NO GLOBALIZATION WITHOUT REPRESENTATION

U.S. Activists and World Inequality

Paul Adler

PENN

UNIVERSITY OF PENNSYLVANIA PRESS

PHILADELPHIA

Published by
University of Pennsylvania Press
Philadelphia, Pennsylvania 19104-4112
www.upenn.edu/pennpress

Printed in the United States of America on acid-free paper

10 9 8 7 6 5 4 3 2 1

A catalogue record for this book is available from the
Library of Congress.

ISBN 978-0-8122-5317-7

For My Parents

CONTENTS

ABBREVIATIONS

ACA	Action for Corporate Accountability
AFL-CIO	American Federation of Labor–Congress of Industrial Organizations
ART	Alliance for Responsible Trade
CAP	Consumers' Association of Penang
CTC	Citizens Trade Campaign
DCN	Debt Crisis Network
EDF	Environmental Defense Fund
FAO	Food and Agriculture Organization
FAT	Frente Auténtico del Trabajo (Authentic Labor Front)
FTAA	Free Trade Area of the Americas
G-77	Group of 77
GATT	General Agreement on Tariffs and Trade
GTW	Global Trade Watch
HAI	Health Action International
IATP	Institute for Agriculture and Trade Policy
IBFAN	International Baby Food Action Network
ICCR	Interfaith Center on Corporate Responsibility
IFG	International Forum on Globalization
IFPMA	International Federation of Pharmaceutical Manufacturers' Associations
ILWU	International Longshore and Warehouse Union
IMF	International Monetary Fund
INBC	International Nestlé Boycott Committee
INFACT	Infant Formula Action Coalition
IOCU	International Organization of Consumers Unions
IPS	Institute for Policy Studies
MAI	Multilateral Agreement on Investment
MODTLE	Mobilization on Development, Trade, Labor, and Environment
NAFTA	North American Free Trade Agreement

NAM	Non-Aligned Movement
NEPA	National Environmental Protection Act
NIEO	New International Economic Order
NIFAC	Nestlé Infant Formula Audit Commission
NIRO	New International Regulatory Order
NRDC	Natural Resources Defense Council
NWF	National Wildlife Federation
PAN	Pesticide Action Network
PNTR	Permanent Normal Trade Relations
PRI	Partido Revolucionario Institucional (Institutional Revolutionary Party)
RMALC	Red Mexicana de Acción Frente al Libre Comercio (Mexican Free Trade Action Network)
TWI	Third World Institute
TWN	Third World Network
UE	United Electrical, Radio, and Machine Workers
UNICEF	U.N. International Children's Fund
UNITE	Union of Needletrades, Industrial, and Textile Employees
USAS	United Students Against Sweatshops
USBIC	United States Business and Industrial Council
WHA	World Health Assembly
WHO	World Health Organization
WTO	World Trade Organization

Introduction

A few blocks from the imposing dome of the U.S. Capitol lies a nondescript, grey, three-story building tucked among restaurants, coffee shops, and offices. From outside, this edifice's occupants seem clear—the Hunan Dynasty restaurant and a Wells Fargo branch. Look closer and you'll notice a small, golden plaque to the right of a door, etched with the words "Public Citizen." Walk in and climb to the top of the stairs and you'll find the cramped offices of a decades-old, liberal advocacy nonprofit, full of frenzied, often young, staffers. Walking through the halls, you'll see people diving into complex public policy documents, writing press releases, planning protests, editing grant applications, and more. From 2005 to 2007, I was one of them, working as an entry-level staffer at Public Citizen's Global Trade Watch division.

During my time there, amid the chaos, I encountered something unexpected. Every week, we gathered for our staff meetings in a long, rectangular fishbowl of a room, inexplicably raised several feet off the floor. On the surface, these meetings were what you might expect, filled with reports about upcoming free-trade bills and strategy brainstorms. What surprised me was how staff meetings also acted as history seminars. These gatherings offered as good an advertisement as I can imagine for why remembering and grappling with the past is important—from discussions of long-ago fights with other progressive groups to analyses of legislators' voting records to summaries of social struggles from around the world.

Yet, as much as I learned, many questions remained only partially answered. How did the "corporate" or "neoliberal" globalization we opposed come into being and evolve? What reasons accounted for progressives' marginal status in the U.S. political scene? Why did various intra-activist tensions exist? And what roles did the small nonprofits that we (and so many of our dearest friends) were throwing our energies into have to play in the great debates of the moment?

My path to working at Public Citizen (and writing this book) began in the early 2000s, when agitation against neoliberal globalization occupied a central place in national and global politics. In the United States, considerations about these issues peaked in the last days of 1999. During the "Battle in Seattle," forty thousand demonstrators took over the streets, helping to catalyze the implosion of a meeting of the World Trade Organization (WTO). The Seattle protests garnered an avalanche of media coverage and generated intense public discussion and activist mobilization.

To the extent a mainstream public memory of this upsurge exists in the United States, it recalls Seattle as the beginning of a blip of activism that ended on September 11, 2001.[1] What mostly remains are faint memories and lingering questions. To cite but one example, most activist movements have a few widely used names ("civil rights movement," "labor movement," etc.) Yet, to this day, no single name identifies the groups that fought—and, in many cases, continue to confront—institutions such as the WTO or deals such as the North American Free Trade Agreement (NAFTA). Were they antiglobalization? Pro–fair trade? Members of the Global Justice movement? Parts of the alterglobalization movement?[2]

This book attempts to lift some of this haze by telling a longer history of challenges to late twentieth-century globalization. To be clear, this book is not a chronicle of the entirety of the mobilizations, organizations, and movements that, even just in the United States of America, took on global neoliberalism. Rather, this work focuses on one important node of that opposition within the United States—the history of what I call public interest progressivism.[3] Put succinctly, public interest progressive groups were (and are) professionalized advocacy nonprofits. They rely on lobbying, lawsuits, and other "insider" tactics to bring about social change. Like their predecessors in the Progressive and New Deal eras, they believe that the private sector's pursuit of profit causes social ills, from unsafe products, to a degraded environment, to economic and democratic inequalities. Public interest progressives, who hit the heights of their influence in the late 1960s and early 1970s, aimed to rejuvenate the regulatory state and revive U.S. liberalism.

Accounts of public interest progressives are relatively absent from histories of late twentieth-century U.S. politics.[4] To find them, one has to look to histories of particular issue-based mobilizations, such as consumer rights or environmentalism.[5] However, as this book shows, public interest progressivism deserves study as a coherent and influential policy and political formation.

In the last decades of the twentieth century, public interest progressives became key critics of the political and economic changes sweeping the globe. We will start this story in the 1970s, when activists such as socialist feminist Leah Margulies joined forces with two Midwest farm boys, Doug Johnson and Mark

Ritchie, to ignite a global boycott of Nestlé. The impulse to tackle global inequalities continued through the 1980s, as policy intellectuals such as John Cavanagh of the Institute for Policy Studies grappled with the rise of neoliberalism. These waves of advocacy grew stronger in the 1990s, when people such as Public Citizen's Lori Wallach, an energetic lawyer and activist, mobilized against what they saw as the deprivations of a new era of globalization.

In focusing on the history of dissenters against the policies of late twentieth-century economic globalization, public interest progressives were crucial not only for their own actions but for their roles as conveners of larger coalitions. They helped build alliances of labor unions, farmers' groups, grassroots activists, and others, creating what I call the fair globalization coalition. I use the term *fairness* to invoke the ultimately reformist politics of most of these groups.[6] Calling this formation a coalition rather than a movement is also deliberate. Most of the organizations involved did not arise to confront global neoliberalism. From trade unionists to farmers to advocacy nonprofits, these groups tended to divide their attentions among many issues. With the brief (and complex) exception of the period between the Battle in Seattle and the September 11, 2001 terrorist attacks, they did not possess the "high degree of shared collective identity" that many scholars argue defines social movements, such as labor or feminism.[7] Rather, fair globalizers formed a coalition because they shared common enemies, coordinated on distinct campaigns, and created organizations to tie disparate constituencies together.

Highlighting public interest progressives does not diminish the importance of other U.S.-based advocates and activists in recent globalization struggles. Other parts of the wider set of mobilizations against neoliberalism have, and continue to receive, substantial scholarly attention. This work builds upon these already rich and growing literatures concerning political forces, such as organized labor and grassroots leftists and radicals.[8]

Understanding the fair globalization coalition requires examining what animated their activism. This necessitates engaging with ongoing debates about globalization. Examining the coalition's mobilizations reinforces the argument that, rather than some uncontrollable force of nature, globalization is a set of processes shaped by and (at least) partially governed by institutions. As Mark Ritchie, an activist whose career spans the entirety of this book's story, declared at the Seattle protests, "We now have come to understand that the need for global governance is a necessary topic for us in confronting globalization."[9]

Governance can be defined as the web of laws, norms, and institutions that set the rules and establish the processes molding how societies function. While the idea of "governance" connotes government, as political scientist Mark Bevir notes, the term applies more broadly. Multilateral institutions (such as the United Nations and World Bank), private corporations, and nongovernmental organizations (NGOs) also participate in governance.[10] Fundamentally, questions of governance hinge on power: who has it, who does not, how those who have it use it, and how power imbalances can change.[11]

While particular individuals and NGOs in the fair globalization coalition engaged with questions of global economic governance starting in the mid-1970s, in the coalition's time as a political force, fair globalizers have struggled against neoliberal governance. Neoliberalism remains a hotly debated concept. In some academic discussions and popular narratives, neoliberalism is often defined, as explained by historian Daniel Stedman Jones, as a "free market ideology based on individual liberty and limited government that connected human freedom to the actions of the rational, self-interested actor in the competitive marketplace."[12] From this starting point, it might seem that neoliberals would look askance at governance, which, after all, connotes ideas of regulation and bureaucracy. In the words of one historian, neoliberals "denied the desirability of any robust international governance of the global economy."[13]

Certainly, neoliberalism, especially in its proponents' public rhetoric, decries attempts to oversee or shape the workings of capitalist markets. However, this does not mean that neoliberals disdain governance: in fact, governance lies at the core of the neoliberal project. What distinguishes neoliberalism most from older notions of classical liberalism does not lie in its followers' devotion to notions of the free market. Rather, neoliberalism's distinctiveness stems from the proactive role its backers imagine for governmental, intergovernmental, and multilateral bodies in structuring the economic order.

Neoliberalism arose as a rejection, starting in the late nineteenth century, of mass political forces—socialism, trade unionism, communism, social democracy, and so on—that sought to reform or overturn capitalism. Instead, neoliberals believed in the need to create governmental (and especially legal) instruments to protect capitalism from the masses. As historian Quinn Slobodian has convincingly demonstrated, the "real focus of neoliberal proposals is not on the market per se but on redesigning states, laws, and other institutions to protect the market."[14] In other words, at its core, neoliberal politics uses mechanisms of governance to protect and promote the prerogatives of private enterprise.[15]

To confront international neoliberal governance naturally requires global agitation.[16] Of course, the fair globalizers were far from the first U.S. activists to engage in internationalism.[17] While they rarely invoked older moments of cross-border solidarity, they faced many of the same challenges as past mobilizations in forging and maintaining relationships with friends and foes around the world. While this book primarily concentrates on how U.S.-based activists attempted to become "global citizens," it is vital to remember that these tales are but pieces of larger international histories.[18]

Advocates from the U.S. fair globalization coalition were not the only U.S. NGO staffers trying to become internationally influential at the twentieth century's close.[19] During the 1970s, the number of nonprofit advocacy groups that focused on issues of torture, censorship, and other attacks on civil and personal liberties grew rapidly, as seen in the rise of such organizations as Amnesty USA and Human Rights Watch. For those taking part in the human rights revolution, individual rights served as the rallying cry and governments as the chief villains. Meanwhile, fair globalization activists, while supportive of individual rights, emphasized socioeconomic questions. Over the past two decades, a blossoming of scholarship on human rights has often portrayed discourses and politics of human rights as overshadowing or even replacing those of social welfare. However, a fuller narrative shows that economically minded discourses did not disappear. Instead, they became one of many languages of international social justice.[20]

Even within the realm of U.S.-based nonprofits engaging with socioeconomic inequalities between the Global North and the Global South, fair globalizers also differed from many of their contemporaries.[21] The majority of U.S.-based humanitarian and development nonprofits (which often predated public interest progressive groups), whether major foundations such as Rockefeller and Ford or large relief NGOs such as CARE, have tended to agree with, rather than contest, development orthodoxies.[22] While these groups preached the gospel that development involved a series of technocratic challenges, activists in the fair globalization coalition countered that inequality and politics are inseparable.[23] They argued that greater worldwide social welfare would not result from reifying technology or markets or through paternalistic aid programs, but rather would grow from respect for local particularities and fighting to restrain global capitalism.

Histories of how people in the United States act in transnational and global fields are deeply intertwined with histories of racism.[24] As a slowly diversifying, post-1960s, predominantly white political force, public interest progressives believed in an anti-racism that was not often introspective or self-critical. In approaching economic governance issues at home and abroad, public interest advocates often embraced what American Studies scholar Eric Larson calls "colorblind anti-corporatism." As Larson describes, this worldview pits "the people" against "corporations," without disentangling the unequal ways that corporate activities or larger political economic structures affect communities of color versus white communities.[25] Public interest progressives hoped that anticorporate politics could unite disparate communities around shared problems. However, the lack of emphasis on inequities suffered distinctively and disproportionately by marginalized and oppressed communities limited the fair globalization coalition's ability to profoundly confront societal inequalities.[26]

At the same time, public interest progressives' philosophies, especially among the most internationalist groups, did not ignore multiple vectors of oppression. Public interest advocates believed in using their relative privilege within the U.S. political system to diminish or remove what they argued were harmful influences from the U.S. government and multinational companies on peoples in the Global South. Such actions often followed the advice of Global South activists, who indicated that the best solidarity U.S. organizations could provide was making change "at home." As this book shows, Global South activists confronting international neoliberalism refused to follow a script of being the subordinated victims of condescension from the Global North. They negotiated with, maneuvered around, and pushed back on their colleagues in the North—forging imperfect but relatively effective international networks.

Accounts of resistance to neoliberal globalization point to many start dates for this agitation—some as early as the Book of Genesis.[27] My book embraces a more modest timespan, seeing the 1970s as a turning point.[28] It begins with an early episode of public interest progressives tackling global inequality: the Nestlé boycott launched in 1977. Started by a ragtag group of activists in New York City and Minneapolis, the boycott grew into a powerful international force. It also inspired a wave of global campaigns aimed at winning regulations for other industries, such as pesticides and pharmaceuticals. Yet, over the course of the 1980s, the ambitions of public interest groups to remake global economic governance collapsed under the weight of the debt crisis, the decline of the left around the world, and the rising power of corporations and rich countries' governments. From the mid-1980s to the early 1990s, think tanks such as the Institute for Policy Studies and individuals such as Nestlé boycott cofounder Mark Ritchie tried to comprehend a rapidly changing world economy.

By the late 1980s, rather than fighting for a better future, public interest progressives devoted themselves to preventing an unacceptable present from becoming a horrifying future. No conflict more starkly illustrated the new political landscape than the battle over the North American Free Trade Agreement. Because it directly affected organized labor, farmers, environmentalists, and public interest groups in the United States, NAFTA crystalized the formation of the fair globalization coalition. Represented by such umbrella groups as the Citizens Trade Campaign and the Alliance for Responsible Trade, the fair globalization coalition made the effort to pass NAFTA into one of the bitterest legislative fights of recent decades.

Following the passage of NAFTA and the coalition's failure to halt the creation of the World Trade Organization, public interest advocates and their allies regrouped. They spent the mid-1990s refining their understandings of the world economy and reenergizing their coalitions. These efforts bore fruit, as fair globalization advocates scored three major wins in 1998 and 1999. Domestically, advocates succeeded in blocking Fast Track, legislation vital to passing future free-trade agreements. The second win happened globally, as activists defeated the Multilateral Agreement on Investments, a proposed treaty to expand the rights of multinational corporations.

The fair globalization coalition's third victory came with the Battle of Seattle. Following the Seattle victory, there came a moment when questions of globalization and development dominated headlines and inspired massive protests from Quebec City to Genoa, Italy. Briefly, the fair globalization coalition became part of a wider mass movement. Yet, soon after, the September 11 attacks all but ended (in the United States) the budding movement.

The U.S. fair globalization coalition's work continues to the present day. Fair globalization advocates hold a permanent place in the policy dialogue. Most recently, they played a crucial role in making support for the Trans-Pacific Partnership politically untenable across much of the political spectrum. Some groups also helped to shape the rewriting of NAFTA into the U.S.-Mexico-Canada Agreement. More broadly, the questions of global inequality raised by fair globalizers have only become more pressing, especially as climate change intensifies. How we reached this historical juncture is the story to which we shall now turn.

Prologue

The Good Parts of the System to Beat the Bad

Putting aside tired clichés about small groups of people changing the world, the fact that nonprofits such as Public Citizen or the Institute for Policy Studies became influential players globally is, on its surface, a confounding one. Understanding this trajectory starts with a slightly earlier tale—the rise of public interest progressives in domestic U.S. politics.

As good a place as any to begin is November 16 and 17, 1970. Over the course of these two days, the U.S. Senate's Labor and Public Welfare Committee held hearings on public interest progressives. The question at hand was "the right of public interest law-firms and other charitable organizations to engage in litigation in the public interest."[1] Responding to threats from the Internal Revenue Service to rescind their tax-exempt statuses, representatives from a flood of organizations—from the Center for Law and Social Policy to the Natural Resources Defense Council (NRDC) to the American Civil Liberties Union—pled their case (successfully, as it turned out). Amid all the verbiage, one phrase sticks out. Spoken by then former Sierra Club leader and Friends of the Earth founder David Brower, it encapsulated public interest progressivism's politics. "We . . . are convinced," Brower stated, "it is possible to use the good parts of the system to beat the bad parts of the system."[2]

These words illustrated public interest progressivism's reformist heart. Hailing from a political lineage running from late nineteenth- and early twentieth-century muckrakers and consumer advocates through the technocratic foot soldiers of the New Deal, public interest progressivism emerged in the 1960s determined to confront challenges both familiar and distinct.[3] As with their forebears, they viewed the power of "Big Business" as society's greatest challenge. Business writer Hazel Henderson outlined this perspective in the *Nation*, noting that corporate power was "encountered daily by millions of citizens who attempt to fight polluted air, oil-smeared beaches . . . rampant freeways, deceptive advertising," and more.[4] Or as the most influential public interest progressive, Ralph Nader, stated in February 1970, big business represented the country's "most powerful, consistent, and coordinated power grid."[5]

Of course, criticism of large corporations did not start with Ralph Nader. Concerns about business influence date back as far as corporations have existed.[6] What differentiated public interest progressives' worldviews and approaches stemmed from their historical moment. Their political ancestors in the Progressive and New Deal eras fought to create government agencies and legal frameworks to constrain business power. By the 1960s, a robust array of regulatory agencies existed, including the Securities and Exchange Commission, the Department of Labor, and the Federal Trade Commission. Public interest progressives became active at a moment in which the question of *whether* the federal government would regulate private enterprise appeared settled. Instead, the question hanging over 1960s reformers asked if the regulatory state could remain vigorous over the long term.

The health of the federal regulatory state weighed on a few young liberals in the mid- to late 1960s. They lauded the positive effects of past governmental actions to hold business accountable. But they also found troubling realities within the federal regulatory apparatus. Many agencies had been "captured" by private interests; as staff from the Center for Law and Social Policy stated in 1969, government "agencies cannot be relied upon to resolve all policy questions in the public interest when the only advocates before them are the articulate spokesmen of private interests."[7] Even when agencies (or at least parts of them) operated effectively, lack of funding and bureaucratic malaise weakened their efficacy. Furthermore, much work remained in ensuring workplace, consumer, and, ecological protection.

Surveying this landscape, some liberals in the late 1960s felt "frustration, anger, [and] loss of confidence in the future."[8] As Charles Halpern, a leading public interest attorney, explained, many who became public interest progressives believed in New Deal liberalism. Reflecting decades later, Halpern stated that such people, if they had been coming of age "in the 1930s instead of the 1960s . . . would have looked to the federal government for solutions." However, the 1960s were not the 1930s. Now many liberals believed that "the federal government was not on its own going to be the effective source of innovation and reform."[9] They longed for a different form of politics.

Some scholars have claimed that public interest progressives' politics entailed putting a liberal sheen on Reagan-style neoliberalism. One such historian castigated Nader for embracing a "slash-and-burn rhetoric . . . [that] planted an antigovernment legacy that coarsened political discourse and undermined popular support for social democratic solutions."[10] What such critiques seem to miss is that not all criticism of government cuts from the same cloth. When public interest progressives lambasted the regulatory state, it was for falling short or for serving corporate interests, not for being too aggressive in checking corporate power. At a few times, such skepticism resulted in some public interest champions advocating deregulation of certain sectors (such as airlines and trucking). Yet, when measured against their overall legislative records and the consistent hostility of large corporations and right-wing activists to their advocacy, it is hard to see public interest progressives as mere unwitting shills for conservatism or neoliberalism.

Public interest progressives' critiques of government also arose from the larger horrors inflicted by the U.S. government during the 1960s, especially its war in Southeast Asia. The U.S. war in Vietnam intensified distrust of government and, with such liberals as John Kennedy and Lyndon Johnson residing in the White House, prompted reconsiderations of liberalism. However, as opposed to radicals who saw the war as a manifestation of the nation's imperialist soul, public interest progressives viewed the conflict as a betrayal of both "American" and liberal values.

Disillusionment with mid-century liberalism inspired progressive and liberal-minded people in the United States to embark on several paths. A few tried to keep one foot in the liberal world and one in the radical New Left world.[11] The epicenter of this approach arose in the offices of the Institute for Policy Studies (IPS), a left-wing think tank. While frequently frustrated or enraged with mainstream liberalism, IPS's staff did not reject it outright. Instead, as IPS fellow Arthur Waskow explained, those working at the Institute for Policy Studies hoped to unite the "generation of liberal reformers with the sit-in generation" by developing policy ideas that were both pragmatic and transformational.[12]

Most public interest progressives followed a distinct path from IPS, modeling their work on the example set by Ralph Nader. In the 1960s and 1970s, Ralph Nader was one of the most respected people and effective political actors in the United States.[13] Leaping onto the national stage in 1965 with his best-selling book *Unsafe at Any Speed*, Nader epitomized public interest progressives' confrontational and reformist politics. He called for a "new kind of citizenship" in which everyday people engaged in sustained efforts to keep government responsive and to challenge business power.[14] Answering a question about society's "evils," Nader noted that "evils are an inevitable result of concentrated power that's insulated from broader human value . . . no matter where [power] is located, it's going to be abused if the pathways are not open for a broader spectrum of values."[15]

In trying to open those "pathways," Nader helped to found numerous nonprofits, including Public Citizen, the Public Interest Research Group, and the Center for Responsive Law. While Nader proved prolific at starting organizations, the growth of public interest advocacy went beyond just him. Kicking off in the mid-1960s, the number of public interest groups ballooned in a process that political scientist Jeffrey Berry calls the "advocacy explosion."[16] This growth reached its zenith in the last years of the 1960s and first years of the 1970s; as a survey of eighty-three major public interest nonprofits started before 1972 showed, almost half emerged between 1968 and 1972.[17] Many of these new groups quickly became leaders in their fields: of twelve major national environmental groups founded between 1892 and 1972, five of them were created between 1967 and 1972.[18]

Within a short time, public interest progressives' influence became impossible to deny. On the consumer front, of the forty-seven major federal consumer safety laws enacted between 1890 and 1972, more than half took effect between 1966 and 1972, peak years of public interest agitation.[19] Concurrently, environmental advocates assisted in writing, passing, and implementing a raft of laws, such as the Clean Water Act and the Clean Air Act of 1970. Reflecting on this legacy, historian Meg Jacobs characterizes the advances in environmental protection alone as marking "a new era of business regulation . . . at least as momentous as the Progressive and New Deal eras."[20] The effectiveness of public interest advocacy inspired intense disdain and mobilization by significant parts of the business community. In the 1971 "Powell Memorandum," which became the informal and later infamous manifesto for the modern U.S. corporate lobby, Lewis Powell described Nader as "perhaps the single most effective antagonist of American business."[21]

Several factors gave coherence to public interest progressivism. One was its demographics. Public interest groups consisted of middle-class individuals, often boasting a master's or a law degree from a prestigious university. Most public interest progressives were white. At first, the staff tended to be majority male, but by the early 1970s, more and more women joined the ranks. The staffs of these groups viewed social change as both a calling and a profession.[22]

Organizationally, the professionalized nonprofit served as their chosen vehicle. As Institute for Policy Studies cofounders Richard Barnet and Marc Raskin explained in 1962, it was "imperative to have institutions outside the government, thinking, planning, and suggesting alternatives" while simultaneously staying "intimately in touch with the decision making process."[23] To that end, relying on foundations and individual donors for funding, activists created nonprofits. Frequently either based in or gravitating toward Washington, D.C., their offices impressed only in the towers of papers filling every corner and the collections of "second-hand desks and hand-me-down chairs" occupying their workspaces. The number of full-time staffers could vary from less than ten to around fifty, with many groups operating at the lower end of that spectrum.[24]

From the moderates at the Environmental Defense Fund (EDF) to the leftists at the Institute for Policy Studies, public interest groups' day-to-day work lay at the intersections of expertise, "responsible militancy," and participation. To wield power, public interest groups first gained and applied expertise about how government and business operated. Large companies kept their internal workings secretive. Government ostensibly had to be open, but as lawyers from the Center for Law and Social Policy noted, the operations of federal agencies were often "so complex and demanding" as to be almost unintelligible. In both cases, the sheer weight of technical procedures and papers could easily overwhelm, especially to anyone without the time, "resources, and skills to make their voices heard in agency decision-making."[25]

This is where public interest advocates entered. They saw themselves as the people's experts. From Nader's early 1960s forays into auto safety onward, advocates proved adept at interpreting and translating highly complex policy language into comprehensible prose. Advocates disseminated their analyses widely—through articles, books, appearances in media, and more. Individuals, media outlets, congressional offices, and federal regulatory officials soon began turning to public interest advocates to help explain and advise on complex matters. As Environmental Protection Agency deputy administrator John Quarles Jr. noted in 1973, "On occasions too numerous to mention . . . [public interest] groups have surfaced weaknesses or errors in the governmental activities, bringing such problems to the attention of high officials where corrective action might be taken."[26]

As important as technical knowledge could be, advocates recognized that to achieve change, "it is necessary to use political action."[27] To turn their values into policy, public interest progressives embraced approaches that NRDC cofounder John Adams called "responsible militancy."[28] Many of these tactics grew from advocates' policy expertise. For example, reaching out to news media did not merely convey information. As with Progressive-era muckrakers, public interest progressives expected news coverage to energize everyday people to mobilize and act.[29] Seeing article after article on a given controversy—and the resulting public anger—made legislators fearful that public interest progressives could, in the words of former Federal Trade Commission head Michael Pertschuk, exact "political retribution if they [Congress] failed . . . to address the sources of that outrage."[30]

Public interest progressives also engaged in more proactive actions. Following the lead of older legal advocacy groups, especially the American Civil Liberties Union and the National Association for the Advancement of Colored People's Legal Defense Fund, their essential tool became the lawsuit. "Sue the bastards!" served as public interest progressives' unofficial motto.[31] Advocates benefited from legal changes in the 1950s and early 1960s that made legal action easier to take. One of the most critical changes involved expansions in standing rights—the ability of a person or group to claim a grievance and to sue for damages—which gave advocates greater ability to use legal remedies.[32]

If aggressive lobbying and lawsuits represented the "militant" part of "responsible militancy," the "responsible" part pointed to public interest groups' avoidance of more confrontational tactics. As EDF leader Charles Wurster reassured *Sports Illustrated* readers in 1969, "We don't block traffic. We don't sit in. We don't riot."[33] Public interest progressives emphasized what they deemed pragmatism and measurable accomplishments. As Sierra Club executive director Michael McCloskey explained, "One can have heady dreams of sweeping revolutions, but revolutions are not made in the dream world." Instead, he insisted, change happened when people entered "the political process" and showed their willingness "to suffer all its frustrations and limitations" to win concrete achievements.[34]

McCloskey's call for more people to enter the political process spoke to the third pillar of public interest progressivism: the idea of "participation." Positioning their work within U.S. history, one set of public interest advocates declared that "much of the history of this nation could be written around movements by the public-at-large to democratize those institutions exercising political and social power over them."[35] Practically speaking, achieving widened participation meant increasing the number of access points through which citizens (or the public interest groups serving as the "people's" ostensible representatives) could have a say in policy makers' deliberations.

While public interest progressives endorsed citizen participation in businesses and government, they were often ambivalent about public participation within their own organizations. Some public interest groups did not try to grow grassroots memberships. Others built grassroots support; however, membership often consisted of little more than signing petitions, donating money, and being on a mailing list. "We won't waste your time and money . . . on anything but *getting results*," boasted an NRDC recruitment letter. It also promised they would "send you our quarterly Newsletter and periodic bulletins about crucial environment issues in which you can become involved—*but only if you want them.*"[36]

Scholars and activists have bemoaned public interest groups' downplaying of the grassroots; arguing as political scientist Theda Skocpol has, that while "classic membership federations built two-way bridges across classes and places . . . in a civic America dominated by centralized, staff-driven advocacy associations, such bridges are eroding."[37] Yet painting a dichotomy of elitist public interest groups against genuine grassroots activists oversimplifies matters. Public interest groups' organizational structures and tactics did not simply flow from a decontextualized elitist disdain of grassroots organizing. Rather, they reflected the political moment of the mid-1960s to mid-1970s. As seen in early victories, like Nader's mid-1960s triumphs, public interest advocates found that they could win without the years-long work of nurturing a grassroots base. Instead, again and again a few hard-charging advocates informed and cajoled their way to victory.

Many factors contributed to the historical conjuncture facilitating public interest progressives' successes. As scholars such as Kim Phillips-Fein have shown, the business community remained largely demobilized on Capitol Hill from the late 1930s until the mid-1970s. Conversely, organized labor (which supported many regulatory initiatives) flexed substantial lobbying muscle in these years. As late as 1974, labor unions boasted 201 political action committees, while all U.S. businesses together claimed only 89.[38] Supporters of new consumer and environmental regulations also benefited from the differentially polarized partisan politics of the time—one in which many Democrats and Republicans could collaborate on consumer and environmental issues.[39] This, and the sense (both real and imagined) that it would require too much time and expertise for large numbers of people to follow every complex bureaucracy and piece of legislation, created a situation where public interest groups viewed their theories of change as effective.

Moreover, a typology that pits mass movements against elite NGOs freezes public interest groups historically, failing to recognize later changes. Certainly, in their early years, with vibrant radical movements to their left, most public interest groups expended little energy cultivating grassroots memberships. However, as time passed, shifts occurred. One major change came with the collapse of many New Left groups by the mid-1970s. Contrary to portrayals of hippies turning into yuppies, many New Left activists stayed politically engaged.[40] One of the refuges they found were public interest groups, which former New Leftists often infused with an emphasis on mobilization and protest.[41]

Thus, public interest groups became durable repositories for liberal and even left-wing thinking and agitation in a time when few other options seemed to last.[42]

Most public interest progressive groups devoted themselves to domestic concerns. However, building on their commitment to rein in corporate power, beginning in the mid-1970s, some public interest progressives began looking to the global stage. Here again, the U.S. war in Vietnam weighed heavily. Beyond furor about the violence and critiques of the destructive naiveté of U.S. policy makers, some activists also began identifying how corporate power functioned internationally. Some U.S.-based activists went further by protesting U.S. businesses' overseas operations. In 1965, Students for a Democratic Society members launched a sit-in at Chase Manhattan Bank to oppose loans to South Africa, and antiwar protesters frequently targeted Dow Chemical for supplying napalm to the U.S. military.[43]

Appropriately enough, Ralph Nader offered an early voice calling for public interest groups to go global. Speaking before a U.N. commission in September 1973, he lamented that the "largest 10 'worldcorps' (by sales) are bigger than some 80 nations (by GNP)." He damned multinationals' exploitation of workers and consumers, decrying how the companies' power "vastly exceeds their accountability to these people they so deeply affect."[44] Nader also offered a path forward. "The best ideas in the world are not going to catch hold . . . unless a larger number of the world's people are brought to a focus of concern on these issues," he counseled, urging a "public jolting" of multinational corporations.[45] It did not take long for wish to become reality.

PART I

Don't Buy Nestlé

CHAPTER 1

Of Big Business and Baby Bottles

October 1979, Geneva, Switzerland. Sitting in a meeting hall in the headquarters of the World Health Organization (WHO), Doug Johnson, Leah Margulies, Andy Chetley, and Anwar Fazal made for a ramshackle team. Johnson, a former Boy Scout; Margulies, a firebrand from New York City; Chetley, a Canadian journalist-activist; and Fazal, a pensive internationalist from Malaysia, were in Geneva to discuss breast-milk substitutes and global economic governance.

Reaching this metaphorical (and literal) table required years of mobilizing against a behemoth of multinational private enterprise: Nestlé. To this day one of the world's richest companies, in 1978, Nestlé reported annual sales larger than the annual gross domestic products of more than one hundred countries.[1] Meanwhile, the principal U.S. activist group confronting Nestlé had $9,685.13 in the bank.[2]

Despite these resource imbalances, in October 1979, the activists were winning. At the close of this WHO- and UNICEF-sponsored meeting, the two U.N. agencies agreed to create the International Code of Marketing of Breast-Milk Substitutes. The meeting also left activists with an established role in global governance. Thierry Lemaresquier, who worked as an NGO liaison with the United Nations, stated that the meeting confirmed "the very real socio-political power" of NGOs, while Artemis Simopoulos of the U.S. National Institutes of Health praised activists for being "most eloquent and very well versed."[3]

Margulies, Chetley, Fazal, and Johnson traversed a difficult path to reach this moment. They experimented with different forms of political mobilization and action. They went from novices to experts in everything from public health policy to the United Nations' inner workings. They confronted many hurdles and made many mistakes. They also achieved many successes. At the time of the Geneva meeting, activists had forged an effective international boycott, an accomplishment that, decades later, author and activist Naomi Klein anointed the "granddaddy of modern brand-based actions."[4]

Indeed, the breast-milk substitutes marketing fight played an important role in the histories of U.S. and global activism on Global South-North economic affairs in four main ways. First, the campaign saw public interest groups bring the attention of fellow NGO advocates, bureaucrats, politicians, and publics to the importance of multinational enterprises in shaping international economics and society. Second, the campaign forced activists to learn how to navigate across local, national, and global terrains to exert maximum influence. Third, the experiences accrued and the connections made by activists built linkages that blossomed into a multi-issue, global justice network. Finally, while the campaign started as a standard consumer boycott, over time it morphed into something grander. As activists plunged deeper into the world of international advocacy, questions of global governance became ever more prominent. In this brief moment during the late 1970s and early 1980s, discussions of governance took on a different tenor than that found in most of our story. Rather than combating what advocates saw as institutions and ideas that intensified inequality, progressives imagined something else: global economic governance in the service of the people.

*   *   *

More than perhaps anyone else in the United States of America, Leah Margulies brought the mixture of strategic savvy and systemic thinking that gave rise to and propelled the Nestlé boycott. Born in New York City on April 12, 1944, Margulies seemed destined to become a left-wing activist like her parents before her. Her father worked for the International Ladies' Garment Workers' Union; he and Leah's mother met and fell in love as members of the Young People's Socialist League.[5] Growing up in this milieu, Margulies became an activist at a young age; by middle school, she was churning out essays on the crimes of the Ku Klux Klan. Attending Boston University in the early 1960s, she marched in picket lines against racist hiring practices at Woolworth's department stores and other actions in support of the Black freedom struggle.[6]

As the years passed, Margulies began encountering a problem common for women involved in civil rights and anti–Vietnam War activism: sexism from some male comrades. While activism permeated her days, she also felt "pretty out of it, in large part because women were just not really valued in the movement."[7] In 1968 Margulies relocated to New Haven. She had recently married and moved to be with her husband, a PhD economics student at Yale University. In

New Haven, Margulies's activist fire began to rekindle. She jumped into a multitude of feminist activist projects—from helping to organize consciousness-raising groups to playing flute in the New Haven Women's Liberation Rock Band.

The following year, while at home one day, Margulies picked up when the phone rang. On the other end was Yale economics professor Stephen Hymer, calling to recruit Margulies's husband to be his research assistant. Margulies immediately declared Hymer's question "the most sexist thing I've ever heard: he doesn't want a job and I'm the one who needs one." Hymer's response: "Okay Leah, you're hired." This brief conversation set the course for the rest of Margulies's life.

By the late 1960s, Hymer had earned the reputation as the "father of international business theory."[8] In her role as his assistant, Margulies learned how to research multinationals, picking up tips such as "read specialized business journals and not academic articles," while also developing a deep understanding of international business operations. Her curiosity was piqued when examining corporate activities in the Third World. The amount of raw information Margulies learned overwhelmed her. She could soon think of little else than multinational corporations and how "these people are taking over the world!"[9]

These interweavings of First World companies and Third World societies were in and of themselves nothing new. As modern corporations arose in Europe and the United States in the nineteenth century, some businesses turned their sights abroad, investing in cash crops, mining, and transportation, particularly in Latin America.[10] These trends intensified in the wake of World War II and the collapse of formal European empires. Accounting for 8 percent of the total gross national product in non-Communist countries in 1950, multinationals accounted for 22 percent by 1974.[11] As a U.N. report concluded, "The value-added by each of the top ten multinational corporations in 1971 was . . . greater than the gross national product of over 80 countries."[12]

Though most multinational investment occurred among Global North companies and countries, by 1973 "about a third of the total estimated stock of foreign direct investment" went to the Global South. Certain sectors received the most attention: resource extraction accounted for 50 percent of multinational investments in the Third World, with a significant additional portion going to agriculture.[13] However, economic growth in parts of the Third World during the 1950s and 1960s attracted multinationals not just to the possibilities of producing goods in the Global South but also of selling consumer products.

For nationalist and leftist intellectuals, political movements, and governments across Africa, Asia, and Latin America, multinationals' investments were, in the words of Chilean president Salvador Allende, "undermining the genuine interests of the developing countries."[14] As many leftists argued, multinationals acted like imperial governments: they extracted the wealth found in the Third World and exported it, engorging the wealth of the affluent and impoverishing the deprived. As Ghanaian president Kwame Nkrumah wrote in 1965, the "result . . . is that foreign capital is used for the exploitation rather than the development of the less developed parts of the world."[15]

Building on such assessments, a network of economists and sociologists, many hailing from Latin America and Africa, produced a body of scholarship known as dependency theory. According to these thinkers, the structures of global capitalism perpetuated and deepened inequalities, both within individual nation-states and between the "core" of the First World countries and the "periphery" of the Third World. Taking a historical view, they attributed this state of affairs to the social, economic, and political structures built by colonialism and continued by forms of neoimperialism.[16] These factors explained why many countries' entire economies—their transportation systems, labor forces, and so on—revolved around the production and export of a few products such as sugar or bauxite. In trying to comprehend the persistence and growth of inequality, dependency theorists looked to multinationals as "institutional structures . . . which underlie and reinforce the mechanisms of dependence."[17]

Dependency theory added intellectual weight, analytical precision, and linguistic framing to sentiments flowing around the world, including in the late 1960s United States. Some intellectuals and progressive activists in the United States read dependency theory thinkers and started incorporating those analyses into their own worldviews.[18] At the same time, anticorporate sentiments were on the rise during the 1960s, from Black freedom activists targeting Woolworth's, to environmentalists confronting Union Oil, to consumer groups blasting General Motors. Coupled with rising labor unrest in the early 1970s and critiques of companies as promoting social conformity, big business's popularity plummeted in the United States. Whereas in 1966, public "confidence in the heads of large corporations" stood at 55 percent, by 1975 that number had dropped to 15 percent.[19]

Margulies entered this ferment pondering how U.S. activists could confront globe-spanning corporations. During the first years of the 1970s, she worked with grassroots projects to educate activists, especially in the feminist movement, about multinationals.[20] She and her husband divorced, leading Margulies to return to New York City. After again working as a researcher, in 1974, she accepted a job with the Interfaith Center on Corporate Responsibility (ICCR). A public interest nonprofit, ICCR channeled the moral and financial power of Catholic orders and mainline Protestant churches to press large corporations to embrace social responsibility.[21] ICCR hired Margulies to build a program dealing with multinationals and global poverty.[22] She tested several campaign ideas with ICCR member congregations, such as ones challenging the ecological and social effects of the Green Revolution.[23] She also explored an issue familiar to her from past research: corporate marketing of breast-milk substitutes in the Global South.[24]

The question of breast-milk substitute marketing spoke directly to an interlocking set of inequalities. Breast-milk substitutes, like infant formula, arose as one of many nineteenth- and early twentieth-century attempts coming from white Europeans and settlers to "improve" human lives through technology. The desire for human betterment was often quite genuine. For instance, Justus von Liebig, who invented the first breast-milk substitute, undertook this work because of his grandchildren, whose mother could not breastfeed. Yet, as the industry grew, it increasingly relied on marketing to overcome health and nutritional concerns. The products went international, with Nestlé selling substitutes in Australia, Europe, and the Americas by the 1870s. A century later, when Margulies began mobilizing the campaign, breast-milk substitutes were big business, with worldwide sales estimated at $2 billion by the early 1980s.[25]

As use of the substitutes increased, breastfeeding declined in many places: in Brazil alone, the percentage of mothers solely breastfeeding dropped from 96 percent in 1940 to 39 percent in 1974.[26] What made substitutes controversial were the health risks associated with their use in some circumstances of impoverishment. The risks ranged from not having the income to buy sufficient substitutes to dangers posed by lack of access to clean water and refrigeration. In particular, without basic sanitation, using products such as infant formula increased newborns' risks of suffering from malnutrition or disease, as well as dying.[27] Paying for breast-milk substitutes also extracted money from families with little to spare, with studies from countries ranging from Brazil to Pakistan showing that a single day's supply of infant formula often cost around half of a family's daily wages.[28]

Of course, great nuances existed regarding breastfeeding and substitutes. Some mothers found breastfeeding painful or could not breastfeed at all for various reasons. Others found freedom in using formula. However, companies selling these products did not stop at advertising to these specific groups. To entice as many families as possible, businesses such as Nestlé advertised their products as markers of modernity. The companies' advertising in the Global South emphasized their products' scientific sophistication, with one Nestlé ad boasting, "Lactogen with Honey is specially prepared by Nestlé's child nutrition experts."[29] Building on these claims, Nestlé's and other companies' promotional materials suggested use of substitutes would facilitate "a release from the kin obligations of the traditional cultures."[30] The companies marketed in many venues, from purchasing ads in local medical journals, to offering free samples to medical personnel, to producing "baby books" aimed at women to teach them about child-rearing. Most controversially, companies also hired "milk nurses"—salespeople sent to newborn wards to gin up customers.[31]

Margulies followed in a decades-long lineage of people trying to raise the alarm about breast-milk substitute marketing. Beginning in the 1930s, pediatrician Cicely Williams tried for decades, with little success, to make the issue into a scandal. As time passed with minimal progress, frustrations mounted. In 1974, renowned tropical medicine doctor Derrick Jelliffe declared that some "groups may have to take a more aggressive, Nader-like stance" to force the companies to respond.[32] In the United Kingdom and Sweden, activists embraced this call. The British antipoverty nonprofit War on Want sponsored an influential pamphlet, *The Baby Killer*, and Swiss activists launched a lawsuit against Nestlé. However, by the middle of 1975, these efforts stalled, leaving room for Margulies to take the lead.[33]

Speaking before church groups and other activist communities, she became ever more convinced that the breast-milk substitute controversy presented an "excellent example of the . . . harmful effects of corporate expansion into Third World food systems." As she noted in a report on her activities, the issue combined "1) a glaring problem that demands immediate concern and action with 2) the possibility for a more in depth analysis as to why this kind of injustice would occur."[34]

In part, the issue's "excellence" stemmed from the ease with which it could be explained and the anger it provoked. Margulies later explained that women's groups in particular responded to her presentations. As activists would discover, the eventual boycott could not have happened without the dedication of women's divisions within different churches. In talking with these constituencies, Margulies found opportunities for popular education.[35] The controversy illustrated larger dynamics about multinationals' influence on social and economic development found in dependency theory. As Margulies explained to *Mother Jones*, "corporations operate in the Third World in a way that creates overall economic dependency as horrifying, impoverishing, and unnatural as the dependency of a healthy mother on expensive powdered milk."[36]

By late 1974, Margulies convinced ICCR's leadership to let her focus exclusively on a campaign around breast-milk substitute marketing. At first, Margulies deployed the typical tactics of public interest advocates. She mobilized several congregations that owned shares in American Home Products and

Figure 1. Nestlé advertisement in Rhodesia, 1977. Courtesy of the Wisconsin Historical Society.

Bristol-Myers (the two biggest U.S. companies selling substitutes abroad) to submit shareholder resolutions requesting information on the companies' marketing practices.[37] While American Home Products quickly acquiesced, Bristol-Myers resisted, urging its shareholders to oppose the resolution, which received 5 percent of the vote.[38]

Frustrated, Margulies ramped up ICCR's effort. In the spring of 1976, she arranged for the Sisters of the Precious Blood, a small order of nuns based in Chicago, to deploy that most sacred of public interest tools: the lawsuit. This lawsuit charged Bristol-Myers with issuing "false or misleading material statements or omissions in proxy materials" in violation of Securities and Exchange Commission rules.[39] It produced few results. After nearly two years of litigation, Bristol-Myers agreed to improve reporting on its marketing but did not agree to any policy changes. Even before this happened, Margulies had decided to move beyond standard public interest tools, searching for ways to escalate the campaign. However, to do so, she would need new allies, ones eager to take more aggressive action.[40]

CHAPTER 2

A Strong Boycott Is One Way

In November 1976, Margulies's quest took her to the southeastern Texas town of Palacios.[1] There, at a YMCA retreat center, activists gathered to discuss expanding the work of the National Coalition for Development Action, which aspired to be a "citizen's movement on development issues."[2] Late 1976 was a propitious time for such aims. For this was the era of international debates over the possibility of a New International Economic Order, or NIEO.[3]

By the early 1970s, a rising critique from some in the Third World insisted that, with political decolonization mostly complete, economic decolonization represented the next stage of liberation. A vast literature, stretching from the structuralism of economist Raúl Prebisch to Marxist dependency theorists, outlined how structures built by colonialism continued to produce socioeconomic inequalities.[4] Third World institutions, such as the Non-Aligned Movement (NAM) and the Group of 77 (G-77), became sites for governments and policy thinkers to deliberate about these challenges.[5] These discussions led to certain demands: stabilizing commodity prices, increasing foreign aid, expanding Third World influence in global institutions, and the "right of every country to adopt the economic and social system that it deems the most appropriate."[6]

In December 1973, preparation met opportunity. In that month, the Organization of the Petroleum Exporting Countries (OPEC) instituted a fourfold increase in oil prices. For many in the Global South, OPEC's success was revelatory.[7] All of a sudden, a group of Third World states had forced the First World to accede to their economic demands. Leaders such as Jamaica's Michael Manley and Tanzania's Julius Nyerere called for organizing OPEC-like producer associations for other commodities that would act, in Nyerere's words, as "trade unions of the poor."[8]

Flush with policy proposals, organized through the NAM and the G-77, and now boasting a (seemingly) plausible strategy for winning real changes, some Third World states pressed their case. G-77 and NAM members successfully lobbied for a Special Session of the U.N. General Assembly, which opened in April 1974. Weeks of talks closed with the passage of the Declaration on the Establishment of a New International Economic Order on May 1, 1974. The resolution committed the United Nations to aiding in the construction of a new order. As Pakistani economist and U.N. official Sartaj Aziz recalled about many of his Third World colleagues, "We all felt very good and we agreed that . . . the New International Economic Order could become a reality in a few years."[9]

Pro-NIEO states viewed the United Nations as both the best venue to negotiate a new order and as the most promising home for new forms of global economic governance. For instance, pro-NIEO governments lobbied for a U.N. agency to "regulate and supervise the activities of transnational corporations."[10] In 1976, this advocacy led to the formation of the U.N. Centre on Transnational Corporations. The new agency was charged with researching multinationals and formulating a code of conduct to supervise corporate behavior.[11]

Watching from Washington, D.C., the Ford administration decided to avoid major policy concessions to the Global South while maintaining cordial relations with pro-NIEO states, especially Cold War allies such as Iran. As Secretary of State Henry Kissinger stressed, "We are not asking the LDCs [less developed countries] to endorse our system and do not believe they should expect us to endorse all of their positions."[12] This decision to avoid confrontation arose from calculations articulated by a 1975 Central Intelligence Agency report which stated that if the "developing-country caucus is to be persuaded of the value of dialogue, the industrialized nations will probably have to make concessions."[13]

At the same time, in the United States a constituency arose open to the overall call of the NIEO for a fairer world order. During the mid-1970s, a disparate array of grassroots anti–world hunger efforts began agitating. Inspired by a mix of Peace Corps experiences, religious convictions, and books like Frances Moore Lappé's best-seller *Diet for a Small Planet*, grassroots activists held teach-ins and fundraisers, collected petitions, and lobbied Congress. New organizations, many of them tied to faith communities (for example, Bread for the World), took policy action to bolster and reform U.S. foreign aid. To varying degrees, participants in this antihunger and antipoverty wave rejected notions of charity. Their analyses often emerged from or resonated with dependency theory. To combat hunger, they sought to change policies and structures.[14]

Leah Margulies went to Palacios to tap into this energy.[15] Picked up by a friend at the airport, Margulies discovered she was sharing the ride with a fellow Palacios attendee, Doug Johnson. Also a veteran of 1960s student activism, Johnson followed a different path than Margulies to a life of activism. Where Margulies grew up in a New York Jewish leftist family, Johnson's childhood milieu was a family of apolitical farmers outside of Kansas City. Johnson had been a Boy Scout and high school debater before going to Minneapolis's Macalester College in the fall of 1967. There, he immersed himself in the antiwar movement before dropping out of school to travel throughout Asia. Journeying to India, he visited Mohandas Gandhi's *ashram*. The impoverishment Johnson saw shocked him, and he developed a deep passion for combating exploitation.[16]

Returning to Minneapolis in the early 1970s, Johnson became director of the Third World Institute (TWI), a small center based at the University of Minnesota. At TWI, he arranged educational programming and service trips focused on Third World poverty. Initially excited by the work, within a few years, Johnson and other volunteers increasingly wanted "to learn through action." These feelings crystallized for Johnson during a trip to Guatemala, when a Guatemalan friend remarked to him that, while "we love to see you here, remember your job is in the belly of the monster." Johnson and his colleagues needed a campaign. Casting about, he invited a stream of speakers to Minneapolis, hoping for a spark of inspiration.[17]

Among those he brought to Minneapolis included Joe Collins, the head of the international economics division at the left-wing think tank, the Institute for Policy Studies. In 1975, IPS cofounder Richard Barnet cowrote an early and influential book on multinational corporations titled *Global Reach*.[18] IPS staff traveled the country to promote the book. After Collins's address, Johnson wrote him a thank-you letter. In it, Johnson presciently wrote that he was "particularly intrigued by . . . the need for citizens to begin evolving global responses" to multinational corporate power.[19]

Johnson was thus primed when Margulies, after describing her work, boasted, "If you join this campaign, I swear you'll never be bored again."[20] Margulies and Johnson continued talking throughout the conference. They also met up with a third individual who played a critical role in the campaign (and much later activism), Mark Ritchie.[21] Born and raised on a farm in Iowa, Ritchie's fascination with issues of world hunger and poverty developed early. His father served in the U.S. Marines in China shortly after World War II, where he witnessed extreme deprivation that moved him to devote his life to researching livestock diseases.

During his youth, Ritchie went to a Methodist church that emphasized missionary work and a social gospel message. After attending Iowa State University and living in Alaska, Ritchie moved to San Francisco where he became active in the burgeoning food justice community.[22] Ritchie also involved himself in a different anti-Nestlé campaign, this one focused on cheese imports. Interested in both local and international activism, Ritchie attended the Palacios gathering to meet with Margulies about her anti-Nestlé work. To Johnson and Ritchie, Margulies divulged her "fantasy" for the campaign's next step: a consumer boycott. The two men greeted the idea enthusiastically.[23]

After the Palacios meeting, Margulies, Johnson, and Ritchie began recruiting. They started with activist groups interested in global inequalities, such as Clergy and Laity Concerned, which had initially formed to mobilize faith leaders against the U.S. war in Vietnam.[24] In early January 1977, a small group, including Margulies, Johnson, and Ritchie, gathered and created the Infant Formula Action Coalition (INFACT).[25] Over the next few months, INFACT activists held public education meetings in houses and church basements. Their most effective tool proved to be a documentary titled *Bottle Babies*. Made by a West German director, *Bottle Babies* vividly laid out the case against the breast-milk substitute industry. The film carried an emotional punch, ending with a montage of corporate jingles and images of colorful ads juxtaposed with scenes of a graveyard for infants where formula cans and bottles served as gravestones.[26]

Despite their initial excitement, INFACT's leaders did not immediately leap into mobilizing a boycott. Questions of organizational capacity and potential effectiveness lingered. Plus Margulies was still involved in campaigns against several U.S. companies. It would be the emerging grassroots that convinced activist leaders to pursue the boycott. Attending meeting after meeting, they found people declaring that while it was "great you're doing stuff on Abbott or Bristol-Myers, this movie is about Nestlé and I'm not going to buy their products anymore."[27]

By May 1977, INFACT leaders decided to launch a boycott of Nestlé. This target and this approach appealed to them for three reasons. First, Nestlé accounted for around one-third of all sales of breast-milk substitutes, including the largest share in the Global South.[28] Thus, if Nestlé changed its practices, other companies might follow. Second, given Nestlé's status as a Swiss company, its corporate structure, and its deep coffers, tactics such as shareholder resolutions or lawsuits held little promise.[29] Third, unlike other corporations selling substitutes, Nestlé was (and is) a "consumer facing" company. This meant that significant portions of its profits came from sales of mass consumer goods, such as chocolate and coffee. At the time, Nestlé also owned restaurant and hotel chains under its Stouffer's brand. Thousands and thousands of people chose daily whether or not to purchase Nestlé goods. Thus, the potential of consumer pressure to get results appeared high.[30] Deciding on a boycott, mobilizing intensified in preparation for the July 4, 1977, launch.[31]

Starting in Minneapolis, the Nestlé boycott rapidly expanded nationwide. Employing personal networks at first, INFACT mobilized public actions. Boycott organizers sent supporters and potential supporters thousands of note cards with lists of Nestlé products, prewritten postcards to mail to Nestlé, and texts of model resolutions to be introduced at church, union, and other civic groups' meetings aimed at garnering institutional endorsements of the boycott.[32] In cities with the most active local campaigns, such as Chicago, Denver, and Baltimore, grassroots boycotters also conducted informational pickets outside grocery stores and Stouffer's hotels and restaurants.[33] Drawing from many supporters' experiences in the antiwar movement, INFACT supporters mounted theatrical street actions as well, such as the "Boston Nestea Party" in which activists dumped twenty (empty) crates of Nestlé products into Massachusetts Bay.[34]

As with any campaign, one ingredient in the recipe of motivating people involved articulating compelling language. In explaining the controversy, the story U.S. activists told emphasized a few messages. Tapping into pervasive anticorporate feelings, INFACT emphasized the campaign as a challenge to "the unethical business practices of some of the largest enterprises in the world."[35] More viscerally, campaign materials commonly featured images of mothers holding dead infants, tiny caskets, and dead babies floating in milk bottles.

In framing the campaign, activists had to answer a seemingly straightforward question: why did so many people in the Third World abandon breastfeeding for products like infant formula? Activists blamed multinationals for playing "upon [mothers'] fears . . . of losing status by appearing 'primitive.'"[36] Yet portrayals of mothers in the Global South as hapless victims, gullible consumers, or "Madonna-like" ideals of premodern idyllic living reinforced patronizing tropes.[37] While activist literature tried to situate mothers' decisions within larger societal frameworks, an underlying assumption emanating from the more visceral imagery still (potentially) conveyed the message that impoverished people could not make thoughtful decisions.[38] Given the predominantly white and middle-class backgrounds of the activists, such portrayals easily fit into a long line of paternalistic Global South-North efforts.[39]

However, INFACT staff members did not unquestioningly present such images. Rather, they recognized complexities and grappled with them.

Commenting on a proposed campaign image, organizer Doug Clement complained about the use of "another starving baby picture."[40] In a 1978 discussion, boycott leaders discussed whether they were, in effect, "blaming or denigrating poor mothers? Are our positions perceived as racist, classist, or sexist?"[41] Engaging with such concerns, INFACT publications challenged rich countries claims to superiority, mocking the idea that "West is Best" or that people in rich countries "have nothing to learn from Third World peoples."[42] Publications backing the boycott highlighted the struggles mounted in Global South countries against breast-milk substitute marketing. U.S. activists, whether in newsletters or public addresses, often cited the experiences and research of Global South health professionals. Talking points distributed to the grassroots lauded moves by Third World activists and governments to restrict or ban advertising.[43]

Yet language that framed mothers in the Third World as victims persisted. This was an intentional decision. It arose from the assessment by some boycott leaders that they needed to "appeal to a broader constituency, including those who have never heard the word 'multinational.'"[44] Furthermore, the boycotters believed recent history showed the effectiveness of this approach. As Doug Clement asserted, shocking imagery "worked for Biafra and Bangladesh" because "damn it, the starving baby is what this is all about."[45]

Ultimately, INFACT leaders tilted toward emphasizing speed in mounting the campaign over the slower and more profound work of deeper public education and inclusive organizing. These tactical calculations mixed with a belief among activists that their very campaigning was a stand against complacency and privilege. As Margulies and her colleague at ICCR, Ed Baer commented in a major strategy memo, U.S. boycott supporters were, by the fact of where they lived, "beneficiaries of the exploitation of the Third World." With that in mind, and given that the energy of so many people in the Global South was "consumed by the struggle to survive," U.S. activists thus saw themselves as bearing a "RESPONSIBILITY to speak against the harmful effects of corporations, where ever they are."[46]

Overall, disputes over linguistic and visual framing occupied relatively little space in the deliberations of boycott leaders. Much of their work aimed at recruiting support from an array of civil society groups. Of the constituencies they reached out to, the most critical proved to be churches, especially mainline Protestant ones. Having national religious organizations and local congregations on board gave the boycott a wide reach, access to material resources, and the validation of endorsement by crucial moral voices.

Many churches responded enthusiastically to the boycott, as throughout the 1970s, many mainline Protestants became increasingly involved in social justice work.[47] Within two years, the boycott received the blessing of the national Presbyterian and Unitarian Universalist churches, and most important, the National Council of Churches, U.S. mainline Protestantism's principal coordinating body.[48] Mobilizations among congregants secured many of these successes, as church leaders often "felt forced to become more involved by pressure from local church people."[49] The participation of churches supercharged the boycott, as seen in a revealing document. More than a decade after the boycott's launch, Nestlé executive Geoffrey Fookes met with cigarette company officials facing off with INFACT. Discussing what Nestlé learned, Fookes emphasized that the "involvement of the churches" proved "difficult to tackle."[50]

While religious groups formed the core of the grassroots boycott, INFACT also solicited support from liberal-left constituencies, such as labor unions and feminist organizations. These groups' levels of participation varied, from adding their name to a letterhead to serious mobilizations.[51] Progressive celebrity endorsements spread awareness, including from figures such as feminist writer and activist Gloria Steinem, labor and civil rights leader Cesar Chavez, and Ralph Nader. Nader saw in the boycott the realization of his earlier hopes around challenging global corporations, praising it as a "major cause in the corporate responsibility movement throughout the world."[52]

College and university students also added vitality to the campaign. At colleges and universities across the country, young activists hosted debates, mobilized to remove Nestlé products from their campuses, and protested—including a thirty-six-day hunger strike by a student at the University of Minnesota.[53] Students won concrete victories, as when the Corp, a student-run company at Georgetown University, stopped selling Nestlé goods in April 1978.[54]

Public health professionals made up a third constituency wooed by INFACT organizers. Wishing to legitimize their case against the companies, activists recruited figures such as Dr. Benjamin Spock, author of the best-selling *The Common Sense Book of Baby and Child Care*, to make the medical case for the boycott.[55] The most important public health endorsement arrived in 1981, when the American Public Health Association, the nation's leading organization for public health workers, backed the boycott.[56] This support lent credibility to INFACT and brought material aid. As institutions, public health groups could inflict financial pain on Nestlé, such as when the Catholic Health Assembly pulled its annual conference from a Nestlé-owned hotel.[57]

Victories such as these continued strengthening the boycott. However, to force real change would require an expanded array of approaches.

CHAPTER 3

From Grassroots Boycotters to
Global Advocates

The people who started the Nestlé boycott did not begin as standard public interest progressives. Margulies's political influences drew from the "old left" of socialist and labor activism, from the civil rights movement, and from late 1960s radical feminism.[1] Johnson, Ritchie, and many of those mobilizing at local levels boasted experiences in various 1960s and 1970s protest movements. Yet, within two years, the boycott's heads acted as public interest professionals, whether appearing before the U.S. Senate or the United Nations. Their journeys say much about the exigencies and complexities of grassroots mobilizations and public interest advocacy.

When boycott leaders and grassroots participants gathered in November 1977 for the first National INFACT Conference, the spirit of 1960s New Leftism suffused the proceedings. While the boycott grew quickly, at this point the main participants were people who already self-identified as activists. Over two days, many of them expressed distrust of hierarchy and conventional politics. One person warned participants to "keep [the] system from changing you." Others worried about aspects of campaigning that "take expertise." Meanwhile, Ann Arbor organizer Bill van Wyk insisted that the grassroots "be heavily involved in decision making—absence is devastating."[2]

Perspectives such as these reflected powerful currents emerging from particularly student and youth activism. For many, a core element of their political engagement was, as one attendee at the INFACT conference explained, that "structure reflects commitment to process."[3] In other words, any serious organized effort to overturn inhuman bureaucracies and democratize society needed to ensure that its own organizations did not replicate hierarchical or oppressive structures. Feminists in particular expressed such critiques, many having suffered through paternalistic and misogynistic leadership structures in other leftist causes (like antiwar).[4] Within INFACT, these currents translated into resistance to hierarchy. Rather than a small advocacy nonprofit, many activists wanted INFACT to be a "national clearinghouse, facilitating work that is already going on, not a national structure."[5]

While sympathetic to these ideas, boycott leaders such as Johnson and Margulies expressed skepticism about what they viewed as a near zealous antagonism to all forms of hierarchy or even structure. They worried that the absence of clear leadership or roles would leave INFACT "so dispersed that nothing moves." In combating a major corporation, Johnson further argued that the "steering committee needs to be able to meet quickly and easily."[6] Such views were also rooted in experience. People like Johnson and Margulies felt that many radical experiments in "horizontal" or leaderless forms of organization had failed. Such concerns received a wide airing in an influential 1972 article by feminist Jo Freeman called "The Tyranny of Structurelessness." In it, Freeman discussed how "structurelessness" often produced informal hierarchies and power relations, while also leaving activists "incapable of mounting" nationwide campaigns.[7]

However, for the first few years of INFACT's existence, the "horizontalists" won. While Johnson served as INFACT's ostensible director, its leadership consisted of a body called the Decision Making Group (DMG). Members of the DMG lived across the country and operated on a consensus decision-making model. As time passed, frustrations mounted. Proposed projects continued failing to materialize as "nobody took responsibility for doing anything," reflecting a widespread "hesitation among leadership to take leadership."[8] Ambiguities over responsibility led to many decisions happening in an "ad hoc and seats-of-the-pants" manner.[9]

Meanwhile, hanging over INFACT's work was the specter of fundraising, which consumed copious amounts of leadership time.[10] The organization's small budget limited its ability to operate, from producing materials to hiring staff.[11] The reasons for INFACT's financial woes stemmed from its difficulties in garnering foundation grants, along with the economic slump of the late 1970s, which meant that "people just can no longer part with money for groups like us." In 1979, for example, INFACT fundraising director Moe Rodenstein submitted proposals to six foundations requesting a total of $95,000. Only $6,000 came in.[12]

In some cases, foundations saw INFACT's work as outside their programmatic missions. Others prioritized smaller, community-based organizations for their giving. And still others "felt that it might not be appropriate . . . to give to an anti-corporate campaign."[13] Even as INFACT tried different fundraising techniques, the belief pervaded that a campaign breakthrough would ease these challenges; as activists argued, "Money doesn't create program, program creates money."[14]

* * *

Of course, money alone could not buy success. While this observation proved banal for the boycotters, it came as an unexpected lesson for Nestlé's wealthy executives. Right after the boycott's launch, Nestlé public relations staff attempted to engage INFACT leaders in conversation to deescalate.[15] However, while they desired conversation, engaging in real negotiation was not on the table. While conceding breast milk's nutritional superiority, Nestlé official statements asserted, "It is widely recognized that infant formula plays a crucial role in the total infant nutrition picture." They further dismissed claims that the company bore any blame for infant malnutrition or death.[16] Beyond defenses of breast-milk substitutes' health benefits, Nestlé also boasted that its operations helped the Global South in broader ways— from nutrition to jobs to transfers of needed capital and technologies to poor countries.[17]

After initial, less contentious maneuvers to resolve the conflict were rebuffed by the boycotters, Nestlé began its counterattacks. Company representatives criticized the boycott on several fronts. Nestlé materials framed the conflict as one of rational businesspeople being attacked by emotional activists who supported "some sort of 'back to nature' crusade."[18] Nestlé executives further dismissed the boycott as exemplifying the 1970s "age of activism." Attributing psychological rather than policy motivations to boycotters, Nestlé assistant secretary Henry Ciocca said the *real* reason for the campaign stemmed from a loss of "confidence in traditional beliefs and institutions" that was coursing through society in the wake of the 1960s rebellions.[19]

Not all Nestlé officials merely complained about and pathologized activists. Others tried to defeat the boycott. These officials hoped their public messaging might encourage divisions between what they saw as two boycott factions. On one side, company officials viewed groups such as INFACT as "activists . . . concerned with political objectives, such as the . . . promotion of the New International Economic Order."[20] Nestlé leaders believed the "activists" could not be reasoned with; thus the company needed to discredit and marginalize them. Nestlé officials identified the second boycott faction as the "critics of conscience," namely, the churches. These critics, many in the company believed could be convinced to "reexamine the issue in a fair and unemotional way."[21]

To counter the boycott, Nestlé representatives attended forums and debates at churches, on college campuses, and in the media, while also responding to reams of proboycott letters. To manage its counteroffensive, Nestlé hired in succession two of the world's largest public relations firms—first, Hill & Knowlton and then Edelman.[22] Typical of the sort (although not the scale) of Nestlé's actions, in 1978, the company mailed (at Hill & Knowlton's urging) a twenty-four-page booklet outlining its case to more than 300,000 clergy members.[23] However, the company's inability to show convincing self-reflection, along with activists' able organizing, meant that the boycott continued gaining momentum.[24]

Even as Nestlé's public relations efforts fell flat, INFACT and ICCR leaders pondered their next moves. Although the boycott appeared successful, it was a tactic, not a strategy. "Our goals need to reflect our growing understanding," an ICCR status report in August 1978 commented, "that in order to change social and political realities, you can't just say, 'No, don't do such and such.' You need to suggest positive programs that *can be implemented by real people in the real world*; in this case by governments and health institutions."[25]

In search of a path forward, in early 1978, Doug Johnson temporarily moved to Washington, D.C. There he tried to stir up interest for a Senate hearing on the breast-milk substitute marketing controversy. Initially, he targeted Senator Frank Church. By this point, Church was the Senate's greatest foe of shadowy power centers. During the 1970s, he led intensive hearings uncovering the sordid misdeeds of U.S. multinational companies (such as bribery of foreign officials) and U.S. intelligence agencies (ranging from illegal surveillance to assassinations).[26] Concurrently, as a "back-up," Johnson contacted Senator Ted Kennedy's staff.[27] When Church eventually declined, Kennedy— who was receiving fifty letters a day from INFACT supporters urging him to hold a hearing—said yes.[28]

On May 23, 1978, the hearing convened. INFACT and ICCR diligently prepared. They assembled a substantial roster of health experts and practitioners from Global South countries where they knew "promotion to be bad."[29] These voices moved the senators, as they brought the controversy to life. Filipina doctor Navidad Clavano, for example, reported the results of a two-year study she had worked on, which concluded that newborns fed only breast milk had a 47.7 percent lower mortality rate than those fed breast-milk substitutes.[30]

While health professionals from the Global South provided powerful testimonies, ironically, no witness aided the boycott more than Oswald Ballarin, Nestlé's spokesman. Ballarin opened his testimony by dismissing the boycotters' charges as "misleading," declaring the anti-Nestlé campaign an "indirect attack on the free world's economic system."[31] Immediately, a wave of derisive laughter erupted throughout the room. Senator Kennedy told Ballarin that he "could not seriously expect us to accept that on face value."[32] While witnesses from other corporations performed more ably, the damage from Ballarin's missteps (which received significant media attention) cast a shadow over them all.[33] Making this turn of events all the more ironic was the fact that while Ballarin wrongly implied that anti-Nestlé voices did not care about mothers and children, his assessment of the boycotters' ideology was largely correct. After all, the activists behind the campaign saw the boycott as an experiment in combating multinational corporate power.

Following the hearing, Kennedy discussed pathways forward with the activists and the companies. Given that the U.S. Congress could not directly regulate a Swiss company, Kennedy searched for an alternative.[34] From these deliberations emerged the idea of reaching out to the World Health Organization. Kennedy sent a letter to WHO director-general Halfdan Mahler requesting that Mahler host a meeting to establish a "meaningful, uniform code of ethics" for advertising of breast-milk substitutes. Mahler soon agreed. Partnering with the U.N. International Children's Fund (UNICEF), the WHO began planning for a fall 1979 gathering.[35]

The decision of leaders at two important U.N. agencies to take on the breast-milk substitute marketing question fundamentally altered the campaign. A third party would now enter the fight between activists and corporations. At first, this prospect provoked worry and ambivalence among boycott leaders, as expressed in strategy memoranda from late 1978 and early 1979. On the "minus" ledger, boycott leaders identified two main concerns. First, they worried about the "locus of activity . . . moving exclusively into institutional channels beyond our influence."[36]

Such a move threatened activists' main power source: the boycott. A consumer boycott emphasized action by everyday people; now an important campaign current would rest on the shoulders of a few leaders. The grassroots nature of the boycott excited many as a declaration that movement politics still existed almost a decade after the 1960s ended.[37] It felt like a stand against the societal drift from solidarity toward individualism happening in U.S. culture and politics. For example, after seeing the hit film *Saturday Night Fever*, Margulies's colleague Ed Baer criticized the film as emblematic of these trends, as it encouraged "Travolting, not revolting."[38]

Beyond these broader concerns, activists worried that even if they could successfully lobby the WHO and UNICEF, these efforts might end in a pyrrhic

Figure 2. Leah Margulies and Doug Johnson, U.S. Senate, 1978. Courtesy of the Wisconsin Historical Society.

victory. The official rhetoric coming from U.N. personnel expressed, at best, ambiguity over whether concrete policies would emerge from the fall 1979 meeting. WHO and UNICEF invitations stressed scientific and investigative goals, using cautious language.[39] As Anthony Hewitt, information officer for UNICEF, stated, "We don't expect a code of ethics to emerge. . . . Some sort of consensus is likely to emerge from the meeting . . . but those will not amount to a set of rules and regulations that any international organizations could set down for individual companies or governments."[40] Such proclamations prompted Margulies to state that the "problem will be enforcement and monitoring."[41]

Ironically, questions about the United Nations' influence partly stemmed from the ongoing fight by G-77 and NAM governments for a New International Economic Order. By 1979, prospects for rewriting the rules governing the world economy looked dim. Although some Western European governments took the NIEO demands seriously, the United States, the United Kingdom, and West Germany opposed all but the most modest proposals. This created a situation in which many U.N. staff wanted to move past Global North-South conflicts. Given U.N. officials' sense of being trapped between First and Third World interests, Nestlé boycott leaders worried that these U.N. agencies would thus "end up doing very little . . . because they exist right smack in the middle of the international class war."[42]

On top of all these apprehensions, INFACT and ICCR staff also feared that negotiations gave Nestlé an ability to undermine the boycott. Specifically, they predicted that Nestlé would use the meeting as a rhetorical cudgel to demand the boycott's termination.[43] On this point, they were correct. In May 1979, Nestlé mailed a letter to thousands of pastors asking them to "join us in support of this conference and its goals," while in private Nestlé officials praised moving the conflict to the United Nations as "the right approach as far as . . . depoliticizing" the controversy.[44]

For all the trepidation about moving from national boycott to international public interest advocacy, one inescapable fact confronted the boycotters. With or without them, the WHO and UNICEF would be engaging the issue. And as Margulies and Baer noted, "Reaching the international agencies and forcing them to participate is a major victory!" Inspired by their successes thus far, activists concluded that they should keep pushing. "We do not need to accept the implied limits of WHO, we need to try to expand WHO's mandate," proclaimed Margulies and Baer.[45] Here boycotters adopted an attitude toward the WHO that resembled the approach of past U.S. public interest groups to federal regulatory bodies. These agencies and bureaucracies were far from ideal.

Their enforcement powers were limited and they were susceptible to corporate influence. However, the primary missions of the WHO and UNICEF were laudable. And activists, through their support and critique, could make these institutions better. "Undoubtedly," wrote ICCR's Ed Baer in April 1979, "the industry has means of making its voice heard within WHO. We should strive to do the same."[46]

CHAPTER 4

Evolving Global Responses

In deciding to fully engage with the United Nations, activists entered the world stage at a fluid moment in international political economics. Even a few years earlier, they would have encountered a world where the governments backing a New International Economic Order possessed greater sway. However, in the late 1970s, two trends pointed to possibilities for activists: recent changes in the WHO's mandate and the rise of an international consumer rights politics.

During the 1970s, the World Health Organization underwent an internal shift, embracing a social justice–focused approach. In the 1950s and 1960s, the World Health Organization focused on "technical" matters around combating specific diseases. By the late 1960s, the WHO moved to emphasize health equity. A major driver for this change came from its director-general, Halfdan Mahler. Becoming director in 1973, Mahler, a charismatic physician, entered office with what a U.K. government memorandum characterized as "missionary zeal."[1] By the mid-1970s, the WHO reframed its mission as building a "new international health order" whose "characteristics . . . are precisely those demanded by the NIEO."[2] This included concentrating on promoting primary health programs and tackling questions of "appropriate technology." The latter clearly related to the breast-milk substitute controversy, with Mahler declaring it "more important for developing countries to . . . apply health technologies suitable for them than to receive from the affluent countries ready-made solutions whose worth in many cases has not been proved."[3]

A second cause for hope derived from the fact that U.S. groups would not go to the WHO-UNICEF meeting alone. By 1979, a global network had emerged focused on breast-milk substitutes, both as an important issue in its own right and as a proxy for challenging multinational corporations. Crucial to this alliance was a contact Margulies made years before.

In the summer of 1975, still early in the campaign, she flew to Mexico City for the World Conference on Women.[4] Not having organized a panel, Margulies went to the location designated for civil society events. There, she posted a sign with a room number and an open invitation to anyone who wanted to talk about multinational companies. She later indicated that one hundred people swung by, including Anwar Fazal, the Asia regional director for the International Organization of Consumers Unions (IOCU).[5]

No story of late twentieth-century Global South-North activism is complete without examining Fazal and his home: the Malaysian state of Penang.[6] Penang's status as a locus for global activism derives from its long history as a trading center.[7] Located mostly on an island off the coast of western Malaysia, Penang offered a natural midpoint for travelers going between southern and eastern Asia. Its position helped facilitate Penang to become (although not without conflicts), a cosmopolitan hub where Muslims, Hindus, Christians, and Confucians coexisted. Throughout most of its history, Penang remained distant from the seats of wider political power, whether that of the Kedah Sultanate, the British Empire, or the postcolonial Malaysian state. This contributed to a distinct independence in Penang's political culture, one that nurtured dissent.[8]

One manifestation of these dynamics emerged in 1969 with the formation of the Consumers' Association of Penang (CAP). Started during a time of heightened government repression following violence targeting ethnic Chinese, CAP sought to appear "apolitical," according to Fazal. "Nothing could have seemed less calculated to upset authority" than consumer activism, he later explained.[9] However, from its start, CAP's vision used consumer product safety as an entry point to broader analyses. "We all share the responsibility to ensure that exploitation and unfairness in our society is removed," proclaimed CAP president S. Mohamed Idris in 1973. Under his leadership, CAP embraced grassroots organizing and a broad economic justice agenda, including tackling ecological degradation and labor abuses.[10]

Amassing an impressive list of victories, by the mid-1970s, the Consumers' Association of Penang attracted the attention of the IOCU. Founded in 1960, the IOCU started as a network of large, Global North–based consumer advocacy groups.[11] However, by the late 1960s, the IOCU started reaching out to "groups working against great odds in developing countries."[12] Unfortunately, these were dire times for civil society in much of the Third World. During the 1970s, the "Global Cold War" intensified, dominated by coups, moves toward greater authoritarianism, and armed conflicts across many countries in Africa, Asia, and Latin America. Repressive regimes did not look kindly on communities engaging in economic or political advocacy, making forging such organizations difficult and dangerous.[13]

Malaysia, and Penang more specifically, proved a partial exception. This environment helped nurture activists such as Anwar Fazal. Born in 1941, Fazal embodied many of the best traits often associated with Penang, such as cosmopolitanism and dedication to social justice. He received his primary education at the Penang Free School, a diverse institution that encouraged freethinking. As a university student, he became an activist leader, joining debates over neo-colonialism and consumption. After attending university, he worked as a civil servant in George Town and ran the Penang library. As he searched for a path, Fazal connected with people doing activist organizing, such as S. Mohamed Idris.[14]

Soon, working at the Consumers' Association of Penang, Fazal achieved a meteoric rise. In his first years, he helped facilitate contacts between CAP and the IOCU. By 1974, the IOCU successfully recruited him to serve as its Asia regional director. After four years at that post, Fazal made history, becoming the first person from the Global South elected as president of the IOCU. Fazal saw his role as broadening the organization's mandate.[15] To him, consumer rights entailed more than safe products; they also encompassed economic equity and ecological harmony. As president, Fazal committed himself to strengthening Third World civil society and to building robust Global South-North alliances. Furthermore, he viewed this work as another front in the fight for the New International Economic Order.[16] Fazal believed Global South activists needed to simultaneously fight for the NIEO and improve it, by ensuring everyday people would share in its future benefits, not just elites.[17] The breast-milk substitute marketing controversy offered an opportunity for Fazal. The campaign provided him a chance to speak about the injustices of the world economy to a large, global audience. It also would allow NGOs around the world to "strengthen their co-operation and collaborate in practical terms."[18]

*   *   *

From October 9 to 12, 1979, Fazal joined allies from around the globe in Geneva to test whether global public interest agitation could produce substantive results. The Joint WHO-UNICEF Meeting on Infant and Young Child Feeding brought together government officials, company representatives, NGO advocates, and U.N. staff as (at least formally) equals.[19] The meeting saw delegates divide among five committees, discussing everything from the status of women to promoting breastfeeding. Unsurprisingly, the main fireworks exploded in the session on corporate marketing.[20] Industry representatives repeatedly antagonized most of the other delegates. Company representatives attempted to stall the talks, nitpicked over linguistic specifics, and distributed a "points of agreement" document they hoped would allow them to take control of framing the meeting. Moreover, no industry representatives attended the sessions dealing with health issues and women's rights. By the second day, according to British journalist Andy Chetley, "It was clear that few delegates had any sympathy left for industry's tactics."[21]

Activists entered the final plenary of the meeting bullish about their prospects. As the different working groups each announced their consensus conclusions, they eagerly awaited word about the final subject: company marketing and a potential code of conduct. When it arrived, the language adopted by the WHO and UNICEF excited the boycotters. The two agencies proclaimed that there "should be no sales promotion, including promotional advertising to the public" of breast-milk substitutes. The final statement from the WHO and UNICEF further declared "there should be an international code of marketing."[22] WHO head Halfdan Mahler even proclaimed that there was "no way industry can get away with what they have been doing in the past and say they have our blessing."[23]

On top of these policy victories, activists also scored an organizational triumph. Having spent the last few years building informal ties among groups in the United States, Western Europe, parts of sub-Saharan Africa, the Caribbean, Southeast Asia, and more, they now decided to formalize these connections. During the meeting in Geneva, activists met frequently and founded a new organization, the International Baby Food Action Network (IBFAN). Activists had long hoped to create an international coordinating body, and one evening "after a few beers," they did. Aware of the monetary and communications limits they faced, IBFAN's founders envisioned the new organization as a "paper tiger." Its power would derive from its ability to "intimidate industry with the façade of a large, powerful, tightly-organized pressure group."[24]

This new network's first challenge hit immediately. With the start of the code-drafting process in Geneva, activists found themselves overwhelmed. In the United States, INFACT and others now had to simultaneously manage a national boycott, become experts on international regulation, and learn to be effective national and international lobbyists. Balancing these efforts became the central concern for INFACT and IBFAN, as they pondered how to "maximize the credibility gains from the WHO process" without "shackling" themselves as the "loyal and relatively powerless opposition."[25]

Entering the negotiations, the activists decided to stake out maximalist positions. They demanded that the code be "developed on the basis of what health workers and policy makers consider optimal steps" and that it "should not be the result of negotiations with industry, which will certainly seek to weaken the code."[26] In taking this position, they hoped to fortify the United Nations to push back against company pressures. Somewhat unexpectedly, they found sympathy for this approach from within the U.N. bureaucracy. During a meeting between WHO assistant director-general David Tejada and the activists, Tejada explained that "WHO positions will represent an arithmetic average of extreme positions." He urged the boycotters to maintain a hard line, stating that activist "pressure can move the point of compromise in a constructive direction."[27] UNICEF senior deputy director Eric Hayward echoed this request, asking activists to "use our networks in any way possible to bring pressure" on the WHO and UNICEF to balance corporate influence.[28]

By the time a final version of the WHO-UNICEF code appeared in November 1980, it had gone through four significant drafts. During this process, debates raged over everything from the wording of the preamble to the conditions under which health professionals could recommend breast-milk substitutes. Activists flew frequently to Geneva for both private lobbying visits and public meetings.[29] At times, the process resembled a spy drama, as each side tried to outdo the other in obtaining as much insider intelligence as possible.[30]

The negotiations forced INFACT to operate more as a public interest group than a grassroots activist one, just as many had feared. The organization's power now emanated not just from the public boycott but also from its professional staff's expertise and connections. This shift accentuated tensions between national leadership and some of the grassroots activists, who felt that INFACT now paid only "lip-service" to them.[31] Tensions reached a point where one Denver activist proposed that the grassroots groups break away from INFACT to form a separate entity.[32] Conversely, at the same time, other boycott endorsers seemed ready to quit, believing the campaign to be at the cusp of victory.[33] Even among the Decision Making Group, criticisms of INFACT's direction increased, with one member asking "why 10 people . . . had to go to Geneva" for a WHO meeting.[34] While INFACT's core leaders moved to put out these fires, they punted on addressing many of the critiques, instead focusing on the immediacy of the code-writing talks.

In mounting a global campaign, activists enjoyed the (relative) good fortune of not having to also wage a full-scale battle against the U.S. government. Internationally, the administration of President Jimmy Carter tried to promote a U.S. foreign policy sensitive "to the new reality of a politically awakening world," including by being more open than Nixon or Ford to aspects of the NIEO.[35] Carter's administration, which received generally good marks from consumer groups on domestic issues, declared their "full support of the recommendations" emerging from the WHO-UNICEF meeting.[36] However, as the code drafting neared completion, concerns surfaced. Some in the State Department worried that it could set a "precedent . . . which would allow [U.N.] secretariats to control the drafting of codes."[37] A U.S. move to complicate the process started.

The conflict hit in May 1980 at the World Health Assembly (WHA) in Geneva. The World Health Assembly (which is the WHO's governing body) meets annually to make major decisions through a one-country, one-vote process, giving the Global South a distinct numerical advantage.[38] At the 1980 WHA, the United States tried to slow code-related discussions.[39] Using connections in Congress and with major liberal groups, boycotters quickly pressed the Carter administration to reverse course, joining their pleadings with those of Global South governments. These efforts worked. Surveying the diplomatic scene, a State Department cable announced that the "chances of . . . getting the desired changes are virtually zero. . . . Our tactic is interpreted as a device to delay progress . . . by a country seeking to protect multinational corporations."[40] In the end, the U.S. delegation voted in favor of proceeding with the code. For the rest of Carter's term, the United States ceased attempts to undermine the process. Activists celebrated a victory against business and the U.S. government.[41]

However, the Carter administration's reversal came after it achieved an important success of its own. While activists and many Third World governments wanted the code to take the form of a legally binding regulation, the United States, joined by several other rich, capitalist states, insisted on making it a non-legally binding recommendation.[42] On this point, the United States and other Global North countries played hardball. They deemed a legally binding code "unrealistically extreme."[43] Desperate to avoid conflict that, from his perspective, might collapse the entire process, WHO head Mahler eventually publicly endorsed a voluntary code, all but sealing the deal.[44]

Afterward, contemplating their many accomplishments in strengthening the code language and their failure to make it legally binding, ICCR's Ed Baer and Dutch organizer Annelies Allain asked their compatriots to think into the future: "Do we want to become a sort of international public interest group? Do we want to fade away, leaving the ball in the hands of the bureaucrats to fight the companies?"[45] The answer from most was "no." Rather, figures such as Doug Johnson insisted that activist NGOs needed "to focus on industry and whether or not they . . . will implement the code." After all, even a legally binding code would fail without enforcement, which activists doubted the WHO could provide by itself.[46] Activists thus viewed the WHO-UNICEF code as providing the framework and consumer and other activist groups as providing the accountability muscle.[47]

Just as activists began to imagine their place in global economic governance, the dilemmas for progressives in the United States became starker. On November 4, 1980, Carter lost to conservative Republican Ronald Reagan by more than eight million votes.[48] This development worried the boycotters greatly. Pondering the election's ramifications, INFACT board member Mark Ritchie warned that "our ability to influence public policy" would suffer and that the coming "national rightward shift" would bring an "improved climate for business" that would "mean more aggressive tactics on their part."[49] Looking specifically to the Nestlé boycott two months later, INFACT staffer Leslie Knowles cautioned that activists needed to gird themselves as "there are indications that the Reagan administration may launch an attack on WHO in an attempt to torpedo the code."[50] Such omens would come true in the 1980s, but they would prove neither quick to implement nor mark a complete defeat for public interest progressivism.

*   *   *

In October 1980, as talks over a final version of the code proceeded, Anwar Fazal published a call to arms titled "Brave and Angry: The International Consumer Movement's Response to Transnational Corporations." In it, Fazal took stock of civil society efforts to bring attention to the "inability of our economic and political system to protect the consumer from . . . transnational companies." He praised the Nestlé boycott as a powerful step forward, declaring, "No issue demonstrates better the muscle of the international consumer movement than the campaign against the promotion of infant formula." Fazal's words captured the spirit of the Nestlé boycott at this moment.[51]

However, the path forward would not be easy. The Nestlé boycott benefitted from a confluence of factors. Domestically, these included its arrival years after the height of 1960s organizing, but at a time when feminist activists, former antiwar protesters, and others were still mobilized and searching for new causes. Globally, the brief ascent of the Third World as a political bloc meant that multinational companies and rich-country governments could not easily brush aside critiques from "below." Entering the 1980s, however, many of these elements would begin to dissipate. Going forward, INFACT and its allies would now be operating in the framework of the nascent neoliberal era.

PART II

A New International Regulatory Order?

CHAPTER 5

You Must Keep the Struggle Visible

In 1983, two years into her term as the first woman to serve as U.S. ambassador to the United Nations, Jeane Kirkpatrick penned an article for *Regulation*, a journal produced by a leading U.S. conservative think tank, the American Enterprise Institute.[1] The article was entitled "Global Paternalism: The UN and the New International Regulatory Order." Kirkpatrick wrote it as a warning. In it, she coined the term "New International Regulatory Order," or NIRO, to identify what she saw as a vital goal of the New International Economic Order agenda.

Explaining its contours, Kirkpatrick defined the NIRO as a plan for "restricting and discrediting multinational/transnational corporations" by creating U.N. codes of conduct and other international regulatory mechanisms. Identifying the NIRO's backers, Kirkpatrick singled out an "'iron triangle' of nongovernmental organizations, third world representatives (particularly of the radical third world countries), and ideologically sympathetic international bureaucrats."[2]

Kirkpatrick's assessment of activists' goals might sound hyperbolic, but she was essentially correct. Such individuals as Anwar Fazal, Leah Margulies, and Doug Johnson dreamed of a New International Regulatory Order—although they did not use the phrase. Envisioning their long-term future in late 1983, activists from INFACT articulated a transformative plan, imagining goals for two years, five years, fifteen years, twenty-five years, and fifty years out. At its core, their plans posited a growing role for activist NGOs in world economic governance. While at two years they aspired to have "won the Nestlé boycott," within five years they hoped to be setting the "agenda for international organizations to deal with transnationals." Looking twenty-five years ahead, they dreamed of a world in which "transnational investments [were] so discredited that political regulation with consumer involvement is [the] norm." In fifty years, they fantasized of a world where economic activity happened through a "transnational cooperative system."[3]

While in retrospect, this plan appears optimistic to the point of myopia, at the time it represented serious commitments. Riding on the heels of the Nestlé boycott's successes, in the first years of the 1980s, new activist networks formed. Aiming at pesticides and pharmaceuticals, public interest groups around the world mobilized to restrict the power of these industries.

Of course, despite all their efforts, a New International Regulatory Order did not happen. Just as the Nestlé boycott's accomplishments inspired progressives, they also triggered multinational corporations and the Reagan administration to resist. The U.S. government took a leading role, battling in the United Nations to slow regulatory initiatives. Cuts in U.S. contributions to the United Nations undermined agencies such as the WHO and helped block momentum for any sort of New International Regulatory Order.

At the same time, public interest progressives faced massive hurdles in pressuring corporations. Seen from the outside, INFACT appeared fearsome. Behind the curtain, internal problems from fundraising to maintaining grassroots energy constantly threatened the boycott's viability. Furthermore, INFACT leaders' sense of their imperatives also catalyzed significant fights between U.S. boycott groups and allies around the world. Finally, activists, whether they boycotted Nestlé or tried to hold other multinational industries accountable, increasingly realized how "limited" even their greatest victories proved. This demonstrated that, as tough as winning could be, the harder work came protecting and building upon accomplishments over the long term. Thus, activists found themselves running into the very dynamics on the global stage that helped give rise to public interest progressivism in the United States.

*   *   *

Entering 1981, activists viewed the newly elected Reagan administration as an unambiguous foe. However, they recognized that the administration had a very narrow window to affect talks over the International Code of Marketing of Breast-Milk Substitutes (the WHO-UNICEF code's official name). By the time people such as Jeane Kirkpatrick assumed office, the code's language was set. The only decision left for the Reagan administration was whether the United States would vote for or against it.

Somewhat surprisingly, within the administration, no consensus existed on this question. Some urged a U.S. abstention or even a yes vote—provided the code stayed non-legally binding. Among this faction included such officials as the deputy assistant secretary for international health at the Department of Health and Human Services, John Bryant, and several U.S. Agency for International Development staffers, who argued that a "reasonable code is needed which . . . regulates any blatantly inappropriate practices."[4] In both houses of Congress, bipartisan majorities favored a "yes" vote; as a group of eminent Democratic and Republican senators insisted, "Opposition . . . would damage our relations with other nations, including important U.S. allies."[5]

Kirkpatrick disagreed. Joining with compatriots such as influential Reagan counselor Ed Meese and Undersecretary of State for International Organization Affairs (and future Iran-contra conspirator) Elliott Abrams, she urged a "no" vote. This faction argued that the code represented a dangerous infringement on businesses' free-speech rights. However unenforceable or weak the proposed code might be, they saw it as the first step on a slippery slope.[6] As Secretary of State Alexander Haig cautioned, "This Code could set a precedent for other Codes," leading to a global regulatory body overseeing all multinational enterprises.[7] Some in the "no" faction tied the code to Third World demands for a New International Economic Order. Eventually, these voices won out. Mere days before the vote at the World Health Assembly, the administration announced it would vote no, citing as a "central basis . . . serious concerns about WHO's involvement in commercial codes."[8]

The Reagan administration's opposition produced a firestorm of disapproval. Two high-ranking public health officials with the U.S. Agency for International Development resigned, with one denouncing the Reagan administration's stance as "contrary to the best interests of my country, inexplicable to my professional colleagues . . . and damaging to the health and growth of the world's children." During the next weeks, around 1,600 articles and opinion pieces appeared in newspapers across the United States, most condemning the Reagan administration.[9] As for the code itself, U.S. opposition ultimately mattered little. In the end, 181 countries voted in favor, with the United States casting the lone "no" vote.[10]

At Nestlé headquarters, a sense of bewilderment pervaded in the vote's aftermath, followed by introspection. As Nestlé executive Geoffrey Fookes admitted years later, the company's leadership "got it wrong" regarding how to engage the boycott's first years.[11] Following the WHO-UNICEF code's passage, company officials faced the reality that Nestlé "lacked credibility, was on the defensive . . . and had no strategy for resolving the conflict on acceptable terms."[12]

Grasping to retake the initiative, Nestlé placed its public relations in the hands of Rafael Pagan Jr. A former army intelligence officer, Pagan had been advising multinational corporations since 1970.[13] A shrewd operator, he pushed the company to embrace an approach "based on the fundamental decision that we had to deal with the issue not the critics."[14] The company would henceforth admit that problems existed with its marketing and make changes accordingly. Ultimately, Pagan argued, this course of action would undermine the boycott coalition, triggering a "breakthrough" that would cause an "erosion of support for the boycott."[15]

Nestlé inaugurated its new strategy on March 16, 1982. On that date, the company announced it would comply with the code. To prove its commitment, Nestlé released a seventy-page set of instructions for employees on implementing the WHO-UNICEF code. On examination, however, the Nestlé instructions actually provided a road map showing employees how to avoid implementing the code. The instructions proved dubious enough to elicit a rare public chastising from UNICEF director James E. Grant, who demanded that Nestlé not "use the name of UNICEF . . . in any way which suggests our endorsement of Nestlé's instructions."[16]

Despite this rebuke, Nestlé's antiboycott plan continued. On May 3, 1982, the company introduced its masterstroke: the Nestlé Infant Formula Audit Commission (NIFAC). Also the brainchild of Rafael Pagan Jr., the company pitched NIFAC as an independent accountability body designed to "apprise the Company of any problems it discovers . . . in its application of the WHO or National Codes."[17] With public health experts and religious leaders as its commissioners, NIFAC reviewed Nestlé documents and submissions from outside groups to judge whether the company was abiding by the code.[18] To head the commission, Nestlé recruited former Democratic senator and Carter administration secretary of State Edmund Muskie. Convincing Muskie to chair the commission served the company's purposes brilliantly. As a senator, Muskie had been an ally of public interest groups, giving him credibility with many boycott supporters.[19]

INFACT wasted no time in attacking NIFAC. They viewed Nestlé's move as a way to coopt the governance mission now embraced by the WHO and UNICEF. Boycotters aimed to discredit NIFAC, insisting that the fact it was "wholly funded by Nestle" offered "sufficient [reason] to make its every ruling and report suspect."[20] Activists tested NIFAC's credibility by submitting evidence of Nestlé violations of the code and producing reports questioning the commission's conclusions. The activists believed such pressure would show that NIFAC systematically excused Nestlé violations.[21]

However, to the activists' chagrin, NIFAC demonstrated just enough independence to muddy such charges. NIFAC's commissioners criticized Nestlé, chiding the company for taking "a superficial attitude or disregard" toward the commission.[22] As Doug Johnson later admitted, despite NIFAC's "severe limitations," it "provided a channel through which Nestle . . . made changes in policy."[23] Yet this did not mean Nestlé achieved a clean bill of health or that NIFAC alone changed the company's practices. Nestlé representatives still distributed free samples of infant formula to health care providers and pressed Global South legislatures to weaken proposals aimed at turning the code into national law.[24]

Still, the creation of NIFAC produced uncertainty where clarity had previously existed for grassroots boycotters. An August 1982 survey of local boycott leaders asked, "Does your group find itself having to remind people that the boycott is still on?" Most organizers answered yes. The reason for the confusion was the "Nestle impetus in March and April," that is, NIFAC.[25] The commission thus spurred demobilization. With the WHO-UNICEF code in place and Nestlé making changes to its marketing, many boycott backers concluded that they had won. Combined with the exhaustion resulting from years of intensive volunteer mobilization, by September 1982, INFACT national organizers Betty La Sorella and Scott Sommer warned that local groups were "burning out," reporting steep declines in boycott activities.[26]

NIFAC's formation also intensified the difficulties of maintaining and expanding the boycott's institutional base. Already, by early 1982, a growing list of churches began informing Margulies that they wanted "to get out of the boycott."[27] Around this time, INFACT also suffered its biggest letdown in recruiting religious institutions. From the start, boycotters dreamed of getting the United Methodist Church, the nation's largest mainline Protestant denomination, onboard. As the years passed, they steadily garnered support within different sectors of the United Methodist Church, winning the endorsements of thirty state, regional, and national church bodies by 1982.[28] However, the top hierarchy of the church hesitated. Instead of an endorsement, they established a committee to investigate whether the church should join the boycott. After a two-year review, and citing NIFAC positively, the United Methodist Church's leadership decided against endorsement. In a statement released in September 1982, they declared that Nestlé had "made significant changes" and was "acting responsibly."[29] This left the boycotters with the work of preserving the mainline Protestant support they had rather than gaining additional institutional backing.

Compounding these external challenges, INFACT leaders also faced institutional near-disaster. Fundraising from foundations dried up. By mid-1982, INFACT recorded a deficit of $80,000. The monetary situation became so bad that in July, INFACT's Board of Directors wrote to Johnson declaring a state of "organizational crisis" and demanding a cessation of "all non-essential . . . work" to concentrate on fundraising.[30] Worsening the boycott's plight, national INFACT postponed a major grassroots training session five separate times before finally holding it. When it happened, debates between participants and facilitators became so contentious that eight attendees walked out. Failures such as these "really hurt the morale," especially of many longtime, left-leaning grassroots activists.[31] By late 1982, the boycott appeared on the road to collapse.

The hardships of 1982 intensified INFACT national leadership's move to professionalize the organization. Brought in to evaluate INFACT's leadership in August 1982, an independent consultant described a myriad of problems— with their principal critiques seemingly lifted straight from Jo Freeman's article, "The Tyranny of Structurelessness." The consultants observed that there existed a "reluctance" among the leadership "to recognize and affirm organizational realities: that there *is* a 'management group.'" They further concluded that INFACT's "ad-hoc" nature produced situations where "operational job descriptions are apparently absent," creating a climate of intense insecurity, "anxiety, and low morale." Unsurprisingly, all of these issues resulted in a work climate in which "fairly serious interpersonal conflicts" persisted.[32]

The findings of the consultants triggered changes. The staff leadership redoubled their efforts to ensure that INFACT's organizational systems struck "a good balance between reliance on trust and reliance on known structures and procedures."[33] Planning became more concrete, with terms such as "S.A.M." (specific, attainable, and measurable) appearing regularly in documents.[34] Job roles were clarified and channels of communication improved. By March 1983, an INFACT planning retreat reported that the "staff is settled down and performing professionally without major conflict for the first time in history."[35] Such a judgment proved somewhat premature; in April, an INFACT board meeting reported "personnel issues not attended to" and "departmental structure faltering." Yet, even amid these cautionary words, the report still concluded that "morale improved."[36]

It is tempting to see in these shifts the larger transformations that some social movement scholars attribute to neoliberalism—of moves toward "professionalization" and a narrowing of democratic vistas.[37] Yet, in many ways, what happened to INFACT represented a dynamic wider than its historical moment. As many social movement theorists point out, maintaining high levels of intense participation in activism, such as protests or boycotts, is almost impossible. Various combinations of success, defeat, repression, and/or exhaustion invariably set in. By late 1982, five years into the boycott, INFACT confronted just such a moment. Nestlé boycotters in the United States faced the additional hurdle that, for most of its participants, they did not have a direct material stake in the campaign. Given these obstacles, INFACT's leaders decided that professionalization appeared the most realistic path to hold the campaign together.[38]

Surmounting this moment became the core mission of INFACT. Fortunately, for them, in the last months of 1982, good news arrived. INFACT received several foundation grants. Recovering from the previous year, activists treated these gains as temporary boosts for a "hard to maintain" campaign.[39] Entering 1983, INFACT defined its primary goal as "re-activating the Nestle Boycott to serve as a *visible* and *calculable* force."[40]

In rejuvenating the campaign, INFACT's leadership began seriously addressing problems they had left festering. Chief among these were relationships between the grassroots and the national staff. INFACT's national leaders took on these tensions partly by directing newly available funds to the grassroots. The leadership also sought ways to return the campaign to its moral underpinnings; as United Farm Workers organizer Jessica Govea advised them, "Whether or not Nestle abides by specific articles of the Code is important to us, but what is important to people . . . is what happens to babies."[41] Discussions with Govea formed one part of a larger effort by INFACT leadership to deeply engage with the example of the United Farm Workers' boycotts. During 1982 and 1983, INFACT leaders reached out to farmworker veterans, such as Govea, Marshall Ganz, and Fred Ross, for advice.[42]

These conversations played an essential role in formulating a new plan: the Taster's Choice instant coffee boycott. By targeting Nestlé's most profitable single product in the United States, INFACT's heads believed they could make Nestlé "fear permanent loss of market share." They would start with coffee and then expand, with boycotters targeting a growing "long list of products." INFACT leaders felt that this approach would force Nestlé to negotiate in good faith.[43]

In two cities, Chicago and Boston, INFACT invested substantial resources, including, for the first time, hiring local activists as full-time organizers. In Chicago, the Taster's Choice campaign launched in March with picketing outside of grocery stores, and within a few months, organizers gathered 50,000 petition signatures.[44] Boston showed Chicago to be no fluke. There, organizers

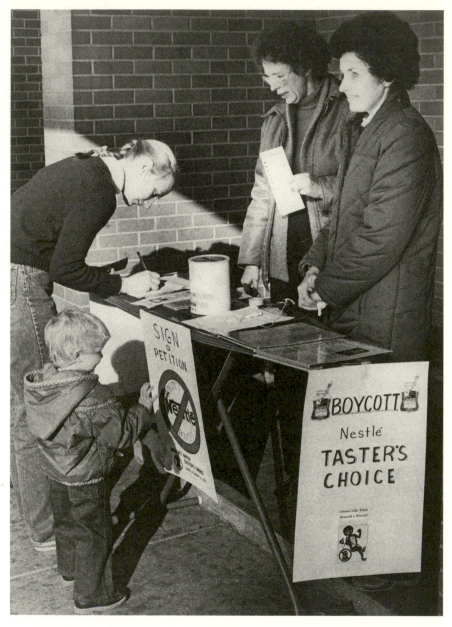

Figure 3. Activists tabling for the Taster's Choice campaign. Courtesy of the Wisconsin Historical Society.

focused on house meetings, which Johnson cheekily labeled a "Tupperware party . . . with a social justice bent." The Boston effort kicked off to great success, hosting 131 house parties attended by 850 people and netting a significant number of newly committed boycotters.[45] The new energy permeated outside of these cities—from a Girl Scouts troop in Geneva, Ohio, to the Berkeley co-op board, to incarcerated individuals at Attica State Prison, fresh anti-Nestlé efforts arose.[46]

The Taster's Choice campaign brought further tangible improvements in the national-grassroots relationship. As early as January, Ohio organizers commended INFACT's national staff for "moving toward better local/national relations. . . . This is great and I hope to see even more of it."[47] At the Denver Justice and Peace Committee, long one of the local groups most critical of INFACT national leadership's treatment of the grassroots, activists now declared the national staff's "focus on 'people power'" as "great!"[48] Concretely, INFACT allowed local groups to use the national body as a tax-exempt "fiscal agent," an idea championed by INFACT's Washington, D.C., chapter for years. This change allowed grassroots organizations greater ability to conduct their own fundraising.[49] From near-disaster, the boycott seemed revived. However, doubts persisted about how long this energy could be maintained. Plus boycotters still needed an answer to the question posed to them by organizer and social movement theorist Marshall Ganz: "What are you trying to win?"[50]

CHAPTER 6

A Mixture of Relief, Anger, Joy, Sadness

In June 1983, International Baby Food Action Network coordinator Andy Chetley wrote to Doug Johnson praising the "exciting news that INFACT is pursuing new approaches to community organizing," referring to the Taster's Choice campaign. Simultaneously, Chetley's letter expressed concern. He asked "that the international aspect of INFACT's work is not weakened in the process" of reviving the U.S. boycott.[1] Here, Chetley addressed one of the core pressures of the campaign: the attempt to balance national and international dynamics and interests. These tensions would nearly explode in early 1984, as stresses in different corners of the world campaign collided, suffusing a seeming moment of victory with intense ambiguity.

The May 1981 passage of the WHO-UNICEF code gave the growing international campaign around breast-milk substitute marketing a major boost. A new division of labor between Global North and South soon emerged. Groups in the Global North took on two main tasks. One was continuing to use their greater resources to lobby at international levels and to fund and conduct research. The second task was to maintain the boycott. As Peruvian IBFAN activist Margarita Segura explained, companies' "habits do not disappear simply because an executive . . . says they will."[2] This made it imperative, in Anwar Fazal's words, to "use the momentum" of the WHO-UNICEF win "to keep the boycott going."[3] Acknowledging this dynamic, in the early 1980s, INFACT worked to export the boycott throughout the Global North (i.e., where the bulk of Nestlé consumers were). By October 1982, boycotts existed in seven countries: the United States, Canada, West Germany, the United Kingdom, Ireland, Sweden, and Australia, with new initiatives percolating elsewhere in Western Europe and in Japan.[4]

Unfortunately for activists outside of the United States and Canada, the other boycotts proved relatively small for a few reasons.[5] The first was timing.

Many European groups began their boycotts shortly before the formation of the Nestlé Infant Formula Audit Commission. The veneer (and to some extent, reality) of NIFAC demonstrating Nestlé's willingness to change dampened activist enthusiasm abroad as much as it did in the United States.[6] A second set of factors arose from differing cultures of activism and opportunity structures in various countries. For example, West German organizers explained their campaign's weakness as rooted in a lack of "experiences with boycotts. For many people it is very difficult to believe that they have some power with a boycott."[7] In other countries, legal structures governing nonprofits threw up hurdles. Reporting from the United Kingdom, the Baby Milk Action Coalition noted its serious monetary challenges arising from "charity laws that prevent any financial support for political activities—and boycotting is always considered as a political . . . activity."[8] Compounding these troubles was a long list of other, familiar factors: lack of funds, trouble convincing people to become involved, and more.[9]

Simultaneously, IBFAN swung into action. After the May 1981 code passage, IBFAN focused on two main initiatives: the "gathering of information from the Third World on current promotional activities of infant formula companies" and "building . . . citizen pressure campaigns" to turn the code into laws in individual countries.[10] These foci reflected shifts in IBFAN's membership. Initially, the network threatened to be a Global North operation. Of its founders, only Anwar Fazal hailed from the Third World. However, with time, it diversified. By February 1982, seven of its sixteen coordinators came from Global South countries.[11]

The 1980s were a propitious moment for a group such as IBFAN. In the 1980s, civil society and social movements flowered in many places. From indigenous rights to human rights and feminists to trade unions, civil society both benefited from and in many cases drove the waves of protests that swept away dictatorships throughout Africa, Asia, and Latin America.[12] Some of these groups fed into IBFAN. New consumer, public health, and especially women's organizations became IBFAN regional leaders.[13] Combining with the Global North boycotts, activists hoped IBFAN could ignite a "never-ending spread of brushfires," leaving industry "on guard at all times."[14] As activist Hazel Brown, a powerful feminist intellectual and activist from Trinidad and Tobago proclaimed, IBFAN would "go to parliaments, we'll go to the courts, we'll go to corporate headquarters, we'll go to the streets."[15]

Southern IBFAN members confronted a myriad of challenges. Some derived from logistics, as many countries still possessed impoverished communication and travel infrastructures resulting from colonial legacies and the realities of corruption and neoimperialism. Coordinating advocacy thus proved painstaking.[16] IBFAN organizers also encountered skepticism about the organization. From mothers to government officials, many questioned whether IBFAN represented another "savior," promising much and delivering little. For African coordinator Margaret Kyenkya, this challenge led her to take "great pains to emphasize . . . that IBFAN was *not* another international organization yet again sending experts . . . [but] a network on whose behalf I was extending the hand of co-operation."[17]

Coping with logistical issues seemed easy compared to codifying the code into national law. Summarizing efforts in southern and eastern Asia, IBFAN's Choong Tet Sieu reported that navigating the "widely differing political systems under which the groups are working" posed significant challenges.[18] As of January 1983, only four countries—Argentina, Portugal, Trinidad, and Yugoslavia—had laws based on the WHO-UNICEF code, with eleven other countries claiming laws with provisions weaker than those in the code.[19] Yet successes did happen. In India, the government established a commission to study turning the WHO-UNICEF code into law. Nestlé soon started targeted donations, including to the president of the Indian Academy of Pediatrics, to water down this effort. India's leading consumer advocacy group quickly publicized these payments, causing the pediatrics' association to reject Nestlé donations. In the end, Nestlé's intervention backfired, aiding advocates in winning a stronger law passed in late 1983.[20]

Growing bonds of solidarity linked Global South and North groups together. Testifying in a U.S. House of Representatives hearing, Leah Margulies highlighted the story of the Indian Academy of Pediatrics to further pressure Nestlé and to celebrate activist responses.[21] Fazal also ramped up his efforts to build South-South and South-North networks. The IOCU helped IBFAN activists and groups secure funding, including from the United Nations, for regional and global conferences on code enforcement.[22] Such gatherings produced results. For example, in a grant application, Jeanine Velasco (a Peruvian IBFAN coordinator), described an April 1983 gathering of IBFAN members funded by UNICEF as a "decisive step" in catalyzing work across Latin America.[23]

Even as these efforts proceeded, simmering tensions between INFACT and IBFAN heated up. Recalling bad experiences from INFACT's first years, activists such as Doug Clement and ICCR's Ed Baer complained that IBFAN "lacked clear objectives and coordinated strategy."[24] They, at times, tried to move IBFAN in different directions. While U.S. activists saw their recommendations as wise counsel, others viewed these critiques as another example of

U.S. groups asserting themselves as leaders, not partners. At the IBFAN Congress in May 1981, Third World groups criticized northern activists for "telling others what to do."[25] These internal conflicts stayed manageable, however, mainly due to IBFAN's dispersed nature. With different organizations concentrating on their own domestic or regional operations, the need for close coordination globally was limited, limiting the opportunities for conflicts to erupt.[26]

*   *   *

Manageable as these global relations were, the seeds of greater conflict germinated over the course of 1983. By the middle of the year, despite the shot in the arm provided by the Taster's Choice campaign, INFACT still faced a "lack of enthusiasm for intensifying and/or continuing the boycott" within the United States.[27] The malaise did not reside at any one level: from the volunteers weekly picketing their local grocery store to Leah Margulies and Doug Johnson, exhaustion prevailed. Many churches' flagging enthusiasm posed an especially acute challenge. Margulies and Ed Baer at the Interfaith Center on Corporate Responsibility took point in communicating with the churches. Many church representatives expressed desires for the boycott to end. Some churches even dropped out.[28] These dynamics partly reflected larger political shifts. As part of the mobilization of the U.S. Christian Right, many mainline Protestant churches experienced "intensifying struggle . . . for dominance by both left and right," that dampened enthusiasm for taking controversial stands.[29]

Sensing a need to "create [a] climate anticipating victory," in December 1983, INFACT prepared its "final four demands." The demands zeroed in on provisions of the WHO-UNICEF code still not enforced by Nestlé: placing hazard warnings on labels, revising company literature for doctors and mothers, halting "gifts" to health workers, and stopping distribution of free supplies except for infants who medically needed them.[30] If Nestlé complied with these demands, INFACT said, the boycott would end.

As preparations continued for publicly announcing the demands in early 1984, Doug Johnson took a train to New York City from Washington, D.C. Onboard, he recognized a fellow passenger: Nestlé executive Niels Christiansen. The two struck up a conversation, with Johnson explaining INFACT's demands and Christiansen expressing the company's desire to reach a final resolution. The two ended their chat by pledging to continue their discussions.[31] While Nestlé and activists had engaged in irregular conversations from January 1982 to the spring of 1983, this dialogue produced nothing substantive.[32]

Yet, with most people at INFACT and Nestlé tired of the conflict, and with officials from UNICEF willing to mediate, new negotiations bore fruit.

On January 20, 1984, after weeks of talks, Nestlé agreed to implement INFACT's final four demands. As Doug Johnson later recalled, the full weight of this breakthrough "only started to sink in when I got home and started to cry—a mixture of relief, anger, joy, sadness."[33] Four days later, Nestlé vice president Carl Angst and William Thompson, the head of the International Nestlé Boycott Committee (INBC), the boycott coalition's negotiating body, appeared at a joint press conference. The two men publicized Nestlé's agreement to follow the final four demands and the INBC's reciprocal pledge to "suspend" the boycott.[34]

Stirring as the moment was, it also ignited one of the most intense internal debates of the entire campaign. In dashing to reach an agreement, INFACT's leaders maintained, at best, inconsistent contact with their Western European and Global South allies. Most foreign activists first heard about the boycott suspension in their local newspapers the day after its announcement.[35] Understandably, European and Global South activists responded with shock and anger, particularly as the U.S. activists' decision suggested they did not feel it "important to listen to [the] 3rd world."[36]

This charge stung INFACT's leaders. As recently as October 1983, guaranteeing an "opportunity for 3rd world to influence 1st," had topped their list of priorities.[37] Yet at the moment of decision, these principles bent to the point of breaking. In part, this reflected the speed with which the talks evolved and the inconsistent communications among organizations in different countries. At the same time, U.S. groups prioritized their own self-assessed needs over the interests and opinions of their global partners. Feeling the U.S. boycott collapsing around them, they seized an opportunity to end it.

These tensions erupted at the beginning of February 1984 in Mexico City, site of the International Baby Milk Campaign: Strategies for Action conference. This gathering marked the first time that groups from every corner of the Earth working on the issue assembled in one place. While seeing this conference "as a springboard to build and solidify . . . international grassroots relationships," INFACT's leaders also (privately) insisted that "despite any other public pronouncements, the conference must serve INFACT goals."[38] At the conference, U.S. leaders spoke with a mix of pride and caution; Leah Margulies urged activists to celebrate a "great victory," while Doug Johnson declared, "Victory means many things to many people but it belongs to all of us."[39]

Quite understandably, such sentiments came off as patronizing and dismissive of the anger and critiques articulated by many other meeting attendees.

From a Filipino participant to a delegate from Kenya, many "had just started trusting the network" when they heard of the boycott suspension. Some arrived with reports of recent violations by Nestlé, which they hoped would inspire the boycott's continuation. Others did not necessarily disagree with INFACT's action but wanted democratic consultation first. At one point, Latin American delegates issued a statement summarizing the extreme frustration felt by European and Global South groups, declaring, "We do not need to be instruments of the campaign but active participants of it."[40]

Following the speeches, a series of small strategy groups met to hammer out the campaign's future. On completing their deliberations, the committees presented their conclusions publicly. The last group to speak was the Nestlé Campaign Strategy Group. The committee's members opened by acknowledging that they had "been through a deep, intense struggle" and that "at times it was not at all clear" that agreement would happen. The strategy group then offered their proposal, which was subsequently accepted by all. European and Global South NGOs would accede to the boycott suspension, while being guaranteed equal voice in all future decision making. The European and Third World groups also emphasized that suspension did not equal termination. If Nestlé "violated" the agreement, they would move for "the potential resumption of the Boycott."[41]

Despite these compromises, European and Global South groups remained rightfully resentful over their exclusion from the January talks, with West German activists refusing to end their boycott.[42] While soothing relations with the Europeans, U.S. groups also tried to reinvigorate efforts to aid Global South partners.[43] One of these initiatives involved a program called "twinning," which would "match a single U.S.-action group with a single Third World group, each group providing practical and moral support for its 'twin.'"[44] However, preparations dragged on for months, and "fundraising by the U.S. groups" went "far slower than . . . hoped," leading Clement to recommend that INFACT "not set overambitious goals."[45]

The failure of twinning emerged from several dynamics. Over the course of 1984, within INFACT, fierce debates emerged over the organization's future. A substantial faction, many of them newer to the boycott, pushed INFACT to switch its attentions. They advocated for a campaign aimed at the nuclear arms race, specifically through a boycott of General Electric, due to its participation in manufacturing nuclear weapons. The boycott suspension created space for these debates, sucking out most of the remaining grassroots energy for the Nestlé boycott. From abroad, IBFAN leaders expressed concerns about being abandoned (again) by their U.S. comrades.[46] Some of the founders of the U.S.

boycott tried to keep INFACT's attention turned to breastfeeding but with minimal luck.[47]

By September 1984, individual U.S. groups began terminating their boycotts, and many more expressed desires to "have the Boycott over."[48] At INFACT's top levels, the leaders read this confluence of events as a sign that there was "not enough momentum left and it was good to stop now before Nestlé had time to notice."[49] Nestlé, under new leadership, also wished more than ever to end the boycott. Beginning in January, top executives had started negotiating the purchase of the Carnation Corporation, a major U.S. food company. Representing what up to that point would be the largest non-oil corporate merger in U.S. history, Nestlé wanted to clear as many obstacles and tamp down on any controversies as possible to ensure the deal went smoothly.[50]

Finally, a settlement happened. While Nestlé demurred on a few issues, overall the company pledged to follow the WHO-UNICEF code. On Thursday, October 4, 1984, the two sides held a press conference in Washington, D.C., closing seven years of conflict. Both sides offered conciliatory remarks, with Doug Johnson acknowledging "Nestlé has taken some risks" and Nestlé's Carl Angst stating that "we learned quite a bit." Yet this agreement proved more of a truce than a final peace, with Johnson observing, "We're sitting up on the platform together. We don't yet share a world view."[51]

CHAPTER 7

Our New Way of Global Organizing

For many public health professionals and public interest advocates, the boycott's end represented the amazing finale to a campaign that had already become an inspiration. As Anwar Fazal explained in 1982, the "infant formula campaign gave us a model for global organizing. It involved people at the community level in protest against a Nestlé outlet . . . and at the international level enabled us to take on directly the U.N. agencies and the trade associations of multinationals." Fazal believed replicating this model could lead to "a global consumer movement that is the strongest ever in history. With our new way of global organizing, and with our new power, multinationals will have to change. . . . They have no choice."[1]

Fazal's confidence seemed warranted. At the time he outlined this vision, not only was the Nestlé boycott gaining strength globally, but two sibling campaigns targeting the pesticide and pharmaceutical industries had just launched. If they could also succeed, a model would exist for future activist initiatives. Industry by industry, it seemed, they could construct a world economy that did less harm and more good for the great majority of people.

While significant differences existed among these industries, activists selected pesticides and pharmaceuticals because of the power of linking public health dilemmas to corporate activities demonstrated by the breast-milk substitute marketing fight. All three of these industries boasted of selling products that brought modernity to "backwardness." All three were booming industries. Between 1971 and 1985, imports of pesticides to Latin America increased by 48 percent, to Africa by 95 percent, and to Asia by 261 percent. Meanwhile, every four years, starting in the 1960s, Third World countries doubled their purchases of pharmaceuticals.[2]

As with breast-milk substitutes, pesticides and medicines seemed, on the surface, to be positive products. Yet, throughout the 1970s, scandal after scandal emerged, implicating both industries in the creation of new forms of dependency and exploitation. During the 1970s, the WHO, environmental groups, and public health experts released reports revealing that at least 500,000 people suffered annually from poisoning by pesticides.[3] Controversies also emerged around medicines whose uses had troubling, even lethal effects. Aside from health risks, the high prices charged by companies presented a real drag on public health efforts, with many Third World states spending nearly half of their health budgets on drugs by the early 1980s.[4]

Challenging both industries presented ripe opportunities to test Fazal's "new way of global organizing."[5] While many Third World states championed Green Revolution technologies in the 1960s, by the early 1980s, calls intensified for regulations to rein in unsafe uses of pesticides.[6] If anything, medicines inspired even greater skepticism. In 1976, the issue of improving Third World access to pharmaceuticals was incorporated into the New International Economic Order, as the Non-Aligned Movement demanded "the preparation of a list of priority pharmaceutical needs of each developing country."[7] Two years of research by the WHO led to the publication of a "Model List of Essential Drugs," naming two hundred medicines shown to be "therapeutically effective." Patents did not protect many of these drugs. This made them cheaper to buy and permitted Third World states to manufacture them domestically. In subsequent years, the WHO assisted nations in implementing "essential drugs" policies, much to the chagrin of the multinational pharmaceutical companies.[8]

Drawing energy from the Nestlé boycott's successes, an inchoate band of public health professionals, scientists, and activists concerned about pesticides and pharmaceuticals began to network. Many of these figures reached out to Anwar Fazal, who used the resources of the International Organization of Consumers Unions to nurture new campaigns. In late May 1981, an IOCU-convened meeting on pharmaceuticals took place in Geneva, happening shortly after the World Health Assembly that created the WHO-UNICEF code. Fifty individuals from twenty-seven countries met in a gathering that one U.N. staffer described as full of "enthusiasm . . . confidence and power." By its close, the delegates agreed to create a new NGO coalition, Health Action International (HAI).[9]

Simultaneously, public health experts and activists approached Fazal, asking him to "do something about pesticides like you have done about breastfeeding and about pharmaceuticals."[10] Thus, a year after the formation of HAI, a band of twenty advocates from sixteen countries gathered under the IOCU's auspices in Penang to form the Pesticide Action Network (PAN).[11] Some overlaps existed among these different coalitions, but they also each recruited new allies. Environmentalist NGOs, such as Greenpeace and Friends of the Earth, joined the Pesticide Action Network. From the beginnings of HAI and PAN, unlike with the breast-milk substitute marketing campaign, Third World activists played essential roles.[12] This emphasis partly came from the experiences of IBFAN. Both PAN and HAI based their structures and activities on IBFAN and grew rapidly, with PAN counting three hundred member groups from fifty countries by 1986 and HAI having fifty members by 1985.[13]

The births of two new global public interest networks and the creation of the WHO-UNICEF code in one year sent chills through corporate boardrooms. The business press blamed the Nestlé boycott. The leading journal *Business International* advised companies to "closely examine the long saga of the infant formula controversy" for insights into the tactics that activists had "learned and perfected."[14] A confidential report produced by one industry association about public interest groups found them "moving from strength to strength" as their "hardcore leaders thoroughly understand the internal functioning of a multinational company." Resignedly, the report concluded that the "activist phenomenon is here to stay for a while," suggesting "that companies use extreme caution and keep a cool head."[15] Seeking to spread these insights, writers for business school textbooks began including case studies of the Nestlé boycott in their works, turning it into "business ethics folklore."[16]

Over the next years, the pesticide and pharmaceutical companies took differing approaches to containing activist demands. Pesticide companies tried placating and coopting the campaigns, while pharmaceutical firms followed Nestlé's more confrontational stance. Regarding pesticides, in the early 1980s, the industry's main representative body, the International Group of National Associations of Manufacturers of Agrochemical Products (known as GIFAP), decided that all-out opposition to regulation would prove futile. Rather, they pushed for future U.N. oversight to fall under the auspices of the Food and Agriculture Organization (FAO) rather than the World Health Organization. Where the WHO staff and leadership seemed energized to challenge private enterprise, the FAO had a reputation for tilting toward agribusiness. Thus, the pesticide companies maneuvered to have the code-writing process occur in their favored U.N. agency.[17] They succeeded. With this victory in hand, pesticide companies took an accommodationist stance toward activists, even acceding to one of their critics, Oxfam Great Britain staffer David Bull, being allowed to write the code's first draft.[18]

Looking for ways to win a strong code by pressuring both the companies and the FAO, in 1985 the Pesticide Action Network initiated an "international public education and media effort" dubbed the "Dirty Dozen Campaign."[19]

Through reports, legislative initiatives, and protests, PAN highlighted twelve pesticides seen as "demonstrative of the problem as a whole." Activists initially hoped to win regulations or even bans on such products as DDT and paraquat.[20] Individually, Dirty Dozen–inspired initiatives achieved mixed results, with some nations banning certain pesticides while others continued to be widely employed.[21]

The Dirty Dozen's launch came only months before the culmination of the FAO's negotiations on a code of conduct. During the talks over the code, activists spoke enthusiastically of it being "a major step towards achieving . . . minimum international standards to govern the distribution and exchange of pesticides."[22] Yet, as time passed, PAN's expectations sank. The eventual ratification of the text in November 1985 generated frustration, with Oxfam's David Bull calling it "full of loopholes, rife with internal contradictions, totally lacking in legal force, and far short of what most pesticide activists would wish for."[23] However, over time, PAN members managed to strengthen aspects of the code, such as winning the inclusion of language about prior informed consent.[24] Over the next decades, the decentralized organizing done by PAN groups helped produce the 2001 Stockholm Convention on Persistent Organic Pollutants—a legally binding treaty aimed at restricting and banning various dangerous substances. Even with this treaty and PAN groups' attempts to support governmental regulatory efforts, the dilemmas of pesticide use remain far from settled.[25]

Meanwhile, the fight over a code of conduct for pharmaceuticals became more divisive and ideological. In the first years of the 1980s, the prospects for winning a robust code overseeing medicines looked promising. The WHO claimed indisputable jurisdiction over drugs. Alarmed by what *Business International* described as "increased cooperation between activists and the UN on . . . the New International Economic Order," the drug companies initially tried to "repel this predictable campaign" through co-optation.[26] In August 1981, the International Federation of Pharmaceutical Manufacturers' Associations (IFPMA) released a voluntary code of conduct. This attempt to blunt activist energies quickly failed. The drug companies' code relied on vague language and contained no enforcement mechanism, causing advocates and WHO officials to dismiss it as "a distraction."[27]

Marching ahead, Health Action International activists felt confident they could win a code of conduct. The May 1982 World Health Assembly saw nations from the Global North and South speak in favor of a WHO code patterned after the breast-milk substitute code.[28] Shortly thereafter, on May 29, 1982, a major upset occurred in the international politics of medicine. On that day, the Bangladeshi government announced a new policy banning almost

1,700 drugs, introducing price controls, and initiating an industrial policy to encourage domestic pharmaceutical production. The government's maneuver aimed to consolidate popular support for the military regime of Lieutenant General Hussain Muhammad Ershad, who had seized power in a coup less than two months before. Making this move all the more relevant to ongoing global debates, the Bangladeshis made it clear that their policies were modeled on the WHO's essential medicines initiative.[29]

The new law induced a harried response from the global pharmaceutical industry and the U.S. government. Companies and rich nation governments alike feared that Bangladesh's example would become a precedent for other Third World states. Within hours of the law's passage, the U.S. ambassador to Bangladesh called Ershad, demanding the law's reversal. Over the next months, such warnings persisted. Companies and the U.S. government inundated Bangladesh with letters and delegations pronouncing a common message—that "these regulations may inhibit future foreign investment in Bangladesh."[30]

Jumping into the fray, Anwar Fazal declared that the Bangladeshi government "must be supported."[31] U.S. public interest groups and international networks such as HAI sent letters and met with policy makers, insisting they back off the Bangladeshis. Ultimately, pressure from the pharmaceutical industry and Global North governments failed to overturn the Bangladeshi law. In the years that followed, studies by the United Nations and other groups concluded that the law decreased the use of unsafe drugs, lowered Bangladesh's import bills, and seeded a flourishing domestic medicine industry.[32] While the Bangladeshi government's steadfastness was by far the most important reason its policy survived, pressure from HAI and U.S. public interest groups contributed. As one of the Bangladeshi officials who created the law, Nural Islam, stated in 1984, "Without the support . . . from health care people throughout the world, they [the Bangladeshis] might have succumbed to tnc [transnational corporate] pressure."[33]

The resilience of the Bangladeshi government instilled further confidence among the activists at HAI. Its members identified the 1984 World Health Assembly as an important opportunity to advance the cause of a code, dispatching twenty lobbyists from thirteen nations to the meeting.[34] Activists left this gathering satisfied, as the WHA requested that a meeting of experts be convened the following year to encourage rational drug use.[35] Activists analogized this meeting to "the 1980 WHO-UNICEF meeting on infant and young child feeding," which had catalyzed the creation of the breast-milk substitute marketing code.[36] It seemed another victory for global economic governance based on reining in corporate power was at hand.

CHAPTER 8

The Limitations of Victories

Coming out of the 1984 World Health Assembly, a marketing code for pharmaceuticals appeared quite likely. This provoked grave concerns in the corporate community. *Business International* lamented that, despite corporations' "stiff resistance efforts," they had failed to slow activists' momentum.[1] Within the Reagan administration, the 1984 WHA compounded worries. Administration officials still felt the sting of having been, as described by U.S. deputy ambassador to the United Nations Kenneth Adelman, "clobbered" by the WHO-UNICEF code vote.[2] In 1982, Adelman further warned that the WHO-UNICEF code seemed to be "the opening skirmish in a much larger campaign."[3] For officials in business and the Reagan administration, something needed to change.

Intellectually, the foundations for confronting the push for what Jeane Kirkpatrick dubbed the New International Regulatory Order began in the offices of the New Right's premier think tank: the Heritage Foundation.[4] In 1982, the foundation initiated a new program: the United Nations Assessment Project.[5] Over the next years, Heritage Foundation staff and fellows produced numerous memos, briefing books, and reports premised on the idea that multinational companies were the "First Victim of the U.N. War on Free Enterprise."[6] Bolstering Kirkpatrick's claims about an "iron triangle" of forces trying to overturn the free market, analysts working with Heritage saw the United Nations as the linchpin in efforts bent on "creating new institutional structures . . . to govern the world economy."[7] The Heritage Foundation name-checked such groups as IBFAN, HAI, and PAN as essential players, describing them as leaders in a "'new wave' of extremist, anti-free enterprise consumer organizations" threatening to "swell the anti-capitalist chorus."[8]

Many Heritage Foundation publications in the early to mid-1980s painted the idea of a New International Economic Order as a looming threat. Certainly, some Third World states still proclaimed their "determination to pursue . . .

the establishment of a new international economic order." However, by this point, few believed the NIEO could ever happen.[9] Rather, as the director of the Institute for Policy Studies concluded in March 1981, the NIEO debate was "hopelessly stagnant."[10]

An autopsy of the NIEO reveals multiple causes of death. The pro-NIEO coalition of countries resembled an impressionistic painting—coherent from afar and a blurry mess up close. With governments ranging from right-wing dictatorship in the Philippines to the socialist government of Tanzania and with economies ranging from those dependent on a single agricultural commodity to more diversified ones, finding commonalities of interest and making concrete progress on negotiations proved difficult. Buoyed at first by OPEC's power and support, as divisions among oil-exporting states and changes in the global market weakened OPEC, the pro-NIEO coalition's main source of economic power dropped from the scene. The debt crises of the late 1970s and early 1980s also undermined the bargaining power of key countries such as Jamaica in pressing for a new order.[11]

The early 1980s demise of the NIEO also stemmed from the conservative turn in the governments of West Germany, the United Kingdom, and the United States between 1979 and 1982.[12] In October 1981, a conference in Cancún, Mexico, to reenergize the Global North–South dialogue led nowhere, as Reagan derided those who "claim massive transfers of wealth somehow, miraculously, will produce new well-being." Instead, Reagan chided countries for not having faith that "free people build free markets that ignite dynamic development."[13]

Reagan, Margaret Thatcher, and other conservatives did not just talk ill of the NIEO. They acted. To block further corporate regulation and the broader NIEO, the Reagan administration and its allies directed their fire at the United Nations. The administration embraced intransigent positions in negotiations within the U.N. system over aspects of the NIEO, like the Law of the Sea or the Integrated Program for Commodities. The U.S. government also withdrew (or threatened to withdraw) from U.N. agencies such as UNESCO and pushed for the weakening of agencies such as the U.N. Conference on Trade and Development that had nurtured the NIEO.[14] U.S. stonewalling also ended an attempt to devise a generalized U.N. Code of Conduct for multinational corporate activities. Begun in the mid-1970s after a blip of excitement, by the late 1970s, this initiative fell into the drudgery of interstate negotiations, showing little progress.[15]

Watching these events unfold, INFACT cofounder Mark Ritchie saw a clear move to "undercut the powers of United Nations agencies . . . which worked for regulation of transnational corporate abuses."[16] Activists understood that without robust U.N. agencies, their ability to participate in world economic governance would diminish substantially. Conservatives realized this too, with the Heritage Foundation observing that what gave "IOCU and similar groups muscle is the legitimacy which they achieve through their association with the U.N."[17] While the primary strategy for blocking NGO advocacy came through targeting U.N. agencies, the Reagan administration also attacked activists more directly. For instance, in 1984, the administration moved to label Esther Peterson—a longtime U.S. labor and consumer activist, a former aide to Presidents Lyndon Johnson and Jimmy Carter, and then U.S. representative to the IOCU—a "foreign agent," thus impeding her ability to meet with U.S. government officials.[18]

The most damaging strike aimed at the United Nations originated in Congress. In 1983, Republican senator Nancy Kassebaum of Kansas, complaining of the "tyranny of the Third World majority in the United Nations," introduced an amendment to cap future U.S. contributions at no more than 20 percent of any U.N. agency's budget.[19] In 1985, Kassebaum maneuvered passage of a version of her amendment, which Reagan signed into law. Soon after, the spigot of U.S. dollars started running dry, throwing the United Nations into the worst financial crisis in its history to that point.[20]

While Kassebaum's amendment did not expressly target the World Health Organization, neither did the WHO escape U.S. pressure. In 1986, the United States only paid $10 million out of its "assessed contribution" of $62.8 million to the WHO and gave no sign it would soon reverse course. In public, the United States claimed its funding cuts would nudge U.N. agencies to streamline their operations through greater fiscal prudence.[21] Yet public interest advocates suspected ulterior motives. At meeting after meeting of the WHO, U.S. government representatives repeated their "strong position" that the United Nations "should not be involved in efforts to regulate or control the commercial practices of private industry."[22] Meanwhile, the Heritage Foundation recommended that the United States "reconsider its membership" in the WHO if the agency continued work on commercial codes.[23]

Among the WHO staff, many viewed the cuts as a warning against enacting a code of conduct for pharmaceuticals.[24] The WHO director-general Halfdan Mahler bolstered such claims with a few choice words in a 1987 speech. In his address, Mahler alluded to meetings in which government officials "hint that a positive response on my part is the key to voluntary contributions to WHO." Mahler even speculated that some of the pressure ultimately derived from the "influence of commercial lobbies who falsely believe that WHO is blocking their expansion"—likely a reference to the pharmaceuticals industry.[25]

It is unclear whether the Reagan administration intended a direct tie between budget cuts and the WHO code. However, intentions mattered less than perceptions and the material results of the cuts. In the second half of the 1980s, the WHO saw its budget slashed by a quarter. An institution often praised for being "very tightly managed . . . with little waste to cut" now suffered. The real victims were people assisted by the WHO. The United States' budgetary cuts certainly killed people who otherwise might have lived. One result of the drying up of funds was the WHO scaled back efforts on HIV/AIDS and eliminated or reduced initiatives such as a massive global child immunization program.[26]

Simultaneously, the U.S. funding cuts intensified existing wariness within the WHO about pursuing a medicines code. While proud of the WHO-UNICEF code and critical of multinational corporations, Mahler also felt that the WHO becoming a battlefield over global economic governance created a "difficult climate in which to maneuver and keep its vision straight."[27] Sharing Mahler's sense of the situation, many WHO staff, even if they sympathized with public interest groups, also felt that "recourse to ideological campaigns" represented a "dangerous, counterproductive undertaking."[28]

Given these factors, by the middle of 1985, advocates at Health Action International understood that they could not overpower or outwit the companies and the U.S. government. They decided to bid a tactical retreat by deemphasizing advocacy for a code of conduct. As leading HAI member Charles Medawar bluntly observed, given the complexity of the pharmaceuticals issue, the fervent opposition to enacting a code of conduct, and the WHO's limitations, it seemed "unrealistic to expect WHO to become involved in formal, full-scale international regulation."[29] Instead, he recommended that advocates emphasize support for the WHO's essential drugs program, since "reducing the number of drugs must come first. There is no point in trying to control the promotion of . . . drugs that are not wanted in the first place."[30] However, in public, advocates continued to lobby for a code of conduct, in part hoping to misdirect the companies and in part hoping that political dynamics might change and make the code viable.[31]

Then, in late November 1985, the WHO-convened Conference of Experts on the Rational Use of Drugs met in Nairobi, Kenya. When first announced, activists dreamed that this gathering would mirror the 1979 meeting that initiated the writing of the WHO-UNICEF code. World Health Organization officials also looked to that 1979 meeting as a model. Except for them, it was a model of everything *not* to do. Officials ensured that the format would minimize NGO contributions and the chance for fights between activists and companies.[32] Mahler further declared in his closing remarks, "There is no place for supranational regulation of drug promotion by WHO."[33]

Cementing the defeat, in May 1988, an Ethical Criteria for Medicinal Drug Promotion passed in a vote at the World Health Assembly. According to HAI, these criteria were "considerably weaker than many industry voluntary codes."[34] This disappointment came on the heels of the ascension of Hiroshi Nakajima as the WHO's new director-general. While not a free-market ideologue, Nakajima craved calm and wanted a "dialogue with industry." Moreover, Nakajima was no friend to public interest advocates. During a private audience with drug company representatives, he called for improving relations between the WHO and companies, stating that it "will be hard because your counterparts (the consumer groups) are so strong, but I'll try." Industry responded to Nakajima favorably, with one company official telling him that while "the late 70's and early '80s might have been characterized as a period of confrontation . . . now we are entering a period of accommodation."[35] Perhaps only coincidentally, as the 1980s closed, the Reagan administration paid $20.5 million in arrears to the World Health Organization.[36]

*   *   *

In the late 1980s, public interest progressives who targeted multinational corporations learned difficult lessons. A moment that crystallized this education through action came on June 28, 1988. On that day, former INFACT director Doug Johnson appeared at a press conference, lamenting that "until recently . . . [I] believed that I would never stand again in a press conference making a statement about a Nestlé boycott. But the fact is, Nestlé has not kept the promises it made."[37] Three months after Johnson uttered those words, people around the world restarted the boycott of Nestlé.

The boycott's resumption arrived after years of disappointment. As far back as 1979, Leah Margulies cautioned that the true "problem" with the campaign would be "enforcement and monitoring."[38] Despite the tireless efforts of the International Baby Food Action Network since the boycott's end in 1984 and real improvements in people's lives, advocates kept hearing of new marketing abuses. Companies skirted the code through offering free samples while other firms continued direct marketing, with one Indian pediatrician reporting that in "certain maternity hospitals in Bombay almost all the newborns are introduced to the formula in the first two to three days of life."[39]

While resurrecting the boycott appeared a logical step after years of fruitless dialogue, activists cautioned that such a campaign had to be "clear" and "winnable," as "calling a Boycott a second time is difficult enough—to lose it would be a disaster."[40] At the same time, strong sentiments persisted that the

Nestlé boycott's victory (or apparent victory) needed defending, otherwise "a message will be sent that as long as corporations are able to outlast and out-spend us, they will prevail."[41] Thus, on October 4, 1988, the newly formed non-profit, Action for Corporate Accountability (ACA), declared that companies "leave us no choice" but to relaunch the boycott.[42]

Initiated once again in the United States, the renewed Nestlé boycott failed to attract the same passion and commitment as the first one. Two main reasons explain the difference in outcomes. The first relates to the inability of the ACA organizers to mobilize supporters, especially among institutions in the United States. Most devastating was the lack of excitement from the churches that had formed the base of the initial boycott.[43] In part, this was because many churches felt that talks rather than picket lines could resolve what they now viewed as a technical matter. The enervated church response was also due to the weakening and relative depoliticization of many mainline Protestant churches during the 1980s. Second, Nestlé learned from the first boycott. The company's public re-lations machine operated much more smoothly, avoiding the kind of petty and overly confrontational approaches that failed in the late 1970s. Moreover, the company again relied on the Nestlé Infant Formula Audit Commission to show its commitment to solving (or at least whitewashing) the issue.[44]

Overseas, however, the boycott fared better. Within a year of its relaunch, boycotts existed in Ireland, Finland, Mauritius, Mexico, Norway, and Sweden, with an especially strong campaign in the United Kingdom.[45] These efforts won some victories, such as Nestlé's 1992 announcement that it would end free and subsidized samples of infant formula to doctors.[46] In 1994, the U.S. campaign won a symbolic victory when the Clinton administration reversed Reagan's "no" vote, putting the U.S. government on record supporting the code.[47] Yet, for all these accomplishments, the issue remains unresolved to this day. In the United States, an inability to fundraise forced ACA to shutter its doors in the mid-1990s.[48] Meanwhile, the International Baby Food Action Network continues to operate, doing much the same work it has since 1981. Every year it diligently issues reports detailing how "companies continue to undermine breastfeeding" and IBFAN's efforts to minimize such actions.[49]

Observing these dynamics over the years, the woman who did so much to make these fights a reality, Leah Margulies, felt a sense of pride despite the set-backs. Analyzing the code in a 1997 law journal article, she commented that the fight for corporate accountability "is a drama that is continuously unfold-ing."[50] Organizers saw victory and saw defeat, but what Margulies was sure of was that the boycott marked an important step forward. After all, while she cared deeply about the issue, the campaign from its start was meant partly as an experiment to gauge whether small nonprofits could affect international economic policy. "In 1980–81 it was innovative for NGOs to be present at intergovernmental negotiations. Now it is common," she noted.[51] Indeed, the campaign demonstrated the power of NGO advocates to push the world's most powerful institutions to do things they did not want to. Activists did so by employing a wide array of tactics. They conducted studies useful to policy makers. They put pressure on governments, corporate heads, and bureaucrats through meetings, lobbying, and more direct activism. They established powerful global networks that paved the way for future fights.

However, the inadequacies and defeats suffered by groups trying to push a New International Regulatory Order have led some scholars to mischaracterize the activists' ideology and policy goals. As one historian has declared, "Rather than generating political mechanisms to limit the power of corporations, activists now called for an ethical market in which multinational corporations would regulate their own practices."[52]

Such an analysis seems to arise from conflating activists' tactical compromises with their ideological aspirations. Leading public interest progressives never subscribed to the idea that the answer to corporate malfeasance or economic inequality was corporate self-regulation. Rather, they believed that consumer and other nonprofit advocacy groups needed to hold companies to account. They hoped that governments and multilateral agencies could play substantial parts in this quest. Public interest activists' lack of full faith in intergovernmental or governmental bodies' ability to regulate industry stemmed not from a preference or even acceptance of the free market but rather from their lived experiences with the inadequacies and failings of regulatory bodies. Indeed, as one scholar recently noted, groups such as INFACT are not especially well "equipped or designed to transform the state" into a power strong enough to take on multinational capital (though not for a lack of trying).[53] As seen in such examples as Health Action International's defense of the Bangladeshi government or IBFAN members' work to create national legislation, public interest progressives tried to make the regulatory state work. Their emphasis on "technical fixes and restrictions on the market" came not from ideology but from cold assessments of their abilities and limitations.[54]

In the late 1970s and through the 1980s, public interest advocates discovered a powerful truth about the global economy: governance matters. Yet they came onto the scene right when a massive shift in the politics of governance occurred. The U.N. was increasingly disempowered. Deregulation reigned throughout much of the world. Public interest groups would grow stronger in the 1980s and the 1990s, but this strength would now turn toward playing defense.

PART III

Revolution Within the World
Capitalist System

CHAPTER 9

Economic "Freedom's" Awful Toll

On May 2, 1991, John Cavanagh, an economist at the Institute for Policy Studies, stood before a gaggle of reporters at the National Press Club in Washington, D.C. Cavanagh began his remarks by gesturing to the banner behind him, a large white canvas held up with tape and string, on which appeared the words "Mobilization on Development, Trade, Labor, and Environment." He acknowledged that the "acronym for our mobilization up here behind me spells out the word 'motley,' which is how the *Wall Street Journal* has taken to referring to our group." Cavanagh jovially added that MODTLE's members were "anything but motley," assuring reporters that the coalition included major labor unions, family farm groups, faith organizations, and consumer and environmental lobbies.[1]

Cavanagh felt a sense of accomplishment in this moment. For the past decade, he and a band of allies had dreamed of building a "citizen's lobby of enormous strength to combat world economic inequities."[2] Their work took inspiration from other recent internationalist campaigns, including the Nestlé boycott, the antiapartheid movement, and opposition to U.S. imperial interventions in Central America. At the same time, U.S.-based activists drew ideas and leadership from partners in the Global South. A principal fount for such guidance continued to be Penang, Malaysia, where disciples of Anwar Fazal labored throughout the 1980s to forge regional, transnational, and global alliances.

The ascent of neoliberalism drove this networking. Writing at the decade's close, one of Cavanagh's colleagues argued that the "greatest transformation in world politics of the last fifty years . . . , the emergence of an integrated global economy," would be the legacy of the 1980s. Public interest progressives did not look kindly on these changes, criticizing the philosophies undergirding the new world economic order as rooted in a "fanatical adherence to an ideology of free markets and privatization."[3] As the 1990s began, the term *neoliberalism* increasingly appeared in left-leaning activists' vocabulary as a descriptor for the contemporary economic order.

Activist definitions of neoliberalism tended to highlight its ideological mission. The "neoliberal model is based on coercion, strength, control and cultural assimilation," insisted the International NGO Forum on World Bank and IMF Lending, a gathering of mainly Global South activists from sixty countries in September 1990.[4] During the 1980s, critics of neoliberalism identified its manifestations around the globe, from the breaking of strikes and trade unions to privatization and austerity. Yet it took time for most progressives to identify these phenomena as parts of what IPS economist Michael Moffitt presciently described in 1978 as a "revolution within the world capitalist system."[5]

The ascent of neoliberalism shifted ideas, practices, and institutions engaged in global economic governance—and thus altered how public interest progressives approached these questions. During the 1970s and 1980s, their campaigns aimed at multinational companies' activities in the Global South and attracted some grassroots attention in the United States. However, these efforts were mainly framed around humanitarianism or solidarity, not self-interest. This would not be the case in the 1990s. In the eyes of family farmers, union workers, and many others, the Uruguay Round (which created the WTO) and NAFTA embodied their fears about Reaganism at home magnified on a global scale. These agreements made concrete the larger processes of neoliberal globalization that threatened livelihoods and swelled wealth disparities within and between countries. Simultaneously, consumer and environmental advocates saw NAFTA and the WTO as amplifying threats to the regulatory state. However, broader pain and greater fears also opened possibilities for alliance building among disparate constituencies. The 1980s ushered in neoliberalism and created the fair globalization coalition.

*   *   *

It was no accident that John Cavanagh and the Institute for Policy Studies took center stage at that May 1991 press conference. From the 1970s on, the IPS led the way among U.S. public interest progressives in grappling intellectually with world economic inequalities. The institute itself arose in the early 1960s, born of an awkwardly timed laugh. In 1961, two mid-level national security experts, Richard Barnet and Marcus Raskin, attended a meeting on nuclear weapons at the Pentagon. At the meeting's start, one official declared that "if this group cannot bring about disarmament, then no one can." Both Barnet and Raskin chuckled. Despite serving in government, they believed the policy makers in the room embodied the world's problems, not their solutions. Both men managed to suppress their laughter and, in doing so, noticed one another. They soon formed a lifelong friendship and partnership.[6]

Believing most policy think tanks "serve only to reiterate what the government wants to hear," Barnet and Raskin built the IPS as an alternative.[7] Initially, the institute's staff tended to be liberals who "had come to Washington believing that the American governing process was mostly responsive to . . . public needs." Yet, as the 1960s unfolded, the politics of the War on Poverty, the Black freedom struggle, and especially the U.S. war in Vietnam caused most of the IPS staff to gravitate toward leftist analyses of domestic and international injustices.[8]

In confronting U.S. imperialism and global wealth inequalities in the early 1970s, the institute's staff invariably took note of events happening in Chile. On September 4, 1970, Chilean elections led to the victory of the Unidad Popular, a coalition of leftist political parties famously headed by Salvador Allende. Allende's team included a dapper and energetic economist named Orlando Letelier, who became ambassador to the United States.

While living in Washington, D.C., Letelier befriended people at the Institute for Policy Studies, one of the few organizations in town actively supporting the Unidad Popular. As economic near-collapse and political turmoil engulfed Chile in early and mid-1973, Letelier returned home, serving at different moments as the foreign minister and defense minister. Then came the tragedies of September 11, 1973, when reactionary forces led by General Augusto Pinochet overthrew the Unidad Popular in a vicious coup. Letelier survived and was thrown into prison on remote Dawson Island.[9]

Intense international pressure from human rights activists and governments led to Letelier's release in 1974. The following year, he accepted a job offer from Barnet and Raskin to work at IPS on international economic policy. Letelier received the task of mobilizing an international think-tank network to support progressive Third World governments advocating for a robust New International Economic Order.[10] Letelier and his colleague, IPS economist Michael Moffitt, leapt into the work, making substantial progress in a short time. They met with policy experts and political figures the world over, wrote a booklet about the NIEO, and helped launch research networks and initiatives.

Meanwhile, Letelier became an internationally renowned and highly effective leader in the global campaign confronting Pinochet's regime.[11] Letelier brought to this work his interest in economics. In late August 1976, the *Nation* published an article of his dissecting a then unusual socioeconomic experiment:

the implementation of neoliberal policies by the Chilean junta.[12] Titled "Economic 'Freedom's' Awful Toll," Letelier's article showcased an analytically sharp critique of neoliberalism. In it, he not only demonstrated how neoliberal policies increased immiseration, but also dissected the rhetoric of neoliberalism. Letelier argued that neoliberal intellectuals' insistence on the obvious truth of market rationality "provided an appearance of technical respectability to the *laissez-faire* dreams and political greed" of economic elites.[13]

Letelier's effectiveness as a leader of global anti-Pinochet forces put him in grave danger. On the morning of September 21, 1976, he picked up his colleagues Michael Moffitt and IPS fundraiser Ronni Karpen Moffitt to drive to work. As they rounded Sheridan Circle, a bomb placed on the bottom of the car exploded. Letelier and Ronni Karpen Moffitt died soon after, while Michael survived. Unsurprisingly, the assassins worked for Pinochet's intelligence services, operating as part of an international murder program called Operation Condor run by several South American right-wing dictatorships.[14]

After a period of mourning, the IPS directors decided to hire an interim director for the international economics project. They approached Howard Wachtel, a longtime activist and economics professor teaching at American University. Wachtel, a friend of Letelier's, accepted. Initially, he planned to continue Letelier's pro-NIEO work.[15] Then came the morning of January 19, 1977. As Wachtel drank his coffee and flipped through the *International Herald Tribune*, his comprehension of the world economy transformed. Skimming the pages, he paused on an article about massive protests occurring in Egypt. Reading further, Wachtel took note of the cause: an austerity program negotiated between the International Monetary Fund and the Egyptian government meant to reduce that country's debts.[16]

Reading about the protests thrust Wachtel deep into study of international finance and institutions. He insisted on redirecting the IPS's international economics work from the moribund NIEO toward exploring debt and finance. While acknowledging that "debt is nothing new to the Third World," he highlighted the unprecedented levels of Global South debt.[17] In his 1977 booklet, *The New Gnomes*, Wachtel traced Third World debt to structural economic factors dating to European colonialism and to a more recent phenomenon: increased lending by multinational banks to Third World states. As Wachtel observed, in 1967, 28 percent of non–oil producing Third World countries' debts originated from private bank loans. By 1976, that number stood at 40 percent and rising.[18] The growth in private lending resulted from oil-producing countries' elites depositing large sums of money in U.S. and European banks following the 1973 OPEC oil price hike. Flush with unexpected funds, private banks lent billions to governments from Peru to Zaire. Many Third World governments were eager for these often low-interest, minimal conditions loans, as they tried to deal with sharp increases in prices for most goods resulting from higher oil and dropping commodity prices.

While governmental and private-sector elites debated the wisdom of so-called petrodollar recycling, relatively few in Global North progressive circles paid much attention, despite books and articles such as Cheryl Payer's 1974 book, *The Debt Trap*, warning about debt as a renewed form of imperialism.[19] Wachtel made it his mission to spread the word as far and wide as possible. *The New Gnomes* sold thousands of copies worldwide and was translated into four languages. Wachtel also traveled widely to promote its findings.[20] These actions helped establish the IPS as a hub for left-leaning explorations of international political economy.

Beyond questions around individual countries' debts, during the late 1970s, a small team of left-leaning economists worldwide (including Wachtel), deliberated over broader structural questions. They perceived deep changes happening in the workings of international finance. As Egyptian economist Ismaïl-Sabri Abdalla noted, the multinational banks had neither the power nor the international legitimacy to impose policy conditions on countries. They needed an international, intergovernmental body to do this. Enter the International Monetary Fund.[21] As Wachtel stated, by the late 1970s, the IMF had developed a "pre-fab austerity formula" it recommended to indebted governments across Africa, Latin America, and Asia. Wachtel compared the fund's influence to the British Empire's heyday. His colleague Michael Moffitt put it even more succinctly, calling the IMF "capitalism's new policeman."[22]

Putting these elements—debt, the growth of international finance, and the raised profile of the IMF—together, Wachtel and a few others began describing the emergent debt crisis as a bridge between eras of political economy. They argued that, as Global South countries' debts mounted, governments' policies shifted toward austerity and capitalist integration.[23] This did not seem a fluke or a temporary condition. Rather, the planet seemed to be marching toward a "reconstructed world economic order."[24]

The processes that Wachtel described—debt paving the way for neoliberal policies—became one of the most important worldwide trends of the 1980s. While individual countries (for example, Egypt) approached debt disaster throughout the 1970s, in the early 1980s, the crisis became an undeniable phenomenon. This happened from a mix of causes, including simmering financial challenges, the two major oil price hikes in the 1970s, and spikes in interest rates.

The unofficial "start" of the Third World debt crisis arrived in August 1982, when Mexico came within days of defaulting on its debts. By the end of 1982, thirty-five sub-Saharan African and Latin American states informed their creditors that they were on the edge of default.[25] The crisis only worsened in subsequent years. During the 1980s, Third World states paid $1.62 trillion in interest and repayments, while more than sixty countries experienced substantial decreases in per-capita income.[26]

Debt crises all but silenced not only demands for a New International Economic Order, but individual countries' attempts to chart development paths based on using government as more than a security net and booster of private enterprise. A microcosm of this history unfolded in Mexico, a nation that became central to debates about globalization in the 1990s. Throughout the twentieth century, the Mexican state acted as an early innovator and test subject for a myriad of economic development ideas. The Mexican Revolution bequeathed land reform as an important consideration in fighting poverty. In 1938, at the urging of labor unions and leftists, President Lázaro Cárdenas nationalized U.S. and British energy holdings. This act set important legal and policy precedents for future nationalizations around the globe. Throughout much of the century, Mexico attempted to build domestic industries through government aid and high tariffs, policies collectively known as import substitution industrialization.[27] Internationally, Mexican officials played important roles at the 1944 Bretton Woods conference, helping to shape such institutions as the World Bank and IMF. Mexican governments also asserted themselves as leaders among the Third World. In the 1970s, Mexican president Luis Echeverría became a major voice backing the NIEO.[28]

Then, in the 1980s, Mexico became a test case for neoliberalism. During most of the decade, national economic policy making centered on debt management. Desperate to reverse economic freefall, successive governments instituted harsh austerity measures along with trade liberalization and privatization. However, neither President José López Portillo nor his successor Miguel de la Madrid zealously adhered to all tenets of the liberalized capitalist gospel. Along with austerity, the Mexican state also (temporarily) nationalized its banking sector and imposed capital controls, policies not usually associated with a dedication to free markets.[29]

At the same time, Mexico experienced a new form of program administered by the IMF (and later the World Bank), one whose name quickly entered popular parlance across the Third World: structural adjustment. Structural adjustment plans called for countries to accede to dramatic changes, from privatization of state-owned industries, to liberalization of financial markets, to austerity and cuts to social welfare programs. To its proponents, the aim was clear. As the IMF executive board concluded at its meeting in 1983, "Structural adjustment called for open and liberal international markets, so that market forces could operate fully."[30]

Whether structural adjustment "worked" is the subject of ongoing scholarly and policy debate.[31] What is certain is that in such countries as Mexico, the decade of debt and austerity brought substantial increases in inequality and impoverishment. In Mexico, austerity led to a 29.6 percent cut to education and a 23.3 percent reduction in health spending.[32] Meanwhile, between 1984 and 1992, Mexico's Gini coefficient—a measure of income inequality—increased by 10.7 percent, with the number of billionaires soaring from one in 1987 to twenty-four in 1994.[33] As they often do, numbers ably obscured the lived experiences of people. In real terms, austerity meant that Martha Hernandez de Gonzalez barely scraped by, living alone in a small rural town in Chihuahua while her husband and children worked as undocumented laborers in the United States. It meant that on the outskirts of Mexico City, Gloria Bautista's two oldest children dropped out of school due to cuts to education spending, leaving them to work "odd jobs in the street" despite neither of them being "old enough to work legally."[34]

For women such as Martha Hernandez de Gonzalez or Gloria Bautista, the 1980s also saw the blossoming of one possibility for paid employment: the growth of the maquiladora sector. Starting in the 1960s with the Border Industrialization Program, Mexico courted foreign investors to establish manufacturing operations. This gave rise to the maquiladoras, factories that imported component parts and where workers produced radios, automobiles, textiles, and more for export. In a bid to earn export dollars, during the 1980s, the Mexican state offered incentives to attract foreign investment. Where in 1980 maquiladoras employed 120,000 people, by 1991, more than 460,000 workers (overwhelmingly women) marched daily in lines through dusty streets to massive warehouse buildings, often a stone's throw from the U.S. border.[35]

Spreading production processes worldwide, attracting foreign investment to impoverished regions, giving women new opportunities. To their boosters, these factories, whether in Mexico, the Philippines, or Indonesia, epitomized the benefits of neoliberal development. Indeed, maquiladoras fostered some industrialization, created some economic growth, and offered some women some social and economic opportunities.

These facts proved less impressive when contextualized. While maquiladoras boasted wages higher than the minimum, the actual costs of living, especially for families, well outpaced Mexico's low minimum wage.[36] The owners and managers of the factories' preference for hiring women flowed not from any desire for women's liberation but from misogynistic views ascribing to women physical dexterity and political docility. Abuses in sweatshops run rampant to this day, including firings for pregnancy, exposure to dangerous chemicals, and sexual harassment.[37]

Finally, maquiladoras failed to generate broader and deeper economic growth. Neoliberal aligned columnists and economists argued that, just as textile and other manufacturing had once spurred industrialization in Europe and the U.S., these processes would now happen in countries like Mexico. Yet, with multinational industries spreading out the production process, assembling goods via factories in many locations around the world, the promise that maquiladoras would catalyze the growth of other, domestically rooted industries quickly diminished or simply disappeared.[38]

In the 1980s and 1990s, however, it was an article of faith among neoliberals (and many others), that sweatshops represented an essential engine of economic growth. The "proof" cited for this assertion lay with the development successes of countries in East Asia. Where dreams of self-sufficiency had sparked imaginations across the Third World in the 1960s and 1970s, in the 1980s, aspirational gazes often turned to the "Asian Tigers." A hodgepodge of states including Singapore, South Korea, Taiwan, and Malaysia, these countries achieved incredible economic growth and social development between the 1960s and 1980s. In that time, based on a range of indicators, some leapt from "Third" to "First" World status. By the mid-1980s, a fable arose about these countries. It told the tale of how, starting after World War II, most Third World countries chose poorly by relying on government as the engine of growth. At the same time, so the fable went, the Asian Tigers chose wisely by trusting the free market.

The neoliberal fable elided many crucial explanatory details. In differing ways, the "Tigers" had all made extensive uses of government to spur and manage industrialization. Government further played a key role in promoting and propping up promising export industries. In South Korea and Taiwan, early and dramatic land reforms and investments in primary education were crucial. In Singapore, a large majority of all the housing stock was publicly built and owned. And all of these countries violently suppressed dissent.[39] But, in the early neoliberal era, such inconvenient facts did not get in the way of a good fable.

CHAPTER 10

What's This GATT?

Understanding the core moral of the neoliberal fable—embrace the free market and prosperity will follow—was easy. To dissect and comprehend the intricacies of how the new world of neoliberal governance would operate was not. During the 1980s, scattered around the world, various people tried. Among them was a familiar face in this story: Mark Ritchie. Growing up on an Iowa farm in the 1950s and 1960s, Ritchie never imagined that his life would provide key connective tissue among different eras of U.S. and even global activism, nor that he would become, in the words of one scholar, a "twentieth-century Paul Revere" of global economic governance.[1] He helped to start the Nestlé boycott, but by that campaign's (first) ending in 1984, he was ready to move on. Ritchie now returned to the questions of agriculture and economic justice that first politicized him in the late 1960s.[2] Ironically, his shift to the local would lead him on a transnational quest, ending in his becoming an early expert on a new instrument of global economic governance: the World Trade Organization.

Ritchie returned to agricultural issues at a dire moment. During the 1980s, U.S. farmers plunged into crisis, with many noncorporate farmers facing the worst slump their profession had experienced since the Great Depression. On the international stage, U.S. farmers suffered a 50 percent drop in the value of their exports between 1981 and 1986.[3] A cornucopia of causes explained this downturn, including collapsing global markets exacerbated by the Third World debt crisis. Speaking of how debt forced Third World countries to boost exports for currency, League of Rural Voters director Dixon Terry commented that "it's ironic that we are destroying rain forests in Central America to produce cattle which are then shipped to the United States putting U.S. livestock producers out of business."[4]

Ritchie viewed the stakes of the farm crises as existential. The crisis affected "not merely our weekly food bill . . . but the kind of world we will leave our children."[5] In late 1984, Ritchie decided to leave INFACT but remain in Minneapolis. He accepted a job with the state's Department of Agriculture as a farm policy analyst, specializing in international trade.

Even as his focus turned to the domestic, the experiences of the Nestlé boycott lingered in his thinking. Ritchie understood the boycott's legacy as decidedly mixed. On the plus side, its "victories laid a solid foundation for on-going efforts to challenge corporate power." Yet in looking at the substantive results of those victories, Ritchie could only conclude that they "were also quite limited." After all, the ultimate goal of the Nestlé boycott and the pesticide and pharmaceutical campaigns aimed at constructing "a long-term regulatory mechanism for transnational corporate behavior." Instead, the campaigns had become narrow fights to press companies into adhering to non–legally binding codes of conduct.[6]

While the dream of forging mechanisms to restrain global corporations appeared to be over, the idea of creating new international economic governance institutions proved quite alive—just not among public interest progressives. Ritchie discovered this truth rather unexpectedly. In his work for the Minnesota Department of Agriculture, Ritchie focused on promoting small-scale farming. As he dug into policy details and regularly communicated with federal officials, Ritchie increasingly encountered resistance to some of his ideas based on surprising grounds. "We would go to Washington and we would say we want to adopt this new kind of policy because we think it will get family farm income up and they'd say 'we can't really do that because of GATT,'" Ritchie recalled. "So we all started saying 'what's this GATT?'"[7] Answering that question soon catapulted Ritchie back into the international arena.

Answering the question "what's this GATT?" had never been more complicated than in the mid-1980s. Founded in 1949, the General Agreement on Tariffs and Trade operated as a skeleton version of John Maynard Keynes's post–World War II idea for an International Trade Organization (ITO). That vision called for an institution that would deal with commodity price fluctuations, trade disputes, and workers' rights issues, among others.[8] Failing to receive support (including from the United States), the proposal for an International Trade Organization never materialized. However, the elements of the ITO proposals dealing with tariffs and other specific trade concerns remained, thus giving rise to the GATT. In its slimmed-down form, the new organization facilitated the growth of international trade in manufactured goods. Among its accomplishments, negotiations through the GATT resulted in a drop in the average tariff on manufactured products from 40 percent in 1947 to 5 percent by the late 1990s.[9]

The GATT's mandate focused on industrial manufactured goods. Thus, when Ritchie heard "GATT" as the answer to why certain agricultural initiatives could not be pursued, this response befuddled him. After extensive research based on materials he could find in the United States, Ritchie still felt unsatisfied. Thus, in 1987, he decided to take a leap, moving to Brussels to research the GATT firsthand. Helpfully, this decision assisted two public interest campaigns at once. Ritchie's wife, Nancy Gaschott, whom he met through the Nestlé boycott, was still deeply involved in the breast-milk substitute marketing fight. At the time, she worked as a staff attorney for Action for Corporate Accountability, the group that launched the second Nestlé boycott. Gaschott could work at the International Baby Food Action Network offices located in Brussels, while Ritchie split his time between Brussels and Geneva, the location of the GATT's headquarters.[10]

In Geneva, Ritchie connected with a small circle of people also grappling with the GATT. Of these individuals, no one did more to educate left-leaning activists worldwide than Indian journalist Chakravarthi Raghavan. After decades of being a newspaperman in India, in the early 1980s, Raghavan moved to Geneva. There, he worked as editor in chief for the Special United Nations Service, a left-wing wire service covering U.N. talks relevant to the Global South. Raghavan quickly took an interest in talks occurring within the General Agreement on Tariffs and Trade. Soon, his dispatches bore the tenor of the first ominous tones of a horror film soundtrack. As early as November 1982, he warned that the United States and Western Europe appeared set on using the GATT to orchestrate "a virtual return to the early colonial era with the 'free traders and free booters' of that era being replaced by today's more powerful 'Transnational Corporations.'"[11]

Raghavan's journalism focused on calls emanating from around the world for a new and expanded series of negotiations to commence within the GATT framework. In the past, such rounds had focused on lowering tariffs or tinkering with the organization's operations. That changed in 1986, when GATT members gathered in Punta del Este, Uruguay, to kick off an eighth round of talks. Declaring "our task is more difficult than any that has confronted world trade since the very creation of GATT in 1947," U.S. trade representative Clayton Yeutter proclaimed the need not only to finish a new round of negotiations but also to widen the GATT's mandate. Yeutter advocated for bringing agriculture, services, investment, and intellectual property rights under GATT rules. Doing so was no mere desire; as Yeutter declared, "We cannot envision—nor agree to—comprehensive new trade negotiations that do not include these four issues."[12] An institution previously devoted to one facet of international trade now looked to widen its purview to oversee large swaths of economic activity and policy. In so doing, an empowered GATT would gain increased input not only into international trade but also the domestic laws of countries around the globe.

Far from a mere U.S. or Global North imposition, however, the desire to expand GATT's purview through the Uruguay Round also stemmed from some Global South sources. Governments around the world feared a rise in protectionist policies in the late 1980s that could potentially undermine hopes for recovery from the debt crisis. For Third World countries such as Côte d'Ivoire, ravaged by "the burden of debt service, the reversal of financial flows, the falling trend of raw material prices, and the difficulties of access to export markets," the rise of protectionism appeared "disastrous."[13]

Thus, the prospect of new talks at the GATT to open markets held real promise for Third World states. Moreover, many Global South leaders hoped that agreeing to new GATT rules could help them attract foreign investment, especially given the substantial gaps among Third World countries in investment levels. During the 1980s, only ten countries in the Global South received around 70 percent of all foreign direct investment.[14] Moreover, many Third World negotiators believed that new rules would actually empower them, by creating adjudication mechanisms that would generate a commonly agreed-on set of rules for all states to follow.[15]

Watching these events from the sidelines, Raghavan empathized with Global South governments. After all, their desires to open markets in the Global North and to participate in a legalistic institution that (to some degree) flattened power differentials reflected logical and important goals.[16] In his dispatches, Raghavan highlighted talks where Global South nations (and some northern ones) pushed back on demands by the United States for more liberalization. However, despite these nuances, Raghavan feared that Third World countries would lose a great deal more than they might win from agreeing to whatever resulted from the Uruguay Round.

Poking around Geneva to learn more, Ritchie met Raghavan and the two began talking. In their conversations, the issue of corporate power became the linchpin of their critiques of the Uruguay Round. Both Raghavan and Ritchie feared that rules imposed by a supercharged version of the GATT would empower multinational corporations to challenge and override government regulatory and social welfare policies. For instance, Raghavan worried that a broader GATT mandate would lead to attacks on "local content" provisions, in which countries required foreign companies to use a certain percentage of domestically produced materials in their manufacturing processes—a policy intended to support and induce domestic economic activity.[17]

To draw a simple line between corporate wishes and the eventual creation of the World Trade Organization would oversimplify matters. Many factors played into the talks.[18] Yet internal documents from major corporate lobbies illustrate their interest in the creation of a more muscular version of the GATT. Writing to the head of Pfizer in April 1985, Alex Trowbridge, then president of the National Association of Manufacturers, asserted, "There is a growing feeling in the United States, and indeed among NAM's members, that the rules of the General Agreement on Tariffs and Trade have not kept pace with the realities of international commerce."[19]

Trowbridge and other corporate leaders did not immediately call for a new international governance body. At first, they focused on getting expanded rules under the existing GATT. A document prepared by one of the most powerful U.S. corporate lobbies, the Business Roundtable, echoed U.S. government officials, seeking to place services, government procurement, and other economic questions under the GATT's purview. The Roundtable also supported the creation of new international codes of conduct to promote and protect private enterprise.[20] As the Uruguay Round began, major U.S. businesses, such as Merck, Monsanto, and Warner Communications, formed the Intellectual Property Committee to promote their goals in the Uruguay Round talks.[21]

While corporations lobbied from the outside, some of the key intellectual architects of the transformations of the General Agreement on Tariffs and Trade openly proclaimed their belief in neoliberalism—and their desires to incorporate its tenants into the revised GATT. Such individuals as Ernst-Ulrich Petersmann and Frieder Roessler, lawyers working at the GATT and important figures in the Uruguay Round talks, came into the 1980s perturbed by the fights over the NIEO and 1980s protectionism. They viewed the Uruguay Round as an opportunity to enshrine different norms of international economic governance, drawn from thinkers such as leading neoliberal Friedrich Hayek. The GATT's first director-general, Peter Sutherland, stated in 1994, "In designing a set of rules and institutions to carry out this task, the drafters of . . . the WTO drew on two of Hayek's key insights—the role of the price system . . . and the importance of the rule of law."[22]

For Ritchie, Raghavan, and others, the push to empower private commerce by creating a legal architecture that eased the ability of companies or governments to challenge other countries' laws caused worry. For example, from his work at the Minnesota Department of Agriculture Ritchie had been following an ongoing dispute between the European Community and the United States regarding growth hormones that previewed fears about the WTO. In 1985, the European Community banned six common growth hormones used in livestock, citing possible health ramifications. The United States used the GATT's dispute resolution system to challenge the European Community's ruling as a trade barrier disguised as a safety measure.[23] To Ritchie, this move by the United States represented an attack on all that public interest progressives had accomplished. "Sensing the growing concern of consumer groups everywhere . . . the U.S. government is attempting to move the power to establish these types of regulation into the international arena, where they can then be used to overturn national regulations," he predicted in May 1989.[24]

After gaining a better understanding of the GATT and the Uruguay Round, in 1988, Ritchie returned to Minneapolis. Soon he started making trouble. The U.S. Trade Representative's office blasted him in 1989 for sharing what it claimed were confidential documents about the Uruguay Round with members of the U.S. Congress.[25] Ritchie also tried to recruit the International Organization of Consumers Unions to his cause. These attempts fell short, with Ritchie in 1989 decrying "the silence of IOCU" as "deafening."[26] Ritchie soon returned to his activist roots, helping to found a new public interest group, the Institute for Agriculture and Trade Policy (IATP), which functioned as a think tank and advocacy group.

He also began reaching out globally. Articulating what he had learned over the years in a 1988 speech in Tokyo, Ritchie noted that "in the 1960s and 70s there was a popular slogan . . . 'Think globally, act locally.'" This slogan neatly summarized the philosophy that helped launch the Nestlé boycott. However, Ritchie continued, now "we are learning that we must act globally in order to solve many of our local problems." He called for "global public education campaigns . . . [and] action campaigns to change corporate and governmental policies."[27] Ritchie did not scream into the night with these words. As he well knew, such campaigns and networks were already flowering the world over.

CHAPTER 11

An Independent Voice on Behalf of the Majority

For people like Ritchie who aspired to build "new and workable alternatives" to neoliberal capitalism, finding hope during the 1980s meant looking outside the state.[1] In the Global South, the 1980s saw a blossoming of "new" social movements and NGOs. Amid these activist surges and resurgences, new networks emerged, tying distinct groups together. For fair globalizers, the story of networking and coalition building in this era often involved more thought and connection than action. Advocates pondered the new world order and the failures of the past and began reaching outside their bubbles. The middle to late 1980s thus laid the foundations for future advocacy.

Unsurprisingly, Penang served as a hub for mobilization and campaigning. Its status owed much to the tireless work of Anwar Fazal. By the mid-1980s, Fazal was a veteran of South–South and South–North networks challenging exploitative private and state power. Yet he was also a man adrift. Fazal's work while president of the International Organization of Consumers Unions to move that organization in a more progressive direction, rooted in the Global South, provoked pushback. By the early 1980s, some of the major European and U.S. consumer groups within the IOCU moved to regain control. They maneuvered the IOCU back toward a narrow agenda, as Mark Ritchie discovered. Partly in response, Fazal stepped down as president in 1984, while remaining its Asia regional head.[2]

Fazal now concentrated on nurturing a new generation of Global South activists. One of them was economist and consumer advocate Martin Khor. Born in Penang in 1951, Khor's journey to a life of social justice work took him through the social gospel he discussed as a member of the Young Christian Students to his studies at the Universiti Sains Malaysia to Cambridge University, where he earned a PhD in economics during the peak of the NIEO debates.[3] After obtaining his degree, Khor returned home to work at the Consumers

Association of Penang. There, he further refined his advocacy skills, such as "an ability to translate superficially complex texts into understandable terms" along with his approach to management, "a style of gently encouraging people to deliver their best."[4]

From his perch in Penang, Khor saw disparate activists operating in parallel to one another, often based on particular issue areas. Khor believed a broader analysis and identity was needed for people in the Global South fighting for justice. He, Fazal, CAP director S. Mohamed Idris, and others wanted to facilitate dialogues to produce an overarching Third World vision that could replace the "void on the world stage" left in the wake of the New International Economic Order's defeat.[5]

Certain that there "will be no change in the Third World until Third World peoples begin to stand up and speak for themselves," staff at CAP discussed what they could do. They envisioned building an organization modeled on the International Baby Food Action Network. This new force would devote itself to analyzing and coordinating activism across a multitude of issues besetting the Third World.[6]

Using Fazal's connections, Khor took the lead in organizing a conference, held in Penang in November 1984. Over the course of six days, eighty-five writers, academics, and activists from twenty-two countries met for the Third World: Development or Crisis? conference. By the end, participants had produced an eighty-page manifesto. The document sharply distinguished its participants' worldviews from those expressed through bodies representing Third World governments, such as the Non-Aligned Movement or the G-77. Conference attendees blasted the politics of the NIEO as an "elite dialogue." Proclaiming the NIEO "exists only in name," they outlined how Third World politics in the 1970s had failed to loosen the "industrial countries . . . stranglehold over commodities, trade, industry, and services."[7]

Deconstructing the NIEO marked only the beginning of their critiques. The document further elaborated how deeply Western ideologies and practices permeated the Third World—from sex work catalyzed by tourism to cultural homogenization. The attendees also denounced local Global South elites for facilitating such processes, often through autocratic rule.

Declaring that the "delusion of 'one model for all' must be destroyed," participants celebrated the Third World's "wide spectrum of views."[8] This spectrum included strains of thought from dependency theory, postcolonial studies, environmentalism, and Third World feminism. Given these many strands, the conference did not produce a new, singular Third World vision. Yet much agreement existed. Out of the gathering, a rough consensus emerged on the need for the development of "self-reliant economies" emphasizing eco-logical sustainability, indigenous cultural practices, and careful engagement with the world economy.

Closing out the gathering, Khor vowed to work for the "establishment of a network among NGOs in Third World countries," leading to the 1985 founding of the Third World Network (TWN).[9] Based in Penang and led by Khor, chapters of the TWN soon appeared in Asia and Africa. The network functioned (and continues to operate) as an international public interest group, parlaying influence through strategic use of its staff's expertise about international institutions and policies. The TWN targeted several constituencies, with a crucial one being negotiators from Global South governments. By producing reports, hosting seminars, and sending representatives to U.N., G-77, GATT, and other meetings, TWN staff provided alternative perspectives challenging the views propagated by the legions of multinational corporate lobbyists and Global North experts swarming such gatherings.[10]

By the late 1980s, the TWN joined an array of groups attempting to build South–South alliances. Women from across Asia, Africa, and Latin America gathered in the mid-1980s to start DAWN—Development Alternatives with Women for a New Era. This group argued that "there can be no hope of stopping gender oppression unless there is also a fight against other forms of oppression," with inequitable development policies being their central focus.[11] Policy experts and activists passionate about the intersections of ecological protection, indigenous rights, and sustainable farming founded the World Rainforest Movement. The writings and campaigning from such groups created denser connections and provided some of the main Global South public interest groups' connections to mass movements.[12]

Despite arising in the 1980s, few of these groups came into being with the specific intent of confronting neoliberalism. While the Third World Network's founding document discussed structural adjustment, many of its critiques flowed from a longer historical worldview. Yet, in the 1980s, Global South activists could not avoid increasingly reorienting their work to confront neoliberal policies and politics. Writing to Nestlé boycott leader Doug Johnson in November 1984, Costa Rican feminist Marta Trejos reflected on monitoring the WHO-UNICEF code as part of her work with the International Baby Food Action Network. While stating that her "work for IBFAN continues to be a high priority," she also noted that current events made this "ever more difficult." Trejos then described how organizing against the new conservative Costa Rican government's recent accord with the International Monetary Fund increasingly took up her time. The new austerity plan had unleashed cuts to "programs of social assistance," leaving many "brutally impoverished."[13] Such plans were a response to debt—a cause that inspired many to action.

*   *   *

A few months after the TWN's inception, Consumers' Association of Penang staffer Evelyn Hong received a letter from the United States. In it, Cynthia Obadia of the Quaker Office at the United Nations wrote about hearing of TWN's founding, which, she stated, "interested me greatly." Obadia informed Hong that she was contacting her to inquire about possibilities for collaboration "on behalf of a group which is working on the international debt situation called the 'Debt Crisis Network.'"[14]

Largely forgotten even in activist circles, the Debt Crisis Network (DCN) emerged in the 1980s as an incubator for the fair globalization coalition. Officially launched in 1985, the main force behind the DCN was the Institute for Policy Studies. After Howard Wachtel's return to teaching in 1980, the IPS brought in new staff to continue its global economics work. Among their ranks included John Cavanagh. Earnest and bright, Cavanagh became interested in international economics while interning in the summer of 1974 at the Indo-China Resource Center, an antiwar policy group. Spending time collaborating with Cambodian and Vietnamese antiwar activists, Cavanagh became fascinated and infuriated over Global North–South inequalities.

After earning a master's degree in economics from Princeton University, Cavanagh moved to Geneva in 1978 to work as a researcher, initially for the U.N. Conference on Trade and Development and then for the World Health Organization. While in Geneva, he observed corporate and governmental efforts to beat back the Nestlé boycott and campaigns by the Pesticide Action Network and Health Action International. Cavanagh not only bore witness to these fights; he lived them. During his time at the WHO, he coauthored a report on regulating international alcohol advertising. Ready in October 1982, the report instead sat on the proverbial shelf—likely suppressed due to corporate and U.S. government pressures.[15]

Frustrated by the limitations and pressures at the WHO, Cavanagh left in 1983 to work at the Institute for Policy Studies. He picked up Wachtel's work, maneuvering IPS to become a lead voice in the U.S. supporting debt reduction or cancellation and the end of immiserating World Bank and IMF austerity programs.[16] By the summer of 1984, he convened staffers from progressive think tanks, advocacy arms of mainline Protestant and Catholic churches, and antipoverty NGOs to collaborate.[17] From such meetings arose the Debt Crisis Network.

Figure 4. The Institute for Policy Studies staff, early 1980s. John Cavanagh is second from the left in the back row. Courtesy of the Wisconsin Historical Society.

Members of the DCN began by educating other progressive groups and legislators, as well as the public, about the debt crisis. To these ends, they produced memos and reports, hosted briefings, and even commissioned a comic book.[18] Network members tried to mix pragmatic policy lobbying with bigger aspirations for using the debt crisis as a chance to rewrite the rules of international finance and economic governance. Commissioned to write a report for the DCN in December 1984, staff at the Development Group for Alternative Policies urged the United States to push for major changes: increasing the power of Global South countries in the IMF and the multilateral development banks, promotion of radical land reforms, and deep reductions in military aid.[19]

The Debt Crisis Network's members pondered various techniques for affecting policy—from congressional briefings to corporate campaigns aimed at multinational banks. However, the group proved largely unable to launch sustained initiatives. Groups in the DCN tended to be policy analysis organizations. Few of them claimed the political sway necessary to enact a strategy that could pressure private banks, the IMF, or the World Bank, at least not without help. Their failures to move policy caused tensions in a network already riven with personality disputes. By 1990, the Debt Crisis Network ceased to exist.[20]

While the DCN changed few policies, it laid important groundwork. Amid many lengthy discussions, members pondered the hard reality that "it is more effective to show how the debt crisis hurts US constituents" than to try to mobilize solely around injustices overseas.[21] "Our task is to help the broadest numbers possible see that the causes of their own economic insecurity lie within the system . . . not with other victims," declared one key activist.[22]

The possibilities for organizing large numbers of people around globalization were becoming more promising in the late 1980s. As IPS staff identified in 1989, "Sweeping changes in the world economy have created a number of constituencies that are beginning to realize they must get involved in world economy issues."[23] After all, neoliberalism did not just happen "over there." In the United States during the 1980s, the assaults on labor unions, the regulatory state, and social welfare programs, while rarely called neoliberal, were manifestations of the same politics.[24]

Of all the potential constituencies in the United States to form a new political lobby, none possessed the kind of institutional power that organized labor still wielded. The history of unions' battles over the global economy is, of course, a long one. Starting in the mid-nineteenth century, U.S. unions protested "degraded labor" abroad, worrying that competition with lower-paid European workers would undermine (some) U.S. workers' standard of living.[25] While these fears occasionally led to a desire for internationalist solidarity, more often, U.S. unions' critiques of the world economy proved inseparable from defenses of white supremacy, as seen in U.S. labor backing for immigration restrictions like the Chinese Exclusion Act.[26]

Another shift happened after World War II. With the U.S. manufacturing sector dominant through the world, many unions (both leaders and members) vigorously backed expanding overseas trade. These views coupled with the strident anti-Communism emanating from much of U.S. labor's leadership. During the Cold War, the country's main coordinating body for unions—the American Federation of Labor–Congress of Industrial Organizations (AFL-CIO)—was led by figures from the more conservative ends of organized labor. This was especially the case in the International Department of the AFL-CIO, which focused the federation's efforts overseas on combating leftist and Communist-aligned trade unions in Europe and throughout the Third World more than battling multinational capitalists.[27]

The period of U.S. unions' backing for freer trade closed in the 1970s. As the United States' share of global industrial production shrank and competition from Western Europe and Japan intensified, more and more U.S. unions sought to restrain trade.[28] In the early 1970s, the AFL-CIO aligned with a substantial

number of House and Senate members to promote the Foreign Trade and Investment Act, also known as the Burke-Hartke bill. The legislation proposed a
freeze on imports at mid-1960s levels, the elimination of tax incentives for foreign
investment, and other policies to discourage outsourcing by U.S. companies.
Burke-Hartke met with intense opposition from business, the Nixon administration, and many in Congress, forces whose combined strength ensured the legislation's demise before it came to a vote.[29]

Within a few years of Burke-Hartke's defeat, large swaths of the United States
economy, especially in the Midwest, once buoyed by exports, now hollowed out.
Factories shuttered, and in their shadows arose depression and despair. For such
towns and cities as Youngstown, Ohio, and Flint, Michigan, the factories were
their economic heart.[30] Organized labor suffered major declines in membership,
with the United Auto Workers losing half its membership between 1970 and
1985.[31] Trade was not the only or even most important culprit. Increased efficiency
and new technologies lowered the number of people needed to make as great or
greater quantities of steel, textiles, or automobiles. A new climate of union busting
promoted by companies and growing parts of the Republican Party also contributed to growing inequality and job insecurity.[32] Yet trade clearly had an impact, as
seen in the phenomenon of traceable factory movement from the United States to,
in this era, countries in East Asia and increasingly Mexico.[33]

Thus, public interest progressives, small and family farmers, and unionized
workers all faced a common foe in policies of international neoliberalism. Yet,
as logical as unifying these and other liberal-leaning constituencies might have
seemed, the actual work of doing it posed intense challenges. Late 1980s U.S.
liberalism was not a healthy creature. Many tensions and contradictions of interests (or at least perceived interests) existed, leading to bad blood. These dynamics were exacerbated by the pressures of economic stagnation and the rise
of Reagan and the business lobby, which threw liberals on the defense.

Some of the starkest divides came between trade unions and certain public
interest progressives. Frequent allies, particularly in the early 1970s, by the late
1980s, decades of decline for organized labor put many unions in defensive
postures.[34] Many workers and labor leaders believed they had to side with certain business imperatives (such as opposition to environmental laws) to protect
unionized jobs. These dynamics accentuated conflicts among unions and environmentalists, who clashed over everything from logging in the Pacific Northwest to the Clean Air Act amendments of 1990.[35]

The sniping among progressive groups by no means only originated from
organized labor. Ralph Nader consistently raged against the AFL-CIO, declaring
in a December 1980 article that the "weakness and flatness of most independent

trade unions is turning them into de facto company unions."[36] Some consumer groups also angered organized labor by supporting certain deregulatory measures (as in trucking and airlines), as well as freer trade in the 1980s, believing these changes pushed against corporate consolidation and improved the lives of consumers.[37] Nor did public interest progressives feud only with labor. Conflicts also erupted between grassroots groups such as the National Welfare Rights Organization and public interest lawyers over the best tactics and strategies to achieve change.[38] Even within public interest sectors such as environmentalism, feuds over policy and tactics were common and many of these conflicts worsened in the 1980s, as all progressive constituencies found themselves constantly fighting defensive battles.[39]

Attempts to bridge these divides during the late 1970s and through the 1980s typically went poorly. One such example came in the late 1970s with the Progressive Alliance. Boasting more than a hundred member organizations, from feminists to labor to environmentalists, the Progressive Alliance was the brainchild of United Auto Workers head Douglas Fraser. It hoped to be a single voice for the broad progressive agenda. Yet, after a brief spark of promise, the Progressive Alliance fell to in-fighting and collapsed within three years. In the case of the alliance, one of the major issues stemmed from public interest groups feeling marginalized in the alliance's decision-making process by the bigger labor unions. For many other efforts, the Reagan Revolution did real harm, as progressive groups dug into their individual policy trenches to battle the ascendant conservative movement.[40]

Despite these difficult conflicts, the 1970s and 1980s were not a black hole sucking out any possibility of cooperation among liberal organizations. Naderite groups in Ohio collaborated with labor unions to fight deindustrialization and try to find alternate paths for workers.[41] Subsets of environmentalist and consumer nonprofits found room to cooperate with unions. One of the most promising examples was the Citizen Labor Energy Coalition of the late 1970s and early 1980s, which brought public interest progressives and unions together to advocate for more ecologically friendly energy production policies.[42]

By the end of the 1980s, center-left and leftist forces had been shaken the world over. Despite being in a death spiral for years, the final collapse of the Soviet Union in 1991 brought about notions of an "End to History" that signified the ultimate triumph of capitalism, now often defined as a neoliberal version of capitalism.[43] Conservatives trumpeted this narrative constantly. Thus, entering the 1990s, U.S. progressives faced a tall order. They needed to overcome their conflicts and stitch together a coalition to tackle a new and unfriendly world order.

CHAPTER 12

A Coalescing Coalition

Political coalitions do not simply emerge. They must be built. In the 1980s, the Debt Crisis Network tried but won few policy battles. However, the DCN helped move different organizations toward greater cooperation. In the first years of the 1990s, such efforts found renewed life through an injection of new organizational blood and the clarity of a big legislative fight. For nothing brings groups together like a discrete campaign with a specific end goal. In 1991, that campaign arrived with the mobilization to stop Fast Track.

To reach this point required an already nascent coalition. In late 1980s Minneapolis, Mark Ritchie threw himself into building just such a force. Eager to widen a political base of supporters for a "fair and equitable agreement at GATT," Ritchie established what he called the Fair Trade Campaign, a coalition of family farm organizations and church groups.[1] From his time with the Nestlé boycott, Ritchie possessed both critiques of and experience in coalition building that he applied to this work. Overall, he believed that the "family farm constituency" needed to be "rapidly and continuously extended from family farmers to the activist community and to progressive citizens."[2]

Simultaneously, in Washington, D.C., the public interest progressive community began to pay attention to the Uruguay Round and broader questions of international economic governance. By 1990, "trade" started rolling off the tongues of a small but expanding clique of public interest progressives. Somewhat surprisingly, the first major attempt in Washington, D.C. to bring such groups together originated from within the National Wildlife Federation (NWF).

Why was this surprising? The NWF represented a peculiar kind of public interest progressive institution. Founded in 1936, it did not start as a Washington, D.C., lobby. Rather, it emerged as an organization bringing preservationists, conservation-minded hunters, and more together around saving animal species and "natural" places. However, as with many older conservation groups, in the 1960s and 1970s the NWF built up a presence in Washington as a professionalized lobby. It cultivated a reputation for being uncontentious, a tack that helped it reach a membership in the millions by 1983. In the 1980s, the federation's leadership also embraced certain neoliberal tenets. NWF's president at the time, Jay Hair, sought to make environmentalism more mainstream, looking to collaborate with the "free enterprise system" as a "full and equal partner."[3]

Even as Hair promoted NWF's moderation, a few staff took on controversial campaigns. Beginning in the early 1980s, in coordination with other major U.S. environmental NGOs, the federation's small international department participated in a campaign targeting the World Bank and other multilateral development banks. They criticized these institutions for engaging in socially and ecologically destructive lending practices. As U.S. advocates worked globally, exposure to activists from other countries tended to shift their international staffs toward embracing more systemic and left-of-center views. By 1991, U.S. greens could point to substantial accomplishments, including the World Bank's creation of an environmental department and an independent Inspection Panel.[4]

One of the people in the NWF's international department, Stewart Hudson, wanted to do more. His time on the development banks' campaign acculturated him to think about global economic governance.[5] In the spring of 1989, he started convening semiregular meetings of the Ad Hoc Working Group on Trade and Environmentally Sustainable Development.[6] The working group opened the doors to formal coalition building. Hudson brought various actors together, from the United Food and Commercial Workers union, to the National Farmers Union, to Friends of the Earth.[7]

In early 1991, a new person started attending the meetings, one who would go on, as much as anyone, to make international economic governance a hot button issue in U.S. politics: Lori Wallach. Born in a small town in northern Wisconsin, Wallach grew up as one of the only Jewish kids around. Bullied by some peers, she learned to be scrappy, recalling after one fight in school her mother telling her to "kick your enemies and pick your friends; no one should feel neutral about you."[8] These words would serve as a guiding principle for Wallach from that point forward.

After graduating from Wellesley College, Wallach stayed in Massachusetts to attend Harvard Law School. Already identifying as a progressive, Wallach dove into a mobilization to prevent the shuttering of Harvard Law School's public interest counseling office. These efforts connected Wallach with staff at

Public Citizen, the flagship of Ralph Nader's public interest fleet. These connections, ironically, did the work the counseling office should have. Soon, lawyers at Public Citizen offered Wallach a fellowship at the organization's renowned Litigation Group. In the spring of 1990, Wallach became a staff attorney at Public Citizen's Congress Watch division.[9]

There, Wallach received the charge of following matters of food safety and the "human environment." Attending congressional hearings, she took note of repeated references to the General Agreement on Tariffs and Trade, as well as to an upcoming North American free trade deal. Wallach grew frustrated with her fellow consumer advocates' lack of interest in international issues, with one exception: Mark Ritchie. Hearing of a fellow Midwesterner also fixated on the GATT, she reached out to him and found her suspicions validated—and a long-term work partnership began.[10]

Wallach started pressing her boss, Congress Watch director Michael Waldman, to allow her to spend more time on global economies. Eventually, her prodding resulted in an audience with Ralph Nader himself. Nader still wielded significant influence in Washington, D.C. While winning proactive victories during the Reagan years proved difficult, public interest progressives, with Nader by far their most recognizable spokesperson, cemented themselves as a powerful voice of opposition.[11]

Accompanied by Waldman, Wallach went to Nader's office, filled to the rafters with binders and papers. Sitting at his desk, Nader turned to Wallach and in his gruff, eternally skeptical tone asked her if she really believed that corporations were "using trade agreements to launch what I believe you are calling a 'sneak attack' on consumer regulations and the democratic process." Wallach froze. An effusive individual, she could not discern whether Nader's tone indicated dismissive disbelief or weary acknowledgment. After a pause, she decided to push ahead, declaring, "You're Ralph Nader! I assume you already know all of this. You probably knew that a year before everyone else. I'm glad I finally caught up. What're we going to do about it?" Nader sat for a moment and then looked to Waldman, stating with a smile, "You can go," while asking Wallach to stay and strategize.[12]

Starting with that meeting, Wallach's work portfolio shifted to emphasize international economics. As part of her new focus, she began attending the Ad Hoc Working Group's meetings. Wallach soon grew dispirited. She felt that the gatherings spent too much time pondering and not enough acting. At one point, Wallach told its convener, Stewart Hudson, that "you people don't know how to run a campaign."[13] Wallach herself recounts an early meeting where she "took off [her] shoes, stood on one of the big chairs . . . and said 'Anyone who is interested in actually figuring out how to help [a] political campaign about this issue, see me in the corner.'"[14] Her insistence helped to catalyze coalition building; as Friends of the Earth international staffer Alex Hittle commented, she "took the bull by the horns, got people up and running, counting votes."[15] Wallach also benefited from her position at Public Citizen. Despite the group's clashes over the years with various liberal constituencies, it had also participated in pro-labor, pro–family farm, and pro-environmental struggles. Public Citizen thus possessed sufficient prestige and influence that it could serve as what sociologist Michael Dreiling calls a "bridging organization."[16]

Wallach's sense of urgency owed much to the need for a united front by early 1991. For the first legislative battle in the new globalization wars rapidly approached. This fight would not be over a substantive piece of policy but rather a procedural measure called Fast Track. An innovation of the Nixon administration, Fast Track limited (and still limits) Congress's ability to alter trade agreements. Unlike most legislation, where members of Congress may offer amendments, Fast Track largely eliminates that process. Instead, once government-to-government talks conclude on a trade deal, Congress receives a simple choice: yea or nay.[17]

Subject to frequent renewals, Fast Track would next expire in June 1991. For the administration of George H. W. Bush, obtaining Fast Track authority seemed essential.[18] With the Cold War over, the Bush administration sought to secure U.S. hegemony. Tightened and expanded global economic relations offered one such path, especially as a way for the United States to reassert its standing not just militarily (which it had done with the Gulf War) but also economically.[19]

Thus, in March 1991, the administration commenced its renewal campaign. Over the next months, Bush stumped for the legislation, declaring, "If we lose this Fast Track authority, we lose any hope of achieving these . . . vital agreements."[20] Many in the international economic law and business community agreed. Writing to Wallach and Ritchie, one foundation head described a symposium he attended "of corporate lawyers, law professors, and government trade officials" during which he was "struck by how concerned this large group . . . was for the future of fast track."[21]

Befitting the newer, more holistic types of international economic arrangements symbolized by the Uruguay Round, the Bush administration acknowledged that "issues not typically addressed in trade agreements" were being raised in negotiations.[22] Speaking those words was Carla A. Hills, the head of the Office of the U.S. Trade Representative, which would soon become among the fair globalization coalition's main antagonists. Established in 1962, the office's mandate expanded during the 1970s. The office became the main policy shop for coordinating U.S. international economic engagement, with its head acting as "principal advisor and chief spokesperson to the President on international trade policy."[23]

Hills recognized that free trade was becoming increasingly controversial. Speaking to the president of Colombia only a few days before Bush officially asked Congress for Fast Track renewal, Hills cautioned that anyone who might think "this is a situation where we ask and Congress acts, this is not the case."[24]

Confirming Hills's worries, one week after Bush's March 1 request, the chairpersons of the House Ways and Means and Senate Finance committees, Democrats Dan Rostenkowski and Lloyd Bentsen, wrote to President Bush. Although both men backed Fast Track, they warned of mounting opposition in Congress. They knew that many of their colleagues were pondering issues only recently being incorporated into trade talks, including environmental standards, health and safety concerns, and labor rights. They requested that the administration deliver by May 1, 1991, an "action plan" answering criticisms about labor, environment, and consumer safety.[25] The deadline gave the Bush administration roughly six weeks to allay these concerns.[26]

The growing skepticism in Congress owed much to the work of public interest advocates and their allies. Soon after Wallach began challenging the Ad Hoc Working Group, Stewart Hudson dropped his and the National Wildlife Federation's role in it. Wallach and Public Citizen soon assumed leadership over the group. Their first task was to convince some of the participants to jump onboard the Fast Track fight. Many advocates were not paying attention, with Mark Ritchie admitting that he "didn't even think about a fast-track fight, partly because I think I expected . . . that fast-track would never be . . . an issue" that generated controversy.[27] Fast Track was just the kind of boring, administrative procedure that public interest progressives studied closely, understood as a crucial political battleground, and had experience turning into a vibrant political fight. As Ritchie reflected, Wallach made a major contribution by bringing "the perspective of the Nader good government" forces to the campaign.[28]

Even as the Bush administration and some public interest groups mobilized, a shared question dangled before them all. Both sides knew that Fast Track's passage hinged in large part on two major constituencies: organized labor and large environmental lobbies. The trade unions seemed a lost cause for the pro–Fast Track side. During the Reagan-Bush years, despite implementing some protectionist measures, these administrations leaned more into policies promoting deindustrialization and undermining unions. Labor tried to push back. In 1987, for instance, the AFL-CIO fought a losing battle for legislation to ameliorate factory closings.[29] Recent GOP trade politics, combined with the overall increasingly hostile relationship between unions and the Republican Party, made the Bush administration winning over labor an impossibility. "The center of the debate is over who is going to get hurt and who is going to be helped," stated AFL-CIO secretary treasurer Tom Donahue, adding the victims would clearly be "the workers of the United States."[30]

Organized labor's opposition to Fast Track did not mean it would collaborate with other foes. Many in the labor hierarchy wanted to maintain their own party line and political connections. As United Food and Commercial Workers lobbyist Segundo Mercado-Llorens (who *did* work closely with public interest groups) later recalled, many labor leaders "were leery of getting involved with environmental groups" because of past disputes. "And they were no particular friends of Ralph Nader's," he added.[31] Thus, while specific unions and union officials coordinated with the nascent fair globalization coalition, much of U.S. organized labor waged a parallel struggle.

While courting labor was a nonstarter for the Bush administration, picking off some environmentalists from the anti–Fast Track coalition appeared plausible. Recognizing that the "environment is going to be a big issue," several staffers at the Environmental Protection Agency made the case that environmentalists' demands around trade "create an opportunity for us."[32] This message fit Bush's 1988 electoral promise to be the "environmental president." Unlike most of today's Republican Party, in the late 1980s, a substantial number of GOP members identified as environmentalists. This meant that Republicans could still win the confidence of certain green lobby groups.[33] Bush counted on his EPA director, William Reilly, to accomplish this. A Republican conservationist, Reilly served in the Nixon administration, working on environmental issues. During the mid-1980s, he became president of one of the nation's largest green groups, the Conservation Society.[34]

Reilly recognized that he did not have to win over the entire environmental community. More left-leaning groups, such as Friends for the Earth, which decried Fast Track as a "virtual license to kill environmental protections," could not be swayed.[35] Even moderate groups sided with anti–Fast Track forces at first. However, Reilly's familiarity with the U.S. environmental community gave him an "in." He singled out Jay Hair, president of the NWF, whom he knew from his days at the Conservation Society, as a promising target.

During the next two months, leaders from moderate green lobbies met with members of Congress and the Bush administration. In these discussions, representatives from several big environmental groups (such as the NWF and the Environmental Defense Fund [EDF]) came away feeling that the administration took their concerns seriously. These large public interest groups were accustomed to working within the system. The Bush administration's entreaties seemed promising after years spent in the policy desert of Reaganism.

The hook for some green groups to alter their positions came with the release on May 1, 1991 of a White House letter outlining the administration's plans to address regulatory and labor issues in future trade talks.[36] The proposal mixed vague pronouncements with concrete offerings. It stated that the U.S. would "not agree to weaken U.S. environmental and health and safety laws and regulations" and assured the "design . . . of an integrated plan to clean up the U.S.-Mexico border" as part of any future U.S.-Mexico trade deal. Most concretely, the plan spoke to public interest groups' long-standing demands for input into policy making by promising to place two green representatives on each of six different advisory committees.[37]

For groups within the emerging fair globalization coalition, the Bush letter created a "choose your own adventure" moment. Most public interest groups and unions viewed the May 1 plans as "wholly inadequate" and a "docile dog."[38] Yet a few major environmental groups (such as the NWF and EDF) disagreed. For them, the letter proved sufficient to win their public endorsement. Jay Hair took to the *New York Times*' opinion page, boasting, "For the first time in free trade history, an environmental review will be part of the negotiations."[39] Concurrently, other groups, such as the Natural Resources Defense Council, did not openly support Fast Track but muted their criticism, stating that they were "disinclined to block pursuit of new agreements on a procedural vote."[40] The split among the greens offered a scaffolding for wavering Democratic members of Congress to support Fast Track. Other Democrats swung due to administration promises to assist in protecting industries in their districts, such as by barring Japanese firms from placing bids on federally financed construction projects.[41]

The most important argument to win over wavering Republicans and Democrats focused on procedure, not policy. "The fast track process has proved workable and highly successful in past trade negotiations because of active and regular consultations . . . and we fully intend for that to be the case with the Uruguay Round [and] NAFTA," promised Carla Hills in letters to members of Congress.[42] The Bush administration's lobbying efforts climaxed on May 23, 1991, with Fast Track's passage. Over 85 percent of congressional Republicans voted for the measure, along with a strong minority of Democrats, with the House voting 231 to 192 in favor of Fast Track. The Senate followed the next day, voting 59 to 36 in support.[43]

The nascent fair globalization coalition lost its first fight, but this was not a discouraging result. Few had expected Fast Track to encounter any hurdles at all. Now, the previously "unthinkable" notion that either or both the Uruguay Round and NAFTA could fail seemed a distinct possibility.[44] However, expressions of optimism were necessarily tempered. Many questions remained: when would either GATT or NAFTA land in Congress's lap? Would the environmental community split again? Would disparate lobbies be able to better coordinate? As Wallach noted in a late July 1991 letter, only one certainty existed: that many "angst-laden weeks" lay ahead.[45]

*   *   *

The Fast Track fight opened a new period of struggle in the United States over the world economy's governance. During the 1980s, public interest progressives watched as their already modest hopes to constrain global capitalism and improve the livelihoods of millions disappeared. The death of the New International Economic Order and the eruption of the debt crisis ended (at least for a while) the possibilities of Third World governments spearheading reforms. With blame for the Global South's travails pinned by many elites (and others) not on legacies of colonialism or neoimperialism but rather on Third World governments' overreach, the door opened for neoliberals "to lock-in the deregulatory trade policies that many countries adopted in the 1980s."[46]

By the early 1990s, public interest progressives recognized this reality. In the late 1980s and early 1990s, advocates strived to understand the mechanisms and institutions by which neoliberalism was coming into existence. They also appreciated that, alone, the public interest advocacy community could never beat back the rise of neoliberalism. The fight to block Fast Track offered a first test of whether unions, environmentalists, consumer groups, farmers' organizations, and think tanks could pool their resources.

With Fast Track, these constituencies started coordinating to combat the same enemies. To become an actual coalition, however, required much more work—work that needed to happen fast. As advocates regrouped after Fast Track's passage, the Uruguay Round and North American Free Trade Agreement talks continued "rushing forward at a whirlwind place."[47] By the summer of 1992, clarity arrived: the next fight would be over the future of North American economic relations.

PART IV

We Fought Big Against
NAFTA and Lost

CHAPTER 13

What Do You All Export?

January 15, 1991, seemed a suboptimal day to host a congressional briefing devoted to "Opening Up the Debate: Agricultural, Environmental, and Labor Dimensions of North American Integration." After all, war in the Middle East seemed imminent. Five months earlier, Iraqi dictator Saddam Hussein's military had stormed into neighboring Kuwait, occupying the oil-rich kingdom. Months of negotiations followed, as a massive international military coalition assembled on Kuwait's borders. In late November 1990, the U.N. Security Council endorsed a resolution setting January 15, 1991, as the deadline for Saddam's regime to withdraw its troops. Now that the day had arrived, no one knew what would happen.[1]

Meanwhile, in a hearing room on Capitol Hill, Mark Ritchie and Pharis Harvey of the International Labor Rights and Education Fund waited nervously. Harvey's wife brewed enough coffee to caffeinate about a hundred people. Then a minor miracle happened. By the time the event began, they found it impossible to caffeinate everyone. In the end, over four hundred people—public interest advocates, trade lawyers, congressional staffers, and more—packed the hearing room. Attendees heard U.S., Canadian, and Mexican advocates detail the many pitfalls that accompanied a possible North American free trade accord.[2]

The battle that emerged over the North American Free Trade Agreement in the first years of the 1990s illustrated just how heated the politics of free trade could be. In the annals of conflagrations over the U.S. engagement with the world economy, few policies inspired as much raw conflict or public attention as NAFTA.[3] During the debate over congressional approval, NAFTA regularly appeared on the front pages of major newspapers, inspired sketches on *Saturday Night Live*, inflamed grassroots passions across the political spectrum, and generated combined spending by all sides in the tens of millions of dollars.[4]

Fair globalizers saw the North American Free Trade Agreement as a promising target in trying to stem the tide of neoliberalism. Battling NAFTA would allow advocates to make international economic governance questions more concrete for millions of people. Instead of discussions around abstractions such as the "Third World" or the "global economy," focusing on NAFTA meant talking about jobs and regulations at home and foreign investment's effects on people in a single Global South country: Mexico. Moreover, unlike the fights against Nestlé and other companies in the 1970s and 1980s, the battle of NAFTA would happen in the halls of the U.S. Congress. This meant that public interest progressives and their allies would engage on a familiar battlefield. Since NAFTA would affect so many different constituencies, fair globalizers would also have long lists of new potential allies. The conditions for victory seemed ripe.

The campaign against NAFTA facilitated the coalescing of the fair globalization coalition into an assertive policy and political force, one with institutions specifically devoted to the cause. The Debt Crisis Network, the Fair Trade Campaign, the Ad Hoc Working Group, and the mobilization to stop Fast Track started this process. Combating NAFTA, however, necessitated creating new institutions, forging common language and positions, and figuring out how to mobilize to win.

Widening the coalition also brought new limitations. The internationalist orientation of the 1970s and 1980s public interest campaigns dimmed, replaced by a louder focus on neoliberalism's effects within the United States of America, especially job outsourcing. In some rhetorical constructions, the Third World became the opponent—a nebulous "other" whose low labor and environmental standards facilitated the "race to the bottom." Moreover, while the Nestlé boycott or the Debt Crisis Network's agitation highlighted alternative paths for governing the world economy, in fighting NAFTA, the overwhelming focus fell on just saying "no."

The relative parochialism of the NAFTA fights has garnered much criticism over the years from activists and scholars. Critics accuse much of the U.S. progressive opposition to NAFTA of embracing an essentially nationalist politics, one that did not live up to the higher values and imperatives of transnational solidarity.[5] There is much truth to this take. When progressives in the U.S. lambasted NAFTA because it shuttered factories or infringed on national sovereignty, they operated on a rhetorical playing field friendly to nationalist, nativist, and sometimes outright white supremacist political projects. However, it would be simplistic to see U.S. progressives as simply reactionary, even if unintentionally. For such critiques downplay the complex interrelationships at work between domestic and internationalist politics seen in the NAFTA fight.

Understanding these links begins with a short anecdote. In his history of solidarity between U.S. and Latin American leftists, scholar Steve Striffler notes an "oft-told story in solidarity circles." The story goes as follows: U.S. activists ask their Latin American comrades how people in the United States can best aid Latin American liberation struggles. The response tends to be some variation on the following: "The best thing Americans can do is change things in the United States, fix your own country and government."[6]

To varying extents and depending on different groups and individuals, members of the fair globalization coalition followed this advice. As we shall see, many organizations did, to varying extents, espouse internationalism. Perhaps more importantly, the groups forming the fair globalization coalition represented one of the few liberal-left voices in U.S. politics during the 1990s with any real sway on matters of political economy. By helping to prop up the voices of more populist and progressive elected Democrats and by bringing together different progressive constituencies, the fair globalizers helped keep U.S. liberalism on life support. They also worked to slow the encroachment of neoliberalism into Mexico. Some of this work also seeded future internationalism. Some of it did not. All of it contributed to ushering in a new era of debate over the future of global economic governance.

*   *   *

The notion of a free trade pact covering North America germinated for decades before anyone seriously tried to make it happen. In announcing his presidential candidacy in November 1979, Ronald Reagan spent several paragraphs talking about a "North American accord."[7] However, little follow-up happened, as Mexico spent the 1980s grappling with its debt crisis and the Reagan administration tackled other priorities. Then, on February 1, 1990, one meeting highlighted a new phase in hemispheric economic relations.

The occasion was the World Economic Forum, a multiday mix of galas and academic conference for the international economic and political elite, held annually at an exclusive ski resort in Davos, Switzerland.[8] Among the attendees that year was Mexican president Carlos Salinas de Gortari. Salinas arrived in Geneva anxious. The political party he headed, the Partido Revolucionario Institucional (Institutional Revolutionary Party, or PRI), had ruled Mexico since 1929. However, given the party's record of decades of corruption, repression, and autocracy fused with the austerity of the 1980s, it now faced a profound crisis of legitimacy.[9]

The Mexican populace rightfully distrusted the PRI and Salinas in particular. In 1988, he ascended to the presidency under almost comically dubious circumstances. Polls in the lead up to that year's presidential election showed left-wing opposition candidate Cuauhtémoc Cárdenas with a notable lead. Then, on election day, a computer glitch shut down the vote count for a week. When the PRI government finally announced the vote tally, it declared Salinas the winner.[10] Once in office, he dedicated himself to restoring the PRI's strength by deepening neoliberal economic reforms. Salinas prided himself on his ability to lead Mexico to "anticipate the change" sweeping the world economy.[11]

To win in the new world order, he believed Mexico needed to embrace "the great world movement toward free trade" by signing an accord with the United States.[12] This move would, as Salinas later told President George H. W. Bush, "consolidate the new policies for a market-oriented economy," by tying Mexican domestic policy to international agreement. Salinas believed this would incentivize foreign investors to invest in Mexico, confident the government could not heavily regulate or nationalize their businesses.[13] Here was neoliberal governance in action—the push for international agreements designed to protect private industries and capitalist prerogatives. At Davos, along with his secretary of commerce and industrial development, Jaime Serra Puche, Salinas pitched the idea of a free-trade deal to U.S. trade representative Carla Hills. This was the moment when talks over NAFTA became a reality.[14]

It took two years of intense negotiations to hammer out the North American Free Trade Agreement's text. Although bearing the moniker "free trade," NAFTA's provisions extended well beyond the realms of tariffs and quotas. Of twenty-two chapters, only the first five dealt primarily with the elimination of tariffs and other barriers to trade in physical goods. The remaining seventeen chapters concerned NAFTA's purview over other economic sectors, including agriculture, financial services, government procurement, intellectual property rights, and investor protections.

NAFTA's policies reflected the fact that, as leading international business scholar Alan Rugman noted, "The business sector was not just consulted, it wrote the agenda."[15] NAFTA boosted many businesses in various ways, from tightened patent protections to investor-state dispute settlement. The later provision was particularly notable as an expansion of corporate powers. Under NAFTA, a U.S. company (for example) could sue the Mexican or Canadian government via a parallel, international judicial system if the U.S. company felt a Canadian or Mexican law unfairly targeted the U.S. company. NAFTA also promoted business by calling for "national treatment," which limited governments' ability to treat foreign companies differently from domestic ones and by pushing for the opening of previously closed industries, such as Mexico's financial sector, to foreign direct investment. However, NAFTA did not upend every sector, excluding certain sensitive ones, such as Mexico's petroleum sector or Canada's cultural industries.[16]

NAFTA's importance did not stem from its originality. Its calls for tariff cuts echoed processes of greater free trade enacted through bilateral and multilateral agreements and through the General Agreement on Tariffs and Trade. Its investment protections followed in and built on the footsteps of numerous bilateral investment treaties that dated back to 1959.[17] NAFTA's novelty instead derived from amalgamation. Placing so many provisions previously scattered across many agreements inside the same text marked a major step forward in policy making. NAFTA, in effect, would serve as a leap forward in building a global economy governed on neoliberal principles.[18]

*   *   *

NAFTA looks even less novel considering it grew out of the United States–Canada Free Trade Agreement, signed in 1989. Although little noticed in the United States, in Canada, this deal sparked a raucous political fight. On the progressive left, many agreed with famed *Handmaid's Tale* author Margaret Atwood that the agreement possessed "the potential to fragment and destroy the country in a way that nothing else has succeeded in doing."[19] Atwood joined with fellow Canadians to form a fair globalization coalition consisting of unions, public interest groups, farmers, and sympathetic legislators known as the Action Canada Network. Throughout 1987 and 1988, Canadian progressives battled the U.S.-Canada agreement, from lobbying in Parliament to blockading border crossings with tractors. However, these efforts proved futile. With the pro–free trade Progressive Conservative Party holding a majority in Parliament, the agreement passed easily.[20]

In Canada, the fight over free trade went directly to questions of national identity. To be a Canadian patriot in the late twentieth century (for many) meant taking pride in a legacy of social democracy. More pointedly, this form of Canadian pride contrasted values of solidarity against the individualism and greed associated with the United States.[21] Canadian anti–free trade activists launched creative protests asserting their national pride. Such actions included placing U.S. flags over Canadian ones at a trade summit and rewriting Woody Guthrie's most famous ballad with the lyrics:

This land is your land, this land is my land
Despite Mulroney and Reagan's grand plan
We'll fight this free trade, we won't be betrayed
We'll stay Canadian, you and me![22]

Among the Canadian anti–free trade champions, perhaps the most notable was Maude Barlow. Already renowned in Canada as a powerful feminist voice, during the 1980s, she became chair of the Council of Canadians (a large public interest lobby) and a leader in the Action Canada Network. From those positions, she became the public face and a key strategist against free-trade accords.[23] A committed Canadian patriot, Barlow also identified as an internationalist. In the late 1980s and early 1990s, she warned colleagues in North America that the passage of the U.S.-Canada pact offered elites the "power to move to the next step"—a continental free-trade agreement.[24] Barlow worked closely with Tony Clarke, a veteran Christian progressive activist. During the fight, Barlow and Clarke reached out to U.S. activists like Ralph Nader for assistance, but received little.[25]

Barlow found more receptive partners almost three thousand miles to the south. In Mexico, discussions over NAFTA intensified struggles surrounding economic policy and national identity. The battle lines here were encapsulated in a 1991 meeting. Granted a rare audience with a high official—Jaime Serra Puche—a group of Mexican independent unionists, farmer organizers, and policy researchers entered Serra Puche's office. There they waited. Eventually, Serra Puche walked in and sat at his desk. Looking the activists over, he asked, "What do you all export?" knowing that none of them were businesspeople. A long silence ensued. Then, according to one participant, left-leaning economist Carlos Heredia, an activist, looked at Serra Puche and replied to his question: "Un chingo de Mexicanos" (millions of fucking people).[26]

This retort both skewered Salinas's promise that NAFTA would improve the Mexican economy (and thus slow undocumented immigration) and demonstrated the growing spirit of resistance found on the Mexican left. Austerity and the rise of foreign-owned factories in the 1980s bred despondency, but they also spurred agitation. Although Mexico's state-recognized labor movement acted as an adjunct to the PRI government, independent unions became a node of opposition. Unauthorized "wildcat" strikes joined with actions taken by the independent Frente Auténtico del Trabajo (the Authentic Labor Front, or FAT) to inject vibrancy into the Mexican worker struggle and reassert a Mexican identity premised partly on anti-imperialism.[27]

As Salinas's free-trade agenda pushed forward, budding networks of Mexican farmers, policy analysts, independent unionists, and others began to respond.

Helping to catalyze their movement were warnings arising from Canadian colleagues. Mexican leftists heeded these calls based, in part, on decades-old relationships forged through solidarity around labor rights and support for peace and justice in Central America.[28] In early October 1990, twenty-seven Canadian activists, including Maude Barlow, traveled to Zacatecas, Mexico, for the Social Organizations Facing Free Trade meeting. Different as their countries were, Mexican and Canadian activists found commonalities, mainly regarding their shared concerns about the superpower lying in between their borders. In their Final Declaration, activists declared that the "people of Canada and of Mexico, have . . . suffered under the aggressive . . . neo-liberal policies of the United States." Vowing that Canadian and Mexican workers "will not act like strikebreakers for anybody" (meaning they refused to be pitted against one another), the activists proclaimed their intent to "raise our voices against . . . free trade agreements."[29]

Out of these conversations, unionists at the FAT led the way in stringing together the Red Mexicana de Acción Frente al Libre Comercio (the Mexican Free Trade Action Network, or RMALC), launched in April 1991. Its members included the FAT, individual academics and activists, women's groups, farmers' organizations, and more. RMALC believed that enhanced trade with the United States and Canada *could* spur improvements in social welfare. But such an agreement would need to "acknowledge the inequalities among the economies" of the signatory countries. This meant debt cancellation, no privatization of social welfare programs, stringent environmental protections, and democratized Mexican trade unions, among other policies.[30]

RMALC organizers approached their work mindful of the severe limitations they faced. Despite possessing some trappings of a democratic state, Mexico remained under the rule of an autocratic government. Thus, even RMALC's requests that the Mexican government offer some transparency regarding negotiations proved radical in their own way and were rebuffed. However, their relative powerlessness also freed RMALC leaders to think about building a movement working over a longer time horizon for democracy and economic justice.[31]

Simultaneously however, the participants at the Social Organizations Facing Free Trade gathering wanted to stop NAFTA. To do so necessitated connecting with partners in the United States. As one of RMALC's founders, Carlos Heredia, explained, combating NAFTA meant Mexican NGOs and social movements needed to "increasingly work with partners in other countries."[32] For, if nothing else, they recognized that as one RMALC memo stated, "whether or not there will be an FTA [free trade agreement] depends on their [the U.S. government's] decision."[33]

CHAPTER 14

New Schisms and New Alliances

Throughout the NAFTA fight, Canadian and Mexican activist leaders, such as Maude Barlow and Carlos Heredia, traveled regularly to the United States for meetings and speaking tours.[1] In making the rounds, they and their compatriots dealt with two distinct networks representing the U.S. fair globalization coalition. Here was but one example of how the NAFTA fight scrambled lines of division across vast swaths of the U.S. political spectrum—from public interest progressives to conservatives to the Democratic Party.

Many reasons accounted for the existence of two fair globalization factions. One central dividing line between the different networks emerged over how each conceptualized the time spans they were working within. Was fighting NAFTA one episode in a years- or decades-long struggle, in which case the emphasis should go toward the slow work of developing and spreading big ideas and organizing mass social movements? Or were fair globalizers in an immediate fight to win a discrete battle that they hoped would translate into larger changes? How one answered these questions helped to determine which of two networks would seem more appealing in fighting NAFTA: the Alliance for Responsible Trade (ART) or the Citizens Trade Campaign (CTC).

The Alliance for Responsible Trade grew from the ashes of the Debt Crisis Network and the Mobilization on Development, Trade, Labor, and the Environment. In all three of these organizations, John Cavanagh played a leading role. The primary ART members were policy research nonprofits, such as the Development Group for Alternative Policies and the International Labor Rights Education and Research Fund.[2] Steeped in discussions of Global North-South relations and equitable development, these groups feared NAFTA's implications for North American political economy, particularly in Mexico. They looked askance at talk of the "national interest," a term they contended only spoke to "the interests of an elite few." IPS staff argued that U.S. anti-NAFTA activists needed a "globalist perspective [which] fundamentally opposes racism and chauvinism."[3] Otherwise, they believed, opposition to NAFTA could slip into reactionary and nationalist assertions.

The internationalist lens changed how ART activists approached the fight. From a Mexican perspective, fighting NAFTA marked a next stage in a long story. To Mexican leftists, NAFTA appeared as a predictable sequel to the structural adjustment agenda begun at least as early as 1982.[4] Learning from Mexican activists in RMALC, many members of ART argued for patience and long-term thinking in confronting NAFTA. For them, the fight was not just against an agreement but a whole neoliberal political project.

Flowing from this position, ART groups did not see defeating NAFTA as a battle to prevent the end times. While they advocated against the agreement, some in ART also argued that too many progressives placed "an excessive focus on the outcome of the NAFTA vote itself." They viewed NAFTA as a neoliberal propellant but reminded their compatriots that blocking the agreement "would not in itself have halted . . . economic integration."[5]

Based on this analysis, ART members cautioned against an anti-NAFTA campaign based on saying "no." They asserted that framing the campaign only as "against" NAFTA or neoliberalism meant operating on the "premise of defeat." In other words, a solely negative effort tacitly accepted the false notion that progressives had no positive program of their own. Instead, ART groups demanded that progressives "develop an alternative that goes beyond a critique or that simply aims to be an amendment to the proposed NAFTA."[6]

ART members insisted that U.S.-based activists collaborate with Mexican and Canadian representatives to write a joint statement envisioning a just economic integration. In rolling out such a vision, ART members insisted that "people who *are + will be* affected" should be at the center of the conversation.[7] They consistently sought input from Canadian and Mexican partners about what issues the U.S. groups should deal with—or deal with better.[8] Commitments to egalitarianism did not always equate with successes in enacting those values. For instance, several meetings occurred in which Mexican groups felt disrespected or undervalued, as they sent the presidents and executive directors of their organizations while U.S. NGOs dispatched lower-level staffers.[9] However, the Mexican groups did not stay silent. ART members tried to learn from and better address such inequalities. Thus, ART slowly gained trust and recognition as the more "internationalist" U.S. network.[10]

While ART members imagined a different world, CTC members zeroed in on the question of whether they could they stop NAFTA in the U.S. Congress. Whereas ART included many groups without large memberships, the CTC's ranks included major unions, environmental and consumer groups, farmers' organizations, and others with sizable memberships.[11] With groups such as Public Citizen at the head, the CTC mounted what author and activist David Ranney calls a "classic public interest campaign."[12] This meant a focus on Washington, D.C., and mobilizing around Congress specifically. The CTC's approach stemmed from a simple power analysis: only "if we really threaten an agreement's passage or kill one" would fair globalizers' voices gain the "leverage and political space" necessary to advance a different agenda.[13]

CTC groups looked skeptically at ART's desire to elaborate a competing trade plan in the midst of the NAFTA fight because, to them, clarity equaled coalition. Delving into specific ideas for a "different" NAFTA could easily alienate potential allies. This dynamic especially appeared in discussions over a NAFTA "social charter." An idea floated by some in the ART orbit and some members of Congress, the social charter looked to mimic the European Community policies by which new entrants received significant economic aid, aimed at uplifting living standards.[14] CTC-aligned groups greeted the social charter idea skeptically. They questioned whether real enforcement and aid would happen. Tactically, CTC members felt backing a social charter would muddy their message, ultimately providing an excuse for congresspeople to vote for NAFTA. CTC thus rejected the idea, finding it was "dangerous to proceed with a plan not supported by major constituency-supported groups."[15] Instead, they went with the simpler "'kill the NAFTA, it's unfixable' strategy."[16]

Even if unintentionally, the split between ART and the CTC mirrored older conflicts between public interest progressives and more radical activists. One motivating factor for people to join public interest progressive groups in the 1960s came from a desire to be "pragmatic." At the same time, such pragmatism often meant not openly and fully articulating critiques of structural injustices such as racism. The conflicts between these worldviews could at times get personal and unpleasant. As ART coordinator Karen Hansen-Kuhn recalled, representatives from some CTC groups would frequently tell her some version of the sentence, "ART were the thinkers and CTC the doers." As Hansen-Kuhn further noted, "They didn't mean that in a nice way."[17]

That any of these disputes mattered in the larger politics of NAFTA demonstrated the importance of public interest progressives to this fight. This truth in turn raises the question: why were *these* groups headlining the liberal-left anti-NAFTA coalition? The obvious alternative would have been the AFL-CIO. Most unions opposed Fast Track. As talks on NAFTA continued through 1991 and 1992, the federation expressed grave doubts about this "job-gutting" agreement.[18] Nor was the AFL-CIO staunchly against being in any coalitions.

In a pertinent example, beginning in 1989, the AFL-CIO became an important member of the Coalition for Justice in the Maquiladoras, a network of NGOs, unions, and grassroots groups confronting abuses in Mexican factories.[19] And yet the AFL-CIO did not join the CTC or ART, choosing to run its efforts in parallel.[20] The reasons for this are many and highlight the importance and limitations of public interest progressives.

Public interest groups became central to the campaign because of their organizational structures and the incentives those structures created. People such as Ritchie and Wallach devoted their full attention to a single issue. This allowed them a level of policy and political knowledge, as well as pure time to work on one issue, which few other political advocates possessed. Public interest groups' staffs were small, with individual executive directors serving as the main decision makers, making them quicker to act and react. Relatedly, while groups such as Public Citizen had thousands of dues-paying members, these individuals possessed little input into the tactics, rhetoric, and strategies of the organizations they belonged to, creating further flexibility.[21] Put another way, public interest progressives' pinballs faced fewer flippers before going down the drain.

Organized labor functions differently. Unions' mission to defend their members' jobs across many industries and the varied political interests and connections growing from that mission placed them in a thicket of complex relationships. This was especially the case with the AFL-CIO's relationship to the Democratic Party, an alliance of necessity and heartbreaks.[22] Union decision making is much more hierarchical (and at least somewhat more democratic). Given these complexities, many individual unions and the AFL-CIO leadership placed great value on preserving their organizational autonomy.[23] Furthermore, as explained by AFL-CIO economist Greg Woodhead, questions of reputation emerged: "We [organized labor] have to be a little more measured in the way we do things. We try to be more careful [so] that people don't just think we're clownish or into street theater. . . . And besides, we have thirteen million dues paying members. [The CTC and its allies] have some smart lawyers. They don't have the clout and the votes, frankly, even the money. So we didn't disagree with what they were trying to do, but we have to maintain a certain kind of distance."[24]

This did not mean, however, that unions were absent from the fair globalization coalition. From the founding of the AFL-CIO, divisions have ebbed and flowed, and individual unions or groups of them have dissented from the federation's line. In the late twentieth century, these dissents frequently happened around international issues. While the AFL-CIO's leadership backed the U.S.

war in Vietnam, many union members and leaders railed against it. In the 1980s, a coalition of unions broke with the AFL-CIO over U.S. interventions in Central America. Labor activists, with support from some of the biggest unions (e.g., the UAW and the American Federation of State, County, and Municipal Employees), formed the National Labor Committee in Support of Human Rights and Democracy in El Salvador, which worked with other liberal groups to support Salvadoran trade unionists and lobby against Reagan.[25] NAFTA offered yet another chance for individual unions to buck the AFL-CIO's often tepid leadership.

From the start of the NAFTA fight, local labor activists, branches of national unions, and individual unions eagerly sought out coalitions.[26] Helping lead the charge was the Washington lobbyist for the International Ladies' Garment Workers' Union, Evelyn Dubrow. A union organizer since the late 1930s and labor lobbyist since the mid-1950s, Dubrow's work ethic made her a legend, as she "trudged so many miles around Capitol Hill that she wore out 24 pairs of her Size 4 shoes each year."[27]

Decades of experience in a diverse union helped Dubrow appreciate the power of alliance. Teaming up with Lori Wallach, Dubrow frequently invited CTC members for after-work food and drinks at the Democratic Club in D.C. In these informal settings, trust could more easily solidify.[28] Working also with United Food and Commercial Workers' lobbyist Segundo Mercado-Llorens, the CTC became an outlet for unions to operate outside of the AFL-CIO's confines.[29] In turn, the cooperation of such unions as the Amalgamated Clothing and Textile Workers Union, the UAW, and the Teamsters added a political heft that the CTC would not have had otherwise.

*   *   *

Beyond the fair globalizers, patterns of division and convergence swept U.S. politics. On the other side of the political spectrum, NAFTA exposed divisions among conservatives over the United States' place in the world. Mainstream conservatives believed the United States needed to stay "engaged," taking advantage of the USSR's collapse and the Cold War's end to assert U.S. imperial predominance. Supporting free trade would fulfill the dream of conservatives such as Texas senator Phil Gramm to "export capitalism," providing "the missing ingredient for the expansion of freedom" around the globe.[30] President Bush backed the agreement wholeheartedly, making its passage an important plank in his 1992 reelection bid.[31]

Meanwhile, a long dormant strain of conservative thinking awakened with a different view. So-called paleoconservatives rejected U.S. entanglements abroad. Often committed to white nationalist views, paleoconservatives worried about foreign influences sapping and impurifying the nation's strength. Their chief spokesperson was former Nixon and Reagan aide and prominent pundit Patrick Buchanan. An ardent Cold Warrior and free trader, the end of the superpower showdown brought forth Buchanan's paleoconservative soul. He counseled the nation to turn inward after fifty years of being "drained of wealth and power by wars, cold and hot."[32] Buchanan raged against free trade, proclaiming that we "just can't let foreign imports come in here and rob us of American jobs."[33]

Buchanan tested the paleoconservative message by running against Bush in the 1992 GOP primaries. His desire to "Make America First Again" attracted not only fringe right-wing groups but also some white blue-collar and middle-class workers. In addition, Buchanan drew backing from a subset of business interests, like textile companies, who felt besieged by free trade. The Buchanan campaign aggressively courted the latter, holding fundraisers organized by the United States Business and Industrial Council (USBIC).[34] Founded in 1933 to oppose the New Deal, the USBIC transformed into a coalition of small- and medium-sized industries that, in the words of its president John Cregan, tended to "part from our friends in the business community and in the conservative community on trade matters."[35]

The big name in the protectionist business community was textile magnate Roger Milliken. An influential force on the hard right, Milliken virulently opposed organized labor and funded right-wing groups from the John Birch Society to the Heritage Foundation.[36] Yet, as foreign competition cut into his profits through the 1970s and 1980s, he increasingly disagreed with his conservative compatriots on trade, funding protectionist groups and politicians.[37] A small but loud minority of U.S. corporate heads agreed with Milliken. For instance, then real-estate mogul and celebrity Donald Trump derided NAFTA as "only good for Mexico" and proof that "we never make a good deal."[38]

The Bush and Buchanan wings of conservatism articulated coherent worldviews. The same could not be said for another crucial anti-NAFTA figure, Ross Perot. Already a famous billionaire and veterans' rights voice, in 1992 Perot threw his hat in the presidential ring. He reprimanded both parties and promised fiscal responsibility and business common sense. His messages certainly resonated, as at some points he topped the polls.[39] Perot's popularity partly derived from his opposition to NAFTA. This perspective placed him on the same side as 57 percent of the country, according to a September 1992 Gallup poll.[40]

Perot's message lacked Buchanan's rabid nationalism and bigotry. Nevertheless, his appeal significantly derived from his nationalistic message of reversing U.S. decline. On trade, Perot bemoaned how deindustrialization weakened the country and warned of the corrupting influences of foreign lobbyists.[41] He also blasted multinational companies for their profiteering and mistreatment of workers. During the second presidential debate, Perot infamously warned of U.S. jobs disappearing as the "giant sucking sound going south." The full context of Perot's quip merits attention, as he intended it as a rebuke of his CEO peers. "To those of you in the audience who are businesspeople, pretty simple: if you're paying $12, $13, $14 an hour," Perot stated, "and you can move your factory south of the border, pay a dollar an hour . . . and you don't care about anything but making money," then outsourcing would be inevitable.[42]

Although Perot sounded a few populist notes about sticking up for U.S. workers, his fairly conservative platform, his bizarre conspiracy theories, and his status as a third-party candidate ensured that liberals would not back him.[43] With NAFTA negotiations wrapping up in late 1992, this left fair globalizers with one other mainstream option in the election: Arkansas Democratic governor William Jefferson Clinton.

During the Democratic primary, several candidates, including former (and future) California governor Jerry Brown, Virginia governor Doug Wilder, and Iowa senator Tom Harkin opposed NAFTA.[44] Harkin and Brown hailed from the labor-liberal wing of the party. Worried about job loss and deregulation, the labor-liberals formed the backbone of the Democratic Party's anti-NAFTA faction.

Bill Clinton did not identify with the labor-liberals. Instead, he sided with the growing "New Democrats" faction. This group asserted that Democrats during the 1960s and 1970s had tilted too far left. New Democrats worried that the party's base clung to views—whether "softness" on defense, support for antipoverty programs, or advocacy for such "social" issues as abortion or aggressive civil rights policies—that placed Democrats out of the national "mainstream." During the 1980s, New Democrats formed organizations, such as the Democratic Leadership Council and the Progressive Policy Institute, to promote their views. They called for the party to deemphasize state intervention and regulation in favor of collaboration with business, a more hawkish foreign policy, and caution on "social" issues. Politically, New Democrats prided themselves on declaring their "independence" from core Democratic constituencies such as organized labor. By doing so, they showed the party was changing. When Democrats lost every presidential election of the 1980s, many attributed these hardships to the party being too "liberal." This allowed the New Democrats to gain ground within the party. In 1992, Bill Clinton promised New Democrats a ticket to the White House.[45]

Clinton believed in "an opportunity agenda" premised on "economic growth through free and fair trade, as well as investments in new technologies and in world-class education and skills."[46] These beliefs inclined Clinton to back NAFTA. Moreover, regarding poverty and international development, the possibilities for capitalist enterprise to produce social gains enticed Clinton. While governor of Arkansas, he became fascinated by the work of Muhammad Yunus, the Bangladeshi antipoverty entrepreneur whose Grameen Bank brought microfinance (the provision of tiny loans to impoverished people, mainly women) to global attention.[47] As Clinton explained, the Grameen Bank illustrated his belief that "whenever the power of the government can be used to create market forces that work, it's so much better than creating a bureaucracy."[48]

Despite his intellectual proclivities pointing towards a NAFTA endorsement, Clinton did not immediately back NAFTA. He wanted to win, which meant not overly antagonizing organized labor. In running for president, Clinton balanced his centrist views with populism. He blasted the "jetsetters and feather bedders of corporate America" who outsourced U.S. jobs. On NAFTA, he stated that he "supported the negotiation . . . so long as it's fair to American farmers and workers, protects the environment, and observes decent labor standards."[49]

This position did not endear Clinton to the Citizens Trade Campaign or the Alliance for Responsible Trade. To them, Clinton's notion that NAFTA represented a fundamentally sound accord that just needed some socially conscious tweaking proved laughable. Still, Clinton's hedging offered hope. It indicated that he neither fully supported NAFTA nor that he believed that the political dynamics would allow it to pass.[50]

Eventually, Clinton clarified his beliefs. On October 4, 1992, in Raleigh, North Carolina, he delivered an address on "Why I Support the North American Free Trade Agreement." The speech displayed Clinton's classic use of nuance, or dodging, depending on one's views. Going on at length, Clinton explained that although NAFTA was "unpopular with some people and organizations I admire . . . I think we should go forward with it because it advances our interests . . . more than it undermines them if we also do the other things needed to deal with the deficiencies in this agreement." Clinton clarified that he would only back NAFTA if a further round of negotiations led to new labor and environmental protections.[51]

With the election's outcome uncertain, what was clear for fair globalizers was that they needed to prepare for a big legislative fight. However, the nature of that fight would depend on the man in the White House. Writing in October 1992, John Cavanagh hoped for a Clinton victory. Yet, regarding NAFTA, he admitted that Clinton posed complications. "Bush was a fabulous target . . . a clear lightning rod against which we could organize," he observed. Clinton was not. Even as he would "basically accept much of the neo-liberal economic vision," Clinton would offer some fixes to NAFTA. This would "likely . . . create a lot of confusion in our broader ranks," thus weakening the budding fair globalization coalition.[52] A little over two weeks after writing these words, Cavanagh, and many others woke up to face this new, confusing reality.

CHAPTER 15

Our Job Is to Get Him to Bend in Our Direction

On November 3, 1992, the Democratic Party ended its twelve-year exile from the White House. Clinton's win elicited many emotions from U.S. progressives. Some felt jubilant. After more than a decade of GOP presidents and intraliberal fights, many public interest progressives and other liberal groups proclaimed themselves "more interested in making real-world progress than protesting."[1] Others felt ambivalent about the new administration, caught between excitement and trepidation. Mark Ritchie counted himself among this group, stating in December 1992, "I can't tell you how happy I am . . . that in just a couple weeks we'll have a new Congress, a new President, and a new Cabinet," while also declaring that Clinton "can help us or he can hurt us, as George Bush did."[2] And still others, like Ralph Nader, prepared to fight. Nader early on articulated how the fair globalization coalition would approach the new president: "Clinton is like any politician: He bends in the direction of those who cause him the most instability. . . . Our job is to get him to bend in our direction."[3]

Clinton entered office with an enormous policy agenda. In its first months, the administration and its congressional allies barely passed a controversial budget bill, became embroiled in a fight over gays and lesbians in the military, and initiated a massive effort to remake the health care system.[4] As all this happened, a lively debate erupted in the White House over how, or even whether, to promote NAFTA. Somewhat surprisingly, Clinton's U.S. trade representative, Mickey Kantor, sided initially (and privately) with NAFTA skeptics. Kantor, a prominent lawyer with a past representing everyone from large companies to migrant workers, knew Clinton well, having served as his campaign chair. No free-trade zealot, Kantor worried about the politics of NAFTA.[5] Early on, he offered a plan to quietly dispose of it, stating, "All I have to do is be so tough on the environmental side agreements, Mexico and Canada will never agree. We'll look good to Democrats."[6]

Concern over political dynamics led the administration to deprioritize NAFTA until late summer 1993. Their punting worried staff working on NAFTA, who urged Clinton to move "as early as possible—because attacks by NAFTA foes are damaging its prospects."[7] However, while Clinton "continued to express his conditional support," he also "avoided making any public time-specific commitments" to advancing it.[8]

The White House's indecision gave fair globalizers time to either slow down or speed up their mobilizations. For the leaders of the AFL-CIO, Clinton in the White House caused consternation. Publicly, the federation attacked NAFTA as a "disaster . . . based solely on exploitation" that needed to be "rejected and renegotiated."[9] Yet, at the AFL-CIO Executive Council meeting in May 1993, President Lane Kirkland cautioned that full-throated labor opposition would "shut the labor movement out" from possibilities to improve NAFTA, and, perhaps, from influencing other Clinton administration policies.[10]

The AFL-CIO's hesitation also stemmed from Clinton's promise to negotiate a pro-labor side agreement. The administration used this promise as a way to woo different labor leaders. In April 1993, Kantor met with several union presidents, stating, "We believe there is a good chance that we will be able to work closely with Jack Sheinkman [head of the Amalgamated Clothing and Textile Workers Union] in seeking support for NAFTA."[11] While reports like those about Sheinkman proved exaggerated (he himself never wavered in his opposition), the charm offensive accentuated union leadership's anxiety over breaking with the new Democratic president. Thus, the AFL-CIO held back from a full-on effort against NAFTA during the spring and into the summer of 1993. Some in labor further requested that the Citizens Trade Campaign tone down their language, such as requesting that opposition be framed as against "Bush's NAFTA."[12]

Little of this political ambiguity filtered into the ramshackle offices of CTC's nonprofit members. They used the lull to get ready: setting up offices, regularizing meeting schedules, and hiring staff. This included hiring a director, former Indiana Democratic congressman Jim Jontz, who had been a progressive populist champion while in the House.[13] This move was meant to solidify the Citizen Trade Campaign's alliance with the Democratic Party's labor-liberal faction. Meanwhile, publicly, the CTC approached Clinton cautiously, stating they wanted "to be able to work with you to put people and the environment first."[14]

Privately, many in the CTC believed the chances of Clinton shifting to a "no" position or putting forth game-changing side agreements were close to nil. They attempted to logjam the agreement to buy more time to rally opposition on Capitol Hill. Some of these efforts built on earlier initiatives, such as a lawsuit filed by Public Citizen, Friends of the Earth, and the Sierra Club. The lawsuit relied on legislation public interest organizations had used extensively for more than twenty years: the National Environmental Protection Act (NEPA). Passed in 1969, NEPA opened environmental policy making to robust citizen input and required environmental impact assessments before the implementation of some federal legislation and other actions. NEPA epitomized the politics that gave rise to public interest progressives during the late 1960s and early 1970s, in which working "within the system" carried real promise.

The lawsuit charged that the environmental review of NAFTA fell "far short of doing what is required."[15] Launched in July 1991, the lawsuit slowly wound its way through the courts. As late as July 1993, White House senior staff fretted that the lawsuit remained one of the principal factors acting to "complicate NAFTA's timing."[16] Eventually thrown out, the lawsuit found public interest groups using traditional tactics in new ways. Two decades before, a NEPA lawsuit likely would have been the thrust for passing new regulations. In the 1990s, with a revived business lobby and more economically conservative parties, advocates used NEPA to slow down the government in order to do the demanding work of political organizing.[17]

In going to the grassroots, CTC leaders targeted the House of Representatives. They saw little chance of victory in the Senate, whose members favored trade agreements more than their House colleagues.[18] To win, activists needed to wage a "unified campaign" based on close coordination among issue groups and robust contact between grassroots activists and Washington-based organizations.[19] A daunting prospect, it also seemed an eminently plausible one. In the first months of 1993, very few congressional Democrats expressed support for NAFTA. "The votes are not there for approval ... even if you get the best deals for the environment and jobs," lamented Robert Matsui, a leading pro-NAFTA House Democrat.[20] While Speaker of the House Tom Foley backed NAFTA, House Majority Leader Richard Gephardt expressed, at best, cautious agnosticism.[21] His chief trade adviser, Mike Wessel, met regularly with the CTC to keep them apprised of events on the Hill.[22]

One notch down the House Democratic power structure, anti-NAFTA progressives found their best friend in Congress in Democratic whip David Bonior. A mild-mannered, thoughtful, New Deal Democrat, Bonior represented a district outside of Detroit dependent on auto manufacturing—a district ravaged by deindustrialization.[23] A serious Catholic, Bonior's version of the faith tilted towards liberation theology, and he espoused a fervent internationalism and passion for justice in Latin America. During the 1970s and 1980s, Bonior undertook fights on crucial environmental laws and against Reagan-Bush policies in Central America.[24]

These experiences convinced Bonior of the power that could flow from alliances between legislators and outside groups. Bonior opened his offices to ART and CTC groups, hosting regular strategy meetings with representatives of Congress, their staffs, and activist organizations.[25] In these meetings, activists such as Wallach acted like accountants. Information replaced currency, and the "whip list" became the ledger book. Across gridded sheets of paper, names of House members appeared next to a number ranging from one to six. A one signified an enemy; a five, a friend; a six indicated more information needed. A three signified an undecided legislator. "Threes" therefore received the most attention from all sides. Using documents sometimes produced by CTC members, anti-NAFTA members of Congress recorded details from their conversations with colleagues. This information joined notes from CTC organizations' lobbyists and went to the offices of key anti-NAFTA groups and individuals.[26] The sheets also recorded substantive information on individual politicians, such as a September 2, 1993, document commenting that Nancy Pelosi, then a rising star in the party, had "taken a lot of hits on environ. issues."[27]

Within the Citizens Trade Campaign, constant meetings brought constituencies together. At cramped conference tables, activists strategized over how to move individual congresspeople. Was Los Angeles congressman Matthew Martínez still wavering? Contact a textile workers' local in his district and have some union members meet with him to declare, "This will be the end of all our sewing jobs in Los Angeles. Your mom had one of these jobs. That's why you got to go college and now you're in Congress. You can't be for this."[28] Did a member of Congress need to see a flood of ads in their local newspaper? Solicit the input of everyone from animal rights defenders to economists sitting around the same table and inquire who could fund the ad and collectively brainstorm its content.[29]

Such coordination did not happen only in Washington, D.C. Simultaneously, statewide fair-trade coalitions emerged as chapters of the CTC. Fair-trade campaign chapters might include a Sierra Club branch aligned with a steelworkers local coordinating with a National Family Farm Coalition group to prepare a congressional lobby visit. Fair-trade coalitions sometimes engaged in media-grabbing events. In Colorado, a "tractorcade"—a march of tractors—between Colorado Springs and Denver highlighted the plight of small farmers.

In Northfield, Minnesota, union members and allies picketed outside a Sheldahl factory after it announced the outsourcing of 104 jobs to Mexico.[30]

Through it all, national CTC groups held frequent conference calls trying to glue these parts together. The calls allowed activists from across the country to "meet" and to hear "a policy analyst's presentation of a key issue" or the "presentation of a promising local initiative by its organizers."[31] This coordination, combined with the policy expertise of public interest advocates, enriched grassroots mobilization. In turn, in Washington, D.C., the grassroots allowed the professionalized advocates to be more assertive in their demands, including with allies. As Wallach recalled about one meeting between advocates and Gephardt, "It was very useful to say to Gephardt's staff and others, 'what can you do with those crazy field people? . . . I just wanted to warn you that I cannot hold them off much longer.'"[32]

Both nationally and locally, one of the major dilemmas for progressive anti-NAFTA forces centered on how ideologically diverse their alliances should be. At the same time as progressives mobilized, so too did millions of Ross Perot supporters. Since losing in 1992, Perot had devoted his energies to building a substantial grassroots political lobby, United We Stand America. The Texas tycoon believed NAFTA offered the perfect issue to keep his backers energized.[33] In September 1993, he released a book, *Save Your Job*, followed by a national speaking tour, holding eighty-seven rallies in forty-three states.[34] These were no small events, each often attracting thousands of attendees.[35]

Joining Perot among right-leaning NAFTA foes were companies in the U.S. Business and Industry Council and reactionaries affiliated with Pat Buchanan. While the council stuck to talking points about the dangers of foreign competition, Buchanan fought on explicitly xenophobic grounds. In his speeches and op-eds, he often made declarations such as, "We want to remain two distinct nations . . . consistent with our national identities and national character."[36] He also blamed corporate greed for harming the nation, mocking conservative NAFTA supporters for wanting the United States to be "swamped with illegal aliens" because "illegals work cheap."[37] These views found support elsewhere in the country. From comparatively tame rhetoric that "good fences make good neighbors" to letters to Congress exclaiming that the United States must "kick all illegal immigrants out!" opposition to NAFTA facilitated a rise of racist nativism.[38]

Explicit racism mixed with broader nationalistic sentiments. Angst about the United States did not only appear in explicitly conservative bubbles. Polling showed large majorities skeptical of free trade, identifying international commerce as one of numerous factors causing "American decline." One survey by respected liberal pollsters Ruy Teixeira and Guy Molyneux found that "67 percent of Americans favor 'restricting foreign imports to protect American industry and American jobs.'"[39]

From anti-immigrant nativism to general wariness of trade, NAFTA put a spotlight on predominately white working- and middle-class individuals' feelings that the United States was in decline. This was especially true for the manufacturing sector. Since World War Two and the era of mass unionization, many factory jobs became "good" jobs, in that they could provide a middle-class lifestyle. While these jobs became less overwhelmingly white after the 1930s and 1940s, many still saw them as the cornerstone of a white male normality. As the factories closed, new politics arose. This anger sometimes swung decidedly towards right-wing politics, with free trade seen as a surrender to foreign influences in the same ways that abortion rights or increased participation of people of color in the national life marked a debasement of the nation. For others, the decline was mainly about a vanishing middle-class quality of life and a harsher economic order. And for many, all these and other factors mixed together.[40] This mixture could be seen in such documents as a Teamsters flyer that both spoke out against the exploitation of Mexican truck drivers by capitalists and ominously warned that Mexican drivers did not speak or read English or "undergo drug and alcohol testing."[41]

Given these complex overlaps in why people opposed NAFTA, it came as little surprise that some collaborations emerged across political lines at local and state levels. In particular, chapters of Perot's United We Stand America coordinated with state-based and local CTC groups. According to a comprehensive post-NAFTA campaign report on the CTC's activities, roughly one out of every four state fair-trade campaign chapters coordinated in some capacity with United We Stand America.[42]

Such dynamics did not only exist "in the field." Rhetorically, stories of decline frequently framed many CTC groups' critiques. One of the most constant refrains, even if unwittingly, suggested Mexican inferiority. "U.S. corporations love to flee to Mexico so they can hire workers for five dollars a day. . . . Also, the corporations can freely dump their toxic wastes without the interventions of an EPA," declared a full-page advertisement in the *New York Times* sponsored by a large array of progressive anti-NAFTA groups.[43] While most of these critiques were technically correct, without context, they could paint a portrait of Mexico as an inexplicably poorer, less safe place. This decontextualized image of course contrasted sharply with an understanding of Mexico as a country affected by centuries of Spanish colonialism, U.S. invasion, land theft, neoimperialism, and state-sponsored repression. Along with specific rhetoric about

Mexico, some public interest progressives also talked about NAFTA as a foreign assault. "NAFTA . . . imposes an unacceptable international autocratic regime on our democratic processes in the United States," stated Ralph Nader at a press conference, where he stood next to Paul Weyrich, a NAFTA foe and one of the essential architects of the New Right's rise (including helping to found the Heritage Foundation).[44]

Nader's presence at a press conference with someone whose politics (mostly) stood diametrically opposed to his own showed how the drive to win led to distasteful alliances. Staring at endless one-to-six charts of members of Congress, some fair globalizers felt that they needed to coordinate with anti-NAFTA conservatives. Thus, some public interest groups and conservatives (mainly the U.S. Business and Industry Council) shared information. A representative from the CTC frequented meetings of the Roger Milliken–funded No-Name Group, where vote counts were discussed, imported wine was "banned and, at times, the atmosphere turns xenophobic with anti-Mexican slurs."[45] At the same time, progressives steered well away from Buchanan, keeping these relationships quiet and highly tactical in nature.

Along with being unsavory, building such ties carried risks. Throughout the campaign, proponents of NAFTA tried to tie all opponents to the most reactionary antitrade voices. The National Council of La Raza decried anti-NAFTA groups for relying on "smirks, stereotypes, and caricatures" of Mexicans.[46] Many pro-NAFTA business and government representatives and media figures echoed this criticism. The idea that anti-NAFTA sentiments actually arose from racism even made it onto *Saturday Night Live*, with a sketch purporting to be a paid ad from Perot and the AFL-CIO in which actor Rob Schneider played a "crude Mexican stereotype" satirizing anti-NAFTA arguments as rooted in bigotry.[47]

CTC groups knew they needed to address this challenge. As Wallach bluntly wrote in a strategy memo, the threat of progressive anti-NAFTA groups being "cast as selfish xenophobes" demonstrated the "liability of Not Participating in Trinational Work."[48] CTC groups sponsored delegations from Mexico to Canada of legislators and activists. Union leaders from the national to the local level emphasized repeatedly that the unions' fight was not with Mexican workers but with the multinational firms exploiting workers on both sides of the border.[49] These moves were not just about pragmatism. Most CTC leaders believed in internationalism of one kind or another. But they followed their sense of the existing politics in the country rather than hopes for future, better politics.

Of course, for the Alliance for Responsible Trade, Global North-South inequality was central to all discussions. Baked into the core of ART's work was collaboration across borders with RMALC and the Action Canada Network. One of the most prominent enactments of this philosophy came from the United Electrical, Radio, and Machine Workers (UE), the most active trade union in ART. An independent union pushed out of the CIO in the late 1940s for its leftist politics and communist leaders, the UE began allying with the Frente Auténtico del Trabajo, Mexico's main independent trade union organization, in the late 1980s. These bonds included efforts at cross-border solidarity, like a campaign run concurrently in Mexico and the United States targeting General Electric.[50]

Meanwhile, ART's members continued coordinating, among other projects, with the Red Mexicana de Acción Frente al Libre Comercio and the Action Canada Network to create a statement offering a progressive alternative to NAFTA. In March 1993, the groups issued the Just and Sustainable Trade and Development Initiative for North America. The document included callbacks to the demands of the 1970s for a new international order. It endorsed codes of conduct for multinationals, incorporating International Labor Organization standards as the absolute floor for workers' rights, debt relief, and the "right to a toxic-free workplace and living environment" as core parts of any future agreement.[51]

At the Development Group for Alternative Policies, one of the main ART members, advocates invited RMALC economist Carlos Heredia to come to the United States and work for a year. Born in 1956, Heredia's introduction to politics emerged through his involvement with Catholic-based communities rooted in liberation theology. Becoming a significant influence throughout Latin America in the 1960s and 1970s, liberation theology stresses Christian teachings about poverty and inequity and urges its followers to combat injustice in the here and now.[52] During the 1980s, Heredia became involved with popular education programs through the organization Equipo Pueblo. There, he worked with farmers, academics, trade unionists, and others to offer popular education about the policy inner workings of structural adjustment programs imposed by the government and the IMF. This work put Heredia in contact with a broad array of activists who later formed RMALC.

On coming to Washington, D.C., Heredia went on speaking tours, testified before Congress, and produced reports about how NAFTA would undermine Mexican social welfare. He spoke English, Spanish, and French, and he also traveled to Canada. While Heredia was well aware of the split between CTC and ART, he did his best to avoid becoming involved. As he later explained, the idea of interfering in domestic politics was anathema to him as a progressive and a person from the Third World. Moreover, from his and many Mexican activists' perspectives, the exact ideological stances of the CTC and ART mattered less than keeping up good relations with progressive-minded U.S. organizations.[53]

By the time Heredia arrived in Washington, many of the battle lines had been set. However, uncertainty reigned about the Congressional and presidential politics affecting the future of the continent. Few people knew quite what was happening with Bill Clinton's attempts to assuage critics through newly negotiated side agreements. Congressional dynamics seemed to favor anti-NAFTA forces, but that did not mean the battle was over. Then, on August 13, 1993, the Mexican, Canadian, and U.S. governments finished negotiations to add side agreements on labor rights and environmental protections to NAFTA. This marked the start of the final, most intense phase of the NAFTA debate.[54]

CHAPTER 16

NAFTA Is the Future

On December 31, 1992, Katie McGinty, an adviser to incoming Vice President Al Gore, wrote a long memorandum to still "Governor Clinton." In it, she outlined the problems and possibilities of negotiating side agreements to NAFTA with Canada and Mexico. She minced no words, stating "strong supplemental measures . . . will have to be negotiated with the Mexicans and Canadians if the NAFTA is to pass Congressional muster."[1] The administration followed McGinty's advice. From the winter of 1992 to the hottest days of summer 1993, negotiators put together a set of packages on labor, environment, and other trade matters. On August 13, 1993, they went public.

Regarding workers, the negotiators presented the North American Agreement on Labor Cooperation (NAALC), which established institutions and procedures to address labor abuses. The agreement aimed to press governments to obey their own labor laws and made proving that a given abuse happened because of NAFTA (and could thus be taken before the NAALC) quite difficult. Politically, the Clinton administration held out little hope the agreement would swing U.S. unions to support NAFTA. "No labor side agreement, no matter how strong, will be able to peel off any unions," wrote Clinton aide (and Lori Wallach's former boss) Michael Waldman in early August 1993. "However," he continued, "the strength of the side agreement will affect the intensity of labor's opposition."[2]

The side agreement did affect labor's intensity, just not in the direction Waldman hoped for. Among skeptics and opponents of NAFTA, the labor side accord generated disdain. From Mexico City, RMALC denounced the accords as "insufficient," complaining of their government's continuing "antidemocratic" posture.[3] For Mexican activists such as Bertha Luján or Carlos Heredia, hope also arose from this conclusion. They expected that the furor over the side agreements would "certainly make it difficult for NAFTA to pass the U.S. Congress."[4]

Indeed, the conclusion of the side agreement talks offered the final signal needed by the AFL-CIO to, in the words of its president Lane Kirkland, "go for broke."[5] He dismissed the side agreements as "political window dressing." The AFL-CIO now moved to activate a full on "no" campaign.[6] Soon, thousands of letters, packets, bumper stickers, and other anti-NAFTA paraphernalia flowed from the AFL-CIO to its affiliates.

The mobilization plan used by the federation was designed by the head of its task force on trade, Mark Anderson. The effort called on local and statewide union bodies to activate union members to pressure members of Congress through meetings, phone calls, and rallies. Moreover, as Anderson and some others in the AFL-CIO had long advocated, the plan led the AFL-CIO to embrace cooperation with public interest progressives. Anderson belonged to a subset of labor officials who looked at alliances with other progressives as a necessity. Labor officials began communicating more, especially with the Citizens Trade Campaign, letting activists from the coalition use AFL-CIO facilities.[7]

Where the labor accord inspired unanimity in antagonism, the environmental side agreement ignited what journalist Mark Dowie calls "the nastiest internecine squabble" in a century of U.S. environmentalist history.[8] The reasons for this split arose from the interweaving of multiple factors relating to the political moment and the structures of the pro- and anti-NAFTA organizations. Even before NAFTA, as seen in the Fast Track fight, divisions existed within the green public interest lobby. The openness of some environmental NGOs to back trade grew with Clinton's election. Major green groups felt relieved at having enthusiastic White House access after years on the outside. At least twenty-four staff members from groups such as the EDF and NRDC moved into jobs in the administration, with Vice President Al Gore welcoming them, given his own record of championing environmentalism.[9]

Public interest environmentalists wanted concrete wins. As an official from the League of Conservation Voters told *Newsweek* weeks after Clinton's election, "We don't want to ruin what could be a good relationship any sooner than we have to."[10] Measuring how much input into the NAFTA side agreements they could get became an important test of the new administration for such NGOs as the NWF, the EDF, and the NRDC.

In the first months of 1993, these organizations met with Environmental Protection Agency staff, U.S. trade representative Mickey Kantor, and others to advocate regarding the side agreements. As the heads of seven green lobbies wrote to Kantor on May 4, 1993, they would back NAFTA if the administration incorporated their conditions.[11] By late summer, the administration fulfilled enough of these requests to merit endorsement. Under the North American Agreement on Environmental Cooperation, new institutions, both intergovernmental and independent, would hear and address complaints about ecological degradation. After intense arguments, the ability of governments to deploy trade sanctions stayed in the final agreement—although petitioners would have to clear numerous legal and bureaucratic hurdles to activate them.[12]

Even among the NAFTA-friendly environmentalists, few saw the side agreement as a huge victory. Instead, many argued it was sufficient. Moreover, given that "trade will continue with or without the NAFTA," they saw it as an important step.[13] Some environmental lobbies asserted that it would be better for NAFTA and future agreements for environmentalists to make changes to what existed rather than launching a futile campaign to block the agreement. This view fit with past public interest advocacy. After all, U.S. environmental groups had decades of experience helping to pass laws and regulations that started as sufficient, only to strengthen them in following years.

On September 15, 1993, Vice President Gore, Mickey Kantor, EPA head Carol Browner, and Senators Max Baucus and John Chafee joined the heads of the Environmental Defense Fund, the Audubon Society, the World Wildlife Fund, the National Wildlife Federation, Conservation International, and the Natural Resources Defense Council for a press conference. One by one, each praised how a "cranky, irascible, and difficult" group of advocates had worked with the Clinton administration to cement "a really extraordinary package."[14]

Clinton administration staff immediately put the "Group of Seven" to work. Focus groups showed that especially among middle-class liberals, invoking the support of green groups proved "particularly effective" in swaying voters toward backing NAFTA.[15] Pro-NAFTA environmentalists also mounted lobbying efforts on the Hill, bringing grassroots members to help spread the message that "NAFTA is good for the environment."[16]

Unsurprisingly, these actions enraged fair globalizers, especially at the two major anti-NAFTA national green organizations, the Sierra Club and Friends of the Earth. Their fury was matched by the condescension emanating from some leading pro-NAFTA greens. NWF chief Jay Hair relished trashing anti-NAFTA environmentalists, particularly the Sierra Club. At the September press conference, he blasted NAFTA foes for not "having the facts" and "feeding off of misinformation put out by groups like the Sierra Club."[17] When the CTC pointed out that, outside of these seven big green groups, most environmental organizations rejected NAFTA, Hair called the claim "pure baloney."[18] Not all pro-NAFTA greens fought so intensely. As Hair issued his condemnations at the September 15 press conference, a young man to his left, Justin

Ward, representing the NRDC, shifted uncomfortably. As soon as Hair finished, Ward moved to the podium to offer an olive branch, stating that the "perception of a major rift . . . has been given more attention than it deserved and tends to obscure more basic agreements."[19]

Ultimately, the importance of the pro-NAFTA greens did not emanate from persuading flocks of legislators. Almost no member of Congress saw the environmental lobby as their chief friend or foe. Rather, by ensuring, as scholar John Audley describes, that two "equally strong, yet diametrically opposed, perspectives on NAFTA" came from the "'same' constituency," they muddied the waters. This allowed some House members to put aside environmental concerns when making their decisions. Pro-NAFTA greens also offered the agreement a progressive sheen, making it easier for moderate Democrats to support. Finally, it meant that fair globalizers went on defense regarding one of "their" issues. For they were now vulnerable to attacks claiming that *opposing* NAFTA represented the real antienvironmental stance.[20]

The completion of the side agreements came just as the Clinton administration, having won on the budget and retreated on "Don't Ask, Don't Tell," turned its attentions more fully to NAFTA. The administration identified NAFTA as one of three issues, along with health care and "reinventing government," headlining its fall 1993 agenda.[21] Clinton saw health care and NAFTA as complements. Agreements such as NAFTA would grow the economy, leading to some worker displacement. To ease this pain, the administration would enact new social insurance and job-training programs—and thus prove the superiority of the New Democrats' advocacy for using government to simultaneously back business and ameliorate some inequalities.

Rhetorically, administration officials emphasized post–Cold War optimism and concerns about U.S. economic decline through a focus on the "future." "NAFTA is the future," declared one memo. "You can't close your eyes and hope that the global economy will go away. We must compete, not retreat." Complementing the policy reasoning and rhetorical flourishes was the political necessity of winning. "If the Congress rejects NAFTA, the power of the United States and the authority of the President will be weakened. What nation would trust the word of the United States when an agreement negotiated by two presidents can't pass?" proclaimed the NAFTA war-room team to Bill Daley and Rahm Emanuel in a September memo.[22]

From the perspective of pro-NAFTA forces, the Clinton administration's ratcheting up its attention came at just the right time, if not a little too late. As an October 1993 strategy document outlined, the "NAFTA fight is unlike any other legislative campaigns waged by the administration. The goal cannot be to

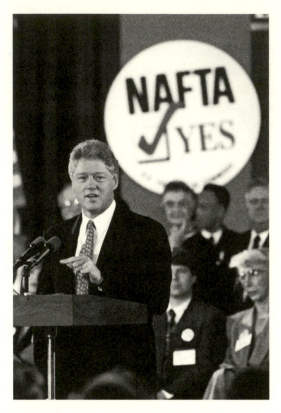

Figure 5. President Clinton promotes NAFTA at the U.S. Chamber of Commerce, November 1, 1993. Courtesy Sharon Farmer, William J. Clinton Presidential Library.

'win over' a majority of the broad public—there's no time, and it's probably not possible." Describing a possible path forward, advisers urged the administration to see NAFTA as a "fight waged principally among elites." Still, the NAFTA war team declared the need "to demonstrate enough popular support so that lawmakers don't fear electoral meltdown if they support NAFTA."[23]

Among those the administration hoped to activate for the fall offensive included corporate lobbyists. With crucial exceptions in some trade-threatened industries, most large businesses and many smaller ones embraced NAFTA. They just did not think much would need to be done about it. Meeting in the spring of 1992, the international trade director for Eastman Kodak, Sandy Masur, asked her colleagues whether the company should devise a pro-NAFTA media strategy. One of her coworkers brushed off this suggestion, stating,

"There'll be two or three articles about the NAFTA. . . . We don't need to worry about the media."[24] That person's premonitions proved quite wrong.

Realizing they had a fight on their hands, in early 1993, members of two of the mightiest corporate lobbies—the Business Roundtable and the U.S. Chamber of Commerce—formed a coalition called USA*NAFTA. By late June 1993, USA*NAFTA boasted more than two thousand member corporations, from the Allegheny Foundry Company to General Electric.[25] However, its heads found it difficult to mobilize businesses. They could get signatures on letters but not much else. One of the main reasons was skepticism of Clinton. The new Democratic administration's drive to sign labor and environmental side agreements did not endear him, or the agreement, to corporate interests.[26]

As the vote approached, however, USA*NAFTA members began worrying. Writing in September, Ernest Pepples of Brown and Williamson Tobacco gave NAFTA "at best, a 50-50 chance of being passed," stating that getting it through the House would be a "battle royale." Pepples noted a further challenge: most companies did not want to stake too much, seeing NAFTA's fate as lying "in President Clinton's hands. He must lead the charge."[27] As if answering Pepples's concerns, on the same day he offered this opinion, the Clinton administration intensified its wooing of business. The administration soon recruited Lee Iacocca, the recently retired chairman of Chrysler and one of the nation's most celebrated businesspeople, as a "telegenic, visible, and articulate" national spokesperson for NAFTA.[28]

USA*NAFTA proved an assertive foe for ART and CTC. In turn, for USA*NAFTA members, countering activists represented an important priority. In one June 1993 memo, the lobby listed as one of its primary goals the preparation of a "point-by-point rebuttal to Citizens Trade Campaign . . . distribute to media and Congress."[29] In another case, the corporate lobby mocked the Alliance for Responsible Trade for its "short-sighted view of the future" and "protectionist and defeatist outlook."[30]

Business elites brought money and raw political power. Yet the Clinton administration also recruited other allies to make "defensible public arguments for the agreement."[31] The day before the environmentalists' press conference, for instance, Clinton held an event in the White House featuring former presidents George H. W. Bush, Gerald Ford, and Jimmy Carter all declaring their support for NAFTA. At a reception that evening, anti-NAFTA congressional leader David Bonior ran into Carter on a balcony. Bonior introduced himself and Carter responded, "I know who you are, David, and I'm very disappointed in you," to which Bonior retorted, "Well, I'm very disappointed in you."[32]

Lobbying by the administration of wavering House members also intensified. Attending a different White House reception, prominent liberal congressman Henry Waxman (still undecided), found himself unexpectedly seated next to singer and actress Barbra Streisand. Before he could speak, Streisand pointedly asked him, "Are you going to be for NAFTA?"[33]

In plotting the path to victory, Clinton faced a tough choice. Part of the president's appeal derived from his willingness (even eagerness) to bash parts of the Democratic base to show his independence.[34] Al From, head of the centrist Democratic Leadership Council, and other New Democrats encouraged him to do more. "I can't tell you how much better it would make your life and how much it would strengthen your presidency for you to beat Bonior and organized labor on NAFTA," From proclaimed in an August 30, 1993, memo. From further stated that winning on NAFTA would make "clear that you, not the Democratic leadership in Congress or the interest groups, set the Democratic Party's agenda."[35]

While From geared up for a fight, other Clinton aides wished to minimize strife within the house of liberalism. Frustrated as they felt with organized labor, they knew union support would be vital for winning health care reform. This made organized labor "politically problematic to attack." Perhaps the only liberal group that the administration saw as even less appealing to snipe with were public interest progressives. As a memorandum for Al Gore explained, certain NAFTA opponents "should not be referenced" due to their credibility with the public. Top on the list was Ralph Nader, who remained "popular" and the opposition's "strongest validator."[36]

Unwilling to fully commit to liberal civil war, the Clinton administration looked for a clear enemy. Fortunately, Ross Perot was still around. By the fall of 1993, Perot emerged as the country's single loudest anti-NAFTA voice. Because of this, the fair globalization coalition and Perot's fates became intertwined. This made the stakes all the higher when on November 4, 1993, the announcement hit that Perot would appear on the popular CNN talk show *Larry King Live* to debate Vice President Gore.[37] For the Clinton administration, Perot represented a welcome foil. His businesses participated in outsourcing jobs, he was no labor champion, he seemed an antiquated nationalist, and he trafficked in conspiracy theories. All of these elements made it easy, according to the memorandum prepared for Gore, to "paint him as protectionist, backward-looking, and small."[38]

The debate devastated the NAFTA opposition. Despite some good moments from Perot, including a surprisingly moving opening in which he talked about the dignity of Mexican *maquiladora* workers, Gore dominated. Perot did okay on substance, but his irritability played poorly against Gore's confidence. Watching the ninety minutes unfold, CTC and ART organizers felt dismayed. In the immediate aftermath, CNN pundits unanimously declared Gore the winner, while calling Perot "crabby." Appearing on CNN right after, Lori Wallach spun the situation as positively as she could, stating that Perot's performance would "jazz up" anti-NAFTA forces.[39] Privately, most progressives' assessment concurred with the AFL-CIO's Mark Anderson, who believed "Perot was the worst thing that ever happened to us."[40]

The Gore-Perot debate boosted the pro-NAFTA forces. In a November 10 letter to Congress, the head of the White House's pro-NAFTA operation, Bill Daley, assured members that "yes" was good politics, stating, "The more Americans know about NAFTA, the more they like the agreement."[41] Yet even this momentum did not convince the administration that they could win. Thus, in the last days before the vote, the "NAFTA Bazaar" (as one scholar labeled it) opened for business. Targeting remaining undecideds, the Clinton administration orchestrated a flurry of deal making. From extra orders of military aircraft partly produced in a certain district, to additional agricultural protections, to promises of heightened immigration enforcement, the largesse poured out. While the exact numbers are unclear, a study by political scientist Diana Evans concluded that "members who received a special benefit from the administration, then supported it on NAFTA."[42]

At the grassroots level, activists scrambled to contact members of Congress. "If you can fax, FAX them right away. Or else call as soon as possible. Do both if you can. Clinton is doing some extreme arm-twisting and bribing. . . . These people need to . . . know that if they vote for NAFTA . . . we will extract an electoral cost," declared Harel Barzilai, a Cornell graduate student in an e-mail to the listserv misc.activism.progressive.[43] Meanwhile, in Washington fair globalizers pondered how to turn the "NAFTA bazaar" to their advantage by depicting NAFTA as synonymous with corruption. Consultants to the CTC suggesting holding a "NAFTA Claus" stunt, in which a person dressed as Santa would sit in a room in the House of Representatives with a bag of "presents" and a sign reading "Admission: One Pro-NAFTA Vote."[44]

On Wednesday, November 17, 1993, the House finally voted. During the day, the pro-NAFTA forces buzzed with energy in the halls of Congress, but as the day progressed, all became quiet. The anti-NAFTA crowd concluded they had lost. Not sure what to do as the final hour approached, two Ohio anti-NAFTA Democratic House members, Marcy Kaptur and Sherrod Brown, marched into the Ways and Means Committee room to find it overflowing with pro-NAFTA lobbyists.[45] A little later, David Bonior walked outside to the

Capitol's east steps. There, Bonior recalled the "emotional occasion" of a candlelight vigil, as Lori Wallach, John Cavanagh, Jesse Jackson, and Ralph Nader joined hundreds of anti-NAFTA activists.[46] The event soon turned into a communal funeral. At 10:36 p.m., the final vote tally in the House of Representatives arrived: 234 votes in favor to 200 against, an "unexpectedly large margin" according to the *Los Angeles Times*.[47] Two days later, NAFTA sailed through the Senate on a vote of 61 to 38.

Progressive foes of NAFTA vented their anger. Ralph Nader framed the vote as an indictment of U.S. liberalism's trajectory, proclaiming that Bill Clinton "threw his lot in with Gingrich Republicanism and the Big Business lobbies," thus forcing Democrats to embrace "crypto-Republicanism."[48] Advocates also framed NAFTA's victory as a triumph of corruption, insisting that because pro-NAFTA forces "could not gain Congressional approval on its own merits," they instead won through what Public Citizen president Joan Claybrook deemed a "multi-billion dollar vote buying operation."[49]

*   *   *

The NAFTA fight set the parameters for future conflicts over global trade and governance in the United States. It forced a motley crew of progressive organizations to form a coalition that existed not just in name but in institution. Battling NAFTA did not only bring these groups together. It showed them the importance and limitations of a myriad of campaigning strategies—from local organizing to transnational coalition building. It also revealed how complicated debates over global economics would be in the United States. Far from falling along strictly partisan or even strictly ideological lines, trade confused these usual demarcations.

For a certain segment of public interest progressives, the NAFTA fight served as an important pivot point. In the 1960s and 1970s, public interest groups honed an insider model of policy advocacy that proved quite effective. In pushing for new laws and new regulatory bodies to oversee those laws, they generally counted on Democratic majorities and liberal Republicans in Congress, as well as allies in the federal bureaucracy, to enact change. While they found deficiencies with the presidencies of Nixon, Ford, and Carter, environmental and consumer groups could still work with them (or at least with allies in the federal bureaucracy) to make change. After the hostility of the Reagan-Bush years and Clinton's election, the question became: were the 1980s a fluke or had twelve years of Republican presidents remade the game?

After the NAFTA fight, the answer was clearly the latter. Public interest groups still possessed friends on Capitol Hill. However, the politics in Washington, D.C. now leaned even more strongly to big business than they had in the 1960s and 1970s. Business had organized and now employed hundreds of powerful political action committees, lobbying outfits, and networks. The Democratic Party had entered a low-level civil war over its economic platform, epitomized by New Democrat Bill Clinton versus New Dealer David Bonior.

In this climate, public interest groups faced a series of choices. Some, like the pro-NAFTA environmentalists, tried to recapture the glory days of twenty years prior, when policy expertise and close relationships with the federal government yielded policy wins. Others, like Lori Wallach at Public Citizen or Brent Blackwelder at Friends of the Earth, staked out a different path. On issues related to the global economy, they discovered that public interest groups could not hope to win legislatively—much less be a voice for economic justice domestically or internationally—without backing from a grassroots power base. Thus, public interest groups started to break out of their silos and ally more deeply with unions and community groups. They retooled their policy analysis skills away from formulating new laws and towards understanding international procorporate initiatives in order to better oppose them.

Combating NAFTA also illustrated the complexity of campaigning around Global North-South solidarity politics in the 1990s. The fact that agreements such as NAFTA affected both the Global North and Global South posed opportunities and risks. The mobilization of self-interest arguments over job loss or weakened consumer and environmental protections could bring thousands, even millions, more voices into play on global economic matters. Yet, zeroing in only on such issues threatened to make every argument over international economic policy into a deliberation just over the homeland.

Of course, defending well-compensated union jobs from outsourcing was not an inherently right-wing or even nationalistic position. But a focus on problems mainly in the United States opened the doors to more nationalist stances—and allies. However, as seen in the catastrophe of the Gore-Perot debate and the constant need for fair globalizers to differentiate themselves from Buchanan, cross-ideological alliances, even at the shallowest of levels, carried major risks. Simultaneously, collaborations across borders showed a different path forward. Cooperation among Canadian, Mexican, and U.S. groups yielded little immediate concrete gains because of the particularities of the politics in Mexico and Canada. But not every future situation would be like NAFTA. The possibilities for cooperation across countries would also soon expand. For upcoming battles would not just be trinational, they would be global.

PART V

Rebuilding to Victory in the 1990s

CHAPTER 17

We Are All Asking, Where Are We?

When the sun rose on Sunday, January 1, 1995, it ushered in perhaps the most dispiriting day of the fair globalization coalition's youthful existence. On that day, NAFTA celebrated its first birthday and the World Trade Organization's doors officially opened for business. A mere two months before, the Republican Party swept the midterm elections, assuming control of both the House and the Senate for the first time in decades. Newly elected House Speaker Newt Gingrich strongly backed free trade, declaring on the day of the NAFTA vote that he would tell his "children and grandchildren I voted for us to do something positive."[1]

Despondency reigned among anti-NAFTA progressives. "We are all asking ourselves where are we after the NAFTA and GATT fights in a new era of Gingriches?" wrote Institute for Policy Studies staffers Sarah Anderson and John Cavanagh in December 1994. Exacerbating the negative mood, many in the fair globalization coalition continued to wonder whether better tactics and strategies might have defeated NAFTA or, even worse, whether they had mounted a fundamentally unwinnable fight. Whatever the particular diagnosis of defeat, Anderson and Cavanagh worried for the future, lamenting that "just as our message becomes ever more critical, a number of us seem disheartened."[2] Or as Citizens Trade Campaign head Angela Ledford pondered, "How do we raise these issues and others in this new Congress without a vote pending? Should we work on trade issues as part of a larger economic package or should we isolate a simpler trade issue ... and make it the centerpiece of a larger campaign?"[3]

Two years later, a different mood pervaded. "The transnational corporate lobby is well-heeled," noted Mike Dolan, lead organizer at Public Citizen's Global Trade Watch division in an e-mail to allies. Yet Dolan continued, the coalition had recently "cornered the market on people power and we seem to be winning this historic debate."[4] Dolan's prognosticative powers did not disappoint. By October 1998, staff at the U.S. Trade Representative's office warned that over the previous year "we played a more defensive role than in previous years. . . . We need to take a step back and evaluate."[5]

How did activists go from multiplying defeats to escalating victories? During 1995 and 1996, the fair globalization coalition reassessed and rebuilt. For the public interest progressives, these years let them focus on what they did best: research, translate technical talk into understandable prose, and publicize their findings. These energies were mainly directed at NAFTA, which served as the public symbol of the harms wrought by what activists increasingly dubbed "corporate globalization." At the same time, Citizens Trade Campaign and Alliance for Responsible Trade groups reached a truce, as the organizations tackled different issues while finding room for cooperation. U.S. activists also deepened their internationalist ties through the creation of an ongoing forum bringing thinkers and activists concerned with neoliberal globalization together.

During these same middle years of the 1990s, the fair globalization coalition remobilized. Through the efforts of people such as Dolan, networks of grassroots activists built during the NAFTA fight reorganized and reenergized. Groups such as Public Citizen and other Washington-based NGOs also committed more resources directly to globalization issues. From both fronts, coalition members used the existence of NAFTA to highlight the real damages of neoliberal globalization. Rather than hypothetical claims, they could now point to actual shuttered factories; actual attacks on health, labor, and environmental regulations; and more to build momentum against neoliberal expansion.

By the last years of the 1990s, the fair globalization coalition came better equipped to fight than it had for NAFTA. In 1997 and 1998, fair globalizers mounted two large campaigns—one mainly domestic and one predominantly international—and won both. At home, the coalition ably took advantage of hardening partisan lines and an energized labor movement to block the latest attempt to renew Fast Track negotiating authority. This helped give breathing space to ART's work deepening connections across Latin America to mobilize against NAFTA expansion. Simultaneously, fair globalizers across the spectrum plunged into a campaign where internationalism was not just a slogan but a successful philosophy, as NGOs around the globe successfully torpedoed negotiations for the Multilateral Agreement on Investment (MAI). These wins cemented the fair globalization coalition as a force to be reckoned with.

*   *   *

Before attaining these triumphs, advocates first slogged through an extended period of defeats. In the weeks following NAFTA's passage, fair globalizers lived in a haze. At the CTC, staff went from the exhausting exhilaration of campaigning to the tedium of "transferring the bookkeeping," moving "administrative files to the CTC office," and "dealing with bill collectors."[6] The organization held about $50,000 in unpaid debts and lacked an executive director. As acting head Angela Ledford highlighted in January 1994, "We are at a critical stage in the life of the Citizens Trade Campaign."[7]

One of the most pressing dilemmas surrounded the upcoming congressional vote on the United States becoming a member of the World Trade Organization. Sliding into the background during the heat of the NAFTA fight, the Uruguay Round talks trudged forward throughout 1992 and 1993. Originally intended to bolster the General Agreement on Tariffs and Trade created in 1947, by the early 1990s the Uruguay Round's ambitions had grown. Now negotiators sought to create a whole new institution to be the hub for global economic governance. With such a far-reaching agenda involving so many different states, the talks' success remained far from certain.

The final Uruguay Round agreement proposed a leap forward for global economic liberalization. Rather than tinkering with the General Agreement on Tariffs and Trade, the Uruguay Round concluded with agreement to establish a new body, the World Trade Organization. As with NAFTA, tariffs and quotas represented only one part of the WTO's mandate. Whereas the GATT focused on manufacturing, the WTO's purview would encompass agriculture and the broadly defined service sector. Its provisions included measures limiting the ability of governments to impose laws and regulations, such as rules meant to promote domestic industries. Other provisions also represented substantial changes. The WTO's Trade-Related Aspects of Intellectual Property Rights regime, for example, set a global standard of twenty years for patent protection of new medicines.[8]

Complementing the wider range of policy areas covered by the WTO was an enhanced legal architecture for resolving disputes between countries. Under the GATT, if one state believed another's policies discriminated against them, the aggrieved party had to go through a slow process that required obtaining consensus to form a panel to consider the dispute. Once that process concluded, consensus was again needed, including from the country potentially under sanction, to adopt the panel's conclusion.

WTO rules streamlined this process. Now, adjudicating the dispute and determining sanctions would happen quickly, with consensus only needed to impose penalties. In principle, this transformation in global governance appealed to Global South countries. For some leaders, the new rules promised to place the rich within a more equitable legal framework. However, by making it easier to bring forth disputes, the new system also created incentives for governments to challenge others, including over consumer and environmental regulations. Plus, countries with more resources would be better equipped to raise and pursue disputes than those without.[9]

Multinational corporate executives looked at the Uruguay Round results favorably. The U.S. Chamber of Commerce emphasized the benefits of substantial worldwide tariff reductions, while pharmaceutical companies praised the intellectual property measures.[10] Not everyone in the business class, however, was satisfied. Some wanted more. For instance, Nestlé CEO Helmut Maucher spoke in favor of implementing even stronger dispute resolution mechanisms, including allowing companies direct access to these mechanisms, as they did through NAFTA, instead of limiting them to governments.[11]

The completion of the Uruguay Round talks presented a challenge to the fair globalization coalition. In the United States, both houses of Congress needed to approve implementing legislation before the country could join the WTO.[12] This meant another round of legislative battles. NGOs within the fair globalization coalition again mobilized, stirring up anti-NAFTA activists with declarations such as "the fact is that the GATT is worse than NAFTA," as one CTC mailing intoned in February 1994.[13] Heated rhetoric like this began to permeate the grassroots, with Angela Ledford reporting to Mark Ritchie that "lots of people want to do field work on GATT." She added, "Give me a call."[14]

One sign of hope came from the halls of mainstream U.S. environmentalism. Even pro-NAFTA groups, such as the Natural Resources Defense Council, eventually opposed the Uruguay Round. As with NAFTA, initially these organizations tried to work on the inside to insert stronger ecological protections. However, pressures on the Clinton administration from business were, if anything, more intense than they had been on NAFTA, given the global scope of the Uruguay Round. When environmentalists' minimum demands were not even met, the groups moved to opposition.[15]

Among public interest voices, none rose higher during this fight than Ralph Nader's. Certain that the Uruguay Round would lead to "an unprecedented corporate power grab," Nader threw himself into lobbying against it. He pulled every string he still possessed, leading Wallach to recall that, in the decades she has spent as a public interest lobbyist, she never met with more senators (as opposed to their staffs) than during this campaign. To attract legislators' and public attention, groups such as Public Citizen used a host of publicity stunts.

Public Citizen distributed pillows to senators with the words "Sleep on It" printed on them. Nader offered $10,000 to the charity of choice of any senator who would read the WTO full legislation and take a twelve-question quiz. Only one, Colorado Republican senator Hank Brown, accepted Nader's challenge. Brown passed Nader's quiz and then made an announcement. While usually a free trader, he declared his opposition to the Uruguay Round based on concerns over U.S. sovereignty.[16]

Brown's change of heart pointed to an important but difficult dynamic. As with NAFTA, reaching the necessary vote margin in the House of Representatives meant relying on more than liberal Democratic votes. The GATT fight saw some in the Citizens Trade Campaign leaning into more nationalistic arguments. For instance, Congress and the president needed to agree on making up the $14 billion of lost tariff revenues that would result from the United States' ascension into the WTO.[17] On this point, the CTC played with right-wing talking points, calling on legislators to "Stop the Clinton Spending Spree! . . . GATT will increase the federal deficit by $28 Billion . . . and force . . . taxpayers to pay more just to fatten the bank accounts of a few foreign corporations."[18] Building on his rhetoric from the NAFTA fight, Nader emphasized the WTO's threats to U.S. sovereignty. "Have you ever heard of São Tomé?" he inquired at a press briefing. He then stated, "They've got a vote like ours in the WTO." Such nationalist rhetoric showed that the internal disputes over pragmatism, nationalism, and internationalism that had split the fair globalization coalition during the NAFTA campaign persisted.[19]

Beyond reinforcing right-wing tropes, these efforts also simply failed in their pragmatic mission. The legislation passed in the House of Representatives by a vote of 288 to 146 and 76 to 24 in the Senate—both substantially larger margins than the NAFTA vote.[20] The reasons for the outcome reflected, in part, a weary opposition coalition. Formerly pro-NAFTA environmentalists opposed the Uruguay Round, but they did not "invest substantial resources in a lobbying campaign . . . given the apparent likelihood that the treaty will pass easily in Congress."[21] To Nader, who tended to explain success and failure as solely the function of how dedicated an individual or group was to the cause (rather than consider more structural factors), the explanation for the defeat was a deficit of defiance. He lashed out at allies, accusing the AFL-CIO (for example) of "throwing in the towel."[22]

One of the structural factors at play during the debate was that other, big events dominated many peoples' attentions. Unlike with NAFTA, the Uruguay Round never pierced the public consciousness. After all, 1994 was the year of the O. J. Simpson murder trial and the Clinton health care reform debacle.

According to a Gallup Poll, three-fifths of people surveyed "didn't know enough about the international trade treaty to have an opinion," while 23 percent backed it and only 14 percent opposed it. The eventual vote came during the "lame duck" session after the November elections and before the new Congress took hold, when many members (like those who had lost) felt most comfortable making unpopular votes.[23]

Those paying the most attention to the Uruguay Round resided in the Clinton administration. After the collapse of health care reform, Clinton needed a policy victory. Administration officials leaned on the business lobby to ensure congressional Republicans chose corporate wishes over the GOP's desire to inflict legislative losses on Clinton. At a closed-door meeting with business executives, deputy U.S. trade representative Rufus Yerxa stated, "I know that Republicans tend to listen to industry voices." He asked participants to "urge the Republicans to avoid the trap" of partisanship, cautioning that political pressures could otherwise "drive the Administration into the hands of some Democrats who have some wild ideas"—that is, the David Bonior New Dealer faction.[24]

Indeed, some anti-NAFTA congressional voices did mobilize against the WTO. Frustrating as this opposition was for the administration, it also played to its favor internationally. Throughout the Uruguay Round talks, U.S. negotiators used the threat of congressional rejection to press other countries into compromises that favored U.S. positions. Thus, in a way, the very effectiveness of the anti-NAFTA forces helped to ensure the United States' embrace of the WTO.[25]

Emerging from this defeat, some activists tried to keep the energy up. Writing to CTC members, Wallach acknowledged, "It can be hard to see beyond the congressional result, and speaking from personal experience, easy to get fed up and depressed." Yet she continued, "After a little spleen-venting, sleep, and reflection, what we have accomplished actually is no less than astounding."[26] Such fighting words did not necessarily resonate. Traveling to Miami in December 1994, Institute for Policy Studies staffer Sarah Anderson found herself immersed in the brave new world of the "Washington Consensus," a term increasingly popularized to signify neoliberal governance. Attending the Summit of the Americas, which brought together heads of states to discuss a possible hemisphere-wide free-trade deal, she watched elated corporate and government officials celebrate NAFTA, the WTO, and the future. The experience left her utterly "demoralized."[27]

CHAPTER 18

Exposing the Entire Free-Trade Model

Rebuilding in the aftermath of two losses within a year started with interpersonal relationships. In 1996, reflecting on his almost twenty years of internationalist agitation, Mark Ritchie wrote an essay reminding his colleagues of the "importance of personal relationships. . . . It is the people that matter."[1] During the mid-1990s, many fair globalizers' took this advice to heart. Without a major campaign to wage, they used the pause to ask deeper questions and to build and strengthen personal and interorganizational relationships.

Taking the lead on one critical initiative was Jerry Mander, a former corporate advertising star, who left the for-profit realm in the 1960s. Mander went on to cofound one of the country's first nonprofit ad agencies, Public Media Communications, whose clientele included the Nestlé boycotters.[2] In the early 1990s, Mander connected with his friend Edward Goldsmith, the founder of the *Ecologist*, around their shared disdain for the direction of global capitalism.

Goldsmith's worldview did not easily fit into conventional ideological slots. An environmental thinker, activist, and journalist, he possessed radical critiques of society's focus on ideas of "progress." He was an earlier thinker in "deep ecology," believing that the Industrial Revolution represented a fundamentally wrong turn in human history. He embraced "tradition" as an ideal, including a deep admiration and support for precapitalist indigenous peoples' ideas and societies, an emphasis on the value of small communities, but also potentially retrograde views.[3] Goldsmith and Mander's discussions led to the formation of the International Forum on Globalization (IFG).

Composed initially of sixty people representing sixty groups from twenty-five countries, the IFG included public intellectuals, think tank researchers, grassroots agitators, and public interest advocates. When IFG members

gathered, their meeting minutes resembled the scrambled notes of a graduate
school sociology seminar more than a policy strategy session. Broadly speaking, as Mander explained, most of its participants believed "economic globalization amounts to a kind of Corporate Utopian scheme, which will do harm to
all other sectors." Mander further explained that "most among us feel the process is unreformable and *not inevitable*" and that the "only eventual solution
must lie with a process of re-localization."[4]

After those broad points of consensus, however, complex disagreements
over analysis and solutions arose, as demonstrated in the meeting notes from a
January 1995 IFG gathering. The notes show members recognizing the intellectual morass they found themselves in. This partly reflected the international
left's post–Cold War ideological vacuum. Attendees at the meeting admitted
that "nothing [was] ready to replace communism," which had at least offered
"something to be for rather than something to be against." As Council of
Canadians leader Maude Barlow stated, the "new ideology is that there is no
ideology."[5]

However, that was not entirely true. Everyone possessed ideas, and one
main intellectual faction emerged within the IFG, consisting of the forum's
founders and some key members. This grouping identified with varying philosophies of deep ecology, indigenous environmentalism, and ecofeminism.
They asserted that the only way out of the crises of economic inequality and
ecological devastation lay in a return to the "community-based economy."
Many of them looked at "modern" science and technology as antagonists, with
Goldsmith declaring there was "more to discover than invent—Don't need new
tech, new science." The views of many in this group partly arose from explicit
examinations of colonialism's effects on indigenous peoples. As Seneca historian and activist John Mohawk insisted at one meeting, activists needed to
"challenge Western science as a tool of Western capital." The focus on indigenous practices led to many insights about the profundity of global inequities. It
also reflected serious considerations about ecology, pointing out that the fundamental oppression of the Global South by the Global North grew from the
extraction of "biological resources."

Many espousing these views, particularly those not from indigenous backgrounds, rooted their worldviews in a decontextualized romanticism that removed indigenous peoples from their historical specificities and complex
societal politics. Few in this group seemed to interrogate ideas of "tradition,"
"community," or the "local." Thus, questions over how "traditional" values,
local communities, or small business enterprises could function as oppressive
forces remained underexplored. Or, as IFG participant Leah Wise of the

Southeast Regional Economic Justice Network pointedly asked, "Who is the we; the community we are reclaiming?"[6]

Perhaps the most heated discussions among IFG members concerned what Indian ecofeminist Vandana Shiva dubbed the "good vs. bad globalization" debate. Figures such as Shiva and Goldsmith, who highlighted traditional societies, doubted the very idea of global governance. They believed that such concepts as "fair trade" ended up "legitimizing [the] whole global system." Even some of the more "pragmatic" activists shared such doubts, asking whether critics of neoliberal globalization, in Maude Barlow's words, spent "too much time putting into governments how to claim rights back."

Indeed, the options seemed few. For those in the United States, a major challenge revolved around winning a political fight versus an ideological one. While a growing number in the Democratic Party might oppose specific trade deals, most U.S. liberals still advocated the underlying ideas of capitalist integration that many in IFG rejected. Meanwhile, at a global scale, "countries who used to lead the fight against TNCs [transnational corporations] now grovel for investment," bemoaned Martin Khor, recalling the vanished era of a mere twenty years earlier, when many Third World states called for global transformation, whether a New International Economic Order or Marxist revolution.[7]

These doubts did not stop some advocates from speaking up for reform or global governance. Filipino activist Walden Bello reminded IFG members that they could not just "yield" the international arena to neoliberals. Khor, Cavanagh, and others echoed this point, arguing that discussions of localization would fail without attention to new global rules.[8] However, even among those arguing in favor of greater global economic governance, rifts emerged. Martin Khor railed against introducing "workers rights" into international fora, seeing this move as "clearly prompted not by feelings of goodwill towards Third World workers, but by protectionist attempts to prevent the transfer of jobs from the North to the South."[9] Simultaneously, Chilean environmentalist Sara Larrían made the opposite argument regarding environmental regulations, stating, "Opposition to environmental standards as imperialist [from people in the Third World] comes from pol. Parties—not enviros."[10]

Given all this, unsurprisingly, a single coherent vision for alternative economics and global governance did not emerge from the IFG. However, a useful set of commonly agreed-upon notions about core problems did. Chief among these was the argument, as explained by Canadian campaigner Tony Clarke, that the "real power to rule is being exercised not by governments and their agencies but by transnational corporations."[11] Thus, the framing for many campaigns shifted, portraying corporations as the puppet masters and governments as (to varying degrees) their servants. Furthermore, across the spectrum of IFG factions, critiques of corporations' harms to ecology and to workers expanded to encompass questions of culture, emphasizing homogenization, with "consumer" replacing other identities as the new global norm. And, amid the more philosophical discussions, IFG also offered a space for many technical discussions of policies such as the WTO's intellectual property rights regime.[12]

U.S. public interest advocates came to the IFG with varying degrees of enthusiasm. Commenting on U.S. fair globalizers (especially from the CTC), Mark Ritchie observed that while they understood "issue specific fights," they remained "very weak" on understanding the "overall policy changes required to bring about fundamental change."[13] Many at the Alliance for Responsible Trade talked up the IFG as a place to have serious, long-term conversations outside the strictures of a campaign. Unsurprisingly, many from the Citizens Trade Campaign approached the IFG skeptically, viewing it as a "loosey-goosey" assortment of "lots of conceptualizers, few producers." The value some from the CTC derived from the forum stemmed less from ideas than connections. The IFG opened space such that "once personal relationship is established," specific groups of activists were "all thrilled to off road"—that is, activists met and then began scheming about new campaigns and projects.[14]

Outside of these private conversations, members of the IFG prepared public education initiatives. Along with publishing books, the main method for spreading their message consisted of public teach-ins. In 1995 and 1996, the IFG sponsored speaking tours across the United States featuring a cavalcade of activists, including Wallach, Barlow, Shiva, Khor, Bello, Brent Blackwelder, and more. At their best, the IFG's traveling lecture series gathered hundreds, even thousands of people, equipping them with knowledge and rhetoric for future campaigns.[15]

*   *   *

IFG members were not alone in raising the specter of corporate globalization in the mid-1990s. In 1994, the same year as the fight against the creation of the World Trade Organization, many NGOs affiliated with the Alliance for Responsible Trade, in collaboration with small organizations working in solidarity with struggles in particular countries, came together to form the 50 Years Is Enough coalition. The name nodded to the half-century birthdays of the International Monetary Fund and the World Bank in that year. While the organization's name and many of its members sought these institutions' abolition, the coalition officially demanded "far-reaching changes in the lending policies, internal processes and structure" of the two institutions.[16] 50 Years Is Enough joined existing environmentalist campaigns targeting the World Bank and the IMF, using U.S. government appropriations as leverage.[17]

While 50 Years Is Enough focused on multilateral bodies, other groups went straight at big business. In 1996, a small nonprofit, the National Labor Committee (NLC) published a report on horrid conditions in Honduran sweatshops, highlighting the employment of laborers as young as fifteen working seventy-five-hour weeks.[18] This was not the NLC's first publication, but it garnered much greater attention than they had ever received. The reason was the news hook of implicating a celebrity.[19] Among the people and companies that the NLC identified as profiting from sweatshops included Kathie Lee Gifford, then cohost of *Live! with Regis and Kathie Lee*, one of the nation's most popular television programs.

The scandal exploded across the airwaves. In the next years, building partly on the NAFTA fight's focus on *maquiladoras*, "sweatshop" became a household word. Making much noise on the issue was the Union of Needletrades, Industrial, and Textile Employees (UNITE). During the mid-1990s, UNITE dispatched members to do awareness-raising actions at stores selling apparel made in sweatshops. UNITE also helped nurture what became one of the most vibrant student organizations ever to appear on the U.S. left: United Students Against Sweatshops. In the wake of the Kathie Lee Gifford revelations, autonomous student organizations protesting sweatshop labor appeared on several campuses. A group of students interning at UNITE helped stitch these independent groups together. Students began rallying around demands that university administrations pass codes of conduct and support attempts to monitor labor conditions in factories producing apparel for colleges and universities.[20]

The sweatshop controversies, although focused on Central America and Indonesia, built on the debates aired during the NAFTA fight. To help keep debate alive, groups such as Public Citizen and the Institute for Policy Studies produced regular reports tracking NAFTA's effects. In 1995, Public Citizen published *NAFTA's Broken Promises: Job Creation Under NAFTA*, a study claiming that of sixty-six specific corporate pledges that NAFTA would increase jobs, fifty-nine had not come true.[21] The study displeased corporate officials. "Although traditionally, NIKE ignores most of Public Citizen's views . . . *NAFTA's Broken Promises* . . . contained such a gross inaccuracy about NIKE's operations that I am compelled to ask that you issue a correction," wrote Nike lobbyist Brad Fogel.[22] Both the Business Roundtable and the U.S. Commerce Department also denounced the report.[23]

NAFTA's Broken Promises was one of many studies undertaken by groups such as Public Citizen and the IPS under the banner of "NAFTA Accountability." Activist groups started watchdogging NAFTA's impacts immediately after its passage. On Capitol Hill, fair globalization groups' reports provided backing for legislators to continue drumming up opposition to the already-existing agreement and future expansions of it.

What no one expected, however, was how quickly questions of NAFTA's effects on Mexico would hit the front pages. First, on January 1, 1994 (the day NAFTA took effect), the Ejército Zapatista de Liberación Nacional (Zapatista Army of National Liberation, or EZLN) initiated an armed insurgency. Arising in the southern Mexican state of Chiapas, the Zapatistas declared NAFTA a "death sentence" and seized several towns. While their armed rebellion lasted a short time, the Zapatistas and their leader, Subcomandante Marcos, quickly became global leftist heroes. Zapatista writings on neoliberalism and their work to build an autonomous, noncapitalist society acted as an ongoing rebuttal to neoliberalism.[24]

The next strike against narratives of NAFTA's success hit in late 1994. As the first year of NAFTA implementation came to a close, multinational financiers and banks that had poured money into Mexico suddenly fled. Almost overnight, Mexico faced the potential of grappling with its worst economic downturn since the 1930s.[25] Where only weeks before, Clinton had planned to celebrate NAFTA's one-year anniversary, he now demurred. Instead, the administration hunkered down to win support for a $40 billion "stabilization" package to salvage Mexico's economy.[26]

The Zapatista uprising and the "peso crisis" reinvigorated U.S. fair globalizers. As a joint CTC–ART press release proclaimed, while NAFTA did not create the peso crisis, it "encouraged a climate wherein Mexico's stock market became a casino for short-term investors."[27] By renewing the spotlight on Mexico's economy in U.S. political discourse, the crisis enhanced fair globalizers' ability to keep NAFTA in the headlines. Amplifying their critiques, anti-NAFTA forces in Congress also highlighted the peso crisis. "The truth of the matter is, we're not gleeful to say that we were right about NAFTA," declared a gruff congressman with an unmistakably working-class Brooklyn accent named Bernie Sanders in late January 1995.[28]

One of the groups most deeply committed to "NAFTA Accountability" was Public Citizen, whose work highlighted the organization's leadership within the fair globalization coalition. During the NAFTA and WTO fights, the point person on globalization, Lori Wallach, worked under the auspices of Public Citizen's Congress Watch division. Now she successfully lobbied her superiors to form a new division within Public Citizen. Launched in 1995, Global Trade Watch (GTW) immediately became a crucial space for policy analysis and political mobilization within the fair globalization coalition.[29]

One of the most important early actions undertaken by GTW involved investing significantly in grassroots activism. As Wallach noted in a lengthy May 1995 memorandum, "We have made our trade critiques politically relevant, but as the votes showed, not politically determinative." The answer was "a major shift in public perception."[30] This meant keeping up and growing the grassroots. For Public Citizen, this led to the hiring of a new field organizer: Mike Dolan.

Boisterous, charismatic, and effective, Dolan fit well into the Public Citizen culture, which mixed 1960s New Leftism with older liberal politics. Before joining the group, he had spent years learning from veterans of the United Farm Workers, organizing for political candidates, and serving as the field director for Rock the Vote.[31] Living in San Francisco when he accepted the job at Public Citizen, Dolan pitched a novel idea to introduce himself to the grassroots members of the Citizens Trade Campaign. Rather than immediately moving to Washington, D.C., he would rent a U-Haul adorned with a large "'NAFTA: Bad Then, Worse Now—Demand NAFTA Accountability" banner on the side and drive across the country, stopping all over to meet "the field."[32] Dolan tied his road trip to a proposed piece of legislation, the NAFTA Accountability Act, a bill demanding a review and possible withdrawal from NAFTA by the United States. Crisscrossing the nation, Dolan found CTC-affiliated groups dissipating but not completely gone. Dolan moved swiftly to revivify them. After arriving in Washington after many conversations, he instituted a regular series of fax messages to CTC affiliates, containing detailed information about policy and politics and clearly spelled-out action items, such as lobby days or letters to the editor.[33]

This constant drumbeat of anti-NAFTA messaging helped to shape a broader growing discontent with the accord. By early 1997, Gallup found 37 percent of people in the United States held favorable opinions of NAFTA, as compared with 47 percent with negative opinions.[34] Dissatisfaction with NAFTA even filtered into popular culture, as witnessed in a March 1995 episode of the wildly popular television show *The Simpsons*. In the episode "A Star Is Burns," hypervillainous corporate tycoon Montgomery Burns wishes to commission an epic cinematic biography of himself. Burns barks at his assistant, Waylon Smithers, to "Get me Steven Spielberg!" Told that Spielberg is "unavailable," Burns commands Smithers, "Then get me his non-union, Mexican equivalent!" The resulting biopic includes a scene where Burns promises Mexican villagers that he will "close plants in America and bring work here."[35]

In the realm of electoral politics, however, dissatisfaction with North American free trade encountered something of a vacuum. Electorally, this energy had little place to go on the left. While Ralph Nader ran for president as an independent in 1996, he put little energy into the effort and received little in return. Among Democrats, none of the labor-liberals challenged Clinton in the primary. While Ross Perot ran again, he did not spark the same energy as four years before.

Into this void entered Patrick Buchanan. Without abandoning his ongoing rhetorical and political war against gays, lesbians, people of color, and Latin American immigrants, Buchanan's second shot at the White House uplifted economic nationalism more explicitly. Announcing his candidacy for the Republican Party presidential nomination, Buchanan quickly turned to trade, promising that he would ensure "there will be no more NAFTA sellouts of American workers. There will be no more GATT deals done for the benefit of Wall Street bankers. . . . We start looking out for America First."[36] At first, this message resonated more than expected. Buchanan won the first four GOP primary contests, culminating in victory in the all-important state of New Hampshire.[37]

Buchanan's campaign helped crystallize a challenge for progressives. Starting with the NAFTA fight, some fair globalizers had formed alliances with right-wing interests such as the U.S. Business and Industry Council. Buchanan's attacks on international bodies having power over U.S. domestic laws and legislatures paralleled critiques by fair globalizers. Unsurprisingly, people at ART, who tended to highlight questions of racism, urged a response to Buchanan in order to draw a sharp dividing line. Writing to progressive public relations expert David Fenton, Cavanagh observed that "the early success of the Buchanan campaign" had "polarized" the trade debate as portrayed in mass media into a binary between "unconditional support of free trade vs. Pat Buchanan's racist protectionism."[38]

Fair globalizers tried to distinguish the two and present a third option. In a February 1996 press release, the CTC pointed to the "widespread disenchantment with the promises made by 'free trade' politicians" that helped propel Buchanan to his early wins. Yet, the CTC affirmed, Buchanan's proposal for constructing a wall on the U.S.-Mexico border was "shortsighted and mean spirited," and they further reaffirmed the importance of solidarity, declaring that "only by working with our Mexican allies will we be able to throw off the yokes of . . . oppressive trade agreements."[39]

Buchanan's popularity momentarily shook up the politics of trade within the Republican Party. While GOP frontrunner Bob Dole remained committed to free trade, he also began publicly criticizing past agreements. Championing this move was Robert Lighthizer, later to become President Donald Trump's U.S. trade representative. In the mid-1990s, Lighthizer had already served as deputy U.S. trade representative and now acted as Dole's campaign treasurer. A defender of U.S. industrial prerogatives over unrestricted trade, Lighthizer urged Dole to "slash the 'free' out of free trade."[40] At the Republican convention, Dole proclaimed that the United States must "commit ourselves to a trade policy that does not suppress pay and threaten American jobs . . . and [does] not let our national sovereignty be infringed by the World Trade Organization."[41] Yet Dole's trade agnosticism did not go far, especially after Buchanan dropped out of the race. A mere two months after the convention, while debating Clinton, Dole affirmed, "I supported the President's trade policy."[42] He blamed job loss not on NAFTA but on weak enforcement of its provisions. Still, that Dole believed he needed to fire off a few anti–free trade broadsides showed the instability of globalization politics.

Meanwhile, in the Clinton camp, optimism about the international economy prevailed. Free trade represented a key stepping-stone on the president's "bridge to the twenty-first century," a vision for a prosperous, globalized U.S. future. Clinton advisers, such as Mark Penn and Dick Morris, insisted that Clinton owed his 1996 win to his appeal to upwardly mobile suburbanites who favored deregulation and free trade.[43] With his next four years secured, Clinton wanted to "take advantage of the extraordinary opportunities presented by the growing global economy."[44] Yet the administration soon discovered that they could not long run from the budding anger and resistance inspired in large part by NAFTA's legacies.

CHAPTER 19

Derailing Fast Track

Shortly after Clinton's reelection, his Council of Economic Advisers released a report on the United States' place in the world economy. With the U.S. economy seemingly booming, the sense of decline that permeated the early 1990s now faded. As part of continuing to assert U.S. preeminence, the document called for expanding NAFTA. "Market opening and integration in the West hemisphere, which began with . . . NAFTA, is approaching its culmination in ongoing talks on creating a Free Trade Area of the Americas [FTAA]," the report boasted.[1] Unsurprisingly, the desire of Clinton and leaders across the Americas to sign onto the NAFTA agenda energized both the Alliance for Responsible Trade and the Citizens Trade Campaign. In an example of how an activist division of labor can minimize conflict and maximize outcomes, the two networks challenged the oncoming FTAA with distinct approaches.

For those at ART, the proposed Free Trade Area of the Americas became their top issue. Their dedication to combating the FTAA arose largely because Mexican and other Latin American activist groups identified its defeat as *their* main priority. Mere weeks after NAFTA's approval, RMALC's membership gathered to discuss the future. They warned that NAFTA's passage "opened the door to the rest of the continent" for neoliberal expansion.[2] In response, Mexican activist Carmen Valadez declared during a hemispheric activist gathering in March 1994 that opponents of the NAFTA "model" needed to "develop our *own* continental ties."[3]

Even as FTAA talks moved forward, activists more immediately worried over negotiations for a U.S.-Chile Free Trade Agreement, seen as a building block to a hemispheric agreement.[4] In Chile, the Red Chile de Acción para una Iniciativa de los Pueblos (the Chilean Action Network for Peoples' Initiatives), modeled on the Mexican anti-NAFTA coalition, began preparing. In May 1997, they hosted the Foro Ciudadano Hemisférico Frente a la Globalización (the

Citizen Hemispheric Forum on Globalization), offering space for anti-FTAA organizers from across the Americas to talk in-person.[5]

Of the two U.S. fair globalization networks, the Alliance for Responsible Trade took the lead in engaging with this transnational organizing. ART leader Karen Hansen-Kuhn helped run *Our Americas*, a newsletter covering policy and political developments in the FTAA negotiations. ART and RMALC produced documents about the anguish NAFTA was causing Mexican farmers and laborers.[6] Activists in ART viewed their approaches to the NAFTA fight as bearing fruit. To them and many in Latin America, it now seemed clear that long-term, cross-border organizing was the key to eventual success. Moreover, unlike with NAFTA, for the FTAA, they wanted to be sure a detailed alternative developed by left-leaning civil society existed. This would be a long, grueling process fraught with ideological, tactical, and strategic disagreements.

The initial wave of this fervent, Americas-wide mobilization peaked with the creation of the Hemispheric Social Alliance, launched in May 1997 at a meeting in Belo Horizonte, Brazil. Spearheading this initiative were union federations: the AFL-CIO and, especially, the Brazilian Central Única dos Trabalhadores (the Unified Workers Federation). These union federations, operating under the umbrella of a seeming Cold War relic—the Inter-American Regional Organization of Workers—decided that unions needed relationships with NGOs and social movements in order to beat the FTAA. Thus, for the first time in its history, the Inter-American Regional Organization invited non-union groups to participate in a meeting. Out of this gathering arose a manifesto for the anti-FTAA coalition and the Hemispheric Social Alliance.[7] The document displayed the growing prevalence of antineoliberal arguments centered on ideas of governance, stating that "so called free trade is actually trade regulation that increases the advantages of international capital."[8]

While organized labor played a significant role, the very fact of their outreach to social movements and NGOs demonstrated the emergent influence of these groups. U.S.-based members of ART neither led these efforts nor were bit players in them. Representatives from ART groups attended Hemispheric Social Alliance meetings, offering input, expertise, and perhaps more important, greater access to the centers of power located in Washington, D.C.[9] ART invited leaders from major South American unions and social movements to the United States, including for briefings to members of Congress and their staff.[10] Meanwhile, in a U.S. context, ART understood itself as the tendency within the fair globalization coalition focused on helping "to build a hemispheric social alliance around the positive social vision." Simultaneously, as ART leader

David Ranney reflected, there also existed the need "to defeat neo-liberal pro-posals." To do so, he continued, "requires single minded dedication to that end. That work is being ably done by the Citizens Trade Campaign."[11]

For the CTC, defeating NAFTA expansion meant diving into a brewing procedural fight: the renewal of Fast Track, the legislation that smoothed the path for trade deals by limiting the role of Congress in trade negotiations. The last Fast Track renewal happened in 1991. In that moment, the fight helped spur the fair globalization coalition's formation. The legislation had lapsed in late 1994. With its growing free-trade agenda, in early 1997, the Clinton ad-ministration decided to push for renewal.[12] In his February 1997 State of the Union address, Clinton declared he needed "the authority now to conclude new trade agreements."[13]

As they charted a path forward, many Clinton administration officials be-lieved they had at least one advantage absent during the NAFTA fight. Orga-nized labor, still the most potent left-of-center force opposing new free-trade pacts, seemed (potentially) uninterested in repeating the all-out offensive they eventually launched against NAFTA. The White House's confidence partly stemmed from the giant upset that rocked the U.S. labor movement in 1995. For the first time in the history of the AFL-CIO (or its predecessor, the Ameri-can Federation of Labor), the expected next president of the federation lost an election. Instead John Sweeney, formerly president of the Service Employees International Union, who ran an insurgent campaign, took the reins. Along with him came a slate of candidates for other offices, all running under the banner of "New Voice." Many New Voice leaders identified as left critics of the AFL-CIO leadership. They had fought for years within their unions and in the federation for more resources to go toward organizing workers. Many in New Voice wanted to move away from the defensive and reactive postures the fed-eration had embraced for decades. Some were particularly interested in global issues, having waged battles to alter the AFL-CIO leadership's foreign policy positions.[14]

At first, officials in the Clinton administration hoped the New Voice leaders might actually step back from trade fights. Unlike the manufacturing union representatives who had previously dominated the AFL-CIO, key members of the New Voice's leadership arose from service-sector unions. A janitor or a checkout clerk faced many challenges, but fear of their job being offshored was not one. Furthermore, an article in the New Republic in April 1997 reported that, privately, Sweeney scoffed at the amount of resources poured by the AFL-CIO into combating NAFTA.[15] It seemed to the Clinton administration that an opening existed for détente over trade between centrist Democrats and organized labor. As one White House aide urged, "We need to go to Sweeney. . . . Be positive, no threat."[16]

For the heads of the Citizens Trade Campaign, anything that calmed the White House concerned them. Among CTC members, fear arose that the AFL-CIO was "effectively . . . ceding the field" to the pro–free trade side. Rumors spread that certain high officials at the AFL-CIO wanted to move the federation toward neutrality or even support for future free-trade pacts in order to improve relations with Clinton. In response, CTC leaders worked back channels, urging labor to stay firmly in the opposition camp.[17] The AFL-CIO did issue a statement in February 1997 attacking NAFTA's "inadequacies" and stated further that it would oppose Fast Track unless the renewal included strong worker and environment protections.[18]

Meanwhile, the CTC prepared for its first big fight in two years. This would test whether Mike Dolan and countless regional and local organizers had indeed reconstructed and solidified networks from the NAFTA fight. Reporting to the CTC's Executive Committee in March 1997, Dolan noted that the campaign could count on 413 activist leaders in 17 states.[19]

The CTC's NGO leaders stayed in close touch with the heads of large national groups to coordinate messaging and strategy. New technologies streamlined and expanded the mobilization. Organizers now relied on technologies including "blast fax" and e-mail, which allowed for rapid communication with large numbers of people. More so than e-mail, for Dolan, the "blast fax" impressed; as he later recounted, this system made it so the "last thing before I went home, I could push a button and first thing in the morning everyone from local labor councils to Sierra Club chapters would have a fax *from me*."[20]

The core message in Dolan's blast faxes and other CTC communiqués was simple: they wanted to ensure that no one could hear the phrase "Fast Track" and not immediately think "NAFTA." As Teamsters press person Steve Trossman argued, the message "should be very simple: NAFTA has failed for working families."[21] Here, public interest groups' policy expertise became a lobbying weapon. They distributed press releases, memos, and reports on how NAFTA had weakened food safety, increased job outsourcing, and otherwise (according to them) harmed livelihoods.

As they geared up for their own campaign, the Clinton administration faced a quandary. Both NAFTA and the Uruguay Round passed when Democrats controlled both houses of Congress. Now the GOP held the majorities. Although most Republicans backed free trade more vigorously than did most Democrats, they were also dedicated to inflicting as many political defeats on Bill Clinton as possible. Moreover, they possessed an actual policy disagreement on Fast Track. The Clinton administration wanted to include labor and environmental language in the Fast Track negotiating objectives, either within the main text or as side agreements. Gingrich scoffed, declaring that Republicans "would be willing to look at [fast track] as long as we aren't mandating a social contract."[22]

Republican pressure helped kill hopes among some liberals that the new Fast Track might include provisions making it (and future free-trade deals) more palatable to labor and other progressives. Indeed, as the side agreement talks had done with NAFTA, discussions of new policies within Fast Track temporarily eased organized labor's response. As Thea Lee, an economist who had been in the fair globalization trenches for years (and was now the AFL-CIO's deputy chief of staff) announced in an August 1997 memo, "As soon as the administration releases legislation, we will stop debating the merits of different fast track bills and go into opposition mode. I have heard no rumors that are our demands are likely to be met." However, Lee noted, "Our strategy for attacking will depend on how far the administration goes to placate moderate Democrats."[23]

Lee received her answer on September 16, 1997, when President Clinton unveiled his Fast Track bill. The bill included a call for labor and environmental protections to be included in future trade accords. However, such provisions would only be applicable for abuses of ecology and employees that could be "directly related" to the effects of future free-trade agreements.[24] This language left a gaping hole, as almost any scandal involving environmental or worker issues could be attributed to reasons not "directly related" to the trade bill.

Clinton still held out some hope for calm between his administration and labor. On September 24, 1997, he spoke at the AFL-CIO Constitutional Convention. There, Clinton admitted, "I know we don't see eye to eye on Fast Track, but I think I owe it to you to tell you exactly why I feel so passionately. . . . And I think I've earned the right to be heard." Unionists listened but did not agree with the president's reasoning. In a stinging rebuke shortly after his speech, the AFL-CIO's Subcommittee on the Global Economy reported on awful labor conditions in countries such as Guatemala. Kicking off the next morning, Sweeney declared, "We want the world to know how strongly we oppose NAFTA expansion and Fast Track."[25]

Soon after, the AFL-CIO and many of its constituent unions went to red alert. The United Steelworkers alone generated 160,000 handwritten letters to Congress opposing Fast Track. Union locals placed dedicated cell phones at workplaces so that individual workers could call members of Congress on their breaks.[26] This intensity owed much to fears of a NAFTA repeat. Writing to CTC organizers, Dolan reminded them, "This time in '93 we thought we had

NAFTA beat and still yet the First Free Trader did his 'comeback kid' schtick and . . . well, you remember."[27]

Fortunately for fair globalizers, winning over congressional Democrats proved much easier than it had for NAFTA. For one, after 1994, there were fewer congressional Democrats—and more of those who remained identified with the labor-liberal faction of the party over the Clintonite New Democrats. Electorally, Democrats knew that in the lead-up to the 1994 midterms and afterward, many rank-and-file union members had stayed home, unable to stomach backing pro-NAFTA Democrats. Unions also hit pro-NAFTA Democrats where it hurt by decreasing their donations and support.[28] Thus, by the time Clinton began seriously pushing Fast Track, a sizable portion of the Democratic congressional caucus opposed the president, including previously pro-NAFTA members.[29]

Boxed in on the left, little promise was to be found on Clinton's right. The business lobby backed the bill, but Fast Track's procedural nature and Clinton's sluggishness in advocating for it depressed corporate enthusiasm. In late July 1997, several leaders of the Business Roundtable wrote a memo to their members. In it, the CEOs of General Motors, Procter & Gamble, and Boeing (among others) lamented that Fast Track's "prospects" looked "uncertain." They attributed this predicament to "opposition by organized labor, human rights groups, protectionists, isolationists, and environmental groups," whose efforts had taken their "toll" on free-trade backers. These executives further admitted that fair globalization groups commanded the public discourse, as many congresspeople spoke of fast track renewal as a "referendum on NAFTA, which is remembered on Capitol Hill" as a "difficult vote."[30]

Even as business tried to mobilize, dissension also brewed among some House Republicans. The relative success of Patrick Buchanan's primary campaign in 1996, the continuing strength of Perot's United We Stand America, and GOP conflicts with Clinton on other matters all sapped energy from the caucus. Republicans threatened to prevent the legislation from going to a vote unless Democrats could sway at least eighty of their members to vote "yes"—an impossible task.[31] Waiting on the vote, U.S. Trade Representative Charlene Barshefsky remembered telling her husband, "Either I pray this bill fails, or we withdraw it, but it's now a liability."[32] Clinton chose the latter of Barshefsky's options. Around 1:15 a.m. on November 10, 1997, only hours before the scheduled vote, he called Gingrich and asked for an indefinite postponement of the vote. Gingrich concurred.[33]

On hearing the news, jubilation mixed with caution among fair globalizers. "Almost certainly, Clinton will make another go," Wallach noted in a late

November 1997 memo. In the interim, the Citizens Trade Campaign would profusely thank its congressional allies, heap praise or pressure (depending on their trajectories) on wavering members, and punish its foes.[34] In the meantime, they celebrated. Especially heartening was the media narrative that emerged about Fast Track's demise. Analyzing the outcome in the *Washington Post*, reporters Thomas Edsall and John Yang concluded, "In the politics of the Democratic Party, the winner in the fast-track outcome is the growing alliance of diverse interests that includes AFL-CIO president John Sweeney, Ralph Nader, [and] the Sierra Club."[35]

Within a few months, celebrations went on hold. By early 1998, Clinton again raised the possibility of Congress approving Fast Track. Speaking to small-business owners in Santiago, Chile, in April 1998, Clinton assured them, "I will continue to work hard with Congress to build support for Fast Track."[36] Simultaneously, Gingrich felt his own pressures. Annoyed by the emphasis on social conservatism among congressional Republicans, corporate leaders at the U.S. Chamber of Commerce and the Business-Industry Political Action Committee signaled their frustration at the lack of progress on business's agenda. To get Gingrich moving, corporate lobbies began shifting their donations to a more even spread between Democrats and Republicans.[37] U.S. multinational heads worried that the "continued lack of fast-track is leaving the United States on the sidelines" of global economic competition, with the Business Roundtable declaring Fast Track "even more important now than it was last year."[38]

On June 25, 1998, during a bipartisan press conference focused on the plight of U.S. farmers, Gingrich seized the moment to announce his goal of holding a Fast Track vote by September. Yet Gingrich's timing actually gave Democrats opposed to the bill more leverage than ever. The fall of 1998 marked the apex of the effort by leading congressional Republicans to impeach and remove President Clinton from office over the Monica Lewinsky affair. To thwart this crusade, Clinton knew he needed the absolute support of the whole Democratic Party and its activist allies.[39] Wary of angering such groups as labor and public interest progressives, Clinton deprioritized Fast Track. Meanwhile, Gingrich and GOP leaders hoped to use this dynamic to their advantage. Knowing that some Democrats wanted to back free trade (especially those from export-reliant districts), they tried to force those members to choose between their party and the business community. "Whose interests are you representing— ours or the Washington labor union bosses?" asked Republican National Committee spokesperson Mary Crawford.[40]

With a vote set for late September 1998, the White House yielded to the need to maintain harmony in its base. Reports swirled of Clinton administration

Figure 6. Dan Seligman (Sierra Club), Brent Blackwelder (Friends of the Earth), Lori Wallach (Public Citizen), and Kathy Ozer (National Family Farm Coalition), September 23, 1998. Courtesy of Scott J. Ferrell and Getty Images.

officials urging pro–Fast Track Democrats to temper their support of the bill.[41] Fair globalizers mobilized to shore up their supporters and gain more backers in Congress. When Fast Track finally came to a vote, only 29 Democrats supported it, while 171 voted "no." Whereas in 1993, 41 percent of House Democrats backed NAFTA, now only 14 percent supported Fast Track. Even on the GOP side, it appeared that free trade's popularity was waning; 151 House Republicans voted "yes," but 71 said "no."[42]

With the calling of the vote count, at Global Trade Watch's headquarters a few blocks away, anticipation exploded into glee. "Congratulations!! Yippee!! Yahoo!!" started a memo sent by Wallach to allies and friends.[43] Victory opened space not only to breathe but to contemplate alternatives. If the current model of Fast Track now appeared too politically toxic, clearly significant alterations would have to happen. As Wallach noted in a memorandum to the United Auto Workers, "We need to lay out the mechanisms that ensure we get the contents we want," such as enforceable labor and environmental protections with equal standing to investment provisions.[44] Even if those negotiations faltered, however, the fair globalization coalition's victory proved something basic: they could win a political brawl over international economic governance.

CHAPTER 20

We Seem to Be Winning

The consequences of Fast Track's demise registered far beyond U.S. borders. In April 1998, just as Gingrich tried to revive Fast Track, a summit of (almost all) the governments of the Americas met in Santiago to continue negotiations over the Free Trade Area of the Americas. Uncertainty permeated, with several Caribbean and Latin American countries' negotiators registering their frustration over the failures around renewing Fast Track.[1]

At the same time, gathered across the street, a thousand or so anti-FTAA activists met for the People's Summit of the Americas. For them, Fast Track's ambiguous future generated excitement, for it left the Clinton administration coming to Santiago "naked" and unable to make progress.[2] Yet simultaneously many at the People's Summit worried over other developments. As one anti-FTAA newsletter observed, one "important and alarming topic of discussion . . . was the Multilateral Agreement on Investment," which activists dubbed a "coming attraction."[3]

The Multilateral Agreement on Investment started as both a policy overreach and a retreat. The vision of its creators was to write an international legal framework enshrining expansive protections for multinational enterprises from government interference. While, in the 1970s, activists, such as Anwar Fazal and Leah Margulies, called for a new international regulatory order, the MAI embodied a vision for a new international *deregulatory* order. Its immediate origins lay in the early 1990s at the Organization for Economic Cooperation and Development (OECD). Founded in 1961, the OECD represented the rich and soon-to-be-rich countries. During the 1970s, the OECD acted as a counterweight to organizations representing the Third World, such as the Non-Aligned Movement and the G-77.[4]

In the early 1990s, U.S. representatives began calling for the OECD to create a framework for governing international commerce and uplifting multinational enterprises. In May 1995, OECD representatives circulated a proposal to deal with the "dramatic growth and transformation of foreign direct investment" in recent years.[5] The proposal looked to add new rules but also to standardize and expand existing agreements. Throughout the previous decades, governments had signed hundreds of bilateral investment treaties with one another. While these treaties often resembled each other in broad terms, the little differences counted. Thus, the desire to standardize the rules also drove the push for an MAI.[6]

In the mid-1990s, the newly formed World Trade Organization seemed a promising venue for such efforts. U.S. and E.U. negotiators urged the new body to bring corporate investment rules under its jurisdiction. Yet many Global South governments, cautious about the WTO, spoke against expanding its mandate so quickly.[7] Rather than picking a fight, groups such as the U.S. Council on International Business called for talks to occur at a more favorable venue, such as the OECD, before going to the WTO.[8]

In formulating proposals, negotiators worked closely with the Business and Industry Advisory Committee, the OECD's official mechanism for soliciting corporate input.[9] The advisory committee held to a maximalist stance over what measures should go in a future investment treaty. Outlining their goals for the MAI talks, in 1995 the U.S. Council on International Business stated that investors needed protection "from the arbitrary seizure of their assets, whether directly through nationalization or indirectly through costly discriminatory taxes or other measures."[10]

The members of the Business and Industry Advisory Council knew what such provisions could look like. After all, they already existed in some bilateral investment treaties and, crucially, in NAFTA. One of the main tools for protecting multinationals from regulation would be an investor-state dispute settlement mechanism. Including this provision would allow an "aggrieved investor to proceed to arbitration . . . without depending on the co-operation of the host state." This meant a company could take direct legal action against a government through the MAI, ignoring local or national courts.[11] Relatively uncontroversial at first, by the late 1990s, investor-state dispute settlement received increasing publicity, and not in ways that benefited pro-MAI voices.

The controversies mainly arose from the North American Free Trade Agreement. By 1997, NAFTA's investment protections came under greater scrutiny as the first cases became public. One, emanating from Canada, belied NAFTA proponents' claims that the agreement protected environmental laws. In September 1996, the U.S.-based Ethyl Corporation sued Canada's government after the Canadians banned the import of the gas additive MMT, citing worries about its toxicity. Angered by this move, the Ethyl Corporation (which produced and sold MMT), used NAFTA's investor-state language to launch a $250 million lawsuit against the Canadian government, claiming that the ban constituted an action "tantamount to expropriation."[12] Ongoing at the time of the MAI talks, the Ethyl case became a rallying cry for fair globalizers, especially the lawyers at groups such as Public Citizen. They followed the case closely and briefed grassroots supporters and legislators about its implications. Meanwhile, in Paris, negotiators looked to place even more sweeping investor-state language within the MAI.[13]

As talks proceeded from May 1995, with the goal of concluding by May 1997, negotiators kept a low profile. They consulted extensively with private enterprises and discussed the broad outline of the Multilateral Agreement on Investment with staff from some labor unions and large, international NGOs such as the World Wildlife Federation.[14] Nevertheless, few details emerged for the wider public, making the MAI into a kind of phantom agreement. Council of Canadians head Maude Barlow reached out to her government contacts, who rebuffed her, accusing her of being a "conspiracy theorist."[15] Some progress came in late 1996, when Mark Ritchie's group, the Institute for Agriculture and Trade Policy, heard from an unnamed, "particularly concerned" Global South diplomat about negotiations at the OECD.[16] Then Martin Khor scored the first break. He obtained a partial text through contacts in Geneva that only further heightened concerns.

Not long after, a breakthrough happened. In February 1997, someone close to the negotiations leaked a copy of the text to opponents. Global Trade Watch and the Council of Canadians were the first to see the complete draft. Tony Clarke, a veteran of free-trade fights dating back to the 1980s in Canada, and GTW's Lori Wallach began furiously poring over the document. Clarke, in collaboration with Maude Barlow, started putting together a report, while Wallach busied herself creating an annotated copy of the text.

On April 7, 1997, fair globalizers publicly released the document.[17] The ease and breadth with which they could spread it testified to the power of new communications technologies. As Wallach recounted, even a few years earlier, distributing the MAI text globally would have required spending hours at a photocopier before rushing to Dulles Airport to load copies on mail flights, taking days to arrive around the world.[18] In April 1997, the same task merely involved uploading the MAI text using a technology that, at the time, still inspired curiosity and even an eye roll or two: the internet. The internet allowed them to share information and plot actions almost instantaneously. Not only did public interest organizations use the internet; so did grassroots activists, with the principal anti-MAI listservs recording around forty new posts every day during the height of the campaign.[19]

To defeat the MAI, U.S. activists hit not only the information superhighway but also the physical highways and byways. In the United States, Wallach, Thea Lee of the AFL-CIO, Scott Nova of the recently formed progressive think tank the Preamble Collaborative, and others started speaking across the country.[20] Other OECD countries also saw quick and strong mobilizations by groups that had previously worked against the WTO or on other questions of international political economy.[21]

Within a few months of the launch of anti-MAI campaigns in several countries, officials at the OECD and some of its member governments concluded they could not ignore critics. They proposed holding a conference between themselves and the opposition in Paris in October 1997.[22] To many activists, the offer smacked of a trap. They warned that the meeting might be a "fig leaf'" meant to "cover the completely undemocratic nature of the MAI negotiations."[23] Moderate groups countered that such meetings were necessary if outside groups were to have any impact. Most of the NGO leaders in the MAI campaign, such as Barlow and Wallach, took a position closer to the hardliners but with a nuance. They agreed that the October meeting between the OECD and critics should happen, but they also made it clear that the MAI needed to be stopped, not amended.[24]

This position became near-consensus among public interest groups as the year progressed. Discussions among NGOs led many moderate groups to realize a simple fact: they could not influence the OECD "solely by our own individual pressure, because you have to absolutely have public pressure."[25] Moreover, moderate groups already felt that the OECD negotiators were not taking them seriously. Thus, in the lead-up to the October meeting between the OECD and NGOs, moderate (and many previously pro-NAFTA) U.S. groups, such as the National Wildlife Federation, joined Public Citizen and others to ask the U.S. Trade Representative's office to insist that the OECD give critics more than three hours of time.[26] They also asserted that unlike with NAFTA, side agreements would not suffice to win their acquiescence, much less their support.[27]

On October 27, 1997, the long-awaited meeting happened. Barlow recalled the consultation occurring "in an enormous high-ceilinged boardroom of the former Rothschild estate with red velvet chairs, crystal chandeliers, and gold leaf paneling around a very large board table—the government negotiators at one end, us at the other."[28] The conversation quickly grew testy, with terse exchanges and occasional snide remarks flying back and forth. OECD negotiators stated that the meeting saw a "constructive exchange of views" and affirmed their interest in studying NGO proposals.[29] On the other side of the table, however, few saw a future in conciliation.

After October, a fully formed international resistance to the MAI arose. With so many national networks linked through the internet and by growing personal connections, the alliance looked for a common strategy. They found it in an approach devised by and dubbed "monkeywrenching" by Tony Clarke, a term used by novelist and radical environmentalist Edward Abbey in his book *The Monkey Wrench Gang*. Clarke likely took some inspiration from Abbey's tale of a scrappy few breaking the infrastructures upholding injustice.[30] As he explained in a January 1998 memo, monkeywrenching entailed activists working to intensify disagreements among their governments' negotiators. "If Canada's negotiators are demanding a total exemption for culture under the MAI, then it would be strategically important to get Jack Valenti and the U.S. entertainment industry stirred up to publicly denounce such a move," he proffered as an example.

Instigating and intensifying such conflicts would hopefully lead to a "moratorium or at least another extended delay" in talks, building to the ultimate objective: "to kill the MAI."[31] In late January 1998, in Amsterdam, advocates from seven countries gathered. There, the monkeywrenching strategy received a full hearing. Clarke asked all those present to "look at your country's reservations [i.e., what issues their government felt reluctant about negotiating] and assess how serious they are." The assembled activists liked what they heard. They approved Clarke's idea and began formulating resources and mobilizing their constituencies.[32]

Within the United States, the subfederal level became the main site for mobilization. Since no final text existed, members of Congress had nothing to vote on and therefore fairly little leverage. However, at the local and state levels, activists started building opposition designed to trickle up to the federal level. The key campaign, devised in good part by Scott Nova, the head of the Preamble Center (and later of the CTC) involved supporting "MAI Free Zones." This initiative sought to put local and state governments on record opposing the MAI. It received a jolt of energy when, in April 1997, the Western Governors' Association, representing states from Kansas to Hawaii, issued a report on the Multilateral Agreement on Investment's potential effects at subfederal levels. The report concluded that a range of laws—from ones promoting microbreweries to protections for wetlands—could all come under threat. The Western Governors' Association included both Democrats and Republicans, a fact that made the report especially powerful, allowing MAI opponents to avoid strict partisan lines.[33]

Building on this momentum, the Citizens Trade Campaign mobilized. In San Francisco, Juliette Beck, working with the California Fair Trade Campaign, set an early precedent. With a handful of activists, Beck "marched down to the city hall one day" and started speaking with legislative staff. Fair globalizers managed to get one of their allies on the Board of Supervisors to introduce a resolution declaring the city's opposition to the MAI. With a bill now available, Beck and others mobilized local activists to lobby their representatives on the board. Activist numbers were minuscule—only four people showed up to one phone bank—but without business lobbies or the Clinton administration offering a counterpoint, Beck and her colleagues helped pass the resolution unanimously.[34] A number of cities followed in becoming "MAI Free," including Berkeley, Boulder, and in a preview of coming attractions, Seattle.[35]

At the federal level, MAI inspired, at best, mixed feelings. Some in the U.S. government agreed (at least partially) with critics. An Environmental Protection Agency memo cautioned that the MAI would "unduly restrict the U.S. government's ability to protect health, safety, and the environment."[36] In February 1998, Stuart Eizenstat of the U.S. Department of State and Jeffrey Lang from the U.S. Trade Representatives' office jointly acknowledged that it was "clear to us" that the April deadline for completing talks "cannot be done."[37]

Outside the United States, different countries' anti-MAI coalitions kicked in at different moments. Using the internet, they shared information quickly, empowering distinct groups. Teach-ins, briefings, and protests became commonplace across the OECD countries, as activists raised awareness and tried to show popular dissatisfaction.[38] The Canadians organized mass petitions and phone banks calling members of Parliament.[39] In Japan, environmentalist NGOs attended open government meetings about MAI. They pressed the sometimes underinformed negotiators to learn more about recent NAFTA investor-state dispute decisions, helping sow doubts.[40] In Finland, environmentalists helped convince Ministry of Economic Affairs officials to reexamine the text in light of concerns about potential future challenges to Finnish regulatory laws.[41]

The combined pressures on OECD governments worked. On April 28, 1998, negotiators announced they would be taking a "period of assessment and further consultation between the negotiating parties and with interested parts of their societies."[42] This move mollified almost no one. Among the financial commentariat, the retreat sparked fretful prognostications about the MAI fight signaling a dim future for neoliberal globalization. Citing the infamous line from *Butch Cassidy and the Sundance Kid* in which, doggedly pursued by unknown riders, the titular outlaws constantly ask, "Who are those guys?" *Financial*

Times writer Guy de Jonquières laid out these fears. He called opponents of the MAI a "horde of vigilantes" and quoted a "veteran trade diplomat" saying the MAI fight marked a "turning point" for nonstate actors' influences on global economic governance.[43]

Displaying the complexities of international campaigns, the positive momentum of the anti-MAI campaigners sparked concern among allies in the Global South. From Penang, Martin Khor cautioned that talks on investment protections might now return to the World Trade Organization, where, if approved, they would immediately cover the poor nations, not just the rich.[44] Northern colleagues in groups such as Public Citizen and Friends of the Earth quickly prepared a letter opposing (and more importantly, publicizing the potential of) such a move. Mobilizations in OECD countries only grew and intensified, with French, U.S., Swiss, Belgian, and Canadian groups organizing a September "International Action Week" to ensure the MAI stayed in the public spotlight.[45]

Among OECD governments, the French felt some of the strongest heat. French negotiators feared the fallout if a future MAI paved the way for attacks on government culture policies, such as a law requiring a majority of films shown in the country to be French in origin. As the government pondered its options, Prime Minister Lionel Jospin quietly commissioned a study of the politics of the MAI. He recruited French politician (and then member of the European Parliament) Catherine Lalumière and Inspector General of Finances Jean-Pierre Landau to head the investigation.

From July to September 1998, Lalumière and Landau interviewed people and researched. Their findings were blunt. Rather than affirming OECD members' public statements that technical disagreements among governments explained the MAI's woes, they instead credited (or blamed) "perfectly well informed" NGOs advancing "criticisms well argued on a legal level." The MAI fight, they concluded, showed that "the emergence of a 'global civil society' represented by NGOs" was a "doubtless irreversible" trend that global elites ignored at their own peril.[46]

Between international NGO pressure, domestic opposition, and disputes among OECD member governments, the French decided to end their participation in MAI talks. On October 14, 1998, Jospin addressed the French parliament. He announced France's withdrawal from further talks, citing the Lalumière report's conclusions as one reason.[47] Jospin's announcement did not immediately tank the MAI. In mid-October, delegates met again in Paris. Though this gathering showed some self-reflection, it made little progress. By mid-November 1998, no amount of spin or renegotiation could mask the truth. "The EU will not negotiate without France," declared Strobe Talbott, the U.S.

deputy secretary of state, in a cable to all U.S. embassies in OECD countries. The MAI died—and to this day remains dead. As Talbott concluded, the "controversies that have arisen in the MAI will not go away. They relate to the very process of globalization."[48]

*   *   *

Recounting the MAI fight years later, Maude Barlow recalled her sentiment in late 1998: "We tasted victory. And we liked how it tasted."[49] The fair globalization coalition in the United States and the worldwide network against corporate globalization certainly had much to cheer about in this moment. Stopping Fast Track and the MAI dampened the rush to cement neoliberalism as the North Star of international economic governance. In the Americas, the Hemispheric Social Alliance continued building strength to fight the FTAA.

Reaching this moment took time and effort. After the crushing blow of NAFTA's passage, followed by the formation of the World Trade Organization, U.S. fair globalizers seemed lost. Fortunately for them, many of the critiques they circulated during those fights remained or only grew in salience. Years of lived experience with NAFTA often seemed to confirm activists' critiques. These realities built a basis for reorganization and reinvigoration. The core of the U.S. fair globalization coalition also took time to refine their ideas and their politics, especially through international relationships. Across the U.S. fair globalization coalition, the value of such internationalism was now clear, ideologically and programmatically.

In both the case of Fast Track and that of the MAI, fair globalizers correctly analyzed that, underneath the sheen of an emergent neoliberal consensus, differences existed. Newt Gingrich and Bill Clinton might actually agree on some big matters, but partisanship still existed and created room for action. Rich country governments all might want deregulation, but localized politics still existed. Thus, by the late 1990s, U.S. fair globalizers and activists globally refined and proved the effectiveness of monkeywrenching.

Amid the celebrations, one tough reality remained. These wins were defensive in nature. Stopping Fast Track allowed fair globalizers more time to work against the FTAA. Blocking MAI reduced the number of battlefields, but it did little to slow the momentum of the principal new instrument of neoliberal global governance: the World Trade Organization. Confronting that institution would lead fair globalizers to the most kinetic week of many of their lives.

PART VI

You Must Come to Seattle!

CHAPTER 21

Everybody Clear Your Calendars

Anticipation hung in the air on the morning of January 25, 1999. With MAI talks recently finished, the future of the World Trade Organization came to dominate discussions of global governance. And now, after months of negotiations, the Clinton administration would finally unveil which U.S. city would host the next WTO Ministerial. Occurring every other year, World Trade Organization ministerials bring together member states for talks about expanding the organization's mandate. Press accounts reported three cities as the top contenders: San Diego, Honolulu, and Seattle. Then the announcement arrived: it would be Seattle.

This pronouncement generated acclaim across the political spectrum, from the most pro to the most anti-WTO groups. For the Clinton administration, which wanted to signal the United States' continuing commitment to free trade after the Fast Track and MAI defeats, Seattle seemed perfect. After all, as Microsoft head Bill Gates wrote in a *New York Times* op-ed, "Perhaps more than any other city in America, Seattle illustrates the benefits of global commerce."[1] The presence of major multinational corporations, such as Starbucks, Microsoft, Boeing, and Amazon, in the city offered persuasive evidence for Gates's case.[2]

Of course, the city of Seattle was more than headquarters of large corporations. Its residents included a sizable number of union members.[3] In the city, and even more so around the Pacific Northwest, a robust collection of environmentalist communities existed—from Sierra Club volunteers to ecoanarchists.[4] Overall, Seattle boasted a progressive-leaning population. On issues of globalization, it was one of the largest U.S. cities to become an "MAI Free Zone." Little wonder then that on the day following Clinton's announcement, an e-mail flew among Global Trade Watch's staff exclaiming, "Everybody clear your calendars. We're going to Seattle at the end of November."[5]

Eleven months later, the Battle in Seattle began. During five days of rallies, marches, teach-ins, tear gas, smashed windows, and lobbying, disparate bands of activists managed to place issues of global inequality at the center of world debate. In preparation, public interest progressives found themselves dealing with old allies in new ways and people they had not previously talked to, namely, activists for whom the halls of Congress or negotiators' offices in Geneva represented foreign territory. The relationships of different types of organizations—unions, national public interest groups, anarchists, grassroots activists, and more—profoundly shaped conflicts over the mobilization and the actual protests. Yet, despite these challenges, the protests largely worked. They helped to scuttle the WTO Ministerial by utilizing every tactic short of armed insurgency. And for a moment, it seemed, Seattle marked a birth date, one in which the fair globalization coalition might have helped give rise to a veritable mass movement.

*   *   *

The moment the news hit that Seattle had been selected, the offices of Global Trade Watch erupted. Staff picked up their phones and logged on to the internet, with everyone racing to reserve every hotel and motel room, youth hostel space, and meeting venue in Seattle that they could.[6] As recalled by Global Trade Watch organizer Alesha Daughtrey, she and her colleagues did not have specific plans for what to do with these spaces. Rather, they felt confident that "if we weren't going to use them, someone else would, and if we didn't get in immediately, all of these spaces would get snapped up by the WTO Host Committee."[7]

At the Citizens Trade Campaign, organizer Mike Dolan (on loan from his usual job at Global Trade Watch), sprang into action. The chance to be at the center of large-scale demonstrations thrilled the always excitable Dolan. He quickly hired two organizers and contacted key people at allied organizations, both in Seattle and nationally. Dolan's fieldwork against Fast Track and the MAI had netted him contacts and relationships across the country. Global Trade Watch thus established itself as the key national public interest nonprofit preparing for Seattle.[8]

One of the first challenges faced by fair globalizers was that few people outside of particular elite policy worlds knew much about the World Trade Organization. Unlike NAFTA, the WTO's inception garnered little public attention in the United States. Fortunately, for the purposes of mobilization, in the years following its formation, the WTO offered plenty of fodder for skeptics of neoliberal governance.

Commencing operations in 1995, the WTO became a hub for international economic negotiations and dispute resolution. Countries joining the WTO agreed to abide by rules over everything from tariff rates to nontariff barriers to trade, including regulatory laws. Anyone questioning this new body's ambitions to be the powerhouse of global economic governance only needed to hear Director-General Renato Ruggiero's declaration that "we are no longer writing the rules of interaction among separate national economies. We are writing the constitution of a single global economy."[9] Some in the WTO made even more brazen statements, with one former official characterizing it as "a place where governments collude in private against their domestic pressure groups."[10]

During its first years, several cases came before the WTO that appeared to confirm the fears of its progressive critics. In 1998, a ruling came down on the "shrimp-turtle case." In this instance, several governments charged the United States with discriminating against their exports because of a 1989 amendment to the Endangered Species Act banning imports of shrimp caught using nets that also captured and killed turtles. As of 1999, the United States appeared to have lost the case. This decision came on top of the United States' defeat in a case trying to defend provisions of the Clean Air Act challenged by Venezuela.

While these cases undermined the very kinds of regulations that public interest progressives had long supported, other cases suggested that the WTO's governance would further Global South-North inequalities. One such example stemmed from the WTO's challenge to the 1976 Lomé Convention, a trade agreement between the European Union and the African, Caribbean, and Pacific Group of States. The Lomé Convention gave trade preferences to former European colonies. Several Latin American states, which were not parties to Lomé and where major U.S.-based multinationals (like Chiquita) operated plantations, sought to overturn the convention. The United States and a few Latin American states sued, and the European Union lost. The Europeans agreed to alter Lomé but not to the extent recommended by the WTO. This prompted the U.S. government to impose sanctions on certain E.U. goods in retaliation. Meanwhile, farmers in countries that had benefited from Lomé endured greater hardships, as their previously secure markets dried up. In the words of Jamaican trade unionists, what was "at stake is the very stability—economic, political, and social—of our region."[11]

Even when formal cases did not arise, the WTO could act to chill future regulation. One such example served as a fitting epitaph for activists' dreams in the 1970s and early 1980s of a new international regulatory order. In the first half of the 1990s, as the Uruguay Round approached completion, Gerber, one of the largest multinational corporations selling infant formula, saw a chance to employ a new tool in an old case. In 1983, Guatemala passed legislation modeled on the WHO-UNICEF International Code of Marketing of Breast-Milk Substitutes. Over the next decade, the Guatemalan government pressured Gerber to comply with the law. As the WTO approached its formal inception, Gerber signaled to the Guatemalans its intention to lean on a government friendly to the company to use new WTO intellectual property rights provisions to challenge Guatemala's law. In response, the Guatemalan government changed the law to apply only to domestically produced infant formula. These examples and more led activists to believe the WTO was a growing behemoth that, at a minimum, needed to be slowed, deeply reformed, or possibly just abolished.[12]

*   *   *

For public interest groups headquartered in Washington, D.C., the reality of an upcoming WTO meeting in a major U.S. city posed many questions; most basically, what should they do in response? Given recent successes against Fast Track and the MAI and the presence of robust progressive communities in Seattle, the idea of getting people into the streets soon entered the conversation. On February 12, 1999, twenty-two representatives, mainly from public interest groups with a few unionists, gathered in Washington, D.C., to begin discussing options.

At this moment, most of those assembled imagined a conventional set of actions. A main focus would be on lobbying of government officials within the meeting. However, everyone at the meeting also wanted to see more public display, such as educational events and permitted marches. The goal of these would be to register dissent and to spread awareness of the WTO. Throughout the meeting, questions around intended audience pervaded. Dan Seligman, the point person on globalization issues for the Sierra Club, urged CTC groups to create "a clear, widely appealing message, probably focused on an American audience due to the upcoming presidential race (we could affect election debate on trade)."[13] This meant reaching out to "soccer moms and kind of regular folks on the street" as the "target audience"—in other words, the primarily white, middle-class people making up the public interest progressive base.[14] Reaching these constituencies would require tightly coordinating the protests' message. In the words of the Alliance for Democracy's Ruth Caplan, they needed to develop "a united voice for the CTC, so there's no organizational competition between coalition members."[15]

Activists gathered at these meetings did not envision a totally placid set of events. Some amount of spectacle appealed to many of the participants. As

Marceline White from Women's EDGE stated, "We spoil surprise element of actions, etc. if USTR knows too much." Consensus soon backed White's proposal to keep "individual NGOs' plans secret. . . . This allows law enforcement to be ready for our numbers and reasonable in dealing with us, without being so 'ready' that they restrict our movements or protest areas."[16]

While only three representatives from organized labor attended the February 12 meeting, public interest advocates knew the protests would not succeed without major union involvement. They worried that mounting a large-scale demonstration represented what Njoki Njoroge Njehu of 50 Years Is Enough called a "big challenge in the US!" given the widespread "apathy and disinterest."[17] Realistically, only labor possessed the numbers and resources to put thousands of bodies on the streets. Thus, the day after the WTO announced Seattle as the meeting location, Dolan scribbled in his notebook that he needed to "hook w/AFL-CIO."[18]

Doing so led him to Joe Uehlein, then head of the federation's Strategic Campaigns division. Uehlein wanted unions to embrace a more community-rooted and deeply progressive "social movement unionism" that went beyond winning "bread and butter" fights for members.[19] As a supporter of the New Voice contingent that won power in the AFL-CIO in 1995, Uehlein felt hopeful for labor's future. Hearing about the multiconstituency mobilizing happening for Seattle excited him. Nevertheless, it did not mean the AFL-CIO hierarchy would sign on. The big question under deliberation at the top concerning whether to put resources toward Seattle revolved around size: "Will it be big enough to warrant a mass effort" on labor's part?[20]

A few months of discussions passed, while Uehlein communicated both with nonlabor allies and with Ron Judd, president of the King County Labor Council (the primary labor institution in Seattle). During these conversations, it became clear that other progressive organizations planned to make the World Trade Organization meeting into a dramatic display of people power. Some in the union movement agreed, as more militant leaders and the rank and file wanted labor to show its power. Asked about his own vision for protesting the WTO, Judd stated that "in a perfect world we'd repeat 1919," referring to the general strike that shut down Seattle in that year.[21]

The counsel of such individuals helped assure AFL-CIO president John Sweeney's support for the federation playing a major role in Seattle. After all, one of Sweeney's promises as AFL-CIO president was to better integrate the organization into a larger progressive movement.[22] The gears of the federation's mobilization machine now started. Thea Lee in the AFL-CIO's Public Policy Department coordinated with Wallach and other NGO activists on the federation's policy stances. Organizers traveled to union locals and central labor councils, sometimes using fact sheets and pamphlets developed by groups such as Global Trade Watch, to educate union members about the WTO. The mundane necessities of protest took time, as hours went by coordinating logistics to charter buses and even airplanes to transport union members to Seattle.[23]

The energy spiked in mid-August at the Washington State AFL-CIO's convention. There, Uehlein proclaimed labor's intent to get "15,000 union members onto the streets of Seattle." Keynoting the event, John Sweeney delivered a similar pledge, with one difference. Instead of promising 15,000 union members on the streets, he instead proclaimed labor planned to bring 50,000. Soon after Sweeney concluded, Uehlein ran into him. Uehlein asked about the number Sweeney cited, saying, "Our goal is 15,000." "Well, now it's 50,000," Sweeney replied.[24]

*   *   *

In much of its public discourse leading up to Seattle, organized labor (at least at official levels) abandoned the more nationalistic rhetoric of the past. Speaking before the AFL-CIO convention, President Sweeney declared, "We must not let greedy multinational corporations who dominate our global economy forget. We make no distinction between working families in Peking, working families in Pakistan, and working families in Pittsburgh."[25]

Internationalism was a language not only expressed in words, however. While the street protests are the best remembered part of the Battle in Seattle, another, less heralded piece is crucial: the role of NGOs, especially ones hailing from the Global South. At all levels, the Battle in Seattle was not a "made in the U.S.A."–only event. Locally in Seattle, the Filipinx group Sentenaryo ng Bayan led the way in putting together the People's Assembly, a gathering of foreign activists happening right before and during the demonstrations.[26] The AFL-CIO funded several trade unionists from the Global South to attend as well. The International Forum on Globalization brought many of its highest-profile Third World members, such as Martin Khor and Vandana Shiva, to Seattle. Their numbers would be relatively small but their imprint large.

Along with these public actions, a parallel operation moved forward. For much of 1999, this work focused not on Seattle but on Geneva, the home of the World Trade Organization. There, Lori Wallach, Mark Ritchie, Martin Khor, and others saw the chance to again use monkeywrenching to repeat the success seen battling MAI. Coordinating with the same group of allies, they planned to "build international governmental consensus towards the 'no new

round–assessment' position." The goal would be for some Global South governments to demand that instead of piling more policies onto the WTO's docket,
the Seattle meetings should instead examine and reassess existing agreements.[27]

Activists counted one major advantage in mobilizing for Seattle in contrast
to fighting the MAI. At the WTO, almost every country on Earth would be
represented, not just the rich ones. Playing on a larger field meant that activists
benefited from already existing tensions within the WTO, especially between
the richest and some of the poorest countries. In agreeing to a whole slew of
new rules when the WTO first came online, Third World countries found
themselves struggling with the costs and logistics of implementing those policies. Global South countries had also consented to postponing discussions on
some of their pressing issues, such as reducing rich-country agricultural subsi-
dies. Increasingly, such decisions seemed like defeats of the marginalized by
the strong rather than compromises among constituents of an equitable organization.[28]

Global North-South conflict found a human focal point in the spring of
1999. Having been appointed to a four-year term, WTO director-general Renato Ruggiero left in May 1999. With no consensus replacement candidate, a
race emerged. Two individuals took the lead: former New Zealand trade minister Mike Moore and Thai deputy prime minister and minister of commerce
Supachai Panitchpakdi. Supachai emerged as the early favorite, with many
African and Asian governments backing him. However, Moore did not let early
setbacks restrain him. He resembled a Kiwi Bill Clinton, identifying with the
center-left, he believed that a mix of liberalization, competition, and some
safety nets for those who fell behind equaled prosperity. As New Zealand's
trade minister during the later 1980s, he spearheaded privatization and liberalization policies. His track record and politics appealed to the Clinton administration, who decided to back him over Supachai. In a hotly contested race, riven
with backroom dealing, Moore eventually triumphed. To soothe tensions,
Moore and Supachai agreed to split the six-year term, with Moore taking the
first three years.[29]

Despite the compromise, the election exacerbated simmering discontent
among negotiators, especially from sub-Saharan African and Caribbean countries. Compounding these concerns were the structural challenges of power
and numbers. While governments at the WTO possessed formal equality (such
as in voting), disparities showed in other ways. One such inequality related to
the number of people assigned to negotiations. The United States could dispatch
hundreds of experts to bolster their negotiators, while a Third World state might
only have two or three. This made it difficult for Global South negotiators to

quickly process all the information being thrown around and make informed decisions.[30]

These inequalities provided international public interest groups, such as the Third World Network, an opportunity. TWN director Martin Khor culti-vated relationships with negotiators and used the organization's expert staff to generate policy knowledge and act as a policy and political strategy resource for Global South states. By the late 1990s, more and more negotiators from Global South governments turned to the TWN for advice during WTO talks. Their work became prominent enough that Canadian economist and policy-maker Sylvia Ostry deemed them the "virtual secretariat."[31] In recognition of the Third World Network's efforts, in 1996, the Group of 77—the organization of Global South countries that helped lead the NIEO fight—awarded the TWN its South-South Cooperation Award for "providing analyses that have enabled these [poor] countries to adopt common positions on these issues."[32]

Going into Seattle, Khor believed Third World states might have some le-verage.[33] In September 1999, he gave a speech before the Ministerial Meeting of the G-77. Khor implored the government officials to stay firm in the upcoming talks. "Developing countries must unite and persuade first themselves and

Figure 7. Martin Khor (center) with other international advocates, including Meena Raman (right) of the Third World Network. Behind her is Lori Wallach. Undated, Global Trade Watch Papers.

then the developed countries that this is the time to review the WTO and not to expand its scope further," he stated.[34] At the meeting, the G-77's chairman, Guyanese minister of foreign affairs Clement J. Rohee, supported calls from some Global South states for Seattle to be a "review, repair, and reform" round.[35]

In the United States, public interest groups followed the lead of Global South representatives, many of whom they had deepened relationships with at meetings of the International Forum on Globalization. When requested, Wallach jetted to Geneva to add her policy expertise.[36] At the Institute for Agriculture and Trade Policy, Nestlé boycott veteran Mark Ritchie and his staff, especially Kristin Dawkins, also plugged away. In late November 1998, Dawkins coorganized a forum on the WTO's intellectual property rights with representatives from the South Centre, an intergovernmental organization providing policy expertise to Global South countries.[37]

How all this would play out in Seattle remained an open question. For Khor, the inside work needed its complement. The "people in the North" needed to take action, he stated at one meeting. The poor could not do this alone, "because the people of the South have no control over their government."[38] Fortunately for Khor, many people were preparing to take action. And not all of them came from the often restrictive worlds of Washington, D.C. or Geneva based lobbying.

CHAPTER 22

Shut Down the WTO!

Over the course of 1999, Citizens Trade Campaign and Public Citizen organizer Mike Dolan lived a bifurcated existence. When in Washington, D.C., many union officials and public interest advocates viewed him, at least in his words, as an "axe swinging radical." Yet, when he went back to Seattle, he and many of the national fair globalization coalition groups were viewed in a very different light. In Seattle, Dolan was a "reviled . . . reformist."[1] These sometimes blurry, and often contentious dividing lines separating large, bureaucratic liberal organizations from smaller, often more militant groups, deeply shaped the Battle in Seattle.

Within days of the announcement that Seattle would host the WTO, people in the city mobilized. One of the main people building bridges between the national liberal groups and local activists was Sally Soriano. Born and raised in Seattle, Soriano grew up in a politically active family; her dad was a member of the left-wing International Longshore and Warehouse Union (ILWU). Soriano campaigned for Jesse Jackson in the 1988 primaries, excited by his ambitious and progressive vision for U.S. liberalism's future.[2] After the election, she continued working with the Rainbow Coalition, Jackson's activist organization. In that capacity, she became involved in anti-NAFTA and then anti–Uruguay Round work.

Soriano soon linked up with the Citizens Trade Campaign. For the fight against the Uruguay Round in 1994, she became the coordinator for the CTC's Washington State affiliate, the Washington Fair Trade Campaign. From that post, Soriano threw herself into all the major trade fights of the 1990s, leading the way against Fast Track and playing a powerful role in making the city an MAI Free Zone. When the announcement about the WTO coming to Seattle hit, Soriano quickly looked to Global Trade Watch's educational materials to learn about the institution.[3]

Then Soriano received a call from Mike Dolan.[4] During their conversation, the two agreed that a meeting in Seattle needed to happen soon to begin coordinating between local activists and national and international organizations. One month after their call, Dolan, Soriano, and eighty other people gathered at the Labor Temple, a red-brick rectangular building that housed many Seattle local unions' offices. The assembled individuals identified with many causes, from animal rights to sustainable farming to workers' rights. Energy and excitement buzzed throughout the room. No one knew exactly *what* should happen, but broad agreement existed that they should do more than a few rallies.

Unsurprisingly, tensions among different factions started to surface. These disagreements proved reminiscent of conflicts between the New Left and the Naderites from the 1960s and between leaders of INFACT and some grassroots supporters during the Nestlé boycott. On one side were such figures as Dolan. Coming from union and public interest backgrounds, they insisted on a formalized professionalism in day-to-day operations. As Dolan described, this "model of organizing is hierarchical. I demand accountability from my organizers. I want numbers. I want updates. And I'm going to get it."[5] The values underlying this model emphasized clearly articulated "deliverables" that could be easily documented in a memo or, perhaps more important, in a grant proposal to a major foundation.

Conversely, a wider diversity of approaches existed among the Seattle-based groups. Some hailed from local branches of national organizations, from United Steelworkers locals to Sierra Club chapters. Members of these groups might not always agree with those above them in the hierarchy of their organizations, but they still tended to operate similarly to the national public interest and labor groups. However, echoing debates from the Nestlé boycott, others in Seattle identified with nonhierarchical models, many rooted in 1960s activism. As Anne Slater from Seattle Radical Women explained, there existed "a history in Seattle of coalitions . . . having open discussion and debate." Deliberations that might seem wasteful or indulgent by D.C. advocates were seen by these grassroots activists as vital to coalition building and maintenance over the long haul.[6] Moreover, as leftists were frequently not concerned about needing to remain "respectable" to retain their access in parts of Washington, D.C., they felt freer to espouse radical ideas.

One early field of conflict among these factions revolved around messaging. Much as national public interest figures disdained the WTO, they argued that the message needed to call for its reform, not its dissolution. Trying out slogans in his organizing notebook in late February 1999, Dolan put down "Assessment, No New Round Turn Around, What's the Rush?" as possibilities.[7]

On the other hand, many in the Seattle activist community exhibited no trepidation about demanding the WTO's abolition. "No to WTO" served as their rallying cry. One moment of tension between these conflicting instincts came when Sally Soriano sent an organizing packet to the CTC offices in Washington, D.C. to show off the work being done in Seattle. The packet was titled "No to WTO," and it sparked a firm pushback.[8] Disagreements over the name of the coalition inspired weeks of debates. Dolan and others advocated for the name "People for Fair Trade" while many others wanted "No to WTO." As recalled by activists on both sides, this debate became a two-month slog that ended in the "ultimate wishy-washy compromise": calling the group People for Fair Trade/No2WTO.[9]

While choosing a name might seem a slight matter, it offered a window into other, more serious issues. One of the most contentious dilemmas for those organizing the protests revolved around representation, diversity, and accountability. The Sierra Club, Public Citizen, and others drew most of their support (and staffs) from white, middle-class professionals. Though Seattle's population was predominantly white, there were significant communities of color, including Filipinx, Black, Chinese, Chicanx and Mexican, and indigenous peoples.[10]

Many of the most politically involved people from the communities of color were radicals. Their analyses of inequality centered on white supremacy and the legacies of slavery and colonialism in the United States and abroad. They saw a range of oppressions and issues as deeply interconnected and in need of inclusion in the protests' messaging and actions. They also wanted to push past critiques of neoliberalism as something extraordinary or unprecedented. Instead, they understood this newest phase of political economy as the most recent iteration of colonialism and imperialism, forces to be understood not as problems of the past but as lived realities into the present.

For example, Ace Saturay, who organized with the Filipinx community action group Sentenaryo ng Bayan linked agitation against the WTO to the century-long history of U.S. colonialism and neoimperialism in the Philippines. Brown Collective organizer Denise Cooper argued that calls to transform the criminal justice system should be included, viewing law enforcement suppression of anti-WTO demonstrators as a natural outgrowth of a long history of law enforcement repression of communities of color.[11] In trying to insert such issues into the coalition, few worked harder than Lydia Cabasco, a Seattle local and the only woman of color and only queer person of color on the staff of People for Fair Trade/No2WTO.[12]

Attempts by radical activists of color and their allies to connect the WTO to such critiques proved a nonstarter with the big, predominantly white groups.

Public interest groups also assiduously avoided discussion of immigration, seeing it as a "divisive" issue for their white working- and middle-class bases.[13]
Cabasco and some other organizers of color argued that these decisions made
mobilizing people of color quite difficult. Frustrating as well was the tokeniza-
tion that activists of color experienced. Cabasco, for instance, remembered being placed "in charge of people of color, whatever that meant."[14] She proposed
creating popular education tools that showed how the WTO's decisions affected "what a person utilizes throughout his or her day," from breakfast cereal
to clothing, as a way of making it more tangible for more communities, but her
idea received relatively little support.[15] Recollecting later, local immigrant and
labor activist Juan Bocanegra argued that some of the disdain from white activists "was overt and some of it was innate to those types of groups. They're
racist, liberal, bullshitting groups."[16]

 Of course, people of color across Seattle did not profess a single, monolithic
political view. While Cabasco tried to engage with white-dominant groups,
other organizations beat their own paths. Ace Saturay noted that his organization remained "friends with Mike Dolan, also, because, as a coalition, we
have to work together." Yet, at the same time, he noted, "We have to carry our
own message," and Sentenaryo ng Bayan organizers worked diligently in their
own communities to take action.[17] Regino Martinez of El Centro de la Raza
similarly accumulated his share of criticisms, but declared that, for this particular action, "You know what? We're going to look past our differences, because
this goes beyond differences. . . . This goes to justice and equality for people in
the world."[18] However, the fact that many of the radical, people of color led
groups had to, yet again, bite their tongues and go around the liberal mainstream further showed how the "pragmatic" politics of Washington, D.C. constrained more transformative visions.

*   *   *

Concurrent with the mobilizations happening in Seattle, another cohort of activists began planning something grand: direct action to shut the WTO down.
At the center of this group was the Art and Revolution Collective, a loose-knit
set of activists and artists who experimented with creative protest visuals and
tactics. Soon after news of the WTO meeting in Seattle became public, many in
Art and Revolution, such as cofounder David Solnit, pondered what role they
could play.[19] After initially failing to garner much interest, in the summer of
1999, Solnit and others (especially in the Bay Area) rounded up activists for
serious planning. They reached out to two West Coast–based NGOs, Global

Exchange and the Rainforest Action Network, for logistical and financial assistance.[20]

Global Exchange, founded in 1988, worked on human rights and economic equity issues and was involved in lobbying, public education, social justice tourism, and selling "fair trade" products. The Rainforest Action Network combined elements of public interest advocacy with dramatic direct actions of the sort often associated with Greenpeace.[21] These organizations filled an essential bridging role. Both of them had their "public interest" components, staffed with professional activists who knew policy in great detail and were involved in formalized lobbying and advocacy. However, both also participated in disruptive protests, with the Rainforest Action Network in particular becoming famous for its creative direct actions, from hanging banners off buildings to disruptions of meetings and other corporate and governmental events.

As these preparations commenced, another organization, the Ruckus Society, entered the picture. Cofounded by Mike Roselle, a prolific radical environmentalist who helped start the Rainforest Action Network as well as Earth First! the Ruckus Society began in 1995 as a vehicle for training environmentalists in nonviolent, direct-action protests. Then, in 1998, Ruckus branched out to begin training people from a variety of left-leaning movements. Ruckus emphasized media-grabbing dramatic actions, with Roselle explaining, "The content will get totally passed over if the image is lost."[22]

Gathering for meetings around San Francisco, this loose collection of groups founded a coordinating body, the Direct Action Network (DAN). They drew inspiration from the Zapatista movement in southern Mexico. After their short-lived armed insurgency in the mid-1990s, the Zapatistas transformed significant parts of Chiapas into a liberated zone, in which rural, indigenous people eked out a noncapitalist existence. Intensely attuned to the outside world, in 1998, the Zapatistas helped launch People's Global Action, an international network of activist groups. The Zapatistas' militancy and their calls for activists around the world—spread through pamphlets, books, and postings on internet listservs—infused the DAN activists with a radical analysis and a belief that profoundly radical social change was possible.[23]

People clustering around the Ruckus Society and DAN did not hide their aims from the world. "We are planning a large scale, well organized, high visibility action to *shut down* the World Trade Organization. We will nonviolently and creatively block them from meeting." To do so, they would employ "affinity groups," packs of between five and fifteen people acting through consensus decision making and following principles laid out by DAN. Among those principles included commitments against property destruction and to avoiding "violence, physical or verbal towards any person." Invoking these principles as a "basis for trust," DAN also made clear its commitment to tactical pluralism.[24]

For Mike Dolan and GTW, the growing involvement of activists who emphasized civil disobedience over lobbying created a challenging situation. On the one hand, as leaders in the CTC and established Washington, D.C., policy players, they needed to keep more cautious organizations onboard. Groups such as the National Wildlife Federation expressed nervousness that the trade debate was becoming too polarized, warning against "those who want to trash [the WTO]."[25] Meanwhile, at the AFL-CIO, concerns filtered throughout the bureaucracy that that arrests and disturbances might "screw our march up."[26]

Simultaneously, the more time Dolan spent on the West Coast, the more excitement he felt about the possibilities for civil disobedience. Hearing resistance from some in D.C. to greater militancy, Dolan encouraged them "to go out there and see the energy."[27] As he commented in his organizing notebook, protests by such groups as Ruckus and DAN create "more political space" for the liberals. Just as INFACT activists during the Nestlé boycott made World Health Organization officials seem more "reasonable" in their calls to regulate industry, having radicals on the street, Dolan believed, would empower established organizations and Global South governments.[28] Thus, quietly, Dolan tried to help more militant activists. Writing about the labor mobilizations, Dolan urged Global Trade Watch supporters to pay attention to the left-leaning ILWU and the Washington State Labor Council. "We like them," he wrote in an e-mail to one of GTW's organizing listservs. "They are more militant than the current position of the largest labor organization."[29]

As the principal link between Washington, D.C., and the West Coast, Dolan and Public Citizen found themselves in a strong position to act as broker. While the direct-action folks voiced many critiques of Dolan and the D.C. groups, seeing them as imperious, they did not forswear links with them. There existed a crucial set of activists on both sides of the anarchist–direct action and organized labor–public interest divides who recognized the need to find ways to actively cooperate without becoming embroiled in a likely futile attempt to achieve "unity" or a singular message. Instead, these individuals possessed a modest but crucial goal: make sure no one stepped on others' toes. This philosophy led Dolan at one point to call the AFL-CIO to check in about the direct-action activists' plans. When he did not get a response, Dolan left a message: "The Direct Action people want to do something on Tuesday morning. . . . I need to get right back to them." Dolan waited a few hours but did not receive a reply. He then called David Solnit at the Direct Action Network, informing him, "They didn't get back to me. So I guess you have the tacit, you know, agreement."[30] Public Citizen also quietly passed a few thousand dollars to DAN to help defray their organizing expenses.[31] In this way, Public Citizen not only acted as a traditional public interest NGO, translating technical policy and distributing to grassroots organizations; it also assumed the role of intermediary between direct-action groups on the ground and professional organizations inside the Beltway. Yet this was not necessarily a permanent role. Rather, it reflected the dynamics of what scholars Margaret Levi and Gillian Murphy term an "event coalition"—a "short-lived" political formation "created for a particular protest or lobbying event."[32]

By the beginning of November 1999, a near-finalized schedule of events coalesced. On each day of the week, starting on Monday, November 28, marches, teach-ins, and other events would highlight a theme ranging from labor standards to women and democracy. Starting the previous weekend, education and training gatherings combined with rallies and marches would run almost nonstop. Tuesday, the first day of the WTO Ministerial, would see the most spectacular actions. Labeled "Labor Rights, Human Rights, and Standards of Living" day, it would kick off at 7:00 a.m. with DAN activists physically shutting down the ministerial. Three hours later, tens of thousands of union members would march through downtown.[33]

Not all events were fully coordinated. Organized labor, for instance, still only had a general notion of what the Ruckus and DAN folks would do. Moreover, even as these parallel mobilizations brewed, yet another group of activists also planned to make Seattle into an unforgettable few days. Often labeled the "Black Bloc," these groups' version of anarchism was distinct from those found in the Direct Action Network or Ruckus Society. With a base in Eugene, Oregon, these individuals wanted no part in the ongoing mobilizations and had no real contact with any other activists. "Tilting at the excesses of the system never gets down to the rotten, death-culture foundations. . . . Phony half-measures and pseudo-critiques and submissive demos [demonstrations] are no advance at all," proclaimed the *Black-Clad Messenger* zine.[34]

What particularly distinguished the Black Bloc was a willingness, even eagerness, to damage private property. To them, private property embodied a system of capitalist violence; moreover, physical objects were not people and thus destroying "things" did not constitute "violence." As one activist told a *Chicago Tribune* writer, the world's inequalities are "just so extraordinarily absurd that it should just seem obvious to everyone that we need to dismantle private property. And that begins by breaking the spell. And that's what a smashed window does."[35]

While scholars and activists debate the exact origins of the Black Bloc, the actions of West German *Autonomen* provided an important precursor. A community of anarchists who formed during the 1980s, the *Autonomen* rejected working with establishment groups such as unions or political parties. Dressed in black, they engaged in street fights with neo-Nazis and with law enforcement, often during environmentalist protests. A network of zines (small, self-published magazines) and punk bands helped spread the word about their philosophy and approach to activism throughout Western Europe and the United States. In the United States, this philosophy attracted a few radical environmentalists in the Pacific Northwest fighting against logging the region's last old-growth forests. While some of these groups took some inspiration or had connections with better-known national groups such as Earth First! others represented autonomous, localized nodes of resistance. Consisting predominantly of white people in their mid-twenties, the Black Bloc and its allies emerged as a numerically small but important part of the activist scene in the Northwest.[36] Soon, however, their relative obscurity—and the relative obscurity of a whole host of neoliberal globalization opponents—would end.

CHAPTER 23

Battling in Seattle

Activists were, of course, not the only ones spending 1999 preparing for the WTO meeting. Law enforcement across many levels also readied themselves for that winter week. Yet a key part of the success of the Battle in Seattle would derive from law enforcement's failures. In the wake of the Battle in Seattle, many wondered why the police and others seemed so unprepared to contain the demonstrations. The Seattle police and the Federal Bureau of Investigation knew of planning for large disruptive protests. However, their attention was focused elsewhere. In the wake of the 1995 Oklahoma City bombing by domestically-based, white, right-wing terrorists and the bombings of two U.S. embassies in East Africa by al-Qaeda on August 7, 1998, much of the security work leading up to the WTO Ministerial focused on a possible terrorist attack.[1]

It took until late April 1999 for the possibility of "disturbances, riot, or mass protest" to begin creeping into FBI correspondence.[2] By mid-summer, law enforcement took note of the general mobilization aimed toward Seattle; after all, it was publicly and widely broadcast over the internet. As the date approached, police and the FBI ramped up their activities, requesting criminal background checks on speakers at the International Forum on Globalization's planned teach-ins. The FBI also compiled a thorough list of upcoming protest actions, including DAN and Ruckus Society plans to shut down parts of the city.[3]

Even as U.S. law enforcement and intelligence services tried to game out possible disruptions, at the U.S. Trade Representative's office and in the White House, other concerns predominated. Not only had Fast Track and the Multilateral Agreement on Investment been defeated, but the Asian financial crisis shook many peoples' faith that ever-expanding liberalization would solve the world's problems.[4] The crisis exploded in the summer of 1997, hitting the "Asian Tigers," those most economically successful of Global South countries.

These countries had liberalized their financial sectors during the 1990s, which brought in large investments. In 1997, a panic occurred leading to rapid capital flight. While somewhat under control by 1999, the Asian financial crisis shook the foundations of the neoliberal "Washington Consensus," leaving the Clinton administration (among others) worried about backing more financial and economic liberalization.[5]

From his 1992 presidential campaign onward, Clinton had advocated an aggressive agenda of worldwide economic liberalization coupled with policies to address inequality. As the Seattle meeting approached, Clinton understood the increasing power of the fair globalization coalition, who as aides pointed out, "have fundamentally different views about whether or not WTO rules ... adequately protect our domestic ... regulations." Clinton wanted his message in Seattle to highlight the idea of "putting a human face on the global economy."[6] For those concerned with workers' rights, Clinton proposed a working group and enhanced cooperation between the International Labor Organization and the World Trade Organization. As for environmentalists, the administration put forth ideas about environmental reviews and other safeguards to be inserted into the WTO.

Overall, as the Seattle Ministerial approached, Clinton administration aides stated that they had "a substantive and credible set of negotiating objectives and a reasonable shot at achieving them."[7] Yet U.S. Trade Representative Charlene Barshefsky privately expressed skepticism that WTO talks would succeed. Barshefsky's worries covered many issues. For one, new Director-General Mike Moore had only assumed his post in early September. The meeting in Seattle would be the first time many in his quickly assembled team met in person. Negotiations meant to deal with hard issues before the actual ministerial meeting made little progress.[8] Rich countries clashed over several concerns. The Europeans wanted to focus on investment and competition issues, the Japanese on antidumping, and the United States on a range of matters, including social ones. Moreover, within the Global North, governments differed over how strongly they wanted to push an ambitious agenda, with the United States hoping for a more restrained round.[9] As these problems stacked up, Barshefsky's concerns grew. She even inquired about the possibility of canceling the meeting, which proved impossible.[10] In public, she stayed optimistic. "There is a pattern to these things," Barshefsky counseled, "Everyone knows that failure is not an option, so it will come together."[11]

The weekend before the ministerial's start, uncertainty dominated across the full spectrum of people heading to Seattle. Mark Ritchie, whose IATP helped organize educational events, approached Seattle in a reflective mood. It had been more than twenty years since he first jumped on board the Nestlé boycott. Looking at the crowd during one rally, he spoke about the past and future. "We have to stop this exploitation. . . . We have to stop thinking that national governments are the only, or the single, or even the most important building block of that global governance. Global governance must start with the will of the people brought out in public movements . . . on a global basis."[12] Here, Ritchie identified the long-term, big-picture question: could a different way of structuring the world economy come into existence? The answer to that question however, seemed to depend on a more immediate conundrum posed by Global Exchange leader Kevin Danaher: could a "big-tent with abolitionists and reformers together" successfully slow or block the WTO ministerial?[13] Starting early in the morning of Monday, November 28, 1999, the test began.

∗   ∗   ∗

At 4:00 a.m., a group of activists from the Rainforest Action Network and the Ruckus Society gathered at a construction site. Aided by lights left on by the building crew but otherwise bathed in darkness, they scaled a 170-foot-high crane. It took several hours of climbing, moving along the thin long arm, and repelling off the sides, for the protestors to get into position. Then, as morning traffic rushed into downtown, the activists unfurled a massive banner. On it appeared two arrows pointing in opposite directions. Inside each arrow appeared a word: "WTO" aimed one way, "Democracy" the other.[14] This was the opening note of the protest symphony.

At noon, around 3,500 environmentalists marched downtown.[15] One NGO, the Earth Island Institute, prepared 500 large turtle costumes, referencing the WTO decision on fishing nets. As they proceeded, a host of union workers joined them. Among their number included Brad Spannon, a longshoreman from nearby Tacoma, who waved a sign declaring "Teamsters and Turtles: Together at Last!"[16] The slogan instantly became a favorite among the anti-WTO demonstrators. Then, a few minutes before the environmentalists' march ended, a few people dressed in black turned over some newspaper dispensers and attempted to break the windows at the NikeTown store. Many demonstrators chanted "nonviolence" at them and even formed a line in front of the store. As police approached, the Black Bloc fled.[17]

Monday otherwise unfurled without much drama. Teach-ins ran constantly as demonstrators and delegates continued flooding in. That evening featured two major public interest group events. Jubilee 2000, a new faith-based network lobbying for the cancellation of debts owed by Global South states to the IMF, World Bank, Global North governments, and multinational banks, brought thousands together to encircle the Washington State Convention Center for a vigil.[18] Soon after, the People's Gala commenced. A kind of protest variety show, it featured bands, comedy troupes, and speakers. The emcee for the event was supposed to be Michael Moore—the acclaimed progressive documentarian, not the director-general of the WTO. Among those speaking included Seattle's mayor Paul Schell. Recounting his days protesting the Vietnam War, Schell made one request of the demonstrators: "Be tough on your issues, but be gentle on my town."[19]

The morning of Tuesday, November 30, opened in classic Seattle fashion—with gray skies and early morning rain that turned into a light drizzle.[20] The field of conflict for the week centered on the massive convention center, located in the city's downtown. However, the WTO Ministerial's organizers opted to use the Paramount Theater, located just a few doors from the convention center, as the site for the opening ceremonies. Expecting protesters to mount an action at the Paramount, police surrounded it with city buses and a mesh fence. They thought this would contain the protest. It did not.

At 7:00 a.m., affinity groups fanned out over a several-block radius, encircling the Paramount Theater. Once in position, they proceeded to blockade roughly a dozen separate intersections. In the middle of the streets, affinity groups of around twenty-five people sat in circles, their arms spread out and linked together through plastic and PVC pipes. Inside the pipes, activists placed specially crafted chains and locks, allowing each participant to lock themselves to the person to their right and left. To undo these mechanisms, police would need to cut through the pipes, a task both difficult and fraught with the danger of seriously injuring people. Simultaneously, larger groups of demonstrators surrounded those locked down, providing the sheer numbers to stop (or at least slow down) anyone from breaking through the blockades. None of these actions should have surprised anyone, given DAN and Ruckus's weeks of publicizing the action and past meetings between activists and the Seattle Police Department.[21]

Those committing civil disobedience started on Tuesday, expecting the police to conduct orderly, if time-consuming, arrests.[22] Yet this did not happen. Rather, police panicked, surprised by the sheer number of protesters who turned out. The law enforcement presence in Seattle, both city cops and Washington State police, totaled only 340 officers. They now faced off against thousands of demonstrators.[23] This made it impossible to conduct arrests at a sufficient scale to undermine the blockade.

This confluence of circumstances—protesters' careful planning and law enforcement's failures—made real the activists' dream of shutting down the

WTO. All along the perimeter established by direct-action activists, hundreds of delegates found it impossible to reach the Paramount Theater. In many cases, they could not even leave their hotels, as protesters swarmed through downtown, preventing people from getting out of the buildings. In some cases, negotiators tried to shove their way through. In others, they paused and talked to demonstrators. Back in the hotel suites, dignitaries such as U.S. secretary of state Madeleine Albright seethed.[24]

By 10:00 a.m., WTO leaders decided to postpone the opening ceremonies, and the word went out for delegates to stay in their hotels.[25] Simultaneously, about a mile from the convention center, at Memorial Stadium, tens of thousands of union members converged. Rick Bender of the Washington AFL-CIO took the mic first, cheekily telling those assembled, "Welcome to Washington, the first, and probably after today, the last state to host the WTO." The stadium, built for 25,000 people, overflowed, as thousands who could not enter milled about outside.[26] For a little over two hours, a cavalcade of speakers barnstormed against the WTO, an unfair global order, and (sometimes) capitalism itself. Many speakers were older, white male presidents of individual unions. Interspersed, however, were some speakers from foreign unions or workers themselves—a presence owed in part to pressure from local activists of color like Cindy Domingo of the Northwest Labor and Employment Law Office.[27]

While tens of thousands gathered to hear the speeches, back in the city's downtown, the direct action activists began encountering significant resistance. Police, angry and unnerved by their failure to stop the activist blockades, attacked. That unleashed pepper spray on the crowds, sometimes taking a second to rip off a protestor's protective wear, like goggles, before blasting chemicals straight into their eyes. The air filled with a horrid mist as some protesters yelled "Shame! Shame!"[28] The Battle in Seattle was now fully engaged.

Even as the police began employing force, the World Trade Organization meeting continued to falter. Inside the Paramount Theater, WTO director Mike Moore tried to rally the attendees, declaring the Seattle Ministerial "doomed to succeed."[29] Moore's bluster was belied by the fact that only a few people were in the theater to hear his assertion. Among those few were activists from Global Exchange, including former California Fair Trade Campaign staffer Juliette Beck. At one quiet moment, she and two of her comrades mounted the stage and asked if anyone wished to discuss the global economy's future. No one accepted, and police rapidly kicked them out.[30]

Eventually, with most delegates still unable to reach the Paramount, Moore, Barshefsky, and others decided to cancel the opening ceremonies. This marked an important achievement for protesters. While the delays might seem merely

Figure 8. Seattle police pepper-spray protesters, November 30, 1999. Courtesy Steve Kaiser and Flickr Commons.

symbolic or just a nuisance, these setbacks held real policy implications. Every minute the attendees were not in session, every minute that protests distracted, frustrated, or inspired them, was another minute that the business of the WTO did not advance. In particular, as Wallach later noted, the delays meant that rich-country negotiators had less time to pressure those from the Global South.[31]

At the same time the WTO Ministerial suffered its first defeat, the AFL-CIO rally wrapped up. For a moment, the next step was uncertain. As recalled by Vinnie O'Brien, from the AFL-CIO's Department of Field Mobilization, some "discussion about not having a march" transpired, given the disturbances near the convention center. However, with so many rank-and-file members, plus other activists and demonstrators raring to march, thoughts of cancellation quickly dissipated.[32] However, key organizers did decide to alter the march route. Originally, the unions planned to go down Pine Street, taking them directly past the Paramount Theater.[33] To minimize conflict, union members acting as marshals received instructions to change routes, turning back unionists to the stadium early.[34] Ready to move forward, the cry of "Power! Power! Power to the People!" echoed as tens of thousands of trade unionists began parading downtown. It was noon on November 30, 1999.[35]

At almost the exact same moment, a few blocks from the convention center, on Pine Street, Black Bloc members smashed windows of large corporate stores

Figure 9. Part of the labor march, November 29, 1999. Courtesy of the Seattle Municipal Archives, Image Identifier 176886.

and punctured the wheels of parked police cars. Videos of these actions would soon circulate the globe, and become for many, their main impression of the protests. Many non-Black Bloc demonstrators felt outrage over these actions. Activists such as Fred Miller from the local chapter of Peace Action, saw the Black Bloc's property destruction as serving only to further antagonize the police. The Black Bloc later countered by pointing out that the tear gas and pepper spray started flying for two hours before anyone smashed a window.[36] Shouting matches broke out between different groups of protesters, with many yelling at the Black Bloc to "take off your fucking masks and join the rest of us!"[37]

To leaders of public interest groups, large environmental NGOs, and national labor unions, the Black Bloc presented a dilemma. Only a few weeks earlier, when asked about the possibility of property destruction occurring, Mike Dolan assured an interviewer that "none of that is going to happen."[38] Now it had. Mainstream groups quickly denounced those breaking windows. "Why didn't the police identify and arrest the vandals early on?" inquired Dolan in a press release on Tuesday evening. "If they had, the ugliness in the afternoon and my own substantial discomfort would have been avoided. We didn't come to trash Seattle, we came here to expose the trashy reputation of the WTO."[39] In some cases, public interest activists and others went further. Medea Benjamin of Global Exchange rallied protesters to stand in front of NikeTown and other large corporate outlets to prevent further property damage. Wallach and some others in the CTC and allied unions dispatched union members not only to protect stores but to try and capture anyone committing property destruction and hand them to the police.[40]

Even as this drama played out, the massive labor parade slowly moved toward downtown. The closer they came to the convention center, the clearer it became that downtown had erupted. Union marshals now began directing the tens of thousands of unionists away from the fracas. However, in a rather remarkable and spontaneous moment, thousands of union marchers and allies decided not to follow the marshals. As Barbara Dean, a member of the California State Employees Association recalled, she and others "left the path of the parade to join in support" of the direct-action folks. As they closed on the convention center, a scene of chaos beckoned them, with the "mighty militia of police in riot gear, wearing gas masks, shooting individuals point blank with rubber bullets, dousing them with pepper spray, and lobbing exploding canisters of tear gas into the group."[41] Soon, clumps of rank-and-file union members started splitting off the main march to join in solidarity with and reinforce the direct-action activists.

The next few hours proved some of the most harrowing of the whole week, as police violence intensified and militant demonstrators smashed more windows and set dumpsters on fire. Under intensive pressure from the Clinton administration, at 4:30 p.m., Mayor Schell declared a state of emergency and imposed a curfew. Around 5:30, the police launched an offensive to push demonstrators out of downtown. This led to police waging their fight in residential neighborhoods. For hours, the deafening cracks of flashbang grenades and the searing pain wrought by tear gas filled the air of significant parts of downtown Seattle.[42] Eventually, however, the situation calmed—for the night.

CHAPTER 24

A Messy Miracle

With the city under security lockdown, at 1:30 a.m. on Wednesday, December 1, Air Force One taxied onto the tarmac at Boeing Field. Alone, President Bill Clinton descended the stairs, entered a limousine, and rode into the city. Clinton struck a careful tone when he spoke later in the morning. "I condemn the small number who are violent," he told gathered delegates, "but I'm glad the others showed up. Because they represent millions of people who are now asking questions. . . . And we ought to welcome their questions and be able to give an answer."[1]

Clinton's remarks showed nuance but also political calculation. An election year was coming up. Clinton's Vice President, Al Gore, needed the Democratic base on his side, especially organized labor.[2] Thus, he not only offered conciliation through words but through a controversial proposal. While talking with the *Seattle Post-Intelligencer*, Clinton raised the idea of putting new labor rights mechanisms into the World Trade Organization's rules. Specifically, Clinton floated a plan for allowing governments to use trade sanctions through the WTO against countries that did not crack down on violations of core labor rights. Many Global South negotiators rapidly denounced Clinton's idea. Even Barshefsky and others in the administration expressed skepticism about it.[3]

Clinton retreated on this idea and from much of the conference. Even as Air Force One had descended into the city, millions in Seattle, the United States, and worldwide waited—eager, frightened, or thrilled. Their anticipation was not about Bill Clinton's musings. Rather, they wanted to know what would happen on the streets of Seattle on Wednesday, December 1. At 8:00 a.m.., Mayor Schell issued Local Proclamation of Civil Emergency Order Number 3, which instituted a "limited curfew" around the WTO meeting site. This amounted to a no-protest zone.[4] On the streets, police received orders to "arrest all the protestors."[5] With additional police officers and a few hundred

National Guard soldiers deployed in Seattle, the big question was: would the protesters show up again?

The answer came around 6:30 a.m., as thousands of people descended into the downtown no-protest zone. Singing "On the streets of justice / We won't turn around" and yelling "peacefully assemble!" hundreds of people pushed into the curfew area.[6] Unlike Tuesday, police instigated mass arrests early on, carting off protesters in city buses. Yet the demonstrators kept coming.

While the enhanced law enforcement presence dashed hopes of again physically blockading the conference, the protests still had an effect. Although in many places, the police used force; in others, the sheer number of protesters changed the calculus. At the Westlake Center Plaza, just a short walk from the convention center, after overseeing wave after wave of arrests, one field commander told his men, "We're out of here," and ordered his officers to abandon the plaza to protesters.[7]

Amid the chaos, preplanned actions also continued, meant to highlight distinct themes relating to neoliberal globalization. Wednesday, December 1, was "Women/Democracy/Sovereignty/Development" day, which despite the name, specifically highlighted gendered critiques of neoliberalism. Spearheading the programming for this day was a newer, Washington, D.C.–based advocacy group, the Women's EDGE Coalition (founded in 1998).[8] Women's EDGE conducted research on the gendered inequities produced by neoliberalism, pointing out that the WTO and other global governance bodies had "no gender perspective or analysis," as well as few women in their upper echelons.[9] Women's EDGE and individual women in public interest groups, including Global Trade Watch, the Alliance for Democracy, and the Catholic group Center for Concern, wanted to highlight and challenge the absence of discussions around gender and neoliberalism. First, however, they had to fight in the public interest ranks for a themed day for women, as some activists argued that December 1 should have two distinct themes. Women activists, including GTW's Margrete Strand-Rangnes successfully pushed back, arguing "It would send a poor signal if the day slotted for women's concerns is the only day that is slotted for two themes."[10]

Over the next months, women working at various Washington, D.C., public interest groups reached out to women activists around the world. Their discussions often centered on showing how women fit into existing narratives. A "general point to make," wrote GTW staffer Michelle Sforza, was that "as women are second-class economically, anything that the WTO does that hurts working families and poor people, will hurt working women and poor women more."[11] By December 1, a full schedule of panels and workshops along with a march was organized. While the crowds in Seattle often lacked diversity, the participants on this day hailed from all over the world—from the U.S.-based "raging grannies" to indigenous Filipina activists.[12]

Scheduled activities such as the Women/Democracy/Sovereignty/Development day teach-ins and march, along with more spontaneous marches, continued through Thursday and Friday. However, the intense drama of Tuesday and Wednesday subsided. In the latter days of the demonstrations, many direct-action activists switched their attention from the WTO to local law enforcement. On Thursday, marches continued, climaxing with around one thousand people heading to the King County Jail in downtown, the building then holding many arrested protesters. Shouting "Let Them Go!" they encircled the jail until the evening, when word came of an apparently reasonable agreement on how to proceed in getting the arrested out.[13]

While the action on the streets captured most of the media attention, within the Washington State Convention Center, key figures from the International Forum on Globalization orbit lobbied whomever they could. The activists on the inside were veterans of such advocacy, with experiences stretching back to NAFTA and even the Nestlé boycott. Credentialed to enter the convention center were such people as Mark Ritchie, Lori Wallach, and Martin Khor, who wandered the halls, talking to delegates, especially from Global South governments.[14] As the hours passed, they sensed rising frustration, especially from sub-Saharan Africa and Caribbean negotiators, whose small delegations struggled to keep up with all that was happening in the talks.

On the morning of Thursday, December 2, Barshefsky declared, "I reserve the right to also use a more exclusive process to achieve a final outcome," further stating that as the meeting chair, it was her "right" to do so.[15] This statement signaled the intensification of the use of "green room" sessions. The name referred to a process by which representatives from Global North governments brought in negotiators from specific middle-income or poor countries for discussions, hoping that a mix of promises and pressure would be most effective in a smaller setting. In the weeks leading up to Seattle, many Third World negotiators had complained about the green rooms. Their reappearance in Seattle only intensified frustrations, especially among some African and Caribbean negotiators.[16]

Waiting in hallways, unsure what to do, some Global South negotiators ended up watching CNN, where images of the protests played on an interminable loop. This gave them a visceral, albeit indirect, connection to the ongoing demonstrations. While most initially dismissed the protesters, as time passed, delegates adopted a range of views. Some sympathized. As one delegate from an unnamed Pacific Island country told *Institutional Investor*, a "lot of what the demonstrators say is what we think."[17] Others welcomed the demonstrations as a firm display that U.S. public opinion did not unanimously support more economic liberalization. Chatting with members of the Thai delegation, Mark Ritchie recalled that the protests "empowered and emboldened" them to feel able to resist rich governments' demands.[18]

As rich states' pressures mounted, representatives from several European NGOs, the World Wildlife Fund, and the Third World Network pled with delegates to "not sign any document without obtaining a prior expert opinion." They urged Third World officials to demand "suspensive clauses" for new agreements, allowing leeway to get out of new policies if needed. Some organizations provided translation services for French-speaking delegations, given that WTO officials were releasing important documents in English.[19]

While far from the main driving factor for African and Caribbean negotiators, the advice and assistance coming from national and global public interest groups helped to fortify their positions.[20] On the evening of Thursday, December 2, some African negotiators made a bold move. Speaking through the Organization for African Unity, they declared that there existed "no transparency in the proceedings and African countries are being marginalized and generally excluded on issues of vital importance."[21] For this reason, they continued, "Under the present circumstances we will not be able to join the consensus required to meet the objectives of this Ministerial conference." Soon after, a group of Caribbean and Latin American states put out a similar document listing reasons they too would not join in consensus.[22] These statements all but ended the negotiations. Even if the United States and the European Union could come to terms, demands for consensus meant that Global South nations held real spoiler power.

It took a good deal of Friday, December 3, for this reality to sink in. The U.S. delegates approached Mayor Schell about prolonging the meeting. The mayor, unsurprisingly, said "no." Demonstrating just how decisive he was, Schell further suggested that he might remove police protection from the convention center if the WTO outstayed its scheduled time. Here again, the protests had an impact. Whatever differences might have existed, especially between the European Union and the United States, the protests ensured there would not be sufficient time to iron them out.[23]

With the option of extending the ministerial off the table, Moore brought in representatives of the European Union, Singapore, Egypt, South Africa, and Brazil to see if anything could be salvaged. The assembled delegates concluded it could not. At 10:30 p.m., Barshefsky told ministers that "it would be best to take a time out."[24] The Seattle Ministerial ended without any new agreements.

Sitting in anticipation inside the convention center, Wallach, Khor, and others waited for word of the meeting's fate. When they got the news of the collapse, Wallach quickly radioed Dolan, exclaiming, "Trade team! Trade team! We did it! The WTO expansion is stopped! We have won!" Dolan listened intently through the "crackling static," and then his whole face "lit up." Grabbing a megaphone, he faced the crowds and shouted, "We won!" Cheers suffused with relief and disbelief erupted throughout the streets of Seattle. Inside the convention center, activists scrambled to prepare a press conference.[25] Not long after, demonstrators picketing outside of the facilities imprisoning most of the arrested demonstrators heard the news. "I'm reading this off my pager. This is direct information. A complete collapse. There will be no new Millennium Round," declared one activist, followed by an explosion of cheers from inside and outside.[26] Soon after, law enforcement released hundreds of demonstrators with no charges pressed.[27]

*   *   *

In the weeks and months following the Seattle protests, multiple narratives arose to explain why the ministerial failed. A rush began among those in governments and multinational companies to ensure that protesters received zero credit. Neither Moore's nor Barshefsky's statements explaining the meeting's end even mentioned the demonstrations.[28] "As an aside," declared National Foreign Trade Council head Frank Kittredge at a U.S. congressional hearing, "the protest activity was not the reason for the lack of final agreement."[29] Nor was the uprising of Global South states given much credence. Rather, differences between the European Union and the United States received the bulk of the blame.

That was the public spin. In private, elites talked about the demonstrations differently. At a meeting of the Global Business Forum, someone close to the WTO Secretariat acknowledged that many in the WTO "were taken aback by the reactions of the demonstrators in Seattle—the position of NGOs that the WTO is bad. . . . That was a very negative factor in affecting their morale."[30] In one gathering, an official who had served in Margaret Thatcher's conservative government, surrounded by U.S. policy-making elites, declared, "We must never have another WTO meeting on U.S. soil." Discussions occurred over how to delegitimize NGO activists in the future and boost the WTO's public image.[31]

The fear of the elites was the joy of the public interest groups, leftists of all stripes, and international activists who made the Seattle protests happen. The demonstrations awakened for many in the United States a sense that the heady days of 1960s-style radical protest might return. Speaking at a rally outside the King County Jail demanding protesters' release in the midst of the Battle in Seattle, Tom Hayden—a former leader of Students for a Democratic Society, one of the "Chicago 7," and an overall infamous 1960s leftist—made the connection explicit: "I never thought the time would come," he declared, "that a new generation of activists would part the waters, the waters in which your idealism is supposed to be drowned, and come to the surface."[32] Reflecting years later, essayist and activist Rebecca Solnit pondered the legacy of the protests for the left. "Seattle is sometimes misremembered as an Eden," she mused, before noting that it "was just a miracle, a messy one that won't happen the same way again."[33]

The idea of Seattle, from the perspective of WTO critics, as a "messy miracle" is apt. Seattle did not mark a triumph of unity, no matter how many times people chanted "Teamsters and Turtles, Together at Last!" Certainly, given the small participation of people of color, the protest fell short of being an unambiguous triumph of progressive or leftist politics in the United States. In reality, many of the different constituencies did not really unite but rather ran in parallel.

Yet this last point was actually crucial to the demonstration's successes. Rather than insisting on a pretense of consensus, what made the protests work was that organizations functioned in tandem and each did what they do best. As Sierra Club staffer Dan Seligman noted, "There was a powerful synergy between the civil disobedience and the permitted activities. The civil disobedience created a lot of energy and images, but the permitted activity created the message."[34] This "diversity of tactics" meant that direct-action activists temporarily shut down the meeting, labor flexed its muscles, and NGO policy wonks such as Wallach and Khor provided their assistance to Global South delegates. This appeared to mark a powerful turning point for the U.S. fair globalization coalition. For almost a decade, a coalition of established organizations had worked, mostly legislatively, to fight neoliberalism. Now, at the end of the millennium, U.S. fair globalizers celebrated their third defeat of a neoliberal initiative in a little over one year's time. Perhaps the moment had arrived for a next leap, from a coalition on the defensive to a mass movement on offense.

Coda

A Multiheaded Swarm of a Movement

Following the Battle in Seattle, mainstream journalists fanned out, trying to discover who these protesters were who captured the world's attention in Seattle. Reporting for the *New Yorker*, writer William Finnegan decided to profile a twenty-seven-year-old veteran of campaigns around Fast Track, "MAI Free" cities, and the WTO: Juliette Beck. As Finnegan recounted, amid their conversations during the early months of 2000, Beck surprised him with a request. "We need a name," she stated. "For the movement as a whole. Anti-Corporate Globalization isn't good enough. What do you think of Global Citizen Movement?"[1]

Beck's inquiry spoke to the excitement and uncertainty of the moment. Almost overnight, organizationally and ideologically disparate coalitions (such as the Citizens Trade Campaign) and networks (such as the Direct Action Network) had become something greater. In the year and a half between the Battle in Seattle and the September 11, 2001, terrorist attacks, activists produced a volume and an intensity of dissent that marked a new era in U.S. antineoliberal agitation. Moreover, as Beck's question showed, many activists were beginning to self-identify as members of a movement.

This last step was crucial. As many scholars of political movements and activism argue, forming a "collective identity" is an "essential" feature of social movements, one that distinguishes them from networks or coalitions. "Indeed, a social movement process is in place when collective identities develop that go beyond specific campaigns and initiatives," note movement theorists Mario Diani and Ivano Bison.[2] This was now happening. Following the spirit of Beck's question, activists tried out different names, ranging from "anti-globalization" to "alter-globalization" to the more popular "global justice movement."[3]

The global justice movement was never a tightly integrated entity. Rather, as one of its wisest theorists, chroniclers, and participants, Naomi Klein, observed in July 2000, global justice was a "decentralized, multiheaded swarm of a movement." Klein further described its currents as "intricately and tightly linked to one another, much as 'hotlinks' connect their websites on the Internet."[4] This was an apt description, but one that actually showed how the global justice movement mirrored many past movements in its structures and actions. After all, just look (for example) at the alphabet soup of organizations making up the 1970s feminist movement or the 1950s-1960s Black freedom struggle and any notion that social movements are typically highly integrated tactically or institutionally will quickly be disabused.[5]

Several factors collided in the late 1990s to give rise to a movement that especially attracted young, mainly (but by no means exclusively) white, and often middle-class people. The mix of economic prosperity and rising inequality characterizing the decade proved vital. After the recession of the early 1990s, the U.S. economy boomed through the rest of the decade. Unemployment fell to less than 4 percent, real wages increased, and the stock market soared.[6] At the same time, wealth and income inequalities, rising since the 1970s, only grew starker.[7]

Positive statistics could not fully sedate uncertainties about and critiques of 1990s capitalism. As Naomi Klein wrote in her book *No Logo* (which became an unofficial movement manifesto), some people in the richer countries felt trapped in a "global web of logos and products . . . couched in the euphoric marketing rhetoric of the global village."[8] Many young people thus felt they lived in a kind of fake world. Or, as Tyler Durden, the lead character in the 1999 film *Fight Club* declared, "Advertising has us . . . working jobs we hate so we can buy shit we don't need. We're the middle children of history, man, no purpose or place."[9] Some corners of culture spoke to and encouraged critical thinking about such anxieties. From zines to *The Simpsons* to alternative hip-hop, some young people learned from art how to satirize (and thus critique) the "new branded world."[10]

Absorbing culture (itself often highly commercialized) was, at best, just a start. But the choices for doing more seemed slim in the 1990s. Partisan politics offered an apparent wasteland. The center of the Republican Party continued marching rightward. The Democrats presented an unappealing alternative. The embrace by the Democratic mainstream of neoliberalism, spearheaded by Clinton and the New Democrats, may have yielded electoral successes, but it also alienated some.[11]

Few offered louder jeremiads against the partisan politics of the era than Ralph Nader. Fed up with what he viewed as Clinton's betrayals (especially on free trade), in 2000, Nader embarked on a controversial third-party presidential bid under the Green Party ticket. He dismissed the Democrats and Republicans as feeding "at the same corporate trough. They are . . . two heads of one political duopoly: the DemRep Party."[12] Some embraced this message. When the tallies came in, Nader garnered almost three million votes, running especially well with young people.[13]

Action outside of electoral politics also seemed futile. For many recently politicized people, the idea of joining a mass movement seemed like silly 1960s nostalgia. Certainly, people still protested, sometimes quite successfully, as with ACT-UP's forcing the U.S. government to take action on HIV/AIDS.[14] But, as historian Lisa Levenstein argues about 1990s feminism, most people "expected activism to look like the iconic black-and-white photographs from the 1960s."[15] And they did not see such events or movements happening. Popular culture reinforced these anti-activist messages. Movies such as *Forrest Gump* presented 1960s activism as a naïve wrong turn.[16] Even those dreaming of a leftist revival could not imagine it actually happening. "I wish it was the Sixties/I wish we could be happy/I wish/I wish/I wish that something would happen," belted the popular (and politicized) alt-rock band Radiohead in 1995.[17]

The Battle in Seattle offered a public repudiation of such hopelessness. It replaced anxiety with the promise of community and action. "I have a little more understanding of how something like the Vietnam War protests shaped a whole generation," wrote one participant.[18] Now there seemed a movement to join—and at least three principal currents one could dive into to join the fight against neoliberalism.

First were the mass street demonstrations. Of course, protests against neoliberalism were nothing new in 1999. But they had not happened before in the United States of America to anywhere near the scale of the Battle in Seattle. The successes of those days launched a race for repetition. As Naomi Klein described, an "odd sort of anxiety . . . set in" about street protests. "Was that it? When's the next one? Will it be as good, as big . . . 'the next Seattle'?"[19] For a time, hundreds of thousands labored to answer "yes" to the last question.

Protesters faced verdant fields of opportunity in trying to replicate Seattle. In what became known as "summit hopping," anytime those who governed the world economy gathered (and they did so frequently), thousands descended to demonstrate against them.[20] The first test of the movement in the United States came with the "A16" protests in April 2000 against the annual IMF–World Bank meetings. Over three days, between 10,000 and 15,000 people marched, blocked intersections, and rallied. The IMF and World Bank meetings proceeded, but law enforcement's harsh measures—including mass arrests legally

Figure 10. Global justice activists block streets during "A16," April 16, 2000. Courtesy Jeremy Hogan and Alamy Stock Photos.

dubious enough that Washington, D.C. eventually paid $13 million in settlement money in a class action lawsuit—only poured fuel on the global justice movement fire.[21]

The next major mobilization for U.S. activists came with the Summit of the Americas, held in late April 2001 in Québec City. This meeting featured all the heads of state of the Americas (except Fidel Castro) to continue negotiations over the Free Trade Area of the Americas. Canadian fair globalizers, active since their mid-1980s mobilization against the U.S.-Canada Free Trade Agreement, readied a welcome. Thousands from the United States, particularly college students and rank-and-file union members, came north to join in. Months of preparation went toward the protests, as people formed affinity groups, taught themselves about the FTAA, and readied for action.[22] The summit itself occurred in a section of downtown that law enforcement barricaded behind a tall wire fence. This move produced surreal scenes resembling a mix of a medieval siege and *Mad Max*, as activists marched toward the fence while police fired tear-gas canister after canister into the crowds. Many residents joined the protests. Québec independence sentiments ran strong and many were angry that the national Canadian government decided to hold the summit in the heart of the province. While demonstrators could not shut the summit down, turnout matched Seattle's roughly 40,000, showing the movement's sustained energy.[23]

Organizing these demonstrations displayed the often-decentralized approaches of the movement's protest-centered arm. At times, as in Québec, established organizations, such as trade unions, actively participated. However, the bulk of organizing came from smaller groups and ad-hoc coalitions, often with more radical, anarchistic politics than the fair globalizers. Sometimes these were established groups, and at other times, new coalitions emerged, such as the Washington, D.C.–based Mobilization for Global Justice. The internet made it easier to spread the word. One did not have to be connected to an organization but, rather, just needed internet access and some ability to either join an organized trip or get to a protest spot themselves.[24]

In the midst of all this activity, U.S. global justice activists took heart from feeling part of a global movement. They cheered as Bolivian farmers and urban workers beat back water privatization in Cochabamba.[25] They celebrated the IMF's and World Bank's inability to find peace overseas, as thousands marched against the meeting of these institutions in Prague in September 2000. They mourned the police killing of twenty-three-year-old protester Carlo Giuliani, one of more than 100,000 people who overwhelmed the streets of Genoa, Italy, in July 2001, to counter a meeting of the Group of Eight leaders.[26]

None of these actions disrupted these meetings in the way Seattle had. Yet they still advanced movement goals. Most simply, the marches recruited new activists. "These demonstrations create teachable moments," explained Mike Prokosch of United for a Fair Economy. "People hear what we're doing and they want to know about it."[27] A second effect happened in the realm of public discourse, by forcing media to listen to a wider range of voices.

One key moment came when former World Bank chief economist and future Nobel laureate Joseph Stiglitz published an article in the establishment magazine *New Republic* entitled "The Insider."[28] Stiglitz began by summarizing activist critiques, starting each sentence with "they'll say," as if preparing to lambaste protesters. Then, he swerved, declaring, "And they'll have a point," before offering a blistering critique of the IMF.[29] Stiglitz and other economists critical of neoliberalism offered a sharp contrast with most contemporaneous mainstream punditry. Before Seattle, op-ed writers tended toward smug dismissals of critiques of neoliberalism, calling critics "economic quacks peddling conspiracy theories," in the inevitable words of *New York Times* writer Thomas L. Friedman.[30]

For all that marches could accomplish, they were also limiting. Sheer distances constrained people's ability to participate. So did issues of physical ability, as shown by one participant-scholar's recollection of summit hopping as "physically intense and thrilling . . . often highly athletic, but occasionally hazardous to one's health."[31] Risks arising from confrontations with law enforcement varied, especially depending on racialized backgrounds, with Black and indigenous activists being at higher risk of police violence.

Such realities increasingly sunk in for the predominately white activists. Inspired by activist and writer Elizabeth Martínez's widely circulated article, "Where Was the Color in Seattle?" discussions about racism within activist spaces picked up. In the Bay Area especially activists of color and white activists began addressing questions of inclusion through deliberation and action. These discussion led to the formation of the Catalyst Project, based in San Francisco. Catalyst organized curricula and workshops about white supremacy and antiracism mainly for white activists, work that continues to the present.[32]

Fears of disproportionate police violence were one specific reason not everyone would leap onto the streets. However, as with nearly all movements, direct action was not the only form of engagement. One other avenue involved changing consumer behavior. As the Nestlé boycott had demonstrated, store shelves offered a potential alternative space for organizing. One such avenue ran through fair-trade products. The fair-trade model bypassed normal supply chains. Instead, businesses purchased goods, such as coffee or fruits or craft objects, directly from cooperatives in the Global South and sold them to consumers, guaranteeing higher prices for the producers.

The spread of fair trade grew out of organizing. Organizations such as Equal Exchange, Oxfam, and Global Exchange, mounted campaigns targeting stores like Starbucks, demanding they carry more fair-trade products. Sales of these goods showed a notable uptick after the Seattle protests and have continued since then, although controversies persist over certification processes and how much impoverished communities actually benefit.[33]

Concurrently, another, more radical form of (partially) consumer-based activism swept college campuses. Targeting the production of college apparel and offering radical and intersectional analyses, United Students Against Sweatshops ballooned. From January to mid-April 2000, USAS activists occupied the offices of the presidents of the flagship schools of the Universities of Iowa, Kentucky, Michigan, Oregon, and Wisconsin, along with Macalester, Purdue, SUNY–Albany, and Tulane.[34] By mid-2001, USAS boasted two hundred chapters nationwide.[35] As USAS activist Jessica Champagne declared, students posed a simple question to their school administrations: would they "really commit to empowering these workers to have a voice and make sustainable changes in the industry" or would they "run for cover"?[36]

USAS pushed college and university administrations to agree to independent monitoring of their apparel supply chains, financial support for workers' rights advocacy, and use of schools' purchasing power to push multinationals such as Nike to improve labor standards. They also ran independent solidarity campaigns with workers' struggles abroad. Further, throughout 1999 and 2000, USAS activists conceived of and, with trade union and other allies' support, founded a new global governance body: the Worker Rights Consortium. To this day, the consortium acts as watchdog and mobilizer in solidarity with apparel workers around the globe.[37]

From the streets to the shelves, the most dramatic actions of this era ran in parallel to ongoing fair globalization coalition initiatives. Even during the height of the protest moment, linkages between fair globalizers and more radical activists remained sporadic, ad hoc, and often contentious. Yet, whether they liked it or not, their fates and actions became increasingly intertwined.

In their public discourse, fair globalizers praised most protesters, distancing themselves mainly from those who damaged property. Speaking to a crowd of mostly young protesters in Washington, D.C., in April 2000, United Steelworkers president George Becker celebrated that activists "represent what is best in your generation."[38] Responding to questions about the protests in Québec

City, Wallach noted that "until a handful of kids decided to push over a fence, it's not really considered the news that the rest of the world who'll live with the results gets to know."[39]

Beyond celebratory words, public interest groups and protesters found productive overlap in education. Since the 1960s, one of public interest progressives' main contributions to politics and policy came from their translation services, turning technical language (like what Wallach called "GATTese") into understandable prose.[40] Organizations such as Global Trade Watch produced pamphlets, fact sheets, and websites used by activists around the country (and beyond) to learn about institutions and policies of global economic governance.[41] Fair globalizers sought to make such information readily available. As an example, right before the April 2000 IMF–World Bank demonstrations, the International Forum on Globalization hosted an all-day teach-in attended mainly by hundreds of young, new activists.[42]

Such moments of symbiosis, however, were easily matched by points of tension. As happened in Seattle, radical groups, especially those with stronger analyses of race, class, and gender intersections, criticized fair globalizers for excluding such perspectives. In particular, some radicals blasted certain fair globalizers for not taking racism more seriously.[43] Older alliances by fair globalizers now proved even more troublesome, as ties between groups such as Public Citizen and right-wing businessman Roger Milliken came under fire from a few leftists, with accusations flying that Milliken personally financed some of Public Citizen's operations.[44] Tactics on the streets also inspired fierce debate: whether property destruction counted as "violence," whether to distinguish "good" and "bad" protesters, and wider debates over the efficacy of different approaches. These arguments happened in more venues and more quickly than in perhaps any previous movements' history, as listservs became instant debating spaces for differing interpretations of these questions.[45]

Public interest groups engaged with these criticisms at times and brushed them aside at others. "I have to go back to my real work of confronting the corporate elite," stated Mike Dolan when asked about his skipping the A16 protests.[46] Dolan's sentiments pointed to the primary reason such groups as GTW and the Sierra Club did not participate in these mobilizations in any great depth. For the CTC, in particular, long-term movement building needed to wait, as after Seattle no issue loomed larger than stopping the People's Republic of China from joining the WTO.

Looking to score one last victory on globalization before leaving office, President Clinton threw himself into ensuring that the United States granted

China "permanent normal trade relations," or PNTR. China underwent regular congressional reviews and votes to maintain its "most favored nation" trading status with the United States. As China moved to join the WTO, Clinton, the corporate community, many Republicans, and some Democrats saw a need to change this. They pointed out that without PNTR, the United States would be unable to trade with China under WTO rules. The corporate lobby, seeing "tremendous business opportunities," made this fight a top priority.[47] Beyond economic arguments, PNTR supporters asserted that the agreement would improve overall U.S.-China relations.

For the CTC and the AFL-CIO, PNTR for China threatened to further legitimize and strengthen the WTO. They also objected to the Chinese government's record on human rights. Moreover, questions of fair globalizers' political influence, whether real or perceived, haunted many advocates. "If we lose, it will undo all our victories in recent years. . . . The media very much wants to present Seattle as a fluke. . . . A defeat on the China fight will enable them to do so," warned a CTC memorandum.[48]

In their mobilization, some fair globalizers moved away from the Battle in Seattle's progressive internationalism. Combating China's PNTR status often drew on nationalism and even xenophobia. Dolan, for instance, called Veterans of Foreign Wars halls to rile up Korean War veterans in order to get more calls in to Congress. The Teamsters, major participants in Seattle, invited Pat Buchanan to speak at a rally in Washington, D.C. Throughout, rhetoric aimed not at neoliberalism or global governance but rather at "China" as a nightmarish place flew freely. Some activists pushed back. "It is unfortunate that the first major post-Seattle legislative battle is over China and the WTO," wrote John Cavanagh, Sarah Anderson, and Bama Athreya. Walden Bello, a key participant in global activism added that attempts to ally with the U.S. right "splits the post-Seattle transnational progressive movement."[49]

In the end, it was for naught. Arguments from supporters of PNTR on economics and foreign policy grounds persuaded many in Congress. Despite a major mobilization by labor unions, environmentalists, and others, and a strong parallel mobilization on parts of the right, PNTR passed in the Senate by 83 to 15 and in the House by 237 to 197.[50] For fair globalizers, the defeat hurt. "In 2000, the empire struck back," wrote CTC organizers.[51] In the years to come, they could take no solace in having been right, as China's gaining permanent normal trade relations proved catastrophic for the U.S. manufacturing sector, with recent studies showing the agreement played a leading role in the disappearance of millions of jobs.[52]

The intense negativity of the China PNTR fight also did no favors to activists trying to show that the movement had positive ideas.[53] In fact, the campaign against PNTR helped crowd out a parallel legislative struggle in which fair globalizers *did* imagine what a better international economic governance law might look like. This effort started in 1997, when the Clinton administration unveiled the African Growth and Opportunity Act, a trade deal for sub-Saharan African countries.

In response, public interest groups hunkered down with new allies, notably the TransAfrica Forum, and produced an alternative bill: the Human Rights, Opportunity, Partnership, and Empowerment for Africa Act, or HOPE for Africa. Sponsored by Representative Jesse Jackson Jr., HOPE for Africa called for debt cancellation, encouragement for local production in sub-Saharan African countries, U.S. pressure to end IMF–World Bank structural adjustment programs, and protections for African countries' production of generic drugs. Jackson, working closely with fair globalizers, secured support from seventy-four of his House colleagues. However, the bill went no further, and the African Growth and Opportunity Act eventually passed.[54]

Despite the setbacks of the China PNTR fight, by late summer 2001 in the United States and around the world, the global justice movement sailed with the wind at its back. In the United States, marches, teach-ins, and localized campaigns continued activating more people. Mainstream media now offered at least grudging respect to activists' critiques. The time seemed right for a big display of dissent, with many activists looking to late September 2001. The IMF and World Bank would again meet in Washington, D.C. "It is imperative that supporters of global economic justice send a clear message: the movement for global justice continues to grow," stated a coalition of groups including 50 Years Is Enough and Global Exchange.[55]

As preparations continued, the September mobilization started building excitement. Early signs indicated that distinct parts of the global justice movement would come together in ways not seen since Seattle. Most prominent was the AFL-CIO's intensified participation. Since Seattle, the federation had endorsed global justice protests but had not mobilized its members to turn out for them. This was about to change. "America's unions will unite with a broad range of activists from around the world to insist on transforming the rules and institutions of the global economy to ensure that they work for working people," the AFL-CIO proclaimed.[56] Many public interest groups also planned to increase their participation.[57] Reports from law enforcement and protesters estimated that the crowds would reach or perhaps exceed 100,000 people.[58]

Preparations continued into the morning of September 11, 2001. On that clear and bright day in Washington, D.C., a phalanx of environmental, faith, and public interest advocates converged mere blocks from the White House, at the AFL-CIO's headquarters for meetings about the demonstrations. Later that day, they planned to hold a press conference in front of the U.S. Capitol to announce their intentions for the protests.

The press conference never happened. Waiting outside AFL-CIO president John Sweeney's office, activists received word of hijacked airliners slamming into the Twin Towers. Immediately, activists scattered, rushing to figure out how they would respond to these world-shaking events.[59] In Mike Dolan's organizing notebook, usually bursting with names and notes, not a word appeared on the page for September 12.[60]

The September 11 terrorist attacks upended the emergent U.S. global justice movement. In the hours and days following the attacks, speculation over who carried them out included some accusations against "anti-globalization" activists.[61] While few latched onto such conspiracy theories, the drive to national unity in the face of foreign terrorism and the swelling of support for President George W. Bush was intense. An ardent free trader, Bush promoted free trade as a key tool for fighting terrorism: "In every region, free markets and free trade and free societies are proving their power to lift lives. . . . We will demonstrate that the forces of terror cannot stop the momentum of freedom."[62] The power of Bush's words came from the context; dissent suddenly became riskier, even dangerous. Not only would disruptive marches court intensified state repression, but they also would likely alienate large majorities of everyday people.

It was therefore unsurprising that in the days following the attacks, fair globalizers pulled back. Within a few short days, most organizations gearing up to protest the IMF and World Bank stopped. A few thousand people still came, crying into the wilderness against potential U.S. military retaliations.[63]

As the months and years passed, many wondered, if not for 9/11, what might have happened? Certainly, one could point to factors suggesting that the global justice wave in the United States would have dissipated even absent the September 11 attacks. The movement was riven with tactical and ideological fissures. Sustained mass mobilization, especially around international issues (except for opposing war or other imperial military intervention) would have been difficult no matter the other circumstances. However, none of these analyses are slam dunk cases for the movement's inevitable demise. After September 11, some in the movement adapted in ways that answered these challenges, by mixing localized and global activism. United Students Against Sweatshops moved toward aiding campus workers in organizing trade unions while also continuing their international work. Campaigns to push various institutions to boycott bonds that helped finance the World Bank illustrated the movement's ability to innovate. In short, no one will ever know whether the global justice movement could have become a sustained social movement in the United States. We only know that the politics of war and fear snapped shut a moment of possibility.

Conclusion

On September 12, 2001, Mark Ritchie wrote a heartfelt call to activists. "It is now up to the citizens—individually and in the organized groups that make up our civil society—to find the ways to justice."[1] Some tried to follow in the spirit found in Ritchie's words, keeping up the struggle against neoliberal governance. However, many others shifted from globalization to focus on opposing the U.S. invasions of Afghanistan and Iraq, or to other causes, or to just dropping out. By 2007, what headlines still appeared about the global justice movement invariably came with such headlines as "Where Have All the Anti-Globalization Activists Gone?"[2]

Few could deny that in the United States, mass protests against neoliberal globalization faded after September 11, 2001. A few sparks still flew. In February 2002, in New York City, a few thousand demonstrated against the World Economic Forum. In Miami, in November 2003, a gathering of hemispheric leaders to continue Free Trade Area of the Americas talks attracted at least ten thousand protesters, as well as a particularly brutal police clampdown that likely dissuaded future actions.[3] In the subsequent years, everdwindling numbers turned up at meetings that once attracted tens of thousands of protesters.[4]

These trends led many to pronounce the end of antineoliberal agitation in the United States. Such statements reveal an impoverished definition of activism in which public protest is the only metric. For many of the nonprofits, unions, and other groups in the Citizens Trade Campaign and the Alliance for Responsible Trade, the post–9/11 era did not end their work but rather, in a way, transported them back in time. They reverted to the positions they held at the end of 1998: an influential policy and political force, but a coalition, not part of a social movement.

For the next decade and a half, fair globalizers rode an advocacy seesaw, going from defeat to victory to defeat. Domestically, fair globalizers mobilized against new free-trade agreements and renewals of Fast Track. In most cases, their efforts ended in defeat. At other times, they showed real muscle. In two of the most contentious legislative fights—Fast Track renewal in 2001–2002 and the Central American Free Trade Agreement in 2005—each bill passed by a single vote in the House of Representatives. Heartbreaking for activists, the closeness of these votes demonstrated fair globalizers' sustained influence. In particular, these conflicts showed fair globalizers' sway within the Democratic Party, as rarely more than a handful of House Democrats supported new trade legislation.[5]

Internationally, the scene looked brighter during the 2000s. Soon after September 11, the World Trade Organization convened in Doha, Qatar. There, the round of talks meant to finish in Seattle finally came to completion. What no one knew at the time was that for at least the next twenty years, Doha would be the last successful WTO Ministerial.[6]

The next WTO Ministerial happened in September 2003, in Cancún, Mexico. As it approached, many who had fought the MAI, joined under the umbrella of groups such as the Our World Is Not for Sale network to coordinate activism in their home countries and internationally.[7] Activists from around the world also benefited from years of gatherings of the World Social Forum, a kind of "counter Davos," where hundreds of people from around the globe met annually to share ideas and plans for resisting neoliberalism and imperialism.[8]

Efforts to scuttle the WTO talks received a major boost when, leading up to Cancún, the European Union and United States rejected many Global South governments' policy requests, including from Brazil and India. In Cancún itself, mass demonstrations happened—including a suicide committed by South Korean farmer, Lee Kyung Hae, as a protest against WTO agricultural policies. After last-ditch efforts by the European Union to salvage the gathering failed, Kenyan negotiator George Oduor proclaimed "the conference is ended," followed by a walkout of African states' delegates.[9] Many in the mainstream press and government officials declared that NGOs "deserve much of the blame" for Cancún's failure.[10] While definitely an overstatement, NGO lobbies "stiffened the spines of unsteady national governments of the South," in scholar Vijay Prashad's words, showcasing public interest groups' importance in global governance.[11]

Meanwhile, U.S. fair globalizers, spearheaded by the Alliance for Responsible Trade, continued mobilizing with Latin American social movements against the Free Trade Area of the Americas. In the early 2000s anger across much of Latin America over impoverishment and inequalities exacerbated by neoliberalism catalyzed a surprising political transformation. During the decade, many Latin American electorates voted left-wing populists and socialists into power, including in Venezuela, Brazil, Argentina, and Bolivia. Representing some of the region's largest economies, these governments were, at best, skeptical of the FTAA. In 2005, leaders including Venezuela's Hugo Chávez and Argentina's Nestor Kirchner rejected further talks, ending the dream of an Americas-wide free trade zone.[12]

Win. Lose. Win. Lose. In the United States for much of the 2000s and into the 2010s, it seemed that all this had happened before and would happen again. Of course, no one predicted how 2016 would upend shibboleths across the political spectrum—with few issues debated more strikingly than globalization and free trade.

In 2015 and 2016, the great question in the United States around international neoliberalism related to the Trans-Pacific Partnership. Heralded as the future largest free- trade zone in the world, passing TPP had all the makings of a sequel to the NAFTA fight.[13] It appeared that a Democratic president, either Barack Obama or Hillary Clinton, would get it to squeak through Congress with mainly Republican votes. Then, the GOP and Democratic presidential primaries began, and the politics of trade exploded.

Among the Democrats, longtime fair globalization champion Bernie Sanders shocked everyone with the robustness of his primary bid. In challenging Hillary Clinton, Sanders used his consistent record of opposition to free-trade deals as a key marker of difference.[14] Free trade became a major substantive and symbolic dividing line between left-leaning and more centrist factions of the party more broadly. And it seemed the left was winning. In a surprising move, Clinton, who as Obama's secretary of state helped negotiate the TPP, now spoke against it. While few doubted that this move arose from political calculation more than principle, the very fact that such calculations led to opposition to TPP spoke to both generalized concerns about free trade and the strength of fair globalizers.[15]

While Sanders and Clinton surprised, Donald Trump shocked. Democrats were supposed to be the party of ambivalence on trade, with economic nationalism relegated to the GOP's fringes. Yet here was the Republican Party nominee exclaiming that "NAFTA is the worst trade deal maybe ever signed anywhere."[16] In his rhetoric, Trump strongly echoed Pat Buchanan but with far greater success. As president, Trump showed a fair degree of seriousness. He quickly pulled the United States out of TPP talks and appointed people committed to reforming U.S. trade policy, like Robert Lighthizer and Peter Navarro, to important positions.

The Trump administration launched various trade "wars" and also completed one of the only bipartisan initiatives of the first term, the renegotiation of NAFTA. The new version of NAFTA was called the U.S.-Mexico-Canada Agreement or USMCA. Some of the players in this book—Global Trade Watch, the Sierra Club, and more—had an important role in its conceptualization. Many of these groups differed sharply on the renegotiation, revealing the changing but steady nature of debates over tactics and strategies among coalition members.

*   *   *

As I finished this book in the summer of 2020, the politics surrounding fair globalizers and neoliberal globalization were intensely uncertain, multiplied by questions of how the COVID-19 pandemic would reshape world economics and politics. Yet core questions raised by the story of fair globalizers and global justice advocates remain relevant, namely, the question of power: how to get it and how to wield it.

Public interest progressives' conceptions around how to obtain and use power are, as with most political forces, historically rooted. In their case, public interest advocates' organizational structures and "theories of change" are still in many ways rooted in the late 1960s and early to mid-1970s. In the 1960s and through much of the 1970s, the institutional pillars backing liberal reforms, both domestic and international, appeared strong. Therefore, public interest advocates did not concentrate on building and exerting raw political power. They did not grow large memberships, become directly involved in elections, or embrace disruptive protest. Instead, they understood themselves as policy catalysts, cajoling powerful institutions to implement reform. Equally important, advocates viewed themselves as external watchdogs. From experience, they knew that large private enterprises and state bureaucracies would never on their own protect the public. Such bases of institutional economic and political power, public interest progressives argued, needed constant observation and prodding from experts on the outside.

Embracing these perspectives limited public interest progressives' worldviews in many cases. Certainly, some individuals and groups within the public interest progressive community (like the Institute for Policy Studies) situated themselves as critics working toward radical transformation. But most public interest progressives held to a shorter timeline. They believed it more important to win something tangible—a new law, a regulation—sooner rather than (in their minds) making themselves noisy nuisances who could show no concrete policy accomplishments. In some cases, this pragmatism was wholly sincere. At other times, it represented a resigned sense that more change might be impossible, with the fall of New Left movements weighing heavy.

During the 1960s and 1970s, public interest progressives' "responsible militancy" offered real results. It is hard to deny that their advocacy has over the years saved and improved lives, with examples ranging from seatbelts to cleaner air to safer consumer products. During the 1970s particularly, there seemed little reason to fundamentally question the model. Certainly, public interest progressives experienced political disappointments and failures. However, these defeats usually arose from lost offensive fights aimed at expanding the scope and efficacy of the regulatory state.

By the beginning of the 1990s, this was no longer the case. At home, the rise of a more conservative politics in the Republican Party (and the Democratic Party) and the resurgence of the business lobby transformed the policy scene. Internationally, the advent of the WTO and agreements such as NAFTA signaled that even the modest hopes of the late 1970s and early 1980s for fairer global economic governance were gone.

Amid these uncertainties, public interest progressives were thrust into a political role they were ill-equipped for. To understand the role of public interest progressives in larger U.S. politics from the early 1980s until recently, one might imagine the liberal-left in the United States as an edifice, held up by a series of differently sized pillars. These pillars represent distinct constituencies: organized labor, religious organizations, community groups, public interest nonprofits, and so on. During the 1980s and 1990s, the pillars representing institutionalized movements, such as labor, civil rights, or the liberal wing of the Democratic Party, weakened precipitously. Public interest progressives suddenly found themselves with much greater responsibility for holding up the edifice of U.S. liberalism than they had before.

Organizationally and especially demographically, this was not a role for which public interest groups were well suited. They did not have the mass memberships or political influence to simply replace labor or mainline Protestant churches. This led to the formation of coalitions, like the Citizens Trade Campaign. However, at the same time as they carried more weight, the work of liberal reform became much harder. Public interest progressives had relied on other actors to place the kinds of pressure on politicians that come, for example, from being able to threaten their reelection. Meanwhile, public interest progressives' lack of large, demographically diverse, and activated grassroots memberships also diminished their capacities. If organizationally, public interest progressives were suboptimal, demographically they made even less sense as liberal leaders, as seen by the lack of people of color in Seattle.

Fortunately for U.S. liberalism and the left, events in the past few years point to the movement of public interest progressives from center stage. In the early and mid-2000s the "Netroots," a collection of groups like MoveOn.org brought a more assertive voice to liberal and Democratic politics. In the aftermath of the 2008 financial crash, a series of leftist uprisings and organizations have sprung up, including the short-lived Occupy moment, Black Lives Matter, immigrant rights organizing, the surge of the Democratic Socialists of America, renewed worker militancy, and climate justice turning into a mass force.[17] Public interest progressivism no longer carries a disproportionate amount of the weight in keeping U.S. liberalism (much less the left) aloft.

This is not to say they have no role. Take climate change, a topic that fair globalizers in the United States and global justice activists around the world have become particularly involved in. Achieving any sort of global regime that addresses the climate crisis will require incredible strides in international governance. After all, millions of peoples' lives already depend (and will rely more in the future) on the decisions made by international governance bodies, such as the United Nations and the World Bank. And, of course, the question of how to influence these bodies, as well as national governments, by working across borders will only grow in salience. As Brandon Wu, of the progressive international nonprofit ActionAid has stated, "We have a scientific reality where we need to deal with this problem urgently, and then we have a political reality where we can't. And we need to shift that political reality."[18]

Fair globalizers will likely find a role in this effort. The question remains, what will their role be? In recent years, in many progressive and left-wing spaces, metaphors of ecology have gained popularity in explaining how different constituencies might best interact.[19] The idea, popularized by the Momentum training institute and movement incubator, behind "movement ecology" is that forces for political change—whether they be networks, coalitions, or movements—interact in complicated ways. Ideally, distinct philosophies and approaches of activism find their niches, creating a degree of harmony among potential allies. This metaphor is not only useful for the future but also the past. Through its lens, public interest progressivism's historical and political virtues and deficiencies become clearer. Public interest progressives' often single-minded devotion to a particular cause or set of institutions can harm their ability to be part of a larger whole. However, it also allows them to focus, identifying challenges others do not. Their emphasis on expertise limits them, but also acts as a source of power. Their reformism and often narrow horizons become an ideological and political trap but also give them the ability to weather dramatic political changes over decades, during which many more radical groups disappear. For now, the fair globalizers' work, in Rebecca Solnit's words, of "painstaking mastery of arcane policy, stubborn perseverance year after year for a cause, empathy with those who remain unseen, and outrage channeled into dedication" appears set to continue.[20]

NOTES

Introduction

1. Noah Smith, "The Dark Side of Globalization: Why Seattle's 1999 Protestors Were Right," *Atlantic*, January 6, 2014, https://www.theatlantic.com/business/archive/2014/01/the-dark-side-of-globalization-why-seattles-1999-protesters-were-right/282831/.

2. Manfred B. Steger and Erin K. Wilson, "Anti-Globalization or Alter-Globalization? Mapping the Political Ideology of the Global Justice Movement," *International Studies Quarterly* 56 (2012): 439–454.

3. In using this phrase, I am both indebted to and modifying the term "public interest liberalism" coined by political scientist Michael W. McCann. The word "progressive" better captures the political breadth of these groups: some viewed themselves as mainstream liberals, but others understood themselves as leftists. See Michael W. McCann, *Taking Reform Seriously: Perspectives on Public Interest Liberalism* (Ithaca: Cornell University Press, 1986).

4. Michael Kazin and Maurice Isserman, *America Divided: The Civil War of the 1960s*, 4th ed. (Oxford: Oxford University Press, 2012); Kevin Kruse and Julian E. Zelizer, *Fault Lines: A History of the United States Since 1974* (New York: W. W. Norton, 2019); Jonathan Bell and Timothy Stanley, eds., *Making Sense of American Liberalism* (Urbana: University of Illinois Press, 2012); Jeffrey Bloodworth, *Losing the Center: The Decline of American Liberalism, 1968–1992* (Lexington: University of Kentucky Press, 2013).

5. Lizabeth Cohen, *A Consumers' Republic: The Politics of Mass Consumption in Postwar America* (New York: Knopf Doubleday, 2008); Lawrence B. Glickman, *Buying Power: A History of Consumer Activism in America* (Chicago: University of Chicago Press, 2009). Recent histories of contemporary U.S. environmentalism include James Morton Turner, *The Promise of Wilderness: American Environmental Politics Since 1964* (Seattle: University of Washington Press, 2012); Jennifer Thompson, *The Wild and the Toxic: American Environmentalism and the Politics of Health* (Chapel Hill: University of North Carolina Press, 2019); Robert Gottlieb, *Forcing the Spring: The Transformation of the American Environmental Movement*, rev. ed. (Washington, DC: Island, 2005).

6. Peter Beilharz, "Social Democracy and Social Justice," *Journal of Sociology* 25, no. 1 (1989): 85–99.

7. Jonathan A. Fox, "Coalitions and Networks," in *International Encyclopedia of Civil Society*, ed. Helmut Anheier and Stefan Toepler (New York: Springer, 2009), 487.

8. On labor and globalization, see Jefferson Cowie, *Capital Moves: RCA's Seventy Year Quest for Cheap Labor* (New York: New Press, 2001); Ronaldo Munck, *Globalisation and Labour: The New Great Transformation* (London: Zed, 2002); Kim Scipes, ed., *Building Global Labor Solidarity in a Time of Accelerating Globalization* (Chicago: Haymarket, 2016); Kate Bronfenbrenner, ed., *Global Unions: Challenging Transnational Capital Through Cross-Border Campaigns* (Ithaca: Cornell University Press, 2007). On grassroots leftist opposition to neoliberal globalization, see David Solnit and Rebecca Solnit, eds., *The Battle of the Story of the Battle of Seattle* (Oakland, CA: AK, 2009); Todd Wolfson, *Digital Rebellion: The Birth of the Cyber Left* (Champaign: University of Illinois Press, 2014); Luis A. Fernandez, *Policing Dissent: Social Control and the Antiglobalization Movement* (New Brunswick, NJ: Rutgers University Press, 2008), 35–68; A. K. Thompson, *Black Bloc, White Riot: Anti-Globalization and the Genealogy of Dissent* (Oakland, CA: AK, 2010); Jeffrey S. Juris and Alex Khasnabish, eds., *Insurgent Encounters: Transnational Activism, Ethnography, and the Political* (Durham, NC: Duke University Press, 2013); L. A. Kauffman, *Direct Action: Protest and the Reinvention of American Radicalism* (London: Verso, 2017), 135–162.

9. Mark Ritchie, "Peace and International Systems," speech at the World Trade Organization and the Global War System Conference, November 28, 1999, https://ratical .org/co-globalize/WTOandGWSfp.html.

10. Mark Bevir, *Governance: A Very Short Introduction* (Oxford: Oxford University Press, 2013), 3–4.

11. Mark Mazower, *Governing the World: The History of an Idea* (New York: Penguin, 2012); Stephen Buzdugan and Anthony Payne, *The Long Battle for Global Governance* (New York: Routledge, 2016); Glenda Sluga, *Internationalism in the Age of Nationalism* (Philadelphia: University of Pennsylvania Press, 2013); Simon Jackson and Alanna O'Malley, eds., *The Institution of International Order: From the League of Nations to the United Nations* (New York: Routledge, 2018).

12. Daniel Stedman Jones, *Masters of the Universe: Hayek, Friedman, and the Birth of Neoliberal Politics* (Princeton: Princeton University Press, 2014), 2. See also David Harvey, *A Brief History of Neoliberalism* (Oxford: Oxford University Press, 2005); Naomi Klein, *The Shock Doctrine: The Rise of Disaster Capitalism* (New York: Picador, 2007); Angus Burgin, *The Great Persuasion: Reinventing Free Markets Since the Depression* (Cambridge, MA: Harvard University Press, 2012).

13. Victor McFarland, "The New International Economic Order, Interdependence, and Globalization," *Humanity* 6, no. 1 (Spring 2015): 219.

14. Quinn Slobodian, *Globalists: The End of Empire and the Birth of Neoliberalism* (Cambridge, MA: Harvard University Press, 2018), 6.

15. Amy C. Offner, *Sorting Out the Mixed Economy: The Rise and Fall of Welfare and Developmental States in the Americas* (Princeton: Princeton University Press, 2019); Massimo De Angelis, "The Political Economy of Global Neoliberal Governance," *Review (Fernand Braudel Center)* 28, no. 3 (2005): 229–257; Stephen Gill, "New Constitutionalism, Democratisation, and Global Political Economy," *Pacifica Review: Peace Security and Global Change* 10, no. 1 (1998): 23–38.

16. On transnational activism, see Margaret E. Keck and Kathryn Sikkink, *Activists Beyond Borders: Advocacy Networks in International Politics* (Ithaca: Cornell University Press, 1998); Jackie Smith, Charles Chatfield, and Ron Pagnucco, eds., *Transnational Social Movements and Global Politics: Solidarity Beyond the State* (Syracuse, NY: Syracuse University Press, 1997); Sidney Tarrow, *The New Transnational Activism* (Cambridge: Cambridge University Press, 2005).

17. Steve Striffler, *Solidarity: Latin America and the US Left in the Era of Human Rights* (London: Pluto, 2019); Penny M. Von Eschen, *Race Against Empire: Black Americans and Anticolonialism, 1937–1957* (Ithaca: Cornell University Press, 1997); Carol Anderson, *Bourgeois Radicals: The NAACP and the Struggle for Colonial Liberation, 1941–1960* (Cambridge: Cambridge University Press, 2014); Van Gosse, *Where the Boys Are: Cuba, Cold War America, and the Rise of a New Left* (London: Verso, 1993).

18. François Polet, ed., *Globalizing Resistance: The State of Struggle*, trans. Victoria Bawtree (London: Pluto, 2004); Ligaya Lindio-McGovern and Isidor Wallimann, eds., *Globalization and Third World Women: Exploitation, Coping and Resistance* (New York: Routledge, 2016); Sara C. Motta and Alf Gunvald Nilsen, eds., *Social Movements in the Global South: Dispossession, Development and Resistance* (New York: Palgrave Macmillan, 2011).

19. Akira Iriye, *Global Community: The Role of International Organizations in the Making of the Contemporary World* (Berkeley: University of California Press, 2002).

20. Samuel Moyn, *The Last Utopia: Human Rights in History* (Cambridge, MA: Harvard University Press, 2010); Akira Iriye, Petra Goedde, and William I. Hitchcock, eds., *The Human Rights Revolution: An International History* (Oxford: Oxford University Press, 2012); Barbara J. Keys, *Reclaiming American Virtue: The Human Rights Revolution of the 1970s* (Cambridge, MA: Harvard University Press, 2014); Sarah B. Snyder, *From Selma to Moscow: How Human Rights Activists Transformed U.S. Foreign Policy* (New York: Columbia University Press, 2018). On human rights and social welfare, see Samuel Moyn, *Not Enough: Human Rights in an Unequal World* (Cambridge, MA: Belknap Press of Harvard University Press, 2018).

21. In this book, I use the terms "Global North" and "Global South" and "First World" and "Third World" interchangeably. In this, I am mirroring the usage of such phrases by the historical actors I examine, including those from African, Asian, and Latin American countries. See Marlea Clarke, "Global South: What Does It Mean and Why Use the Term?," *Global South Political Commentaries*, August 8, 2018, https://onlineacademiccommunity.uvic.ca/globalsouthpolitics/2018/08/08/global-south-what-does-it-mean-and-why-use-the-term/; "Concepts of the Global South—Voices from Around the World," Global Studies Center, University of Cologne, Germany, https://core.ac.uk/download/pdf/33335548.pdf; Martin W. Lewis and Kären E. Wigen, *The Myth of Continents: A Critique of Metageography* (Berkeley: University of California Press, 1997).

22. Brian H. Smith, *More Than Altruism: The Politics of Private Foreign Aid* (Princeton: Princeton University Press, 1990); Heike Wieters, *The NGO Care and Food Aid from America 1945–1980: "Showered with Kindness"?* (Manchester, UK: Manchester University

Press, 2017); Rachel M. McCleary, *Global Compassion: Private Voluntary Organizations and U.S. Foreign Policy* (Oxford: Oxford University Press, 2009).

23. Erez Manela and Stephen Macekura, eds., *The Development Century: A Global History* (Cambridge: Cambridge University Press, 2018); Corinna R. Unger, *International Development: A Postwar History* (London: Bloomsbury Academic, 2018); Sara Lorenzini, *Global Development: A Cold War History* (Princeton: Princeton University Press, 2019).

24. Robert Vitalis, *White World Order, Black Power Politics: The Birth of American International Relations* (Ithaca: Cornell University Press, 2017); Mimi Thi Nguyen, *The Gift of Freedom: War, Debt, and Other Refugee Passages* (Durham, NC: Duke University Press, 2012); Michael H. Hunt, *Ideology and U.S. Foreign Policy* (New Haven: Yale University Press, 1987); Linda Haywood, Allison Blakely, Charles Stith, and Joshua C. Yesnowitz, eds., *African Americans in U.S. Foreign Policy: From the Era of Frederick Douglass to the Age of Obama* (Urbana: University of Illinois Press, 2015).

25. Eric Larson, "'Where Was the Color in Seattle?' White Populism and 'Colorblind Anti-Corporatism' in the 1990s," paper presented at the America's Newest History: The Nineties in Historical Perspective conference, Purdue University, West Lafayette, IN, March 2, 2017.

26. For a leftist critique of professionalized nonprofits, see Dylan Rodríguez, "the political logic of the non-profit industrial complex," in *The Revolution Will Not Be Funded: Beyond the Non-Profit Industrial Complex*, ed. Incite! Women of Color Against Violence (Boston: South End, 2007), 21–40.

27. Robin Broad and Zahara Heckscher, "Before Seattle: The Historical Roots of the Current Movement Against Corporate-Led Globalisation," *Third World Quarterly* 24, no. 4 (August 2003): 714.

28. Niall Ferguson, Charles S. Maier, Erez Manela, and Daniel J. Sargent, eds., *The Shock of the Global: The 1970s in Perspective* (Cambridge, MA: Harvard University Press, 2010).

Prologue

1. Senate Committee on Labor and Public Welfare, *Tax Exemptions for Charitable Organizations Affecting Poverty Programs*, 91st Cong., 2nd sess., 1970, 1.

2. Senate Committee on Labor and Public Welfare, *Tax Exemptions for Charitable Organizations*, 273. On Brower, see Tom Turner, *David Brower: The Making of the Environmental Movement* (Berkeley: University of California Press, 2015).

3. Michael McGerr, *A Fierce Discontent: The Rise and Fall of the Progressive Movement in America, 1870–1920* (Oxford: Oxford University Press, 2003), 147–182; Landon R. Y. Storrs, *Civilizing Capitalism: The National Consumer's League, Women's Activism, and Labor Standards in the New Deal Era* (Chapel Hill: University of North Carolina Press, 2003); Jennifer Klein, *For All These Rights: Business, Labor, and the Shaping of America's Public-Private Welfare State* (Princeton: Princeton University Press, 2006).

4. Hazel Henderson, "Politics by Other Means," *Nation*, December 14, 1970, 618.

5. *Congressional Record*, 91st Cong., 2d sess., February 24, 1970, 4699.

6. Sarah Soule, *Contention and Corporate Social Responsibility* (Cambridge: Cambridge University Press, 2009); Marcel Van Der Linden, ed., *Workers of the World: Essays Toward a Global Labor History* (Leiden: Koninklijke Brill, 2008).

7. "The Center for Law and Social Policy," October 1, 1969, Box 194, Folder 1256, RG 3.1, Rockefeller Brothers Fund Archives, Rockefeller Archive Center, Sleepy Hollow, New York (hereafter RBF). On regulatory capture, see Daniel Carpenter and David A. Moss, eds., *Preventing Regulatory Capture: Special Interest Influence and How to Limit It* (Cambridge: Cambridge University Press, 2014).

8. "Project on Corporate Responsibility: Proposal for Support," June 1, 1971, M97-170, Box 12, Folder 2, Stern Fund Records, Wisconsin Historical Society, Madison (hereafter SFR).

9. Charles Halpern, interview by Thomas Hilbink, April 17–18, 2003, quoted in Thomas Miguel Hilbink, "Constructing Cause Lawyering: Professionalism, Politics, and Social Change in 1960s America" (PhD diss., New York University, 2006), 353.

10. Judith Stein, *Pivotal Decade: How the United States Traded Factories for Finance in the Seventies* (New Haven: Yale University Press, 2010), 252, 152. See also Reuel Schiller, "The Curious Origins of Airline Deregulation: Economic Deregulation and the American Left," *Business History Review* 93 (Winter 2019): 729–753.

11. Van Gosse, *Rethinking the New Left: An Interpretive History* (New York: Palgrave Macmillan, 2005); John McMillian and Paul Buhle, eds., *The New Left Revisited* (Philadelphia: Temple University Press, 2003). On New Leftists and liberals, see Doug Rossinow, *Visions of Progress: The Left-Liberal Tradition in America* (Philadelphia: University of Pennsylvania Press, 2008), 195–261.

12. Paul Hoffman, "Coalition Formed to Back New Left at November Polls," *New York Times,* June 10, 1966, 1. On IPS, see Brian S. Mueller, "A Think Tank on the Left: The Institute for Policy Studies and Cold War America, 1963–1989" (PhD diss., University of Wisconsin–Milwaukee, 2015), 31–121.

13. Darren K. Carlson, "Public Perceptions of Ralph Nader," *Gallup Brain*, March 2, 2004, https://news.gallup.com/poll/10828/gallup-brain-public-perceptions-ralph-nader.aspx. On Nader, see Patricia Cronin Marcello, *Ralph Nader: A Biography* (Westport, CT: Greenwood, 2004).

14. *Cong. Rec.*, 91st Cong., 2d sess., February 24, 1970, 4699.

15. Eileen Shanahan, "Reformer: Urging Business Change," *New York Times*, January 24, 1971, F1.

16. Jeffrey M. Berry, *The Interest Group Society*, 3rd ed. (New York: Longman, 1997), 17–43.

17. Jeffrey M. Berry, *Lobbying for the People: The Political Behavior of Public Interest Groups* (Princeton: Princeton University Press, 1977), 34.

18. Robert Cameron Mitchell, Angela G. Mertig, and Riley E. Dunlap, "Twenty Years of Environmental Mobilization: Trends Among National Environmental Organizations," in *American Environmentalism: The U.S. Environmental Movement, 1970–1990*, ed. Riley E. Dunlap and Angela Mertig (Philadelphia: Taylor & Francis, 1992), 13.

19. Teresa M. Schwartz, "Consumer Product Safety Commission: A Flawed Product of the Consumer Decade," *George Washington Law Review* 51, no. 1 (November 1982): 34.

20. Meg Jacobs, "The Politics of Environmental Regulation: Business-Government Relations in the 1970s and Beyond," in *What's Good for Business: Business and American Politics Since World War II*, ed. Kim Phillips-Fein and Julian E. Zelizer (Oxford: Oxford University Press, 2012), 212.

21. Lewis F. Powell to Mr. Eugene B. Sydnor Jr., "Attack on American Free Enterprise System," August 23, 1971, https://scholarlycommons.law.wlu.edu/powellmemo/1. On public interest groups' influence, see Benjamin C. Waterhouse, *Lobbying America: The Politics of Business from Nixon to NAFTA* (Princeton: Princeton University Press, 2014), 38–39; Cohen, *Consumers' Republic*, 354–362; Kim Phillips-Fein, *Invisible Hands: The Businessmen's Crusade Against the New Deal* (New York: W. W. Norton, 2009), 150–212.

22. Julius Duscha, "Stop! In the Public Interest!" *New York Times Magazine*, March 21, 1971, 12; McCann, *Taking Reform Seriously*, 33–35; Judy Harkison, "A New Breed of Lobbyist: They Argue for the Public's Cause," *New York Times*, September 3, 1971, 33; Lily Geismer, *Don't Blame Us: Suburban Liberals and the Transformation of the Democratic Party* (Princeton: Princeton University Press, 2014).

23. Marcus Raskin and Richard J. Barnet, "A Proposal for an Institute for Policy Studies," July 19, 1962, Box 104, Folder 38, Institute for Policy Studies Papers, Wisconsin Historical Society, Madison (hereafter IPSP); Marc Raskin to Hallock Hoffman, May 29, 1962, Box 79, Folder 31, IPSP.

24. Duscha, "Stop! In the Public Interest!" SM14. See Joel F. Handler, Betsy Ginsberg, and Arthur Snow, "The Public Interest Law Industry," in *Public Interest Law: An Economic and Institutional Analysis*, ed. Burton A. Weisbrod, Joel F. Handler, and Neil K. Komesar (Berkeley: University of California Press, 1978), 49–60.

25. "The Center for Law and Social Policy," October 1, 1969, Box 194, Folder 1256, RG. 3.1, RBF.

26. John R. Quarles Jr. to Marshall Robinson, September 28, 1973, Box 696, Folder 4168, RG. 3.1, RBF.

27. James W. Moorman quoted by Raymond J. Sherwin, "Law, Politics, and the Environment: An Address for the Centennial Observance of the Alabama Law School," November 9, 1972, Container 281, Folder 62, Sierra Club Records, BANC MSS 71/103 c The Bancroft Library, University of California, Berkeley (hereafter SCR).

28. John Adams, "Responsible Militancy: The Anatomy of a Public Interest Law Firm," *Record of the Association of the City of New York* 29 (1971): 632.

29. Louis Filler, *The Muckrakers* (Stanford: Stanford University Press, 1968).

30. Michael Pertschuk, *Revolt Against Regulation: The Rise and Pause of the Consumer Movement* (Berkeley: University of California Press, 1982), 32.

31. Paul Sabin, "Environmental Law and the End of the New Deal Order," *Law and History Review* 33, no. 4 (November 2015): 972.

32. Richard B. Stewart, "The Reformation of American Administrative Law," *Harvard Law Review* 88, no. 8 (June 1975): 1723–1748.

33. Gilbert Rogin, "All He Wants to Save Is the World," *Sports Illustrated*, February 3, 1969, 24.

34. Michael McCloskey, "Keynote Address: 'Earth Day' University of Minnesota," April 22, 1970, Container 132, Folder 24, SCR.

35. "Project on Corporate Responsibility: Proposal for Support," June 1, 1971, M97-170, Box 12, Folder 2, SFR.

36. John H. Adams to Friend of NRDC, October 1972, Container 156, Folder 30, SCR. See also McCann, *Taking Reform Seriously*, 176–208.

37. Theda Skocpol, *Diminished Democracy: From Membership to Management in American Civic Life* (Norman: University of Oklahoma Press, 2003), 226.

38. Jerome L. Himmelstein, *To the Right: The Transformation of American Conservatism* (Berkeley: University of California Press, 1990), 142.

39. Jacob S. Hacker and Paul Pierson, *Winner-Take-All-Politics: How Washington Made the Rich Richer and Turned Its Back on the Middle Class* (New York: Simon & Schuster, 2010), 95–116; Waterhouse, *Lobbying America;* Phillips-Fein, *Invisible Hands*.

40. Jack Whalen and Richard Flacks, *Beyond the Barricades: The Sixties Generation Grows Up* (Philadelphia: Temple University Press, 1989).

41. Harry C. Boyte, *The Backyard Revolution: Understanding the New Citizen Movement* (Philadelphia: Temple University Press, 1980), 87–92, 204–205. See Jane F. McAlevey, *No Shortcuts: Organizing for Power in the New Gilded Age* (Oxford: Oxford University Press, 2016), 9–12, for a discussion of advocacy, mobilizing, and organizing.

42. Michael Kazin, *American Dreamers: How the Left Changed a Nation* (New York: Alfred A. Knopf, 2011), 209–276; Rossinow, *Visions of Progress*, 253–260; Howard Brick and Christopher Phelps, *Radicals in America: The U.S. Left Since 1945* (Cambridge: Cambridge University Press, 2015), 173–323.

43. David Vogel, *Lobbying the Corporation: Citizen Challenges to Business Authority* (New York: Basic, 1978), 40–68.

44. United Nations Department of Economic and Social Affairs, *Summary of the Hearings Before the Group of Eminent Persons to Study the Impact of Multinational Corporations on Development and on International Relations* (New York: United Nations, 1974), UN Doc. ST/ESA/15, p. 91.

45. United Nations Department of Economic and Social Affairs, *Summary*, 97.

Chapter 1

1. "The World's Largest Public Companies: 2019 Ranking," *Forbes*, https://www.forbes.com/global2000/list/#tab:overall; Susan George, "Nestlé Alimentana SA: The Limits to Public Relations," *Economic and Political Weekly* 13, no. 37 (September 16, 1978): 1591.

2. Infant Formula Action Coalition, "Financial Summary: Fiscal Year Jan. 1, 79–Dec. 31, 79," M93-263, Box 6, INFACT Records, Wisconsin Historical Society, Madison (hereafter IFR).

3. Thierry Lemaresquier, "Beyond Infant Feeding: The Case for Another Relationship Between NGOs and the United Nations System," *Development Dialogue* 1 (1980): 121;

House Committee on Foreign Affairs, *Marketing and Promotion of Infant Formula in the Developing Nations*, 96th Cong., 2nd sess., 1980, 13.

4. Naomi Klein, *No Logo: Taking Aim at the Brand Bullies* (New York: Picador, 2000), 336.

5. "Leah Margulies—Civil Rights Feminist and Anti-Corporate Activist, Founding Member of the New Haven Women's Liberation Rock Band and Movement, and Single Mother," *Veteran Feminists of America*, https://www.veteranfeministsofamerica .org/legacy/LEAH%20MARGULIES.htm. On the International Ladies' Garment Workers' Union, see Daniel Katz, *All Together Different: Yiddish Socialists, Garment Workers, and the Labor Roots of Multiculturalism* (New York: New York University Press, 2011).

6. Maggie May, "45 Years, Millions of Lives: An Interview with Leah Margulies," *Philanthropy Women*, August 5, 2019, https://philanthropywomen.org/women-leaders/45 -years-millions-of-lives-an-interview-with-leah-margulies/.

7. May, "45 Years, Millions of Lives." On sexism in New Left movements, see Sara Evans, *Personal Politics: The Roots of Women's Liberation in the Civil Rights Movement and The New Left* (New York: Vintage, 1979); Ruth Rosen, *The World Split Open: How the Modern Women's Movement Changed America* (New York: Viking, 2000), 94–143; Benita Roth, *Separate Roads to Feminism: Black, Chicana, and White Feminist Movements in America's Second Wave* (Cambridge: Cambridge University Press, 2004), 47–76.

8. *Contributions to Political Economy* 21, no. 1 (December 2002), a special issue devoted to Steven Hymer.

9. Most of these biographical details come from Leah Margulies, interview with author, New York City, July 20, 2011.

10. Alfred D. Chandler Jr. and Bruce Mazlish, eds., *Leviathans: Multinational Corporations and the New Global History* (Cambridge: Cambridge University Press, 2005); Franco Amatori and Geoffrey Jones, eds., *Business History Around the World* (Cambridge: Cambridge University Press, 2003).

11. James M. Cypher, "The Transnational Challenge to the Corporate State," *Journal of Economic Issues* 13, no. 2 (June 1979): 514.

12. United Nations, *Multinational Corporations in World Development* (New York: Department of Economic and Social Affairs, 1973), 13.

13. United Nations, *Multinational Corporations in World Development*, 9, 10a.

14. Salvador Allende, "Address to the United Nations General Assembly," in *The Salvador Allende Reader: Chile's Voice of Democracy*, ed. James D. Cockcroft and Jane Carolina Canning, trans. Moisés Espinoza and Nancy Nuñez (Melbourne: Ocean Press, 2000), 211.

15. Kwame Nkrumah, *Neo-Colonialism: The Last Stage of Imperialism* (New York: International Publishers, 1965), x.

16. Omar Sánchez, "The Rise and Fall of the Dependency Movement: Does It Inform Underdevelopment Today?" *Estudios Interdisciplinarios de América Latina y el Caribe* 14, no. 2 (2003): 31–50.

17. Norman Girvan and Cherita Girvan, "The Development of Dependency Economics in the Caribbean and Latin America: Review and Comparison," *Social and Economic Studies* 22, no.1 (March 1973): 10.

18. Fernando Henrique Cardoso, "The Consumption of Dependency Theory in the United States," *Latin American Research Review* 12, no. 3 (1977): 7–24.

19. Roy W. Morano, *The Protestant Challenge to Corporate America: Issues of Social Responsibility* (Ann Arbor: UMI Research Press, 1982), 14.

20. Leah Margulies and Judith Miller, "The Image of Women," in *Connecticut Conference on the Status of Women* (Washington, DC: National Education Association, 1972), 44–48.

21. Margulies interview, July 20, 2011. On ICCR, see Lynn D. Robinson, "Doing Good and Doing Well: Shareholder Activism, Responsible Investment, and Mainline Protestantism," in *The Quiet Hand of God: Faith-Based Activism and the Public Role of Mainline Protestantism*, ed. Robert Wuthnow and John H. Evans (Berkeley: University of California Press, 2002), 343–364.

22. Leah Margulies, "Report of the Eco-Justice Task Force," June 1976, Box 3, Action for Corporate Accountability Records, Minnesota Historical Society, St. Paul (hereafter ACA).

23. Nick Cullather, *The Hungry World: America's Cold War Battle Against Poverty in Asia* (Cambridge, MA: Harvard University Press, 2013); Vandana Shiva, *The Violence of the Green Revolution: Third World Agriculture, Ecology, and Politics* (London: Zed, 1992).

24. Leah Margulies, "Report of the Eco-Justice Task Force," June 1976, Box 3, ACA.

25. Stephen Solomon, "The Controversy over Infant Formula," *New York Times,* December 6, 1981. On the history of breast-milk substitutes, see Rima D. Apple, "'Advertised by Our Lovely Friends': The Infant Formula Industry and the Creation of New Pharmaceutical Markets, 1870–1910," *Journal of the History of Medicine and Allied Sciences* 41 (1986): 2–23; Paige Hall Smith, Bernice L. H. Hausman, and Miriam Labbok, eds., *Beyond Health, Beyond Choice: Breastfeeding Constraints and Realities* (New Brunswick, NJ: Rutgers University Press, 2012).

26. Derrick B. Jelliffe and E. F. Patrice Jelliffe, *Human Milk in the Modern World* (Oxford: Oxford University Press, 1978), 218–219, quoted in Andrew Chetley, *The Politics of Baby Foods: Successful Challenges to an International Marketing Strategy* (New York: St. Martin's, 1986), 7.

27. Benjamin Mason Meier and Miriam Labbok, "From the Bottle to the Grave: Realizing a Human Right to Breastfeeding Through Global Health Policy," *Case Western Law Review* 60, no. 4 (2009–2010): 1082.

28. Nancy Ellen Zelman, "The Nestlé Infant Formula Controversy: Restricting the Marketing Practices of Multinational Corporations in the Third World," *Transnational Lawyer* 3, no. 697 (1990): 709.

29. From an advertisement quoted in Senate Committee on Human Resources, *Marketing and Promotion of Infant Formula in the Developing Nations*, 95th Cong., 2nd sess., 1978, 581.

30. "The Infant Formula Controversy: A Nestlé View," November 1978, Box 25, ACA.

31. Caryn L. Finkle, "Nestlé, Infant Formula, and Excuses: The Regulation of Commercial Advertising in Developing Nations," *Northwestern Journal of International Law and Business* 14, no. 602 (1994): 602–619; Mary C. Gilly and John L. Graham, "A Macroeconomic Study of the Effects of Promotion on the Consumption of Infant Formula in Developing Countries," *Journal of Macromarketing* 8, no. 1 (1988): 21–31.

32. D. B. Jelliffe and E. F. P. Jelliffe, "Food Supplies for Physiologically Vulnerable Groups," in *Human Rights in Health: CIBA Foundation Symposium*, ed. Catherine Elliott and Julie Knight (Amsterdam: Associated Scientific Publishers, 1974), 144.

33. Rita Catherine Murphy, "The Facts of INFACT: How the Infant Formula Controversy Went from a Public Health Crisis to an International Consumer Activist Issue" (master's thesis, University of Minnesota, Minneapolis, 2012), 32–55.

34. Leah Margulies, "Report of the Eco-Justice Task Force," June 1976, Box 3, ACA.

35. Margulies interview, July 20, 2011.

36. Barbara Garson, "The Bottle Baby Scandal," *Mother Jones* 2, no. 10 (December 1977): 60.

37. "Chronology: The Infant Formula Controversy," May 16, 1980, Box 5, ACA.

38. Vogel, *Lobbying the Corporation*, 190.

39. Barbara C. Hewson, "Influencing Multinational Corporations: The Infant Formula Marketing Controversy," *International Law and Politics* 10 (1977–1978): 147.

40. Leah Margulies, "Infant Formula Campaign Report," September 1976, Box 28, ACA.

Chapter 2

1. Margulies interview, July 20, 2011.

2. Michael Moffitt to Bob Borosage, "Draft of the Planning Paper IPS/TNI Program on International Economic Order," January 18, 1978, Box 23, Folder 31, IPSP.

3. On the NIEO, see the special edition of *Humanity Journal* 6, no. 1 (Spring 2015).

4. Edgar J. Dosman, ed., *Raúl Prebisch: Power, Principle and the Ethics of Development* (Buenos Aires: Inter-American Development Bank and the Institute for the Integration of Latin America and the Caribbean, 2006).

5. Peter Willetts, *The Non-Aligned Movement: The Origins of a Third World Alliance* (New York: Nichols, 1978); Karl P. Sauvant, *The Group of 77: Evolution, Structure, Organization* (New York: Oceana, 1981).

6. U.N. General Assembly, Sixth Special Session, *Declaration on the Establishment of a New International Economic Order*, A/RES/S-6/3201, May 1, 1974, http://www.un-documents.net/s6r3201.htm; Craig Murphy, *The Emergence of the NIEO Ideology* (Boulder: Westview, 1984).

7. Christopher R. W. Dietrich, *Oil Revolution: Anticolonial Elites, Sovereign Rights, and the Economic Culture of Decolonization* (Cambridge: Cambridge University Press, 2018).

8. Julius Nyerere, "A Trade Union of the Poor," *Bulletin of Atomic Scientists* 35, no. 6 (June 1979): 38–39. On Manley and Nyerere's visions for the NIEO, see Adom Getachew,

Worldmaking After Empire: The Rise and Fall of Self-Determination (Princeton: Princeton University Press, 2019), 142–176.

9. Thomas G. Weiss, Tatiana Carayannis, Louis Emmerij, and Richard Jolly, *UN Voices: The Struggle for Development and Social Justice* (Bloomington: Indiana University Press, 2005), 227.

10. U.N. General Assembly, Twenty-Ninth Session, *Charter of Economic Rights and Duties of States,* A/RES 29/3281, December 12, 1974, http://www.un-documents.net /a29r3281.htm.

11. Tagi Sagafi-nejad with John H. Dunning, *The UN and Transnational Corporations: From Code of Conduct to Global Compact* (Indianapolis: Indiana University Press, 2008), 89–124.

12. "Memorandum of a Conversation," September 5, 1975, Doc 299, U.S. Department of State, *Foreign Relations of the United States, 1969–1976,* vol. 31, *Foreign Economic Policy, 1973–1976* (Washington, DC: U.S. Government General Printing Office, 2009), 1025 (hereafter FRUS).

13. Central Intelligence Agency, "Prospects for the 7th Special Session of the UN General Assembly, August 27, 1975, Doc 27, *FRUS,* Volume E-14, Part 1, *Documents on the United Nations, 1973–1976,* http://static.history.state.gov/frus/frus1969-76ve14p1/pdf /d27.pdf. On U.S. foreign policy and the NIEO, see Daniel J. Sargent, *A Superpower Transformed: The Remaking of American Foreign Policy in the 1970s* (Oxford: Oxford University Press, 2015), 131–198; Michael Franczak, *The North-South Dialogue: Global Inequality and American Foreign Policy, 1971–1984* (Ithaca: Cornell University Press, forthcoming).

14. Boyce Rensberger, "A Growing Clamor for a Well-Fed World," *New York Times,* October 19, 1977, C1; Arthur Simon, *The Rising of Bread for the World: An Outcry of Citizens Against Hunger* (New York: Paulist, 2009); Laura Roper, ed., *Change Not Charity: Essays on Oxfam America's First 40 Years* (Boston: Oxfam America, 2010), 23–91; Frances Moore Lappé, *Diet for a Small Planet, 20th Anniversary Edition* (New York: Ballantine, 1991), xv–1.

15. Margulies interview, July 20, 2011.

16. Doug Johnson, "Notes for Discussion with Nestlé Management," October 7, 1985, Box 25, ACA.

17. Doug Johnson, interview with author, Minneapolis, MN, May 5, 2011.

18. Richard J. Barnet and Ronald E. Müller, *Global Reach: The Power of the Multinational Corporations* (New York: Simon & Schuster, 1974). On *Global Reach's* influence, see Stephen Zamora, "Book Review," *Catholic University Law Review* 26, no. 2 (Winter 1977): 449–456.

19. Doug Johnson to Joe Collins, March 11, 1975, Box 6, Folder 44, IPSP.

20. Margulies interview, July 20, 2011.

21. Johnson interview, May 5, 2011.

22. Jonathan Kauffman, *Hippie Food: How Back-to-the-Landers, Longhairs, and Revolutionaries Changed the Way We Eat* (New York: HarperCollins, 2018).

23. Mark Ritchie, phone interview with the author, February 17, 2016.

24. Mitchell K. Hall, *Because of Their Faith: CALCAV and Religious Opposition to the Vietnam War* (New York: Columbia University Press, 1990).

25. "Meeting to Discuss Infant Formula Abuse," January 8, 1977, Box 1, ACA.

26. Howard Z. Lorber and Margo Cornelius, "Grave Markers: *Bottle Babies*," *Jump Cut: A Review of Contemporary Media* 27 (July 1982): 33–34.

27. Johnson interview, May 5, 2011.

28. Chetley, *Politics of Baby Foods*, 18. There are conflicting figures for Nestlé's sales of breast-milk substitutes in Global South nations in this period. See Kathryn Sikkink, "Codes of Conduct for Transnational Corporations: The Case of the WHO/UNICEF Code," *International Organization* 40, no. 4 (Autumn 1986): 826, for the low number; and T. Beauchamp, "Marketing Infant Formula," in *Governments and Transnational Corporations*, ed. Theodore H. Moran and John H. Dunning (London: Routledge, 1993), 154, for the high number.

29. Maggie McComas, "The US Campaign," in *Infant Feeding: Anatomy of a Controversy, 1973–1984*, ed. John Dobbing (London: Springer-Verlag, 1988), 60.

30. Magnus Boström, Michele Micheletti, and Peter Oosterveer, eds., *The Oxford Companion of Political Consumerism* (Oxford: Oxford University Press, 2019).

31. Douglas Johnson letter to TWI "friends," May 5, 1977, Box 5, ACA; Gloria Onland, "Nestlé's Infant Formula Marketing in Third World Protested," *Minnesota Daily*, July 5, 1977.

32. Doug Johnson, "Confronting Corporate Power: Strategies and Phases of the Nestlé Boycott," in *Research in Corporate Social Performance and Policy 8*, ed. James E. Post (Greenwich, CT: Jai, 1986), 334; "Model Nestlé Boycott Endorsement," June 22, 1978, Box 6, ACA.

33. "Brief News Roundup," April 9, 1980, Box 6, ACA.

34. *INFACT Update*, Issue 2 (April 1978): 5, M93-263, Box 33, Folder 38, IFR.

35. Form letter from INFACT to potential supporters, undated, Box 5, ACA.

36. Doug Clement, "Infant Formula Malnutrition: Threat to the Third World," *Christian Century* 6, no. 3 (March 1, 1978): 209.

37. Doug C. to Local Organizing and Resources Task Forces, "Re: Nestlé Coupon Collection Drive, Which, by Any Other Name, Would Be as Much Work," December 12, 1978, M93-263, Box 28, IFR.

38. Penny Van Esterik, *Beyond the Breast-Bottle Controversy* (New Brunswick, NJ: Rutgers University Press, 1989).

39. On issues of white supremacy and racism within progressive U.S. movements, see Keeanga-Yamahtta Taylor, ed., *How We Get Free: Black Feminism and the Combahee River Collective* (Chicago: Haymarket, 2017); Michael C. Dawson, *Blacks In and Out of the Left* (Cambridge, MA: Harvard University Press, 2013).

40. Doug C. to Local Organizing and Resources Task Forces, "Nestlé Coupon Collection Drive," IFR.

41. "Infant Formula Subcommittee," April 21, 1978, Box 23, ACA.

42. Doug Johnson, "Bottle Babies," July 3, 1977, Box 5, ACA.

43. "First Draft of Nestlé Debate," undated, Box 24, ACA; Infant Formula Action Coalition, *INFACT Notes* (December 1978), Box 5, ACA.

44. Steve Korsen to Doug, Doug, and TWIRP, December 15, 1977, Box 2, ACA.

45. Doug C. to Local Organizing and Resources Task Forces, "Nestlé Coupon Collection Drive," IFR. On the politics of humanitarian imagery, see Heide Fehrenbach and Davide Rodgono, eds., *Humanitarian Photography: A History* (Cambridge: Cambridge University Press, 2015).

46. Leah Margulies and Ed Baer to Infant Formula Work Group, National INFACT Decision Making Group and Close Friends of the Baby Formula Campaign, "The WHO Strategy," February 14, 1979, Box 26, ACA.

47. Jil K. Gil, *Embattled Ecumenism: The National Council of Churches, The Vietnam War, and the Trials of the Protestant Left* (DeKalb: Northern Illinois University Press, 2011).

48. "Formula for Action: A Background Paper in Support of the Proposed Resolution to Support the Nestlé Boycott for Presentation to the NCC Governing Board," November 2–4, 1978, Box 9, ACA; Marjorie Hyer, "Church Council Backs Boycott of Nestlé Co.," *Washington Post,* November 10, 1978, E18.

49. Becky Cantwell, "Infant Formula Campaign Report," September 29, 1977, M97-182, Box 5, IFR.

50. "Meeting with Geoffrey Fookes—Nestlé," October 2, 1994, Industry Documents Library, University of California, San Francisco (hereafter IDL), https://www.industrydocumentslibrary.ucsf.edu/tobacco/docs/#id=msmp0206.

51. Robert Drinan to Union Presidents, "The Importance of the Nestlé Boycott to the Union Movement," 1982, Box 5, ACA.

52. "Nestlé Boycott Endorsements (Partial List)," 1979, Senator H. John Heinz III Collections, Carnegie Mellon University Archives, Pittsburgh (hereafter JHC), http://digitalcollections.library.cmu.edu/awweb/awarchive?type=file&item=591612; Ralph Nader, "Sales of Baby Formula Stirring Protest," *Washington Star,* October 29, 1977, C3.

53. Harold Grey, "Nestlé Boycott Kept Alive Locally by Restaurant Picket," *Minnesota Daily,* January 5, 1981, 9.

54. Moira Sheridan, "VV to Warn of Nestlés' Boycott," *Hoya* 5, April 28, 1978, 1.

55. Thomas Maier, *Dr. Spock: An American Life* (New York: Basic, 2003).

56. American Public Health Association, "Nestlé Boycott," January 1, 1981, https://www.apha.org/Policies-and-Advocacy/Public-Health-Policy-Statements/Policy-Database/2014/07/10/13/13/Nestle-Boycott.

57. Edward J. Spillane to Constituent Members of the Catholic Health Association, Major Superiors, Health Care Coordinators, and Diocesan Coordinators of Health Affairs, "Relocation: 1979 Catholic Health Assembly," November 21, 1978, Box 7, ACA.

Chapter 3

1. Maurice Isserman, *If I Had a Hammer: The Death of the Old Left and the Birth of the New Left* (New York: Basic, 1989).

2. "November 2–4, 1977 INFACT Conference Minutes," undated, M93-263, Box 28, Folder 57, IFR.

3. "November 2–4, 1977 INFACT Conference Minutes," IFR.

4. "November 2–4, 1977 INFACT Conference Minutes," IFR.

5. "November 2–4, 1977 INFACT Conference Minutes," IFR. On debates over hierarchy in U.S. movements, see Francesca Polletta, *Freedom Is an Endless Meeting: Democracy in American Social Movements* (Chicago: University of Chicago Press, 2002).

6. "November 2–4, 1977 INFACT Conference Minutes," IFR.

7. Jo Freeman aka Joreen, "The Tyranny of Structurelessness," *Second Wave* 2, no. 1 (1972): 5.

8. Decision Making Group Meeting of March 29 to April 1, 1979, Box 1, ACA.

9. Lois to DMG, "Proposed National Coordinating Committee II," August 23, 1979, Box 2, ACA.

10. "Minutes of April 18, 1978, INFACT National Policy Council Meeting," April 1978, Box 1, ACA.

11. Shirley Powell to Moe, December 22, 1979, Box 1, ACA.

12. Moe to DMG, "Big Financial Trouble," undated, M93-263, Box 6, IFR.

13. Moe to DMG, "Big Financial Trouble," undated, M93-263, Box 6, IFR.

14. "November 2–4, 1977 INFACT Conference Minutes," IFR.

15. S. E. Korsen to Doug Johnson, October 14, 1977, Box 24, ACA.

16. "Nestlé Statement of Position," September 24, 1979, Box 24, ACA.

17. "The Infant Formula Controversy: A Nestlé View," November 1978, Box 25, ACA; "Address Given by Mr. Pierre Liotard-Vogt, Chairman of the Board of Directors—Annual General Meeting of 22nd May 1980 in Lausanne," Box 24, ACA. On modernization and international development, see David Ekbladh, *The Great American Mission: Modernization and the Construction of an American World Order* (Princeton: Princeton University Press, 2010).

18. David E. Guerrant to Doug Johnson, May 5, 1978, Box 24, ACA.

19. Henry G. Ciocca, "The Nestlé Boycott as a Corporate Learning Experience," March 18, 1980, Box 25, ACA.

20. Channing W. Riggs, "Speech at the Society of Consumer Affairs Professionals, Toronto, Canada (October 3, 1985)," IDL, https://industrydocuments.library.ucsf.edu /tobacco/docs/#id=kqjb0047.

21. Riggs, "Speech at the Society of Consumer Affairs Professionals"; David Guerrant to All Nestlé Employees, November 8, 1978, Box 24, ACA.

22. S. Prakash Sethi, *Multinational Corporations and the Impact of Public Advocacy on Corporate Strategy* (Boston: Kluwer Academic, 1994), 69–70.

23. Chetley, *Politics of Baby Foods*, 53

24. Kevin Higgins, "Infant Formula Protest Teaches Nestlé a Tactical Lesson," *Marketing News* 17, no. 12 (June 10, 1983): 1, 5; Sethi, *Multinational Corporations*, 68–72.

25. "Status Report: Infant Formula Education/Action Program," revised August 18, 1978, Box 3, ACA.

26. LeRoy Ashby and Rod Gramer, *Fighting the Odds: The Life of Senator Frank Church* (Pullman: Washington State University Press, 1994).

27. "A Revised Update," undated, Box 3, ACA.

28. Sethi, *Multinational Corporations*, 81.

29. Doug J. to Ted, Ed, Leah, Doug C., "RE: Witnesses from Abroad or More Appropriately, Soliciting Written Testimony," May 5, 1978, Box 3, ACA.

30. Senate Committee on Human Resources, *Marketing and Promotion of Infant Formula*, 11.

31. Senate Committee on Human Resources, *Marketing and Promotion of Infant Formula*, 127.

32. Senate Committee on Human Resources, *Marketing and Promotion of Infant Formula*, 128.

33. Warren Brown, "Role of Infant Formula Makers in Developing Countries Hit," *Washington Post,* May 24, 1978, A8.

34. Senator Ted Kennedy to Henry C. Cicocca, July 21, 1978, Box 36, ACA.

35. Sethi, *Multinational Corporations*, 91; Senator Ted Kennedy to Henry C. Cicocca, July 21, 1978, Box 36, ACA.

36. "Trip Report of Edward Baer, ICCR to Geneva Switzerland June 19 Through 21, 1979," undated, Box 38, ACA.

37. Kauffman, *Direct Action*, 35–81.

38. Ed Baer to Leah Margulies, "Hi," July 16, 1978, 10pm, Box 25, ACA. On class politics, solidarity, *Saturday Night Fever,* and the 1970s, see Jefferson Cowie, *Stayin' Alive: The 1970s and the Last Days of the Working Class* (New York: New Press, 2010).

39. H. Mahler and Henry R. Labouisse to War on Want, March 15, 1979, Resource Center for Baby Milk Action, http://archive.babymilkaction.org/pdfs/whoinvite79.pdf.

40. *United Methodist Reporter,* July 20, 1979, quoted in Interfaith Center on Corporate Responsibility, "What We Believe About the WHO/UNICEF Meeting: Plans and Actions," September 1979, Box 28, ACA.

41. "Transcription of Notes: Nestlé Boycott Co-ordinating Meeting," September 11, 1979, Box 1, ACA.

42. Margulies and Baer, "WHO Strategy."

43. Leah Margulies to Dr. Manuel Carballo, July 25, 1978, Box 3, ACA.

44. David Guerrant, "Dear Pastor," May 8, 1979, Box 24, ACA; Douglas A. Groner to Alan Berg, March 14, 1979, Box 36, ACA.

45. Margulies and Baer, "WHO Strategy."

46. Edward Baer to Key Friends of the Infant Formula Campaign, "Latest News on the WHO Meeting," April 26, 1979, Box 28, ACA.

Chapter 4

1. Report, Steering Committee on International Organizations, WHO, Report on the 27th WHA, Geneva, May 7–23, 1974, Department of Health and Social Security, July 19, 1974, FCO 61/1208. U.K. National Archives, quoted in Nitsan Chorev, *The World*

Health Organization Between North and South (Ithaca: Cornell University Press, 2012), 58.

2. "Technical Discussions on the Contribution of Health to the New International Economic Order," A33/Technical Discussions/1, Geneva, WHO, quoted in Chorev, *World Health Organization Between North and South*, 56.

3. Dr. Halfdan Mahler, "World Health Is Indivisible," May 9, 1978, Chronological files (incoming)—Chrons 20, 1771809, WB IBRD/IDA 03 EXC-10-4542S, General Correspondence, Records of President Robert S. McNamara, Records of the Office of the President, World Bank Group Archives, Washington, D.C.

4. Jocelyn Olcott, *International Women's Year: The Greatest Consciousness-Raising Event in History* (Oxford: Oxford University Press, 2017).

5. Leah Margulies to Otto Follin, undated, Box 23, ACA.

6. Marina Emmanuel, "Penang: A Paradise to Be Regained," *New Strait Times*, April 22, 1999, 5.

7. Kunda Dixit, "Development: Penang—Island Magnet for Activists," *Inter-Press Service*, October 30, 1995.

8. Yeoh Seng Guan, Loh Wei Leng, Khoo Salma Nasution, and Neil Khor, eds., *Penang and Its Region* (Singapore: NUS, 2009).

9. Interview with Anwar Fazal, conducted by Jeremy Seabrook, July 17, 1997, quoted in Matthew Hilton, *Choice and Justice: Forty Years of the Malaysian Consumer Movement* (Pulau Pinang: Universiti Sains Malaysia Press, 2009), 19.

10. Encik S. M. Mohd Idris, "The Fight Against Rising Prices," June 8, 1973, in *Consumerism: The Penang Experience* (Penang: Consumers' Association of Penang, 1973), 7.

11. Matthew Hilton, *Prosperity for All: Consumer Activism in an Era of Globalization* (Ithaca: Cornell University Press, 2009), 102–112.

12. "Letter from Florence Mason to Colston E. Warne, May 27, 1968," in *IOCU on Record: A Documentary History of the International Organization of Consumers Unions 1960–1990*, ed. Foo Gaik Sim (Yonkers, NY: Consumers Union of United States, 1991), 66–68.

13. Odd Arne Westad, *The Global Cold War: Third World Interventions and the Making of Our Times* (Cambridge: Cambridge University Press, 2006), 158–331.

14. Opalyn Mok, "10 Things About: Datuk Anwar Fazal, the Change Maker," *Malay Mail*, July 24, 2016, https://www.malaymail.com/news/malaysia/2016/07/24/10-things -about-datuk-anwar-fazal-the-change-maker/1167679; Hilton, *Choice and Justice*, 20.

15. Hilton, *Prosperity for All*, 84, 107–108, 130–132.

16. "In Search of Social Justice: The Population/Food/Environment Perspective," address by Mr. Anwar Fazal, Regional Director for Asia and the Pacific, International Organisation of Consumers Unions at the 1976 General Conference of the International Council of Voluntary Agencies (ICVA), Leysin, Switzerland, December 6–11, 1976, http:// www.anwarfazal.net/speech-SocialJustice.php.

17. "Consumerism: The Developing Challenge," address by Anwar Fazal, Regional Director for Asia and the Pacific, International Organization of Consumers Unions at the

Mauritius National Consumer Congress, Port Louis, Mauritius, May 28–29, 1976, http://www.anwarfazal.net/speech-Consumerism.php.

18. "A Time of Opportunity and a Time for Action: A Comment on Consumer Responses to the Current World Crises," text of an address by Anwar Fazal, Regional Director, International Organization of Consumers Unions Office for Asia and the Pacific, 2nd All India Consumer Conference, Bangalore, India, December 15–18, 1974, http://anwarfazal.net/speech-Time.php; Fazal, "In Search of Social Justice."

19. Interfaith Center on Corporate Responsibility and INFACT, "What We Believe About the WHO/UNICEF Meeting: Plans and Actions," September 1979, Box 28, ACA.

20. Sethi, *Multinational Corporations*, 175.

21. Andy Chetley, "Notes, Observations, and Comments on the WHO/UNICEF Meeting on Infant and Young Child Feeding, Geneva, 9–12 October, 1979," undated, Box 37, ACA; Sethi, *Multinational Corporations*, 176.

22. *Joint WHO/UNICEF Meeting on Infant and Young Child Feeding, Geneva, 9–12 October 1979: Statement, Recommendations, and List of Participants* (Geneva: World Health Organization, 1979), 28–29, http://www.who.int/iris/handle/10665/62980.

23. Edward Baer and Leah Margulies, "Infant and Young Child Feeding: An Analysis of the WHO/UNICEF Meeting," *Studies in Family Planning* 11, no. 2 (February 1980): 75.

24. Doug Clement to DMG, November 1979, Box 31, ACA.

25. Ed Baer and Annelies Allain to Our Geneva Team, "Re: Code Discussion," August 26, 1980, Box 37, ACA.

26. Leah Margulies to Dr. Mahler, January 16, 1980, Box 3, ACA.

27. "Notes on Meeting, May 21, 1980," June 2, 1980, Box 25, ACA.

28. "Notes on Meeting with James Grant, Executive Director of Unicef, Eric Hayward, Senior Deputy Director, Doug Johnson, Leah Margulies, and Edward Baer, at UNICEF Headquarters in New York on Wednesday, February 13, 1980," Box 37, ACA.

29. Judith Richter, *Holding Corporations Accountable: Corporate Conduct, International Codes, and Citizen Action* (London: Zed, 2001), 60–70.

30. Douglas Johnson to INFACT DMG, Interested Friends, "RE: Consultation on Third Draft of WHO/UNICEF Code of Marketing," September 10, 1980, Box 37, ACA.

31. Denver Area Justice and Peace Committee and 8th Day Center for Justice to DMG Members, "Don't Buy Nestlé Action Campaign," October 1980, Box 6, ACA.

32. Mary Anne Fiske to Elaine Lamy, September 24, 1980, Box 6, ACA.

33. "Operations Committee Decisions," December 12, 1980, Box 1, ACA.

34. Barbara Hurst, "Monthly Check In," June 1980, Box 1, ACA.

35. Jimmy Carter, "Address at Commencement Exercises at the University of Notre Dame," May 22, 1977, online by Gerhard Peters and John T. Woolley, American Presidency Project (hereafter APP), https://www.presidency.ucsb.edu/documents/address-commencement-exercises-the-university-notre-dame. On Carter's foreign policy, see Betty Glad, *An Outsider in the White House: Jimmy Carter, His Advisors, and the Making of American Foreign Policy* (Ithaca: Cornell University Press, 2009).

36. Senate Committee on Human Resources, *Marketing and Promotion of Infant Formula*, 14; Glickman, *Buying Power*, 278–279.

37. U.S. Mission, Geneva to SECSTATE Washington, D.C., "Subject: Infant Feeding Issue," May 22, 1980, Box 37, ACA.

38. Gian Luca Burci and Claude-Henri Vignes, *World Health Organization* (The Hague: Kluwer Law International, 2004), 35–45.

39. Chetley, *Politics of Baby Foods,* 77.

40. U.S. Mission, Geneva to SECSTATE Washington, D.C., "Subject: Infant Feeding Issue."

41. Chetley, *Politics of Baby Foods,* 79; Julius B. Richmond to H. Mahler, July 31, 1980, Box 37, ACA.

42. Burci and Vignes, *World Health Organization,* 131–146.

43. Memorandum, "Draft International Code of Marketing of Breastmilk Substitutes," External Affairs, July 15, 1980, RG25, vol. 14977, file 46–4-WHO-1, part 9. Canada National Archives, quoted in Chorev, *World Health Organization Between North and South,* 107.

44. Sikkink, "Codes of Conduct for Transnational Corporations," 832; Chorev, *World Health Organization Between North and South,* 107–108.

45. Edward Baer and Annelies Allain to Our Geneva Team, "Code Discussions," August 26, 1980, Box 37, ACA.

46. Douglas Johnson to INFACT DMG, INBC, Friends, December 5, 1980, Box 37, ACA.

47. Doug Johnson to Leah Margulies, February 23, 1981, Box 37, ACA.

48. Jeffrey D. Howison, *The 1980 Presidential Election: Ronald Reagan and the Shaping of the American Conservative Movement* (New York: Routledge, 2013).

49. Mark and Irene to Everyone Involved in the Up-and-Coming DMG Meeting, "About a Proposal for Structuring the First Part of the DMG Meeting," November 16, 1980, Box 1, ACA.

50. Louis L. Knowles to Members of the International Nestlé Boycott Committee, January 29, 1981, Box 35, ACA.

51. Anwar Fazal, "Brave and Angry: The International Consumer Movement's Response to Transnational Corporations (TNCs)," October 1980, http://www.anwarfazal .net/speech-BraveAngry.php.

Chapter 5

1. On Kirkpatrick, see John M. Rosenberg, "Spear Carriers for Empire: The Alliance for American Militarism After the Vietnam War, 1967–1988," (PhD diss., Brown University, 2015), 206–257.

2. Jeane J. Kirkpatrick, "Global Paternalism: The UN and the New International Regulatory Order," *Regulation* (January/February 1983): 21.

3. "Infant Formula Campaign Strategy Meeting," November 29–December 2, 1983, Box 1, ACA.

4. Carol Adelman to Elliott Abrams, "Infant Formula Marketing Code," April 8, 1981, quoted in House Committee on Foreign Affairs, *Implementation of the World Health Organization (WHO) Code on Infant Formula Marketing Practices,* 97th Cong.,

1st sess., 1981, 22; Morton Mintz, "Administration Urged to Back Strict Code on Breast-Milk Substitutes," *Washington Post*, May 3, 1981, A3.

5. Mark O. Hatfield, Patrick J. Leahy, John C. Danforth, Daniel K. Inouye, Robert Dole, and Alan Cranston to Alexander Haig, April 29, 1981, Box 28, ACA.

6. Vernie Alison Oliveiro, "The United States, Multinational Corporations, and the Politics of Globalization in the 1970s" (PhD diss., Harvard University, 2010), 240–245.

7. "Confidential Cable from U.S. Secretary of State Haig to U.S. Missions," 1981, Box 38, ACA.

8. Elliott Abrams, "Infant Formula Code: Why the U.S. May Stand Alone," *Washington Post*, May 21, 1981, A27; Ambassador Gerald Helman, "U.S. Statement on WHO Infant Formula Code," May 20, 1981, quoted in *Cong. Rec.*, 97th Cong., 1st sess., June 16, 1981, 12526.

9. Bruce van Voorst, Kurt Anderson, and Barbara Dolan, "The Battle of the Bottle: In Geneva It Was the U.S. Against the World," *Time* 117, no. 222 (June 1981): 29; House Committee on Foreign Affairs, *Implementation of the World Health Organization (WHO) Code on Infant Formula Marketing Practices*, 97th Cong., 1st sess., 1981, 102.

10. Regina Murphy, "Report on the World Health Assembly Discussion of the International Code of Marketing of Breastmilk Substitutes," May 1981, Box 28, ACA; Sethi, *Multinational Corporations*, 181–196.

11. "Meeting with Geoffrey Fookes—Nestlé," October 2, 1994, IDL, https://www.industrydocumentslibrary.ucsf.edu/tobacco/docs/#id=msmp0206.

12. Rafael D. Pagan Jr., "The Nestlé Boycott: Implications for Strategic Business Planning," *Journal of Business Strategy* 6, no. 4 (1986): 14.

13. "Rafael D. Pagan, 67, Adviser to 5 Presidents," *Washington Times*, May 5, 1993, B6.

14. Rafael D. Pagan, "The Shaping of an Issues Strategy: Remarks Before the Public Relations Student Society of America," October 25, 1983, Box 24, ACA.

15. Pagan, "The Nestlé Boycott," 16.

16. James P. Grant to Rafael Pagan, May 10, 1982, Box 37, ACA. On James Grant, see Adam Fifield, *A Mighty Purpose: How Jim Grant Sold the World on Saving Its Children* (New York: Other Press, 2015).

17. "The Nestlé Infant Formula Audit Commission—(NIFAC) Charter, May 1982, Box 26, ACA.

18. Edmund S. Muskie and Daniel J. Greenwald III, "The Nestlé Infant Formula Audit Commission as a Model," *Journal of Business Strategy* 6, no. 4 (1986): 19–23; Sethi, *Multinational Corporations*, 263–291.

19. Nestlé News, "Nestlé S.A. Has Announced the Acceptance by Former Secretary of State, Edmund Muskie, to Be Chairman of Its Infant Formula Audit Commission," May 3, 1982, Box 26, ACA.

20. Kelly Balogh to INFACT Staff, "Summary: Nestlé Infant Formula Audit Commission Charter & By-Laws," August 12, 1982, Box 26, ACA.

21. Doug Johnson to the Hon. Edmund Muskie, October 14, 1982, Box 5, ACA.

22. "Transcript of Proceedings: Press Conference with Hon. Edmund S. Muskie and Dr. Carl Angst," April 21, 1983, Box 26, ACA.

23. International Nestlé Boycott Committee and IBFAN, "Record of Proceedings: The International Baby Milk Campaign: Strategies for Action," February 2–5, 1984, M97-182, Box 1, Folder 33, IFR.

24. International Nestlé Boycott Committee, "Promises, Promises . . . A Summary Critique of Nestlé's October 1982 Policy Statement," May 20, 1982, Box 31, ACA.

25. Richard L. Ulrich to Scott, August 26, 1982; Mary Tonnes to Scott, August 26, 1982; Denver Justice and Peace Committee to Scott, August 26, 1982, all in Box 6, ACA.

26. Scott and Betty La Sorella to Doug Johnson, "Action Groups: Analysis and Recommendations," September 1982, Box 1, ACA.

27. Leah Margulies and Ed Baer to Jonathan Churchill and James Post, March 31, 1982, M93-263, Box 17, Folder 41, IFR.

28. Sethi, *Multinational Corporations*, 243.

29. *UMCom News,* September 13, 1982, Box 7, ACA.

30. Jurg Gerber, "From Bottles to Bombs: The Role of Success and Occupying a Unique Niche in Organizational Transformation," *Sociological Focus* 24, no. 3 (August 1991): 238–239; "Statement of the Board of Directors," July 12, 1982, Box 1, ACA.

31. Leadership Group (Rob, Betty, Elaine, Scott) to National Chair, INFACT, "Re: C.A.B. History," July 9, 1982, M97-182, Box 5, Folder 39, IFR; "Statement of the Board of Directors, INFACT," July 12, 1982, Box 1, ACA; Mary Tonnes to INFACT, August 26, 1982, Box 6, ACA.

32. Richard Melton and Ann DeGroot to INFACT, "Re: Consultation Report," December 7, 1982, Box 2, ACA.

33. Ed Baer to Participants in the March 18–20 INFACT Planning Workshop," March 11, 1983, Box 2, ACA.

34. "Minutes of INFACT Board of Directors Meeting, September 21–23, 1984," M96-084, Box 1, Folder 40, IFR.

35. Edward Baer to Participants in the March 18–20 INFACT Planning Workshop, "Context of the Planning Workshop," March 11, 1983, Box 2, ACA.

36. "Campaign Center Strategy Workshop," April 1983, M97-182, Box 5, IFR.

37. Peter Dauvergne and Genevieve Lebaron, *Protest Inc.: The Corporatization of Activism* (Cambridge: Polity, 2014).

38. Frances Fox Piven and Richard A. Cloward, *Poor People's Movements: Why They Succeed, How They Fail* (New York: Vintage, 1979), xxi; Sidney G. Tarrow, *Power in Movement: Social Movements and Contentious Politics* (Cambridge: Cambridge University Press, 2011), 206; Donatella Della Porta, *Where Did the Revolution Go? Contentious Politics and the Quality of Democracy* (Cambridge: Cambridge University Press, 2016), 52.

39. "Notes from Washington Office Planning Meeting for Period January thru June 1983," November 20, 1982, Box 1, ACA.

40. Campaign Department to INFACT DMG, "Proposals for a Special Strategy Meeting for the Local Action Section of the Nestlé Boycott Campaign," November 8, 1982, Box 6, ACA.

41. "Summary Report on the International Nestlé Boycott Meeting," May 27–29, 1983, Box 35, ACA.

42. "Lessons from the U.F.W. Boycotts: Notes on a Talk by Jessica Govea," May 28, 1983, Box 35, ACA; DJ to INFACT Strategy Team, "Notes on Meeting with Marshall Ganz Relevant to Workshop," April 7, 1983, M97-182, Box 5, Folder 39, IFR. On the United Farm Workers (UFW), see Matt Garcia, *From the Jaws of Victory: The Triumph and Tragedy of Cesar Chavez and the Farm Worker Movement* (Berkeley: University of California Press, 2012); and Miriam Pawell, *The Union of Their Dreams: Power, Hope, and Struggle in Cesar Chavez's Farm Workers Movement* (New York: Bloomsbury, 2009). On the UFW's influences on other social justice causes, see Randy Shaw, *Beyond the Fields: Cesar Chavez, the UFW, and the Struggle for Justice in the 21st Century* (Berkeley: University of California Press, 2010).

43. INFACT letter to grassroots activists, February 25, 1983, Box 2, ACA; DJ to INFACT Board, "RE: Future Directions," May 17, 1983, Box 5, ACA.

44. "Chicago Campaign Pressures Retailers to Get Taster's Choice off the Shelves," *INFACT Update,* April 1983, Box 18, ACA; Doug Johnson to Eleanor Vendig, July 12, 1983, M97-182, Box 2, Folder 49, IFR.

45. Kathleen Selvaggio, "Activists: Reflections on a Year's Work," *Multinational Monitor* 5, no.1 (January 1984), http://www.multinationalmonitor.org/hyper/issues/1984/01/review-activists.html.

46. "Exciting News, June 6, 1983," Box 6, ACA.

47. Nancy Bartter (Columbus INFACT and OPIRG) to INFACT Board and Staff, "Re: National/Local Relations," January 15, 1983, M97-182, Box 2, Folder 19, IFR.

48. Jerry Stookey to Betty La Sorella, May 5, 1983, Box 6, ACA.

49. Douglas Johnson to Lucy Richardson, "RE: Financial Relationship of Local/National Organization," February 10, 1983, Box 6, ACA.

50. DJ to INFACT Strategy Team, "Notes on Meeting with Marshall Ganz Relevant to Workshop," April 7, 1983, M97-182, Box 5, Folder 39, IFR.

Chapter 6

1. Andy Chetley to Doug Johnson, June 1, 1983, Box 31, ACA.

2. Margarita Segura to Members of INBC, July 10, 1983, Box 35, ACA.

3. Anwar Fazal to U.S. Supporters of INFACT, November 22, 1982, M97-182, Box 3, Folder 34, IFR.

4. Chetley, *Politics of Baby Foods*, 54.

5. "Summary Report on the International Nestlé Boycott Meeting," May 27–29, 1983, Box 35, ACA.

6. "Minutes of Meeting with Nestlé-Findus Concerning Marketing of Mother's Milk Substitutes," August 25, 1983, Box 35, ACA.

7. Aktionsgruppe Babynahrung (AGB) to INFACT, November 17, 1982, Box 35, ACA.

8. Baby Milk Action Coalition to Grace and Doug, "BMAC Quarterly Review," September 1983, Box 35, ACA.

9. Dietlind Stolle and Michele Micheletti, *Political Consumerism: Global Responsibility in Action* (Cambridge: Cambridge University Press, 2013).

10. Douglas Clement to "Dear Friends," February 29, 1980, Box 31, ACA.

11. "Participants in the IBFAN Coordinating Council Meeting," February 24–27, 1982, Box 31, ACA.

12. Jorge G. Castañeda, *Utopia Unarmed: The Latin American Left After the Cold War* (New York: Vintage, 1993), 203–236; Larry Diamond, Marc F. Plattner, Yun-han Chu, and Hung-mao Tien, eds., *Consolidating the Third Wave Democracies: Themes and Perspectives* (Baltimore: Johns Hopkins University Press, 1997).

13. Jeanine Anderson Velasco, "International Baby Food Action Network Latin America: Two-Year Work Plan," December 1, 1983, Box 31, ACA.

14. Annelies Allain, "IBFAN: On the Cutting Edge," *Development Dialogue* 2 (1989): 17.

15. IBFAN, "Baby Food Action Groups Celebrate Code Victory, Intensify Pressure," May 27, 1981, Box 33, ACA. See "Fearless Politics: The Life and Times of Hazel Brown" (UWI St. Augustine, 2015), https://sta.uwi.edu/conferences/15/fearlesspolitics /documents/NOTICE_of_HazelBrownConference.pdf.

16. Marta Trejos to Doug, March 6, 1984, Box 31, ACA.

17. Margaret Kyenkya to ICC Members, B.I.G., "Country Visit Report," August/September 1983, Box 31, ACA.

18. "IBFAN Coordinating Council Meeting—London 24–27 February 1982," Box 31, ACA.

19. IBFAN, "Between the Lines: An Analysis of International Code Implementation," January 1983, Box 38, ACA.

20. "Milk Lobby Upsets Doctors," *New Scientist* 89, no. 1241 (February 19, 1981): 462; Chetley, *Politics of Baby Foods,* 106.

21. House Committee on Foreign Affairs, *Implementation of the World Health Organization (WHO) Code on Infant Formula Marketing Practices*, 97th Cong., 1st sess., 1981, 97–98.

22. Anwar Fazal to IBCOCO (and Friends), "RE: UNICEF Support for Sub-regional Workshops Organized by the International Organisation of Consumers Unions (IOCU)," May 15, 1983, Box 31, ACA.

23. Velasco, "International Baby Food Action Network, Latin America: Two-Year Work Plan."

24. Doug Clement and Ed Baer to IBFAN Coordinating Council, "A Coordinated Action Plan for IBFAN," November 3, 1981, Box 31, ACA.

25. Allain, "IBFAN: On the Cutting Edge," 15.

26. Annelies Allain to Lise Munck, July 28, 1981, Box 33, ACA.

27. Dick Ullrich and John Springer to Ed Baer, Leah Margulies, Betty LaSorella, Pat Young, and Regina Murphy, "RE: Status of Nestlé Boycott," May 16, 1983, Box 6, ACA.

28. Chetley, *Politics of Baby Foods*, 129.

29. Victoria Van Slyke, "Four Hour Briefing with Leah Margulies, September 16–17, 1983," undated, Box 5, ACA; Victoria Van Slyke, "Two Day Briefing with Rick Hoye, September 15–16, 1983," undated, Box 5, ACA. On mainline Protestantism, see *The Future of Mainline Protestantism in America*, ed. James Hudnut-Beumler and Mark Silk (New York: Columbia University Press, 2018).

30. Johnson, "Confronting Corporate Power," 339.

31. Fred Clarkson, "The Taming of Nestlé: A Boycott Success Story," *Multinational Monitor* 5, no. 4 (April 1984), http://www.multinationalmonitor.org/hyper/issues/1984/04/clarkson.html.

32. Sethi, *Multinational Corporations,* 295; Johnson interview, May 5, 2011.

33. INBC and IBFAN, "Record of Proceedings: The International Baby Milk Campaign: Strategies for Action," M97-182, Box 1, Folder 33, IFR.

34. "Joint Statement of INBC and Nestlé," January 24, 1984, Box 24, ACA.

35. Chetley, *Politics of Baby Foods,* 131.

36. "IBFAN Internal Conference," January 31, 1984, Box 35, ACA.

37. Victoria Van Slyke, Doug Johnson, and Doug Clement, "Planning Session on the 'International Conference,'" October 18, 1983, Box 35, ACA.

38. Van Slyke, Johnson, and Clement, "Planning Session."

39. INBC and IBFAN, "Record of Proceedings" IFR.

40. INBC and IBFAN, "Record of Proceedings," IFR.

41. INBC and IBFAN, "Record of Proceedings," IFR.

42. "INBC Europe Meeting, Copenhagen," August 24–26, 1984, Box 35, ACA.

43. "IBFAN African Breast Feeding Conference Overwhelming Success," undated, Box 31, ACA.

44. Carol-Linnea Salmon and Jackie Orr to Pawan, July 23, 1984, Box 2, ACA.

45. Doug Clement to Janice Mantell, Thomas Koch, Wolfgang Sutter, Margaret Bennet-Alder, "Re: Twinning," November 21, 1984, Box 5, ACA.

46. "Minutes: IBFAN 'Sub-Committee' Meeting—3 Aug. 1984, London," undated, Box 33, ACA.

47. Doug Clement, "Dear Nancy," July 8, 1985, Box 17, ACA. On INFACT's shift in focus, see Gerber, "From Bottles to Bombs."

48. "Planning Meeting—DJ & DC," September 5, 1984, M97-182, Box 5, Folder 9, IFR.

49. "Notes About an Action Planning Meeting of the PM/Tampere Action Group," October 9, 1984, Box 31, ACA.

50. Nestlé Holdings Inc. v Commissioner, 70 TCM 682 (1995), http://www.leagle.com/decision/199575270entcm682_1609; Mark Potts, "Nestlé to Buy Rival Carnation for $3 Billion," *Washington Post*, September 5, 1984.

51. "Minutes of Press Conference," October 4, 1984, Box 24, ACA.

Chapter 7

1. "Consumers Take the Offensive Against Multinationals: An Interview with Anwar Fazal, International Organization of Consumers Unions," *Multinational Monitor* 3, no. 7 (July 1982), http://multinationalmonitor.org/hyper/issues/1982/07/interview-fazal.html.

2. David Naguib Pellow, *Resisting Global Toxics: Transnational Movements for Environmental Justice* (Cambridge, MA: MIT Press, 2007), 155; Organisation for Economic Cooperation and Development, *The Pharmaceutical Industry: Trade Related Issues*, Paris (1985), quoted in Vincent Tucker, "Drugs and the Distortion of Health Priorities in Developing Countries," *Trócaire Development Review* (1990): 90.

3. Karen A. Goldberg, "Efforts to Prevent Misuse of Pesticides Exported to Developing Countries: Progressing Beyond Regulation and Notification," *Ecology Law Quarterly* 12 (1985): 1025–1051.

4. Charles Medawar, *Drugs and World Health: An International Consumer Perspective* (London: IOCU/Social Audit, 1984), 9.

5. "Consumers Take the Offensive Against Multinationals."

6. Robert L. Paarlberg, "Managing Pesticide Use in Developing Countries," in *Institutions for the Earth: Sources of Effective International Environmental Protection*, ed. Peter M. Haas, Robert O. Keohane, and Marc A. Levy (Cambridge, MA: MIT Press, 1993), 320–321.

7. *Fifth Summit Conference of Heads of States or Government of the Non-Aligned Movement*, Colombo, Sri Lanka, August 16–19, 1976 (NAC/Conf.5/S/Res 25, Annex IV), 150.

8. Michael R. Reich, "Essential Drugs: Economics and Politics in International Health," *Health Policy* 8 (1987): 39–57.

9. Andrew Chetley, *A Healthy Business? World Health and the Pharmaceutical Industry* (London: Zed, 1990), 71. The quote from the U.N. official is from a "tape recording of a talk given by Surendra Patel at a HAI international meeting held in Penang, Malaysia, in January 1988," quoted in Chetley, *Healthy Business*, 74.

10. "Of PAN, Passion and Vision for Our Future: Interview with Anwar Fazal," *Pesticide Monitor* 9, no. 1 (April 2000), http://www.anwarfazal.net/interview-PAN.php.

11. Matthew Rothschild, "New Coalition Forms to Combat Pesticide Use," *Multinational Monitor* 3, no. 7 (July 1982), http://www.multinationalmonitor.org/hyper/issues /1982/07/rothschild.html.

12. Peter Hough, *The Global Politics of Pesticides: Forging Consensus from Conflicting Interests* (London: Earthscan, 1998), 84; Hilton, *Prosperity for All*, 141–144.

13. Monica Moore, "PAN: The International Grassroots Organization for Pesticide Reform," *Journal of Pesticide Reform* 6, no. 1 (Spring 1986): 10; *IOCU: Giving a Voice to the World's Consumers*, undated, MC 450, Box 106, Folder 2090, Esther Peterson Papers, 1884–1998, Schlesinger Library, Radcliffe Institute, Harvard University, Cambridge, (hereafter EPP).

14. "Infant Formula Critics Now Planning Big Offensive Against Drug and Health Firms," *Business International* 28, no. 26 (June 26, 1981): 201, 205.

15. Corti-A, *INFOTAB*, "Special Interest Groups/Report on the Strategy of Activists and How to Respond to That Strategy," September 23, 1982, IDL, https://industrydocuments .library.ucsf.edu/tobacco/docs/gxmf0146.

16. Andrew Crane and Dirk Matten, *Business Ethics: Managing Corporate Citizenship and Sustainability in the Age of Globalization* (Oxford: Oxford University Press, 2007), 354.

17. Khalil Sesmou, "The Food and Agriculture Organization of the United Nations: An Insider's View," *Ecologist* 21, no. 2 (March–April 1991): 47–56.

18. Paarlberg, "Managing Pesticide Use," 320–321.

19. Clare Hilliker to Gary Taylor, "Meeting with S. Jacob Scherr, NRDC, Washington, D.C., Friday, February 3, 1984," February 15, 1984, Container 2, Folder 21, Sierra Club International Program Records, BANC MSS 71/290 c, Bancroft Library, University of California, Berkeley (hereafter SCIP).

20. United Nations International Business Council, "Summary of Discussion Meeting Thursday, 851024 10:00–11: 40 AM 870 United Nations Plaza Suite 20-C, New York, NY. The Pesticide Action Network: Its Dirty Dozen Campaign," November 6, 1985, IDL, https://industrydocuments.library.ucsf.edu/tobacco/docs/#id=zzkc0114.

21. "Pesticide Action Network's First 20 Years: An Interview with Monica Moore," *Global Pesticide Campaigner* 12, no. 1 (May 2002): 18.

22. Barbara Bramble to William H. Mansfield, October 30, 1984, Container 11, Folder 5, SCIP.

23. David Bull, "The New International Pesticides Code: Unprecedented Tool for Activists," *Journal of Pesticide Reform* 6, no.1 (Spring 1986): 20.

24. Paarlberg, "Managing Pesticide Use," 323–330; Erika Rosenthal and Monica Moore, "The Dirty Dozen: Banned but Rarely Banished," *Global Pesticide Campaigner* 5, no. 3 (September 1995).

25. Stephen Zavestoski, "Environmental Health Organizing in a Globalizing World: The Emergence of a Global Anti-Toxics Movement and Its Political, Legal, and Economic Challenges," in *Health and Environment: Social Science Perspectives*, ed. Helen Kopnina and Hans Keune (New York: Nova Science, 2010), 255–273.

26. "Infant Formula Critics Now Planning Big Offensive," 205; Harry Schwartz, "A Drug-Code Warm-Up," *Pharmaceutical Executive*, August 1981.

27. IFPMA Code of Pharmaceutical Marketing Practices Supplementary Statement, March 2, 1982, Box 105, Folder 2068, EPP; "The WHO and the Pharmaceutical Industry—HAI Briefing Paper for the 35th World Health Assembly," May 1982, Box 106, Folder 2091, EPP.

28. Virginia Beardshaw and Charles Medawar, "Health Activists Seek U.N. Code on Drug Company Marketing Practices," *Multinational Monitor* 3, no. 7 (July 1982), http://www.multinationalmonitor.org/hyper/issues/1982/07/beardshaw.html.

29. Michael R. Reich, "Bangladesh Pharmaceutical Policy and Politics," *Health Policy and Planning* 9, no. 2 (1993): 132–133.

30. Penny Chorlton, "U.S. Is Aiding Drug Companies in Bangladesh," *Washington Post*, August 19, 1982, A1; Zafrullah Chowdhury, "Bangladesh: A Tough Battle for a National Drug Policy," *Development Dialogue* 1 (1995): 104, 109.

31. "The Right Pharmaceuticals at the Right Prices: Some Consumer Perspectives—Presented by Anwar Fazal International Organization of Consumers Unions (IOCU) at UNCTAD, Geneva Switzerland, 7 September 1982," http://www.anwarfazal.net/speech-RightPharmaceuticals.php.

32. Milton Silverman, Mia Lydecker, and Philip R. Lee, *Bad Medicine: The Prescription Drug Industry in the Third World* (Stanford, CA: Stanford University Press, 1992), 125–145.

33. Annie Street to Friends of Supporters of the 1982 Bangladesh Drug Reform Ordinance, "Urgent Request for Support of Bangladesh Drug Reform," May 14, 1984, Box 105, Folder 2068, EPP.

34. "World Health Assembly 7–21 May, 1984: An Observer's Report," undated, IDL, https://industrydocuments.library.ucsf.edu/tobacco/docs/#id=fmhm0078.

35. "Editorial: The Rational Use of Drugs and WHO," *Development Dialogue* 2 (1985): 1.

36. Virginia Beardshaw, "HAI Goes to the World Health Assembly," undated, Box 106, Folder 2086, EPP.

Chapter 8

1. "WHO Moves Closer to Code for Drug Industry: Who Will Be Next?" *Business International*, May 25, 1984, 164.

2. Kenneth Adelman to Ed Meese, "Law of the Sea Treaty Follow-Up," June 29, 1982, *1981–1988*, vol. 41, *Global Issues II*, FRUS, https://history.state.gov/historicaldocuments/frus1981-88v41/d166.

3. Kenneth L. Adelman, "Biting the Hand That Cures Them," *Regulation* (July/August 1982): 16.

4. Jason Stahl, *Right Moves: The Conservative Think Tank in American Political Culture Since 1945* (Chapel Hill: University of North Carolina Press, 2016).

5. "Introduction," *The U.N. Under Scrutiny* (Washington, DC: Heritage Foundation, 1982), v. On the Heritage Foundation's U.N. Assessment Project, see Jennifer Bair, "Taking Aim at the New International Economic Order," in *The Road from Mont Pèlerin: The Making of the Neoliberal Thought Collective,* ed. Philip Mirowski and Dieter Plehwe (Cambridge, MA: Harvard University Press, 2009), 373–378.

6. Roger A. Brooks, "Multinationals: First Victim of the U.N. War on Free Enterprise," *Heritage Foundation Backgrounder* 227, November 16, 1982, 1–24.

7. Brooks, "Multinationals," 8.

8. Brooks, "Multinationals," 20; Burton Yale Pines, "The U.S. and the U.N.: Time for Reappraisal," *Heritage Foundation Backgrounder* 293, September 29, 1983, 15.

9. *Proceedings of the United Nations Conference on Trade and Development, Sixth Session: Volume I, Report and Annexes* (New York: United Nations Publications, 1984), 80.

10. Bob Borosage to TNI Fellowship, "Planning Paper," March 2, 1981, Box 107, Folder 4, IPSP.

11. Vijay Prashad, *The Poorer Nations: A Possible History of the Global South* (London: Verso, 2012), 15–85.

12. Mark T. Berger, "After the Third World? History, Destiny and the Fate of Third Worldism," *Third World Quarterly* 25, no. 1 (2004): 25.

13. "Excerpts from Reagan Speech on U.S. Policy Toward Developing Nations," *New York Times,* October 16, 1981, A12.

14. Steven G. Livingston, "The Politics of Agenda-Setting: Reagan and North-South Relations," *International Studies Quarterly* 36, no. 3 (September 1992): 313–329.

15. Sagafi-nejad and Dunning, *UN and Transnational Corporations,* 119–121.

16. Mark Ritchie and Douglas Clement to Martin Teitel and Ann Fitzgerald, February 17, 1986, Box 17, ACA.

17. Pines, "U.S. and the U.N.," 15.

18. Keith B. Richburg, "Esther Peterson, Foreign Agent?" *Washington Post,* November 1, 1984, 23.

19. *Cong. Rec.,* 99th Cong., 1st sess., 1985, 131, pt. 11, 14937.

20. Robert H. Sprinkle, *Profession of Conscience: The Making and Meaning of Life-Sciences Liberalism* (Princeton: Princeton University Press, 1994), 148.

21. U.S. Library of Congress, Congressional Research Service, *World Health Organization: Effects of Reduced U.S. Contributions,* by Lois B. McHugh, CRS Report 87-108 (Washington, DC: Office of Congressional Information and Publishing, February 25, 1987), 1–3.

22. Quoted in Anita Hardon, "Consumers Versus Producers: Power Play Behind the Scenes," in *Drugs Policy in Developing Countries,* ed. Najmi Kanji, Anita Hardon, Jan Willem Harnmeijer, Masuma Mamdani, and Gill Walt (London: Zed, 1992), 61.

23. Juliana Geran Pilon, "For the World Health Organization, the Moment of Truth," *Heritage Foundation Backgrounder* 507, April 30, 1986, 11.

24. Theodore M. Brown, Marcos Cueto, and Elizabeth Fee, "The World Health Organization and the Transition from 'International' to 'Global' Public Health," *American Journal of Public Health* 96, no. 1 (January 2006): 67.

25. "World Health for All: To Be!" Address by Dr. H. Mahler, Director-General of the World Health Organization in Presenting His Report for 1986 to the Fortieth World Health Assembly, May 5, 1987, WHA40/DIV/4, IDL, https://industrydocuments.library.ucsf.edu/tobacco/docs/#id=hkkn0191.

26. U.S. Library of Congress, *World Health Organization: Effects of Reduced U.S. Contributions,* 7; Philip Revzin, "U.N. Health Agency Finds Funds Shrinking While Work Expands," *Wall Street Journal,* April 7, 1988, 1.

27. WHO Document, 1981, EB67/SR/24. WHO Library, quoted in Chorev, *World Health Organization Between North and South,* 110.

28. John M. Starrels, "The World Health Organization: Resisting Third World Ideological Pressures" (Washington, DC: Heritage Foundation, 1985), vii.

29. Charles Medawar, "International Regulation of the Supply and Use of Pharmaceuticals," *Development Dialogue* 2 (1985): 29.

30. Medawar, "International Regulation of the Supply and Use of Pharmaceuticals," 26.

31. Chetley, *Healthy Business,* 86.

32. Chetley, *Healthy Business,* 85.

33. World Health Organization, *The Rational Use of Drugs: Report of the Conference of Experts, Nairobi, 25–29 November 1985* (Geneva: World Health Organization, 1987), 12.

34. Quoted in Hardon, "Consumers Versus Producers," 61.

35. Antonietta Corti to INFOTAB Members, March 17, 1988, IDL, https://www
.industrydocuments.ucsf.edu/docs/#id=hsny0039.

36. "WHO Notes and News," *World Health Forum* 9, nos. 178–184 (1988): 473.

37. Doug Johnson, "Statement to the Press," June 28, 1988, Box 22, ACA.

38. Leah Margulies, "Response to the Boycott—WHO Expectations," September 11, 1979, Box 1, ACA.

39. Dr. R. K. Anand, "Statement to the Press," October 4, 1988, Box 22, ACA.

40. JM to AA, GIFA, MK, January 28, 1988, Box 33, ACA.

41. "Taking on the Multinationals," undated, Box 22, ACA.

42. Janice Mantell, "Statement to the Press," October 4, 1988, Box 22, ACA.

43. "Action for Corporate Accountability Boycott Endorser List," January 14, 1994, Box 20, ACA.

44. Annelies Allain to Esther Peterson, September 20, 1989, Box 104, Folder 2047, EPP.

45. Baby Milk Action, "Annual Report October 1992–September 1993," Box 104, Folder 2053, EPP.

46. International Nestlé Boycott Committee, "Boycott Forces Partial End of Free Formula Supplies," January 30, 1993, Box 22, ACA.

47. Karlyn Sturmer, "We Did It!" June 1994, Box 22, ACA.

48. Johnson interview, May 5, 2011.

49. *Breaking the Rules, Stretching the Rules 2017* (Penang: IBFAN sdn Bhd, 2017), vi.

50. Leah Margulies, "The International Code of Marketing of Breastmilk Substitutes: A Model for Assuring Children's Nutrition Rights Under the Law," *International Journal of Children's Rights* 419 (1997): 419.

51. Margulies, "International Code of Marketing of Breastmilk Substitutes," 428.

52. Tehila Sasson, "Milking the Third World? Humanitarianism, Capitalism, and the Moral Economy of the Nestlé Boycott," *American Historical Review* 121, no. 4 (October 2016): 1224.

53. Striffler, *Solidarity*, 201.

54. Sasson, "Milking the Third World," 1224.

Chapter 9

1. Mobilization on Development, Trade, Labor, and the Environment, "Press Conference on the North American Free Trade Agreement," May 2, 1991, C-SPAN, video, http://www.c-span.org/video/?17795-1/north-american-free-trade-agreement.

2. John to IPS Staff and Program Council, "TNI, 1986: The Challenge," May 15, 1986, Box 29, Folder 24, IPSP.

3. Institute for Policy Studies, "Working Group on World Economic Integration Project Proposal for Fiscal Year 1989–1990," Box 16, Folder 23, IPSP; John Cavanagh and Jerry Sander, "The United States in the World Economy: Aid, Debt, Trade," in *Winning America: Ideas and Leadership for the 1990s* (Boston: South End, 1989), 342.

4. International NGO Forum on World Bank and IMF Lending, "Continuing the Challenge: Report on the 1990 International NGO Forum," undated, Container 7, Folder 13, Mark Dubois Papers, BANC MSS 2003/314 c, Bancroft Library, University of California, Berkeley (hereafter MDP).

5. Michael Moffitt to Robert Borosage, Saul Landau, and Peter Weiss, "Future of the IEO Project," December 18, 1978, Box 54, Folder 29, IPSP.

6. Joe Holley, "Richard J. Barnet Dies, Founder of Institute for Policy Studies," *Washington Post,* December 24, 2006.

7. Marc Raskin to Hallock Hoffman, May 29, 1962, Box 79, Folder 31, IPSP. On IPS and U.S. foreign policy, see Mueller, "Think Tank on the Left," 121–309.

8. Institute for Policy Studies, "Beginning the Second Decade: 1963–1973," Box 98, Folder 13, IPSP.

9. On Letelier, see Alan McPherson, *Ghosts of Sheridan Circle: How a Washington Assassination Brought Pinochet's Terror State to Justice* (Chapel Hill: University of North Carolina Press, 2019), 11–22, 29–43, 64–72, 87–101. On Chile during this period, see Tanya Harmer, *Allende's Chile and the Inter-American Cold War* (Chapel Hill: University of North Carolina Press, 2011).

10. "TNI Planning Board Meeting Minutes," October 20–23, 1975, Box 106, Folder 27, IPSP.

11. Kim Christiaens, Idesbald Goddeeris, and Magaly Rodríguez García, eds., *European Solidarity with Chile 1970s–1980s* (Munich: Peter Lang, 2014); Heidi Tinsman, *Buying into the Regime: Grapes and Consumption in Cold War Chile and the United States* (Durham, NC: Duke University Press, 2014).

12. Juan Gabriel Valdés, *Pinochet's Economists: The Chicago School in Chile* (Cambridge: Cambridge University Press, 1995).

13. Orlando Letelier, "Economic 'Freedom's' Awful Toll," *Nation,* August 28, 1976, 142.

14. McPherson, *Ghosts of Sheridan Circle.*

15. Howard Wachtel, "New International Economic Order Project: Draft Discussion Paper 1," October 14, 1976, Box 16, Folder 5, IPSP.

16. Howard Wachtel, interview with author, Washington, D.C., February 2, 2012; Khalid Ikram, *The Political Economy of Reforms in Egypt: Issues and Policymaking Since 1952* (Cairo: American University in Cairo Press, 2018), 205–261.

17. Howard M. Wachtel, *The New Gnomes: Multinational Banks in the Third World* (Washington, DC: Transnational Institute, 1977), 11.

18. Wachtel, *New Gnomes*, 11.

19. Cheryl Payer, *The Debt Trap: The IMF and the Third World* (New York: Monthly Review, 1975).

20. Howard Wachtel and Robert Borosage, "Conference on the International Monetary Fund: Proposal for Funding," undated, Box 4, Howard Wachtel Papers, Special Collections, American University, Washington, D.C. (hereafter HWP).

21. Ismaïl-Sabri Abdalla, "The Inadequacy and Loss of Legitimacy of the International Monetary Fund," *Development Dialogue* 2 (1980): 50. On the IMF during the

1970s, see Margaret Garritsen de Vries, *The International Monetary Fund, 1972–1978: Cooperation on Trial* (Washington, DC: International Monetary Fund, 1985).

22. Howard M. Wachtel, "Dancing for the IMF: He Who Pays the Piper Calls the Tune," July 1978, Box 4, HWP; Michael Moffitt to IEO Meeting, "Conference Proposal," June 22, 1978, Box 54, Folder 29, IPSP.

23. Dan Morgan, "Much IMF Help Goes to Repay Commercial Loans, Study Finds," *Washington Post*, June 25, 1977.

24. Wachtel, "Dancing for the IMF." On IPS and 1970s international political economy, see Paul Adler, "'The Basis of a New Internationalism?': The Institute for Policy Studies and North-South Politics from the NIEO to Neoliberalism," *Diplomatic History* 41, no. 1 (September 2017): 665–693.

25. Robert E. Wood, "The Debt Crisis and North-South Relations," *Third World Quarterly* 6, no. 3 (July 1984): 703.

26. Maggie Black, *Children First: The Story of UNICEF, Past and Present* (Oxford: Oxford University Press, 1996), 149. On the debt crisis, see Karin Lissakers, *Banks, Borrowers, and the Establishment: A Revisionist Account of the International Debt Crisis* (New York: Basic, 1991); Lex Rieffel, *Sovereign Debt: The Case for Ad Hoc Machinery* (Washington, DC: Brookings Institution, 2003); David M. Wight, *Oil Money: Middle East Petrodollars and the Transformation of US Empire, 1967–1988* (Ithaca: Cornell University Press, forthcoming).

27. John Waterbury, "The Long Gestation and Brief Triumph of Import-Substituting Industrialization," *World Development* 27, no. 2 (1999): 323–341.

28. Christy Thornton, *Revolution in Development: Mexico and the Governance of the Global Economy* (Berkeley: University of California Press, 2020).

29. Sarah Babb, *Managing Mexico: Economists from Nationalism to Neoliberalism* (Princeton: Princeton University Press, 2004), 171–199; Jeffrey L. Bortaz and Salvador Mendiola, "El impacto social de la crisis económica de México," *Revista Mexicana de Sociología* 53, no. 1 (January–March 1991): 43–69.

30. International Monetary Fund, "Minutes of Executive Board Meeting 83/93," June 29, 1983, p. 5, International Monetary Fund Digitized Archival Collections, https://imfbox.box.com/shared/static/xv1nsdhjmsoqw2jpu1f884jav0qhobgs.pdf. See also Patrick Sharma, "Bureaucratic Imperatives and Policy Outcomes: The Origins of World Bank Structural Adjustment Lending," *Review of International Political Economy* 20, no. 4 (August 2012): 667–686; Paul V. Kershaw, "Averting a Global Financial Crisis: The US, the IMF, and the Mexican Debt Crisis of 1976," *International History Review* 40, no. 2 (2018): 292–314.

31. Pamela Sparr, ed., *Mortgaging Women's Lives: Feminist Critiques of Structural Adjustment* (London: Zed, 1994); William Easterly, "What Did Structural Adjustment Adjust? The Association of Policies and Growth with Repeated IMF and World Bank Adjustment Loans," *Journal of Development Economics* 76 (2005): 1–22; James Raymond Vreeland, *The IMF and Economic Development* (Cambridge: Cambridge University Press, 2003).

32. John Minns, *The Politics of Developmentalism: The Midas States of Mexico, South Korea and Taiwan* (New York: Palgrave Macmillan, 2006), 112–113.

33. Diana Alarcón González, "Trade Liberalization, Income Distribution, and Poverty in Mexico: An Empirical Review of Recent Trends," in *NAFTA in Transition*, ed. Stephen J. Randall and Herman W. Konrad (Calgary: University of Calgary Press, 1995), 133; Carmen Boullosa and Mike Wallace, "40 Years Ago the United States Sent Mexico into a Financial Crisis and It Transformed the Narcotics Industry," *Business Insider*, September 15, 2015, https://www.businessinsider.com/40-years-ago-the-us-sent-mexico-into-a-financial-crisis-and-it-transformed-the-narcotics-industry-2015-9.

34. Carlos Heredia and Mary Purcell, "Structural Adjustment in Mexico: The Root of the Crisis" (Washington, DC: Development GAP, 1995), http://www.hartford-hwp.com/archives/46/013.html.

35. Manab Thakur, Gene E. Burton, and B. N. Srivastava, *International Management: Concepts and Cases* (New Delhi: Tata McGraw-Hill Education, 1997), 334. On the internationalization of sweatshops, see Ellen Rosen, *Making Sweatshops: The Globalization of the U.S. Apparel Industry* (Berkeley: University of California Press, 2001).

36. Kathryn Kopinak, "The Maquiladorization of the Mexican Economy," in *The Political Economy of North American Free Trade*, ed. Ricardo Grinspun and Maxwell A. Cameron (Montreal: McGill-Queen's University Press, 1993), 156.

37. Devon G. Peña, *The Terror of the Machine: Technology, Work, Gender, and Ecology on the U.S.-Mexico Border* (Austin: University of Texas Press, 2014); Altha J. Cravey, *Women and Work in Mexico's Maquiladoras* (New York: Rowman & Littlefield, 1998); Hester Eisenstein, "The Sweatshop Feminists," *Jacobin*, June 17, 2015, https://www.jacobinmag.com/2015/06/kristof-globalization-development-third-world/.

38. Ha-Joon Chang, *Kicking Away the Ladder: Development Strategy in Historical Perspective* (London: Anthem, 2003); Dani Rodrik, "Work and Human Development in a Deindustrializing World," *UN Human Development Report Office Think Piece* (2015), hdr.undp.org/sites/default/files/rodrik_hdr_2015_final.pdf.

39. Masahiko Aoki, Hyung-Ki Kim, and Masahiro Okuno-Fujiwara, eds., *The Role of Government in East Asian Economic Development: Comparative Institutional Analysis* (Oxford: Oxford University Press, 1996); Robert Wade, *Governing the Market: Economic Theory and the Role of the Government in East Asian Industrialization* (Princeton: Princeton University Press, 1990).

Chapter 10

1. Susan Ariel Aaronson, *Taking Trade to the Streets: The Lost History of Public Efforts to Shape Globalization* (Ann Arbor: University of Michigan Press, 2001), 143.

2. Ritchie interview, February 17, 2016.

3. Barry J. Barnett, "The U.S. Farm Financial Crisis of the 1980s," in *Fighting for the Farm: Rural America Transformed*, ed. Jane Adams (Philadelphia: University of Pennsylvania Press, 2011), 168.

4. Dixon Terry, "Soil and Water Conservation the Global Food Price Wars," October 6, 1987, Institute for Agriculture and Trade Policy Document Library, Minneapolis (hereafter IATPDL), https://www.iatp.org/sites/default/files/soil-water-conservation-age-global-food-price-wars.pdf.

5. Mark Ritchie and Kevin Ristau, "Political History of U.S. Farm Policy" (Minneapolis: League of Rural Voters, January 1986), https://www.iatp.org/sites/default/files/2018-01/Political%20History%20of%20U.S.%20Farm%20Policy.%20By%20Mark%20Ritchie%20%26%20Kevin%20Ristau.%20January%201986_0.pdf.

6. Mark Ritchie and Douglas Clement to Martin Teitel and Ann Fitzgerald, February 17, 1986, Box 17, ACA.

7. "Talking About GATT: A Conversation with Mark Ritchie," October 25, 1991, Institute for Agriculture and Trade Policy, YouTube, video, https://www.youtube.com/watch?v=ZJPrZz_grq8&noredirect=1.

8. Daniel Drache, "The Short but Significant Life of the International Trade Organization: Lessons for Our Time," Centre for the Study of Globalisation and Regionalisation, University of Warwick, U.K., November 2000, http://wrap.warwick.ac.uk/2063/1/WRAP_Drache_wp6200.pdf.

9. Herman M. Schwartz, *States Versus Markets: The Emergence of a Global Economy*, 2nd ed. (New York: St. Martin's, 2001), 265.

10. Ritchie interview, February 17, 2016.

11. Chakravarthi Raghavan, "Third World—Gains and Losses," *Inter-Press Service*, November 30, 1982, http://www.sunsonline.org/trade/process/during/82/11300282.htm.

12. "United States: Statement by Ambassador Clayton Yeutter, Trade Representative, at the Meeting of the GATT Contracting Parties at Ministerial Level," MIN (86)/ST/5, September 15, 1986, WTO Documents Online (hereafter WTOD), https://docs.wto.org/gattdocs/q/UR/TNCMIN86/ST5.PDF.

13. "Cote d'Ivoire: Statement by H.E. Mr. Ambassador Amadou Traore, Head of the Delegation, at the Meeting of the GATT Contracting Parties at Ministerial Level, 15–19 September 1986, Punta del Este, Uruguay," MIN (86)/ST/6, September 15, 1986, WTOD, https://docs.wto.org/gattdocs/q/UR/TNCMIN86/ST6.PDF.

14. *World Investment Report 1992: Transnational Corporations as Engines of Growth* (New York: United Nations, 1992), 3.

15. Amrita Narlikar, *The World Trade Organization: A Very Short Introduction* (Oxford: Oxford University Press, 2005), 23–25, 43–45.

16. Chakravarthi Raghavan, "No Evidence Third World Exports Disrupt Industrial Markets," *SUNS*, March 20, 1984, http://www.sunsonline.org/trade/process/during/8485/3world/03200084.htm.

17. Chakravarthi Raghavan, "GATT Negotiations on TRIM Not Open-Ended," *SUNS*, April 7, 1987, http://www.sunsonline.org/trade/process/during/uruguay/trims/04070087.htm; Ritchie interview, February 17, 2016.

18. Narlikar, *World Trade Organization*, 22–42; Martina Piewitt, "The Creation of the World Trade Organization and the Establishment of an Advocacy Regime," *Journal of Public Affairs* 15 (2015): 65–78.

19. Alexander B. Trowbridge to Mr. Edmund T. Pratt Jr., April 16, 1985, IDL, https://www.industrydocumentslibrary.ucsf.edu/docs/#id=rkyy0048.

20. Business Roundtable Task Force on International Trade and Investment, "Getting from Here to There: Preparation for a New Round of Multilateral Trade Negotiations," April 1985, IDL, https://www.industrydocumentslibrary.ucsf.edu/docs/#id=qkyy0048.

21. Carol J. Bilzi, "Towards an Intellectual Property Agreement in the GATT: View from the Private Sector," *Georgia Journal of International and Comparative Law* 19, no. 2 (1989): 343–351; Sharon Beder, "Business-Managed Democracy: The Trade Agenda," *Critical Social Policy* 30, no. 14 (2010): 496–518.

22. Peter Sutherland, "A New Framework for International Economic Relations," Third Hayek Memorial Lecture to the Institute of Economic Affairs, London, June 16, 1994, GATT/1640, https://www.wto.org/gatt_docs/English/SULPDF/91790168.pdf. See Slobodian, *Globalists*, 218–262.

23. Tim Josling, Donna Roberts, and Ayesha Hassan, "The Beef-Hormone Dispute and Its Implications for Trade Policy," Stanford University, 2000, http://iis-db.stanford .edu/pubs/11379/HORMrev.pdf.

24. Mark Ritchie to Organizations and Individuals Concerned with Food Safety/ Consumer Issues, "Potential Impact of GATT Agricultural Talks on Consumers," May 15, 1989, Global Trade Watch Papers, Washington, D.C. (hereafter GTWP).

25. Tim Pugmire, "Who Is Mark Ritchie?" *Minnesota Public Radio News*, December 14, 2007, https://www.mprnews.org/story/2007/12/13/ritchieprofile.

26. Mark Ritchie to Rhoda Karpatkin, Michel van Hulten, Ann Davison, Esther Peterson, Eileen Nic, Anwar Fazal, and Ursula Paredes, July 20, 1989, Box 105, Folder 2075, EPP.

27. Mark Ritchie, "Impact of GATT on World Hunger: Speech to the International Symposium on Food Self-Sufficiency, Tokyo, Japan," August 1988, IATPDL, https://www .iatp.org/sites/default/files/GATTFOODSECURITY.pdf.

Chapter 11

1. *Third World: Development or Crisis?* (Penang: Third World Network, 1985), 4.

2. Hilton, *Prosperity for All,* 197–202.

3. Andrew Ng Yew Han, "Tribute to Martin Khor (1951–2020)," YouTube, April 1, 2020, https://www.youtube.com/watch?v=Dkao841j-C8; N. Trisha, "Former Third World Network Director Martin Khor Dies of Cancer," *Star*, April 1, 2020, https://www.thestar .com.my/news/nation/2020/04/01/former-third-world-network-director-martin-khor -dies-of-cancer; John Cavanagh, "A Thank You to Martin Khor, Champion of Global Equity," Inequality.org, April 7, 2020, https://inequality.org/research/martin-khor-global -equity/.

4. Walden Bello, "Martin Khor: The Making of a Global Activist," *Foreign Policy in Focus*, April 6, 2020, https://fpif.org/martin-khor-the-making-of-a-global-activist/.

5. Wayne Ellwood, "Global Coalition Seeks to Create a New Voice for the Third World," *Inter Press Service,* May 18, 1985.

6. Ellwood, "Global Coalition Seeks to Create a New Voice."

7. *Third World: Development or Crisis?* 12.

8. *Third World: Development or Crisis?* 12.

9. *Third World: Development or Crisis?* 79.

10. Graham K. Brown, "'Stemming the Tide': Third World Network and Global Governance," in *Yearbook of International Co-operation on Environment and Development*, ed. Olav Schram Stokke and Øystein B. Thommessen (London: Earthscan, 2003), 73–77.

11. Tone Bleie and Ragnhild Lund, eds., "Proceedings from Dawn's Bergen Meeting," (Fantoft: Department of Social Science and Development, 1985), 53. On DAWN, see Ashwini Tambe and Alissa Trotz, "Historical Reflections on DAWN: An Interview with Gita Sen," *Comparative Studies of South Asia, Africa, and the Middle East* 30, no. 2 (2010): 214–217.

12. Thomas Davies, *NGOs: A New History of Transnational Civil Society* (Oxford: Oxford University Press, 2014), 149; Vandana Shiva, *The Vandana Shiva Reader* (Lexington: University of Kentucky Press, 2015), 1–4; Jeremy Brecher, John Brown Childs, and Jill Cutler, eds., *Global Visions: Beyond the New World Order* (Boston: South End, 1993).

13. Marta Trejos, "Dear Doug," November 28, 1984, Box 31, ACA. On Costa Rica and neoliberalism, see Marc Edelman, *Peasants Against Globalization: Rural Social Movements in Costa Rica* (Stanford: Stanford University Press, 1999). On Marta Trejos, see Jan Spence, "CEFEMINA: A World Inside a World," *Share International*, April 1996, https://www.share-international.org/archives/social-justice/sj_jscefemina.htm.

14. Cynthia Obadia to Evelyn Hong, February 14, 1984, John Cavanagh Personal Papers, Washington, D.C. (hereafter JCP).

15. John Cavanagh, interview with author, December 14, 2011, Washington, D.C.; Morton Mintz, "Alcohol, Inc: Bartenders to the World," *Washington Post*, September 4, 1983, C2.

16. "Campaign on the Debt Crisis: Working Paper on Initial Tasks," July 25, 1984, JCP.

17. "Notes from July 25, 1984 Meeting on Feasibility of a Debt Crisis Campaign," undated, JCP.

18. *A Journey Through the Debt Crisis* (Washington, D.C.: Debt Crisis Network, 1988).

19. Fantu Cheru, Doug Hellinger, and Kelly Yencer, "Solutions to the Debt Problem," (Washington, D.C.: Development Group for Alternative Policies, December 1984), http://www.developmentgap.org/uploads/2/1/3/7/21375820/solutions_to_the_debt_problem.pdf.

20. John to DCN Coordinating Committee, April 11, 1988, JCP; Elizabeth A. Donnelly, "Proclaiming the Jubilee: The Debt and Structural Adjustment Network," U.N. Vision Project on Global Public Policy Networks, 6–8, http://www.worldhunger.org/articles/hn/debtcrisisnet.pdf.

21. "Notes from July 25, 1984 Meeting on Feasibility of a Debt Crisis Campaign," undated, JCP.

22. Carol to DCN Coordinating Ct., "On Strategy," July 21, 1988, JCP.

23. Institute for Policy Studies, "Working Group on World Economic Integration Project Proposal for Fiscal Year 1989–1990," November 1989, Box 16, Folder 23, IPSP.

24. Doug Rossinow, *The Reagan Era: A History of the 1980s* (New York: Columbia University Press, 2015), 31–66; Marisa Chappell, *The War on Welfare: Family, Poverty, and Politics in Modern America* (Philadelphia: University of Pennsylvania Press, 2011), 199–241; Alberto Alesina and Geoffrey Carliner, eds., *Politics and Economics in the Eighties* (Chicago: University of Chicago Press, 1991).

25. Jonathan A. Glickstein, *American Exceptionalism, American Anxiety: Wages, Competition, and Degraded Labor in the Antebellum United States* (Charlottesville: University of Virginia Press, 2002), 185.

26. Marianne Debouzy, ed., *In the Shadow of the Statue of Liberty: Immigrants, Workers, and Citizens in the American Republic, 1880–1920* (Urbana: University of Illinois Press, 1992).

27. Edmund F. Wehrle, *Between a River and a Mountain: The AFL-CIO and the Vietnam War* (Ann Arbor: University of Michigan Press, 2005); Robert Anthony Waters Jr. and Geert Van Goethem, eds., *American Labor's Global Ambassadors: The International History of the AFL-CIO During the Cold War* (New York: Palgrave Macmillan, 2013).

28. James Benton, "Fraying Fabric: Textile Labor, Trade Politics, and Deindustrialization, 1933–1974" (PhD diss., Georgetown University, 2016), 292–457.

29. Oliveiro, "United States, Multinational Corporations, and the Politics of Globalization," 21–77.

30. Jefferson Cowie and Joseph Heathcott, eds., *Beyond the Ruins: The Meanings of Deindustrialization* (Ithaca: Cornell University Press, 2003); Tracy Neumann, *Remaking the Rust Belt: The Postindustrial Transformation of North America* (Philadelphia: University of Pennsylvania Press, 2016).

31. Erik Loomis, *Out of Sight: The Long and Disturbing Story of Corporations Outsourcing Catastrophe* (New York: New Press, 2015), 47.

32. Joseph A. McCartin, *Collision Course: Ronald Reagan, the Air Traffic Controllers, and the Strike That Changed America* (Oxford: Oxford University Press, 2011); Nelson Lichtenstein, *State of the Union: A Century of American Labor* (Princeton: Princeton University Press, 2012), 212–246.

33. David Kucera and William Milberg, "Deindustrialization and Changes in Manufacturing Trade: Factor Content Calculations for 1978–1995," *Review of World Economics* 139, no. 4 (September 2003): 601–624; Cowie, *Capital Moves*.

34. Scott Dewey, "Working for the Environment: Organized Labor and the Origins of Environmentalism in the United States, 1948–1970," *Environmental History* 3, no. 1 (January 1998): 45–63; Pertschuk, *Revolt Against Regulation*, 100–110.

35. Brian K. Obach, *Labor and the Environmental Movement: The Quest for Common Ground* (Cambridge, MA: MIT Press, 2004).

36. Ralph Nader, "Labor Leadership Faltering," in *In the Public Interest*, December 20, 1980, https://nader.org/1980/12/20/labor-leadership-faltering/.

37. David Vogel and George Nadel, "Who Is a Consumer? An Analysis of the Politics of Consumer Conflict," *American Political Science Quarterly* 5, no. 1 (January 1977): 39–42.

38. Sabin, "Environmental Law and the End of the New Deal Order," 998–999.

39. Jennifer Thompson, "Surviving the 1970s: The Case of Friends of the Earth," *Environmental History* 22, no. 2 (April 2017): 246–249.

40. Andrew Battista, "Labor and Coalition Politics: The Progressive Alliance," *Labor History* 32, no. 3 (Summer 1991): 401–421.

41. Austin McCoy, "No Radical Hangover: Black Power, New Left, and Progressive Politics in the Midwest, 1967–1989" (PhD diss., University of Michigan, Ann Arbor, 2016), 212–273.

42. Andrew Battista, "Labor and Liberalism: The Citizen Labor Energy Coalition," *Labor History* 40, no. 3 (1999): 301–321.

43. Francis Fukuyama, "The End of History?" *National Interest* 16 (Summer 1989): 3–18.

Chapter 12

1. "Dear Senator," March 4, 1991, JHC, http://doi.library.cmu.edu/10.1184/pmc/heinz /box00161/fld00017/bdl0016/doc0001; League of Rural Voters Education Project, "Trading Our Future?" Spring 1990, IDL, http://industrydocuments.library.ucsf.edu/tobacco /docs/nzhy0148.

2. Polly Agee to Carolyn Mugar, "Thoughts and Recommendations Concerning Development of a Public Support Base for the National Committee to Save the Family Farm," January 23, 1986, IDL, https://www.industrydocuments.ucsf.edu/docs/#id =grvf0045.

3. Gottlieb, *Forcing the Spring*, 212–215; John Lancaster, "The Environmentalist as Insider," *Washington Post*, August 4, 1991.

4. Paul Adler, "Planetary Citizens: U.S. NGOs and the Politics of International Development in the Late Twentieth Century" (PhD diss., Georgetown University, 2014), 164–202, 238–278.

5. House Committee on Appropriations, *Foreign Operations, Export Financing, and Related Programs Appropriations for 1989*, 100th Cong., 2nd sess., 1988, 397–400.

6. Rhonda Lynn Evans, "The Rise of Ethical Trade Advocacy: NAFTA and the New Politics of Trade" (PhD diss., University of California, Berkeley, 2002), 142–143.

7. Aaronson, *Taking Trade to the Streets*, 123.

8. Moisés Naím, "Lori's War," *Foreign Policy* 118 (Spring 2000): 31.

9. *Public Citizen: The Sentinel of Democracy* (Washington, DC: Public Citizen Foundation, 2016); Ava Alkon, "Late 20th-Century Consumer Advocacy, Pharmaceuticals, and Public Health: Public Citizen's Health Research Group in Historical Perspective" (PhD diss., Columbia University, 2012), 121–165.

10. Evans, "Rise of Ethical Trade Advocacy," 144.

11. Burt Schorr and Christopher Conte, "Coming of Age: Public Interest Groups Achieve Higher Status and Some Permanence," *Wall Street Journal*, August 27, 1984, 1.

12. Lori Wallach, interview with author, Washington, D.C., August 9, 2016.

13. Frederick W. Mayer, *Interpreting NAFTA: The Science and Art of Political Analysis* (New York: Columbia University Press, 1998), 84.

14. Personal communication with Lori Wallach of Public Citizen (May 7, 1998), quoted in Evans, "Rise of Ethical Trade Advocacy," 174.

15. Bruce Stokes, "The Trade Debate's Guerrilla Warrior," *National Journal*, February 13, 1993, 413.

16. Michael C. Dreiling, "Forging Solidarity in the Struggle over the North American Free Trade Agreement: Strategy and Action for Labor, Nature, and Capital" (PhD diss., University of Michigan, Ann Arbor, 1997), 80, 69.

17. Hal S. Shapiro, *Fast Track: A Legal, Historical, and Political Analysis* (Ardsley, NY: Transnational, 2006).

18. Mayer, *Interpreting NAFTA*, 67–68.

19. Alfred E. Eckes Jr. and Thomas W. Zeiler, *Globalization and the American Century* (Cambridge: Cambridge University Press, 2003), 238.

20. George Bush, "Remarks at a White House Briefing for the Associated General Contractors of America," April 15, 1991, APP, http://www.presidency.ucsb.edu/ws/?pid =19467.

21. Dale Wiehoff to Mark Ritchie and Lori Wallach, "Fast Track," December 12, 1991, GTWP.

22. House Committee on Ways and Means, *President's Request for Extension of Fast Track Trade Agreement Implementing Authority*, 102nd Cong., 1st sess., 1991, 16.

23. Jae Wan Chung, *The Political Economy of International Trade: U.S. Trade Laws, Policy, and Social Cost* (Lanham, MD: Lexington, 2006), 103–104.

24. "Memorandum of Conversation with President Cesar Gaviria of Colombia," February 26, 1991, George Bush Presidential Library (hereafter GBPL), https://bush41library .tamu.edu/files/memcons-telcons/1991-02-26—Gaviria%20Trujillo.pdf.

25. Lloyd Bentsen and Dan Rostenkowski to George H.W. Bush, March 7, 1991, GTWP.

26. Mayer, *Interpreting NAFTA*, 82.

27. Personal communication with Mark Ritchie of the Institute for Agriculture and Trade Policy (June 11, 2001), quoted in Evans, "Rise of Ethical Trade Advocacy," 178.

28. Stokes, "Trade Debate's Guerrilla Warrior," 413.

29. Timothy J. Minchin, *Labor Under Fire: A History of the AFL-CIO Since 1979* (Chapel Hill: University of North Carolina Press, 2017), 137.

30. House Committee on Ways and Means, *President's Request for Extension of Fast Track Trade Agreement*, 97.

31. Personal communication with Segundo Mercado-Llorens of the United Food and Commercial Workers Union (May 11, 1998), quoted in Evans, "Rise of Ethical Trade Advocacy," 175.

32. Mayer, *Interpreting NAFTA*, 80.

33. Christopher Sellers, "How Republicans Came to Embrace Anti-Environmentalism," *Vox*, June 7, 2017, https://www.vox.com/2017/4/22/15377964/republicans-environmentalism.

34. "Reactions Vary on Reilly's EPA Appointment," *Wilmington Morning Star*, December 27, 1988, 5C.

35. Michael S. Clark, "Trade Agreements and the 'Fast Track' Process," March 20, 1991, GTWP.

36. John J. Audley, *Green Politics and Global Trade: NAFTA and the Future of Environmental Politics* (Washington, DC: Georgetown University Press, 1997), 56–57.

37. Senate Committee on Finance, *President's United States–Mexico Free Trade Letter*, 102nd Cong., 1st sess., 1991, 33–35.

38. House Committee on Public Works and Transportation, *Fast Track Authority and North American Free Trade Agreement*, 102nd Cong., 1st sess., 1991, 169; Michael S. Clark, "Re: Lawsuit to Force the United States Trade Representative to Do an Environmental Impact Statement on Trade Agreements According to the National Environmental Policy Act," August 1, 1991, GTWP.

39. Jay D. Hair, "Nature Can Live with Free Trade," *New York Times*, May 19, 1991, E17.

40. John Adams to Ralph Nader, May 15, 1991, GTWP.

41. James Shoch, *Trading Blows: Party Competition and U.S. Trade Policy in a Globalizing Era* (Chapel Hill: University of North Carolina Press, 2001), 144–149.

42. Carla Hills to Henry Hyde, May 24, 1991, GTWP.

43. Shoch, *Trading Blows*, 148.

44. Rod to Public Citizen, June 26, 1992, GTWP.

45. LW to MW, PG, "Trade Issues," July 28, 1991, GTWP.

46. "Remarks of Ralph Nader Before the 13th World Congress of the International Organization of Consumers Unions," July 8, 1991, GTWP.

47. "A Citizens Campaign on Trade: Proposal for Support," August 1991, GTWP.

Chapter 13

1. Andrew J. Bacevich and Efraim Inbar, eds., *The Gulf War of 1991 Reconsidered* (New York: Routledge, 2013).

2. Mayer, *Interpreting NAFTA*, 76–77.

3. Marc-William Palen, *The "Conspiracy" of Free Trade: The Anglo-American Struggle over Empire and Economic Globalisation, 1846–1896* (Cambridge: Cambridge University Press, 2016); Susan Ariel Aaronson, *Trade and the American Dream: A Social History of Postwar Trade Policy* (Lexington: University Press of Kentucky, 1996).

4. John Schmitt, "NAFTA, the Press and Public Opinion: The Effect of Increased Media Coverage on the Formation of Public Opinion," *International Journal of Public Opinion Research* 7, no. 2 (1995): 178–184; "Search Results for NAFTA," *Saturday Night Live*, http://www.nbc.com/saturday-night-live/search/nafta; *The Trading Game: Inside Lobbying for the North American Free Trade Agreement* (Washington, DC: Center for Public Integrity, 1993).

5. Striffler, *Solidarity*, 143–156; Jefferson Cowie, "National Struggles in a Transnational Economy: A Critical Analysis of US Labor's Campaign Against NAFTA," *Labor Studies Journal* 21 (Winter 1997): 3–32; Joel Stillerman, "Transnational Activist Networks and the Emergence of Labor Internationalism in the NAFTA Countries," *Social Science History* 27, no. 4 (Winter 2003): 577–601.

6. Striffler, *Solidarity*, 6.

7. "Ronald Reagan's Announcement for Presidential Candidacy," November 13, 1979, Ronald Reagan Presidential Library Digital Archives, https://www.reaganlibrary.gov/11 -13-79.

8. "WEF: A History," *African Business* 343 (2008): 42.

9. Robert A. Pastor, "Exiting the Labyrinth," *Journal of Democracy* 11, no. 4 (October 2000): 21. On the PRI, see *Partido Revolucionario Institucional 1946–2000: Ascenso y Caída del Partido Hegemónico*, coord. Víctor Manuel Muñoz Patraca (Ciudad de Mexico: Siglo XXI Editores, 2006); William Beezley and Michael Meyer, eds., *The Oxford History of Mexico* (Oxford: Oxford University Press, 2010), 407–635.

10. Randal Sheppard, *A Persistent Revolution: History, Nationalism, and Politics in Mexico Since 1968* (Albuquerque: University of New Mexico Press, 2016), 143–172.

11. "Discurso del president México, Carlos Salinas de Gortari, en la cena ofrecida en su honor por la primera ministra de la Gran Bretaña, Margaret Thatcher," *Revista Mexicana de Política Exterior* 27 (Verano 1990): 88.

12. Carlos Salinas, *Mexico: The Policy and Politics of Modernization* (Barcelona: Plaza y Janes, 2002), 41.

13. Memorandum of Telephone Conservation Between George H. W. Bush and Carlos Salinas de Gortari, March 8, 1990, GBPL, https://bush41library.tamu.edu/files /memcons-telcons/1990-03-08—Salinas.pdf. For more on the Mexican government's side of the negotiations, see Hermann von Bertrab, *Negotiating NAFTA: A Mexican Envoy's Account* (Westport, CT: Praeger, 1997); Carlos Alberto Contreras, "Bankruptcy to NAFTA: Mexico's Foreign Policy Opens to the World, 1982 to 1994" (PhD diss., University of California, Los Angeles, 2008), 146–185; Malcolm Fairbrother, *Free Traders: Elites, Democracy, and the Rise of Globalization* (Oxford: Oxford University Press, 2020), 76–94.

14. Salinas, *Mexico*, 45–48; "President Carlos Salinas," *NAFTA at 10: Progress, Potential, and Precedents* (Washington, DC: Woodrow Wilson International Center for Scholars), 27–28.

15. Alan M. Rugman, "NAFTA, Multinational Enterprise Strategy and Foreign Investment," International Studies Association annual convention, Chicago, 1995, 2, quoted in Imtiaz Hussain, *Reevaluating NAFTA: Theory and Practice* (New York: Palgrave Macmillan, 2012), 34.

16. Maxwell A. Cameron and Brian W. Tomlin, *The Making of NAFTA: How the Deal Was Done* (Ithaca: Cornell University Press, 2002); *Private Rights, Public Problems: A Guide to NAFTA's Controversial Chapter on Investment Rights* (Manitoba: International Institute for Sustainable Development, 2001).

17. Kenneth J. Vandevelde, *Bilateral Investment Treaties: History, Policy, and Interpretation* (Oxford: Oxford University Press, 2010); Taylor St. John, "Institutional Entrepreneurship and the Forgotten Origins of Investment Treaty Arbitration," *GEG Working Paper 2014/94* (Oxford: Global Economic Governance Programme, 2014), 19–24.

18. Nicola Ranieri, "NAFTA: An Overview," in *Regionalism in International Investment Law*, ed. Leon Trackman and Nicola Rainieri (Oxford: Oxford University Press, 2013), 118.

19. Margaret Atwood, "Blind Faith and Free Trade," in *The Case Against Free Trade: GATT, NAFTA, and the Globalization of Corporate Power* (San Francisco: Earth Island, 1993), 92.

20. Jeffrey Ayres, *Defying Conventional Wisdom: Political Movements and Popular Contention Against North American Free Trade* (Toronto: University of Toronto Press, 1998), 21–93.

21. Maude Barlow, "Trade Pact Robs Canadians of Right to Control Their Future," *Edmonton Journal*, December 23, 1992, A10. See also Nazeer Patel, "Rethinking the 'Canadian' in Canadian Social Democracy: Does Nationalism Undermine Social Justice?" *Canadian Social Democracy Study* (2013), http://www.canadiansocialdemocracy.ca/blogs/patel.

22. "This Land Is My Land" lyrics, quoted in Sophia Huyer, "What Is a Social Movement? The Action Canada Network and Free Trade Opposition in Canada, 1983–1993" (PhD diss., York University, 2000), 477.

23. Maude Barlow, *The Fight of My Life: Confessions of an Unrepentant Canadian* (Toronto: HarperCollins Canada, 1999).

24. Maude Barlow, interview with author by telephone, August 18, 2016; Fairbrother, *Free Traders*, 58–76.

25. John W. Foster, "The Trinational Alliance Against NAFTA: Sinews of Solidarity," in *Coalitions Across Borders: Transnational Protest and the Neoliberal Order*, ed. Joe Bandy and Jackie Smith (Lanham, MD: Rowman & Littlefield, 2005), 210–211; Barlow interview, August 8, 2016.

26. Carlos Heredia, interview with author by Skype, May 27, 2016.

27. Kevin J. Middlebrook, *The Paradox of Revolution: Labor, the State, and Authoritarianism in Mexico* (Baltimore: Johns Hopkins University Press, 1995); Dale A. Hathaway, *Allies Across the Border: Mexico's "Authentic Labor Front" and Global Solidarity* (Cambridge, MA: South End, 2000), 109–149.

28. Marie-Josee Massicotte, "Mexican Sociopolitical Movements and Transnational Networking in the Context of Economic Integration in the Americas" (PhD diss., York University, 2004), 226–228.

29. "Canada-Mexico Encuentro: Social Organizations Facing Free Trade Final Declaration," October 5–7, 1990, JCP.

30. RMALC, "For a Free Trade Agreement That Conforms with a National and Popular Plan," August 2, 1992, JCP.

31. Massicotte, "Mexican Sociopolitical Movements," 211–282.

32. "The Other Side of the Mexican Story: An Interview with Carlos Heredia," *NAFTAThoughts: A Newsletter on the North American Free Trade Agreement* 3, no. 2 (May 1993): 3.

33. Red Mexicana de Acción Frente al Libre Comercio, "Los acuerdos complementarios del TLC, insuficientes," August 13, 1993, GTWP.

Chapter 14

1. Barlow interview, August 18, 2016; Heredia interview, May 27, 2016.

2. Michael Dreiling, *Solidarity and Contention: The Politics of Security and Sustainability in the NAFTA Conflict* (New York: Routledge, 2000), 36.

3. Institute for Food and Development Policy and the Institute for Policy Studies, "An Activist's Guide to North American Free Trade," undated, JCP.

4. "IPS Trustees—NAFTA," undated, JCP.

5. "Conference Report for Beyond NAFTA: Toward Equity and Sustainability," October 6–11, 1994, p. 17, GTWP.

6. John Cavanagh, "Conclusions and Recommendations: Strategy Session," July 3, 1991, JCP.

7. "US/Mexico/Canada Mtg in NY," undated, JCP.

8. "MODTLE Statement on Development and Trade Strategies for North America," September 12, 1991, JCP.

9. Pharis Harvey to Members of MODTLE, "Urgent!" October 22, 1991, JCP.

10. Marisa von Bülow, *Building Transnational Networks: Civil Society and the Politics of Trade in the Americas* (Cambridge: Cambridge University Press, 2010), 142–145.

11. Dreiling, *Solidarity and Contention*, 36.

12. David Ranney, *Global Decisions, Local Collisions: Urban Life in the New World Order* (Philadelphia: Temple University Press, 2003), 204.

13. Citizen Trade Executive Board, "Discussion of Social Charter/Goold Draft," Composite Minutes: January 23, 1992; February 22, 1992; March 11, 1992; March 16, 1992, GTWP.

14. Sheldon Friedman, "The EC vs. NAFTA: Levelling Up vs. Social Dumping," *Chicago-Kent Law Review* 68, no. 3 (June 1993): 1421–1426.

15. Citizen Trade Executive Board, "Discussion of Social Charter/Goold Draft," GTWP.

16. Executive Board to Working Groups, "Suggestions for Work Plans," October 1, 1992, GTWP.

17. Karen Hansen-Kuhn, interview with the author, Washington, D.C., July 14, 2015.

18. John R. Oravec, "Job-Gutting Trade Policies Scored," *AFL-CIO News* 37, no. 5 (March 2, 1992): 1.

19. Tamara Kay and R. L. Evans, *Trade Battles: Activism and the Politicization of International Trade Policy* (Oxford: Oxford University Press, 2018), 62.

20. Dreiling, "Forging Solidarity," 72.

21. Skocpol, *Diminished Democracy*, 227–229.

22. Taylor Dark, *The Unions and the Democrats: An Enduring Alliance*, rev. ed. (Ithaca: Cornell University Press, 1999).

23. Dreiling, "Forging Solidarity," 222.

24. Personal communication with Greg Woodhead of the AFL-CIO, April 7, 1998, quoted in Evans, "Rise of Ethical Trade Advocacy," 300.

25. Andrew Battista, "Unions and Cold War Foreign Policy in the 1980s: The National Labor Committee, the AFL-CIO, and Central America," *Diplomatic History* 26, no. 3 (Summer 2002): 419–451.

26. Rand Wilson, "Winning Lessons from the NAFTA Loss," *Labor Research Review* 1, no. 22 (1994): 27–37.

27. "Women's History Month Interview with Evelyn Dubrow," *DemocracyNOW*, March 27, 1997, https://www.democracynow.org/1997/3/27/womens_history_month _interview_with_evy; Steven Greenhouse, "Evelyn Dubrow, Labor Lobbyist, Dies at 95," *New York Times*, June 22, 2006.

28. Wallach interview, August 9, 2016.

29. Dreiling, *Solidarity and Contention*, 33–69; Kay and Evans, *Trade Battles*, 105–108.

30. Senator Phil Gramm, "Exporting Capitalism," *Heritage Lectures* 123 (March 18, 1987): 3. On post–Cold War conservative thinking, see Meenekshi Bose and Rosanna Perotti, eds., *From Cold War to New World Order: The Foreign Policy of George H. W. Bush* (Westport, CT: Greenwood, 2002).

31. Amy Kaslow, "Bush Sees Campaign Boost from Free-Trade Issue," *Christian Science Monitor*, October 7, 1992.

32. Patrick J. Buchanan, "America First, Second, and Third," *National Interest* 19 (Spring 1990): 81.

33. John B. Judis, "The Tariff Party," *New Republic*, March 30, 1992, 23. On Buchanan, see Timothy Stanley, *The Crusader: The Life and Tumultuous Times of Pat Buchanan* (New York: St. Martin's, 2012).

34. Steven A. Holmes, "The Checks Are in the Mail, and Made Out to Buchanan," *New York Times*, February 24, 1992, A16.

35. House Committee on Small Business, *The North American Free Trade Agreement*, 102nd Cong., 2nd Sess., 1992, 6.

36. Jonathan M. Katz, "The Man Who Launched the GOP's Civil War," *Politico Magazine*, October 1, 2015, http://www.politico.com/magazine/story/2015/10/roger-milliken -republican-party-history-213212?o+O.

37. Bob Davis, "How a U.S. Textile Manufacturer Came to Embrace Free Trade," *Wall Street Journal*, May 4, 2015, https://www.wsj.com/articles/how-a-u-s-textile-maker-came -to-embrace-free-trade-1430793654.

38. Andrew Kaczynski, "Donald Trump Spoke Forcefully Against NAFTA at a 1993 Conference," *BuzzFeed*, February 29, 2016, https://www.buzzfeed.com/andrewkaczynski /trump-spoke-against-nafta-at-1993-convention?utm_term=.crneDpgQQ#.hkK4wR233.

39. Albert J. Menendez, *The Perot Voters and the Future of American Politics* (Amherst, NY: Prometheus, 1996).

40. John B. Judis, "The Divide: History vs. NAFTA," *New Republic*, October 11, 1993, 32.

41. Sara Fritz, "Perot Tactics May Be Too Unconventional to Have an Impact," *Los Angeles Times*, October 7, 1992.

42. Commission on Presidential Debates, "The Second Clinton-Bush-Perot Presidential Debate," October 15, 1992, http://www.debates.org/index.php?page=october-15-1992 -first-half-debate-transcript.

43. For example, Perot believed that the North Vietnamese had hired the Black Panthers to murder him—a claim for which he offered zero proof. See Michael Kelly, "Perot Shows Penchant for Seeing Conspiracy," *New York Times*, October 26, 1992, A12.

44. William A. Orme, *Understanding NAFTA: Mexico, Free Trade, and the New North America* (Austin: University of Texas Press, 1996), 78.

45. Kenneth S. Baer, *Reinventing Democrats: The Politics of Liberalism from Reagan to Clinton* (Lawrence: University Press of Kansas, 2000).

46. Bill Clinton, *My Life*, 1st ed. (New York: Alfred A. Knopf, 2004), 366.

47. Lily Geismer, "Agents of Change: The Clintons, and the Long History of Microfinance in the United States and the World," Harvard University Workshop on the History of American Capitalism, March 11, 2016, 33–40.

48. Jann S. Wenner, Hunter S. Thompson, William Greider, and P. J. O'Rourke, "Bill Clinton: The Rolling Stone Interview," *RollingStone*, September 17, 1992, http://www .rollingstone.com/politics/news/the-rolling-stone-interview-bill-clinton-19920917.

49. Bill Clinton speeches quoted in John R. MacArthur, *The Selling of "Free Trade": NAFTA, Washington, and the Subversion of American Democracy* (Berkeley: University of California Press, 2001), 144, 146.

50. Lori Wallach to Citizen Trade Executive Board Colleagues, "Developing a Campaign Plan," September 29, 1992, GTWP.

51. Governor Bill Clinton, "Expanding Trade and Creating American Jobs," October 4, 1992, https://www.ibiblio.org/pub/academic/political-science/speeches/clinton.dir /c151.txt.

52. John Cavanagh to Bob King and Natasha Kadic, "RE: A few initial thoughts on how a Clinton presidency could affect work on the neo-liberal agenda in Latin America," October 18, 1992, JCP.

Chapter 15

1. Art Levine and Amy Cunningham, "Post-Triumph Trauma: For the Long-Suffering Left, Winning Can Feel Weird," *Washington Post*, November 29, 1992, C2.

2. Mark Ritchie, "Speech," December 1, 1992, IATPDL, https://www.iatp.org/sites /default/files/451_2_103947.pdf.

3. Levine and Cunningham, "Post-Triumph Trauma," C2.

4. Patrick J. Maney, *Bill Clinton: New Gilded Age President* (Lawrence: University Press of Kansas, 2016), 45–72.

5. Keith Bradshaw, "Mickey Kantor," *New York Times*, December 12, 1993, 255–259.

6. Mickey Kantor, interview, June 28, 2002, William J. Clinton Presidential History Project, Miller Center, University of Virginia (hereafter CPHP).

7. Michael Waldman, Bob Boorstin, Marla Romash, and Jody Greenstone to George Stephanopoulos, David Gergen, and Mark Gearan, "Draft Communications Memo for Monday Meeting," July 23, 1993, Clinton Digital Library (hereafter CDL), https://clinton .presidentiallibraries.us/items/show/14478.

8. Mark Gearan, Bob Boorstin, Michael Waldman, Marla Romash, and Rahm Emanuel to David Gergen, Mack McLarty, and George Stephanopoulos, "Fall Calendar," July 19, 1993, CDL, https://clinton.presidentiallibraries.us/items/show/44846.

9. "The North American Free Trade Agreement," statement by the AFL-CIO Executive Council, February 17, 1993, GTWP.

10. AFL-CIO Executive Council Minutes, May 4–5, 1993, 8, Box 105, AFL-CIO Papers, quoted in Minchin, *Labor Under Fire*, 196.

11. Michael Kantor to Chief of Staff, "USTR Activities, April 12–18," April 19, 1993, CDL, https://clinton.presidentiallibraries.us/items/show/89783.

12. Lauren Rothfarb to Lori Wallach, "A Message That All CTC Members Can Live With," March 29, 1993, GTWP.

13. Ray E. Boomhower, *The People's Choice: Congressman Jim Jontz of Indiana* (Indianapolis: Indiana Historical Society Press, 2012).

14. Citizens Trade Campaign to President Bill Clinton, March 16, 1993, GTWP; Mayer, *Interpreting NAFTA*, 224–226.

15. "Statement of Michael McCloskey, Chairman of the Sierra Club on the National Environmental Protection Act Lawsuit Against the Office of the United States Trade Representative," August 1, 1991, GTWP.

16. Michael Waldman, Bob Boorstin, Marla Romash, and Jody Greenstone to George Stephanopoulos, David Gergen, and Mark Gearan, "Draft Communications Memo for Monday Meeting," July 23, 1993, CDL, https://clinton.presidentiallibraries.us/items/show/14478.

17. Taunya L. McLarty, "The Applicability of NEPA to NAFTA: Law, Politics, or Economics?" *Maryland Journal of International Law* 19, no. 1 (1995): 121–157.

18. David Karol, "Does Constituency Size Affect Elected Officials' Trade Policy Preferences?" *Journal of Politics* 69, no. 2 (May 2007): 483–494.

19. Ken Deutsch to Jim Jontz, "Accountability and Supervision of Trade Field Staff," May 24, 1993, GTWP.

20. "Kantor Is Told NAFTA Won't Pass House Fast," *Women's Wear Daily*, March 12, 1993, 13.

21. Joyce Barrett, "Gephardt Lightens Up on NAFTA," *Women's Wear Daily*, March 24, 1993, 2.

22. Citizens Trade Campaign Legislative Working Group, "Agenda," March 9, 1993, GTWP.

23. Beth Donovan, "Anti-NAFTA: Essential for Bonior," *Congressional Quarterly*, September 11, 1993, 2374.

24. David Bonior, interview with author, Washington, D.C., January 4, 2017.

25. Wallach interview, August 9, 2016; Bonior interview, January 4, 2017.

26. Deb Allery to Trade Staffers, "Anti-NAFTA Caucus," May 4, 1993, Box 1235, Folder 6, Patsy T. Mink Papers, Manuscript Division, Library of Congress, Washington, D.C. (hereafter PMP).

27. "U.S. House of Representatives—103rd Congress Positions on NAFTA," September 2, 1993, GTWP.

28. This is a paraphrase as recalled during author's interview with Lori Wallach, August 9, 2016.

29. "North American Free Trade Agreement: Citizens Trade Campaign," C-SPAN, video, September 15, 1993, https://www.c-span.org/video/?50402-1/north-american-free-trade-agreement.

30. "National Week of Actions for Fair Trade: May 1–9," undated, GTWP.

31. Dan Goldrich, "Report to Activists of the Citizens Trade Campaign: Reflections on the Struggle over NAFTA," July 1994, GTWP.

32. Lori to Joan, "Trade Coalition Reorganization," December 18, 1992, GTWP.

33. Mayer, *Interpreting NAFTA*, 230.

34. Charlyne Berens, "Amplifying the Giant Sucking Sound: Ross Perot and the Media in the NAFTA Negotiations," *Newspaper Research Journal* 20, no. 2 (Spring 1999): 96.

35. "Nation in Brief: Michigan—Perot Blasts NAFTA at Lansing Rally," *Los Angeles Times*, September 19, 1993.

36. "North American Free Trade Agreement," C-SPAN, video, August 27, 1993, https://www.c-span.org/video/?49450-1/north-american-free-trade-agreement.

37. Patrick J. Buchanan, "America First, NAFTA Never," *Washington Post,* November 7, 1993, C1.

38. Pamela Warren to Patsy Mink, November 9, 1993, Box 1235, Folder 9, PMP; Cornelia Radich to Patsy Mink, June 24, 1993, Box 1225, Folder 9, PMP.

39. John B. Judis, "The Divide: History vs. NAFTA," *New Republic*, October 11, 1993, 26.

40. Susan Faludi, *Stiffed: The Roots of Modern Male Rage* (New York: Perennial, 2000); Dana Frank, *Buy American: The Untold Story of Economic Nationalism* (Boston: Beacon, 2000).

41. International Brotherhood of Teamsters, "The 'Free Trade' Deal Will Drive Away Good Jobs—and Threaten Highway Safety," undated, GTWP.

42. Goldrich, "Report to Activists of the Citizens Trade Campaign," GTWP.

43. "8 Fatal Flaws of NAFTA," *New York Times*, September 22, 1993, A17.

44. "North American Free Trade Agreement," C-SPAN, video, November 4, 1993, https://www.c-span.org/video/?52065-1/north-american-free-trade-agreement. On Weyrich, see Ruth Murray Brown, *For a Christian America: A History of the Religious Right* (Amherst, NY: Prometheus, 2002), 131–137.

45. Bruce Ingersoll and Asra Q. Nomani, "Hidden Force: As Perot Bashes NAFTA, a Textile Titan Fights It Quietly with Money," *Wall Street Journal*, November 15, 1993, A1.

46. National Council of La Raza, "National Hispanic Leader Seeks Repudiation of 'Politics of Race Baiting' as NAFTA Heats Up," June 10, 1993, GTWP.

47. "Mexican Stereotype," in *Saturday Night Live*, NBC, video, November 13, 1993, https://www.nbc.com/saturday-night-live/video/mexican-stereotype/n10486.

48. Lori Wallach to Citizen Trade Executive Board Colleagues, "Developing a Campaign Plan," September 29, 1992, GTWP.

49. Tamara Kay, *NAFTA and the Politics of Labor Transnationalism* (Cambridge: Cambridge University Press, 2011), 79–86.

50. Hathaway, *Allies Across the Border*, 175–181. On the UE, see Ronald L. Filippelli and Mark McColloch, *Cold War in the Working Class: The Rise and Decline of United Electrical Workers* (Albany: State University of New York Press, 1995).

51. Mexican Action Network on Free Trade, Alliance for Responsible Trade, and Citizens Trade Campaign, with Action Canada Network, "A Just and Sustainable Trade and

Development Initiative for North America," in *Global Backlash: Citizen Initiatives for a Just World Economy*, ed. Robin Broad (Lanham: Rowman & Littlefield, 2002), 129–135.

52. Lilian Calles Barger, *The World Comes of Age: An Intellectual History of Liberation Theology* (Oxford: Oxford University Press, 2018).

53. Heredia interview, May 27, 2016.

54. Stuart Auerbach, "U.S., Mexico, Canada Break NAFTA Impasse," *Washington Post*, August 13, 1993.

Chapter 16

1. Katie McGinty to Governor Clinton, "Environmental Issues Relevant to NAFTA," December 31, 1992, CDL, https://clinton.presidentiallibraries.us/items/show/77377.

2. Michael Waldman to Mark Gearan and David Gergen, "NAFTA Briefing Yesterday," August 3, 1993, CDL, https://clinton.presidentiallibraries.us/items/show/89783. On the labor side agreement, see Kay, *NAFTA and the Politics of Labor Transnationalism*, 105–122.

3. RMALC, "Los Acuerdos Complementarios del TLC, Insuficientes," and RMALC, "Declaracion de Presna Sobre la Terminacion de las Negociaciones de los Acuerdos Paralelos al TLC," August 16, 1993, GTWP.

4. RMALC, "Los Acuerdos Complementarios del TLC."

5. Frank Swoboda, "Kirkland: No Compromise on NAFTA," *Washington Post*, September 1, 1993.

6. John R. Oravec, "Side Deals Fail; AFL-CIO Fights NAFTA," *AFL-CIO News* 38, no. 18 (August 23, 1993): 1.

7. Minchin, *Labor Under Fire*, 197–199; Evans, "Rise of Ethical Trade Advocacy," 269; John R. Oravec, "'No NAFTA' Drive Takes Broad Aim at House Vote," *AFL-CIO News* 38, no. 23 (November 1, 1993): 5.

8. Mark Dowie, *Losing Ground: American Environmentalism at the Close of the Twentieth Century* (Cambridge, MA: MIT Press, 1996), 187.

9. Dowie, *Losing Ground*, 177–179.

10. John Barry, "Facing the Powers That Be," *Newsweek*, November 29, 1992, http://www.newsweek.com/facing-powers-be-197080.

11. House Committee on Agriculture, *North American Free Trade Agreement*, 103rd Cong., 1st sess., 1993, 352.

12. Barbara Hogenboom, *Mexico and the NAFTA Environment Debate: The Transnational Politics of Economic Integration* (Utrecht, Netherlands: International Books, 1998), 215–219; Kevin P. Gallagher, *Free Trade and the Environment: Mexico, NAFTA, and Beyond* (Stanford: Stanford University Press, 2004).

13. NWF ActionAlert, September 21, 1993, GTWP.

14. "North American Free Trade Agreement and the Environment," C-SPAN, video, September 15, 1993, https://www.c-span.org/video/?50391-1/north-american-free-trade-agreement.

15. Burston-Marsteller, "Focus Group Analysis: Opinions Toward Proposed Advertising on Mexico," October 14–15, 1993, CDL, https://clinton.presidentiallibraries.us/items/show/44908.

16. "NAFTA Communications Plan," undated, CDL, https://clinton.presidentiallibraries.us/items/show/44899; National Wildlife Federation, "Working Agenda for NAFTA Lobby Week," October 18, 1993, GTWP.

17. "North American Free Trade Agreement and the Environment."

18. "Interview: A Resounding 'Yes' on NAFTA from the NWF," *Greenwire*, September 21, 1993, 6.

19. "North American Free Trade Agreement and the Environment."

20. Audley, *Green Politics and Global Trade*, 100.

21. Mark Gearan, Bob Boorstin, Michael Waldman, Marla Romash, and Rahm Emanuel to David Gergen, Mack McLarty, and George Stephanopoulos, "Fall Calendar," July 19, 1993, CDL, https://clinton.presidentiallibraries.us/items/show/44846.

22. Michael Waldman, Chris Dorval, Jay Ziegler, Arthur Jones to Bill Daley and Rahm Emanuel, "Communications Strategy for NAFTA—Presidential and Surrogates," September 11, 1993, CDL, https://clinton.presidentiallibraries.us/items/show/44899.

23. "NAFTA Communications Plan," undated, CDL, https://clinton.presidentiallibraries.us/items/show/44899.

24. "North American Free Trade Agreement," C-SPAN, video, November 8, 1993, https://www.c-span.org/video/?52169-1/north-american-free-trade-agreement.

25. "USA*NAFTA Membership," June 22, 1993, CDL, https://clinton.presidentiallibraries.us/items/show/44492.

26. Mayer, *Interpreting NAFTA*, 234; USA*NAFTA to Mickey Kantor, June 4, 1993, GTWP.

27. Ernest Pepples, "NAFTA," September 2, 1993, IDL, https://www.industrydocumentslibrary.ucsf.edu/tobacco/docs/#id=mkpy0203.

28. Ambassador Mickey Kantor, "Memorandum to the President," September 2, 1993, quoted in Tim Hanrahan, "Clinton-Era Memo: Get Iacocca to Pitch NAFTA," *Wall Street Journal*, April 18, 2013, http://blogs.wsj.com/washwire/2014/04/18/clinton-era-memo-we-need-lee-iacocca-to-pitch-nafta/.

29. "USA*NAFTA Progress Report," June 9, 1993, CDL, https://clinton.presidentiallibraries.us/items/show/44492.

30. "USA*NAFTA Challenges IPS Report," July 28, 1993, JCP.

31. Waldman, Dorval, Ziegler, Jones, "Communications Strategy for NAFTA."

32. Bonior interview, January 4, 2017.

33. Representative Henry Waxman, interview with author, Washington, D.C., August 3, 2016.

34. David H. Bennett, *Bill Clinton: Building a Bridge to the New Millennium* (New York: Routledge, 2013), 40–41, 58.

35. Quoted in Al From with Alice McKeon, *The New Democrats and the Return to Power* (New York: St. Martin's, 2013), 206, 207.

36. "Gore-Perot Debate: The Message," undated, CDL, https://clinton.presidential libraries.us/items/show/44900; Burston-Marsteller, "Focus Group Analysis: Opinions Towards Proposed Advertising on Mexico," October 14–15, 1993, CDL, https://clinton .presidentiallibraries.us/items/show/44908.

37. Mayer, *Interpreting NAFTA,* 311.

38. "Gore-Perot Debate," CDL.

39. "Larry King Live: The NAFTA Debate," Vanderbilt University Television News Archive, November 9, 1993, https://tvnews-vanderbilt-edu.ezp-prod1.hul.harvard.edu /broadcasts/650199.

40. Quoted in MacArthur, *Selling of "Free Trade,"* 248.

41. William M. Daley to Members of Congress, November 10, 1993, Box 1244, Folder 4, PMP.

42. Diana Evans, *Greasing the Wheels: Using Pork Barrel Projects to Build Majority Coalitions in Congress* (Cambridge: Cambridge University Press, 2004), 158.

43. Harel Barzilai to misc.activism.progressive, "NAFTA: **Action** on 'Swing Votes,'" November 12, 1993, https://groups.google.com/forum/#!searchin/alt.politics .greens/nafta$20%22action$20on$20swing$20votes%22%7Csort:date/alt.politics.greens /unD9yGJa6mQ/96va5su-cQ8J. On progressive activists' early use of the internet, see Kevin Cooke and Dan Lehrer, "The Whole World Is Talking," *Nation,* July 12, 1993, 62.

44. Greer, Margolis, Mitchell, Burns and Associates, Inc. to Citizens Trade Campaign Executive Board, "Recap on the Week, Strategy for Next Week," November 4, 1993, GTWP.

45. MacArthur, *Selling of "Free Trade,"* 273.

46. David E. Bonior, *Whip: Leading the Progressive Battle During the Rise of the Right* (Westport, CT: City Point, 2018), 366.

47. MacArthur, *Selling of "Free Trade,"* 274; James Gerstenzang and Michael Ross, "House Passes NAFTA, 234–200," *Los Angeles Times,* November 18, 1993.

48. "Statement by Ralph Nader on President Clinton, NAFTA, and the House of Representatives," November 18, 1993, GTWP.

49. Public Citizen, "NAFTA Debate Made History," November 18, 1993, GTWP.

Chapter 17

1. "Newt Gingrich on House Passage of NAFTA," C-SPAN, video, November 17, 1993, https://www.c-span.org/video/?c4608699/newt-gingrich-house-passage-nafta. On the 1994 election, see Linda Killian, *The Freshmen: What Happened to the Republican Revolution?* (Boulder, CO: Westview, 1998).

2. John Cavanagh and Sarah Anderson to ART, CTC, "Rethinking NAFTA" meeting participants, and other friends, "Beyond the NAFTA and GATT Struggles: Some Thoughts on Next Steps in the Fair Trade/Economic and Environmental Justice Work," December 21, 1994, GTWP.

3. Angela Ledford to CTC Executive Committee, "Where Do We Go from Here?" January 26, 1994, GTWP.

4. Mike Dolan to tw-list@essential.org, "Business Leaders Gear Up Lobbying and Ad Campaign for 'Fast-Track' Bill," September 19, 1997, http://lists.essential.org/tw-list /msg00055.html.

5. Liz Arky, David Kim, and Mike Williams to Ambassador Barshefsky through Nancy LeaMond, "Congressional Wrap-Up," October 30, 1998, GTWP.

6. Susan Denzer to Executive Committee and Angela Ledford, "Proposal to Complete Administrative Tasks from the NAFTA Campaign," December 14, 1993, GTWP.

7. Ledford, "Where Do We Go from Here?"

8. Anna Lanoszka, *The World Trade Organization: Changing Dynamics in the Global Political Economy* (Boulder, CO: Lynne Rienner, 2009), 47–77; Carlos M. Correa, *Health Economics: The Uruguay Round and Drugs* (Geneva: World Health Organization, 1997); Nitsan Chorev, "The Institutional Project of Neo-Liberal Globalism: The Case of the WTO, " *Theory and Society* 34 (2005): 317–355; Jagdish Bhagwati and Mathias Hirsch, eds., *The Uruguay Round and Beyond: Essays in Honor of Arthur Dunkel* (Ann Arbor: University of Michigan Press, 1998).

9. Jürgen Kurtz, *The WTO and International Investment Law: Converging Systems* (Cambridge: Cambridge University Press, 2016).

10. U.S. Chamber of Commerce, "Pass the Uruguay Round (GATT) Legislation This Year," September 23, 1994, IDL, https://www.industrydocumentslibrary.ucsf.edu /tobacco/docs/#id=hrjl0047; Pharmaceutical Manufacturers Association, "PMA Supports GATT, but Serious Flaws Demand Continued Bilateral Efforts," January 24, 1994, GTWP.

11. Helmut O. Maucher, "International Business Issues in View of Globalisation and Regional Integration," in Bhagwati and Hirsch, *The Uruguay Round and Beyond*, 160.

12. Nitsan Chorev, *Remaking U.S. Trade Policy: From Protectionism to Globalization* (Ithaca: Cornell University Press, 2007), 159.

13. "Citizens Trade Campaign Update," February 17, 1994, GTWP.

14. Angela Ledford to Mark Ritchie, "Lots of Stuff," undated, GTWP.

15. Audley, *Green Politics and Global Trade*, 2.

16. Lisa Romano, "The Reliable Source," *Washington Post*, October 27, 1994, D3; Lisa Romano, "The Reliable Source," *Washington Post*, November 29, 1994, D3.

17. Peter Behr, "As Trade Triumphs Fade, Clinton Faces Series of Tough Fights," *Washington Post*, May 14, 1994, C1.

18. "Senator Sasser: Stop the Clinton Spending Spree!" undated, GTWP.

19. Helene Cooper, "World Trade Organization Created by GATT Isn't the Lion of Its Foes or the Lamb of Its Backers," *Wall Street Journal*, July 14, 1994, A12.

20. Robert E. Baldwin and Christopher Magee, *Congressional Trade Votes: From NAFTA Approval to Fast-Track Defeat* (Washington, DC: Peterson Institute for International Economics, 2000), 5–8.

21. John H. Adams to Ralph Nader, March 3, 1994, GTWP.

22. Ralph Nader to Tom Donahue, December 3, 1994, GTWP.

23. Lydia Saad, "GATT Still a Mystery to Most Americans," *Gallup Poll News Service* 59, no. 29 (December 2, 1994): 1.

24. "Confidential GBF Client Use Only: Luncheon Discussion Meeting on 'The Uruguay Round Package, Possible Amendments to the Text, and Outlook for Congressional Approval' with Ambassador Rufus Yerxa," February 9, 1994, IDL, https://www.industry documentslibrary.ucsf.edu/tobacco/docs/#id=kjbd0196.

25. Craig VanGrasstek, *The History and Future of the World Trade Organization* (Geneva: World Trade Organization, 2013), 63.

26. Lori Wallach, "What We Have Accomplished," December 12, 1994, GTWP.

27. Sarah Anderson, interview with the author, July 13, 2015, Washington, D.C.

Chapter 18

1. Mark Ritchie, "Cross-Border Organizing," in *The Case Against the Global Economy: And for a Turn Toward the Local*, ed. Jerry Mander and Edward Goldsmith (San Francisco: Sierra Club Books, 1997), 499.

2. "Jerry Mander," Schumacher Center for a New Economics, http://www.center forneweconomics.org/people/jerry-mander.

3. Walter Schwartz, "Edward Goldsmith," *Guardian*, August 27, 2009, https://www .theguardian.com/environment/2009/aug/27/obituary-edward-goldsmith.

4. Jerry Mander to David Fenton, April 22, 1996, GTWP.

5. "IFG, 1/95," undated, GTWP. On the post–Cold War international left, see Castañeda, *Utopia Unarmed*; Kristen Ghodsee, *Red Hangover: Legacies of Twentieth-Century Communism* (Durham, NC: Duke University Press, 2017).

6. "IFG, 1/95." For texts examining questions of authenticity, indigeneity, and community, see Regina Cochrane, "Rural Poverty and Impoverished Theory: Cultural Populism, Ecofeminism, and Global Justice," *Journal of Peasant Studies* 34, no. 2 (2007): 167–206; Miranda Joseph, *Against the Romance of Community* (Minneapolis: University of Minnesota Press, 2002).

7. "IFG, 1/95," GTWP.

8. "IFG, 1/95," GTWP.

9. Martin Khor, "Why GATT and the WTO Should Not Deal with Labour Standards," April 1994, GTWP.

10. "IFG, 1/95," GTWP.

11. Tony Clarke in collaboration with other members of the IFG working committee on TNCs, *Dismantling Corporate Rule: A Set of Working Instruments for Social Movements* (San Francisco: International Forum on Globalization, 1996), 3.

12. "IFG, 1/95," GTWP.

13. "IFG Solutions: From 'Ought To' to 'Can Do,'" discussion paper from Colin Hines, Convenor of IFG's Alternatives/Solutions Working Group, December 20, 1996, GTWP.

14. Handwritten notes, undated, GTWP.

15. Natalie L. Schafer, "Strategies and Visions for Change: An Activist Challenge to the Existing Economic Paradigm" (PhD diss., California Institute of Integral Studies, June 1997), 54–55.

16. "50 Years Is Enough Platform," undated, Container 6, Folder 22, MDP.

17. "Notes from the General Meeting of the U.S. 50 Years Is Enough Campaign," September 8, 1994, Container 6, Folder 6, MDP.

18. Steven Greenhouse, "A Crusader Makes Celebrities Tremble," *New York Times*, June 18, 1996, B4.

19. Battista, "Unions and Cold War Foreign Policy in the 1980s," 419–451.

20. Lane Windham to Southern Regional Staff and Others, February 27, 1997. Document provided by Lane Windham. On United Students Against Sweatshops, see Purnima Bose, "From Agitation to Institutionalization: The Student Anti-Sweatshop Movement in the New Millennium," *Indiana Journal of Global Legal Studies* 15, no. 1 (Winter 2008): 213–240; Matthew S. Williams, *Strategizing Against Sweatshops: The Global Economy, Student Activism, and Worker Empowerment* (Philadelphia: Temple University Press, 2020).

21. "Report: NAFTA Breaks Promise of Jobs," *UPI*, September 4, 1995, http://www.upi.com/Archives/1995/09/04/Report-NAFTA-breaks-promise-of-jobs/2198810187200/.

22. Brad Fogel to Ralph Nader, September 22, 1995, GTWP.

23. John Boidock to the Washington Representatives of the Members of the Business Roundtable, "NAFTA's Broken Promise: Job Creation Under NAFTA," September 28, 1995, GTWP; "Statement by Commerce Secretary Ronald Brown on Public Citizen's NAFTA Statement," September 4, 1995, GTWP.

24. Nick Henck, *Subcommander Marcos: The Man and the Mask* (Durham, NC: Duke University Press, 2007); Gloria Muñoz Ramírez, ed., *The Fire and The World: A History of the Zapatista Movement* (San Francisco: City Lights, 2008); Shannon Speed, R Aída Hernández Castillo, and Lynn M. Stephen, eds., *Dissident Women: Gender and Cultural Politics in Chiapas* (Austin: University of Texas Press, 2006).

25. Juan Carlos Moreno-Brid and Jaime Ros, *Development and Growth in the Mexican Economy: An Historical Perspective* (Oxford: Oxford University Press, 2009), 199–203.

26. National Security Council, Speechwriting Office, and Antony Blinken, "Mexico Peso Crisis—Drafts—1/18/95," CDL, https://clinton.presidentiallibraries.us/items/show/9150.

27. Citizens Trade Campaign and the Alliance for Responsible Trade, "To Those Concerned with the Mexico Bailout," April 7, 1995, GTWP.

28. "Rep. Bernie Sanders (I-VT) on the Global Economy and Bailouts," C-SPAN, video, January 31, 1995, https://www.c-span.org/video/?c4546042/rep-bernie-sanders-global-economy-bailouts.

29. Lori Wallach to Peter Buckley, April 4, 1995, GTWP.

30. Lori Wallach to Board of Directors of Public Citizen Inc. and Public Citizen Foundation, "Mid-Fiscal Year Report," May 10, 1995, GTWP.

31. Mike Dolan, interview with the author, July 17, 2015, Washington, D.C.

32. Dolan interview, July 17, 2015; "Area Leaders Rally for NAFTA Controls," *Toledo Blade*, December 16, 1995, 30.

33. Dolan interview, July 17, 2015; Michael Dolan to Trade Activists and Organizers, October 9, 1995, GTWP.

34. "Americans Split on Whether NAFTA Is Good or Bad for US," *Gallup*, February 24, 2017, http://www.gallup.com/poll/204269/americans-split-whether-nafta-good-bad.aspx.

35. *The Simpsons*, "A Star Is Burns," directed by Susie Dietter, written by Ken Keeler, Fox Broadcasting, March 5, 1995.

36. Patrick J. Buchanan, "Announcement of Candidacy," *CNN All Politics*, March 20, 1995, http://www.cnn.com/ALLPOLITICS/1996/candidates/republican/withdrawn/buch.announcement.shtml.

37. Stanley, *Crusader*, 229–282.

38. John Cavanagh to David Fenton, "Some Talking Points for Media Work on International Forum on Globalization Teach-In," April 21, 1996, GTWP.

39. Brent Blackwelder, "Free Trade and Pat Buchanan," February 21, 1996, GTWP.

40. Bob Davis, "Lighthizer, Dole's Idea Man, Attempts to Derail Buchanan with Trade Issue," *Wall Street Journal*, February 28, 1996, A16. On Lighthizer, see Quinn Slobodian, "You Live in Robert Lighthizer's World Now," *Foreign Policy*, August 6, 2018, https://foreignpolicy.com/2018/08/06/you-live-in-robert-lighthizers-world-now-trump-trade/.

41. "Text of Robert Dole's Speech to the Republican National Convention," *CNN All Politics*, August 15, 1996, http://www.cnn.com/ALLPOLITICS/1996/conventions/san.diego/transcripts/0815/dole.fdch.shtml.

42. "October 16, 1996 Debate Transcript," Commission on Presidential Debates, https://www.debates.org/voter-education/debate-transcripts/october-16-1996-debate-transcript/.

43. Maney, *Bill Clinton*, 179–181.

44. "Remarks Prepared for Delivery by USTR Charlene Barshefsky Before the Council on Competitiveness," March 20, 1997, CDL, https://clinton.presidentiallibraries.us/items/show/33319.

Chapter 19

1. "American Economic Leadership in the New Emerging Global Economy," January 9, 1997, CDL, https://clinton.presidentiallibraries.us/items/show/45431.

2. Red Mexicana de Acción Frente al Libre Comercio, "Relaciones Internacionales," January 28–29, 1994, GTWP.

3. LAWG, SolidarityWorks, Fronteras Comunes/CECOPE, CIEP, MaM, *Report to the Continental Forum on Economic Integration: Organizing for Alternatives,* March 11–13, 1994, LAC0016, Series 1, Subseries 3, Box 70, Folder 6, United States Labor Education in the Americas Project Records, Special Collections Research Center, Gelman Library, George Washington University, Washington, D.C. (hereafter LEAPR).

4. Anthony Faiola, "Chile Takes Its Trade Elsewhere," *Washington Post*, December 25, 1997, A29.

5. Dante Donoso, *Notas para un estudio del ALCA* (Santiago de Chile, October 1998), 34, GTWP.

6. Hansen-Kuhn interview, July 14, 2015; Manuel Pérez-Rocha, interview with the author, Washington, D.C., July 15, 2015; "NAFTA and the Mexican Environment" and "The Impact of NAFTA on Mexican Agriculture," undated, GTWP.

7. Von Bülow, *Building Transnational Networks*, 88–89.

8. "Building a Hemispheric Social Alliance to Confront Free Trade," May 15, 1997, http://www.developmentgap.org/uploads/2/1/3/7/21375820/building_a_hemispheric _social_alliance_to_confront_free.pdf.

9. Steve Suppan, Director of Research, Institute for Agriculture and Trade Policy, "Intellectual Property Rights in the Free Trade Area of the Americas Discussion," November 1997, Subseries 4, Box 4, Folder 4, LEAPR.

10. "Alternatives for the Americas: After the Fast Track Defeat—A New Vision for Western Hemispheric Integration," November 20, 1998, GTWP.

11. David Ranney, "Discussion Draft: Organizational Structure Needed to Implement Alternatives for the Americas: Building a Peoples' Hemispheric Agreement," October 23, 1998, GTWP.

12. I. M. Destler, *Renewing Fast-Track Legislation* (Washington, DC: Institute for International Economics, 1997), 16–29.

13. William J. Clinton, "Address Before a Joint Session of the Congress on the State of the Union," February 4, 1997, APP, https://www.presidency.ucsb.edu/documents/address -before-joint-session-the-congress-the-state-the-union-9.

14. Bill Fletcher Jr. and Fernando Gaspian, *Solidarity Divided: The Crisis in Organized Labor and a New Path Toward Social Justice* (Berkeley: University of California Press, 2008), 69–83.

15. John Maggs, "Trading Places," *New Republic*, April 14, 1997, 15.

16. Domestic Policy Council and Elena Kagan, "Fast Track-General," undated, CDL, https://clinton.presidentiallibraries.us/items/show/26221.

17. "AFL-CIO's Position, or Lack Thereof, on Trade: Signs of Major Problems?" February 1997, GTWP.

18. AFL-CIO Executive Council, "Fast Track Negotiating Authority," February 20, 1997, https://aflcio.org/resolution/fast-track-trade-negotiating-authority.

19. Michael F. Dolan to CTC Executive Committee, "CTC Field Inventory," March 12, 1997, GTWP.

20. Dolan interview, July 17, 2015.

21. Steve Trossman to Bob, Lori, Steve W., "Thoughts on Clinton's July 1 Report," July 11, 1997, GTWP.

22. Joyce Barrett, "Gingrich Tells House to Act on Trade Issues," *Women's Wear Daily*, April 30, 1997, 14.

23. Thea Lee to Mike Tiner, Peggy Taylor, Ken Grossinger, Denise Mitchell, David Smith, Gerry Shea, Barbara Shailor, "Current Fast-Track Issues," August 27, 1997, GTWP.

24. "Fast Track Pushes Labor, Environment into WTO hands," *Bridges* 1, no. 34 (September 23, 1997), http://www.ictsd.org/bridges-news/bridges/news/fast-track-pushes -labor-environment-linkage-into-wto-hands.

25. *AFL-CIO 1997 Convention Proceedings: 22nd Constitutional Convention, September 22–25, 1997, Pittsburgh* (Washington, DC: American Federation of Labor–Congress of Industrial Organizations, 1997), 225, 249–250.

26. David Glenn, "How Fast Track Was Derailed," *Dissent* 45, no. 4 (Fall 1998): 47–52.

27. Mike Dolan to Fair Trade Organizers and Activists, "Fast Track Count Down," October 23, 1997, GTWP.

28. Minchin, *Labor Under Fire*, 209–210.

29. Lindsay Sobel, "NAFTA Supporters Desert Clinton on Fast Track," *Hill*, November 12, 1997, 8.

30. Donald V. Fites, Philip M. Condit, John E. Pepper Jr., John F. Smith Jr., Robert J. Eaton, and Joseph T. Gorman to the Business Roundtable, "Proposed Strategy," July 24, 1997, GTWP.

31. Paul Blustein, "'Fast Track' Bill Clears House Panel," *Washington Post*, October 9, 1997, E3.

32. Charlene Barshefsky, March 2, 2005, CPHP, 27.

33. Ken Kerot, "The Politics of Trade: Fast Track's Failure Derails the New Economy," *Policy Perspectives* 5 (1998): 15.

34. Lori Wallach, "Safeguarding Our Intermediate Fast Track Win to Ensure Final Victory: Field, Press, and DC Strategy through April 1, 1998," November 20, 1997, GTWP.

35. Thomas B. Edsall and John E. Yang, "Clinton Loss Illuminates Struggle Within Party," *Washington Post*, November 11, 1997, A6.

36. "Remarks to Business Leaders, Santiago, Chile," April 16, 1998, CDL, https:// clinton.presidentiallibraries.us/items/show/9812.

37. Shoch, *Trading Blows*, 223.

38. The Business Roundtable, "Fast Track: Even More Important Now," July 24, 1998, GTWP.

39. Steven M. Gillon, *The Pact: Bill Clinton, Newt Gingrich, and the Rivalry That Defined a Generation* (Oxford: Oxford University Press, 2008), 223–239.

40. Jonathan Peterson, "Democrats Call House Defeat of Fast-Track Trade Bill Bid to Humiliate Them," *Los Angeles Times*, September 26, 1998.

41. Jim VandeHei, "White House Tells Democrats to Sit Out 'Fast Track' Debate," *Roll Call*, August 3, 1998, 1.

42. Baldwin and Magee, *Congressional Trade Votes*, 7, 33.

43. Lori Wallach to Friends, "Fast Track Victory," September 28, 1998, GTWP.

44. Lori to Alan, "Beckman Memo on 'New Trade Negotiating Authority,'" December 17, 1998, GTWP.

Chapter 20

1. Alejandro Bendaña, "Santiago People's Summit: A Report," undated, Series 1, Subseries 4, Box 84, Folder 4, LEAPR.

2. Sarah Anderson to Fellow Peoples Summiteers, "Summit Coverage," April 29, 1998, Series 1, Subseries 4, Box 84, Folder 3, LEAPR.

3. *Beginnings of a New Hemispheric Social Alliance in the Americas: A Report on the Peoples' Summit in Santiago,* Series 1, Subseries 4, Box 84, Folder 4, LEAPR.

4. Peter J. Muchlinski, "The Rise and Fall of the Multilateral Agreement on Investment," *International Lawyer* 34, no. 3 (Fall 2000): 1034–1039.

5. *A Multilateral Agreement on Investment: Report by the Committee on International Investment and Multinational Enterprises (CIME)/and the Committee on Capital Movements and Invisible Transactions (CMIT)* (Paris: Organization for Economic Cooperation and Development, May 1995), DAFFE/CMIT/CIME(95)13/FINAL, Multilateral Agreement on Investment Documents from the Negotiations (hereafter MAIDN), http://www1.oecd.org/daf/mai/htm/cmitcime95.htm.

6. Kevin D. Archer, "Complex Multilateralism and the Question of Global Governance: The Defeat of the Multilateral Agreement on Investment" (PhD diss., University of Denver, 2005), 114–116.

7. "Statement by H.E. Mr. Frédérk Nzabampema, Minister for Trade, Industry and Tourism, Burundi," December 12, 1996, WTOD, https://www.wto.org/english/thewto_e/minist_e/min96_e/st125.htm.

8. Edward A. Fogarty, *States, Nonstate Actors, and Global Governance: Projecting Politics* (New York: Routledge, 2013), 104.

9. Richard Woodward, "Towards Complex Multilateralism? Civil Society and the OECD," in *The OECD and Transnational,* ed. Rianne Mahon and Stephen McBride (Vancouver: University of British Columbia Press, 2008), 81.

10. Stephen J. Canner, "The Multilateral Agreement on Investment: The Next Challenge for Global Interdependence," in *Foreign Ownership and the Consequences of Direct Investment in the United States: Beyond Us and Them,* ed. Douglas Woodward and Douglas Nigh (Westport, CT: Quorum, 1998), 369.

11. Negotiating Group on the Multilateral Agreement on Investment, *Dispute Settlement (Note by the Chairman),* November 21, 1995, MAIDN, http://www1.oecd.org/daf/mai/pdf/ng/ng959e.pdf.

12. Kent W. Royalty and Dianna Ross, "NAFTA Chapter 11: 'Tantamount to Expropriation'—Tantamount to Explosive," *International Trade Journal* 21, no. 3 (2007): 299–327; Ray C. Jones, "NAFTA Chapter 11 Investor-to-State Dispute Resolution: A Shield to Be Embraced or a Sword to Be Feared," *Brigham Young University Law Review* 2 (2002): 527–560.

13. Jürgen Kurtz, "A General Investment Agreement in the WTO? Lessons from Chapter 11 of NAFTA and the OECD Multilateral Agreement on Investment," *University of Pennsylvania Journal of International Law* 23, no. 4 (2014): 761–768.

14. Catherine Schittecatte, "Contested Future(s): The Social Opposition to the OECD-MAI" (PhD diss., Dalhousie University, 2001), 78–81.

15. Barlow interview, August 18, 2016.

16. "OECD Proposes WTO Link," *Trade News* 5, no. 11 (May 28, 1996).

17. Rob Weissman, Lori Wallach, and Tony Clarke, "News Release: Secret Text of Multilateral Agreement on Investment (MAI) Released on the World Wide Web: NGOs 'Liberate' Draft Text of Extreme Treaty," April 7, 1997, GTWP.

18. Naím, "Lori's War," 33.

19. Ronald J. Deibert, "International Plug 'n Play? Citizen Activism, the Internet, and Global Public Policy," *International Studies Perspectives* 1 (2000): 261–262.

20. "National Speakers Come to Boston for Citizens' Conference on MAI," May 22, 1997, alt.save.the.earth, https://groups.google.com/d/msg/alt.save.the.earth/lVlspnWaGHk /zFs5TE2g03YJ.

21. Wallach interview, August 9, 2016.

22. Katia Tieleman, "The Failure of the Multilateral Agreement on Investment (MAI) and the Absence of a Global Public Policy Network," Case Study for the UN Vision Project on Global Public Policy Networks, (Berlin: UN Vision Project on Global Public Policy Networks, 2000): 15.

23. Lisa McGowan, Mark Vallianatos, and Andrea Durbin to ctaylor@citizen; juhasza@smtp; etc., "draft agenda for mai consultation," October 7, 1997, GTWP.

24. Schittecatte, "Contested Future(s)," 84.

25. Schittecatte, "Contested Future(s)," 86.

26. Mark Vallianatos, Chantelle Taylor, David Schorr, John Audley, Daniel Seligman, Lisa McGowan, Steven Porter, Scott Nova, and Jake Caldwell to Alan Larson and Wendy Cutler, undated, GTWP.

27. Schittecatte, "Contested Future(s)," 83–85.

28. Barlow, *Fight of My Life*, 213.

29. Negotiating Group on the Multilateral Agreement on Investment, *Summary Record: Meeting on 29–30 October 1997*, November 19, 1997, MAIDN, http://www1.oecd.org /daf/mai/pdf/ng/ngm978e.pdf.

30. Ursula McTaggart, "Literature That Prompts Action: Edward Abbey's *The Monkey Wrench Gang* and the Formation of Earth First!" *ISLE: Interdisciplinary Studies in Literature and Environment* 0, no. 0 (2019): 1–20.

31. Tony Clarke to Lori Wallach, "Operation Monkey Wrench," January 12, 1998, GTWP.

32. CTaylor@citizen.org to mstrand@citizen.org, "FWD: Minutes from MAI Strategy Session 24 January 1998 Amsterdam," July 15, 1998, GTWP.

33. Kevin Danaher and Jason Mark, *Insurrection: Citizen Challenges to Corporate Power* (New York: Routledge, 2003), 264–265.

34. Julietbeck@aol.com via Sheila Goldner, "San Francisco is an MAI Free Zone!!!!!!" July 19, 1998, http://club.ugr.be/rugr0045/mai.html.

35. "Seattle Declares Itself 'MAI-Free Zone,'" Third World Network, undated, https:// www.twn.my/title/zone-cn.htm.

36. Daniel B. Magraw, Director International Environmental Law Office to Addressees, "Draft EPA Memorandum on the MAI Takings and General Treatment Provisions," October 2, 1997, GTWP.

37. House Committee on International Relations, *Multilateral Agreement on Investment: Win, Lose, or Draw for the U.S.?* 105th Cong., 2nd sess., 1998, 2.

38. Andreas Rockstein to Margrete Strand-Rangnes, "Briefing on German Anti-MAI Campaign [Part II]," August 11, 1998, GTWP.

39. The Council of Canadians, "Action Alert on the Multilateral Agreement on Investment (MAI)," March 2, 1998, GTWP.

40. Tamoko Sakuma to ADHOC-L@SMPT, "News from NO to MAI Japan Campaign," September 17, 1998, GTWP.

41. Margrete Strand-Rangnes to Chantell Taylor, "FWD: Minutes from MAI Strategy Session 24/1 Amsterdam," July 15, 1998, GTWP.

42. Ministerial Statement on the Multilateral Agreement on Investment, OECD/SG/COM/NEWS(98)50, para. 3 (28 April 1998), quoted in Jonas Ebbesson, "Environmental Assessment of the OECD Multilateral Agreement on Investment," in *Environmental Assessment of Trade Agreements and Policy,* ed. Ole Kristian Fauchald and Mads Greaker (Copenhagen: TemaNord, 1998), 53.

43. Guy de Jonquières, "Network Guerrillas," *Financial Times,* April 30, 1998, 20.

44. Martin Khor to Those Interested in the MAI, "The Need to Oppose the Emergence of an MAI in the WTO," May 5, 1998, GTWP.

45. Margrete Strand-Rangnes to mai-not@essential.org, "Against the MAI: International Week of Action September 21–29," July 28, 1998, GTWP.

46. Catherine Lalumière and Jean-Pierre Landau, "Report on the Multilateral Agreement on Investment," September 1998, http://www.oocities.org/w_trouble_o/lumier.htm.

47. Charan Devereaux, Robert Z. Lawrence, and Michael D. Watkins, *Case Studies in US Trade Negotiation, Volume 1: Making the Rules* (Washington, DC: Institute for International Economics, 2006), 175.

48. U.S. Department of State Cable from SECSTATE WASHDC to All OECD Capitals, "Guidance on Multilateral Agreement on Investment Developments and Follow-Up in the OECD," DOC_NBR: 1998STATE210161, November 10, 1998, GTWP.

49. Barlow interview, August 18, 2016.

Chapter 21

1. Bill Gates, "Shaping the Future in Seattle," *New York Times,* November 29, 1999, A25.

2. Kathy Schwartz, "The Buildup," *SeattleMet,* October 19, 2009, https://www.seattlemet.com/articles/2009/10/19/wto-tenth-anniversary-1109.

3. Jonathan Rosenblum, "Building Organizing Capacity: The King County Labor Council," in *Central Labor Councils and the Revival of American Unionism: Organizing for Justice in Our Communities,* ed. Immanuel Ness and Stuart Eimer (Armonk, NY: M. E. Sharpe, 2001), 163–188.

4. Douglas Bevington, *The Rebirth of Environmentalism: Grassroots Activism from the Spotted Owl to the Polar Bear* (Washington, DC: Island, 2009), 41–155.

5. Greg Miller, "Internet Fueled Global Interest in Disruptions," *Los Angeles Times*, December 2, 1999.

6. Lori Wallach, interview by author, Washington, D.C., December 29, 2016.

7. Alesha Daughtrey, interview by April Eaton, August 17, 2000, transcript, WTO Oral History Project, Harry Bridges Center for Labor Studies, University of Washington, Seattle (hereafter OHP): 3.

8. Michael F. Dolan, "1/26," Organizer Notebook, November 12, 1998–March 15, 1999 (hereafter MDN). See also Margaret Levi and Gillian H. Murphy, "Coalitions of Contention: The Case of the WTO Protests in Seattle," *Political Studies* 54 (2006): 658–660.

9. "UNCTAD and WTO: A Common Goal in a Global Economy," October 7, 1996, TAD/INF/PR 9628, http://unctad.org/en/pages/PressReleaseArchive.aspx?Reference DocId=3607.

10. de Jonquières, "Network Guerrillas," 20.

11. Jamaica Confederation of Trade Unions to John Sweeney, August 14, 1998, Series 1, Subseries 1, Box 203, Folder 8, LEAPR.

12. Jan Hancock, *Environmental Human Rights: Power, Ethics, and Law* (New York: Routledge, 2019), 101. For more on the WTO's dispute resolution system, see Kati Kulovesi, *The WTO Dispute Settlement System: Challenges of the Environment, Legitimacy, and Fragmentation* (Alphen aan den Rijn, Netherlands: Kluwer Law International, 2011).

13. "CTC Working Group Meeting on the WTO Ministerial, 12:00–2:00 p.m.," February 12, 1999, GTWP.

14. Dan Seligman, interview with April Eaton, August 17, 2000, OHP: 5.

15. "CTC Working Group Meeting on the WTO Ministerial," GTWP.

16. "CTC Working Group Meeting on the WTO Ministerial," GTWP.

17. "CTC Working Group Meeting on the WTO Ministerial," GTWP.

18. Dolan, "1/25," November 12, 1998–March 15, 1999, MDN.

19. Lowell Turner and Richard W. Hurd, "Building Social Movement Unionism: The Transformation of the American Labor Movement," in *Rekindling the Movement: Labor's Quest for Relevance in the Twenty-First Century*, ed. Lowell Turner, Harry C. Katz, and Richard W. Hurd (Ithaca: ILR, 2001), 9–27.

20. Joe Uehlein, interview with the author, Takoma Park, MD, July 17, 2016.

21. Ron Judd, interview with Jeremy Simmer, undated, OHP: 6. See Robert L. Friedheim, *The Seattle General Strike*, centennial ed. (Seattle: University of Washington Press, 2018).

22. Andrew Battista, *The Revival of Labor-Liberalism* (Champaign: University of Illinois Press, 2008), 165–191.

23. John J. Sweeney to Members of the AFL-CIO Executive Committee, "WTO Ministerial Meeting in Seattle," July 26, 1999, Box 2, Folder 86, Seattle Ministerial Conference Protest Collection, 1993–2000, University of Washington–Seattle Libraries, Special Collections (hereafter SMCP); Susan Washington to Thea Lee and Greg Woodhead, "Re: Fwd: Labor Track of WTO Training," October 5, 1999, Box 2, Folder 86, SMPC.

24. Uehlein interview, July 17, 2016.

25. *AFL-CIO 1999 Convention Proceedings: 23rd Constitutional Convention, October 11–13, 1999, Los Angeles* (Washington, D.C.: American Federation of Labor–Congress of Industrial Organizations), 35.

26. Ace Saturay, interview with Jeremy Simer, May 4, 2000, OHP.

27. "WTO Ministerial Strategy Goals," undated, GTWP.

28. Fogarty, *States, Nonstate Actors, and Global Governance*, 146–149.

29. Paul Blustein, *Misadventures of the Most Favored Nations: Clashing Egos, Inflated Ambitions, and the Great Shambles of the World Trade System* (New York: PublicAffairs, 2009), 60–64.

30. Rhoda E. Howard-Hassman, *Can Globalization Promote Human Rights?* (University Park: Pennsylvania State University Press, 2010), 73; Amrita Narlikar,"The Politics of Participation: Decision-Making Processes and Developing Countries in the World Trade Organization," *Round Table: Commonwealth Journal of International Affairs* 91, no. 363 (2002): 171–185.

31. Sylvia Ostry, "The Multilateral Trading System," in *The Oxford Handbook of International Business*, ed. Alan M. Rugman and Thomas L. Brewer (Oxford: Oxford University Press, 2001), 249.

32. "Third World Network Gets G-77 Award," *Business Times (Malaysia)*, October 15, 1996, 3.

33. "WTO and the Third World: On a Catastrophic Course—An Interview with Martin Khor," *Multinational Monitor* 20, no. 10 (October/November 1999), http://www.multinationalmonitor.org/mm1999/101999/interview-khor.html.

34. Martin Khor, "Development: South Must Re-examine Trade, Investment Liberalization," *South-North Development Monitor* 45, no. 14 (September 23, 1999), http://www.chasque.net/frontpage/suns/trade/process/followup/1999/09230199.htm.

35. "Statement by His Excellency Clement J. Rohee, Minister of Foreign Affairs of Guyana and Chairman of the Group of 77, at the Opening Ceremony of the Ninth Ministerial Meeting of the Group of 77 Preparatory to UNCTAD-X," September 14–16, 1999, http://www.g77.org/Speeches/091499.html.

36. Wallach interview, August 9, 2016.

37. IATP, "Final Report from the Workshop on TRIPs 27.3(b) Organized by the South Centre and IATP," November 30, 1998, Box 4, Folder 68, SMCP.

38. "International Strategy," undated, GTWP.

Chapter 22

1. Mike Dolan, interview by Steven Pfaff and Gillian Murphy, November 10, 1999, OHP: 5.

2. Ryan Grim, *We've Got People: From Jesse Jackson to Alexandria Ocasio-Cortez, the End of Big Money, and the Rise of a Movement* (Washington, D.C.: Strong Arm, 2019).

3. Janet Thomas, *The Battle in Seattle: The Story Behind and Beyond the WTO Demonstrations* (Golden: Fulcrum, 2000), 111–122.

4. Dolan interview, November 10, 1999, OHP: 3.

5. Thomas, *Battle in Seattle*, 122; Dolan interview, November 10, 1999, OHP: 10.

6. Anne Slater, interview by Gillian Murphy, December 12, 2000, OHP: 4.

7. Dolan, "2/28," November 12, 1998–March 15, 1999, MDN.

8. Thomas, *Battle in Seattle*, 124.

9. Dolan interview, November 10, 1999, OHP: 4; Lydia Cabasco, interview by Monica Gosh, August 15, 2000: 5, OHP; Bill Aal, interview by Miguel Bocanegra, November 11, 2000, OHP: 6; Thomas, *Battle in Seattle*, 124.

10. "Seattle in Focus: A Profile from Census 2000," Brookings Institution, November 1, 2003, https://www.brookings.edu/research/seattle-in-focus-a-profile-from-census-2000/.

11. Saturay interview, May 4, 2000, OHP; Denise Cooper, interview by Steve Pfaff, April 14, 2000, OHP: 6–7.

12. Cabasco interview, August 15, 2000, OHP: 6.

13. Monica Ghosh, "Inside WTO Dissent: The Experiences of LELO and CCEJ," March 3, 2001, http://citeseerx.ist.psu.edu/viewdoc/download?doi=10.1.1.561.3192&rep=rep1&type=pdf.

14. Cabasco interview, August 15, 2000, OHP: 4.

15. Lydia Cabasco to A. Jarman, "Re: WTO Curriculum," July 30, 1999, Box 2, Folder 27, Accession No. 5177-003, World Trade Organization, 1999, SMCP.

16. Juan Bocanegra and Cindy Domingo, interview by Monica Ghosh, August 18, 2000, OHP: 3.

17. Saturay interview, May 4, 2000, OHP: 5.

18. Regino Martinez, interview by Monica Ghosh, April 28, 2000, OHP: 3. See also the excellent article, Elizabeth Betita Martínez, "Where Was the Color in Seattle? Looking for Good Reasons Why the Great Battle Was So White," *Colorlines*, March 10, 2000, http://www.colorlines.com/articles/where-was-color-seattlelooking-reasons-why-great-battle-was-so-white.

19. Katie Renz, "People Power: An Interview with David Solnit," *Mother Jones*, March 22, 2005.

20. David Solnit, interview with Jeremy Simer, March 23, 2000, OHP: 1–4.

21. Lee Hall, "Global Exchange" in *Encyclopedia of Activism and Social Justice*, ed. Gary L. Anderson and Kathryn Herr (London: Sage, 2007), 622; Rainforest Action Network, *Greatest Hits 1985–2010* (San Francisco: Rainforest Action Network, 2010). On Greenpeace, see Frank Zelko, *Make It a Green Peace: The Rise of Countercultural Environmentalism* (Oxford: Oxford University Press, 2013).

22. Richard Worf, "A Ruckus Among Us," *Harvard International Review* 23, no. 3 (Fall 2001): 6.

23. Chris Dixon, "Five Days in Seattle: A View from the Ground," in Solnit and Solnit, *Battle of the Story of the Battle of Seattle*, 74–78. For more on the Zapatistas' global influences and People's Global Action, see Ruth Reitan, *Global Activism* (London: Routledge, 2007), 188–230; Alex Khasnabish, *Zapatismo Beyond Borders: New Imaginations of Political Possibility* (Toronto: University of Toronto Press, 2008).

24. "Nov 30 Shut Down the WTO Mass Nonviolent Direct Action Info," undated, Box 1, Folder 1, SMCP.

25. Mark Van Putten, "Fix Trade, Don't Trash It," *Seattle Times*, November 12, 1999.

26. Bob Gorman, interview with Jeremy Simer, undated, OHP: 9.

27. Dolan interview, July 17, 2015.

28. Dolan, "9/5," 6/28–10/13, 1999, MDN.

29. Mike Dolan to multiple recipients of list TW-LIST, "WTO and the Resolve of Labor," September 2, 1999, Box 3, Folder 2, SMCP.

30. Mike Dolan, interview with Jeremy Simmer, March 3, 2000, OHP: 5.

31. Dolan interview, July 17, 2015.

32. Levi and Murphy, "Coalitions of Contention," 655.

33. People for Fair Trade/Network Opposed to WTO, "WTO Calendar of Events," November 2, 1999, GTWP.

34. "Festival of Impotence or Revolt Now!" *Black-Clad Messenger* 6 (1999): 7.

35. *Breaking the Spell*, directed by CrimethInc Ex-Workers Collective, 1999, https://crimethinc.com/videos/breaking-the-spell. See also Lesley J. Wood, *Direct Action, Deliberation, and Diffusion: Collective Action After the WTO Protests in Seattle* (Cambridge: Cambridge University Press, 2012), 34–36.

36. Francis Dupuis-Déri, "The Black Blocs Ten Years After Seattle: Anarchism, Direct Action, and Deliberative Practices," *Journal for the Study of Radicalism* 4, no. 2 (2010): 45–82; Thompson, *Black Bloc, White Riot*.

Chapter 23

1. National Security Division Domestic Terrorism/Counterterrorism Planning Section, Special Events Management Unit Rm 11741 to National Security, "SEATRADE 99, CT Preparedness—Special Events (DT)," February 25, 1999, in World Trade Organization Ministerial Seattle 12/99, FOIPA Request No 1202765-000 (hereafter FBIF), https://cdn.muckrock.com/foia_files/3-28-13_mr2073_RES.pdf.

2. Seattle to National Security, "Re: 300A-SE-81593," April 26, 1999, FBIF.

3. "Summary of Anti-WTO Activities by Group," November 5, 1999, FBIF.

4. John Dumbrell, *Clinton's Foreign Policy: Between the Bushes, 1992–2000* (New York: Routledge, 2009), 57.

5. Richard M. Samans to Jeffrey A. Shesol, "Speech Material," September 28, 1999, CDL, https://clinton.presidentiallibraries.us/items/show/12140. See Yunpeng Zhu and Hal Hill, eds., *The Social Impact of the Asian Financial Crisis* (Cheltenham, UK: Edward Elgar, 2001); Shalendra D. Sharma, *The Asian Financial Crisis: Crisis, Reform, and Recovery* (Manchester: Manchester University Press, 2003).

6. "Roundtable Discussion with Environmental Leaders," undated, CDL, https://clinton.presidentiallibraries.us/items/show/12234.

7. "The Clinton Administration Agenda for Seattle: Putting a Human Face on the Global Economy," November 29, 1999, CDL, https://clinton.presidentiallibraries.us/items/show/12236.

8. Mike Moore, *A World Without Walls: Freedom, Development, Free Trade and Global Governance* (Cambridge: Cambridge University Press, 2003), 96–97.

9. Jeffrey J. Schott, ed., *The WTO After Seattle* (Washington, DC: Institute for International Economics, 2000).

10. Barshefsky interview, March 2, 2005, CPHP.

11. Mark Suzman, "The First Lady of Trade," *Financial Times*, November 27, 1999, 11.

12. Ritchie, "Peace and International Systems."

13. Alesha Daughtrey to adam@aseed.antenna.nl, etc., "RE: Minutes for Student-WTO Conference Call Monday, July 26, 1999," August 2, 1999, Box 2, Folder 27, SMCP.

14. David Postman, "Environmentalists Scale Crane by I-5—They Prepare Anti-WTO Banner," *Seattle Times*, November 29, 1999.

15. "Day One: November 29, 1999," WTO History Project Timeline, http://depts .washington.edu/wtohist/day1.htm (hereafter HPT).

16. John C. Berg, *Teamsters and Turtles? U.S. Progressive Political Movements in the 21st Century* (Lanham, MD: Rowman & Littlefield, 2003), 1.

17. "Day One: November 29, 1999," HPT.

18. Paul Burks, "My Three Days in Seattle: Deep Ecumenism Meets the WTO," *Earth Light Library: The Magazine of Spiritual Energy*, undated, https://www.earthlight.org /essay_pburks.html.

19. *Trade Off*, directed by Shayna Mercer, Wright Angle Media, 2000.

20. *The Tale of John WTO # 199055676 and My Week in Seattle*, Box 6, Folder 31, SMCP.

21. Rebecka Tilsen, *We Flood Through: My Personal Account, "Prose and Poetry" Shutting Down the World Trade Organization Ministerial Meeting: Seattle Nov. 30th–Dec 3rd* (1999), Box 6, Folder 37, SMCP.

22. WTO Accountability Review Committee, *Preparations and Planning Panel 2*, August 24, 2000, 19–20, http://www.seattle.gov/archive/wtocommittee/panel2final.pdf.

23. WTO Accountability Review Committee, *Preparations and Planning Panel 3* (August 24, 2000), 15, http://www.seattle.gov/archive/wtocommittee/panel3final.pdf.

24. Lynda V. Mapes, "Five Days That Jolted Seattle," *Seattle Times*, November 29, 2009, http://www.seattletimes.com/seattle-news/five-days-that-jolted-seattle/.

25. "Day Two, November 30, 1999," HPT.

26. John Charlton, "Talking Seattle," *International Socialism* 2, no. 86 (Spring 2000), https://www.marxists.org/history/etol/writers/charlton/2000/xx/seattle.htm.

27. Bocanegra and Domingo interview, August 18, 2000, OHP: 8.

28. "Four Days in Seattle," KIRO 7 Special Report, YouTube video, https://www .youtube.com/watch?v=pFamvR9CpYw.

29. Mike Moore, "Seattle Conference Doomed to Succeed," November 30, 1999, WTO News: Speeches: DG Mike Moore, https://www.wto.org/english/news_e/spmm_e /spmm16_e.htm.

30. Paul Hawken, "Skeleton Woman Visits Seattle," in *Globalize This! The Battle Against the World Trade Organization and Corporate Rule*, ed. Kevin Danaher and Roger Burbach (Monroe, ME: Common Courage, 2000), 17.

31. Wallach interview, August 9, 2016.

32. Vinnie O'Brien, interview by Jaelle Dragomir, November 21, 2000, OHP: 2.

33. AFL-CIO, "WTO Rally & March, Nov. 30 in Seattle, Washington," undated, Box 1, Folder 59, SMCP.

34. Patrick F. Gillham and Gary T. Marx, "Complexity and Irony in Policing and Protesting: The World Trade Organization in Seattle," *Social Justice* 27, no. 2 (2000): 220.

35. "Day Two: November 30, 1999," HPT.

36. Thomas, *Battle in Seattle*, 46; "N30 Black Bloc Communique by ACME Collective, 10:48am Sat Dec 4 '99," quoted in scott@prisonactivist.org to abodyke@earthlink .net, "Whose Violence in Seattle," December 4, 1999, Box 6, Folder 34, SMCP.

37. "Four Days in Seattle," KIRO 7.

38. Dolan, November 10, 1999, OHP: 5.

39. Statement of Mike Dolan, Lead Organizer for Public Citizen, "Police Should Reinstate Permits for National Consumer, Environmental, Labor Groups' Peaceful Demonstrations—Failure to Initially Arrest Handful of Roaming Vandals Set Scene for Police Escalation, Attacks on Peaceful Protestors," November 30, 1999, GTWP.

40. Naím, "Lori's War," 49.

41. Barbara Dean, "To Friends of Working People," undated, Box 6, Folder 28, SMCP.

42. "Day One: November 29, 1999," HPT.

Chapter 24

1. Bill Clinton, "International Trade Speech," C-SPAN, video, December 1, 1999, https://www.c-span.org/video/?153935-1/international-trade-speech.

2. Steven Greenhouse, "Seattle Protest Could Have Lasting Influence on Trade," *New York Times*, December 6, 1999.

3. Steven Greenhouse and Joseph Kahn, "U.S. Effort to Add Labor Standards to Agenda Fails," *New York Times*, December 3, 1999, A1.

4. "Exhibit D: Local Proclamation of Civil Emergency Order Number 3 City of Seattle," December 1, 1999, http://www.seattle.gov/Documents/Departments/CityArchive /DDL/WTO/1999Dec6.htm.

5. "Day Three: December 1, 1999," HPT.

6. *This Is What Democracy Looks Like*, directed by Jill Friedberg and Rick Rowley, Independent Media Center and Big Noise Films, 2000.

7. "Four Days in Seattle," KIRO 7.

8. "Women's EDGE," in *Gender, Development, and Trade*, ed. Maree Keating (Oxford: Oxfam GB, 2004), 95.

9. "The WTO: Women Missing in Action," *Notes from the EDGE* 2, no. 3 (April-May 1999), GTWP.

10. Marceline White to Margrete Strand-Rangnes, mriley@coco.org, aspieldoch@ coco.org, rcaplan@icg.org, wb50years@igc.org, July 8, 1999, Box 3, Folder 46, SMCP.

11. Michelle Sforza to Margrete Strand-Rangnes, "Women," October 5, 1999, Box 4, Folder 27, SMCP.

12. "Women Democracy/Sovereignty Development," December 1, 1999, GTWP. For a critical look at gender politics and the protests, see Catherine Eschle, "'Skeleton Women':

Feminism and the Antiglobalization Movement," *Signs: Journal of Women in Culture and Society* 30, no. 3 (Spring 2005): 1741–1769.

13. Danaher and Mark, *Insurrection*, 284; "Four Days in Seattle," KIRO 7.

14. Wallach interview, August 9, 2016.

15. Richard Bernal, "Sleepless in Seattle: The WTO Ministerial of November 1999," *Social and Economic* Studies 48, no. 3 (1999): 71.

16. Martin Khor, "Letter Sent by 11 Countries to WTO Chair Criticising Green Room Process," *News from Geneva*, November 15, 1999, https://www.globalpolicy.org /component/content/article/209/43577.html. On the green rooms, see Ken Jones, "Green Room Politics and the WTO's Crisis of Representation," *Progress in Development Studies* 9, no. 4 (2009): 349–357.

17. Deepak Gopinath, "Our Man in Seattle," *Institutional Investor* 25, no. 2 (February 2000).

18. Ritchie interview, February 17, 2016.

19. Agnes Sinai, "Seattle Turning Point: The Day the South Cut Up Rough," *Le Monde Diplomatique*, January 2000.

20. Chakravarthi Raghavan, "After Seattle, World Trade System Faces Uncertain Future," *Review of International Political Economy* 7, no. 3 (Autumn 2000): 496.

21. Quoted in "Africa: Seattle Aftermath, 12/06/99," University of Pennsylvania, African Studies Center, https://www.africa.upenn.edu/Urgent_Action/apic_12699.html.

22. Aileen Kwa, "From Crisis to Victory for Developing Countries," *Focus on Trade* 42 (December 1999), https://www.iatp.org/sites/default/files/From_Crisis_to_Victory _for_Developing_Countrie.htm.

23. Blustein, *Misadventures of the Most Favored Nations*, 80.

24. Blustein, *Misadventures of the Most Favored Nations*, 80–81.

25. *Public Citizen*, 231.

26. Friedberg and Rowley, *This Is What Democracy Looks Like*.

27. Washington ACLU, *Out of Control: Seattle's Flawed Response to Protests Against the World Trade Organization—A Special Report*, June 2000.

28. WTO Director-General Mike Moore, "It Is Vital to Maintain and Consolidate What Has Already Been Achieved," World Trade Organization press release, December 7, 1999, https://www.wto.org/english/thewto_e/minist_e/min99_e/english/press_e/pres160 _e.htm; "Remarks of Ambassador Charlene Barshefsky, Closing Plenary," December 3, 1999, *India and the WTO: A Monthly Newsletter of the Ministry of Commerce and Industry* 8, nos. 1–2 (November–December 1999), https://commerce.gov.in/publications/newsletter _nov_dec99.htm.

29. House Committee on Ways and Means, *Outcome of the World Trade Organization Ministerial in Seattle*, 106th Cong., 2nd sess., 2000, 96.

30. Global Business Forum, "Meeting Summaries: Conference on the World Trade Organization, Geneva, Switzerland, October 18–19, 2000," undated, IDL, https://www .industrydocumentslibrary.ucsf.edu/tobacco/docs/#id=ztwn0206.

31. Bruce Silverglade to the TACD Food Working Group, April 5, 2000, GTWP.

32. Friedberg and Rowley, *This Is What Democracy Looks Like*. On Hayden, see Tom Hayden, *Writings for a Democratic Society: The Tom Hayden Reader* (San Francisco: City Lights, 2008).

33. Rebecca Solnit, *Hope in the Dark: Untold Histories, Wild Possibilities*, 3rd ed. (Chicago: Haymarket, 2016), 50.

34. Seligman interview, August 17, 2000, OHP: 1.

Coda

1. William Finnegan, "After Seattle: Anarchists Get Organized," *New Yorker*, April 17, 2000.

2. Mario Diani and and Ivano Bison, "Organizations, Coalitions, and Movements," *Theory and Society* 33, no. 3/4 (June–August 2004): 283–284; Fox, "Coalitions and Networks"; Gemma Edwards, *Social Movements and Protest* (Cambridge: Cambridge University Press, 2014).

3. I use the term *global justice movement* in this chapter, as it was the most common phrase used by activists themselves. See Heather Gautney, *Protest and Organization in the Alternative Globalization Era: NGOs, Social Movements, and Political Parties* (New York: Palgrave Macmillan, 2010), 3–4.

4. Naomi Klein, "The Vision Thing," *Nation*, July 10, 2000, 19. On Klein, see Larissa MacFarquhar, "Outside Agitator: Naomi Klein and the New New Left," *New Yorker*, December 1, 2008.

5. Stephanie Gillmore and Sara Evans, eds., *Feminist Coalitions: Historical Perspectives on Second-Wave Feminism in the United States* (Urbana: University of Illinois Press, 2008); Charles Payne, *I've Got the Light of Freedom: The Organizing Tradition and the Mississippi Freedom Struggle* (Berkeley: University of California Press, 1995).

6. Nina Esperanza Serrianne, *America in the Nineties* (Syracuse: Syracuse University Press, 2015), 103.

7. Joseph E. Stiglitz, *The Roaring Nineties: A New History of the World's Most Prosperous Decade* (New York: W. W. Norton, 2003).

8. Klein, *No Logo*, xviii.

9. *Fight Club*, directed by David Fincher, screenplay by Jim Uhls, Fox 2000 Pictures, 1999.

10. Klein, *No Logo*, 4; John McAllister Ulrich and Andrea L. Harris, eds., *GenXegesis: Essays on "Alternative" Youth (Sub)Culture* (Madison: University of Wisconsin Press, 2003).

11. Steve Kornacki, *The Red and the Blue: The 1990s and the Birth of Political Tribalism* (New York: HarperCollins, 2018).

12. "Statement of Ralph Nader Announcing His Candidacy for the Green Party's Nomination for President, February 21, 2000," in *The Ralph Nader Reader* (New York: Seven Stories, 2000), 11.

13. Jeffrey M. Jones, "The Nader Factor," *Gallup News Service*, February 26, 2004, https://news.gallup.com/poll/10798/nader-factor.aspx.

14. Deborah B. Gould, *Moving Politics: Emotion and ACT UP's Fight Against AIDS* (Chicago: University of Chicago Press, 2009).

15. Lisa Levenstein, *They Didn't See Us Coming: The Hidden History of Feminism in the Nineties* (New York: Basic, 2020), 3. See also Elizabeth Martínez, "Whatever Happened to the Chicano Movement?" in *De Colores Means All of Us: Latina Views for a Multi-Colored Century* (London: Verso, 2017), 198–204.

16. Jennifer Hyland Wang, "'A Struggle of Contending Stories': Race, Gender, and Political Memory in 'Forrest Gump,'" *Cinema Journal* 39, no. 3 (Spring 2000): 92–115.

17. Radiohead, "The Bends," on *The Bends*, Parlophone Records, 1995. See Alex Ross, "The Searchers: Radiohead's Unquiet Revolution," *New Yorker*, August 13, 2001.

18. Derek, "Hello Friends," undated, Box 6, Folder 29, SMCP.

19. Klein, "Vision Thing," 20–21.

20. Vinci Daro, "The Edge Effects of Alter-Globalization Protests: An Ethnographic Approach to Summit Hopping in the Post-Seattle Period," in Juris and Khasnabish, *Insurgent Encounters*, 171–199.

21. Vinci E. F. Daro, "Edge Effects of Global Summit Hopping in the Post-Seattle Period, 2000–2005" (PhD diss., University of North Carolina, Chapel Hill, 2009), 46–49.

22. Payal Parekh, "Fighting the FTAA: Quebec City, 2001," *Thistle* 13, no. 4 (June–July 2001), http://web.mit.edu/thistle/www/v13/4/quebec.html.

23. Maxime Lessard-Lachane and Glen Norcliffe, "To Storm the Citadel: Geographies of Protest at the Summit of the Americas in Québec City, April 2001," *Annals of the Association of American Geographers* 103, no. 1 (2013): 180–194.

24. Daro, "Edge Effects of Global Summit Hopping."

25. Jeremy Brecher, Tim Costello, and Brendan Smith, *Globalization from Below: The Power of Solidarity* (Cornwall: Stone Soup, 2000), 27–28.

26. Costas Panayotakis, "On the Self-Understanding of the 'Anti-Globalization' Movement: A View from Genoa," *Capitalism, Nature, Socialism* 12, no. 4 (December 2001): 95–102.

27. "Educated Protestors Plan Next 'Seattle,'" *Washington Times*, April 16, 2001, https://www.washingtontimes.com/news/2001/apr/16/20010416-022035-7485r/.

28. Eric Alterman, "The New Republic Was in Trouble Long Before Chris Hughes Bought It," *American Prospect*, June 16, 2007, https://prospect.org/culture/new-republic-trouble-long-chris-hughes-bought/.

29. Joseph Stiglitz, "The Insider," *New Republic*, April 17 and 24, 2000, 58.

30. Thomas L. Friedman, "Parsing the Protests," *New York Times*, April 14, 2000, A31.

31. Daro, "Edge Effects of Global Summit Hopping," x.

32. Martínez, "Where Was the Color in Seattle?"; Catalyst Project, "Our History," https://collectiveliberation.org/our-organization/193-2/; Mark R. Warren, *Fire in the Heart: How White Activists Embrace Racial Justice* (Oxford: Oxford University Press, 2010), 46.

33. Daniel Jaffee, *Brewing Justice: Fair Trade Coffee, Sustainability, and Survival*, 2nd ed. (Berkeley: University of California Press, 2014).

34. Liza Featherstone, "The New Student Movement," *Nation,* May 15, 2000, 11.

35. Kitty Krupat, "Rethinking the Sweatshop: A Conversation About United Students Against Sweatshops (USAS) with Charles Eaton, Marion Traub-Werner, and Evelyn Zepeda," *International Labor and Working Class History* 61 (Spring 2002): 112.

36. "Kathie Lee Goes on Defensive," *Multinational Monitor* 20, no. 9 (September 1999), http://multinationalmonitor.org/mm1999/99sept/front1.html.

37. Williams, *Strategizing Against Sweatshops.*

38. Nate Blakeslee, "How to Tell If You're in a Movement," *Texas Observer*, May 12, 2000, https://www.texasobserver.org/895-how-to-tell-if-youre-in-a-movement/.

39. "More Protests at Quebec Summit," *ABC News*, April 21, 2001, https://abcnews.go.com/International/story?id=81199&page=1.

40. "Lori Wallach," *Commanding Heights*, pbs.org, https://www.pbs.org/wgbh/commandingheights/shared/minitext/int_loriwallach.html.

41. Frank Ahrens, "For Activists Today, It's Marks, Not Marx," *Washington Post*, April 20, 2001.

42. Blakeslee, "How to Tell If You're in a Movement."

43. Chris Crass, "Beyond the Whiteness—Global Capitalism and White Supremacy: Thoughts on Movement Building and Anti-Racist Organizing," Colours of Resistance Archive, undated, http://www.coloursofresistance.org/492/beyond-the-whiteness-global-capitalism-and-white-supremacy-thoughts-on-movement-building-and-anti-racist-organizing/.

44. Ryan Lizza, "Silent Partner," *New Republic*, January 10, 2000. In my research, I found no hard evidence of any financial connection. See http://home.alphalink.com.au/~radnat/debenoist/alain4.html for a compilation of accusations and responses.

45. See the *Left Business Observer*'s "LBO-Talk Archives," http://mailman.lbo-talk.org/2000/.

46. Marc Cooper, "Less Bank—More World," *LA Weekly*, April 21, 2000, https://www.iatp.org/news/less-bank-more-world.

47. *1999–2000 National Business Agenda: Addressing Policy Priorities of American Business 106th Congress* (Washington, DC: U.S. Chamber of Commerce, 1999), 72, IDL, https://www.industrydocumentslibrary.ucsf.edu/tobacco/docs/#id=gmvv0016.

48. "Campaign Plan to Stop the Push for Permanent MFN for China While Strategically Jamming Up CBI/Africa NAFTA Expansion," undated, GTWP.

49. Dolan interview, July 17, 2015; John Cavanagh, Bama Athreya, and Sarah Anderson, "Don't Strengthen the WTO by Admitting China," *Foreign Policy in Focus*, May 1, 2000, https://fpif.org/dont_strengthen_the_wto_by_admitting_china/; Walden Bello, "Dangerous Liaisons: Progressives, the Right, and the Anti-China Trade Campaign," *Food First Backgrounder* 6, no. 1 (Spring 2000): 1.

50. Devereaux, Lawrence, and Watkins, *Case Studies in US Trade Negotiations, Vol. 1*, 241–299.

51. "Launching a 2-Year 'Trade Democracy' Offensive for Long Term Victory on Globalization-Trade," undated, GTWP.

52. Justin R. Pierce and Peter K. Schott, "The Surprisingly Swift Decline of US Manufacturing Employment," *American Economic Review* 106, no. 7 (July 2016): 1632–1662.

53. "Whose Trade?" *Nation*, December 6, 1999, 13.

54. "H.R.772—HOPE for Africa Act, 106th Congress (1999–2000), Congress.gov, https://www.congress.gov/bill/106th-congress/house-bill/772/text; William G. Jones, "Congress and Africa's Constituency: The Development of the African Growth and Opportunity Act and the Intersection of African American and Business Interests," in *African Americans in Global Affairs: Contemporary Perspectives*, ed. Michael L. Clemons (Lebanon, NH: Northeastern University Press, 2010), 93–118.

55. 50 Years Is Enough, "September 2001 Mobilization," March 22, 2001, https://corpwatch.org/article/september-2001-mobilization.

56. AFL-CIO, "A Call to Action to Globalize Justice," undated, GTWP.

57. Patrick F. Gillham and Bob Edwards, "Legitimacy Management, Preservation of Exchange Relationships, and the Dissolution of the Mobilization for Global Justice Coalition," *Social Problems* 58, no. 3 (2011): 442.

58. Edward Alden and Julia Levy, "Washington Marshals Police Force to Meet a Protest Army," *Financial Times*, August 18, 2001, 7.

59. Lane Windham, interview with the author, July 27, 2016, Takoma Park, Maryland.

60. Dolan, "9/12," September 4, 2001–December 17, 2001, MDN.

61. Faye Bowers and Scott Peterson, "Who Could Have Done It? A Very Short List," *Christian Science Monitor*, September 12, 2001, https://www.csmonitor.com/2001/0912/p1s2-wogi.html.

62. George W. Bush, "Address Before a Joint Session of the Congress on the State of the Union," January 29, 2002, APP, http://www.presidency.ucsb.edu/ws/?pid=29644.

63. Peter Hart, "Covering the 'Fifth Column,'" *Fairness and Accuracy in Reporting*, November 1, 2001, https://fair.org/extra/covering-the-fifth-column/.

Conclusion

1. Mark Ritchie, "People Are the Only Solution to Terror," Nautilus Institute, September 12, 2001, https://nautilus.org/napsnet/special-policy-forum-911/people-are-the-only-solution-to-terror/.

2. Mike Boyer, "Where Have All the Anti-Globalization Activists Gone?" *Foreign Policy*, June 7, 2007, https://foreignpolicy.com/2007/06/07/where-have-all-the-anti-globalization-activists-gone/.

3. Joel Wainwright and Rafael Ortiz, "The Battles in Miami: The Fall of the FTAA/ALCA and the Promise of Transnational Movements," *Environment and Planning D: Society and Space* 24 (2006): 349–366.

4. Mimi Dwyer, "Where Did the Anti-Globalization Movement Go?" *New Republic,* October 25, 2013, https://newrepublic.com/article/115360/wto-protests-why-have-they -gotten-smaller.

5. Shapiro, *Fast Track,* 29–43; Mark B. Rosenberg and Luis G. Solis, *The United States and Central America: Geopolitical Realities and Regional Fragility* (New York: Taylor & Francis, 2007), 83–94.

6. Blustein, *Misadventures of the Most Favored Nations,* 109–130.

7. Reitan, *Global Activism,* 108–148.

8. Boaventura de Sousa Santos, *The Rise of the Global Left: The World Social Forum and Beyond* (London: Zed, 2013); Janet M. Conway, *Edges of Global Justice: The World Social Forum and Its "Others"* (New York: Routledge, 2013).

9. Larry Elliott, Charlotte Denny, and David Munk, "Blow to World Economy as Trade Talks Collapse," *Guardian,* September 15, 2003, https://www.theguardian.com /world/2003/sep/15/business.politics.

10. "The WTO Under Fire," *Economist,* September 18, 2003, http://www.economist .com/node/2071855; Jeremy Smith, "WTO Mood at Cancun Worsened by NGOs—EU's Fischler," *AlertNet,* September 19, 2003, https://www.globalpolicy.org/component /content/article/177/31592.html.

11. Prashad, *Poorer Nations,* 257; Michal Parizek, *Negotiations in the World Trade Organization: Design and Performance* (New York: Routledge, 2020).

12. On the "Pink Tide," see the Winter 2019 special edition of *Dissent* magazine.

13. Kevin Granville, "What Is TPP? Behind the Trade Deal That Died," *New York Times,* January 23, 2017, https://www.nytimes.com/interactive/2016/business/tpp-explained -what-is-trans-pacific-partnership.html.

14. Nicole Gaudiano, "Bernie Sanders Pledges to Rewrite 'Disastrous Trade Deals," *USA Today,* March 31, 2016, https://www.usatoday.com/story/news/politics/onpolitics /2016/03/31/bernie-sanders-pledges-rewrite-disastrous-trade-deals/82473012/.

15. Zeke J. Miller, "Hillary Clinton Haunted by Past Support for Trade Deals," *Time,* July 27, 2016, https://time.com/4426483/dnc-hillary-clinton-trans-pacific-partnership/.

16. Patrick Gillespie, "Trump Hammers America's 'Worst Trade Deal,'" *CNNMoney,* September 27, 2016, https://money.cnn.com/2016/09/27/news/economy/donald-trump -nafta-hillary-clinton-debate/.

17. David Karpf, *The MoveOn Effect: The Unexpected Transformation of American Political Advocacy* (Oxford: Oxford University Press, 2012); Keeanga-Yamahtta Taylor, *From #BlackLivesMatter to Black Liberation* (Chicago: Haymarket, 2016); McAlevey, *No Shortcuts*; Doug Henwood, "The Socialist Network," *New Republic,* May 16, 2019, https://newrepublic.com/article/153768/inside-democratic-socialists-america -struggle-political-mainstream; Laura Wides-Muñoz, *The Making of a Dream: How a Group of Young Undocumented Immigrants Helped Change What It Means to Be American* (New York: HarperCollins, 2018); Brandon B. Derman, *Struggles for Climate Justice: Uneven Geographies and the Politics of Connection* (Cham, Switzerland: Springer Nature, 2020).

18. Brandon Wu, "Did Warsaw Conference Put World on Track Towards 'New Global Climate Regime'?" *PBS NewsHour,* interview by Judy Woodruff, November 27, 2013, http://www.pbs.org/newshour/bb/environment-july-dec13-climatechange_11-27/.

19. "Movement Ecology," Ayni Institute, https://ayni.institute/movementecology/; Benjamin Case, "Social Movement Ecology and Its Implications: Unpacking the Natural Metaphor," *Berkeley Journal of Sociology* 61 (2017): 76-84.

20. Solnit, *Hope in the Dark*, 48.

ACKNOWLEDGMENTS

Just as no campaign is a solo affair, writing a book is a definitively collaborative process. And I had a lot of compatriots in this effort.

I am grateful for the financial support provided by the Georgetown University History Department, the Rockefeller Brothers Fund, and the Cosmos Club. These funds allowed me to visit archives and benefit from the tremendous staffs at the Bancroft Library, the Minnesota Historical Society, the Rockefeller Archive Center, the Arthur and Elizabeth Schlesinger Library on the History of Women in America, the Wisconsin Historical Society, the Library of Congress, and the Special Collections at George Washington University, American University, and the University of Washington.

Georgetown University proved a wonderful launch point for learning to be a teacher and scholar, with support from both my fellow graduate students and the faculty. In particular, thanks are due to Michael Kazin and Joseph McCartin. Both, in their own ways, are exemplars of engaged scholars. Throughout this process, Michael Kazin, with a single, sometimes puckish comment, could always point out fallacies in my thinking and generate fresh thoughts and approaches. Joseph McCartin's sage advice always came in the most reassuring manner imaginable. And I thank Joe further for affirming my desire, at a key early moment, to expand the scope of this book.

At Harvard, I am thankful to Lauren Kaminsky, Jenni Brady, and others for bringing me onboard at the History and Literature concentration. Two colleagues, Angela Allan and Duncan White, deserve particular praise for helping me map out the book, write it, and eat too much ice cream while doing so. Special thanks also to Mike D'Allesandro, Franny Sullivan, Genevieve Clutario, and the wonderful students I met and discussed my research with, especially Nathan Cummings, Kristine Guillaume, and Adrian Horton.

Cambridge is not a bad place to make scholarly connections. My old friend Alex Green and I enjoyed many walks and Indian buffets, where he proffered his fantastic insights on what makes a good book. I benefited immensely from many conversations with the brilliant Megan Black. Quinn Slobodian greatly sharpened my thinking about neoliberalism, Lily Geismer refined my under-standing of U.S. liberalism, Priya Lal helped me think about global politics, and I always enjoyed talking transnational activism with Katherine Marino. I've been fortunate to finish this project while teaching at Colorado College, and thanks goes to all my History Department colleagues, as well as John Gould, Najnin Islam, Eric Popkin, Pallavi Sriram, and Rui Zhou.

When I began my graduate program, an older student urged us to make friends with fellow academics because "your friends aren't going to be inter-ested in what you do." Thankfully, in my case, that advice was irrelevant. I have benefited from conversations with friends, many of whom are involved in one form of activism or another. In particular, I want to thank Judah Ariel, Mehrun Etebari, Amy Faulring, Deen Freelon, Sarah Heydemann, Rob Jackel, Vicki Kaplan, Corey Hope Leaffer, Lisa Leombruni, Seth D. Michaels, Judy Nelson, David Pihl, Josh Rosenthal, Kate Sheppard, Michael Sherrard, Scott Spicer, and Andrew Tirrell. Special thanks to Evin Isaacson for housing me in two different cities and for her sharp and generous feedback.

I'm also especially grateful to Ben Brandzel, Jessica Champagne, Michelle Dixon, Deepa Gupta, Andrew Slack, Taren Stinebrickner-Kaufman, and Max Toth, all exemplary practitioners of internationalist activism, for sharing their thoughts and experiences with me. Brandon Wu and Mary Small went ab-surdly beyond the call of duty as friends, from housing and feeding me in their apartment in Minneapolis for weeks while also providing their incredible in-sights, born of study and on-the-ground experience, on every topic in this book.

I also have made some wonderful friends in the academy whose questions and thoughts have enriched this work. First, I owe much to two professors from my undergraduate years—Eva Thorne and David Cunningham—whose teach-ing inspired me to pursue the topics in this book and a scholarly life. In addi-tion, my thanks to David Ekbladh, Jonathan Fox, Daniel Immerwahr, Sheyda Jahanbani, Paul Kramer, Lisa Levenstein, Stephen Macekura, Simon Toner, Kelsey Walker, and Lane Windham. I am also grateful to folks in Madison who housed, entertained, and enlightened me across multiple research trips: Gen-eviève Dorais, Elena Clare McGrath, Debbie Sharnak, and Naomi Williams. Special thanks also to Stephen Pitti as well as the two anonymous reviewers who provided helpful critiques and suggestions on earlier drafts of this work. And my deepest appreciation to Erik Loomis, who graciously read a late draft of the full manuscript, offering excellent questions and critiques.

For so many reasons, this book would not exist without my former boss at Public Citizen, Lori Wallach, from whom I have learned so much. Years ago, I took on the task of trying to organize the old files of Global Trade Watch. Little did I know how important that time would be or that Lori would one day let me loose to use this invaluable archive. In addition, I am grateful for the wisdom and friendship of a number of former Public Citizen staff members, especially Timi Gerson, Saerom Park, James Ploeser, Chris Slevin, Todd Tucker, and (again) Brandon Wu. Moreover, this book would not be possible without the generosity of many people who graced me with their time: Sarah Anderson, Maude Barlow, David Bonior, Anwar Fazal, Karen Hansen-Kuhn, Carlos Heredia, Doug Johnson, Leah Margulies, Manuel Pérez-Rocha, Mark Ritchie, Margrete Strand-Rangnes, Joe Uehlein, Howard Wachtel, Lori Wallach, Henry Waxman, and Lane Windham. Special thanks to John Cavanagh, who asked wonderful questions, agreed to multiple interviews, and allowed me to rummage through his personal papers, and to Mike Dolan for letting me borrow his personal notebooks and for the all-day epic road trip/oral history.

It's been a long time since I first sat down with my editor, Bob Lockhart, at a meeting of the American Historical Association to discuss an early version of this book. Bob has been a wonderful partner in all of this. From logistics to substance, he has always been patient, thoughtful, and human at every step of the way.

I didn't meet my partner and now wife, Erin Taylor, until late in the writing of this book. Erin is a light of insight, thoughtfulness, nuance, warmth, humor, and principle—and a greater activist than I will ever be. Her love and patience as I marched through the revisions was just amazing—especially her reading of the whole manuscript right before submission.

Finally, my parents, Terrie Gale and Bob Adler, have been an amazing source of strength and love throughout this entire process. Whether assuring me all would be well, reading over early drafts, or sharing their considerable knowledge and perspectives about U.S. and world politics, without them, quite literally, none of this would be possible.

men sick, they were obliged to kill another of their horses. They were weak from lack of food, and Indian cooperation had become essential. To vary their diet, they now began to buy Indian dogs. Clark commented, "All the Party have greatly the advantage of me, in as much as they all relish the flesh of the dogs." Day after day they bought what they could from the Indians—dried fish, roots, berries, acorns, and an increasing number [of] dogs. Fresh fish were now rare, as salmon were out of season.[37]

In the last weeks of October, as they went out of the Sna[ke into] the Columbia, there were signs of improvement. They [...] and one of the party made what was described as "S[...] of the remains of the root bread that had su[...] descended the Columbia, they began to [...] dogs and squirrels. One of the me[...] little bear oil given by an In[...] most delicious fish I ha[...] sea, they saw "great nu[...] ducks, swans, and geese. E[...] from the Indians. Earlier, [...] "most of our people having [...] fish, but prefer dog meat; whic[...]

On the shores of the Pacific, [...] Clark examined the area to decid[...] looked, the men still depended heav[...] son, a variety of waterfowl, and a few [...] dians. They also began to kill elk. The[...] stomach disorders.

The Indians continued to be friendly a[...] advice, the expedition decided to settle for t[...] the Columbia, where there appeared to be a[...] ber, they built crude Fort Clatsop, and they kill[...] Rockies. At one time they had spurned elk in fav[...] but now it was welcome. In the weeks before Ch[...] enough elk and deer for the whole party to return t[...] the men preferred.[39]

Unlike the previous winter in the cold of Fort Mandan, [the...] quite mild, and there was constant rain. Some of the first elk[...] spoiled, and they built a hut to use as a smokehouse. Even afte[...]

37. Ibid., 5:231–96; 10:152–53.
38. Ibid., 5:315, 343; 6:9, 22, 31; 10:153.
39. Ibid., 6:93, 96, 105–9, 114–20.

---

was becoming scarcer. On July 31, when nothing was killed, o[ne of the] men commented in his journal that they were out of fresh meat, an[d it was] very uncommon to us, for we have generally had double as much [as we] could eat." After two days, in which their only kill was one beaver, t[hey] killed and ate two elk, a meat they probably would have avoided a mon[th] before.[30]

On August 12 the explorers reached the Continental Divide. They were no longer seeing buffalo. Their usual kills were deer or antelope, and after the riches of just a few weeks before, the men were disappointed in the quality. Antelope was never a favorite with them, and fish was about to take the place of the constant meat. For a time they went hungry. On Au- gust 13 an Indian gave Lewis a piece of roasted salmon (the first he had seen), and some dried berry cakes given by the Indians, a kind of flour and berry pudding, and flour stirred into a little boiling water.[31]

In the next three months, the party made its way from the Continental Divide to the sea. Gorging on fresh meat, which had been the pattern at meals in the summer of 1805, came to an end. Though they still ate some meat, fish became an essential part of their diet, and the support and friendships of the Indian tribes they encountered became essential. The Shoshone Indians gave the visitors salmon and chokecherries, and, in re- turn, Clark gave them a little salt pork. The Indian trout that they had caught their fresh food was trout, caught on a "sein" made of willow brush. The new pattern became apparent on August 19 and 20. Except for one beaver, plows had no fresh meat, they gave the Indians a good meal of boiled corn and beans and most of over five hundred trout...

that he had bought from the Mandans.[32]

In the following weeks, Lewis also gave the chief a few dried squashes wrote that a group of Indians they met were half-starved. Although the ex- salmon, a beaver, "phesents," grouse, a little parched corn, berries, and no geese, a beaver, "phesents," grouse... prevalent in the United States later in the nineteenth century... these "phesents," were white-tailed ptarmigan, native to the high... had eaten no meat for eight days. On September 3, John Ordway... It was a great treat when they shot a few deer. Clark commented... Pheasants are not native to North America and only b...

30. Ibid., 5:20, 26; 9:199–200.
31. Ibid., 5:74, 83, 87, 95, 97; Chuinard, Only One Man, 307.
32. Moulton, ed., Journals, 5:119, 126, 130, 138, 144.

...that they ate the last of their pork and "lay down wet hungry."[33] ...these weeks in September, the abundance they had enjoyed earlier in the expedition changed to near starvation. On September 14, with their hunters again unsuccessful, the men rehydrated a little of the soup they had brought with them and killed one of their colts. Ordway said that it ate "verry well." On the following days, with the hunters bringing in only pheasants, they killed two more colts and drank a little more of the portable soup. As there was no water, they melted snow to mix with it. On the twentieth, Ordway wrote that they were "half Starved and very weak."[34]

The situation was serious, and Clark and hunters went ahead, out of the mountains, to look for game in level country. That morning the main party finished the rest of a colt, and for dinner there was only condensed soup. They had little left except for a few canisters of soup and a small quantity of bear's oil. The next day they ate only the soup. Several men were suffering from dysentery, and many had boils and other skin eruptions. Before setting out on the frosty morning of September 20, they ate a few handfuls of peas, and "a little bears oil." They were saved by Clark and the rest for the main group.[35]

On September 21 the main party, led by Lewis, ate the remainder of the horse flesh, a few birds, a prairie wolf, and some crawfish. In the ... hunters who killed a crow ...

They gave Clark a little of what they had—a small piece of ... dried salmon, dried berries, and bread made out of ... lowing day when the hunters were unsuccessful ... Clark's advance party reached a village of the Nez Percé ... he had in his pockets for dried salmon, b... provisions were sent back to the mai... roots with a crow they had killed ... Until the explorers reach... finding enough food ... and roots obtain... salmon but ... er 27 was... prov:

---

the meat continued to deteriorate. Christmas dinner consisted of "pore Elk, So much Spoiled we eate it thro' mear necessity, Some Spoiled pounded fish," and a few roots. There was no alcohol left to use for toasts. On the twenty-ninth, Clark commented that the elk had become very disagreeable both to taste and to smell. A guard was ordered to keep fires alight in the smokehouse all the time they had meat there. Even with smoke under it around the clock, there was still difficulty keeping the meat fit for eating, and they now particularly enjoyed any meat from a fresh kill. On December 30, they had "a Sumptious Supper of Elks Tongues & marrow bones."[40]

Elk meat was usually very lean, and rich *fat* meat figured in their dreams. Lewis missed it much more than bread and had reached a point where he was not particular which meat it was. He said that dog meat, horse flesh, and wolf had, from habit, become equally familiar. The men found themselves reminiscing nostalgically about the days when they had been able to get plenty of dogs. Lewis said they had "now become extremely fond of their flesh" and that when they had lived on dogs they had been healthier than at any time since leaving the buffalo country. He thought dog "an agreeable food" and said that he preferred it "vastly to lean Venison or Elk."

In the new year, the eagerness with which the men immediately ate any fresh meat made it necessary to change the method of distribution. Fresh meat had usually been divided among the messes, and it had been left up to them how much to eat fresh, and how much to cure. Often this had meant that it was rapidly used up when fresh. On January 12, when a hunter killed seven elk, it was decided that the meat would be dried before being doled out in small quantities.[41]

A major problem with returning to a largely meat diet was the lack of salt. This, like their other provisions, had been used up. A few weeks before Christmas, Clark went along the seacoast to find a suitable spot to set up a salt camp, and later in December men were sent there with five of the largest kettles to start making salt. This was a long and tedious process of boiling away seawater and gathering up the residue. They were able to make from three quarts to a gallon of salt a day. On January 5, they brought in about a gallon, and Lewis pronounced it "excellent, fine, strong, & white." The party had been out of salt since December 20. Lewis had very much missed it, but Clark announced that it was immaterial to him whether he had it or not.[42]

...id., 6:125–27, 135, 137, 138, 142, 145, 157; 10:184; 11:405, 406.
..., 6:162, 166, 200.
...6:116, 140, 166, 167; 9:262.

Throughout the winter, the explorers continued to have friendly relations with the Indians and supplemented tainted elk by buying roots and berries. The Indians baked, dried, and ground roots to make a type of bread, and they used berries to make a berry soup. Both roots and berries were also boiled with meat. One type of root given to the explorers by both the Chinook and the Clatsop Indians reminded Clark of sweet potato, but the main root they obtained was the wapato.

Wapatos, which come from a plant that grows in low-lying, watery areas and ponds, was extensively used by the local Indians. Like most other roots used by Indian tribes, they were sometimes boiled with meat or dried fish, often dried and pounded to be used in soups or to make a kind of bread, or sometimes simply baked. Clark thought that they were as good as Irish potatoes and a "tolerable Substitute" for bread. Late in December, when the elk meat was badly spoiled, the explorers were very grateful when an Indian chief gave them a half bushel of the roots. In the following days, the explorers bought more. By January 4, they were all gone.[43]

On the following day, the Indians again came to the aid of their visitors. They brought in blubber from a dead whale that had been found on the coast. Lewis described the flesh as white, not unlike pork fat, but spongier and somewhat coarser. He had part of it cooked and found it "very pallitable and tender," with a taste similar to beaver or dog. Joseph Whitehouse wrote that it was "tolerably good eating." When Clark went to visit the Indians who were boiling the blubber from the whale, he found it difficult to persuade them to sell, but he secured about three hundred pounds and a few gallons of oil.[44]

In January and February, both snow and rain caused problems. Late in January, in heavy snow, the hunters killed ten elk and brought in three, but when they went back for the others they could not find them. In February, rain brought more fears of spoiled meat. They jerked elk meat to preserve it but had to carry out the jerking inside because of the constant rain. Elk was now their standard food. Occasionally they killed a deer, but Lewis thought the venison was even poorer in quality than the elk.[45]

In late February, Indians arrived with many small fish. These were probably eulachons, a form of smelt. They look like small salmon and follow the pattern of salmon by coming from the sea into freshwater rivers to spawn. They had begun to run. Lewis liked them cooked Indian-style—simply

43. Ibid., 6:79, 89, 116, 118–19, 139, 142, 147, 165; Chuinard, *Only One Man*, 325; *The Oxford Encyclopedia of Food and Drink in America*, 2 vols. (New York: Oxford University Press, 2004), 2:208.
44. Moulton, ed., *Journals*, 6:166, 183–84; 11:417.
45. Ibid., 6:240–42, 293, 321, 325, 342; 10:191.

roasted in a bunch on a wooden spit. He said they were "superior to any fish I ever tasted." By this time, of course, any fresh fish was likely to taste very good, and the explorers bought half a bushel. The same Indians also brought sturgeon. Lewis pronounced it "good of it's kind." The fish were quickly eaten, and two days later, the party was down to a three-day stock of inferior, tainted dried elk.[46]

Early in March, the situation improved when one of the hunters arrived with fat sturgeons, fresh anchovies, and a bushel of wapato roots. That night the men feasted on anchovies and wapato. The anchovies had to be eaten quickly because they spoiled unless pickled or smoked. The Indians smoked them as they were, with no gutting, and the curing was finished in twenty-four hours. To cook sturgeon, the Indians placed layers of sturgeon and boughs on stones that had been heated in the fire. Water was poured over the stones so that the sturgeon steamed. The Indians also ate both porpoise and flounder. Porpoises were common on the coast, and the Indians sometimes speared them with a gig. Lewis found their flavor disagreeable.[47]

In the weeks immediately before they left Fort Clatsop, the explorers were unable to lay in any provisions for the home journey, but at least they were no longer traveling into the unknown. The mountains would be difficult, but they knew that there was abundance beyond them. On March 23, they left Fort Clatsop. Two days earlier, Lewis had written that they had only one day's provisions on hand. To supplement these, they bought dried anchovies and a dog, and the hunters killed an elk. As they went back up the Columbia, finding enough food was a constant source of anxiety. They managed to kill some deer and elk, and in early April decided to make a halt to dry enough meat to sustain them over the next stage of the journey. In spite of this, they were still heavily dependent on dog meat.[48]

By early May, the explorers were practically out of food. On May 6, when the Nez Percé gave them a young horse in return for treating their sick, it was immediately butchered. The Nez Percé were also helpful in telling the Americans that the Bitterroot Mountains, which they soon had to cross, were then impassable because of snow. For the next month the explorers waited. While waiting, they ate some of their own horses

46. Ibid., 6:342–43.
47. Ibid., 6:368, 378–80, 411–12.
48. Ibid., 6:443, 444; 7:22, 50, 53, 115.

and obtained more from the Nez Percé. They also laid in an extensive store of camas roots and camas bread. Camas root was a staple among the Nez Percé and was used extensively by the Indians of the Pacific Northwest.[49]

By early July, after further delays because of snow, the explorers had crossed the mountains. The two leaders parted for a time to try to find out more about the country, and Lewis's party clashed with Blackfeet Indians, but by then the food shortage had ended. They had reached the buffalo country, and before they came together again, the two parties were slaughtering a variety of game. Late in September 1806, they reached St. Louis, and their epic journey was over.[50]

American explorers crisscrossed the Far West throughout the nineteenth century, but the journey of Lewis and Clark was unique in its breadth, the freshness of much of what the explorers saw and did, and the extent of the expedition's documentation. The men had learned a great deal about the difficulties of taking enough food and killing enough game to avoid food shortages, but these lessons did not prevent other explorers from having similar problems for much of the century.

Nineteenth-century explorers often had difficulty carrying enough food to avoid going hungry. Part of the problem was that they found it difficult to realize that the riches of the plains would disappear in areas farther west, but providing for the future was made difficult in any case by the limits in what could be carried and by the excessive amounts of meat eaten when it was available.

In the fall of 1805, when Zebulon Pike led an expedition up the Mississippi to try to locate its source, he wrote that his party used "the strictest economy." This was strict economy only when compared to the usual quantities of meat consumed by explorers and traders when game was readily available. The ration was two pounds of "frozen venison" a day, sometimes supplemented with flour that the expedition had taken along. Christmas Day was celebrated with two pounds of extra meat, flour, a gill of whiskey, and extra tobacco for each man. On the return journey, when the two pounds of venison was given out fresh rather than frozen, Pike's comment was that it "was scarcely sufficient to keep us alive." He said he was always

49. Ibid., 7:2–3, 215–17, 223–24, 234, 237–50; 10:224–25; Chuinard, *Only One Man,* 362–68; Ambrose, *Undaunted Courage,* 348–55; *Oxford Encyclopedia of Food and Drink,* 1:173.

50. Moulton, ed., *Journals,* 8:84–85, 161–62, 370–71; 10:254; Ambrose, *Undaunted Courage,* 358–94; Chuinard, *Only One Man,* 377–96.

hungry. Just before they arrived back in St. Louis, Pike and his men were delighted to find a great mass of roosting pigeons. They killed hundreds by simply knocking them on the head.[51]

In July 1806, Pike set out again, this time to explore the country between the Arkansas and the Red rivers and to find the origin of the Red River. His experience was very much like that of Lewis and Clark—abundance followed by near-starvation. At first, there was all the meat that anyone could have wanted, and by mid-September, there were herds of buffalo, elks, and antelope on all sides. The men were able to ignore less desirable meat and feast on marrow bones and tongues. The Indians they met were friendly and brought gifts of corn, "grease," buffalo, and bear meat. Pike tried to prepared for the future by drying meat, but by December he had to split the men of his expedition into small parties to increase the chances for successful hunting. Some were lucky and killed game; others nearly starved. Pike's expedition to explore the upper Rio Grande region ended ingloriously when he was expelled from Spanish territory.[52]

There were often more problems if the men of an expedition had to encamp for any long period of time. In 1819, Col. Henry Atkinson and Maj. Stephen Long led an expedition of troops, scientists, and artists up the Missouri. Because the steamboats repeatedly broke down, the men of the expedition had to spend the winter on the west bank of the Missouri, about twenty-five miles from what is now Omaha. Most of them stayed in an area they called Camp Missouri, but Long was in command of a group that was encamped a short distance away near Fort Lisa.

The smaller party with Long survived the winter reasonably well. They received provisions from Camp Missouri and by hunting secured "plenty of venison and other game." When their hunting was unsuccessful, they fell back on salt pork. They were not fussy about the game they ate. Edwin James, who was the botanist and geologist on the expedition, said they sometimes had skunk for dinner "and found it a remarkably rich and delicate food." Far more palatable was the entire hump of a buffalo, cooked "after the manner of the Indians." It was placed in a hole in the ground, covered with cinders and earth, a large fire was placed on top, and it was left overnight. On the next day, it was uncovered, and the men ate a meal of roasted buffalo hump, boiled buffalo meat, two boiled buffalo tongues, sausages made of loin and fat, and the "spinous processes" from the hump

51. Zebulon Pike, *An Account of Expeditions to the Sources of the Mississippi, and through Western Parts of Louisiana . . . in 1805, 1806, 1807* (1810; repr., Ann Arbor: University Microfilms, 1966), 55, 75, 88, 104.
52. Ibid., 111–277.

roasted like spare ribs. For coffee they substituted the seeds of the coffee-tree. This is a tree with seeds that can be said to resemble coffee in flavor. They had no vegetables, but they had good bread made with wheat flour.[53]

The main body of troops at Camp Missouri had a dismal winter. Their lack of fresh vegetables was compounded by much less fresh meat than Long's party and by a shortage of bread. Scurvy became rampant. By March, more than three hundred soldiers had been or were sick, and nearly one hundred had died. But their hunters, who were almost always absent from Camp Missouri, had escaped the disease. It seems likely that they had benefited from food such as raw liver that was often eaten immediately after a kill. This contained the vitamin C that was needed to prevent scurvy. They may also have obtained roots or dried berries from groups of Indians that they encountered.[54]

In the spring, when the snow melted, there was finally some relief. The lack of vegetables was partially alleviated by the collection of large quantities of wild onions and a wild root, somewhat resembling a sweet potato, called the *pomme de terre* by the French-Canadian trappers. This could be eaten either raw or cooked, and a considerable quantity was collected. Major Long had made a trip to Washington in the winter, and when he rode into Camp Missouri late in May the troops had begun to cultivate "extensive gardens" with all kinds of vegetables. There were also about three hundred acres planted with corn and potatoes.[55]

Major Long was now given the task of expanding knowledge of the region south of that crossed by Lewis and Clark. He set out from St. Louis in June 1820 with twenty men and later added two others. For food they intended to rely a great deal on hunting, but they also took with them several hundred pounds of hard biscuits, one hundred and fifty pounds of parched cornmeal, one hundred and fifty pounds of salt pork, twenty-five pounds of coffee, thirty pounds of sugar, and a small amount of salt. They rode horses, while other horses carried their packs and supplies. For cooking, they had two old camp kettles, but they bought two additional small brass kettles from an Indian trader.

Traveling west, they killed their first deer and also began to gather wild onions. At the Pawnee villages, where the Indians grew corn, beans,

53. Edwin James, *Account of an Expedition from Pittsburgh to the Rocky Mountains,* 2 vols. (1823; repr., Ann Arbor: University Microfilms, 1966), 1:180, 191–93.

54. Ibid., 1:76, 195–96; David Meriwether, *My Life in the Mountains and on the Plains,* ed. Robert A. Griffen (1886; repr., Norman: University of Oklahoma Press, 1965), 21, 50–69.

55. Meriwether, *My Life,* 76; John R. Bell, *The Journal of Captain John R. Bell,* ed. Harlin M. Fuller and LeRoy R. Hafen (Glendale, Calif.: A. H. Clark Co., 1957), 89–90.

pumpkins, watermelons, squash, and turnips, the explorers were given corn boiled with buffalo innards. It "relished well," and they filled up on it. A few days later they saw their first buffalo but were unable to make a kill. Game was not as easy to find as they had expected. On June 15, they ate the last meat they had on hand together with some highly seasoned bologna that had been brought from Pittsburgh in the previous year. They had not brought enough corn. Each man's bread ration was set at one half-pound biscuit a day; a few days later this was reduced to three-quarters of a biscuit, and by the end of June, it had been decided that what was left of the bread would be saved for use as a last resort. In its place a small amount of parched corn was issued to be boiled with the meat.[56]

The hunting gradually improved. First there were antelope, and, after the party reached the junction of the North and South Platte, great herds of buffalo. For the time being, they had all the meat they wanted. The party had been divided into three messes, and each mess was given meat along with a little parched corn and a pint of salt a week. They celebrated July Fourth with roasted venison, buffalo meat, and boiled corn soup. Each man was given an extra allowance of corn and a gill of whiskey. Buffalo soon became scarce, but there was still venison. When they came across an area with abundant currants, they all made themselves sick by eating too much unfamiliar fruit.

But, in July, as they pressed on toward the Rockies, the hunters were unable to kill enough meat to satisfy the hunger of the party, and provisions ran low. On July 15, they began an allowance of one pint of cornmeal a man for four days and stopped using salt, except for a little in their soup. They also put a small amount of bologna in the soup to spice it. They still had meat they had jerked earlier in the trip, and they used this when the hunters failed to make a kill.[57]

Late in the month, on the Arkansas River, the party divided. One group continued to follow the Arkansas, while Long led a party in an attempt to reach the Red River before returning to Fort Smith. They divided their surviving provisions. In the following weeks, the men going along the Arkansas lived primarily on meat—buffalo, venison, wild turkey, antelope, and elk. Most of the buffalo meat was from buffalo cows. In August and September, male buffalo were generally rank in taste and practically inedible. When a male buffalo was killed, the men ate only the tongue and marrow bones.

56. James, *Account*, 1:423–26; Bell, *Journal*, 103–21.
57. James, *Account*, 1:429–96; Bell, *Journal*, 106–82.

Apart from the meat, this group's only regular food was a ration of one gill a day of parched cornmeal, which was usually boiled with the meat. It ran out on August 15, and they were left with a small amount of rather moldy crumbled biscuit. This was given out at a rate of a gill a day per man. The men supplemented the diet of meat and moldy biscuit by gathering grapes, plums, and black walnuts (the walnuts were the previous year's growth), and they received some help from the Indians. From the Arapahos they bought salt, some dried and pounded buffalo meat, and "a quantity of small, flat, blackish cakes." These were made of wild cherries, both pulp and stones, pounded together, mixed with buffalo fat, and dried in the sun.

By mid-August game had become very scarce, and the men had only small amounts of jerked meat. When they came across areas where the Indians had planted corn and watermelons, they took some roasting ears, boiled some of the corn, and ate the unripe melons. By August 20 the food situation was worse. The hunters had made no kills, and they were reduced to eating just one meal that day—the biscuit allowance of a gill a man was pooled and boiled in water to make a soup. They were desperate, so when the hunters killed a skunk, they boiled it along with a small amount of jerked buffalo meat and some of the biscuit crumbs.

Two days later, they returned to the ways of their prehistoric ancestors. One of the hunters managed to drag the body of a dead fawn away from the wolves that had killed it. This provided a good meal. In the following days, they killed several turkeys and a hawk, but they were still some two hundred miles from any settlements, and their provisions consisted of six pints of biscuit crumbs and two pints of corn.

On August 25 they stopped for a day to try to find food. The hunters killed three small ducks, and the rest of the men scoured a creek, finding one small turtle, a few small fish, and some fresh water mussels. These they roasted and ate. It was two more weeks before they finally reached the edge of settlement, and they survived on a little game, plums, grapes, "unripe persimmons," and some lean meat. They were also considerably helped by the Osage Indians. At one of the Osage villages, the explorers were given "a large wooden bowl of corn soup," followed by roasted venison, and a soup of corn and pumpkin boiled together. The Indians also gave them meat, a large quantity of blue plums, and salt.[58]

When Long and his men split from the others, they suffered similar problems in finding food. They survived on occasional kills, grapes, plums,

58. James, *Account*, 2:172–254; Bell, *Journal*, 182–272.

fruit from pawpaw trees, honey, and help from the Indians. One morning they breakfasted on grapes mixed with two ounces of sugar. On August 4, when one of them shot a wild horse, they gorged on it until they were stuffed and took the rest with them. They were still eating it on the ninth when, because of the heat, it was beginning to go bad. After they encountered buffalo, they had more meat, but flies prevented them from keeping meat fresh for more than a day. Even eating boiled or roasted buffalo became practically impossible because swarms of flies laid eggs on it as it lay on the grass. For a time they simply made meat soup, leaving the meat immersed until they took it to their mouths.

After they left their companions, they had limited themselves to one fifth of a pint of parched corn a day for each man, but by August 24 they had used it all. Their food was now all meat—buffalo, bear, or elk meat, without salt, and they used turkey or venison "for bread." When they finally reached Fort Smith, they were given a fine breakfast, but they were cautious in eating bread, sweet potatoes, and other items they had done without for so long.[59]

Soldiers on army exploring expeditions often ate anything they could get. In 1849, in the region between San Antonio and El Paso, William Whiting was delighted when an Indian hunter killed a mountain lion. The men were hungry for fresh meat, and Whiting remembered from an earlier experience that young panther was "not bad." On this occasion, he was disappointed, because this was old, lean, tough panther. On the soldiers' trek back to El Paso, Whiting sampled another unusual meat—wild hog. The hams and ribs, which had "a wild, strong flavor," were "very savory." After finding a beehive in a wild oak, the men also had what Whiting described as "the famous frontier meal of a side of venison roasted on a ramrod, basted with bear's oil and dipped in honey."[60]

By midcentury, it should have been easier to provide food for exploring expeditions because of the great increase in commercial food preservation. From the early years of the century, both the English and French had experimented with preserving food. In 1810, in France, Nicolas Appert had published an influential book describing his process of preserving meat, fish, fruit, eggs, and vegetables in bottles. These were made airtight by corks held in place by wires, and put in boiling water for different periods of

59. James, *Account*, 2:10–172.

60. "Journal of William Henry Chase Whiting, 1849," in Ralph P. Bieber and Averam P. Bender, eds., *Exploring Southwestern Trails, 1846–1854* (Glendale, Calif.: A. H. Clark Co., 1938), 282, 334, 348.

time. At about the same time, the English were experimenting with the use of tin cans for preservation.

The early efforts were crude, and often unsuccessful, but by the 1820s commercial canning had spread to America. In both Boston and New York attempts were made to place a variety of foods in either glass or tin containers. By 1840 tin rather than glass had become the norm for commercial food preservation, and there was rapid growth in the 1840s and 1850s. This early canning was a slow process. Tin-plated sheet iron was hand-cut, soldered together, and food put in through a hole in the top before the tin cans were immersed in boiling water. A small hole was left for the steam to escape. This was sealed as soon as the food inside began to boil. The boiling process tended to produce unappetizing foods. By the 1850s the canning of fresh vegetables and fruits was expanding rapidly, and in 1856 Gail Borden obtained a patent for condensing milk.[61]

Although preserved food was becoming available, costs and restrictions in weight often meant that the use of bottles and tins remained limited. Rashness and inadequate preparations also meant that explorers often suffered as they had earlier in the century. John Charles Frémont led five exploring expeditions into the Rockies in the 1840s and 1850s, but he did not learn enough on the first three to prepare him for what he encountered on his fourth and fifth expeditions. The fourth, carried out in 1848–1849, was a complete disaster, and there were major problems on his fifth.

Frémont's father-in-law, Missouri politician Thomas Hart Benton, was interested in the possibility of making St. Louis the eastern terminal of a railroad to the Pacific. Frémont's task was to show that there was a feasible route following the Santa Fe Trail to Bent's Fort on the Arkansas, over the San Juan Mountains into Utah, and on to California. To convince doubters, Frémont unwisely decided to cross the Rockies in winter.

Frémont's party of some thirty men left Westport, Missouri, in late October 1848, and reached Bent's Fort in mid-November. Bent's Fort was a trading post, and a major way station on the Santa Fe trail. Preparations had been inadequate. Frémont brought corn, but in spite of the sufferings of those who had preceded him, he hoped to live largely off the country. This hope quickly proved false. Even before the explorers reached the

61. Edgar W. Martin, *The Standard of Living in 1860: American Consumption Levels on the Eve of the Civil War* (Chicago: University of Chicago Press, 1942), 18, 30–31; Philip D. Armour, "The Packing Industry," in *1795–1895: One Hundred Years of American Commerce*, 386; Edward S. Judge, "American Canning Interests," in *1795–1895: One Hundred Years of American Commerce*, 396–98; Earl C. May, *The Canning Clan: A Pageant of Pioneering Americans* (New York: Macmillan, 1938), 1–11; Richard O. Cummings, *The American and his Food: A History of Food Habits in the United States*, rev. ed. (Chicago: University of Chicago Press, 1941), 67.

Rockies, hunting became nearly impossible because of heavy snows, and the men were reduced to eating their own mules. By early January, when the mule meat was gone, they faced starvation. They boiled all the rawhide they could find in their equipment to get some nourishment. Four men who were sent out to find help became stranded in the mountains. When the others found them, one was already dead, and "the others had eaten part of his body." Ultimately the survivors reached Taos, but by then a third of the party had died.[62]

Frémont's fifth expedition was also designed to prove the feasibility of a railroad route across the San Juan Mountains to the Pacific. Although he was again trying to cross the mountains in winter, he still intended to depend to a great extent on what his hunters could kill. One member of his expedition was a little more imaginative. Artist and daguerreotypist Solomon Carvalho took half a dozen cases of "preserved coffee, eggs, cocoa, cream, and milk." The yokes of the eggs had been beaten to a thick paste and mixed with loaf sugar, the dried milk was also mixed with sugar, and both were hermetically sealed in tin boxes. The manufacturer wanted to test them on this long journey. There was supposed to be nourishment in them to sustain twenty men for a month. The party also had "meat-biscuit," a type of early bouillon, in which flour was saturated with boiled beef juices and baked into biscuits.[63]

The expedition, which consisted of some twenty men, including ten Delaware Indians, left Westport in September 1853. The plains were still rich with buffalo, and soon after crossing the Kansas River, the hunters made their first kill, and the men sat down to buffalo steaks for supper. The Delawares cut the buffalo meat into thin strips, impaled it on green sticks cut from nearby trees, and placed it close to the fire.

Complications arose when Frémont became ill and had to return to St. Louis for treatment. His party encamped and waited over a month for his return. This delay resulted in the squandering of many of the provisions. Carvalho said they lived "sumptuously," with coffee, tea, and sugar three or four times a day. By the time Frémont returned, "the provisions intended for the journey had been lavishly expended and surreptitiously purloined."

62. Charles Preuss, *Exploring with Fremont: The Private Diaries of Charles Preuss, Cartographer for John C. Fremont on his First, Second, and Fourth Expeditions to the Far West,* trans. and ed. Erwin G. Gudde and Elizabeth K. Gudde (Norman: University of Oklahoma Press, 1958), 143–52; Ferol Egan, *Fremont: Explorer for a Restless Nation* (Garden City, N.Y.: Doubleday, 1977), 492–503; Allan Nevins, *Fremont: Pathmarker of the West* (New York: Longmans, Green, 1939), 389–419.

63. Solomon N. Carvalho, *Incidents of Travel and Adventure in the Far West,* ed. Bertram W. Korn (1857; repr., Philadlephia: Kraus Reprints, 1971), 77, 81, 148–49, 151; Nevins, *Fremont,* 463–72.

Most of Carvalho's preserved eggs and milk were gone. Six dozen tin cases had been "wantonly destroyed."[64]

Winter was coming fast, but Frémont set out with inadequate supplies. He expected that there would be ample game on the first part of journey and that he would replenish his supplies at Bent's Fort. At first, all went well. As the explorers neared the Arkansas, Carvalho marveled that they were riding through great herds of buffalo. He estimated that there must have been 200,000 in sight at one time. Bent's Fort was not where they expected it to be. Because of an outbreak of cholera, Bent had moved about thirty miles. At the new post, the expedition obtained a little sugar and coffee and a large amount of dried buffalo meat. Carvalho breakfasted with Bent on dried buffalo, venison steaks, corn bread, and coffee.

Late in November, after a week at Bent's post, the explorers set out along the Arkansas toward the mountains. There was still ample game, both buffalo and deer, and the party lived for several days on the meat of an "enormous" black bear. Carvalho ate only a little of it, because he found it "too luscious and greasy." As they neared the Rockies, Frémont followed the pattern of earlier explorers by halting for several days to hunt and dry meat for use in the mountains. Most of the meat was buffalo and venison.[65]

In the mountains on New Year's Day, 1854, Carvalho produced two boxes containing one pound each of "Alden's preserved eggs and milk." These were all that had survived after the disastrous six weeks the party encamped while waiting for Frémont. Carvalho prepared a "blanc mange," putting the eggs, milk, and arrowroot (sent by his wife in case he was sick) into six gallons of water. The mix also contained the sugar put in the eggs and milk to help preserve them. The resulting treat was a welcome change, because by this time they were killing their horses for food. Their New Year's Day dinner consisted of "our usual horse soup," horse steaks cooked in the remains of tallow candles, and the blanc mange.

The malnourished horses made poor food, and Carvalho noticed the difference when their hunters brought in the choice parts of what they said was a young wild horse. He found the meat to be much more palatable. A little later they discovered that the horse belonged to an Indian woman, and they had to pay for it.[66]

By midcentury, there was often more danger from Indians than in earlier

64. Ibid., 94–96; Egan, *Fremont*, 492–503.
65. Carvalho, *Incidents*, 125, 132–42.
66. Ibid., 148–52.

days, but many Indians were still willing to give help. As the explorers were
now living on horse meat and soup made from the "meat-biscuit" they had
brought with them, they were happy to trade with a party of Indians for a
small amount of venison. Later, as they passed between the eastern fork of
the Colorado and the Green River they also traded for what Carvalho
called "grass-seed." This was a wild grain that the Indian women collected
in the fall, parched, and ground between stones. The Delaware Indians
who were part of the exploring party helped provide variety when they
killed a large porcupine. It was placed on a fire to burn off its quills. The
meat was white and looked like pork. Carvalho found it very fat and said
that his stomach "revolted at it."[67]

Revulsion or not, Carvalho had to eat. One morning, when the frozen
meat of a horse they had killed the night before lay in the snow, he cut out
about half a pound of liver and ate it raw. Earlier in the trek, when food
had been more readily available, he had been revolted to see an Indian eating a piece of raw antelope. The horses they now depended on for food had
little meat on them. Carvalho's opinion was that the taste of a young horse
was "sweet and nutty," but a horse that had almost starved to death had no
flavor and no juices. Even at this time of extremity, Carvalho still turned
his nose up at some food. One day, the hunters returned with coyote. He
had not eaten for twenty-four hours, but he refused coyote meat.[68]

For nearly two months the expedition lived by eating horses, making
use of every part. When a horse gave out, the Delawares slit its throat and
saved the blood in a bucket. The entrails were taken out, "well shaken,"
because there was no water to wash them in, and boiled with snow to produce a "highly flavored" soup. Even the horsehide was roasted to make it
crisp. Carvalho balked only at the bucket of blood. Remembering the horrors of his fourth expedition, Frémont made the men swear that in no case
would they eat anyone who died. This time it did not come to that. In February, they reached a small Mormon community. Carvalho had endured
enough. He left the expedition and went by wagon to Salt Lake City. Frémont eventually pressed on to California.[69]

Although the West was wonderfully rich in game for most of the nineteenth century, explorers discovered that it could never be depended on to
provide a regular supply of food throughout an expedition. This lesson had
been learned by Lewis and Clark nearly fifty years before Frémont continued to hope that he could live off the country.

67. Ibid., 153, 161–70.
68. Ibid., 127, 171–72, 177.
69. Ibid., 189–91; Egan, *Fremont*, 500.

CHAPTER 4

Meat and More Meat

~~~

The flesh of the buffalo is the wholesomest and most palatable of meat
kind.

Zenas Leonard, 1831

T he descriptions of game brought back by the Lewis and Clark
Expedition inspired fur traders to seek pelts along the whole
length of the Missouri, and to cross the plains to tap the beaver
resources in the Rockies at the headwaters of the Yellowstone,
the Columbia, and the Colorado rivers. Determined Blackfoot
resistance at the Three Forks of the Missouri delayed, but did
not prevent, the advance of the fur trade. Beaver was the most desirable
pelt, but the mountain men trapped, hunted, and ate a great variety of
game.

Trader William Ashley's view was that all that was necessary for subsis-
tence in the wilderness was a plentiful supply of good fresh meat: "It is all
that our mountain men ever require or even seem to wish. They prefer the
flesh of the buffaloe to that of any other animal." Ashley reflected a general trapper opinion when he wrote that meat from wild game was "the
most wholesome and best adapted food to the constitution of man." He
claimed "uninterrupted health" for those who "generally eat unreasonable
quantities of meat at their meals."[1]

There was a great belief in the digestibility of buffalo meat. Lewis H.
Garrard, who went west in 1846, commented that a peculiarity of the meat
was that "one can eat beyond plenitude without experiencing any ill-
effects." At midcentury, explorer Howard Stansbury reported that the daily
allowance for a fur company employee was eight pounds of meat a day.

1. Harrison C. Dale, ed., *The Ashley-Smith Explorations and the Discovery of a Central Route to the
Pacific, 1822–1829,* rev. ed. (Glendale, Calif.: Arthur H. Clark Co., 1941), 135.

Often this was all eaten, for "an old mountaineer seldom eats anything else." If available, wrote Stansbury, a mountain man liked a strong cup of coffee with plenty of sugar with his meat, but he never felt "the want either of bread or vegetables." Unless there was a shortage of game, the meat was taken from a buffalo cow because the meat of the bull was considered inferior. Cows were smaller than bulls, but this still meant a great deal of meat. The cows weighed from 750 to as much as 1,000 pounds.[2]

Stansbury described trappers cutting up a buffalo to get the best parts. "These were the 'bass,'" a hump projecting from the back of the neck, which, when boiled, was like marrow, very "tender, rich, and nutritious"; the hump and the hump ribs from just behind the shoulders (some of them were a foot in length); the "fleece," which was the flesh covering the ribs; the "depuis," a flat piece stretching from the shoulders to the tail; the "belly fleece"; the side ribs; the thigh or marrow bones; and the tongue.

This list omitted the liver, which was also highly prized. If hungry, some trappers would eat the liver raw immediately after the buffalo was killed. Nutritionally, this raw liver had great advantages, as it gave the trappers vitamins that otherwise would have had to come from fruit or vegetables. These the trappers often lacked, unless they gathered them wild. Unless there was a shortage of game, much of the buffalo carcass was discarded. Sometimes, only the bass, the hump, and the tongue were taken, or even the tongue alone.[3]

If trappers were traveling from buffalo country into mountainous regions where they could expect difficulty in finding game, they carried buffalo jerky or pemmican in their provisions. The jerky would keep for many months, or even years, although in wet weather there was a danger of its becoming moldy. Trappers chewed it as it was, but they also ate it boiled or roasted. Pemmican, much used by the Indians, was more palatable and more nutritious. Extremely resistant to decay, it lasted much longer than jerky.[4]

All agreed that buffalo meat was desirable, although individual trappers had their own special favorites. After Horace Greeley traveled west in the spring of 1859, he described a discussion among three old mountaineers

2. Lewis H. Garrard, *Wah-To-Yah and the Trail*, intro. A. B. Guthrie Jr. (1850; repr., Norman: University of Oklahoma Press, 1955), 29; Howard Stansbury, *An Expedition to the Valley of the Great Salt Lake* (1852; repr., Ann Arbor: University Microfilms, 1966), 38; Tom McHugh, *The Time of the Buffalo* (New York: Knopf, 1972), 22; *Oxford Encyclopedia of Food and Drink in America*, 1:139–40.

3. Stansbury, *Expedition*, 38; Garrard, *Wah-To-Yah*, 19, 28.

4. McHugh, *Time of the Buffalo*, 66–90; Meriwether, *My Life*, 96–97; Randolph B. Marcy, *The Prairie Traveler* (1859; repr., Williamstown, Mass.: Corner House Publishers, 1968), 160–61.

on the relative merits of various types of meat. Buffalo was the favorite, although Greeley himself thought it "a tough, dry, wooden fiber." He acknowledged, however, that the meat was not at its best in the spring—after a long, hard winter—and that he had not had the best of cooks. The mountaineers he talked with also liked black-tailed deer, mountain hen (grouse), and antelope. They were not as fond of elk or mountain sheep (bighorns). Greeley thought that the antelope he was given was "fresh, fat, and tender." None of Greeley's mountain men liked horse, but they said a slice of cold, boiled dog—"*well*-boiled, so as to free it from rankness," and then thoroughly cooled—was as "tender, sweet and delicate as lamb."[5] George Ruxton, who spent time among the mountain men in the 1840s, described a trapper coming into a village where among the French-Canadians and their Indian wives were some of his old companions. They celebrated his arrival by preparing a "dog feast." Some of the youngest and plumpest dogs were killed, and a coyote, attracted by the smell of blood, also joined them in the pot. In 1844, trader Charles Larpenteur, who was in the West for some forty years, asked a group of Indians in the Rockies to do him the favor of killing and boiling a dog for him—"That I knew would be good."[6]

Ruxton found that "Meat's meat" was a common saying. Mountain men were "starving one day, revelling in abundance the next." Ruxton came away with the impression that the most favored of all meats in delicacy, flavor, and richness was the flesh of mountain lions (cougars), although one mountaineer claimed that beaver tail was unsurpassed by any other kind of meat. Most mountaineers he met rated dog meat second in flavor to mountain lion.

Some trappers grew to like meat to the exclusion of most other food. Two advantages of having a largely meat diet were that game was often abundant, and it was free, except for the cost of the ammunition. The desirability of different foods obviously depended not only on the individual but also on the degree of hunger. Anything that ran, flew, or slithered could be eaten—from buffalo to rattlesnake.[7]

One obvious source of food for trappers who ran out of provisions and could find no game was horse meat. In 1848, Larpenteur traveled for three days without eating anything except the dried buffalo sinew that he kept

5. Horace Greeley, *An Overland Journey from New York to San Francisco in the Summer of 1859*, ed. Charles T. Duncan (1860; New York: Knopf, 1964), 144.

6. Ruxton, *Life*, 97; Charles Larpenteur, *Forty Years a Fur Trader on the Upper Missouri: The Personal Narrative of Charles Larpenteur, 1833–1872*, intro. Milo M. Quaife (Chicago: Lakeside Press, 1933), 176–77.

7. Ruxton, *Life*, 19, 98.

in his bullet pouch to use for mending. Finally, his companion shot a "fine fat" mare that had gone lame in one hip. They each took a piece of the liver and some ribs to cook in the embers of a fire. The liver turned black (presumably burned), and not all of it was edible, but they enjoyed the ribs. Larpenteur thought that the fat was excellent but the lean meat a little insipid. His general conclusion was that "horse meat makes excellent steaks."[8]

When mountain man Jedediah Smith went on a famous exploratory trip from the Great Salt Lake to Los Angeles and back, he and the two men who returned with him depended on horse meat for their survival. They set out with seven horses and two mules and finally reached the Great Salt Lake in the spring of 1827 with one horse and one mule; they had eaten the others to survive. They ate some fresh meat when they made the kills but spread the rest out in the sun to dry so that they could take it with them.[9]

Personal taste and extremity led to the use of strange foods. A Mormon wrote in his journal of a hunter who "roasts the young antlers of the deer and eats them," and David Meriwether described making wolf soup. On a journey from Santa Fe, Meriwether and his party had nothing to eat for three days. Finally, they shot an old wolf and boiled it in the camp kettle. They drank the resulting soup but found the meat too tough to eat until it had boiled all night.[10]

In 1858, a party in the Rockies tired of dried, rock-hard moose meat, which had to be cut into small bits, boiled, and mixed with a little tallow to make it chewable. To provide variety, they killed four ravens and roasted them before the fire. They found that the meat had a smell and flavor so peculiar that two of the four men went back to the dried moose meat. The others picked the tiny raven bones. One of this group said in 1860 that he had gone without vegetables for four years, except for a brief time when he was at an army camp. In all probability he was referring to *cultivated* vegetables available in frontier settlements and was discounting the various roots and other items he was likely to have eaten because of his contact with the Indians.[11]

Ruxton heard of one party of mountain men near the Great Salt Lake

8. Larpenteur, *Forty Years*, 229–31.

9. Dale, ed., *Ashley-Smith Explorations*, 186–90; James H. Maguire et al., eds., *A Rendezvous Reader: Tall, Tangled, and True Tales of the Mountain Men, 1805–1850* (Salt Lake City: University of Utah Press, 1997), 133–34.

10. Ruxton, *Life*, 237; Meriwether, *My Life*, 96–97.

11. Granville Stuart, *Prospecting for Gold: From Dogtown to Virginia City, 1852–1864*, ed. Paul C. Phillips (1925; repr., Lincoln: Univesity of Nebraska Press, 1977), 143, 146–47.

who, desperate for food and water, first ate a few bags of dried ants they found in an Indian village, later killed a horse, drank its blood, ate some of the meat raw, and finally practiced cannibalism after killing an Indian captive.[12] Tales of cannibalism were not uncommon in the mountains; some were fiction, but some were undoubtedly true.

Although most contemporary observers made much of the great dependence of the mountain men on a meat diet, it is clear from surviving journals and other descriptions that trappers were often willing or happy to eat other food when it was available. One factor was that many mountain men married or lived with Indian women who in their own societies were accustomed to a varied diet, including wild roots, fruits, and berries. Camas root, which had become familiar to the men of the Lewis and Clark Expedition, was often eaten by mountain men, and corn was often included in the supplies carried by mountain men in the southern Rockies who had Mexican wives. Cultivated vegetables were rarely seen, but this lack was partially offset by what was gathered in the wild.

In 1834 a Kentuckian who, for his health, went with William Sublette's trading company into the Rockies, described how one fall evening, after they left the rendezvous, they all ate excellent wild plums "to repletion." On Jacob Fowler's trading expedition into the Southwest in the winter of 1821–1822, he described a day when some men hunted while others picked grapes. They bought flour, cornmeal, and bacon when they could. Yet, by far the greatest part of the food that Fowler's party ate came from the game they killed—deer, buffalo, turkey, bear, elk, beaver, goose, and antelope.[13]

A difficulty for the men who were hired by the various trading companies was that the efficiency or generosity of the company could make a big difference in how much they had to eat. Thomas James, who, as a member of the Missouri Fur Company, traveled to the headwaters of the Missouri, and lived there in the winter of 1809–1810, later recalled the problems of food shortages. He complained that in the journey up the river the company officials had supplies but were reluctant to distribute them to the men. After six weeks, most of the provisions that had been distributed had been used up, and the men were living on boiled corn with no salt. After much protest they were given some of the thirty barrels of salt pork

12. Ruxton, *Life*, 81–85, 237.

13. William M. Anderson, *The Rocky Mountain Journals of William Marshall Anderson: The West in 1834*, ed. Dale L. Morgan and Eleanor T. Harris (San Marino, Calif.: Huntington Library, 1967), 205; Jacob Fowler, *The Journal of Jacob Fowler*, ed., Elliott Coues et. al. (Lincoln: University of Nebraska Press, 1970), 13–136.

that were stored on their barge, and matters considerably improved when they began to eat the buffalo and elk that were available in great numbers as they moved up the river.

That winter, on the headwaters of the Missouri, they often went hungry. In February, a small party, including James, was lost for five days without food. When they finally managed to kill some buffalo, their hunger was such that they could not wait for the meat to be cooked and ate most of it practically raw. One problem of winter travel was that heavy snow could cause snow blindness, which made hunting impossible. Because of this, the main party to which James belonged had to eat two horses and three dogs to survive until they could hunt again.[14]

In the spring of 1823, James Clyman went up the Missouri in a party organized by William Ashley. Before they left St. Louis the men, who had been recruited "in grog Shops and other sinks of degredation," lived together in a rented house and were given plenty of bread and pork, which they cooked themselves. At first, they fared reasonably well for food. When they reached Fort Atkinson at Council Bluffs, they even ate vegetables—given to them by the army officers.[15]

That winter Clyman and his companions roamed extensively. Clyman spent much of the winter on the Wind River, where, at first, there was ample game. In one day's hunting with the Crow Indians, more than a thousand buffalo were killed. In February 1824, Clyman moved on to the Sweetwater. Rations were now limited because buffalo were scarce, but Clyman and his companions began to live on bighorns, broiling thin slices of their meat. They stayed in this area in heavy snow for three or four weeks, leaving only when the bighorns began to be scarce. They moved southwest and soon ran out of the dried meat they had brought with them. When at last they killed a buffalo, many of the men ate large slices raw. Again taking meat with them, they went on through South Pass. The only water they had for two weeks was that they could get by melting snow. They killed another buffalo, and, when they reached the Green River, Clyman killed two wild geese. In a few days the geese became plentiful, and they had plenty to eat.[16]

From 1825, when William Ashley concentrated on reaching the central Rockies overland from St. Louis, trappers lived in the mountains on a

14. Gen. Thomas James, *Three Years among the Indians and Mexicans* (1846; repr., New York: Citadel Press, 1966), 12–17, 37–45.

15. James Clyman, *Journal of a Mountain Man,* ed. Linda M. Hasselstrom (1960; repr., Missoula, Mont.: Mountain Press, 1984), 9–10.

16. Ibid., 23–30.

semipermanent basis and were supplied in the spring at an annual rendezvous. Within a few years, Ashley was experiencing extensive opposition from other companies, individual traders, and ultimately from the all-encompassing American Fur Company.

In February 1830, Warren Ferris left St. Louis with a party of American Fur Company trappers traveling overland to the central Rockies. On the first part of the journey they were able to live on food obtained from farmers in Missouri. Corn and "bacon" were bought for the men because they were cheap. They also ate salt pork they had taken with them. Traveling west along the Platte, they found that the first buffalo and antelope they saw and killed were poor and tough, but they were soon in the midst of a great herds of buffalo in good condition. Ferris wrote of feasting "luxuriously on the delicate tongues, rich humps, fat roasts, and savoury steaks." He said that they all came to the conclusion that no meat equaled that of "the female bison, in good condition." They ate it without seasoning and lived on it "solely, without bread or vegetables of any kind." This is a typical mountain man statement, but in the details of his account Ferris reveals that it is an exaggeration.[17]

Ferris described several years of trapping, mostly in the region of modern Idaho, Montana, and Wyoming. Sometimes the trappers went hungry—usually when they had left winter lodges to trap or hunt—but for the most part they seem to have eaten quite well. They laid in a supply of dried buffalo meat for the winter, and Ferris wrote of living "on the best the country afforded," often accompanied by "a large kettle of coffee, and cakes." He does not say whether their "cakes" were simply some type of camas root bread or whether they had some corn or wheat flour to bake on a griddle. It could have been camas, for Ferris describes Shoshone Indian women preparing camas root by cooking it in pits on heated stones. After the camas roots were put in, the pits were covered with earth, and a fire kept burning on top for the best part of a day. The Shoshone Indians also had stocks of salmon and were anxious to exchange them for buffalo meat to vary their usual diet, which was salmon, elks, bighorns, and the camas root. To provide for winter, the Shoshones split, dried, and powdered the salmon, and they also stored large quantities of camas.[18]

Ferris ate a variety of other meats besides buffalo. He and his companions killed black-tailed deer, grizzlies, antelope, elks, a bald eagle, and a goose. They trapped beaver for their pelts, but they also ate the meat. Ferris

17. Warren A. Ferris, *Life in the Rocky Mountains,* ed. J. Cecil Alter (Salt Lake City: Rocky Mountain Book Shop, 1940), 1–39.
18. Ibid., 44, 47, 81–85, 100, 102.

favored beaver "well-boiled." As they traveled along the Salmon River, they killed a fat gray wolf, which "made a tolerable supper." On another occasion, at an Indian camp, Ferris was given a dish of "the choicest morsels" of fat, tender deer and lynx. He thought the flesh of the lynx was far better than that of the deer, and the best he knew except for female bison. Lynx, which are similar to bobcats, were common in Canada and the northern Rockies. They were not often eaten.[19]

When possible, Ferris and his companions added wild fruits and vegetables for variety. On the Lewis River, they found an abundance of both wild onions and a type of lettuce, and on a tributary of the Green River, they ate buffaloberries, which Ferris described as very sour. He mentioned that they were much prized by the Indians as food. Scarlet buffaloberries are borne by two western shrubs—the silver buffaloberry and the Canadian buffaloberry. It is likely his berries were from the smaller Canadian shrub, on which the berries are generally too bitter to eat unless cooked with sugar.

In the summer of 1833, on the Bitterroot River, Ferris and his companions were delighted when Indian women and girls from the Flat Head tribe brought baskets of fruit and provisions. The Indians were preparing to go east on a buffalo hunt, and in the meantime were living on dried buffalo meat, berries, and roots. Horses loaded with berries and several kinds of roots were brought in daily. The most abundant and prized of the roots was one the Indians called "Spathem," the bitterroot that gave its name to the valley. Ferris though it disagreeable for anyone who was unused to it.[20]

In their years of roaming the mountain valleys, trappers acquired a great deal of cumulative knowledge of spots where desirable items could be obtained. Near to the Bear River, there was a favorite gathering spot for waterfowl, particularly geese. In the spring, passing trappers gathered great numbers of eggs. Trappers also took advantage of natural deposits of salt to use with their endless meat. On the surface of "a black stinking mire" near the Green River, Ferris was able to scoop up half a bushel of salt in just a few minutes. It was more difficult to find any regular supply of vegetables. Ferris took considerable pleasure in December 1833, on the Flathead River, in eating vegetables that had been brought from Fort Colville (in the modern state of Washington).[21]

Ferris spent the Christmas of 1833 in a cabin with a French-Canadian and his family. They feasted on buffalo tongues, dried buffalo meat, fresh

19. Ibid., 71, 107–8, 133, 137, 197, 207.
20. Ibid., 159, 171, 173, 211.
21. Ibid., 112, 187, 214; see also Ruxton, *Life*, 76.

venison, wheat flour cakes, buffalo marrow (used as butter), sugar, coffee, and rum. Ferris also enjoyed coffee and cakes to celebrate New Year, but he pointed out that coffee and cake were not the daily fare for the trapping party. He said their usual meal was a piece of boiled venison, with the addition of a piece of fat from a buffalo shoulder. On Sundays they added "a kind of French dumpling." These dumplings were made of minced meat, rolled into little balls, covered with dough, and fried in buffalo marrow.[22]

Zenas Leonard was in the Rockies at about the same time as Ferris but he went much farther afield. He first went to the Rockies in 1831, and both men worked for companies and trapped independently before returning east in 1835. Leonard's account of his experiences shows that mountain men could go hungry even before they reached the mountains, but that a well-organized party could have quite enough to eat even in winter.

In the spring of 1831, Leonard left St. Louis with a large company of trappers and traveled west along the south side of the Missouri. They picked up some provisions and cattle to last them until they reached the buffalo country, which they believed was about two hundred miles away. At the mouth of the Kansas River, they traded with the Kansas Indians for corn and other items, and in June, after traveling through prairies, they reached the Otoe Indians. Again they traded, this time for sweet corn and wild turnips. They also learned that game was scarce and the buffalo much farther away than they had expected.

On June 21 they killed the "last beef," divided it among their messes, and prepared to go hungry. Some wanted to turn back, but they went on, sending hunters out daily. There was little or no game, and they lived mainly on small fish and mussels. With the men still hungry, the leader of the party had two of their horses killed and divided among the messes. In a few days the horse meat was finished, and there was still no game. They decided to leave the Republican River and move toward the headwaters of the Platte. Ten or twelve men stayed with the pack mules, and the rest scattered to hunt. At night they came together to share what they had killed, usually wolves, wildcats, and occasionally antelope.

Soon after they reached the Platte, their troubles temporarily ended. One of the hunters killed two elks, and a few days later the men reached the buffalo country. They quickly killed six or seven buffalo, rested several days to feast, and after their days of hunger decided that "buffalo is the wholesomest and most palatable of meat kind." When they left the Platte,

22. Ferris, *Life,* 188–89, 191.

they moved up the Laramie River, climbing toward the Rockies through plains that at times "were literally covered" with buffalo, deer, bears, elks, prairie dogs, wild goats, bighorns, and antelope.

Late in September, they reached the mountains and decided to winter in the Laramie River valley. They carefully prepared, building cabins and stables and killing buffalo to dry the meat for the winter. The horses were worse off than the men. As there was no feed, the men were forced to let them starve. The trappers, however, did not go hungry. They had camped in an area where buffalo were available even in winter, and in preparation for New Year's Day their hunters killed ten of them. They brought in the fattest hump they could find to roast before the fire.

In mid-January, Leonard and some of the men set out with the intention of making the long journey to Santa Fe to trade beaver skins for new horses, mules, and other items they needed. At first there was ample game, and they killed buffalo and jerked the meat to take with them. It was not enough. They ran out, had nothing to eat for several days, and finally each of the men selected two of the best beaver skins to eat. On the following morning they roasted and ate them. For nine days they lived on beaver skins until finally they killed a buffalo. They stayed for four days to feed on its carcass. Ultimately, fears of hostile Indians drove them to return to their camp in the Laramie valley. They had been away for three months.[23]

Leonard's most ambitious journey was in 1833–1834 when, with a group of trappers and traders, he went through the Great Basin and over the Sierras to California and the Pacific. As the men left the west side of the Great Salt Lake, they killed the last buffalo they saw and were able to take about sixty pounds of dried buffalo meat for each man. In the Sierras they ran out of meat, and there was no game to be found, so they turned to horse meat, first killing a young Indian colt and then two of their own horses. There was soon little need to kill the horses as they were dying daily. When they died, their flesh was preserved for food. Although some of the men eagerly ate the "black, tough, lean, horse flesh," Leonard was repelled. He wrote that "it was the most unwholesome as well as the most unpleasant food I ever eat or ever expect to eat." In all, twenty-four of their horses died, and they ate the best parts of seventeen of them. They also gathered berries and insects and obtained acorns that were in a basket dropped by a fleeing Indian.

As they went down into the San Joaquin valley, game became plentiful.

23. Zenas Leonard, *Adventures of Zenas Leonard, Fur Trader*, ed. John C. Ewers (1839; repr., Norman: University of Oklahoma Press, 1959), 1–28.

There were no buffalo but plenty of deer, elk, grizzlies, and antelope, and they were able to lay in a large supply of venison, elk, and bear meat. Late in November, they reached the Pacific south of San Francisco, went on board a ship from Boston, and ate some food, the like of which they had not eaten for two years, including bread, butter, and cheese. They set out for Monterey and saw game of all types except buffalo. Their hunters killed a great many deer and also wild cattle. These wild cattle, often found in southern California and the Southwest, had usually originated on ranches abandoned by their Spanish or Mexican owners.

After stocking up on provisions and livestock in Monterey, Leonard and his party traveled back over the Sierras. The journey was less harrowing than the trek to California, and by June they were on the Humboldt River. They were, however, still worried about running out of supplies and decided to strike north to the headwaters of the Columbia. They found ample game near the head of the Snake River and laid in a new supply of meat. Early in July, they encountered the first buffalo they had seen since leaving the Great Salt Lake in the previous year. They were able to celebrate the fourth with the choicest parts, together with a little brandy they had undoubtedly picked up in California. A week later, they encamped to await the arrival of provisions from St. Louis.[24]

For many mountain men, the high point of the year for eating, and particularly for drinking, was the annual rendezvous, where pelts were exchanged, and supplies, liquor, and letters were brought in from the east. The men from the different trading companies set up their own camps within a few miles of one another, free trappers mixed in the general throng, and hundreds of Indians arrived to trade. Like sailors returning to port, the trappers often spent much of their earnings in one wild fling. The American Fur Company encouraged drinking at the annual rendezvous because prices were very high, and the employees charged the liquor against the wages. The independent trappers paid in peltries.[25]

The first main rendezvous took place near the junction of Henry's Fork and the Green River in 1825, but the greatest gatherings were in the early 1830s. Apart from liquor, most trappers craved coffee and sugar, and many took the opportunity to buy the first flour that they had seen for many months. Charles Larpenteur said of the 1833 Green River rendezvous, the first he had attended, that he was the only sober man in the camp. "Drinking, yelling, and shooting" went on as he had never heard before. When the

24. Ibid., 65–132.
25. Maguire et al., eds., *Rendezvous Reader,* 204–5; Fred R. Gowans, *Rocky Mountain Rendezvous: A History of the Fur Trade Rendezvous, 1825–1840* (Provo: University of Utah Press, 1975).

drinking finally lessened, the trappers began to prepare their outfits for the coming year.[26]

The rendezvous in 1834 was in June and July on Ham's Fork in what is now Wyoming. William Anderson, who traveled to the rendezvous with William Sublette's supply train, arrived in mid-June. There were a variety of camps scattered along the river and large numbers of independent traders, trappers, and Indians. Anderson said there were "whites of every tongue." Liquor was expensive, but drinking was constant. Later in the month, Anderson commented that there were "drunken songs & brawls every night." For those who did not spend all their time drinking, there was plenty of good food to eat. When he visited the American Fur Company camp, Anderson was surprised to be given the unexpected rarities of both rice pudding and plum pudding.[27]

The wild celebrations remained the same until the rendezvous system came to an end in 1840. At the 1838 rendezvous on the Wind River, Cornelius Rogers said that "the whole time is spent in drinking, gambling, horse-racing, quarreling, fighting &c." The exorbitant prices charged for liquor and the gambling meant that many spent most of their year's earnings in one wild spree. Rogers said that some men spent a thousand dollars in a day or two and that very few had any part of their year's wages left when the gathering broke up. At the same rendezvous, Asa Smith wrote to his parents that it had been "a continual scene of dissipation," even though the liquor was selling for four dollars a pint. Missionaries on their way to Oregon were particularly shocked at the scenes at this 1838 rendezvous. Every night their sleep was disturbed by the drunken carousing.[28]

The best days of roaming the central Rockies to trap for beaver were over by 1840. There were no longer enough beaver to make extensive trapping worthwhile, and the rendezvous system came to an end. Trapping and hunting for pelts continued, but the base for the trappers and hunters reverted to trading posts that had long served the Missouri trade and had also been established in areas all the way south to the Arkansas River. These posts were often referred to as forts and were intended to provide defense as well as shelter and trade, but they were not manned by troops. Some of them only had the post trader and a few helpers—clerks and hunters.

Food was nearly always better and more reliable at the posts than in the

26. Larpenteur, *Forty Years*, 26–27.

27. *Anderson Journals*, 128–38, 140–41, 148; Gowans, *Rocky Mountain Rendezvous*, 142–43.

28. Letter of Cornelius Rogers, July 3, 1838, Asa Smith to his parents, July 6, 1838, in Clifford M. Drury, ed., *First White Women over the Rockies . . . in 1836 and 1838*, 3 vols. (Glendale, Calif.: A. H. Clark Co., 1966), 3:151, 274–75.

high Rockies, and for trappers they were places to trade, get supplies, eat, and drink. As the posts were supply centers, and where the Indians came to trade, the traders tried to keep provisions in store. They also employed hunters to bring in fresh meat and often planted corn or even a few vegetables. At Fort Lisa, an early post on the Missouri in modern Nebraska, the men kept a turnip patch. As these posts could be reached by water, they could be supplied more easily than could trappers in the high Rockies. From the 1820s, steamboats began to supply the posts along the Missouri.

Fort William, near the mouth of the Yellowstone, was built in the late fall of 1833. When it was first occupied in the middle of November, the men were given a few supplies for a special pancake "feast." There was half a pint of flour for each man, and they used buffalo tallow and river water to make thick pancakes. They were also given a small amount of molasses, coffee, and sugar. Charles Larpenteur said he had eaten nothing like it for six months, and "I thought I had never tasted anything so good in my life."[29]

Larpenteur had left Missouri that spring with a party of some fifty men of the trading company of Sublette and Campbell. They went to the rendezvous on Green River before traveling on to the mouth of the Yellowstone to build Fort William. On the first part of their journey, they ate bacon and hard tack, and, very strangely for fur traders, mutton. A drove of sheep had been provided to last them until they reached the buffalo country. The men complained about the mutton, but the first buffalo was brought in three days after they reached the Platte. The meat was boiled, dumped on the grass because there were no pans, and the men sat around with little sacks of salt and long butcher knives, cutting pieces from the meat.

When they met trappers near the Laramie River, "a big drunken spree" took place before they went to the rendezvous and on to the Yellowstone. As they traveled, game became so scarce that they lived on berries and roots for two days, but they soon found more buffalo and were able to resupply themselves at Fort Cass, a trading post at the mouth of the Big Horn. They took two cows to the mouth of the Yellowstone and found abundant game there. In the absence of coffee they drank cow's milk.[30]

The following winter, Larpenteur and the rest of the men at Fort William fared less well. It was a year in which buffalo were hard to find in

29. Meriwether, *My Life*, 36–37; Larpenteur, *Forty Years*, 42–43.
30. Larpenteur, *Forty Years*, 17–40.

the region, and the men depended on their supply of pemmican, to which they added buffalo tallow bought from Indian women. The women put the tallow up in bladders weighing from five to eight pounds each and costing fifty cents. Larpenteur and his partner, a German, bought a bladder. The pemmican was usually eaten at breakfast, and the men had corn for dinner and supper. This was the fare for most of the winter, only occasionally varied by a deer or elk brought in by the hunters.

Fort William had been built by William Sublette, but he quickly sold out to the American Fur Company. The men had to be very careful with extras if they wanted to keep much of their wages. They had to pay one dollar a pint for salt and two dollars a pint for pepper. Each man bought a small amount of salt and pepper, mixed them, and kept them in a small sack. They had no coffee or sugar until a steamer brought them in June 1834, and like the salt and pepper, they were expensive. Men had their purchases debited against their wages.[31]

Daily food at a Missouri River post in the 1830s is well described in a journal kept by Francis Chardon at Fort Clark, a trading post on the Missouri north of what is now Bismarck, North Dakota. Like the trappers in the mountains, the men at Fort Clark leaned very heavily on meat. Chardon frequently left the fort to hunt buffalo with the Indians, and hunters and the Indians often brought fresh meat in to trade. The fort also had its own hunters. In Chardon's first winter of 1834–1835, buffalo meat was plentiful.

In March 1835, Chardon had his first duck of the year, but buffalo continued to be the basic food, and in its absence any meat was eaten. In early May, when the fort had been out of buffalo meat for a few days, Chardon ate a rat for supper. Eating a rat was not out of desperate hunger, because the Mandan Indians had brought several horse loads of fresh meat less than two weeks before. On the day after eating his rat, Chardon was able to go out and kill three buffalo. Rats were a problem at the post. In August that year the men killed 123, and meat was stored on a scaffold in an attempt to keep the rats off.[32]

While meat was central, traders and visitors to Fort Clark sometimes could obtain other food rarely, if ever, seen by the mountain men of the high Rockies. They grew corn at the fort, both to eat and to trade. Barrels of flour were kept in store, and bread and pies were made. They also grew squash. On one evening that summer, Chardon had a supper of coffee and

---

31. Ibid., 48–49.
32. Francis A. Chardon, *Chardon's Journal at Fort Clark, 1834–1839*, ed. Annie H. Abel (Pierre: S.D.: Department of History, State of South Dakota, 1932), 3–4, 18–19, 26, 47, 192.

mince pie, and on another, a very untypical trader's dinner of bread and milk. The mince pie was undoubtedly a traditional one made with meat. The milk was possible because in May 1835 a steamboat brought a cow and a calf to the post. Early in June, Chardon made butter, "the first that has ever been made at this Post." They also kept chickens.[33]

The men at the fort benefited from their contacts with the many Indians in the vicinity. The Indians regularly brought in meat, and they gathered berries throughout the summer. Late in August 1835 Chardon made a rather unusual entry in his journal: "Squaws who went with the war party yesterday returned to day with plenty of Cherries." Sioux and Mandan Indians were often in and out of the post. In September 1835, the Sioux danced a bear dance at the fort and in their village. At their village dance, in order "to imitate the *bear* more thoroughly, they killed a dog and devoured him raw."[34]

The winter of 1835–1836 well illustrated the problem of depending on hunting for regular food. By early January, the men at the fort were out of meat, and in the middle of the month the hunters returned after ten days of hunting to say they had seen no buffalo. There was no danger of real hunger. The fort still had corn, and Chardon was able to send some of it downriver to traders and Indians who were in danger of starving. He was about to send his hunters away to the prairies to fend for themselves when he heard that there were large numbers of buffalo farther up the Missouri. All the hunters were sent after them, and they returned loaded with meat. The difficulties at Fort Clark were over for the winter, and, in March, Chardon rode out to a village of the Gros Ventres Indians to treat them to a feast.[35]

That same month Chardon had a glass of milk with his supper—a "great luxury in this country," and they also collected their first eggs of the season. Food was abundant in the summer of 1836. Fresh meat was brought in with great regularity, and buffalo was varied with ducks and geese. They planted peas and potatoes, and in September Chardon was able to enjoy both at dinner.[36]

On festive days there was always an attempt to dine in some special way. Christmas and July 4 were occasions for extra food, and the French-Canadians at the fort celebrated the feast of Epiphany (Twelfth Night). On Christmas Day in 1834 a large group at the fort, including French-Canadians

33. Ibid., 10, 34, 38, 44, 49.
34. Ibid., 43, 45, 50.
35. Ibid., 52–61.
36. Ibid., 62, 64, 66, 79.

with their Indian families, sat down to meat pies, bread, "fricasseed pheasants," boiled buffalo tongues, and roast buffalo meat. They did not always
have liquor. At Christmas Day in 1836 there was a "feast, of eatables," but
Chardon had no drink to give the men. Two years later, Chardon provided
"a *festin* of Flour, Sugar, & Coffee," and he was also able to give each man
a glass of grog. At Twelfth Night in 1837, one of the men cooked "an excellent dinner" of pudding, pies, fried and roasted meat, and other special
items. Hard liquor was not a constant presence at Fort Clark, but they liked
to have a drink on the fourth and to offer a toast to President Andrew
Jackson. Chardon at times referred to a special meal as "a Jackson dinner."[37]

Wherever they were, most trappers tried to have a special dinner at
Christmas. In 1838 Osborne Russell sat down in an Indian lodge in the
Rockies to have dinner with a French-Canadian and his Indian wife. There
was a variety of courses, beginning with a pan of stewed elk meat and a
dish of deer meat. They also had a "boiled flour pudding" made with dried
fruit, accompanied with a sauce made of the juice of sour berries and sugar.
Finally came "the cakes" (probably some sort of flapjacks), and a great
quantity of strong, sweet coffee. In 1857, at the Rocky Mountain winter
quarters of Capt. Richard Grant and his men, Christmas dinner in Grant's
log cabin consisted of buffalo meat, boiled smoked tongue, bread, a preserve made from chokecherries, and coffee. The bread was undoubtedly
from flour saved for this special occasion.[38]

Throughout his years at Fort Clark, Chardon continued to exchange
feasts with parties of Indians. In April 1837, when a large party of two
hundred and fifty lodges of Arikari Indians arrived with three thousand
buffalo robes and a pack of beaver, they invited Chardon to a feast at
which the main course was dog. Six dogs were killed to provide the meat.
In return, Chardon had his men cook a feast of "ten Kittles of corn" for
the Indians. The Indians also traded for nearly all the corn he had in
store.[39]

Temporary food shortages at the fort could not be avoided. The main
difficulty was the large amount of food consumed both by the personnel
at the post and the frequent visitors. If a shortage of supplies coincided
with a scarcity of game there were problems in finding enough to eat. On
July 4, 1837, they had a celebration dinner, but by the twelfth they had

37. Ibid., 18, 92, 93, 166, 179.
38. Osborne Russell, in Mary E. Jones, *Daily Life on the Nineteenth Century American Frontier*
(Westport, Conn.: Greenwood Press, 1998), 36; Stuart, *Prospecting*, 129.
39. Chardon, *Journal*, 109, 111.

nothing to eat but "a little poor dried Meat" which Chardon had obtained from a steamboat. On the sixteenth, when the hunters arrived with the meat from three buffalo bulls, the cook provided "a Jackson dinner" of "Pot pye, and pudding," but by July 19 Chardon wrote, overdramatically, that with few provisions on hand and thirty mouths to feed they were in "a fair way of starveing." A few days later all the men were out gathering berries. Unlike the men in the high Rockies, the men at Fort Clark were rarely in any real danger of going hungry.[40]

One surprise, in a journal that covers five years in a post on the Missouri, is how seldom Chardon mentions fish. They ate it and Chardon liked it, but it was simply not as important as meat. In August 1835, Chardon mentions having "good fish" for dinner, and on April 16, 1839, a large sturgeon was the "the first fish this year." A week later they caught "several fine cat fish." If they had wanted to, they could have eaten a lot more fish.[41]

Traders going up the Missouri usually called at Fort Clark before pressing on to Fort Union near the mouth of the Yellowstone. For many years, Fort Union was the main American Fur Company post on the upper Missouri. Kenneth McKenzie, who built the post and in its early years ran it for the American Fur Company, lived well. Charles Larpenteur, who for a time was employed as a clerk there, described a meal in the summer of 1834. There was "a splendidly set table with a very white table cloth," and two waiters served. McKenzie, who was well dressed, sat at the head of the table. The main course, as might be expected, consisted of "fine fat buffalo meat," but there was also plenty of fresh butter, cream, and milk. The only restriction was that only two biscuits were allowed to each man. As some of the clerks at the post liked to have a meal just before going to bed, a large kettle of buffalo meat was left boiling for their use. McKenzie "played the nabob," Larpenteur wrote, going to bed late and rising late, and, as nothing was served until he was ready, it was nine before Larpenteur sat down to breakfast.[42]

McKenzie's elegance was not the whole story of Fort Union. At Christmas, drink, not food, dominated the celebrations. The usual fine dinner "was never the case here," and at one Christmas, Larpenteur witnessed a great drunken tumult. It lasted for nearly three days, and there was fighting and stabbing. As a result, two men were initially sentenced to hang, but this was commuted to thirty-nine lashes each. A few years later, when Larpenteur entered Fort Union one night at the beginning of December,

40. Ibid., 120–22.
41. Ibid., 44, 192.
42. Larpenteur, *Forty Years*, 52–57.

he found a large trading party at "the highest pitch of drunkenness" and the company leader and clerks almost as drunk.[43]

Fur-trading posts continued to be used and built through most of the nineteenth century. On the Great Plains, buffalo and other game were still abundant until the 1880s, and in the 1840s trading posts along the main routes to the west were given a great boost by the coming of trans-Continental emigrants. The men at Fort Laramie, in modern Wyoming, a key post for the activities of the American Fur Company, raised cattle and poultry, made butter, and had an abundance of milk. In July 1846 a visitor who ate with officials of the company was given a dinner of boiled corned beef, cold biscuits, and milk. They told him that this was "their usual fare" when they could get flour. When they did not have bread, they lived on fresh buffalo meat, venison, salt beef, and milk. At Fort Bridger, the same traveler found the trappers and hunters "lounging about, making small trades for sugar, coffee, flour, and whiskey." As usual, where trappers gathered, liquor was priced exorbitantly. Two dollars cash was being paid for half a pint, and the visitor heard of a pint selling for a pair of buckskin pants worth ten dollars.[44]

When the great days of the mountain men were over, some continued to trap, and others worked at the trading posts that still existed to accept the diminishing supply of pelts. A few returned to the East, but some married and settled in the small Hispanic towns of the Southwest, where they usually grew a little corn, and hunted for the meat that still provided much of their diet. Others found a living guiding emigrants trekking to the West Coast or set up small trading posts along the trails. There they sold both necessities and luxuries to the hundreds of thousands who crossed the plains from the 1840s to the end of the century.

43. Ibid., 134–35, 150.

44. Edwin Bryant, *What I Saw in California: Being the Journal of a Tour . . . 1846, 1847* (Minneapolis: Ross & Haines, 1967), 109, 112, 144.

Old French Market, New Orleans (courtesy Wisconsin Historical Society)

Fort Union on the Missouri, c. 1832 (courtesy Wisconsin Historical Society)

Herds of bison and elk on the Upper Missouri, c. 1832 (courtesy Wisconsin Historical Society)

Buffalo bull grazing, 1844 (courtesy Wisconsin Historical Society)

Men skinning buffalo, wood engraving from *Harper's Weekly,* 1874
(courtesy Library of Congress)

Herndan Hotel on the Missouri River, 1858 (courtesy Wisconsin Historical Society)

Sketch of Fort Laramie, 1849 (courtesy Wisconsin Historical Society)

Sketch of Pacific Railroad dining car, 1869 (courtesy Library of Congress)

Pilgrims of the plains, 1871 (courtesy Wisconsin Historical Society)

Lithograph of wild turkey shooting, 1871 (courtesy Library of Congress)

Montana cowboys loading the chuck wagon (courtesy Wisconsin Historical Society)

Part 3

Overland Trails

CHAPTER 5

Tortillas and *Frijoles*

⁓

The flesh of the goat is course, but wholesome, and being cheaper than
mutton or beef, it is very freely used by the poor. That of the kid is
hardly surpassed for delicacy and sweetness.

Josiah Gregg, 1844

I n the 1820s and 1830s emigrants from the United States began
to enter the Mexican southwest and California to settle and to
trade. In areas where there were few Spanish, the Americans
simply took their own styles of food and cooking with them,
but in areas where there were already sizeable Hispanic populations, Mexican foodstuffs and Mexican styles of cooking had a
major impact on the American diet. Mexico had established its independence from Spain in the early 1820s, and its borders stretched far into what
is now the American Southwest. The present states of Texas, Arizona,
New Mexico, and California, as well as lower Colorado were all part of
Mexico. Much of this area was Indian country, but there were long-
established Spanish settlements along the Rio Grande, and there were settlements along the Pacific coast as far north as San Francisco.

In the 1820s and early 1830s, the first movement of Americans into
southeastern Texas did not bring any extensive contact with Mexicans. The
immigrants settled in an area that had been little developed by the Spanish. Cotton planters moved in with their slaves, and they were joined by
other, poorer Americans, who hoped for better opportunities in this vast,
undeveloped area. In 1831, an anonymous visitor who sailed from New
Orleans to the mouth of the Brazos River landed in prairies rich in game.
On the waters near the mouth of the river, there were great flocks of wild
ducks, geese, and other waterfowl. The visitor moved up the river to the
small settlement of Brazoria, in an area that had only recently attracted
immigrants, and lodged at what he termed "the principal hotel." The village

had some thirty houses, and the hotel, kept by a son of famous Texas pioneer Moses Austin, consisted of two linked long cabins and had thirty boarders. They ate "excellent" food on a table set in an open passage.

In the woods separating the village from a nearby "estate" there were deer, hogs, and squirrels. The estate grew cotton, but most of its land was used for raising cattle. The owner, who lived in a log house, employed an Indian hunter to keep the family supplied with game, and the visitor was given plentiful food, most of it venison and wild turkey. There was abundant wild honey in hollow trees throughout the area.[1]

As he traveled around Galveston Bay, the visitor was struck by the ample natural resources. There were numerous deer on the prairies, turkeys and wild hogs in the woods, great flocks of waterfowl, many varieties of fish, and tasty oysters. Although there were few settlers, cattle were numerous, and there was abundant milk. The farmers made butter and cheese for their own families. Traveling north of San Felipe, the visitor had a chance to see how some of the poorer settlers were faring. At one house, he was given "cakes made of Indian meal" and milk. In the poorer houses, there was much less meat than in the region's inns, but an old woman, who had very little of anything, gave him a meal of pork, fried with onions "tops and all."[2]

For those who had money, the proximity to New Orleans allowed southeastern Texas to be well supplied for special occasions. English-born Ann Raney was married to John Thomas in Brazoria in 1833, and they had a full day of celebration. Following the ceremony tea, coffee, and cakes were provided, and a dance went on until midnight. The wedding party sat down to supper, the table arranged "with every delicacy that could be procured," including fruit from New Orleans, fowl, meat, more cake, coffee, and plenty of wine.[3]

After their marriage, the new couple moved about thirty miles from Brazoria to a spot where John Thomas already had a cabin, an orchard of peach trees, and "a fine vegetable garden." At her first dinner, the table "was filled with vegetables of all kinds, milk and butter, and the best kind of corn bread." The corn bread was the only disappointment. Ann had only left England in the previous year, and like most of the English immigrants had not taken to corn bread. Her husband promised wheat flour as soon as

1. Anon, *A Visit to Texas: Being the Journal of a Traveller through Those Parts Most Interesting to American Settlers* (New York, 1834), 14–51.

2. Ibid., 90–93, 109–10, 116–17, 226–48.

3. Ann Raney Coleman, *Victorian Lady on the Texas Frontier: The Journal of Ann Raney Coleman*, ed. C. Richard King (Norman: University of Oklahoma Press, 1971), 53–54.

possible. After they moved to settle on the Brazos River, the peaches were replaced by a pecan orchard, and they had a large pond with plentiful ducks, turkeys, cranes, and other fowl.[4]

When Texas gained its independence from Mexico in 1836, the American population of some thirty thousand was still largely confined to the southeastern corner of the state, and even after Texas entered the Union in 1845, the huge area of west Texas was Indian country. Houston in the mid-1850s was very much a frontier town. A central market carried cornmeal, wheat flour brought from Galveston, whiskey, salt pork, veal, mutton, and beef. Pole Kalikst Wolski, who visited Texas at this time, praised Texan hospitality. Settlers around Houston invited all strangers to their table, but, the food, said Wolski, was "not much to boast of." The main items were fried salt pork, corn pancakes, weak black coffee, or strong tea.[5]

Wolski traveled from Houston to live for a time at the French colony of La Réunion. The French were trying to get established near Dallas, which was then a village with only a few hundred residents. On their way from Dallas to the French colony, Wolski and his friends stopped for a night and cooked a meal of soup with rice, accompanied by fried salt pork. When someone came to their camp, they asked him to join them in "that speciality well known to all colonists in Texas, as it is what they live on, pancakes made of corn meal." To drink, they had water "flavored with whiskey."[6]

In Dallas there was a good general store, with "salt pork, whiskey, wine, arak, sugar, salt, coffee, tea, and other articles necessary for life, all scattered chaotically about." Arak is a potent drink usually associated with Asia or the Middle East. Presumably this was a local product that took advantage of the rice production in nearby Louisiana. One version of Arak is distilled from a fermented mash of malted rice and molasses. There was no butcher in Dallas, but settlers brought steers into town, slaughtered them, and sold pieces as they were cut from the carcasses. For much of the year the meat had to be cooked at once before it spoiled. In Galveston, the residents were a little more fortunate, as they cooled their water with ice that was brought "in large quantities from Boston."[7]

That first year, as the French settlers tried to get established near Dallas,

---

4. Ibid., 59–66, 74.

5. Kalikst Wolski, *American Impressions,* trans. Marion M. Coleman (Cheshire, Conn.: Cherry Hill Books, 1968), 154–55.

6. Ibid., 157.

7. Ibid., 143, 180.

they ate in American frontier style. Breakfast consisted of beefsteak (when fresh meat was available in Dallas), or fried salt pork, eaten with beans or lentils (brought from New Orleans), cornmeal pancakes, and black coffee. There was no milk, as the colonists did not have cows when Wolski lived there. Dinner, in midafternoon, consisted of a soup of beef stock (without vegetables, as they had none), meat, wheat bread, and water. Supper, at nine in the evening, usually consisted of corn pancakes and tea. When there was no fresh meat available in Dallas, they had rice soup flavored with salt pork. They did not use butter, as it was "extraordinarily rare" and very expensive.

In the hope of having vegetables, the French settlers planted seeds brought from Europe but found that they would not grow, even though they watered them twice a day with water brought from a spring. The people in Dallas said that vegetables could only be grown if they were planted between rows of corn to shield them from the sun.[8]

While American pioneers in southeastern Texas usually ate in a style typical of the southern frontiers of the United States, those who reached the Mexican settlements in what were to become Arizona and New Mexico experienced a different way of life. In the mainland regions colonized by the Spanish, the Indian occupants had made extensive use of corn, beans, and squash, all plants indigenous to the western hemisphere. These crops played a vital part in the diet of all newcomers to North America, but, in Mexico and the Southwest, Indian foods and cooking had far more impact on the cooking of the Europeans than they did in regions farther north. The difference in influence stemmed largely from the far greater survival of Indian peoples in the general population.

In the British colonies, population growth was so great that the Indian populations were swamped. Most died in wars or from diseases, and the remnants of tribes moved farther west. The Spanish came in fewer numbers. A minority of Spanish held leadership positions and ruled over a population both of mixed Spanish/Indian origin and of Indians who had not mixed with the Europeans. In the British regions, Indian patterns of eating were of great importance for explorers and trappers, but their impact on the incoming European population was primarily through the new food plants of the Americans—particularly corn. In the Spanish regions, varieties of dishes that dated back to pre-European times survived to take an important place in the diet of the region. They blended with foods and

8. Ibid., 181–82.

styles of cooking brought from Spain to produce a distinctive Spanish-Indian eating pattern.[9]

The Spanish introduced animals previously unknown in the Americas—cattle, sheep, pigs, and goats—that also altered the eating patterns of the areas they settled. Mutton had far greater importance in the diet of the Southwest than in that of areas farther north. Although modifications of Mexican and southwestern foods spread throughout the United States in the twentieth century, these foods were strange and exotic to Anglo-Americans when they first moved into the Southwest.

The basic bread was the tortilla. Corn kernels were dried and then cooked in lime and water to loosen the husks for removal. This process released the niacin that was otherwise bound in the corn. The corn was then placed on a large stone (a metate) and finely ground by the use of another stone. Enough water was added to make a dough, and pieces of the dough were flattened and placed on an iron sheet on the fire. The tortillas were used as bread, as a basis for other Mexican foods, and to scoop up the beans (*frijoles*) or other foods placed on the table.

The dark red *frijoles* were as basic to southwestern cooking as tortillas, and together they were a staple of Hispanic diet in the Southwest. In the early 1840s, one American commented that beans, stewed or fried in mutton fat, were eaten at breakfast, dinner, and supper and were used by the Mexicans as potatoes were used by the Irish. The *frijoles* were usually seasoned with red peppers. Peppers, which first became known to the Europeans when Columbus reached Hispaniola, were another constant in southwestern cooking. They grew in many varieties, colors, and flavors, but it was the red, spicy chili peppers that were most favored. Green peppers were often used in salads. Most of the meat dishes were flavored in one way or another with red chili peppers.[10]

The first main contact of the Anglo-Americans with the food of the Southwest came with the opening of the Santa Fe Trail in the early 1820s. Unlike the later trails to Oregon and California, the Santa Fe Trail was primarily a trading route for exchanging American goods for Mexican

9. There is a discussion of the exchange of crops and animals between the eastern and western hemispheres in Alfred W. Crosby, *The Columbian Exchange: Biological and Cultural Consequences of 1492* (Westport, Conn.: Greenwood Press, 1972), and the crops and diet of the Maya, Aztec, and Inca are given extensive treatment in Sophie D. Coe, *America's First Cuisines* (Austin: University of Texas Press, 1994). See also *Oxford Encyclopedia of Food and Drink in America*, 2:146–47; and Alan Davidson, *Oxford Companion to Food*, 207.

10. Magoffin, *Down the Santa Fe Trail*, 157 n. 66; William W. H. Davis, *El Gringo: or, New Mexico and Her People* (1857; repr., Chicago: Rio Grande Press, 1962), 186; Evan Jones, *American Food: The Gastronomic Story*, 2nd. ed. (New York: Vintage Books, 1981), 60–64–66; *Oxford Encyclopedia of Food and Drink in America*, 2:480–82.

silver. Although others had preceded William Becknell into the region, Becknell pioneered a trading route from Boone's Lick in Missouri to Santa Fe and back in the winter of 1821–1822. The early traders across the southwest plains rarely suffered severe hunger while on their journey, which took two months or more. They carried provisions with the trade goods, and ample game was available along large sections of the route.

While on the trail, Becknell was somewhat adventurous in the matter of food. After traveling all day in the sight of buffalo, he killed a prairie dog because he was interested in discovering how it tasted. He roasted a small portion and "found it strong and unpalatable," but he experimented again when he killed an animal that had long shaggy hair and was about the size of a raccoon. In this case, he thought the meat was tender and delicious, but he quickly returned to a diet more normal for Great Plains' travelers by "killing a buffaloe for breakfast." He was near the Arkansas River, and as far as the eye could see the country was "alive with buffaloe and other animals." His party, however, was out of bread and salt for several weeks before it reached Santa Fe early in November.

Although Becknell had been willing to try unknown meat while on the trail, his journal reveals no particular interest in the food being eaten in Santa Fe. He merely commented that corn, rice, and wheat were the main crops grown there and that they had few garden vegetables except onions. Another visitor to Santa Fe at about the same time said the inhabitants raised onions, peas, corn, wheat, and red pepper—"a principal ingredient in Spanish food." Potatoes and turnips, he wrote, were unknown, and though he saw peach trees, he saw no apples, cherries, or pears. Hogs and poultry were scarce, but sheep, goats, and cattle were abundant.[11]

Appreciation of the distinctive food of the Southwest was slow in coming for American visitors. Not until trade became more extensive, and Americans from the north began to live year-round in Santa Fe, did they begin to savor some of the life there. Many Anglo-Americans were highly critical of the inhabitants of northern Mexico and compared them unfavorably with those in their own country. They complained of great gaps between rich and poor, pervasive poverty, the dominant role of the Catholic Church, and what was viewed as a general lack of "enterprise." Even those

11. "Journal of Thomas [William] Becknell," in Archer B. Hulbert, ed., *Southwest on the Turquoise Trail: The First Diaries on the Road to Santa Fe* (Denver: Denver Public Library, 1933), 56–68; James, *Three Years*, 147–48. There is a colorful description of historical recipes on the Santa Fe Trail in Samuel P. Arnold, *Eating Up the Santa Fe Trail: Recipes and Lore from the Old West* (Niwot: University Press of Colorado, 1990).

not blinded by prejudice often at first had difficulty accepting the different food of the Southwest.

In the 1820s James Pattie went through the Southwest and into southern California on extensive trapping expeditions, encountering southwestern food in his trips down the Rio Grande to Santa Fe and beyond. North of Santa Fe, he and his companions were given a dish which he described as "red pepper, ground and mixed with corn meal, and stewed in fat and water." They could not eat it but were able to eat the equally unfamiliar tortillas and milk that were then offered. He described tortillas, probably inaccurately, as thin cakes made of corn and wheat, ground between two flat stones. Most tortillas were made of corn; wheat, which had been introduced by the Spanish, was sometimes used by those who had European tastes.[12]

As Pattie traveled along the Rio Grande from Santa Fe to Socorro, he saw no fenced fields but an abundance of domestic animals. Away from the river, there were great numbers of bears, deer, and turkeys. At St. Philip, he drank the local wine. When he was later in the El Paso region, he saw "magnificent vineyards." In this area, settlements stretched along the river for eight miles, with wheat fields and a great variety of fruit trees.[13]

When Pattie and his companions left the Rio Grande, they hunted through mountain wilderness areas in what are now New Mexico and Arizona. In these travels, they hoped to live on game, but, as so often happened in isolated areas, they alternated between near-starvation and plenty—never managing to take enough meat with them to last when there was no game. On several occasions they ran out of food and ate what they could find, including a buzzard and a raven. After killing an antelope, they immediately drank its blood. They also made use of what they had with them—killing and eating one of their horses and one of their dogs. Surprisingly, although they saw a great many wild hogs, they "could never bring themselves to eat them." Pattie does not explain why they could bring themselves to eat a buzzard or a raven but not a wild hog. Perhaps the wild hogs never appeared when they were desperate.[14]

Pattie and his companions were helped by Indian food. Southwestern Indians made extensive use of the pods of the mesquite trees, which

12. James Pattie, *The Personal Narrative of James O. Pattie of Kentucky*, ed. Timothy Flint and Milo M. Quaife (1831; repr., Chicago: R. R. Donnelley & Sons, 1930), 56; *Oxford Encyclopedia of Food and Drink in America*, 2:481–82.

13. Pattie, *Personal Narrative*, 71–73, 175.

14. Ibid., 73–78, 99–106.

contain seeds rich in protein. The Indians used mesquite pods both green and dried. Fully grown, the pods are as long as six inches and have a sweet pulp around the seeds. When green, they were cooked as they were, and when dried they were ground and either used to make bread or mixed with water to make a drink. Pattie became "very fond" of the bread. The party also obtained dried beans from the Indians, and a group of Navahos gave them various undescribed Navaho dishes, along with dried berries and sweet vegetables.

Later, Pattie traveled through the southwestern deserts to Baja California, where missions founded by the Spanish survived in a weakened state under Mexican rule. There, he encountered Christian Indians who were roasting mescal and "the inside heads of palm trees for food." Pattie found these "very agreeable." He had previously tried an Indian alcoholic drink made from mescal. He thought it tasted like "crab-apple cider."[15]

Mescal, which was popular among both Indians and Mexicans, is made from various species of agave plants (sometimes known as century plants), especially the mescal plant itself. The mescal has a head resembling a cabbage with thick thorny leaves. In the spring Indians and Mexicans cut into it to get a sweet drink. After leaving it to ferment, Mexicans distilled a liquor from it. Like the brandy distilled from grapes, this was often simply called *aguardiente,* but it was also known as *mescal.* The Indians also roasted both the leaves and bulbous roots of mescal and ate them.[16]

For a time Pattie was imprisoned at one of the missions by the Mexicans and was then taken north to San Diego. At first his food was cornmeal mush, given to him once a day, but conditions varied. At one mission, an old steer was killed, and he and his fellow prisoners were given what Pattie thought was a poor meal of boiled meat and corn. When they complained, they were given "a good dish of fat mutton" with tortillas. In prison at San Diego, Pattie was given breakfast and supper of dried beans and corn cooked with "rancid tallow." Pattie was unable to eat it, but the sergeant in charge gave him two other dishes that he described as well cooked and well seasoned.[17]

In the 1830s, as trade along the Santa Fe trail increased, the Southwest became better known to Americans. Josiah Gregg, who traveled the trail extensively in the 1830s, described what had become a well-established

15. Ibid., 85, 92, 187, 265; *Oxford Companion to Food,* 497.

16. Daniel E. Connor, *Joseph Reddeford Walker and the Arizona Adventure,* ed. Donald J. Berthrong and Odessa Davenport (Norman: University of Oklahoma Press), 115–16; Meriwether, *My Life,* 217–18.

17. Pattie, *Narrative,* 266–87.

routine. Wagon trains usually set out from Independence, Missouri, and the traders were often accompanied by trappers heading for the southern Rockies. Even at this early date, there were also often a few "pale-faced invalids" taking the trip for their health. The invalids generally took a few special items—tea, rice, fruit, and crackers—for the first week or two, after which they ate what the teamsters and hunters were eating.

Those who traveled the Santa Fe Trail as teamsters, traders, or hunters were generally well fed. The standard ration for each man for the trip was fifty pounds of flour, fifty pounds of "bacon," twenty pounds of sugar, ten pounds of coffee, and some salt. Beans and crackers were available but were regarded as "*dispensable* luxuries." Water kegs were kept in the wagons for dry areas, particularly the fifty-mile stretch from the Arkansas to the Cimarron River. For cooking there was a frying pan (often a spider), a sheet-iron camp kettle, and a coffee pot. Each man had a tin cup for his coffee and a butcher's knife to take his share of the meat. After the meat was cooked, the men placed the pan and kettle on the ground, sat around them, and used their knives to pick out and cut pieces of meat.[18]

Once traders reached the buffalo range they depended largely on buffalo for meat. They ate all the fresh meat they wanted and made buffalo jerky for use along stretches of the trail when game would be scarcer. At times, they would halt for a day or two to kill as many buffalo as possible and jerk the meat on a scaffold over a fire. Often, the teamsters simply strung strips of buffalo meat on cords along the sides of the wagons to dry in the blazing sun as they continued along the trail.

On Gregg's first trip along the trail in 1831, he and his companions depended heavily on bacon for about a month. Then, when game was readily available, they did not dry enough buffalo meat, and beyond the Cimarron, when game became scarce, they ran short. They used most of the provisions they had taken with them, particularly the flour. Fortunately, they met a Mexican buffalo hunter who sold them a large quantity of dried buffalo meat and bags of "coarse oven-toasted loaves," used by Mexican travelers. The loaves were made by opening up ordinary leavened rolls and toasting them brown in an oven to preserve them. They were very hard but were edible when soaked in water or, preferably, in coffee.[19]

Unlike most visitors from the North, Gregg gave a balanced view of Mexican society in the settlements along the Rio Grande valley. He showed an interest in what the local inhabitants ate and how they prepared

18. Josiah Gregg, *Commerce of the Prairies*, ed. Max L. Moorhead (1844; repr., Norman: University of Oklahoma Press, 1954), 23–24, 39, 49.
19. Ibid., 38, 63–68.

their food, describing the importance of both tortillas and *atole,* which he said had been passed to the Mexicans by the Indians. The Mexican women competed in the thinness of their tortillas, boiling the corn with a little lime, grinding it into paste on a stone, spreading it on small sheet of iron or copper, and putting it over the fire for rapid baking.

Atole is dried, finely ground corn, either made into a mush or mixed with water or milk to make a thick drink. It was eaten at practically every meal. Gregg said that the poorer Mexicans used it more than the Americans used coffee and that together with beans and red peppers it was a main food. Green peppers were served up in different salads and were regarded as "one of the greatest luxuries." At the poorer ranches, the meal was usually eaten without a table. Dishes were served directly out of the kitchen, and each guest balanced a plate on his or her knee. The food was usually hashed or boiled so that it could be scooped up with a tortilla or eaten with a spoon.[20]

Rather than the hogs and cattle, the Mexicans of the Southwest depended on sheep and goats. Mutton was to New Mexicans what pork was to westerners in the United States. Unlike most Americans, Gregg liked mutton. The "immense" flocks of sheep, he wrote, produced a "justly celebrated" mutton with "a peculiarly delicious flavor." As goat's meat was cheaper than mutton or beef, it was much used by the poor. Gregg found ordinary goat meat coarse, but thought the meat of a kid could hardly be "surpassed for delicacy and sweetness." Goat's milk was much more common in the region than cow's milk, and many preferred it. On his first trip along the trail, when Gregg stopped at a sheep ranch north of Santa Fe, he was given goat's milk and "curdle cheese" (a simple type of cottage cheese).[21]

Many New Mexicans added to their stock of meat by traveling north for an annual buffalo hunt, drying the buffalo meat for future use. A German who first went to the Santa Fe region at the end of the 1840s noted that from all parts of the territory the locals would make up yearly expeditions into the buffalo country. They set out in large parties, with wagons scattered among large numbers of two-wheeled Mexican carts (*carretas*) pulled by oxen. Large parties were preferred for protection from the Indians. Expert hunters went with the parties and worked either for wages or, more usually, for shares in the dried meat. The buffalo meat was cut into thin slices and hung on ropes and bushes to dry before being packed into hides

20. Ibid., 76–77, 102–4, 108–11.
21. Ibid., 76–77, 133–36.

for taking back to the settlements. This hunt gave families a reserve of meat for the year, and the surplus was sold to stores in the region. Although the jerky could be eaten dry, it was more usual to pound it into bits and to fry it with fat, chilies, and onions. This custom of providing meat for southwestern settlements did not end until the railroads cut across the plains.[22]

To anyone used to the hard-drinking habits of American westerners, the moderation of the Mexicans of the Southwest was a surprise. Gregg noted that New Mexicans drank a little local wine with their meals but otherwise drank little. Gregg believed that one reason for the higher levels of sobriety in New Mexico was probably the high cost of hard liquor, which placed it beyond the reach of the poorer Mexicans. He was probably referring to whiskey, not the local liquors made from agave plants. William Davis, who lived in Santa Fe in the mid-1850s, also commented on Mexican moderation in drinking and said that at their meals they drank water, coffee, or chocolate. Like most newcomers, he was impressed by the "peculiarly fine" drinking chocolate.

Late in the 1830s, Gregg went south from Santa Fe along the Rio Grande into the region where most wine was made. He drank a "pleasant" wine made from grapes "of the most exquisite flavor," which reminded him a little of Malaga, and a brandy (*aguardiente*) that was agreeably flavored but rather weak. The Anglos referred to the wine and brandy of this region as "Pass wine" and "Pass whiskey." The main source of actual whiskey in New Mexico was the Taos region, where it was distilled primarily from wheat. In the 1850s the wine-growing areas of the Southwest extended all the way from the area directly north of Albuquerque to that beyond El Paso.[23]

The El Paso area provided much of the fruit for the whole region. Along with masses of grapes, there was an abundance of apples and pears, and these were sent, both fresh and dried, both south into Mexico and north to the Santa Fe area, where there was a lack of fruit. Around Santa Fe, Gregg only saw a few inferior orchards of apples, peaches, and apricots. To some extent this lack of cultivated fruit was compensated for by wild fruits, particularly prickly pears. Also a good deal of use was made of the piñon tree. This provided a small, rich pine nut enclosed in an outer shell.[24]

22. Ibid., 67; Franz Huning, *Trader on the Santa Fe Trail: Memoirs of Franz Huning*, ed. Liza Fergusson Browne (Albuquerque: University of Albuquerque, 1973), 26–29.

23. Gregg, *Commerce of the Prairies*, 110, 111, 273; Davis, *El Gringo*, 186, 191–93; George A. McCall, *New Mexico in 1850: A Military View*, ed. Robert W. Frazer (Norman: University of Oklahoma Press, 1968), 44–45; Whiting Journal, in Bieber and Bender, eds., *Exploring Southwestern Trails, 1846–1854*, 310.

24. Gregg, *Commerce of the Prairies*, 111–13, 273, 313.

American travelers usually divided the population of New Mexico into three groups—the Mexicans, the Pueblo or Christianized Indians, and the "wild Indians." Gregg visited the pueblos of the Christianized Indians and said that they were considered the best farmers in the Southwest. Americans were impressed by the quality of the wheat, corn, onions, pumpkins, fruits, and vegetables produced in the pueblos. There were also large herds of cattle and horses.[25]

The food of the Pueblo Indians was much like that of the Mexicans, largely because the general diet of the region depended so much on the corn dishes, including tortillas and *atole,* that had been adopted from the original Indian diet. One type of corn bread that the Indians retained mainly for their own use was *guayave.* This was prepared much like a tortilla, except that the paste was made exceedingly thin, laid on heated stones, and almost immediately peeled off. When the layers were rolled together they formed the *guayave.*[26]

Records of women's perspectives of the Santa Fe Trail and the Mexican Southwest are rarely available for the early years of Anglo contact, but eighteen-year-old Susan Magoffin who in 1846 traveled along the trail with her forty-five-year-old husband, Samuel, a prosperous Santa Fe merchant, wrote a vivid journal describing her new experiences. Mrs. Magoffin was going to the Southwest at a moment of crisis. In May, the United States declared war on Mexico. One of the war's main objectives was the acquisition of the Mexican Southwest and California. For their journey along the Santa Fe trail, the Magoffins accompanied the forces of Gen. Stephen W. Kearny, who had been ordered to conquer the desired Mexican territories.

Samuel Magoffin had obviously made special arrangements for his young bride. She was happy with their conical tent, and her bed was "as good as many houses have." Her journal has a tone that is quite distinct from that of traders' accounts of life along the trail. In mid-June, a week after leaving Independence, Missouri, she left the wagon to pick some of the numerous raspberries and strawberries. There were a great many plums and grapes, but these were not yet ripe. Later in the journey, there were wild black cherries. They seemed sweet-tasting at first but were "as rough as persimons [*sic*]."

25. Ibid., 186–87, 194–95; Magoffin, *Down the Santa Fe Trail,* 151; Joseph K. Mansfield, *Mansfield on the Condition of the Western Forts, 1853–1854,* ed. Robert W. Frazer (Norman: University of Oklahoma Press, 1963), 7–8.

26. Davis, *El Gringo,* 327. See James A. Valasich, *Pueblo Indian Agriculture* (Albuquerque: University of New Mexico Press, 2005).

On July 1, shortly before they reached the buffalo country along the Arkansas, the Magoffins ate a dinner of boiled chicken, soup, rice, gooseberry tart, and wine. Within a week, the men were killing buffalo and stretching the meat out to dry. When they had a soup made from fresh hump ribs, Mrs. Magoffin was as delighted as any hunter. She declared she had never eaten its equal in the best hotels of New York and Philadelphia and thought that the marrow taken from the thigh bones was as good as the sweetest butter. Even in buffalo country, her husband made sure she had variety because later in July she had "a delightful dinner of two roasted ducks and baked beans."

On July 27 they reached Bent's Fort, the main trading post on the trail. It was described by another visitor that year as "a *mélange* of traders, and employers, government officers and subordinates, Indians, Frenchmen, and hunters." Mrs. Magoffin thought it was like an ancient adobe castle. It had over twenty rooms scattered around its inner walls. These included a dining room, a kitchen, a little store, and a billiard room. Good water was available from an inside well, and it tasted especially fine because there was also ice, a rarity for anyone traveling through this region in the 1840s. It had probably been brought from the Rockies in the previous winter and kept in the fort's icehouse. The ice may have been brought out because while Mrs. Magoffin was there she had a miscarriage. The Magoffins stayed at the fort for twelve days, during which time Mrs. Magoffin also had her nineteenth birthday.[27]

The men clearly were trying to be helpful to young Mrs. Magoffin. On the trail again, she was brought two hares, although they still had an antelope to live on for a day or two. The next day, she had a dinner of roast hare with wine. After the meal she walked in the piñon woods and ate some of the nuts. She thought they had a "sweet, rich, oily taste." On this part of the journey, in mid-August, the Magoffins ate much game—turkeys, prairie chickens, and hares. She was promised bear meat, but the men never killed one.

As they neared the Mexican settlements, the Magoffins were met by three rancheros who gave them *aguardiente* (brandy or other liquor), bread, and cheese. The bread was very hard, and the cheese was "clabber," made, said Mrs. Magoffin, like Dutch "smerecase." The "clabber" Mrs. Magoffin knew in the East was probably simply milk that had curdled and thickened. They were now beginning to pass small poor settlements with houses Mrs.

27. Magoffin, *Down the Santa Fe Trail*, 6, 36–37, 43, 56–71, 78; Lewis H. Garrard, *Wah-To-Yah and the Taos Trail*, intro. A. B. Guthrie Jr. (1850; repr., Norman: University of Oklahoma Press, 1955), 42.

Magoffin described as hovels. She said that the food of the inhabitants consisted of cheese, corn bread, and fruit and nuts collected in the mountains. The Magoffins tried to buy a few eggs or a chicken but discovered they were seldom seen in these settlements.

At Las Vegas, Mrs. Magoffin had her first southwestern dinner. It began with tortillas, cheese, and a mixture of what she thought was meat, green peppers, and onions presented in two earthen jugs. There were no knives, forks, or spoons. They ate Mexican-style by doubling up the tortillas and using them to scoop up the chili mixture. It seems likely that the chilies were red as well as green as Mrs. Magoffin ate very little, finding the dish too "strong." Her husband asked for something else for his wife, and she was brought "roasted corn rolled in a napkin." This and an egg completed her meal. On the following day, at Bernal, they stopped at noon for a dinner that she enjoyed a great deal more—fried chicken, corn, and bean soup. When they reached San Miguel their wagon broke, and while it was being mended the villagers brought them tortillas, kid goat's meat stewed with onions, and goat's milk.[28]

At the end of August, the Magoffins reached Santa Fe and moved into a house next to a church. It had four rooms, including the kitchen, all with dirt floors. Young Mrs. Magoffin described it as "quite a nice little place." They arrived too late for dinner to be prepared, but her husband's brother met them at their door, and they dined on oysters and champagne. Oysters were one of the early foods to be preserved in tins, and in the 1840s they found their way from the East Coast to western traders.

In the following days, Mrs. Magoffin began to experience housekeeping in Santa Fe. She was able to buy vegetables—squash, green corn, and green peas from children who came to the door—and there was a market where she could get peaches, "delicious" grapes, melons, and "inferior" apples. She also received four "mammoth bunches" of purple grapes as a gift from two army lieutenants. With snow on the nearby mountains, she found it strange to be living in a valley with excellent fruit and vegetables. Only the apples seemed worse than those she knew at home.

In mid-September, the Magoffins were invited to what she described as her "first entire Mexican dinner." American army officers were present, but they dined southwestern-style with all the men on one side of the table and all the women on the other. The dinner began about 2:00 P.M. and lasted for two and a half to three hours. After only a short time in Santa Fe, Mrs. Magoffin clearly had little idea of what she was eating. She was able to

28. Magoffin, *Down the Santa Fe Trail*, 75, 78, 89–98.

identify a preliminary course of rice flavored with a little butter and salt and covered with slices of boiled eggs, and she recognized the desserts—boiled milk seasoned with cinnamon and nutmeg, "cake pudding," and "fine, cool grapes"—but the major dishes were beyond her knowledge. She knew only that she had meat cooked in various ways.[29]

In the fall, Mrs. Magoffin traveled with her husband south of Santa Fe along the Rio Grande. Their first stop was at a *rancho,* "rather a poor place," with a little corn, beans, a few goats, sheep, asses ("jacks"), and "an abundance of green peppers." Traveling on, they killed and ate sandhill cranes, which had meat as "black as pea fowls." After they were boiled nearly all night, they were "tender and nice." Beyond Albuquerque they stopped to rest and bought eggs, tortillas, grapes, onions, apples, and watermelons from an Indian village on the other side of the river. Here, they found that they could buy all the eggs and fruit they wanted.

Mrs. Magoffin was now beginning to appreciate some of the Mexican food. Camping near a small town, she enjoyed the local tortillas and admitted that with a good dish of beans "one does not eat a bad dinner." When they stayed at a village to help Mrs. Magoffin recover from sickness, she dined at a table for the first time in two weeks, enjoying chilies with mutton, stewed chicken with onions, and a dessert pudding made with bread and grapes. Temporarily, they rented a house furnished in the Mexican manner, and the wife and daughter of the owner came with their own stones and corn to show Mrs. Magoffin how to make tortillas. It involved much more work than she had imagined, although the corn had already been soaked in lye to detach the hull and soften it.[30]

By the time that Mrs. Magoffin went to El Paso in February 1847, she had grown to like southwestern food. For their first two days in El Paso, the Magoffins stayed with a friend of her husband's who was a native-born Spaniard. The house had a garden with an abundance of fruit trees and grape vines, which was typical of houses in the town. It was kept by the owner's twenty-two-year-old daughter. They ate well during their brief stay, with coffee at about 7:30 A.M., breakfast at 10:00 A.M., and dinner at 5:00 P.M. The dishes served were "all Mexican," but it seems likely that they were also influenced by the Spanish origin of the father. All the food served was described as good, and some was "delightful." The meats were boiled rather than roasted, and most were cooked with vegetables—onions, cabbage, and tomatoes, with apples and grapes added. There were four

29. Ibid., 103–14, 130–36, 145.
30. Ibid., 149–76.

courses at dinner and two at breakfast, always ending with beans. Brandy and wine were on the table for each meal.[31]

After two days they moved to the priest's house, which was managed by his two sisters. The priest had been imprisoned by the Americans. Every morning on rising they were given chocolate to drink. Twenty years before, when Gen. George Sibley was on his way from Santa Fe to Taos, he stopped at the village of Santa Cruz and on rising was handed a cup of "very fine, rich chocolate." This was usual at the better homes in the Southwest but largely unknown in American regions to the north. Josiah Gregg thought that the Mexicans had "incomparable chocolate."[32]

In the priest's house, the Magoffins were given breakfast at 10:00 A.M., dinner at 2:00 P.M., chocolate again at dark, and supper at 9:00 P.M. Their meals were served in their rooms and were well prepared and varied. Mrs. Magoffin had decided that she should make a book of recipes to take home, because "the cooking in every thing is entirely different from ours, and some, indeed all of their dishes are so fine 'twoud be a shame not to let my friends have a taste of them too." Young Mrs. Magoffin showed a greater willingness than many Anglos to appreciate what was new in the Southwest.[33]

Although there was war between the United States and Mexico from 1846 to 1848, and the Southwest and California were transferred to the United States, the Santa Fe region retained its Spanish/Mexican/Indian character for much of the century. The number of Anglo-Americans increased, but there were not enough to transform the old customs.

In the mid-1850s, William Davis, a Mexican War veteran, came to Santa Fe as a United States attorney. His description of the region showed that it retained the essential characteristics described by Gregg in the 1830s. Davis believed that there were only about five hundred Anglos in the Santa Fe area. So few obviously had little impact on the food of the region, although Davis noted that tea, coffee, and sugar were becoming more common among "the peasantry," that there had been an increase in the cultivation of vegetables since the Americans had arrived and that barley and oats had been introduced into the region.

Davis liked the food. He thought the local mutton, "the principal article of food of the inhabitants," was "finely flavored." He obviously meant that mutton was the principal *meat*, not the principal article of food. In de-

31. Ibid., 205–6, 211.
32. Ibid., 208; "General Sibley's Santa Fe Diary, 1825–1826," in Hulbert, ed., *Southwest on the Turquoise Trail*, 167; Gregg, *Commerce of the Prairies*, 110.
33. Magoffin, *Down the Santa Fe Trail*, 208–9.

scribing the making of tortillas, he said, more accurately, that tortillas and beans were "the staff of life of all classes of the population." Davis was less fond of goat meat than of mutton, but, like many others, he thought goat's milk, which was in common use, was sweeter and richer than cow's milk.

In the mid-1850s, the supply of foodstuffs at the public market in Santa Fe was barely enough to meet the demands of a population of several thousand. The country people used the market to sell their mutton, red peppers, beans, onions, milk, bread, cheese, and, in season, grapes, wild plums, and wild berries. In winter, Indians and other hunters regularly brought in venison, turkey, and occasionally a bear. The meat was hung on lines and the fruits and vegetables spread out on mats or pieces of board. Onions and beets did excellently in the region and grew to a great size, but potatoes were expensive, and Davis was unsure whether any Mexicans had yet begun to try to cultivate them.[34]

As he traveled in New Mexico, Davis usually commented on his meals. At one inn, the dinner for five men consisted of about two pounds of badly cooked, unrecognizable meat, "half way between a stew and a boil," two small plates of boiled rice, bread, coffee, and "muddy" water. He was less critical when he stopped at a house in a small village on the east bank of the Rio Grande. Although he arrived in the evening, when supper was over, the owner gave him a large dish of *chili colorado* (red peppers and dried buffalo meat stewed together) which flamed "like the crater of Vesuvius," bread, tortillas, and a large pitcher of coffee. For breakfast he was given "*chili, tortillas,* and coffee."

In Penblanca, he ate at the house of one of the large landowners. He called the meal he was given "a true Mexican dinner" and a fair sample of how the better class ate. It began with young, tender, well-flavored mutton and beans. This was followed by a soup that Davis had never tasted before. It had small balls of flour and meat floating in it. The third course was a very hot mutton chili, and the meal was concluded with "stewed beans."

Like most visitors, Davis was impressed by El Paso. He reveled in the lushness of the fruit trees, the vineyards, and the flower gardens and was particularly happy with the only inn in the town. This was kept by a German or Swiss-German landlord. Davis's view was that "his *cuisine* . . . was quite incomparable," and there was a variety of dishes "seldom . . . surpassed in the first hotels in the United States."[35]

34. Davis, *El Gringo*, 47, 66–79, 252–53; Mansfield, *Mansfield on the Condition of the Western Forts*, 3.

35. Davis, *El Gringo*, 172–74, 185–86, 194–95, 213–16.

There was much good living in the El Paso region. Life in a Mexican merchant's family in that area is well described in the memories of Mary Barnard Aguirre. Mary Barnard was an American, born in St. Louis, who married a prosperous southwestern merchant and settled with him in 1863 in Las Cruces, some sixty miles north of El Paso. She traveled the Santa Fe Trail with her husband and three-month-old son, reaching their home in Las Cruces just a week before Christmas. When they sat down to dinner on Christmas Day, she was particularly impressed that one of the foods was "an immense watermelon as fresh & crisp as if it had just been cut." Watermelons, along with bunches of grapes, had been hung in the rafters of the storeroom, and there were grapes packed in chopped straw that were kept until late in the winter. This method of storing fruits and vegetables was typical of the region. A soldiers's wife traveling in New Mexico in the early 1860s remembered long strings of red peppers hanging on the outside of shanties along the way, and big yellow pumpkins adorning dirt roofs.

Mrs. Aguirre's baby son, Pedro, was the first grandson in the family, and great preparations were made for his christening. For three days before the event a baker and two assistants were brought into the house. They roasted fowl and pigs and baked a great variety of cakes and confectionery. The number of eggs used "was a marvel." The baking was carried out in a beehive-shaped adobe oven that opened into the kitchen. It was heated red hot, the coals scraped out, and the various items inserted on shallow pans and pieces of tin. Two hundred guests were invited, some from as far away as El Paso. After the christening, Pedro, who was six months old, was set at the head of the table for the meal, his health was drunk in champagne, and the festive meal was followed by a dance.[36]

Most Anglos who went to settle in the Southwest in the years after the American conquest did not have the comfortable existence of Mary Aguirre. In 1852, as a young girl of eleven, Marian Russell went along the Santa Fe Trail with her mother and brother. Marian's mother had been married, and widowed, twice: her first husband was an army surgeon killed in the Mexican War; her second husband was killed by Indians. An army doctor and two other officers offered the family transportation and provisions from Fort Leavenworth to Fort Union near Santa Fe if the mother would agree to cook for them. The wagon train they rode in was carrying supplies for Santa Fe and Fort Union.

36. Mary Barnard Aguirre, in *So Much to Be Done: Women Settlers on the Mining and Ranching Frontier,* ed. Ruth B. Moynihan et al. (Lincoln: University of Nebraska Press, 1990), 224–25; Lane, *I Married a Soldier,* 97.

After arriving in the Southwest, the family moved to Albuquerque, where Marian's mother rented an adobe house and took in boarders, mostly Indian scouts. These scouts, Marian said, were "white men." At the beginning, her mother did not board Mexicans but was "not long in learning the strange New Mexican cookery." She seems to have served a mixture of Anglo and local dishes. Marian remembered the "ever-present potatoes, gravy and dried apple pie." Potatoes had only come into use in the region with the coming of the Americans, and dried apple pie was a standard American frontier dish. Her mother, however, also served goat meat and mutton, "Indian beans or frijoles," and learned how to make tortillas. One dish the boarders craved was boiled wheat mixed with red pepper pods and cubes of goat meat. All the boarders sat at a homemade wooden table covered with a yellow-patterned oilcloth. They had steel knives and forks with bone handles, tin salt and pepper shakers, and crockery for the plates and cups.

Marian described the Mexican inhabitants of Albuquerque as living on a diet of goat meat and mutton, supplemented with deer and antelope meat, and pinto beans with red pepper. The locals baked tortillas in the ashes of their hearths and "huge loaves of golden brown bread" in outside beehive-shaped ovens. In their gardens they raised beans, peppers, corn, and many kinds of pumpkins and squash. The pumpkins and squash were dried for the winter. They also gathered and dried wild plums and choke-cherries. Marian remembered her mother cooking dried chokecherries, which she thought were all seed and no berry.[37]

Many visitors to Albuquerque in these years remembered the water rather than the food. All that was used had to be taken from the Rio Grande. It was very muddy and had to settle for hours before it was drinkable. An American trader who was there in the mid-1850s said that it was always "more or less oily." William Davis's chief memory of Albuquerque, which he said was "venerable with age," was the "millions" of flies and mosquitoes.[38]

Marian Russell and her mother moved to Santa Fe in the spring of 1854, and they rented a large adobe house on the central plaza and took in military boarders. Like most of the houses, theirs had a garden. Marian worked there, weeding beets and onions and hoeing among the squashes and pumpkins. More vivid in her memory, however, was the candy counter at a local store, which kept its candy in glass show cases, "heaped, piled,

37. Marian Russell, *Land of Enchantment: Memoirs of Marian Russell along the Santa Fe Trail,* ed. Garnet M. Brayer (Evanston, Ill.: Branding Iron Press, 1954), 13–18, 32–39.
38. Davis, *El Gringo,* 194–95; Huning, *Trader,* 55, 57.

and scattered all over." She remembered red candy, white candy, striped candy, licorice, candy hearts with verses, long brown sticks of horehound candy, peppermint candy, wintergreen candy, tiny dots of hot red candy, and candy that looked like shelled corn.

To young Marian Russell, the marketplace, which William Davis thought was marginal in its supplies for the residents, was "a wonder," with heaps of red and green peppers, red and blue corn, and golden melons. She remembered Santa Fe in the mid-1850s as a lively, colorful place. It was a supply center for the whole surrounding country, and there were freight wagons pulling in daily from Fort Union, Texas, and California. Great wagon trains were leaving in all directions, on streets enlivened by chickens, roosters, and goats.[39]

The movement of sizeable numbers of Anglo-Americans into the Southwest did not begin to occur until the development of a mining frontier in the 1850s sent eager gold seekers into the deserts of southern Arizona. After the Civil War, New Mexico became of greater interest when the cattle frontier spread westward out of the Texas panhandle. Even with the increase in Anglos, the Southwest retained its distinctive character and its distinctive foods. Ultimately the food of the Southwest was to have a greater impact on the entire United States than foods of the Anglos had on the Mexican population of the Southwest.

39. Russell, *Land of Enchantment*, 39, 49–56.

CHAPTER 6

On the Oregon Trail

O how I long to feast once more on bread

Elkanah Walker, 1838

From the 1840s to the end of the nineteenth century, hundreds of thousands of settlers went by wagon across the Great Plains to find a new home in the Far West. They had to find a way to feed themselves on a trek that would often last for six months or even more. The first steady stream of emigrants sought the rich agricultural lands of the Oregon region, but these pioneers were quickly followed by others. Some sought isolation and religious freedom on the arid lands near the Great Salt Lake in what is now Utah; others, lured to California by the discovery of gold, hoped to strike it rich. In 1849, a great rush of gold and silver seekers went across the plains to California. Ultimately, gold and silver were sought throughout the Rockies.

A variety of routes were used to reach the Far West. Conditions and dangers varied widely, but, whatever the route, planning the food that would be taken for a journey that would last many months was a major undertaking. Most hoped to supplement their provisions by hunting, and in the Southwest emigrants with money could buy supplies in the towns and villages that dotted part of the route. However, many had to depend on the food they took with them.

In the early years, the most important route was the Oregon Trail. It began on the Missouri River at Independence, Missouri, or some nearby jumping-off point, and stretched westward some two thousand miles to the far northwest. Emigrants plodded west along the Platte to Fort Laramie, past Independence Rock, through South Pass to Fort Bridger, on past Fort Hall on the Snake River, down through the mountains to the Columbia, and into the Willamette valley. Even if all went well, the journey took some six months. At Fort Hall, the trail divided, and some pioneers struck out southwest for California.

127

From the 1840s, guides were available, giving emigrants detailed advice on the best routes on what might be expected on the trails and on what to pack. They gave much the same general advice about what foodstuffs to take, although the amounts varied. An 1845 guide suggested that each individual going to the West Coast needed 200 pounds of flour, 150 pounds of bacon, 10 pounds of coffee, 20 pounds of sugar, and 10 pounds of salt. In addition, chipped beef, rice, tea, dried beans, dried fruit, saleratus (potassium or sodium bicarbonate for raising bread), vinegar, pickles, mustard, and tallow could be taken. Joseph Ware's guide, published in 1849, suggested a barrel of flour or 180 pounds of ship's biscuit, 150 to 180 pounds of bacon, 60 pounds of beans or peas, 25 pounds of rice, 25 pounds of coffee, 40 pounds of sugar, a keg of lard, 30 or 40 pounds of dried peaches or apples, a keg of clear, rendered beef suet (as a substitute for butter), and some molasses, vinegar, salt, and pepper.[1]

In his 1859 guide, army officer Randolph Marcy gave similar suggestions, except that he suggested taking less bacon. Instead, he recommended driving cattle to provide fresh beef. This was quite common when troops were on the march but not typical of western emigrants, although those with children often took a cow to provide milk.

Marcy gave instructions on the best ways to pack and preserve the supplies. While many westerners simply referred to all salt pork as "bacon," army officer Marcy drew a distinction between sides of bacon and barreled pork in brine. Sides of bacon were to be taken in canvas sacks, or, if the bacon had to be protected against extreme heat, in boxes surrounded by bran. If salt pork was taken, it should be removed from the barrels, packed like bacon, and put in the bottom of the wagons to keep cool. Bacon was preferable because it kept better. He also suggested the use of pemmican. If any butter was taken Marcy suggested it should be boiled, the scum skimmed off until it was clear, and the liquid placed in canisters soldered shut. To avoid the sugar getting wet, he recommended putting it in India-rubber or gutta-percha sacks.

Marcy suggested that vegetables could be taken in a dried form. He pointed out that this had proved useful both in the Crimean War and for the American army. To make dried vegetables, fresh vegetables were cut into slices and put into a very strong press to remove the juice. The vegetable cake that remained was then dried in the oven until it became "almost as hard as a rock." When boiled, it swelled. Marcy suggested that

1. Lillian Schlissel, ed., *Women's Diaries of the Westward Journey* (New York: Schocken Books, 1982), 23; Joseph E. Ware, *The Emigrant's Guide to California* (1849; repr., New York: Da Capo Press, 1972), 5–7.

canned vegetables could also be used, but their weight presented a problem. Canned vegetables were becoming more generally available in the 1850s, but the typical emigrant had to consider cost as well as weight.[2]

As a soldier, Marcy was well aware of the problem that scurvy presented for those who took long journeys without fresh fruits or vegetables. The disease had long been recognized, and some had pointed out that fruits and vegetables were needed to avoid it, but many still did not understand how to avoid it. No one yet knew that it was caused by a lack of vitamin C (ascorbic acid), and some of the suggested remedies, such as vinegar, were useless. Marcy wrote, in error, that the antiscorbutic properties of vegetables were not impaired by the process of drying, but he also made the more valuable suggestions that wild onions, grapes, and greens were useful and that, in the absence of vegetables, citric acid could be drunk with sugar and water.[3]

Many emigrants crossing the plains, even if they knew little about scurvy, were protected from it by the many wild berries and currants available along the western trails. Pioneers eagerly awaited the ripening of wild fruits, and in their journals they mention gathering them. In 1844, when mountain man James Clyman went west with one of the first large wagon trains to Oregon, he acted as a guard near Chimney Rock in the valley of the North Platte for "a Beautifull covey of young Ladies & misses while they gathered wild currants & choke chirries which grow in great perfusion in this region." They were not always sure what they were gathering because varieties differed from those at home. In 1847 Elizabeth Smith gathered gooseberries near South Pass, but she was surprised that these, like all the gooseberries she found beyond the Missouri, were smooth.[4]

2. Randolph B. Marcy, *The Prairie Traveler: A Hand-Book for Overland Expansion* (1859; repr., Williamstown, Mass.: Corner House Publishers, 1968), 30–33, 35–36; Alan Davidson, *Oxford Companion to Food,* 718; James E. Nichols, "The Grocery Trade," in *1795–1895: One Hundred Years of American Commerce,* 597. There is an excellent account of food and cooking on the Oregon Trail in Jacqueline Williams, *Wagon Wheel Kitchens: Food on the Oregon Trail* (Lawrence: University Press of Kansas, 1993), 119–20.

3. Marcy, *Prairie Traveler,* 31, 33; Mark Graubard, *Man's Food: Its Rhyme or Reason* (New York: Macmillan, 1943); Joseph R. Conlin, *Bacon, Beans, and Galantines: Food and Foodways on the Western Mining Frontier* (Reno: University of Nevada Press, 1986), discusses scurvy on the routes to California in 1849. See also, Francis E. Cuppage, *James Cook and the Conquest of Scurvy* (Westport, Conn.: Greenwood Press, 1994), 95–101, 124–25; Kenneth L. Carpenter, *History of Scurvy and Vitamin C* (Cambridge: Cambridge University Press, 1985).

4. James Clyman, *Journal of a Mountain Man,* ed. Linda M. Hasselstrom (Missoula, Mont.: Mountain Press Pub. Co., 1984), 97; "Elizabeth Smith Dixon Diary," in Kenneth L. Holmes, ed., *Covered Wagon Women: Diaries and Letters from the Western Trails, 1840–1890,* 11 vols. (Glendale, Calif.: Arthur H. Clark Co., 1983–1993), 1:127.

For cooking equipment, Marcy suggested that every group of six or eight people should take a camp kettle for boiling meat and making soup, a "mess pan" for mixing bread and other uses, a bake pan for baking bread and roasting coffee, a frying pan, a coffee pot, knives, forks, spoons, an extra camp kettle, and a bucket for water. Wagons also carried at least one large water keg. Knives, forks, and spoons were of tin. There were many individual variations on this basic list—many added a Dutch oven and a coffee mill. The frying pan (skillet or spider) usually had short legs and a cover. Those with little equipment used the frying pan for nearly all their cooking, but many women took Dutch ovens, which was a round iron pot with legs and a lid with raised edges so that the coals could be put on top as well as underneath. Another way to cook was to put the fire in a narrow trench about a foot deep and three feet long. Cooking vessels were placed on top of the trench.[5]

Most of the emigrants who went west expected that they would kill game for fresh meat, and they all looked forward to reaching the buffalo country. Many hoped that they would be able to dry enough buffalo meat to support them in the later parts of their journey. Wagons were often seen with strips of buffalo meat dangling from ropes along their sides so that it could dry in the sun. Emigrants also dried meat by the fire on rest days, but they rarely dried enough.

William Taylor, who went in a wagon train from Missouri to Oregon in 1846, said he and his companions saw thousands of buffalo but had a good deal of trouble killing them. They had better luck with antelope, which were all over the plains, and were quite easily killed where they had not previously been hunted. This ease in killing soon changed when the animals became wary, because they were very fast. Taylor and his companions ate little venison. They saw few deer, except for black-tailed deer in the Cascade Mountains, and these were very wild and difficult to hunt. Rocky Mountain sheep had also been scarce and proven difficult to kill. Mountain hares had been very numerous, and Taylor said they were good to eat when no other meat could be found. He had heard, correctly, that there were many bears in the Cascades, though he had not seen any.[6]

When they reached the salmon rivers of the Rockies, emigrants on the way to Oregon usually caught fish, and they traded with the Indians for fresh or dried salmon. This trading is mentioned by most who wrote journals of their trek to Oregon. Rather than being the constant enemies of

5. Marcy, *Prairie Traveler*, 40; Franklin Street, *California in 1850* (Cincinnati, 1851), 55; Williams, *Wagon Wheels*, 79–87; "Journal of Margaret Frink," in Holmes, ed., *Covered Wagon Women*, 2:97.
6. "The Taylor Diary," in Holmes, ed., *Covered Wagon Women*, 1:130–31.

myth, the Indians provided essential support to the pioneers on their trip west.[7]

In the early years of the Oregon Trail and the central trails to California there were very few trading posts to provide essential items or small luxuries that many of the emigrants were lacking. The main posts were Fort Laramie and Fort Bridger, in what is now Wyoming, and Fort Hall, in what is now Idaho. In 1844 there was flour for sale at Fort Hall, but it was very expensive. As the trails west became well established in the late 1840s and 1850s, numerous trading posts were established, some of them mere shacks, but prices were so high that they were beyond the means of most emigrants.[8]

The lack of trading posts was usually offset in the early years by an abundance of game quite close to the trail. In 1844, James Clyman wrote of numerous buffalo, antelope, black-tailed deer, mountain sheep, large stocks of fish in all the tributaries of the Kansas, and prairie ponds rich in wild ducks. The Snake River had numerous trout, but Clyman had difficulty catching them. Even in the 1850s and later, when buffalo were much harder to find close to the trail, emigrants made extensive use of antelope and smaller game.[9]

The greatest problems were usually experienced in the last stages of the journey, particularly if there had been delays due to damage to wagons or bad weather. Ironically, problems and delays were common when emigrants left the main trail in an effort to save time. There was a particular problem if snows began while the emigrants were in the Rockies. When that happened, there was a danger of starvation. Only when things became desperate were the milk cows that were taken by many emigrants eaten, and it was a sign of utter desperation to eat the oxen that dragged the wagons. If that happened, pioneers had to hope for outside help. From the mid-1840s emigrants who had reached Oregon or California formed relief organizations to aid those who were stranded in the mountains, and parties were sent out when it was known that groups were lost in the snows.[10]

Both in 1845 and 1846, emigrants who tried alternate routes into Oregon ran into great difficulties. In 1845, some two hundred families took what was known as the Meek Cutoff beyond Fort Boise, a trading post on

7. Sandra L. Myres, ed., *Ho for California! Women's Overland Diaries from the Huntington Library* (San Marino, Calif.: Huntington Library, 1980), 191–96; Schlissel, ed., *Women's Diaries*, 53; John D. Unruh, *The Plains Across: The Overland Emigrants and the Mississippi West, 1840–1860* (Urbana: University of Illinois Press, 1979), 165.

8. Clyman, *Journal of a Mountain Man*, 99, 111, 115.

9. Ibid., 90–95, 97–98, 114.

10. Unruh, *The Plains Across*, 338–68.

the Snake River. They had great difficulty finding water, many ran out of provisions, and they tried to survive by eating dried grasshoppers and berries obtained from the Indians. Some of the men pressed ahead with packhorses to the Columbia River. Problems were compounded by "a slow lingering fever." Fifty or so died either on the route or shortly after they reached the Columbia.[11]

Some who took the cutoff had a much better experience. They were either lucky or well prepared. Anna Maria King was in a wagon that had enough flour and bacon to last them through the entire trip. Her advice was that it was essential to bring at least 175 to 200 pounds of flour and 75 pounds of bacon for each person. She thought that about two-thirds of those who took the alternate route had run out of provisions and had tried to survive by killing their oxen.[12]

In 1846, the alternate route that caused problems was the Applegate Cutoff. This ran through southern Oregon into the Willamette valley. Many who took this route ran out of provisions and were in danger of starvation. Tabitha Brown, who left Missouri in April that year, wrote that the journey was fine until they passed Fort Hall. With many other families, they made the mistake of taking the advice of a man who said that the Applegate Cutoff would be a better way to go. Some 150 to 200 wagons took that route.

Tabitha Brown's party crossed a sixty-mile desert without grass or water, lost nearly all their cattle, and found a canyon strewn with dead cattle, wrecked wagons, and a variety of personal possessions—everything except provisions. Some died, others survived by eating meat from the cattle lying dead by the side of the trail. With still more mountains to cross, the situation became desperate. They had no bread and had eaten the last of their bacon. Temporarily they were helped when they came up to a party that had fresh venison but soon they were stopped by snow. Their provisions gave out, and they had to shoot one of their best work oxen. They were saved by the arrival of a relief party, and they finally reached settlements in the Willamette valley by Christmas. Another party that ran out of provisions was able to get six "venison hams" from a party of Indians.[13]

Several relief groups came from Oregon to try to help the distressed

11. Keith Clark and Lowell Tiller, *Terrible Trail: The Meek Cutoff, 1845* (Caldwell, Idaho: Caxton Printers, 1966), 44–97, 133, 140–43, 149.

12. Anna Maria King to her mother et al., April 1, 1846, in Holmes, ed., *Covered Wagon Women,* 1:41–42, 44.

13. Tabitha Brown to her brother and sister, August 1854, in Holmes, ed., *Covered Wagon Women,* 1:50–58, "Diary of Virgil Pringle," in Dale Morgan, ed., *Overland in 1846: Diary and Letters of the California-Oregon Trail,* 2 vols. (Georgetown, Calif.: Talisman Press, 1963), 1:185–86.

travelers. Thomas Holt was one of a small party that left in early December. Holt's group originally had two hundredweight of flour. A minister sent another hundredweight and some bacon, and Holt bought some salt pork. Within a few days the relief party began to meet wagons with distressed families. On December 8, Holt found a family who had nothing to eat that day—the children were "crying for bread." He gave them fifty pounds of flour. On the following day, the families in the eight wagons he came up to were all out of provisions, and he gave ten pounds of flour to each family. For the rest of the month, Holt and his small group tried to help families that had run out of food. Often teams of oxen had given out, and families were stranded in their wagons. The relief party continued to hand out flour and were able to kill two deer and divide the meat among distressed families. On the day after Christmas, on the north fork of the Elk River, Holt's party found a group of families that for four days had eaten nothing "but a little tallow boiled in water." Holt gave them three oxen. When he arrived home on January 21, he wrote in his journal that they had "succeeded in relieving many who must have perished."[14]

Stories of disaster, and generalizations about food on the overland trails, cannot, of course, reveal the infinite variety of individual experiences. Emigration to the West Coast by wagon was always an arduous and at times dangerous endeavor, but, in time, travelers gained from the accumulated knowledge of previous emigrants. The trek never became routine, but it became more manageable. It was not a way of escape for the poor or destitute. It has been said that it was mostly "a middle class migration" because of the necessity of providing a wagon, the oxen, and provisions.[15]

The trail to Oregon was pioneered by missionaries who took their wives and families with them. In 1838, Asa and Sarah White Smith went from New England to join Dr. Marcus Whitman, who had already reached the Oregon country. The Smiths experienced the Oregon Trail as it was at the beginning of its history. They left Westport (Kansas City, Missouri) in April and traveled as far as the Wind River with the supply caravan that was going to the annual rendezvous of the fur traders. Most of their equipment and provisions were carried on the backs of mules, although they had a few things in a light wagon. They also took a dozen head of cattle. A cow provided milk, which they had with their tea and coffee.

For the first part of the trip, the Smiths depended on the supplies they took with them, varied occasionally by game. Asa Smith said they lived

---

14. "Diary of Thomas Holt," in Morgan, ed., *Overland in 1846*, 1:190–97. See also Unruh, *Plains Across*, 338–63.

15. Myres, ed., *Ho for California*, 42–43.

mostly on bread and bacon, baking their bread before the fire in a "tin baker." This was a reflector oven, which was open at the front, and had a high, curved back to reflect the heat. Sarah Smith did some baking but said that men (probably those from the supply wagons) were doing most of the cooking. There was not much variety. Among the meals described by Sarah, there was a breakfast of ham, a dinner of ham and corn (eaten sitting in the wagon because it was raining), and a supper of fried ham, bread, and a cup of tea. A gift of a piece of fresh pork was a welcome change. It must have come from a pig that someone had brought along on the trip. There was also a pleasant surprise when someone found some honey. They usually ate sitting on the ground with the food on a table-cloth spread on top of an oilcloth.[16]

Some did not even have bread to vary their diet. Elkanah Walker, another woman in the party, complained that her main food was "fat bacon"—"O how I long to feast once more on bread." Half a wild turkey, which she was given by one of the hunters, was a relief from bacon but was hardly a substitute for bread.[17]

Although they were concerned about having enough food for the whole trip, the Smiths ate reasonably well as they crossed the plains. In mid-May, they still had flour, hard bread, corn they had bought from the Kansas Indians (which they boiled to eat with their meat), smoked pork, and some venison. Their hunters had also brought in an antelope and a goose. A few days later, they reached the buffalo country, and their basic diet changed from salt pork to buffalo meat. At first they were delighted. There was buffalo soup, boiled buffalo, fried buffalo, and sometimes, Sarah said, the men (undoubtedly those from the supply wagons) chopped the meat "& make it appear like sausage." The Smiths were no longer eating bread, as they had decided to save most of their flour for future emergencies. For two weeks they ate buffalo meat for breakfast, dinner, and supper. To drink, Asa had weak coffee and tea with lots of milk. He would have preferred good water, but this could not be found.

Late in June, they reached the rendezvous on the Wind River. Both of the Smiths very much missed vegetables, and Sarah longed for "a crust of brown bread." Asa had diarrhea, and Sarah tried to vary the buffalo meat. On one evening she made a rice pudding, and for another meal she used a little of her flour to make two meat pies. The preparation was difficult. To provide a surface for Sarah to chop the meat, Asa peeled off bark from a

16. "Letters of Asa Smith," in Drury, ed., *First White Women over the Rockies*, 3:142–44; "Diary of Sarah White Smith," in Drury, ed., *First White Women*, 3:71–75.
17. "Diary of Elkanah Walker," in Drury, ed., *First White Women*, 3:263–64.

cottonwood tree. She rolled the crust "with a crooked stick in a hollow bark" and baked the pies at an open fire in the tin reflector oven. They feared eating much of what they had in case the game disappeared. One member of the party ate two cakes which he had kept in a trunk since leaving Connecticut. He said he was "suffering from the disproportionate use of fresh buffalo meat" and found it helpful to have "a small piece of cake from Yankee land dissolved in water."

The wild currants in the area of the rendezvous were still green, but they picked them in the hope that they would be good when cooked. Sarah also made another rice pudding, which she thought was "very nice" even though it had no eggs and very little sugar. To celebrate July 4, she made a "biscuit pudding" for dinner. This was presumably a type of bread pudding. She probably used some of the wild currants to give some flavor to the soaked hard biscuit.[18]

The trading caravan stayed at the rendezvous site, but the missionary party continued their trek to Oregon. A major addition to their diet came when the wild fruits began to ripen. On July 13, they "encamped in a garden of gooseberries." They also made use of natural deposits of salt that they found lying encrusted on the ground, and at Soda Springs they sampled the natural soda water. This was used by countless travelers on the Oregon trail. The soda water made Sarah a little sick, but she found that it made bread "as light as any prepared with yeast." Buffalo was still their basic meat, and they killed many of a great herd they encountered. Most of the meat was dried for future use. Occasionally the hunters killed other game, and the Smiths were given a share of the meat from two bears. Sarah thought it resembled pork.

Late in July they reached Fort Hall and were given supplies sent from Oregon by Dr. Whitman. Soon after leaving the fort, they had a breakfast of "fish & Indian pudding." They ate pudding and dried buffalo meat for dinner and supper. Indian pudding was usually made of corn and molasses. Probably both had been sent by Whitman. Asa went fishing in the Snake River, and on the following day they had pudding with all three meals— at breakfast with fish and at dinner and supper with dried buffalo meat. To drink, they had tea. Near Salmon Falls, they bought salmon from the Shoshone Indians. Sarah said it was "beautiful & we are feasting on it."

In mid-August, they reached Fort Boise and rested for a few days. Sarah baked a pie and biscuits, and they had a rare taste of vegetables. People at

18. "Letters of Asa Smith," 3:144–48; "Diary of Sarah White Smith," 3:75–94; and "Reminiscences of Cushing Ells," 3:299, all in Drury, ed., *First White Women*.

the fort supplied them with pumpkins and turnips, as well as milk. At the end of the month, they finally reached the Whitman mission in Oregon and found that Whitman had about seventeen acres under cultivation. He was successfully growing wheat, corn, potatoes, turnips, garden vegetables in abundance and a great number of melons. This apparently did not distract the missionaries from their preaching. Asa pointed out that Indian women did "most of the work."[19]

The missionaries paved the way, and beginning in 1842 settlers went to Oregon in rapidly increasing numbers. The route became well marked with wagon ruts, discarded possessions, and graves. As life on the trail became better known through guides and letters, many women began their preparations well in advance. Keturah Belknap, who went from Iowa to Oregon in 1848, spent the previous winter spinning and weaving. She made four tablecloths so that she could "live just like I was at home." Early in April, Keturah began to prepare food to last a few days "till we get used to the camp fare." She cooked a chicken, boiled a ham, baked bread and crackers, fried doughnuts, and stewed some dried fruit.

On April 9 they loaded the wagon. First in was a box with bacon, salt, and other items. It fit neatly into the wagon bed and was covered with planks nailed together to serve as a table. Next they put in an old chest packed with clothes, a medicine chest, another box with a few things they were not going to use until they reached Oregon, four sacks of flour, and one of cornmeal, each sack holding 125 pounds. They added a "wall" of small sacks containing dried apples and peaches, beans, rice, sugar, and green coffee. The coffee would be browned in a skillet when they wanted to use it.

For a bed, they planned to level up the sacks and add extra feather bedding, pillows, a whole side of "sole leather," and two comforters. In the corner of the wagon there was just enough room for a washtub, with the lunch basket in it. They also took a churn. The dishes they were going to use along the way were in a basket. Keturah intended to start with "good earthen dishes," and use tin only if the earthenware was broken. Cookware to be used every day was put in a box on the rear of the wagon. The contents were arranged so that an area was left with a chair for Keturah and a space with toys for her daughter, Jessie. They also provided for their child by taking three good milk cows. On the trek, when Keturah milked them at night, she put the milk in covered buckets under the wagon, and

19. "Letters of Asa Smith," 3:157–58; and "Diary of Sarah White Smith," in Drury, ed., *First White Women*, 3:95–108.

in the morning, she removed the thick cream and put it in the churn. She also added some cream from the morning's milking. In the course of the day, as the wagon bumped and rolled along, the churn made its own butter.

When the packing was finished, Keturah's reaction was that the "wagon looks so nice." It was high enough for her to stand up in and had curtains at both ends. On the night before they left, they had milk with "a pot of mush" made by her mother-in-law. This was done to use milk that otherwise would have had to be thrown out. On April 10, the day they set out, Keturah said that "daylight dawned with none awake but me." They had breakfast, put in the dishes and food for lunch, the remaining iron cookware, the churn, the feather bed and pillows, and Keturah's chair. Her husband went for the cattle, and they left.

The Belknaps reached Oregon safely, but the detailed journal that Keturah wrote about their preparations for departure became much sparser when they were on the trail. It finally ended when they reached the Snake River. Her brief comments about food on the trail leave the impression that they fared quite well. Along the Platte, when they killed their first buffalo ("a nice young heifer"), she found the meat rather coarse and dark, but she chopped and cooked it, mixing it with dried apples to make old-fashioned mince pies for lunch. In the Rockies, when they decided to travel all night and take one of the cutoffs to save time, she set about cooking a store of food in advance to make sure they were well provided for. Keturah Belknap was a very capable woman.[20]

In the 1850s, because of the great increase in travel along the Oregon Trail, game was driven away from the main route of the emigrants. The pioneers still tried to hunt for fresh meat, but there was not the abundance of earlier years. Cecilia and Porthenia, married twin sisters who kept a joint journal in 1852, wrote in mid-June on the Platte that though the men had been out most of the time, they had killed only one prairie hen. They often saw antelope, but their hunters were unable to bring in "anything worth speaking of." Antelope were much more wary than they had been just a few years before.

Another problem caused by the great numbers of emigrants was an increasing difficulty in finding fuel. Wood had always been in short supply once the plains were reached, and emigrants depended largely on buffalo chips (large pieces of dried buffalo dung) for cooking. Even these were now becoming scarcer, and the sisters found that after it rained the chips

20. "The Commentaries of Keturah Belknap," in Holmes, ed., *Covered Wagon Women*, 1:189–229.

were difficult to use. In the wet June of 1852, the sisters at times had trouble making a fire to cook the food or to dry what needed drying. On Sunday the twenty-seventh, their party decided to halt for a day, rest the team, and dry everything out. The sisters baked bread, made pumpkin and apple pies, cooked beans and meat, stewed apples, made "dutch cheese" (cottage cheese), and baked suckeyes they had caught "in quantitys sufficient to last some time." The sisters were better-off than many who traveled the Oregon Trail. Their families had been able to buy two hundred pounds of flour in northwestern Missouri. They had also brought cows with them.[21]

In July, more variety was added to their food. In the middle of the month, a week after they had passed Fort Laramie, hunters from the wagon train came in loaded with buffalo meat. To the sisters it was a little disappointing because they thought it tasted "very much like beef." In the following weeks they were able to gather wild berries—strawberries, huckleberries, gooseberries, chokecherries, serviceberries, and some they did not recognize. They also bought potatoes from a man who had groceries to sell. They were the first potatoes they had seen since leaving home. Before they bought the potatoes, the sisters had resisted several other opportunities to buy special items. In the vicinity of Fort Laramie, they had passed a trader who had "a little of everything" in a grocery store he had set up in a tent.

Early in September, the sisters and others in the same wagon train traded with the Indians for a good supply of salmon, and the hunters brought in rabbits. They had hoped to buy provisions at Fort Boise, but there was little available except fish and a little sugar. Some families in the wagon train were now out of flour and could not make bread. It was getting dangerously late in the year, and at the end of the month they were warned by traders from Oregon that they should hurry to cross the remaining mountain areas before the snows came.

The morning of October 2 was very cold, and the sisters could not manage to start a fire to cook breakfast. As they began to go down out of the mountains, they passed broken and abandoned wagons, but they also began to meet Oregon traders. From the Cayuse Indians, "more civilized than any we have seen before," they bought a few potatoes, and by October 22 they had reached the Columbia River.[22]

By the mid-1850s, flimsy traders' shops, groceries, stores, and even crude saloons were scattered sporadically along the trail. The emigrants com-

21. "Journal of Cecilia Adams and Porthenia Blank," in Holmes, ed., *Covered Wagon Women*, 5:253–69.
22. Ibid., 5:270–312.

plained of the prices, but many bought some item of food that they particularly missed—often potatoes. These stores were often of little use to those who were in dire straits for food, because those who had brought a marginal stock of provisions usually did not have the money to buy any more. Those who had ill luck, or had made insufficient preparations, often depended on the goodwill of those in other wagons, which were numerous along most stretches of the trail. In May 1853, Mrs. Amelia Stewart Knight crossed the Missouri to set out for Oregon. A few days later, she noted that "as far as the eye can reach the road is covered with teams."[23]

The great number of emigrants passing along the trail made fuel increasingly difficult to find. At the beginning of June 1852, Polly Coon traveled from Wisconsin with her young daughter to join her husband who was already in Oregon. She began her trek in a group of some twenty emigrants in five wagons, but others joined later. When they reached the Platte River valley at the end of "a very hot dusty day," Polly's wagon had neither wood nor water, but a man in the wagon train gave them a little of both so she could make tea. This tea, with "a little hard bread," was all they had for supper. On the following morning, they had to travel a few miles to find water in order to cook their breakfast.

Polly, or someone else in the wagon train, had a guidebook that warned of a long stretch without wood in the region before Fort Laramie, and for this bad stretch they gathered wood, which they kept in bags, and used buffalo chips whenever they could find them. In the following year, Eliza Butler wrote from Oregon that on their trip they had not suffered much from lack of wood or water, because they "sacked up" enough wood for two hundred miles and filled their water kegs when there was a danger of a lack of water.[24]

While emigrants still ate a good deal of game, buffalo were driven away from the vicinity of the trail by the endless stream of emigrants and hunters. Clarence Bagley, who went to Oregon as a boy in 1852, saw antelope, wolves, jackrabbits, and game birds, but no buffalo. He remembered no problems with food, said they had meat aplenty, and with delight reminisced about the "wonderfully sweet and palatable" bread. His family carried both a reflector oven and a bake kettle (a Dutch oven). They obtained flour from families that had lost members and had flour to sell or throw away. In 1854, Sarah Sutton's party killed antelope, wild geese, sage hens, mountain rabbits, squirrels, a duck, and a snipe. They also caught

23. "Diary of Mrs. Amelia Stewart Knight," in Schlissel, *Women's Diaries*, 205.
24. "Journal of Polly Coon," and letter of Eliza Ground, December 25, 1853, both in Holmes, ed., *Covered Wagon Women*, 5:187–88, 191; 6:20–21.

fish and traded for fish from the Indians, but she wrote on June 13 that "our company have to day killed the only buffalo we have seen."[25]

Among the thousands of emigrants even the most careful preparations could not protect against all the tragedies encountered on the trek west. Sickness regularly took a toll. Seventeen-year-old Abigail Scott went west from Illinois in 1852. Her family was very careful. They prepared all winter, packing bacon, flour, rice, coffee, brown sugar, and hard tack, and even sent more provisions in advance to St. Joseph on the Missouri. These they cooked and packed after they got there. Along the Platte they had ample food, and their main complaints were a shortage of fuel—they had difficulty finding either wood or buffalo chips—and muddy river water. To make the water drinkable, they put in cornmeal, which after a while carried the dirt to the bottom. One night they could find no fuel of any kind and had a dinner of ship's biscuit.

The Scotts passed many graves, but when they heard there was great sickness in other wagon trains, they thought it was diarrhea from drinking bad water. In reality it was cholera, a disease that at times caused great havoc among western emigrants, beginning in the poor sanitary conditions among those gathered in great numbers along the Missouri before setting off and lingering on the trail itself. In late June, soon after they passed Fort Laramie, Abigail Scott wrote in her journal that her mother had died. The rest of the family reached Oregon safely.[26]

In the 1840s and 1850s, those who reached Oregon usually made their way into the Willamette valley, and after the aridity of the plains and the hardships of the Rockies they marveled at a country of such richness. From the earliest days, the Oregon settlements flourished. In 1844, when mountain man James Clyman reached the west bank of the Willamette, there were already settlers, but much of the area was in a pristine state. Pools of mud and water were covered with all kinds of waterfowl—swans, teals, plover, herons, crane, ducks, snipe, and geese. For miles, Clyman wrote, "the air seemed to be darkened with the emmenc [sic] flights that arose as I proceeded up the valley."

The settlers were in "good and prosperous condition," and even the previous year's emigrants had enough for themselves and some to spare for those now on the way. There was plenty of bread, beef, fish, and potatoes,

25. Clarence Bagley, *The Acquisition and Pioneering of Old Oregon* (1924; repr., Fairfield, Wash.: Ye Galleon Press, 1982), 29–31; "Sarah Sutton's Travel Diary," in Holmes, ed., *Covered Wagon Women*, 7:17–76, 49.

26. "Journal of Abigail Jane Scott (Duniway)," in Holmes, ed., *Covered Wagon Women*, 5:21–135.

so much so that the first three were being exported; a brig loaded with wheat and flour was about to leave for Hawaii. The settlements were also sending fish to Hawaii, as well as wheat, flour, and fish to Russian Alaska. The land was remarkably fertile, and Clyman wrote that "the Quantity of small flowering vegettiles [*sic*] is verry remarkable & beyond all conception." A Frenchman already had an apple orchard. Wild strawberries grew in abundance on the prairies, and there was a great variety of other wild berries. Large numbers of cattle were allowed to roam around the settlements in a semiwild state.[27]

Many who came to Oregon were drawn by the rosy reports they received from those who had preceded them. Anna Maria King, who arrived in November 1845, wrote home in the following spring to say that it was "a beautiful country," and "an easy place to make a living." There was an abundance of freshwater springs and "thousands of strawberries, gooseberries, blackberries, whortleberries, currents and other wild fruits." The wheat was the best she had ever seen, and with plenty of mills there was no problem in getting it ground. She said you could raise cattle without it costing a cent, because the grass was green all winter. The cattle were as fat as if they had been fed the whole year round.[28]

Betsey Bayley, who had come out to Oregon in 1845 and was among those who took the disastrous Meek Cutoff, wrote four years later to describe Oregon as "the healthiest country I ever lived in," and "one of the best wheat countries in the world." Vegetables grew well, there was wild fruit in abundance, and the Bayleys had a "fine young orchard" coming along. In 1850, Joseph Geer wrote from Buteville on the west bank of the Willamette that he did not have the room to give a description "of this best country in the world." As soon as he could prepare the ground he intended putting in about ten thousand apple trees and two thousand pear trees. There were excellent fruit trees for sale at $1 for apple and $1.50 for pear.[29]

In February 1852, Mary Colby wrote home to say that the longer she lived in Oregon, the better she liked it. She was living on a section of land one mile square with seven cows, a yoke of oxen, six calves, fifteen hogs, and twenty-four hens. Like so many others, she was particularly delighted that the grass was "fresh and green" all the year round. Their cattle

27. Clyman, *Journal,* 132–64.
28. Anna Maria King to her mother, April 1, 1846, also Rachel Mills to her family, March 3, 1848, in Holmes, *Covered Wagon Women,* 1:41–44; 1:103–8.
29. Betsey Bayley to Lucy P. Griffith, September 20, 1849, and letter of Joseph C. Geer, September 9, 1850, both in Holmes, *Covered Wagon Women,* 1:35–38; 1:152.

in midwinter were fat enough to provide beef to eat. On the previous day she had visited a neighbor who had fresh radishes from his garden and cabbage in blossom. Mary had lived in Massachusetts until 1841, and she said that everything in Oregon in February looked as it did in May at home.

Her letter reads like a promotional brochure. Oregon, she wrote, was a country in which for half of the labor you needed in the East ("the States") you could raise all that you needed to live on and have a good lot to sell. Wheat did not even need to be sowed every year. From one sowing you could get three crops. Vegetables grew to a large size—"turnips as large as a half bushell and beats [sic] as large round as my waist." She said that even prices for nonfood items were not much higher than in Massachusetts. She had brought home a mirror "that I can se [sic] my whole body in for 15 eggs." Like others, she and her husband were waiting for their fruit trees to begin to bear. In the meantime they could get plenty of dried fruit.[30]

In the 1850s and 1860s, orchards spread throughout the Willamette valley. Writing home in 1856, Alfred Stanton said that California provided a market because fruit there was not as good as that in Oregon. This was before California began to use extensive irrigation to expand its fruit production. Stanton expected to have about three hundred bushels of apples in the current year and also had some twenty thousand fruit trees which he intended to sell. The only disturbing factor was that increased settlement in the region had brought about a war with the Yakima Indians, and Alfred Stanton's wife was not as optimistic as her husband. In a postscript she said that her husband was sketching things too rosily—"bettween the indians & grass hoppers we have a continual war." These were only temporary problems. In 1864, it was said of the Willamette valley that there were orchards everywhere. The market in Portland had a variety of "luscious fruits"—"large apples of all varieties, pears, peaches, and plums."[31]

Some of the emigrants who reached the northwest began settlement in what later became the state of Washington. There were a few settlers on Puget Sound as early as 1845, and a few thousand more came in before Washington Territory was separated from Oregon in 1853. Like Oregon, this was a good country for settlers. On New Year's Day, 1852, Abigail Malick, who was from Illinois and had settled on the Columbia River near Fort Vancouver, served up a meal of roast duck, chickens, pork, and

30. Mary M. Colby to her brother and sister, February 8, 1852, in Holmes, *Covered Wagon Women*, 2:49–521.

31. Alfred and Phoebe Stanton to brother and sister, April 13, 1856, and Harriet A. Loughary journal, both in Holmes, *Covered Wagon Women*, 1:90–93; 8:161–62.

sausages, oyster pie, mashed potatoes, bread, pickles, apple pie, mince pie, custard pie, various cakes, apples, gooseberries, greengages, coffee, and tea. Among her winter supplies were a thousand pounds of salmon, one hundred and fifty bushels of potatoes, plenty of cabbage, turnips, sugar, and salt, and a variety of preserves and dried fruit. She said she had never seen the like of the blackberries and raspberries along the Columbia River.[32]

Like Oregon, Washington found a ready market for its food in the tens of thousands of miners who reached California in 1849 and the following years. James Swan, who went to San Francisco in 1850, two years later moved north to what became the state of Washington, living for a time in Shoal Water Bay, north of the Columbia. This was an area that abounded in fish, shellfish, waterfowl, and game. The settlers made a living by collecting oysters for the California market.

Swan described an area of abundant natural resources. The Indians, who were still numerous in the region, had a rich and varied diet. To their basic foods of salmon, game, and roots, they added numerous other items of seafood, including sturgeon, seal, pelican, mussels, and clams. Swan found the flesh of young seals to be "very palatable." He particularly liked young seal liver and thought that when fried with pork, it resembled hog's liver. Swan also tried the seal oil which was skimmed off from the boiled blubber. The Indians ate it with all their food, and Swan thought it was "as sweet and free from fishy flavor as lard." He was less impressed by mussels and pelicans. The mussels, he wrote, were inferior and rarely eaten by the white settlers. Pelicans had "a coarse, fishy, oily flesh."[33]

On July 4, 1853, the oystermen gathered for a celebration. Each of them brought food, including "a great oyster pie," a boiled ham, a cold pudding, doughnuts, pies, and loaves of bread. A neighbor added a half dozen boxes of sardines, and the oystermen feasted around a great bonfire.[34]

In winter, Swan and his friends depended heavily on salmon bought from the Indians. The settlers slightly salted it and smoked it in the tent they used as a smokehouse. They had plenty of vegetables from a garden they planted, and they supplemented their winter fare with ducks, geese, curlews, plover, and snipes. The birds arrived in great numbers whenever the wind blew strongly from the south.[35]

32. Bagley, *Acquisition and Pioneering of Old Oregon*, 22; Lillian Schlissel, et al., *Far From Home: Families of the Westward Journey* (New York: Schocken Books, 1989), 3, 11, 21.

33. James G. Swan, *The Northwest Coast* (1857, repr., Fairfield, Wash.: Ye Galleon Press, 1966), 20, 25–29, 33, 83–84.

34. Ibid., 133–34.

35. Ibid., 142–43.

Swan rarely lacked variety in his food. On one trip to Gray's Harbor, he ate a supper of boiled rice, boiled salmon, boiled and roasted potatoes, roasted crabs and clams, cold raccoon, dried salmon, seal and whale oil, bread, "a pudding made from boiled flour," and huckleberry leaf tea. Oddly, one of the few times he and his friends could not find what they wanted was in the Christmas season of 1854. They had plenty of salt salmon and potatoes in store, but they wanted to celebrate the day with a goose or a duck. For once these were lacking, and they finally made do with two crows. Their friend "the captain" made a "sea pie." The birds were cut up and combined with dumplings, salt pork, potatoes, and onions in an iron pot. It was too tough for Swan. He finished his Christmas dinner with dumplings and potatoes.

The captain was well known for cooking anything he could lay his hands on—eagles, hawks, owls, lynx, seals, otters, gulls, and pelicans. One of his more basic dishes was "fisherman's pudding." It consisted of salt pork, finely chopped and sauteed, to which was added boiling water and molasses. The pot was put on the fire, and cornmeal was gradually added as it boiled.[36]

In the last decades of the century settlers continued to be attracted to the rich regions both north and south of the Columbia River. Emigration by wagon continued even after the coming of railroads to the western plains. It was common in the 1870s and 1880s to travel by wagon along the route of the Union Pacific to the Rockies and the West Coast. Settlement had begun to press out of the prairies into the plains, and, even where settlement had not reached, there were railroad stations to serve as stopping places. Emigrants usually traveled faster than in earlier days because now the wagons were often pulled by horses or mules rather than oxen. Even now, however, some took cattle with them.[37]

In 1878, Lucy Ide went by wagon from Wisconsin to the state of Washington. Her journey took her past numerous farms and towns. She left Mondavi early in May with her husband and children. For supplies, they depended very much on what they obtained along the way. In the first month, they bought oats, codfish, pickles, and a few other items in Dunlap, Iowa, as well as dried peaches from a passing peddler. When they reached Omaha, Mrs. Ide mentioned in her journal that they now needed to get their supplies and go westward. Her list makes somewhat strange

36. Ibid., 274–75, 325–26.
37. Holmes, ed., *Covered Wagon Women*, 8:7–9; 10:7.

reading—"oysters (a case), lobsters flour sugar crackers horsefeed etc." Canning had become quite extensive during the Civil War, and oysters and lobsters had long been among the items canned. Later on the trip, Mrs. Ide mentioned making oyster soup.

Emigrants still gathered greens and fruits, and Mrs. Ide cooked dandelion greens and mustard greens. The mustard greens were from a farm—the woman there offered them all that they wished to pick. Mrs. Ide also picked a few wild ripe strawberries along the Boyer River. Game was much less evident. On June 9, just before they reached Kearny (a town where the old fort stood) she saw six elks, but she said "they were tame ones." Ten days later, near Ogallala, they saw vast herds of cattle. In the 1870s, a great cattle frontier had spread northward through the plains from Texas, replacing the buffalo that were being slaughtered to the edge of existence. On the next day she said she saw nothing but cattle and ponies in every direction.

On July 12, they went through South Pass and two days later met a group of "Princeton NJersey college students." They were in the mountains searching for minerals and petrified woods. The students invited them to see what they had collected and on a Sunday evening came to the Ides' camp. They sang their college songs, and then everyone joined in singing hymns.

At Evanston, Wyoming, the Ides saw another new feature of western life—the Chinese. The Chinese had begun to come into California in the 1850s and were the main labor force on the western stretch of the transcontinental railroad. They had begun to settle in the small towns of the West. The Ides bought supplies in Evanston before going outside to camp, and as they pressed on west they were able to obtain what they needed—provisions in other small towns, fresh beef from a ranch, a bushel of apples when they were camping on the Walla Walla, and all the watermelons they could eat at a farmhouse.[38]

The wagons continued to roll, but it was now more a cross-country trip through populated areas than a trek into the unknown. In 1883, when Sarah Collins went with her husband and children from Kansas to Oregon, passengers on passing trains waved their handkerchiefs at them. Some aspects of the old days remained. On the Platte members of their party killed two antelope, but as they entered Wyoming they were seeing more sheep than game. On Ham's Fork of the Green River, where fifty years before trappers had caroused at the rendezvous, the Collinses camped and fished.

38. "Diary of Lucy A. Ide," in Holmes, *Covered Wagon Women*, 10:59–88.

On July 4 they celebrated with canned strawberries and cake (made without eggs).

In the same year, Mary Surfus took much the same route. Her party bought supplies in towns along the way, killed some game, caught fish, picked wild berries, and explored old forts. The forts she said were "only remnants." In one they found a good bake oven and sheet music for an old song—"I Wandered to the Hills Maggie." The collapsing walls were covered with names and dates left by a host of earlier emigrants.[39] The Oregon Trail was passing into history.

39. "Sarah C. Collins Journal," and "Mary Matilda Surfus Journal," both in Holmes, *Covered Wagon Women*, 10:221–35; 10:236–68.

CHAPTER 7

Water before Every Door

⁓

Citizens can now draw with scanty trouble their drinking water in the
morning, when it is purest, from the clear and sparkling streams that
flow over the pebbly beds before their doors.

Richard Burton, Salt Lake City, 1860

I n 1830, when Joseph Smith organized the Church of Jesus
Christ of Latter-day Saints in western New York, he began a
process that ultimately brought about the settlement of the arid
regions in the Great Basin of the Rocky Mountains. Thousands
of Mormon emigrants crossed the plains to the area around the
Great Salt Lake in what is now Utah, and they had to cope not
only with the problems of providing food on the trail but also with the
major difficulty of settling in an area that was previously thought to be incapable of supporting settlers.

After leaving New York, the Mormons moved several times before settling in Nauvoo, Illinois. There they prospered, but after their prophet,
Joseph Smith, and his brother were murdered by a mob in July 1844,
Brigham Young and the church leadership decided to leave all they had
built in Nauvoo and start their lives again. They sought isolation in the
hope that they could build their own religious community without outside
interference. It was decided that the best chance for this was to settle where
no one else wanted to settle. Survival there depended on a carefully controlled use of all resources, including food.

Preparations for the great emigration were made in the year and a half
after Smith's murder. The first stage began in February 1846 when thousands crossed the Mississippi from Illinois into Iowa. They took with them
great herds of cattle and sheep, as well as pigs, poultry, horses, and mules,
setting up camp a few miles west of the river. When a newspaper reporter
from St. Louis visited Nauvoo in the spring of 1846, he found that some

147

were still in the process of moving, in groups of six to ten wagons. In late September 1846 another visitor to Nauvoo found it deserted. On the other bank of the Mississippi were several hundred emigrants, the last to leave the city.[1]

Under Brigham Young's leadership, the move to Utah was organized with almost military precision, and an attempt was made to divide up the resources fairly between the families. This helped all the emigrants survive, but they lived a Spartan existence. Hosea Stout, one of the leaders, found that several times in the spring and early summer when his family ran out of provisions, he had great difficulty persuading anyone to give him or sell him any more. After receiving some help from a non-Mormon, he was given supplies on the direct order of Brigham Young.[2]

Young decided that to provide for those who had few resources, camps would be established on the route west. At these camps the lands were plowed and planted by advance parties so that those coming later would have crops to harvest. Hundreds of acres were cultivated at different places across Iowa, and a final base was established at Winter Quarters on the west bank of the Missouri, across from Council Bluffs. This was to be the starting point for the great trek into the Rockies. The gathering of extra supplies for the winter of 1846–1847 was helped by the enlistment of the "Mormon Battalion" of five hundred men into the United States Army, which was engaged in fighting a war with Mexico. The Mormon battalion went to the Southwest and eventually to California. Most of their pay went to the church, and Young was able to use it to buy supplies in bulk.[3]

The foresight shown in organizing this massive emigration, and in providing stopping places across Iowa, meant that the trek from Nauvoo to Winter Quarters was accomplished without disaster. By the fall of 1846, thousands of the emigrants were encamped at Winter Quarters. They built hundreds of cabins to live in that winter. On Christmas Eve it was reported that there were nearly thirty-five hundred living at Winter Quar-

1. Leonard J. Arrington, *Great Basin Kingdom: An Economic History of the Latter-day Saints* (Cambridge, Mass.: Harvard University Press, 1958), 18–19; *Daily Missouri Republican*, May 13, 1846, in William Mulder and A. Russell Mortensen, eds. *Among the Mormons: Historic Accounts by Contemporary Observers* (New York: Knopf, 1958), 169–73; "Address by Thomas L. Kane," in Daniel Tyler, *A Concise History of the Mormon Battalion in the Mexican War, 1846–1848* (1881; repr., Chicago: Rio Grande Press, 1964), 64–76.

2. Arrington, *Great Basin Kingdom*, 19; Hosea Stout, *On the Mormon Frontier: The Diary of Hosea Stout, 1844–1861*, ed. Juanita Brooks, 2 vols. (Salt Lake City: University of Utah Press, 1964), 1:125–80.

3. Arrington, *Great Basin Kingdom*, 20–21; Stout, *On the Mormon Frontier*, 1:186. For the Mormon Battalion, see Tyler, *Concise History*.

ters, nearly four hundred of them were sick. Thousands of others were scattered across Iowa in the various camps.[4]

Young's plan was for a pioneer party to leave in mid-April, to be quickly followed by larger emigrant companies. Others would stay to grow crops and help those who would be coming in the following months and years. The pioneer party was a group of nearly one hundred and fifty, nearly all of them men, led by Young. They followed the general route of the Oregon Trail, but to avoid other emigrants, they went along the north rather than the south bank of the Platte to create a new "Mormon Trail." They reached Fort Laramie in early June and went on through South Pass to Fort Bridger. Old mountain man Jim Bridger warned them against settling in the Great Basin, but they pressed on. In July 1847 they entered the valley of the Great Salt Lake. They immediately set to work, plowing, planting, hunting, fishing, and extracting salt from the lake. The hunting and fishing was not very productive, but they were able to plant potatoes, corn, oats, buckwheat, beans, and turnips. They also began to lay out Salt Lake City.[5]

In August, Brigham Young returned to help organize later emigrations, but other emigrants were already on their way. In July, the pioneer party was followed from Winter Quarters by a large caravan of Young's followers: some fifteen hundred emigrants with cattle, horses, sheep, hogs, and chickens. On the way, they were able to supplement their supplies by hunting. Throughout July and August, the men regularly killed buffalo, and the women were able to collect large amounts of berries and currants to make pies. Just before they reached Independence Rock, they were able to use of some of the rich natural deposits of saleratus with corn to make hominy. They reached the Salt Lake Valley in September, and in the first winter of 1846–1847 there were nearly seventeen hundred people living near the Great Salt Lake.[6]

A huge field was prepared, winter wheat was planted, and men were sent to California to buy cows and supplies with some of the money provided by the Mormon Battalion. They returned in spring. Thousands more arrived from Winter Quarters in 1848. Families were assigned land according to the number of members. Problems of insufficient rainfall were dealt with by building an irrigation system. Ditches were dug to bring water from the adjacent Wasatch Mountains, and channels led the water through the city and to the surrounding fields. Strict rules were put into place

4. Stout, *On the Mormon Frontier,* 1:203–47; Arrington, *Great Basin Kingdom,* 21–22.
5. Arrington, *Great Basin Kingdom,* 22, 45–46.
6. Ibid., 22, 45–46; "Diary of Pat Sessions," in Holmes, ed., *Covered Wagon Women,* 1:169–84.

regarding the times for water usage. Water, timber, and minerals were all under public control.

Although irrigation had long been used by the Spanish settlers in the Rio Grande valley, this community use of water and irrigation was a distinctive feature of Mormon settlement. The religious enthusiasm of the Mormons meant that they were willing to accept a type of social control that was usually shunned by more individualistic American pioneers. It was a type of control that had not been seen in most American settlements since the first Puritans had organized themselves to survive in Massachusetts over two hundred years earlier.

In spite of the great efforts of the pioneers, the first two winters were times of great hardship. There was little food. In the winter of 1847–1848, livestock got into and ruined a large part of the planted area, and some of the livestock was lost to predators and to Indians. Food was rationed, and families dug for roots or collected any berries or greens they could find in the barren land near the Great Salt Lake. In the spring of 1848, their growing crops were beset first by frost and then by swarms of crickets eating all in their path. The arrival of seagulls to eat the crickets was viewed by the Mormons as the working of divine providence.

By the winter of 1848–1849, there were over four thousand settlers in the valley. It was a harsh winter. Grain and flour were in very short supply, cattle again were lost, and many people again resorted to scavenging for roots or anything edible that they could find. Some even staved off starvation by eating the hides that had been used as roofing on their cabins. The crisis did not end until the summer of 1849 when the hard work and irrigation resulted in an abundant harvest.[7]

This harvest meant that at last there was sufficient food. The main farming area now stretched some eight miles south from Salt Lake City. A fence separated the fields from pasturelands where settlers grazed their stock in common. There were many cattle, mules, and horses, but few hogs. This meant that there was a shortage of bacon. There was also a lack of anything that could not be produced on a farm. Sugar, tea, coffee, and dried fruit were scarce and expensive. There was a lack of fruit in the early years, and the settlers collected serviceberries from bushes on the mountain slopes. Fortunately, they were sweet enough that they did not need sugar when dried for use in winter.[8]

7. Arrington, *Great Basin Kingdom,* 47–61; Stansbury, *Expedition,* 126–27.

8. Letter of A. P. Josselyn, July 15, 1849, and "The Second General Epistle," both in Mulder and Mortensen, eds., *Among the Mormons,* 235–36, 230; letter of Jerome B. Howard, February 12, 1850, in Elisha Douglass Perkins, *Gold Rush Diary: Being the Journal of Elisha Douglass Perkins on the Over-*

The successful farming had been made possible by the irrigation system, which was a feature that particularly impressed visitors. The city was described as "a City of Gardens" with "a running stream of clear water" in every street. Explorer Howard Stansbury, who came into the valley that fall, wrote of the "unfailing stream of pure, sweet water which, by an ingenious mode of irrigation is made to traverse each side of every street, whence it is led into every garden spot." He also described great flocks of wild geese, ducks, and swans on the Great Salt Lake, and numerous herds of cattle kept in a nearby valley with excellent springs on either side. Cattle wintered there with herdsmen to watch them.[9]

In the summer of 1849, contact with the outside world was greatly increased and the shortage of general provisions somewhat eased, when the Mormons, who had fled to the Great Basin to seek isolation, found themselves directly in the path of the gold rush to California. Thousands of emigrants went through the valley on their way to the mines. They were hungry for vegetables and dairy products and often made purchases or exchanged provisions for fresh food. The gold rush was a valuable source of income for the Mormon settlers, and later, when supply wagons came though carrying goods to California, they were able to buy items in short supply in the settlements. In August 1849, a visitor from Pueblo bought watermelons, radishes, and beets, and commented that "the Mormons are coining gold at this place."[10]

One forty-niner, who reached Salt Lake City in July 1849, slept in his wagon in a Salt Lake City street but arranged to have his meals in a Mormon household. On his arrival, he took some of his provisions there and was cooked "a grand supper." Besides what he was used to, he also was given "*fresh fish, pot cheese, butter, green peas, rye bread & milk & buckwheat cakes.*" The following morning, after the night in his wagon, he went for breakfast and was given buckwheat cakes, rye bread, green peas, salad, onions, radishes, coffee, and milk. Before he left Salt Lake he exchanged a few pounds of his bacon for a few pounds of beef ("pound for pound") and had some of the beef boiled for his dinner and roasted for his supper.[11]

When the settlers celebrated the second anniversary of the arrival of

land Trail in the Spring and Summer of 1849, ed. Thomas D. Clark (Lexington: University of Kentucky Press, 1967), appendix, 176–78; Holmes, ed., Covered Wagon Women, 4:256–58, 269.

9. Howard letter, 177, in Perkins, ed., Gold Rush Diary, 177; Stansbury, Expedition, 100, 18, 128.

10. Arrington, Great Basin Kingdom, 66–68; Letter of O. W. Lipe, August 15, 1849, in Ralph P. Bieber, ed., Southern Trails to California in 1849 (Glendale, Calif.: Arthur Clark Co., 1937), 346–47.

11. Charles Glass Gray, Off at Sunrise: The Overland Journal of Charles Glass Gray, ed. Thomas D. Clark (San Marino, Calif.: Huntington Library, 1976), 62–66.

the original pioneers, long rows of tables were set up outside. They were "loaded with all luxuries of the field and gardens, and nearly all the varieties that any vegetable market in the world could produce." One traveler thought that the Mormon celebration "was very much like one of our temperance meetings." They marched, sang, fired cannons, and "sat down to as fine a dinner as you would find anywhere. . . . They had lots of beans and peas and potatoes, etc." The success of 1849 continued in 1850. In August, when Sarah Davis passed through on her way to California she found "a pleseant place" with "a great deal of vegitation to sell."[12]

One feature of the Mormon settlements that was unusual in newly settled areas was the abundant supply of good salt. John Hudson, who went in the valley in a surveying party in 1850, described the Great Salt Lake "as like a huge pickle tub." The lake was so strongly impregnated with salt that when its waters were driven from the shores by the wind, a salt deposit was left in quantities that could be shoveled.[13]

As early as August 1847, less than a month after the pioneers arrived in the valley, Young and his council had sent a group to get salt from the Great Salt Lake. Between two sandbars they found a large bed of pure salt—enough to fill ten wagons—and in four days were able to obtain 125 bushels of coarse white salt. They also had a barrel of fine table salt, which they had boiled down from four barrels of salt water. They built a bridge over the Jordan River to give them continual access to the lake and put up a year's supply of salt. In July 1849 John Hazlip commented, "They have the finest salt here you ever saw, and any amount of saleratus; they gather it up in a pure state, and it makes splendid bread."

The Mormons waiting at winter quarters for the trek across the plains also benefited from the Great Salt Lake. In January 1848 Martha Haven wrote home that there was plenty of salt and saleratus at Winter Quarters because the pioneers had brought back a considerable amount from the valley. Although families continued to drive to the lake to obtain salt for their own use, Charley White began the commercial manufacture of salt on the shores of the lake in 1850 and in the 1850s expanded his business to supply salt to Mormon settlements throughout the Great Basin.[14]

12. Mulder and Mortensen, eds., *Among the Mormons,* 229, 236; George W. Keys to L. H. Keys, July 15 [25?], 1849, in Bieber, ed., *Southern Trails,* 342–45; "Diary of Sarah Davis," in Holmes, ed., *Covered Wagon Women,* 2:191; Arrington, *Great Basin Kingdom,* 66.

13. John Hudson to his father, July 20, 1850, in John Hudson, *A Forty-Niner in Utah,* ed. Brigham D. Madsden (Salt Lake City: Tanner Trust Fund, University of Utah Library, 1981), 93–94.

14. John A. Clark, "Mormon Church and Utah Salt Manufacture," *Arizona and the West* 26 (1984): 226–30; letter of John B. Hazlip, July 8, 1849, and Martha Haven to her mother, January 3, 1848, both in Mulder and Mortensen, eds., *Among the Mormons,* 234, 214.

Items that could not be produced locally remained difficult to obtain because the Mormons had settled far from any sources of supply. The problem was eased by the steady flow of emigrants along the trail to California, but the settlers also had to rely on what was brought into the valley by commercial freighters and by individuals looking for a quick profit. Beginning in 1849, merchants began to ship goods into Salt Lake City. Sugar and coffee were the basic items, but by the summer of 1850, one shipper was offering canned oysters and sardines, and in the following year a store opened that carried sugar, coffee, and tea, as well as more specialized goods such as raisins, figs, spices, pickles, lemon syrup, and candy.[15]

In 1850, when Margaret Fink was about ten miles from Fort Kearny on her way to the West Coast, her wagon train met two old Santa Fe traders who had a train of wagons "loaded with merchandise" for Salt Lake City. Esther Lockhart, who went across the plains in 1851, later reminisced that, when they were some twelve hundred miles from Council Bluffs, two families in their party left for Salt Lake City. They took with them four big wagonloads of merchandise to sell to the Mormons. It was said that one of them had already shipped forty thousand dollars' worth of goods around Cape Horn to go through California to the Great Basin.[16]

Sugar presented a particular problem for the Utah settlers. It was much desired, but it was expensive and scarce. An attempt was made to ease the problem by planting sugar beets and importing the machinery to process them. A private company organized in 1851 failed two years later, but the church took over the operation. It still was not a success. Both drought and grasshoppers caused problems with the crop, and it was discovered that the beets that were raised could produce molasses but not sugar. Young directed that efforts should be shifted to sorghum cane, and there was an extensive production of sorghum molasses.[17]

From their early days beside the Great Salt Lake, the Mormons were anxious to extend their settlements into new areas and to attract new converts by sending missionaries to the East and across the Atlantic. In the early fall of 1850, the Perpetual Emigration Fund Company was organized, and when it had completed the task of bringing those in the Missouri camps to the Great Basin, it turned its full attention to the problem

15. Henry P. Walker, *The Wagonmasters* (Norman: University of Oklahoma Press, 1966), 156, 159–60; Arrington, *Great Basin Kingdom*, 81–82; "Reminiscences of Esther M. Lockhart," in Holmes, ed., *Covered Wagon Women*, 3:157.

16. "Journal of Margaret A. Fink," and "Reminiscences of Esther M. Lockhart," both in Holmes, ed., *Covered Wagon Women*, 2:78, 3:157; 3:19.

17. Arrington, *Great Basin Kingdom*, 116–20, 122; Holmes, ed., *Covered Wagon Women*, 4:258, 264.

of arranging the emigration of the thousands of Mormons living in England.

Many of the overseas converts did not have the means to reach Salt Lake without help from the church. Representatives in England organized companies, chartered space on vessels, and made detailed plans for their emigration. The emigration fund paid for the expenses of the poorest emigrants. They worked to repay the costs of their emigration when they reached the Great Basin. Those who could afford it, paid part or all of the cost. Food was arranged for by the Mormon agents, but all were expected to bring their own cooking pots and pans.By the end of 1855 nearly 22,000 Mormons had been brought to America from Europe. Providing food for this great mass of emigrants presented major problems.[18]

Most English emigrants who made the trip to Council Bluffs went west in wagons and ate food provided by the perpetual emigration fund. Ten individuals were assigned to one wagon with two yoke of oxen, two cows, and one tent. The amount of available supplies often varied, but, at best, the food allotment for a wagon was one thousand pounds of flour, fifty pounds of sugar, fifty pounds of bacon, fifty pounds of rice, thirty pounds of beans, twenty pounds of dried apples and peaches, five pounds of tea, one gallon of vinegar, twenty-five pounds of salt, and ten bars of soap. There was also milk from the cows and meat from any game that was killed. Emigrants with means also bought such items as dried herrings, pickles, molasses, and more dried fruit and sugar.[19]

Jean Rio Baker, a widow, was a convert who could well afford to pay her own way. She was able to reach the Great Basin before most of the English emigrants. In January 1851, she left London for Liverpool, sailed to New Orleans, and went up the Mississippi to St. Louis. She arrived late in May and bought four wagons and eight yokes of oxen. These were taken by steamboat to Alexandria, then overland to Council Bluffs (Kanesville) to meet up with a Mormon wagon train for the trek to Salt Lake. Mrs. Baker reached Council Bluffs early in July, bought provisions in her two days' stay, and crossed the Missouri on July 5, six months after leaving her home in London. She was traveling in a typical Mormon wagon train. With the supplies she had brought, together with game shot by the hunters and the fish they caught, she was able to eat well on the trip. She had milk from cows that went with the wagon train. Baker was far better off than most

---

18. Arrington, *Great Basin Kingdom,* 97–106; Frederick H. Piercy, *Route from Liverpool to Great Salt Lake Valley,* ed. Fawn M. Brodie (Cambridge, Mass.: Belknap Press of Harvard University Press, 1962), xii–xiii.

19. Piercy, *Route from Liverpool,* 52–53.

emigrants and was also able to buy some of the expensive food that was available at trading posts on the way west, including four "fine hams" and, later, some good bacon.

There were indications, however, that for those without independent funds, rations could be much tighter. In mid-September many of the teamsters driving the wagons went on strike because of the scantiness and poor quality of their rations. Some began to walk away and had to be persuaded to return. When they were promised more food, six of nine agreed to stay. On the day this happened, three provision wagons arrived from Salt Lake City, but they had already sold all they had to other companies. They were continuing east to see if anyone needed help and said that wagons with flour were coming out to meet the wagon train.[20]

Hannah Tapfield King, who came with her family in 1853, was another English emigrant who demonstrated that the Mormons were winning converts among those comfortably off, as well as among the poor. Her family went from Liverpool to New Orleans and up the Mississippi to Keokuk, Iowa. In 1853, this had become the outfitting spot for the Mormon emigration. From Keokuk, Mrs. King went west in a wagon train by way of Council Bluffs. One unusual feature of her trip across the plains was the enjoyment of special drinks. On May 20, when others "dined" with them, she made eggs beaten up with wine and brandy; on June 24 and on July 4 a friend sent her a glass of port; on July 9 they had "a syllabub" (a mixture of milk, cream, wine, and sugar); on July 13 she gave a young man who had been sick, a glass of milk with brandy in it; on August 2 one of her companions gave an Indian "Chief" some whiskey and water; and, finally, on September 8, when Brother Decker arrived with mail from Salt Lake, they gave him wine.[21]

The Mormon opposition to drinking had hardened over the years. In his 1845 journal, the prominent Mormon Hosea Stout referred, without comment, to drinking wine, but that September, President Young made a speech condemning the use of "ardent spirits." This had a powerful effect in limiting the use of alcohol among the Mormons when they arrived in Utah. Explorer Howard Stansbury noted that goods brought into Salt Lake paid a duty of 1 percent, except "spirituous liquors," which had to pay half the price at which they were to be sold. This was to discourage the bringing in of liquor, and Stansbury said that it had "operated to a great

20. "Diary of Jean Rio Baker," in Holmes, ed., *Covered Wagon Women*, 3:201–28, 234–77; Piercy, *Route from Liverpool*, 52.

21. "Journal of Hannah Tapfield King," in Holmes, ed., *Covered Wagon Women*, 6:183–222; Piercy, *Route from Liverpool*, 89, 201.

extent as a prohibition." This was obviously not complete as he mentioned brandy at twelve dollars a gallon and whiskey at eight dollars. In each case, half of the price went to the authorities. Efforts to prevent the use of liquor continued, and it was said in the mid-1850s that "not a tippling house, a gambling house, nor a house of ill-fame" existed within the precincts of Salt Lake and that the city council had repealed all licenses to sell or trade beer and liquor. Yet, in the following years, as the number of Mormons increased, it proved impossible to keep alcohol out of the settlements.[22]

From the entries in Mrs. King's journal, it appears that the Mormon message given by their missionaries in England did not yet include any strong admonitions about drinking. Mrs. King gives no indication that she saw any problem at all in the use of wine or brandy. If she had thought so, she would not have given wine to Brother Decker when he brought mail from Salt Lake City.

In the early 1850s, as emigrants to California continued to pass through the Mormon settlements, some who had only heard anti-Mormon statements were surprised both by the progress that had been made and by the Mormons themselves. One woman who stayed in Salt Lake for the winter of 1852–1853 wrote that "much had been said about them making them out to be a disgrace to the earth but as far as we have seen they are as hospitable & kind as any people I ever met with." She was favorably impressed from the day she arrived. Her family camped opposite a boardinghouse and had a dinner of "green peas, potatoes, roast beef, chicken, bread, butter, cheese & pie." For her, the bread and butter was the greatest treat. Her main complaints about Salt Lake were the high cost of provisions—sugar, coffee, tea, dried fruit—and the lack of fresh fruit. The people where they were boarding were drinking "wheat coffee," which she liked.[23]

Until 1854 the Mormon settlements continued to enjoy dramatic progress. Irrigation had enabled the barren Salt Lake area to produce an agricultural surplus, and expansion into other regions of the Great Basin was achieving success. In 1854, Solomon Carvalho was at Salt Lake City when Brigham Young was about to travel south to sign a treaty with the Indians. Before he left, Young gave "a ball." Carvalho mentioned that on such occasions it was the custom for individuals to bring their own provisions and candles. At the house where he was boarding, the four wives of the owner made pastry, cakes, roasted wild geese and ducks, and garnished

22. Brooks, ed., *On the Mormon Frontier,* 1:50, 69, 75, 77; Stansbury, *Expedition,* 132–33; Piercy, *Route from Liverpool,* 295.

23. "Letters of Lucy R. Cooke," in Holmes, ed., *Covered Wagon Women,* 4:252–64, 269.

hams to take with them. Polygamy had become well established in the Mormon settlements and was soon to be a major source of friction with the United States government.[24]

Carvalho traveled south with Brigham Young's party. It was a large group of about one hundred wagons filled with Mormon leaders with their wives and families. Young rode in the lead wagon with one of his wives, "an accomplished and beautiful lady," who at every camp cooked his meals. In fine weather a white cloth was spread on the grass, and when there was rain a table was set up in the wagon. Beef, venison, eggs, pies, coffee, and other items were served at every meal.[25]

In the mid-1850s, Mormon fortunes temporarily began to change for the worse. A bad harvest in 1855, a particularly harsh winter, and another bad harvest in the following year, brought severe food shortages. A major factor in Mormon surviving these times of crisis was a willingness to share the food that was available through a system of tithing, but the poor crops and the continued immigration of the mid-1850s placed a great strain on Mormon resources.

In September 1855, President Young wrote to the president of the European mission to tell him that the church could not afford to buy wagons and teams and would have to resort to a new way of crossing the plains—the use of handcarts. Emigrants would use the two-wheeled carts to push their possessions across the plains, and a few wagons would be used to carry provisions.[26]

For the voyage across the Atlantic, minimum provisions for passengers were specified by British law, and the amount that had to be provided had recently been increased. For each adult or two children, there had to be at least a weekly ration of one and a quarter pounds of beef, one pound of pork, three and a half pounds of bread, two pounds of potatoes, one and a half pounds of peas, one and a half pounds of rice, one and a half pounds of oatmeal, a pound of sugar, two ounces of tea, two ounces of salt, half an ounce of mustard, one quarter ounce of pepper, and a gill of vinegar. There was also to be three quarts of water for each individual a day, and ten gallons a day for every one hundred persons for cooking.

There was also a regulation list of "Medical Comforts" that each ship

24. Carvalho, *Incidents of Travel*, 221–22.

25. Ibid., 254.

26. Leroy R. and Ann W. Hafen, *Handcarts to Zion: The Story of a Unique Western Migration, 1856–1860* (Glendale, Calif.: A. H. Clark Co., 1960), 29–31; Arrington, *Great Basin Kingdom*, 148–56; Rebecca Cornwall and Leonard J. Arrington, *Rescue of the 1856 Handcart Companies* (Provo: Brigham Young University Press, 1982), 1.

had to carry for every two hundred adults. This would allow special foods to be given to the sick. These supplies included thirty pounds of sugar, twenty-five pounds of sago (a powdered starch made from the pith of sago palms), twenty pounds of pearl barley, fourteen pounds of arrowroot, two dozen pints of milk, one dozen pints of beef soup (presumably in dried form), three dozen half pounds of preserved mutton, two gallons of lime juice, and half a gallon of brandy.[27]

In 1856, some 4,400 Mormon converts went from Europe to the United States. The great majority were from Great Britain, although there were also some 600 from Scandinavia. Of those who crossed the Atlantic, about 2,400 intended to go immediately to the Great Basin, and of these some 1,900 had indicated their willingness to use handcarts to cross the plains. Ships were chartered, and the emigrants sailed from Liverpool to New York and Boston. From there they went by train to Iowa City, which was to be the assembly and outfitting center. In 1856, five handcart companies crossed the plains as well as regular wagon companies.[28]

There were five individuals to each handcart and twenty in each tent. Five tents made up the usual Mormon "hundred." Personal possessions were wheeled in the carts, and the few wagons carried the supplies while cows and steers were driven alongside. A woman in the third company remembered that one of the problems with the carts was that they had no grease for the wheels. When they killed an old buffalo, her husband, a butcher, stayed up all night to boil some of it to get grease, but the buffalo was so old that ultimately there was no grease to be had.

The few wagons meant that supplies were meager, and much depended on successful hunting and on relief wagons when they were within striking distance of the Great Basin. To avoid traveling late into the fall, it was essential to start as soon as possible. In 1856, three of the five companies left Iowa City at the end of the first week in June, two days apart, with about nine hundred emigrants.

The first part of the journey was a trek of about three hundred miles from Iowa City to Florence, Nebraska, through country that was partly settled. It was less threatening than the unsettled regions beyond, but the handcart companies had little money to obtain extra supplies.

Those in the first company quickly found that provisions were in short supply. Archer Walters, an English carpenter in the first company, wrote on June 26 that he was "very faint from the lack of food." He said that they

27. Hafen and Hafen, *Handcarts to Zion*, 38–39.
28. Ibid., 39–49.

were allowed only about three-quarters of a pound of flour each a day and about half a pound of bacon and three ounces of sugar each a week. Those who had no money were "very weak." Once the settled areas were passed, even those who had money had nothing to supplement their rations until hunters with the company brought in game. On July 1, Walters' company received half a pound of flour and two ounces of rice each. He said "my children cry with hunger."[29]

A month later they were still very hungry. Their daily rations were three-quarters of a pound of flour, a few apples, and one and a half ounces of sugar. They assuaged their hunger with shellfish from a creek. A few days later, prospects became better when they reached the buffalo country. Four buffalo were killed, and "hungry appetites satisfied," but soon most of the emigrants were "bad with the diarrhea or purging." On August 23 they were each given one pound of flour, instead of the usual three-quarters of a pound, and Walters said "I was thankful for I never was so hungry in my life." Edmund Ellsworth, the leader of the first company, killed a cow in an effort to relieve the lack of food.

When they reached Fort Laramie, Walters traded one dagger for a piece of bacon and salt and sold another for $1.25. With the money he bought bacon and meal and was so hungry that he began to eat the bacon without cooking it. On the following evening Walters called their bacon and porridge "the best supper for many weeks." Although the company he was in reached the Great Basin successfully, Walters died within two weeks of arriving.[30]

Twiss Bermingham, who was in the second company with his wife and three children, wrote that two families only went ten miles before giving up. They were frightened after getting nothing but "Indian corn stirrabout" for three days. The Bermingham family were usually allowed a pint of milk morning and evening, but at times it was less. On July 31 they were so worn-out at the end of the day that they could not cook. They made do with a "a bit of bread and a pint of milk." A few days later their children were "crying with hunger and fatigue."

By the beginning of September, the ordeal for the first two companies was largely over. Some three hundred miles from Salt Lake they met relief wagons sent from the Great Basin. Each wagon carried one thousand pounds of flour, which had to be paid for at the rate of eighteen cents a pound when the families reached the valley. They still had several weeks

29. Ibid., 57–61, 86, 199, 201, 210, 213, 214; Cornwall and Arrington, *Rescue*, 1–2; Mulder and Mortensen, eds., *Among the Mormons*, 281.

30. Hafen and Hafen, *Handcarts to Zion*, 67–70.

traveling, and it was September 26 before the first two companies reached Salt Lake. About eight miles from the city, they were met by President Young, his counselors, a detachment of Lancers, many inhabitants, and the Nauvoo brass band. When they moved into the city and camped, "provisions of all kinds came rolling in to us."[31]

The third company had about three hundred and twenty emigrants, nearly all of them Welsh. Edward Bunker, the leader of the company, later wrote that "the Welsh had no experience at all and very few of them could speak English." They left Iowa City late in June, and, like the first two companies, were on short rations for the entire trek. Some of the flour was carried in the handcarts, the rest in wagons. The ration each day was about one pound of flour per person, and, while it was available, a little bacon, tea or coffee, sugar, and rice. They also had milk from the cows, a few beef cattle, and were able to kill some buffalo. The bacon and coffee were soon used up. Near the end of the journey they were out of flour for two days before help came from the valley, which they reached early in October.[32]

The first three companies had suffered from short rations but had reached Salt Lake successfully. The last two companies met disaster. These comprised emigrants who had been in ships that were late leaving England. The first left company left Iowa City on July 15 and the second on July 28. The rest of the emigrants who were making the trek to the valley followed in two wagon trains.[33]

As the fourth handcart company (led by James G. Willie) did not have enough room in the wagons for all the flour they would need, each cart carried a ninety-eight-pound sack of flour as well individual possessions. This flour was used first. Forty-five cows and beef cattle added to their rations. One night, near Grand Island, Nebraska, the cattle stampeded, and thirty were lost, many of them oxen. Milk cows now had to help pull the wagons, and the milk and beef ration was sharply reduced.

At the beginning of September, the Willie company reached Fort Laramie. They expected to find provisions there but could get only a barrel or two of hard bread. It was decided to reduce the ration of flour from one pound to three-quarters of a pound, and after Independence Rock it was reduced again—to ten ounces a day. There already had been deaths among the emigrants, and it was now becoming very cold at night. Finally, they ran into a snowstorm. Even now it seemed that rescue was at hand. Two messengers arrived from Salt Lake saying that relief should arrive in

31. Ibid., 62–63, 72–76, 214–15.
32. Ibid., 81–87.
33. Ibid., 91–92.

a day or so. The messengers then rode on east to give the news to the fifth company.

The Willie company struggled on, but the snow was over a foot deep. More cattle died. The last ration of flour was issued. They now used the hard bread from Fort Laramie and killed two of their cattle. Their supplies now consisted of a few pounds of sugar and dried apples, a quarter sack of rice, and twenty or twenty-five pounds of hard bread. They camped while Willie and another man went forward to try to find the relief train. In the camp, they lived on what was left of the hard bread and killed more cattle. Many had dysentery. That, along with the poor diet and hardship, brought further deaths.

Early in October, in Salt Lake City, Brigham Young was surprised to learn that emigrants were still on their way to the valley. On the seventh, the first rescue wagons began to leave Salt Lake with supplies, and many others followed. Families donated large amounts of food, and by the end of October over two hundred teams were on their way east with relief. Progress was slow because of the weather, and in very bad conditions the leading wagons made camp. They were found in camp by Willie and his companion, and on hearing of the distress in Willie's company, they immediately pressed forward. On October 21, several relief wagons reached the Willie company camp with flour, potatoes, onions, and some warm clothing.

The Willie company now continued on toward Salt Lake with about half of the first rescue wagons. Near South Pass they met more rescuers from the valley, encamped with beef hanging frozen on the trees, and at Fort Bridger there were many more rescue wagons. The exhausted survivors were able to ride in wagons for the rest of the trek to Salt Lake. Of the five hundred who had begun the trek, nearly seventy had died.[34]

The fifth handcart company (led by Edward Martin) did not reach Fort Laramie until October 8, and by that time they were on very short rations. Some who had jewelry and watches traded them for a few provisions at the fort. Beyond Laramie, rations were reduced—first to three-quarters of a pound of flour, then to half a pound, and then to even less. In mid-October, when they reached the last crossing of the North Platte (in what is now Wyoming), they were given some help when the two Mormon wagon trains that had left Florence even later, caught up with and passed them. They were still in deep trouble. Soon after they had crossed the

34. Ibid., 93–107, 120–40, 222–27; Mulder and Mortensen, eds., *Among the Mormons*, 282–90; Cornwall and Arrington, *Rescue*, 5–14; Arrington, *Great Basin Kingdom*, 158.

Platte, there were heavy falls of sleet and snow, and within twelve miles they had to halt. They were snowed in. Finally, on October 31, relief reached them. For some it was too late. Of the 576 who had begun the trek with the Martin company, 135 had died. The last emigrants did not reach Salt Lake until the end of November.[35]

To assist in the trek to Salt Lake, the Mormons had a base at Devil's Gate, where the Sweetwater River cut through the mountains, a few miles west of Independence Rock. There was a small stockade and a few log cabins. This was used as an assembly point for the survivors of the last two handcart companies. Many of the possessions—about two hundred wagonloads—were unloaded from the handcarts and stored there while their owners were taken in wagons to Salt Lake City. In the winter of 1856–1857, about twenty men stayed at Devil's Gate to guard the possessions.

Isolated from any help, the twenty men struggled to survive through a harsh winter. They had some cattle in bad condition. These were killed and eaten. They ran out of bread and had only a few crackers. They had no salt. For much of the winter they had to live on what game they could kill—an occasional buffalo and various small animals. When game became scarce, they became so desperate that they ate not only the hides from the cattle they had killed but also wrappings from the wagon tongues, the soles of moccasins, and a piece of buffalo hide that had been used as a foot mat. At first they simply soaked, scraped, and cooked, but this left the glue in, so they adopted a more elaborate procedure—cooking, scorching and scraping the hair off, one hour to extract the glue, then washing and scraping again. After this, they would boil it to a jelly, let it grow cold, and eat it with a little sugar. They also dug thistles from the frozen ground, ate roasted prickly pear leaves, and caught some minnows with a net. Somehow, they managed to survive, helped by food they received from a man carrying mail and by trading with the Indians.[36]

The disaster of 1856 did not end the handcart emigrations. Five more handcart companies crossed the plains from 1857 to 1860. None of them suffered either the hunger or many deaths of the last two companies of 1856, although in 1859 the eighth company, which had over 230 emigrants, ran very short of food. One woman wrote that by the time they were near the Green River "we were literally on the verge of dying of starvation." They were helped by some mountain men and their Indian wives.

35. Hafen and Hafen, *Handcarts to Zion*, 93–116, 218–21; Cornwall and Arrington, *Rescue*, 15–37; Arrington, *Great Basin Kingdom*, 158–59.

36. Daniel W. Jones, *Forty Years among the Indians* (1890; repr., Los Angeles: Westernlore Press 1960), 67–107, 115.

They were given milk and whiskey and a kind of bread. Late in August their worst troubles were over when provision wagons from Salt Lake arrived.[37]

From 1860, there were no more handcarts, but Mormon wagon trains continued. When Mary Lightner, an American Mormon, traveled west in the spring of 1863, she complained that they lived on salt pork, but in her journal she mentioned eating antelope, rabbit, and sage hen, baking bread and shortcake, and drinking coffee and milk. She also felt able to reject bear meat when a large bear was killed. As in most crossings of the Great Plains, the main lack was enough vegetables. She bought some onions and potatoes because they were "getting the canker bad" from the constant diet of salt pork.[38]

In the spring of 1857, arguing that the Mormons were becoming a state within a state, the federal government ordered twenty-five hundred troops to the Great Basin to uphold federal authority. Mormon forces moved east to clash with federal troops, but around Salt Lake City the main disruption came when a peace agreement in 1858 allowed federal troops to enter the valley. Mormon fears were so great that under the direction of President Young most of the inhabitants of Salt Lake City and other northern settlements, some thirty thousand moved south out of the path of the army, leaving only about one thousand behind. When the federal army marched into Salt Lake City, they found it practically deserted. The troops moved into camp some forty miles from the city, and in the summer the Mormon population returned.[39]

The mass exodus limited planting in 1858, but the war with the United States did not permanently hinder Mormon progress. In June 1858, Elizabeth Cumming, the wife of the first non-Mormon governor, was impressed by what she saw when she arrived in Salt Lake City. She described it as "a large, beautiful city, the houses all separate—each with its garden—wide streets, with a pebbly stream running on each side." The gardens were full of flowers and vegetables, and the "promise of fruit." By July she was enjoying vegetables and strawberries. People were pouring back into the city, and the stores were about to reopen.[40]

When Horace Greeley stayed in Salt Lake for over a week in the summer of 1859, he saw gardens filled with peach, apple, and other fruit trees, but his general impression was that the Mormons had a hard life. He

37. Hafen and Hafen, *Handcarts to Zion*, 149–90.
38. Mary Elizabeth Lightner, "Journal," in Holmes, ed., *Covered Wagon Women*, 8:95–108.
39. Arrington, *Great Basin Kingdom*, 171–93; Jones, *Forty Years among the Indians*, 120–22.
40. Letters of Elizabeth Cumming, in Mulder and Mortensen, *Among the Mormons*, 308–11.

thought that many more days' labor were needed to support a family in the Great Basin than in other parts of America. Part of the problem was the expense of importing food supplies that could not be grown locally. Sugar and coffee were expensive, and all types of imported goods "cost twice to six or eight times their prices in the states." Only a small number of the Mormons, he wrote, used tea or coffee, although liquor had become more prevalent since the coming of the United States army.[41]

English traveler Richard Burton visited Salt Lake in the summer of 1860, and, like Greeley, was particularly impressed by the gardens. Although this had been a bad year, with a frost in May severely restricting the production of fruit, great strides had been taken in bringing in kinds of fruit that would flourish in the Great Basin. In Brigham Young's gardens, numerous varieties of apples were being grown. There were also peaches, walnuts, apricots, quinces, cherries, plums, currants, raspberries, gooseberries, and watermelons. In the garden of "Apostle Woodruff," there were apricots from Malta, plum trees from Kew, and French and California grapes.[42]

Burton noticed that a vinery was being planted on the hillside near Brigham Young's residence and thought homemade wine would soon be produced in Utah, but he stressed temperance in his description of the Mormon leader. "His life is ascetic," Burton wrote, "his favourite food is baked potatoes with a little butter-milk, and his drink water; he disapproves, as do all strict Mormons, of spirituous liquors, and never touches anything stronger than a glass of thin Lager-bier; moreover he abstains from tobacco." Burton praised Mormon efforts to curb the use of liquor by taxing importations of liquor at half its price.[43]

Burton, who had traveled extensively in arid regions, was particularly impressed by the way in which irrigation provided a regular supply of water. "Citizens," he wrote, "can now draw with scanty trouble their drinking water in the morning, when it is purest, from the clear and sparkling streams that flow over the pebbly beds before their doors." Water gates enabled the authorities to control the times when residents could draw water.[44]

The late frost of May 1860 had apparently not hurt most of the vegetables, and Burton praised the variety and quality of what was being

41. Greeley, *Overland Journey*, 234–38; also Martin, *The Standard of Living in 1860*, 421.
42. Richard F. Burton, *The City of the Saints: And across the Rocky Mountains to California*, ed. Fawn M. Brodie (New York: Knopf, 1963), 219–21, 297–98, 385, 401.
43. Ibid., 264–65, 279, 297.
44. Ibid., 240.

grown. Potatoes, onions, cabbages, and cucumbers were all "good and plentiful." Tomatoes were "ripening everywhere." In Brigham Young's garden there were Irish and sweet potatoes, squashes, peas, cabbages, beets, cauliflowers, lettuce, broccoli, and newly introduced white celery. In Woodruff's garden, Burton also saw asparagus, and white and yellow carrots. In both of the gardens he saw rhubarb, but he said there was a problem with rhubarb because of the amount of sugar it needed. Sugar was simply too expensive in the Great Basin to be used extensively.[45]

Burton obtained a description and a menu for the "Territorial and Civil Ball" that had been held at the Social Hall on February 7, 1860. It began at 4:00 P.M., and there was a break for food at 8:00. The dinner for 250 consisted of four courses, each with a great variety of foods. It began with a first course of four soups—oyster, oxtail, vermicelli, and vegetable—followed by a widely ranging second course of meats, fish, and vegetables. A variety of items were listed under roast and boiled meats. The roast meats were beef, mutton, mountain mutton, bear, elk, deer, chickens, ducks, and turkeys, and the boiled meats were sugar-corned beef, mutton, chickens, ducks, tripe, turkey, ham, trout, and salmon. Also in the second course were stews and fricassees, oysters, ox tongues, beaver tails, collard head, chickens, ducks, and turkeys. There was also hominy, boiled potatoes, cabbage, parsnips, cauliflower, slaw, baked potatoes, parsnips, and beans. Burton explained, probably mistakenly, that "Slaw" was synonymous with sauerkraut.

The third course consisted of pastry and puddings. The pastries were mince pie, green apple pie, pineapple pie, quince jelly pie, and peach jelly pie. Listed under the puddings were custards, rice, English plum, apple souffle, "Mountain," and "Pioneer." There was also blancmange and jellies. For those with room, there was a fourth course of cakes and fruits. The cakes were pound, sponge, gipsy, and "Varieties"; the fruits were raisins, grapes, apples, and "Snowballs," and there were candies, nuts, tea, and coffee. After supper, dancing continued until 5:00 in the morning. The ball ended, "as it began, with prayer and benediction."[46]

The extent to which the Mormon community was still surrounded by wilderness areas is revealed by the appearance on the menu of a variety of game and fish—mountain mutton, bear, elk, deer, turkeys, ducks, trout, and salmon. There are also indications on the menu that, in spite of the expense of transportation, canned goods were brought out for special

45. Ibid., 221, 299, 309, 401.
46. Ibid., 254–56.

occasions. The oysters and the pineapples must have come from cans. These could be obtained from the increasing number of stores that now were appearing on the main street of Salt Lake City. There was even an ice cream parlor, referred to by Burton as "a kind of restaurant for ice-cream, a luxury which costs $0.25 a glass." Burton, a man of considerable experience, praised the shops: "The stores, I may remark, are far superior, in all points, to the shops in an English country town that is not a watering place."[47]

In the following year, Burton's impression of Mormon prosperity was confirmed by Mark Twain, when he stayed at a hotel in Salt Lake City. He had "a fine supper of the freshest meats and fowls and vegetables—a great variety and as great abundance." Strolling about the city, Twain, like most visitors, admired the "limpid stream rippling and dancing through every street and what seemed to be "a great thriving orchard and garden" behind every house.[48]

When non-Mormon James Miller spent the winter of 1864–1865 in Salt Lake, he described a prosperous community that had grown so much that it was even losing some of its exclusively Mormon character. Miller opened a cigar stand at the corner of a billiard saloon and a restaurant, eating his breakfast at a restaurant in the building and having his dinner and supper brought to the stand. This was not the Salt Lake City of a decade earlier. On December 6 there was a fight in "the Gamblers quarters," and on the seventh the saloon was closed because of the number of drunken gamblers. On Christmas Day, half a dozen men drank all day in the billiard saloon, and this continued on the following day. Miller's Christmas dinner was roast turkey, roast pig, and plum pie but no alcohol. He had plenty of food. In March, he mentioned breakfasting on beefsteak, fried eggs, fried potatoes, and coffee.

Miller was soon to leave Salt Lake. With a non-Mormon element forming an often-unwelcome minority in the Salt Lake population, it is perhaps not surprising that late in 1865 a boycott began against non-Mormon merchants in the city. Miller decided that the time had come to move on.[49]

Mormon difficulties were certainly not over—the practice of polygamy brought a major clash with the federal government in the 1870s and 1880s—but there was no longer a danger of famine. The Mormons had

47. Ibid., 241.
48. Mark Twain, *Roughing It*, ed. Hamlin Hill (1872; repr., New York: Penguin, 1981), 130–31.
49. James K. P. Miller, *The Road to Virginia City: The Diary of James Knox Polk Miller*, ed. Andrew F. Rolle (Norman: University of Oklahoma Press, 1960), 33–61.

created a bountiful land in an area previously regarded as desert. They had been driven to the Great Basin by persecution, but this persecution and their deep religious beliefs had made them willing to accept a high degree of social and economic control. Dedication, cooperation, hard work, and irrigation had enabled them to succeed in an area totally unsuitable for individual settlement.

Part 4

Gold Rush and the Mines

CHAPTER 8

By Land and Sea

Thank the Good god we all got throw [through] and the onely family
that did not eat human flesh.

Virginia Reed, Donner party, 1846

O n the eve of American conquest, the discovery of gold, and the
sudden rush of tens of thousands of miners from the east, California was a largely undeveloped distant outpost of Mexico.
Most of the population was concentrated in the coastal towns.
Inland, there were many ranches with large herds of cattle and
sheep but comparatively few people. Much of the interior
abounded in game. After traveling in California in 1845 and 1846, James
Clyman wrote of plains "litterly [sic] covered with Elk and wild horses," of
deer and grizzlies which could be easily slaughtered, and of skies darkened
by geese and ducks.

The food that Clyman described was like that of the Southwest, with
the addition of large quantities of beef—"fine fat Beef," which was "used
and wasted . . . in the greatest profusion." There was also "fine and fat"
mutton. Fresh beef, beans, and red peppers were cooked together until the
beef was falling apart. Because of the quantity available, and the mildness
of the climate, the beef was nearly always eaten fresh. Red peppers were
used freely "so much so as to nearly strangle a Foringer [sic]." Clyman spent
his time in the interior, and his emphasis was largely on the food to be
found on the ranches.[1]

Those who knew the missions scattered along the coast had different
impressions of California food. William Garner, an Englishmen who lived
in Monterey, wrote of "various kinds of exquisite fruits"—apples, pears,
peaches, pomegranates, plums, nectarines, and oranges—and of the extensive vineyards. Henry Standage, who had come to southern California

1. Clyman, *Journal of a Mountain Man*, 201–34.

with the Mormon battalion of the American army in early 1847, described numerous orchards, large vineyards, and vast herds of cattle.[2]

Most American settlers who came overland to California just before and during the Mexican War followed the Oregon Trail through South Pass and turned southwest to reach northern California by way of the Great Basin. Some, who chose what they hoped would be a speedier trip, left the trail near Fort Bridger and went southwest around the southern edge of the Great Salt Lake on what was usually called the Hastings Cut Off. The great majority continued on the Oregon Trail as far as Fort Hall before striking off to the Southwest. This was a longer route, but emigrants avoided the desert immediately west of the Great Salt Lake. Whichever route was used, there was a problem of dry desert conditions in what was to become western Utah and Nevada and the difficult crossing of the Sierras.

Two of the parties that took the Hastings Cut Off in 1846 had greatly different experiences regarding food. Edwin Bryant was with a wagon train that set out from Independence for California early in May. He traveled with a small group of men, and they engaged another man, who had worked for a trading and trapping company, as their cook and driver. Soon after they started they realized that they had packed their wagon so that they had to remove heavy boxes and trunks before they could get to the flour, bacon, and cooking utensils they needed for their first meal. They browned their coffee beans but could not reach the coffee mill to grind them. After some delay, they had a supper of half-baked corn bread, fried bacon, and coffee.

Bryant and his party were going west in a wagon train of 63 wagons with 119 men, 59 women, and 110 children. On May 12 a committee chosen by the emigrants made an inspection and found they had 58,484 pounds of breadstuffs and 38,080 pounds of bacon. They also had about 700 cattle and 150 horses. On the trail, Bryant was roused at or before sunrise by a trumpet, and by 6:00 A.M. usually breakfasted on bread, fried bacon, and coffee. They were on the march from 7:00 or 7:30 A.M. to midday, when the oxen were rested and they ate something prepared at breakfast. In the afternoon, they trekked on until 5:00 or 6:00 P.M. and made camp. The wagons were put in a circle and the horses and cattle corralled

2. William Roberts Garner, *Letters from California, 1846–1847*, ed. Donald M. Craig (Berkeley and Los Angeles: University of California Press, 1970), 94; "Journal of Henry Standage," in Frank A. Golder, *The March of the Mormon Battalion from Council Bluffs to California* (New York: The Century Co., 1928), 205–38.

in the center. Tents were pitched on the outside, with their openings outward, and camp fires for cooking were lit in front of them.[3]

In the first part of their journey, the emigrants dug up wild onions to cook with their bacon, eased their thirst with berries, brought in several buckets of honey, and caught catfish to vary their diet. One woman, who had brought spices with her, made a jar of pickles from the berries, and when Bryant and a friend gathered several quarts of "ripe strawberries," another of the women in the wagon train served them "with rich cream and loaf-sugar." Bryant described this as "a genuine luxury in this wild region."[4]

At first, they rarely saw any game and depended on their own bacon, but they bought dried buffalo tongues and meat jerky from a small party of Indians. Early in June, on the Little Blue River, they killed a deer, "the first game of any consequence," and now they began to vary their diet with antelope, elk, duck, and plover. Bryant also attended a wedding, complete with wedding cake. It lacked only the icing.

In mid-June, they reached the buffalo country, and Bryant reveled in the meat from fat buffalo cows and heifers, finding it "superior to our best beef." He particularly liked the internal organ called the "marrow-gut" (the chyle, a lymph gland filled with emulsified fat). Bryant thought that, when properly prepared, the "marrow-gut" equaled any delicacy he had ever tasted.[5]

On June 24, at Fort Laramie, Bryant dined with officers of the American Fur Company on boiled corned beef, cold biscuits, and milk. There was plenty of milk as cattle were kept at the post. Good eating continued in the following weeks. A week after leaving Fort Laramie, the married woman in the wagon train who had earlier given them cream and loaf sugar prepared a dish of green peas from wild pea vines and served them with "smoking biscuits, fresh butter, honey, rich milk, cream, venison steaks, and tea and coffee." This was certainly not a typical meal on the overland trails.[6]

They were now eating buffalo, antelope, and sage hens, plus trout for variety. In the Sweetwater valley they were able to obtain milk and buttermilk from a party on the way to Oregon. Bryant expressed concern that all the milk drunk by emigrating parties helped to produce the "febrile

3. Bryant, *What I Saw in California*, 13–32, 74–75.
4. Ibid., 35, 42, 57–60, 62–63.
5. Ibid., 69–70, 72, 78–91, 94–96.
6. Ibid., 112, 118, 248.

complaint known as 'camp fever.'" Most groups, he said, had milk cows with them and sometimes drank it in quarts or even gallons in the course of a few hours. They drank it at every meal and ate fat bacon and buffalo meat.[7]

Bryant and eight of his friends had decided to leave the main wagon train and press on more swiftly, using mules. They took the Hastings Cut Off into the Great Basin, and food now became scarce. Before the Mormons reached the Salt Lake region, the Great Basin was a forbidding and barren wilderness roamed over by parties of Indians scratching a precarious existence from its meager resources. Near the Great Salt Lake, Bryant and the others traded with Indians for a mixture of crushed serviceberries and pulverized grasshoppers, which had been dried hard in the sun.

Even these meager cakes were unavailable as they pressed on into the desert. For about seventy-five miles there was neither water nor grass. On this part of the trip they had only coffee and bread for breakfast as salty bacon made them too thirsty. They were not well prepared for this arid region. Their only container for water was the small, empty powder keg in which they had been carrying their coffee.[8]

Because of concern that they would run out of provisions, they had put themselves on an allowance of one small slice of fried bacon and "a very diminutive piece of bread" twice a day. In the heat of the Great Basin the bacon had become "very rancid," but they were helped when they were able to get flour and bacon from another party of emigrants. At the Truckee River they fished with no luck, but they managed to kill a few ducks. At Truckee Lake they found a "most delicious variety of raspberry."[9]

In the Sierras, they gathered more raspberries, as well as small bitter cherries and red berries, which were known by the Californians as *manzanita* (little apple) berries. They were still short of provisions but managed to kill a deer. As they descended the Sierras, they used the last of their flour. Their only remaining supplies were a pint of rice, about half a pound of rancid bacon, and some coffee. They had been without sugar for two weeks. On August 28, breakfast and supper, which were their only meals, consisted of a cup of coffee without sugar, and on the following day they made a soup for breakfast out of the rancid bacon skins that remained in their provision stack. It produced "a nausea." One of them managed to kill a hare, and they made a soup of it for their supper.

On the thirtieth they came in sight of the Sacramento valley and

7. Ibid., 127, 128, 131, 135, 145, 148, 158.
8. Ibid., 162, 170–72.
9. Ibid., 207, 208, 211, 219–20, 227, 229.

reached a farm owned by an American. They were given cheese and milk and bought flour, fresh beef, cheese, and butter. On September 1 they arrived at Sutter's Fort, a large ranch owned by Swiss-American John Sutter that was a mecca for Americans arriving in these years. For no charge, they were given beef, salt, melons, onions, and tomatoes, and their ordeal was over. Bryant's party had started early in May, had traveled quickly, had reached the Sierras before the coming of winter, and, perhaps most important of all, had good luck. They had run short of food but had reached California safely.[10]

Some were not as fortunate. The most famous western trail disaster—that of the Donner Party—occurred in the same year that Bryant successfully reached California. Though seemingly well prepared, the Donner party took too long, had bad luck, and met disaster in the Sierras. A wagon train of some one hundred emigrants left Illinois in the spring of 1846. On the way it joined with others until there were about two hundred travelers.

The first part of the trip went normally. Tamsen Donner wrote from near the junction of the North and South Platte in the middle of June that the journey "so far, has been pleasant." She said meat was abundant, and there was plenty of butter and milk (they had brought cows with them), but she was a little worried that their preparations for the trip had been inadequate. They had laid in 150 pounds of flour and 75 pounds of meat for each individual, but she said that bread had been "the principal article of food in our camp." This was somewhat unusual as most parties tried to live mainly on game along the Platte and save their flour for future scarcity.[11]

At Fort Bridger the party divided. Most took the usual route by way of Fort Hall but over eighty decided to travel by way of the Hastings Cut Off. This was a fateful decision. It took them much longer than they expected. They did not reach the Sierras until well into fall, and the snows came early that year. In November they were stopped by three-foot snowdrifts at what became known as Donner Lake. They built cabins in an attempt to survive, and they were there until March. They suffered badly from the cold, but worst of all they ran out of food.

Virginia Reed, whose father had earlier pressed on to California in a quest for provisions, later wrote that her family had nothing to eat but "ox hides." They killed their dog and ate him—"head and feet & hide." He lasted a week. Of the fifteen in their cabin, ten starved to death. Virginia and the others survived on hides. Ultimately, some in other cabins began

10. Ibid., 229–47.
11. Tamsen Donner to a friend, June 16, 1846, in Holmes, ed., *Covered Wagon Women*, 1:70.

to eat those who had died. Virginia's comment was that "thank the Good god we have all got throw [through] and the onely family that did not eat human flesh." They were finally saved when a relief party, including Virginia's father, arrived from California.[12]

In 1848, the cession of California to the United States and the discovery of gold in the foothills of the Sierras east of Sutter's Fort transformed the whole region. In the winter of 1848–1849, when news reached the East Coast, many sought to get there with all possible speed. This produced a mass emigration to California in 1849, not only by the traditional northern route along the Oregon Trail to Fort Bridger or Fort Hall but also by sea and by various southern routes.

The gold rush at first produced a different type of emigration. The trek to Oregon had primarily been a movement of families. The 1849 emigration to California was far more a movement of men, some single, some leaving their families in the east in the hope of reaching California rapidly and striking it rich in the goldfields. Some groups of men formed companies and booked space on a ship, others went by land and had a quasi-military organization for the journey, the supplies, and the food. Many individuals simply joined with others at the jumping-off points or went alone on foot, carrying provisions on their backs.

For those along the East Coast, the quickest way to California was by sea. In January 1849, John Shearman wrote that in New York, "Thousands of the best men in Society are going—Indeed, it is only the better class who can go. It requires more money to get there, than the common people can find." It was certainly not only "the best men in Society" who went, but going by sea required more than average resources. For those with the money, there were two main ocean routes: either around the formidable Cape Horn at the southern tip of South America or by ship to Panama, across the isthmus, and by ship up the West Coast.[13]

For the long voyage around Cape Horn, ships carried many of the same provisions—salt pork, flour, hard biscuit, and beans—as were carried on the long journeys by wagon. Fresh food was often provided by keeping pigs, chickens, and sometimes a cow for milk in pens on the deck, and the travelers often caught fish. Complaints were frequent. On the long,

12. Virginia Reed to her cousin, May 16, 1847, in Holmes, ed., *Covered Wagon Women*, 1:74–80; George R. Stewart, *Ordeal by Hunger: The Story of the Donner Party*, rev. ed. (Boston: Houghton, Mifflin, 1960).

13. John Shearman to Benjamin Hudson, January 26, 1849, in Hudson, *A Forty-Niner*, 30; John E. Pomfret, ed., *California Gold Rush Voyages, 1848–1849: Three Original Narratives* (San Marino, Calif.: Huntington Library, 1954), 3–8.

monotonous voyage an undercurrent of discontent at times erupted into active protests. These men were very eager to reach the goldfields, and time passed very slowly. Food from ship to ship varied considerably, depending on the efficiency and honesty of a ship's owners and captain. Both individuals and companies were wise to have their own reserve supplies.

Scanty and bad food rather than starvation was the main problem. Some captains put in at Rio de Janeiro and Valparaiso, but others made no stops during the entire voyage. One man writing from California in September 1849, after a voyage of some six months of "long and comfortless days," said that any man who had been used to a decent standard of living "would find it hard to set to cold salt beef, sea biscuit mouldy and full of living animals, and coffee without sugar, every day morning for breakfast." For dinner, he wrote, every man helped himself from a pan of cold beef, and for supper there was rice boiled in bags, put in a tub, and mixed with water.[14]

Josiah Gregg, who sailed from Mazatlán, Mexico, to San Francisco in the summer of 1849, reported a far happier experience. He said that for the first time he had the opportunity to experience "the delicious preserved meats—beef, veal, mutton—boiled and put up in N. York, in air-tight sealed cans—as also soups—which, being heated, are nearly as good as when first cooked."[15]

C. H. Ellis, who was from Maine, left Boston in January 1849 on a ship carrying thirty-two passengers. The voyage to California took 172 days, including over a month rounding Cape Horn. The ship appears to have been well provisioned, had a good cook, fish were caught on the way, and the passengers varied the provisions with their own supplies, such as nuts and molasses. It was certainly not a voyage of salt beef and sea biscuit, yet, even on this voyage, about half the passengers ultimately pressed the captain for better rations.

For a time the food was quite good. In the first month, at one dinner they had a boiled plum pudding, at another chicken pie and rice soup, and at a third boiled rice and molasses. On a Saturday night they had a substantial meal of pickled tongues, fried pork, potatoes, pickles, pepper sauce, and pancakes. They were carrying both hogs and fowl in pens on the deck, and after the cook butchered a pig they had fresh fried pork for breakfast and roast pork for dinner. Their fowl lasted until near the end of March—

14. Letter from D. Hollister, September. 27, 1849, in Perkins, *Gold Rush Diary,* 163.
15. Josiah Gregg, *Diary & Letters of Josiah Gregg,* ed. Maurice G. Fulton, 2 vols. (Norman: University of Oklahoma Press, 1941–44), 2:348, August 31, 1849.

they had their last chicken dinner on March 25—and they did not kill their last pig until July 3.[16]

From early in the voyage, the provisions were supplemented by fishing. The first big catch was a porpoise weighing about two hundred pounds. The cook served fried porpoise steaks for breakfast, and some of the passengers compared the meat to moose or bullock's liver. Ellis did not like it. He made his breakfast of bread, beef, and coffee.[17]

Hopes of a trouble-free voyage ended at Cape Horn. Gales blocked their progress through the Straits of Magellan, and they were delayed for over a month. For part of the time they lay at anchor, and the ship's captain took the opportunity to send shore parties to replenish their stocks of water and wood. They also killed about fifty sea fowl and caught more fish. The sailors were unsurprised by this delay at Cape Horn, but the prospective miners seethed.[18]

By the end of April, they were in the Pacific, and, as they slowly proceeded up the west coast of South America, tempers became very frayed. Eighteen of the passengers demanded that the captain give them better food, threatening to go to the law in San Francisco if their demands were not met. Ellis was not one of the protesters. On May 19, with the ship's stock of molasses finished, the captain bought some from one of the passengers. As the molasses was in the hold, the hatches had to be opened. Other passengers took the opportunity to take out small private stocks of their own, and at each meal various little bottles and cans were produced to vary the food.

In June, rations were supplemented by bonito and porpoise caught by the captain. Ellis again did not eat the porpoise but tried the bonito. He found it rather dry and not particularly appetizing. Bonito is the strongest-tasting of the various tunas. By June 19, there was no sugar, molasses, or fish, they were eating their last barrel of pork, and the water was "miserable." The lack of molasses was particularly felt because they used it in tea and coffee, on rice and plum duff (a boiled suet pudding with raisins or currants), and even in their water to make it more palatable. The captain had saved one pig and had it killed for "an excellent sea pie" on July Fourth. Less than a week later they reached San Francisco. Although over half of the passengers had become angry about the food, the captain appears to have done quite well. Even the month's delay in rounding Cape Horn had not created insuperable problems.[19]

16. "Journal of C. H. Ellis," in Pomfret, ed., *California Gold Rush Voyages*, 11–20, 35, 92.
17. Ibid., 17.
18. Ibid., 38–63.
19. Ibid., 67–94.

At times, discontent about the food arose earlier in the voyage. Philadel-phian Josiah Foster Flagg, who was in a company that sailed from Philadel-phia in May 1849, had only been at sea for little over a month when he was appointed to visit the captain to discuss the "bad provisions" and other problems on the ship. The complaints to the captain apparently brought about an improvement, and they celebrated July Fourth with a big pot pie. Provisions were supplemented by fishing, and twice Flagg made a meal of freshly caught shark.

The situation was also helped by a call at Rio de Janeiro. Flagg went ashore, visited the market, and bought oranges for preserving. Many ships' captains were willing to pay port charges so that they could buy more pro-visions and ease tensions among both the crew and the passengers. The ship was favored by a comparatively easy passage around Cape Horn and put into Valparaiso, Chile. This was a particular favorite as a port of call, because of its rich variety of fruit—pears, apples, peaches, grapes, and mel-ons—as well as its excellent flour. Flagg bought wine and peaches. Some of the ships they met in Valparaiso harbor had experienced a far worse time rounding the horn—one had been held up for three months. Flagg's ship finally anchored in San Francisco Bay on November 23, 1849. The voyage had taken over six months.[20]

Not surprisingly, travelers on ships that put into ports on their way to California had better memories of their voyage than those cooped up for the entire journey. Franklin Buck, who left the East Coast in January 1849, took ample provisions as well as boxes of books. His comment before he left was that "we are going to live high." He was at sea for most of the time from January to August and particularly enjoyed the stop they made at Rio. He had mint juleps (with ice) and ate unaccustomed cucumbers, water cress, lettuce, oranges, and bananas. On a ride around the bay to visit the botanical gardens, he stopped for "a Brazilian dinner." He was given ham and eggs, omelette, roast chicken, beefsteak, bananas, oranges, guava jelly, citrons, green cheese, claret, Madeira, and coffee.[21]

For those who were prepared to take the chance on maintaining good health across the isthmus, and if they could find a ship on the Pacific coast to take them to California, the quickest route to the goldfields was by way of Panama. In his 1849 emigrants' guide to California, Joseph Ware

20. Josiah F. Flagg Diary, in Josiah F. Flagg Papers, Historical Society of Pennsylvania; see also James Morison, *By Sea to San Francisco, 1849–1850: The Journal of Doctor James Morison*, ed. Lonnie J. White and William R. Gillespie (Memphis: Memphis State University Press, 1977), 12, 21.

21. Franklin A. Buck, *A Yankee Trader in the Gold Rush: The Letters of Franklin A. Buck*, compiled by Katherine A. White (Boston: Houghton, Mifflin, 1930), 28–34.

suggested that, because of its comparative quickness, this should be the route for those who did not have families. The easiest part of the journey was from an East Coast port to Chagres, but there were major difficulties in Panama. From Chagres emigrants went by canoe for nearly fifty miles to Las Cruces. Ware warned travelers that provisions were essential for this journey as none were to be had along the river. In reality, there were places to obtain meals, and these became more common as the number of travelers increased. From Las Cruces, it was a little over twenty miles to the Pacific, and this part of the journey had to be made by mule or horse.

Once the Pacific was reached, the main problem in the early months of 1849 was finding a ship. Shipping lines had not yet been able to react to the sudden rush of forty-niners. Ware warned his readers that a traveler might have to wait for weeks on the Pacific side of the isthmus for a ship to take them to San Francisco, a journey of thirty five hundred miles.[22]

Although Ware thought the Panama route was only suitable for men traveling alone, Mary Megquier helped to pioneer the way across the isthmus when she went to California with her husband early in 1849. They sailed from New York on March 1 and in twelve days were in Chagres. Mrs. Megquier described it as a village of about six hundred people living in huts. At the two hotels you could get beef and fish "by the yard," as well as "stewed Monkeys and Iguanos," which she avoided.[23]

After staying in Chagres for a week, they began their journey across the isthmus, first going a short distance by steamboat to a tiny settlement where they spent the night. On the following morning, they transferred to a canoe paddled by two locals. They stopped at a hut for "a cup of miserable coffee with our biscuit," before spending the night at another tiny settlement. There they sat on the bank of the river and watched canoes arriving with more emigrants, who put up tents, "fried their ham, made their coffee." The settlement was very small, but Mrs. Megquier's party were able to buy a dinner of duck, eggs, and fried plantain. Plantain, a type of banana, if cooked when green, is a useful substitute for vegetables. They had seen no vegetables since leaving the ship.

At 4:00 the next morning they were again on the river, passing through exotic surroundings, with strange birds, monkeys, parrots, and alligators. At one small settlement, they were able to buy coffee and a little milk—the

22. Joseph E. Ware, *The Emigrant's Guide to California* (1849; repr., New York: Da Capo Press, 1972), 48–56.

23. Mary Jane Megquier, *Apron Full of Gold: The Letters of Mary Jane Megquier from San Francisco, 1849–1856*, ed. Polly Welts Kaufman, 2nd ed. (Albuquerque: University of New Mexico Press, 1994), 28.

first milk they had seen on the isthmus—and arrived at Las Cruces to find four hundred Americans camped in and around the town. They had the money to take lodgings at a hotel before visiting friends from the ship who were camped on the river bank. There, they were given biscuits and smoked beef.

After a day in Las Cruces, they left by mule for Panama City, "over one of the roughest roads in the world." Beside the road there were tents "kept by Yankees" where various foodstuffs could be bought. Emigrants who had started for California, but found a long delay in getting a ship for San Francisco, had decided to make money by selling coffee, rice, stewed beans, and pancakes to later arriving emigrants. After a day in the saddle, the Megquiers reached Panama City and lodged in a large hotel. There were about two thousand Americans in the town, practically all of them men. Some had been waiting for weeks. Most were camped out, but some were in hotels.[24]

While they waited, the Megquiers settled into a steady daily routine of meals—up at 6:00 A.M. for coffee and rolls, followed by breakfast at 9:30 A.M., dinner at 4:00 P.M., and nothing more until morning. They were served beef, fowl, eggs, rice, fish, and coffee, but no butter, cheese, good bread, pies, or cake, and the only vegetables were beans and a few expensive potatoes. Now there was more fruit available, but Mary Megquier liked only the oranges and pineapples. Hopes of being able to leave rapidly soon faded. Mrs. Megquier and her husband spent two months in Panama City before leaving for California on May 22 on a ship with some four hundred passengers, fewer than ten of them women. On June 13 they finally reached San Francisco.[25]

Unlike the vessels rounding the Horn, those on the Panama–San Francisco run regularly put in at a number of ports along the route. Acapulco and Mazatlán in Mexico, and San Diego, Santa Barbara, and Monterey in the United States, were frequent ports of call, and others were used as well. These stops meant that provisions were usually better on the west coast vessels than on those making the long journey around the horn, but in the spring of 1849 demand was great and provisions were scarce in all the ports.[26]

In May 1849, Mrs. Jane McDougal sailed from San Francisco to Panama on the steamship *California*. She "had a hard time to get anything

24. Ibid., 15–16, 21, 28–30.
25. Ibid., 18, 21–25, 32–35.
26. See Myres, ed., *Ho for California!* 11; "Captain's Journal," in Pomfret, ed., *California Gold Rush Voyages,* 233–41.

to eat on the steamer." They put in at Santa Barbara, but they could get no fresh provisions for the ship. As Mrs. McDougal could see hundreds of cattle grazing on the hills, and a mission with fine gardens and orchards, she ascribed the lack of provisions to the laziness of the inhabitants. It seems likely that provisions were available but that prices were too high. Mrs. McDougal complained about seasickness and said they had "very little but mutton," but her voyage was hardly arduous. She had a personal servant, who eased the problems of waiting until 9:00 A.M. for breakfast by bringing tea and toast to her cabin.

The voyage improved after they put in to Mazatlán. Mrs. McDougal went ashore. She visited a family she knew and was given fruit and melons with her lunch. Back on ship on the following day, there was champagne and cake for the birthday of another woman on board. After a stop at Acapulco, they met a ship eighty days out from Valparaiso. It was short of water, and the captain of the *California* sent two large casks along with fruit and melons. In return, the ship sent them four large hams and a box of champagne. Their only remaining problem before reaching Panama was that for one day the cook was in irons after clashing with the captain. The captain eased tension on the following day by freely distributing champagne at dinner.[27]

While most forty-niners who came by sea went by way of Cape Horn or across Panama, some either chose or were forced to take other routes. William Perkins was part of a company that was formed in Cincinnati, Ohio. Most emigrants from Ohio traveled overland and took the Oregon Trail to the Rockies before striking out for California. Perkins's group, however, wanted to get to California as quickly as possible by going through Panama. They bought provisions in Cincinnati—mostly kegs of pork and sea biscuit—and took a steamboat down the Ohio and Mississippi to New Orleans. From there they intended to go to Chagres, but the boat they were on sprang a leak and returned to New Orleans. They now decided to go overland across Mexico.

From New Orleans they took a boat to near the mouth of the Rio Grande and on March 8 left Fort Brown to go directly across northern Mexico, by way of Monterey, Saltillo, and Durango. At Durango the governor gave six of them a nineteen-course dinner at which one of the treats was English porter, drunk out of champagne glasses. They pressed on to the West Coast, eating well each night on game, armadillos, wild honey, and tortillas. At Mazatlán they boarded a Danish ship for the trip to San

27. "Diary of Mrs. Jane McDougal," in Myres, ed., *Ho for California!* 9–33.

Francisco but found that the captain had not taken on enough food and water, and what they had was poor. Water was rationed, and the passengers protested bitterly to the captain about wormy bread, putrid jerked beef, and musty rice. This produced somewhat better food, but they also caught sharks to supplement their diet. Finally, they reached San Francisco in late May.[28]

In the twenty years after the great rush of 1849, there was extensive maritime travel between the East and the West Coast by way of Panama. Passengers paid for their food as part of the passage money. The various ports of call, and the route across Panama, were transformed in the years following the gold rush. Supplying the needs of the travelers became a major business. When, In May 1852, William Perkins left San Francisco for Panama on the steamer *Winfield Scott*, it had 800 passengers. On the day they put in to Acapulco, two other ships arrived from San Francisco with another 900 passengers, a ship came from Panama with 1150, and one from Nicaragua had 730. The local inhabitants were making a good profit by selling a great variety of fruit and other items. Every house and hut had a fruit stall, and at night the streets were one great bazaar, with tables and stalls piled high with oranges, cocoa-nuts, mangos, pineapples, plantains, bananas, limes, melons, tortillas, and hot chili dishes.[29]

By the time that newspaper editor Samuel Bowles returned east from San Francisco in 1865, the steamship lines were well established and there was a railway across the isthmus. Bowles said this was now almost the sole route for business and pleasure travel between the East and West coasts, and that two or three thousand passengers passed each way over it every month. There was even competition to the Panama route on a line that went by way of Nicaragua.

The steamship Bowles took from San Francisco carried about a thousand passengers, and he said this was now typical. There were about two hundred in first class, three hundred in second, and some four to five hundred in steerage. First- and second-class passengers ate in the same dining saloon but at different times. Bowles thought the food was good, "even luxurious," almost as good as food at a first-class hotel. Cattle, sheep, chickens, and hogs were slaughtered each day. The journey from San Francisco to Panama took fourteen days, and for most of the time the steamer was in sight of land. They made one stop—at Acapulco. Some went ashore,

---

28. William Perkins, *Three Years in California: William Perkins's Journal of Life at Sonora, 1849–1852,* ed. Dale L. Morgan and James R. Scobie (Berkeley and Los Angeles: University of California Press, 1964), 2–13, 74–84.

29. Ibid., 354–61.

but for those who stayed on board, Mexicans crowded around in small boats selling oranges, bananas, limes, eggs, and many other items. As the Mexicans were not allowed to come on board, the exchange of money and goods was made by lowering and hauling up baskets. Both the passengers and the ship's steward bought food from the boats.

The passengers went by rail across the isthmus to Aspinall and boarded another steamer for New York. The Pacific Mail Steamship Company, which Bowles had taken from San Francisco to the isthmus, had recently taken over the Aspinall-to–New York run and had much improved what had been regarded for years as a bad service. The only deterioration Bowles noticed in the food was that instead of live animals on board, and daily butchering, all the meat for the round trip was taken on in New York and kept on ice. Bowles was pleased with the service and food he received on the whole trip from San Francisco to New York. His only complaint was that the ships were overcrowded.[30]

In the great gold rush year of 1849, although many thousands of emigrants went by sea to California, most traveled overland. The northern route along the Oregon Trail became the choice of tens of thousands. Many who went this way struck out southwest for California near Fort Bridger rather than continuing to Fort Hall, because the route around the south end of the Great Salt Lake had become safer with the coming of the Mormons to Utah.

Many families took the overland trail, but they were far outnumbered by the men who either went alone, with a few friends, or in more formal companies. In early 1849, Charles Glass Gray became a member of the Newark Overland Company, which began with thirty-seven members, most of them from Newark, New Jersey. The party left Newark at the beginning of March and went by train, stagecoach, and steamboat to Independence, Missouri, which they reached at the end of the month. By that time, company members disagreed over the question of whether to have the wagons pulled by oxen or by mules. Oxen were hardier and safer, mules were quicker.

After some men left, the remaining party consisted of twenty-four men in five wagons pulled by oxen. They set out at the beginning of May. As in most of these companies, the men formed themselves into "messes" for eating. Gray was the cook for his mess. On the first part of the trip there

30. Samuel Bowles, *Across the Continent* (1865; repr., Ann Arbor: University Microfilms, 1966), 370–89.

was rain and a lack of even wet wood. A cold dinner on the third was followed on the next day by a breakfast of "cold meat, hard bread & water,"
and an evening meal of baked beans. Over the next few weeks, they killed
only a little game—a few plovers, a snipe (given to the sick), and a turkey—
and were unsuccessful in fishing. The weather was miserable, but Gray
warded it off by opening "a bottle of fine brandy."

On May 15, Gray saw why they were having difficulty finding wood for
their cooking. He stood on a hill and saw "the longest line of wagons I
ever remember." This mass of wagons was typical of 1849. West of St.
Joseph in late April, a young girl noted in her journal that "As far as eye can
reach, so great is the emigration, you can see nothing but wagons."[31]

The numbers clearly concerned Gray's companions. On the following
day, they began to move on before Gray could get the water casks full. They
had enough water to cook with and to wash the dishes that evening but no
water to drink for the rest of the evening or in the morning for breakfast.
At noon the next day, Gray managed to fill two canteens "with dirty water,"
and that night he sat up until 12:00 midnight cooking beans and cleaning
pots and kettles.[32]

One of the wheels on Gray's wagon showed signs of collapsing, and to
try to save it the men threw out many items, including various iron utensils. Two days later the wagon tipped over. The pots and kettles hanging
outside were ruined, and the mess chest was upended, throwing out flour,
coffee, rice, beans, peaches, salt, cutlery and various other items. They must
have been well packed because they were able to put them all back in. Later
in the month, a thunderstorm nearly destroyed their sugar and bread bags
in the front of the wagon, and filled their mess chest four inches deep in
water, soaking their tea, and knocking over "a pot of batter for cakes" that
they kept in there. The loss of cooking utensils was partially offset when
one of them found an iron stove that had been discarded.

Finding fuel continued to be a problem. In the ten days before they
passed Fort Kearny, they carried wood with them. Game was also scarce
but on the twenty-sixth they killed an antelope. A buffalo hunter told them
that they were in the heart of the buffalo country but that the great numbers of emigrants had frightened them away from the trail.

June began inauspiciously. On a wet, cold morning their only breakfast
was "burned bread, greasy oily bacon, cold water & crackers, no fire or coffee & water up to the ankles everywhere we step'd." On the second, they

31. Gray, *Off at Sunrise,* xii–xxix, 1–13; "Sally Hester's Diary," in Holmes, *Covered Wagon Women,*
1:236.
32. Gray, *Off at Sunrise,* 14–16.

finally killed two buffalo bulls but they were a great disappointment. Gray thought it "the most offensive meat I ever tasted." Fishing was now giving some variety to their meals. With a net, they managed to catch half a basketful of fish. Instead of wood, they were now using buffalo chips for their cooking.

As they approached Chimney Rock, they kept finding bacon, flour and cornmeal that had been thrown out by those ahead of them lightening their loads. They picked up some of the provisions and found them superior to their own. Gray was now suffering from "rheumatism" (which he treated with a large dose of brandy) and large blotches on his shoulders. He thought these came not only from bites but also from "living so long on so much fat & grease & salt meats," with no vegetables. He may have been right. A blotchy skin is one of the signs of scurvy. On the day they passed Fort Laramie, they saw "every sort of article abandoned by the gold seekers," including salt, bacon, and flour.[33]

In mid-June, they reached the north fork of the Platte and camped on Deer Creek. Their guide book said the creek had an abundance of fish. This proved true. They caught about 100 with a net, "& made a delicious supper of them." Another break from their daily routine came when, as they approached South Pass, they gathered snow in a pail and ate it. After crossing the summit of the pass, they emptied their wagon to clean it and examine their provisions. They were "sweet & in excellent order." July Fourth brought no special celebration but they caught a few trout in the Green River.

Even in the rush to reach California, many emigrants took the time to celebrate the fourth. In the previous year, one group had made ice cream at South Pass, using sweetened and peppermint-flavored milk. They had made it in a tin bucket inside a wooden bucket, by stirring a mixture of snow and salt between the two buckets. On the southern route, one company bought twenty lambs near Socorro, Mexico, for a celebration dinner. They also had brandy and champagne and invited local women for a dance in the evening.[34]

Gray's party reached Fort Bridger at the end of the first week in July, bought a coffee mill and a few other items, and fished for trout in the adjacent stream. He and some others now decided to leave the trail to Fort Hall and strike out southwest toward Salt Lake City. They found themselves in the minority—seven out of ten teams with them decided to go on

33. Ibid., 17–34.
34. "The Journal of Margaret A. Frink," in Holmes, ed., *Covered Wagon Women*, 2:85–111; Williams, *Wagon Wheel Kitchens*, 176–77, also 164–73 and 179; Bieber, ed., *Southern Trails*, 315–16.

to Fort Hall before turning off for California. Gray and his friends had no problems on the cutoff and reached Salt Lake City in the middle of July. They boarded in a house there, provided some of their own provisions and were given "*fresh fish, pot cheese, butter, green peas, rye bread & milk & buck-wheat cakes,*" as well as salad, onions, and radishes. Gray swapped a few pounds of bacon for a few pounds of fresh beef, pound for pound, and had some of it boiled, and some of it roasted.[35]

On July 19, they were on their way again. Traveling along the northern edge of the Great Salt Lake, they shot many prairie hens and sage hens, but after crossing Bear River they entered a barren desert. Their noon meal was crackers and raw ham—"not a particle of shade, or a quart of water." In the following days water was scarce, but on August 4 they reached the headwaters of the Humboldt River. They were suffering from the thick dust raised by the wagons but were able to shoot a large number of sage hens. For two weeks these were their main source of meat, "with a little bacon to season them." Traveling along the Humboldt, they also shot ducks, mallards, and teal. For breakfast on August 12, Gray ate "a bowl of duck soup, 3 large cups of coffee, & 5 large Slapjacks!"

The region they were in was blazing hot in the day—so much so that their tin utensils were too hot to touch after sitting in the sun—but cold at night. They were nearly out of flour, and they bought some from men in another wagon, with the understanding that it would be given back pound for pound in California. On the following day they used the last of their bacon—"abominable stuff." They tried to buy some from other wagon trains on the road and were unable to do so but were cheered a little by their first rain in two months. It was much needed, for they now had a seventy-mile drive over a scorching desert. To accomplish this task, they traveled, as did most others, at night. On the following day, August 22, they saw dead oxen, broken wagons, and discarded items scattered all over. Gray counted 160 oxen staggering about. They had been left there to die. That night, they camped at a hot spring and were disturbed for most of the night by other teams and pack mules "constantly arriving." When they got up the next morning "as far as we could see the country was cover'd with oxen & mules & horses & men & wagons."[36]

Instead of following the river southward all the way to the Humboldt Sink (the typical route), Gray's party chose to take a route that took them into the Sierras almost to the borders of Oregon before they turned south

35. Gray, *Off at Sunrise*, 38–66.
36. Ibid., 68–85.

into California. Using alternate routes was typical of 1849, as young men tried to get ahead of others on their way to the goldfields. Most travelers they met on this last stretch were, like themselves, short of provisions, but they were now again killing game and catching fish. On October 3 they reached a California ranch, and their ordeal was over. They bought a lot of fresh beef and ate "*several frying pans full of it.*"[37]

Many who followed much the same central route to California as Gray, fared much worse. When they were within two hundred miles of the end of their journey, Gray's party met a man who was driving beef cattle back along the way they had come for the relief of destitute immigrants. He said twenty thousand dollars had been raised in San Francisco for that purpose. A few days later, they saw many travelers on foot. They gave dinner to three of them "as they were entirely destitute—no money—no meat—no bread—no nothing! God only knows what will become of many such." They also saw several graves of people who had perished of scurvy. Gray said those who were suffering with it would give three dollars for a pint of vinegar. Sadly, the vinegar would have been useless. It does not have the vitamin C that the victims of scurvy needed.[38]

In September 1849, Joseph Stephens wrote home to Ohio, "The hardships of the overland route to California are beyond conception." He and his group had started with few provisions, because they had wanted to get along as fast as possible. They were hoping to buy from other wagons on the road. Fifteen hundred miles into their trip, they ran out of provisions and survived by hunting. They still tried to buy from others, but some had already thrown away bacon and bread to lighten their load, others had only enough to last them through, and many would not sell. Stephens wrote of eating raw bacon, powdered crackers, and water for days. At times, there was no water to go with the dry crackers and salt bacon. They repeatedly asked for, and were refused, a cup of coffee. Trying to buy chocolate, they failed at every wagon until an Irish woman *gave* them two pounds.[39]

For those Texans, and many other southerners, who wished to reach the goldfields rapidly the most direct route was by what became known as the Gila Trail, which passed through Texas and a part of northern Mexico to Tucson and Yuma before crossing the desert into southern California. There were various minor variations of this general route, which was used considerably less often than the central route along the Platte River and through the Great Basin. Although there could be problems finding

37. Ibid., 92–117.
38. Ibid., 107, 111, 115.
39. Letter of Joseph L. Stephens, September 6, 1849, in Perkins, *Gold Rush Diary*, 160–61.

enough water in the extreme desert conditions on the southern approach to California, it had the advantage that much of the route was through areas in which there were towns and villages.

One of the earliest gold-seekers who took the Gila Trail was Benjamin Butler Harris, a lawyer from eastern Texas. In the spring of 1849 he left Panola County in a party of some fifty men. They used mules rather than wagons, traveling west through Dallas, then a village of some three hundred, to Johnson Station, the gathering place for those destined for the California mines. Finding that there were too many men there for one company, they formed two—Harris went in the second one under Isaac Duval. The provisions taken by Duval's company were bacon, sugar, *pinole* (parched cornmeal), lard, salt, coffee, sage, and a little sugar. Later, when they passed through Mexico, they added *jigote* (dried meat) as a basic part of their diet. *Blanco jigote* was pounded dried meat flavored with onions and black pepper. For *colorado jigote*, chilies were added.[40]

On April 10, the Duval party left Johnson Station and passed through the area known as the Lower Cross Timbers to the east headwaters of the Colorado of Texas. This was a region abounding in game, and it had "an astonishing quantity of wild-bee trees." They were able to eat fresh buffalo meat before passing into the barren area of extreme west Texas, although salt pork and bread formed a basic part of their diet. Salt pork was an unsatisfactory food in an area where there was a lack of water. They were still killing game, and there was an abundance of wild onions, which they fried.[41]

In the El Paso area, they were able to obtain bushels of ripe apricots, "huge silver-skinned onions," and other garden vegetables from Mexican villages and were greeted with great hospitality. They rested, feasted, and went to Mexican dances, but they also fought among themselves. After an argument about cooking beans, a man who was punched retaliated by stabbing the puncher in the stomach. The man died, but the stabber went free on the grounds of self-defense.

At El Paso they bought dried beef, "dried mule meat," bladders of melted beef fat, and flour. They also drank the local wine. They wanted to buy bacon and lard, but there was none to be had. This was not a region of hogs. Louisiana Strentzel, another Texan who took the southern route to California in 1849, also was unable to buy bacon in El Paso, but his party

40. Benjamin Butler Harris, *The Gila Trail: The Texas Argonauts and the California Gold Rush*, ed. Richard H. Dillon (Norman: University of Oklahoma Press, 1960), ix–x, 6–7, 31 n. See also Bieber, ed., *Southern Trails*, 32–62.
    41. Ibid., 29–45.

bought peaches, pears, apples, grapes, onions, green corn, green beans, wheat, and flour. Another emigrant who passed through El Paso in June found it was difficult to buy provisions at any price.[42]

While in the town, Harris's mess added a cook—an African American barber from Kentucky. He was allowed to travel with the party and given his provisions for serving the mess as cook and barber. He had been left in El Paso by his owner at the close of the Mexican War. Beyond El Paso, the trail went into northern Mexico. Harris's group was well received and ate well, particularly after helping the local inhabitants resist raiding Apaches. As they passed through Guadalupe Pass, moving toward southern Arizona, they saw many wild cattle, and they were able to eat fresh beef. After Spanish control in the region had ended, the Indians had wrought great havoc. Ranches were frequently attacked, many were deserted, and cattle roamed free or were stolen. Hundreds of wild cattle were killed for food by emigrants. Strentzel's party bought peaches, apples, quince, and pomegranates, green corn, and flour at a small village, and they picked peaches and quinces from the trees in a village that had been deserted.[43]

At Tucson, there were hundreds of emigrants on their way to California, and those with money could buy oxen, calves, cows, sheep, mules, green corn, flour, cheese, grapes, and dried beans. Some preparations were necessary in Tucson, for seventy miles of desert lay between there and the Pima Indian villages on the Gila River. Harris's group started at sunset one evening and traveled all night and through the following day. After resting one night, they reached the Gila River. There, they were met by Pima Indians with water, roasted pumpkins, and green corn. Pima agriculture was invaluable to emigrants taking a southwestern route to California.[44]

After leaving the Pima villages, there was a stretch of some two hundred miles, much of it along the Gila River, before the crossing of the Colorado near the mouth of the Gila. There was very little grass, and the only water came from the river or from kegs in the wagons. Harris and his friends caught many "long, slender trout," which they dried on the rocks for future use. The trail was strewn with bacon, lard, and coffee, as well as with cooking utensils that had been discarded by earlier emigrants.

By the time they reached the Colorado River, Harris's whole party found

42. Ibid., 51–58; Louisiana Strentzel to his family, December 10, 1849, in Holmes, ed., *Covered Wagon Women*, 1:254; Bieber, ed., *Southern Trails*, 269–70.

43. Harris, *Gila Trail*, 71–76, 78; Strentzel to his family, in Holmes, ed., *Covered Wagon Women*, 1:255.

44. Harris, *Gila Trail*, 79–82; Strentzel to his family, in Holmes, ed., *Covered Wagon Women*, 1:255–56; also Thomas W. Sweeny, *Journal of Lt. Thomas W. Sweeny, 1849–1853*, ed. Arthur Woodward (Los Angeles: Westernlore Press, 1956), 222–23 n.

themselves very low on provisions. They were living on the parched corn that had been bought for the use of their animals in the desert and the last of the *jigote* they had bought in Mexico. Some messes were completely out. The Yuma Indians who lived here were less friendly than the Pimas, and there was a company of soldiers for the protection of travelers. The first emigrants had reached the Colorado in mid-August and had been streaming by since then.[45]

After crossing the Colorado to the California side, emigrants traveled some fifteen miles to reach wells with a good supply of water. There was no grass, but there were mesquite bushes with clusters of what Strentzel referred to as "muskite beans," known to the emigrants as "bread fruit." These were the pods of the mesquite. Dried and ground, they could be used to make a kind of flour. Strentzel's party rested for three days, gathering as many of the pods as they could. There was another forty-mile desert to cross, but, once that was achieved, there was a relatively easy thirty-five miles to "Warner's Ranch," a place all travelers were glad to see, as it meant that their main difficulties were over.[46]

The Gila Trail was the favorite route for Texans, but southerners north of Texas often went through Santa Fe on their way to California. Fort Smith, Arkansas (and nearby Van Buren), became favorite jumping-off places. In March 1849, the streets of Fort Smith were crowded with California wagons and teams. Area residents were doing extremely well selling provisions. A company that was formed at Fayetteville, Arkansas, advised each person to take 175 pounds of bacon, 140 pounds of flour, and 15 or 20 pounds of salt for the game they hoped to kill. Only stock that would not impede the progress of the company should be taken.[47]

Once the frenetic activity of 1849 was over, emigration to California gradually became more of a family emigration. There were still young men who went alone, some on foot, but family parties became far more typical. Accumulated experience, which was transmitted to those in the East in guidebooks, newspapers, and letters, also enabled emigrants to prepare more effectively for the problems they would encounter on the way.

When Margaret Frink and her husband went from Martinsville, Indiana, to California in 1850 they had a wagon specially built for the trip. The bed of the wagon was divided into small compartments for the

45. Harris, *Gila Trail*, 84–89; Strentzel to his family, in Holmes, ed., *Covered Wagon Women*, 1:256–58.

46. Harris, *Gila Trail*, 89–98; Strentzel to his family, in Holmes, ed., *Covered Wagon Women*, 1:259–60.

47. Bieber, ed., *Southern Trails*, 283–89, 329–31.

provisions and other baggage, with a wooden floor over them, and a mattress on the floor. The mattress was of India rubber and could be filled either with air or water—making "a very comfortable" 1850 water-bed! The Frinks also took a feather bed and feather pillows. The wagon was lined with green cloth, "to make it pleasant and soft for the eye," and it had three or four large pockets on each side to hold personal items such as looking glasses, combs, and brushes.

For provisions, the Frinks took plenty of ham and bacon, apples, peaches, and various other preserved fruits, rice, coffee, tea, beans, flour, cornmeal, crackers, sea biscuit, butter, and lard. Mrs. Frink later said that at that time in Indiana, they had no knowledge of canned vegetables. They were well aware, however, of the problem of scurvy and bought "acid" (one hopes citric) to substitute for vegetables. To hold water for desert crossings they took two five-gallon bottles made of India rubber. Mrs. Frink did not list all the equipment they took with them, but her husband went to Cincinnati and bought a small sheet-iron cooking stove, which was tied on to the back of the wagon. They were better off than many emigrants, and for the first part of the trip they stayed every night at hotels or farmhouses.

The Frinks completed their preparations at St. Joseph on the Missouri River, which was crowded with emigrants preparing to cross the plains. They rented a cabin on the outskirts near the town and stayed for several weeks, waiting for grass to grow on the prairies. They wanted to add pickles, vinegar, potatoes, and other vegetables to their supplies but had difficulty finding what they wanted because of the number of emigrants who had already arrived. Mr. Frink rode for sixteen miles in search of pickled cucumbers before he finally found a bushel. They had to settle for these cucumbers, a peck of potatoes, and some horseradish. Mrs. Frink said she prepared the cucumbers carefully and put them up in kegs with "apple vinegar" as they were to be their main defense against the "dreadful disease" scurvy, "from which the overland emigrants of 1849 had suffered so severely." While apples themselves provide a little vitamin C, apple vinegar has none, and cucumbers practically none.[48]

On May 13 they crossed the Missouri River to begin their trek. A week later in level country Mrs. Frink could see "the long trains of white-topped wagons for many miles." There was a "vast emigration, slowly winding its way westward over the broad plain." Near Fort Laramie, they had to leave their stove. Someone had driven too close to the back of their wagon and

48. "The Journal of Margaret A. Frink," in Holmes, ed., *Covered Wagon Women,* 2:59–76.

smashed the stove with a wagon pole. From that time on, they cooked by digging a narrow trench, building a fire in it, and setting cooking vessels on top.

On June 21 one of their fellow travelers, eager to reach California more quickly, decided to go on alone. They heaped provisions, blankets, and clothing onto his back until he could carry no more, and he set out to walk some fifteen hundred miles to California across the Rockies, the Great Basin, and the Sierras. Some continued to do this in later years. In 1852, soon after her wagon left the Missouri River, another woman was passed by a man going alone to California, pushing and pulling his provisions and clothing in a wheelbarrow. That night he ate raw meat and bread for his supper and slept on the ground in the open air.[49]

The Frinks reached the Rockies by July, and, they celebrated the Fourth by eating the last of their potatoes for dinner. Near Fort Hall, they gathered enough currants to make pies for two or three days. The Frinks had been without any kind of fresh fruit for three months and thought these a great luxury. At an old Hudson's Bay trading post, they were given fresh onions and lettuce, and a day later they traded for fish with Crow Indians. In spite of a setback, when one of their horses got into the wagon and ate all the beans and dried fruit, they were eating better than most.

By August 10, they were nearing the notorious area near the Humboldt River. They met numerous individuals traveling on foot, many of them begging for food. More independent was "a negro woman," who "came tramping along through the heat and dust, carrying a cast-iron bake oven on her head, with her provisions and blanket piled on top—all she possessed in the world—bravely pushing for California." On the fifteenth they entered the desert and passed many dead animals, abandoned wagons, and dumped supplies. With animals dead or wagons broken, the owners had pressed on with what provisions they could carry on their backs.

In this part of their trek, the Frinks met speculative traders, a group that increased rapidly on western trails in the following years. From a wagon loaded with barrels of "pure, sweet water" they bought a gallon for a dollar. At Carson River they found a collection of "dirty tents and cloth shanties" known as "Ragtown." Here, beef, bacon, and flour were sold. The Frinks bought some beefsteak for their breakfast. It was their first fresh meat since they had traded with Indians for antelope nearly a month before. By August 23, even the well-prepared Frinks were living on "short rations," but trading posts were becoming more numerous, and the Frinks

---

49. Ibid., 103; Schlissel, *Women's Diaries*, 189.

still had some money. From a trader they bought five pounds of fresh beef brought over the mountains from California.

As they pressed on into the Sierras, the Frinks continued to meet travelers in desperate situations. One man they passed had rags on his feet instead of shoes, and his total food supply consisted of a pint of cornmeal. Mrs. Frink made him a dish of "gruel" with a little butter and "some other nourishing things" in it. They dug up wild onions, their first fresh vegetables since Fort Hall, and they were able to buy flour from one of the many trading posts they reached as they descended into California. By the first week in September they were in Pleasant Valley, where they found a few miners trying their luck, and their journey was essentially over. It had taken them six months but could be ranked as being as near a comfortable trip to California as could be made.[50]

Like the trail to Oregon, the trail to California continued to be used after the West Coast was connected to the East by rail in the 1860s. Many families continued to pack their wagons with provisions to cross the plains and Rockies to California. Often they would follow the rail tracks so that the stations scattered along the line could serve the same function as the old shacks with provisions had served at an earlier date. As settlement advanced across the plains, emigrants were able to take their wagons from the outskirts of one small town to the outskirts of the next. Even if they had little money to make purchases, few suffered the extreme hardships faced by pioneers of earlier years.

50. "The Journal of Margaret A. Frink," in Holmes, ed., *Covered Wagon Women*, 2:117–56.

CHAPTER 9

Food at the Mines

⌒

Our beans boiling all this while with bacon nicely scored in pot were
fit for supper, a dish savory enough for Jupiter.

Rachel Haskell, Aurora, Nevada, 1867

From 1846 to 1848, American troops arriving in California found
that meat was abundant, but provisions and vegetables were
scarce and expensive. Ranches had great herds of cattle, and the
soldiers lived largely on beef for day after day. There were orchards and vineyards in the southern part of the state, and im-
porters were bringing large quantities of provisions into San
Francisco, but distribution was poor.[1]

In the summer of 1849, when the great mass of gold seekers began to
arrive from the East, San Francisco, the main port of entry, was in turmoil.
Other towns along the coast were eerily empty—Californians had deserted
towns and farms to rush to the mines. Those coming overland by the
southern routes found few people and high prices in the towns. At San
Diego, provisions were very scarce. Only flour could be obtained in any
quantity, and most of that had been brought from Valparaiso in Chile.
Army units and ships' crews were plagued by constant desertions, and the
ranches had lost many of their workers.[2]

San Francisco was totally different. In June, when Mary Megquier and
her husband arrived, she heard that there were six thousand people in the
town without shelter. Her family of five managed to get one small room.
There were not yet enough storehouses for the provisions that were being
imported, and bags of flour, rice, and bread were lying in the streets. The
Megquiers had arrived before most of the forty-niners, and they found

1. John Craig to George Boesinger, October 4, 1847, in Dale L. Morgan, ed., *Overland in
1846: Diaries and Letters of the California-Oregon Trail* (Georgetown, Calif.: Talisman Press, 1963),
1:135–39.
2. Letter of John V. Durivaga, July 1849, in Bieber, ed., *Southern Trails*, 245–46, also 277–79.

that beef, pork, and flour were still as cheap as in the East, but other items, including vegetables, were already "enormously high." In the first three days after they arrived, they had nothing to eat but beef, pickled fish, and bread made from poor flour.

Franklin Buck arrived in San Francisco in August 1849 hoping to make money from supplies he had brought with him. He was disappointed to discover that prices on all items had not yet soared. Flour, one item he had hoped to sell, had come in such large amounts from Chile that it had glutted the market. He found the town chaotic. Large numbers of the houses and stores were simply wooden frames covered with canvas, and there were numerous "grog shops" and gambling saloons. Buck quickly moved closer to the mines, where he knew prices would be higher. At the end of October, when he returned to San Francisco, he found a much larger city, with "a perfect forest of shipping" in the harbor. The canvas houses had vanished and were being replaced by frame and brick buildings. Along with the old "grog houses" there were new saloons "equal to the Broadway saloons and eating houses."[3]

The Megquiers, like Buck, hoped to make money not from mining but from catering to newcomers. Five months after their arrival, prices had soared. Pork, which had been six dollars a barrel was now thirty-five dollars, sugar had gone up from three cents to fifty cents a pound. By November, Mr. Megquier, who was a doctor, was often making fifty dollars a day. The Megquiers were also making money by selling goods, were in the process of building a store, and Mrs. Megquier was cooking for about twenty "boarders" who lived elsewhere.

Writing to her daughter, who had not come to California, Mary Megquier described her "cook room." It was entered through a door from the Megquiers' combined sitting/dining/sleeping room. In one corner there was a chest set on end with shelves; then, in succession, a barrel of sugar; a champagne box on top of a half barrel to serve as a rolling board; a box to hold a candlestick; a large shelf above a barrel of pork, a sack of flour, and a bag of potatoes; a coffee mill; a long board on top of two half barrels, with water pails and a washbasin on top and ironware underneath; a half barrel of apples; and an old chair with washtubs. Hanging on the wall were hatchets, saucepans, gridirons, frying pans, and a variety of other items.

For a time, after they moved into the quarters over their store, the Megquiers had an African American cook. Mrs. Megquier was caustic

3. Buck, *Yankee Trader*, 45–50, 53.

about his performance, but they had a good meal for Thanksgiving. There was roast beef and veal, boiled mutton, fricasseed chicken, potatoes, turnips, onions, beets, mince and apple tarts, three kinds of cake, nuts and raisins, champagne, porter, ale, and wine.

Mrs. Megquier liked San Francisco. Everyone was his own man, she wrote, and you could do as you pleased with no talking about a thing not being respectable. The town was full of noise and confusion. "It is now past midnight," she told her daughter, "I can hear guns firing, music, some calling for help. I think by the sound they are having a drunken row, but it is so common it is of no account."

In the following months, Mrs. Megquier continued to look after their house, the store, and her doctor husband and again took on the cooking for the many boarders. She now had the help of an Irish woman and a boy. After the boy had made the fire, Mrs. Megquier was up at seven to make the coffee and biscuits, fry the potatoes, and broil three pounds of steak or liver. Her woman swept and set the table. From eight to nine they served breakfast.

After breakfast, Mrs. Megquier baked six loaves of bread, four pies, or a pudding. For dinner at 2:00 p.m. they had baked lamb, beef, and pork, baked turnips, beets, potatoes, radishes, salad, and "everlasting soup." For tea, there was hash, cold meat, bread and butter, sauce, and some kind of cake. Mrs. Megquier did all the cooking, washing, and ironing and made six beds. Her woman washed the dishes and carpets, which had to be cleaned every day because the house was so dusty, presumably because of the endless construction. Not surprisingly, Mary Megquier told her daughter in June 1850 that she was "sick and tired of work."

She may have been sick and tired of work, but she still had her enthusiasm for the freedom of California life. She told her mother she had not been to church for a year, but "there is no such thing as slander known in the country no back biting, every ones neighbor as good as himself." At a housewarming she danced all night and then had to work all day, but their building had a fine view of the bay, and she could "stand by the stove and watch the porridge" while looking at the ships "rolling lazily" in the harbor. There was an excitement about life that had been lacking back east.[4]

For those with money, there was plenty to eat in the city. In 1850, William Kelly found hotels and restaurants at every turn. There were American, French, Spanish, and even Chinese restaurants, for the Chinese were beginning to make their way into California. The Chinese, new to

4. Megquier, *Apron Full of Gold,* 34–69.

America, were encountering much hostility. Chinese customs and Chinese food were frequently condemned. Kelly, however, had an unusual tolerance, writing that amid great competition the Chinese "carry off the palm for superior excellence in every particular. They serve everything promptly, cleanly, hot, and well cooked." And apart from "their own peculiar soups, curries, and ragouts, which cannot be even imitated elsewhere," they served the dishes of every nation.[5]

In the following years, a more typical reaction was that of American newspaperman Samuel Bowles. In 1865, he went to an elaborate banquet in one of San Francisco's Chinese restaurants. There were scores of dishes, ranging from bird's nest soup to duck, fried shark's fin, stewed pigeon, and bamboo soup. Bowles admitted it was a magnificent dinner by Chinese standards, but he was obviously disturbed that there were no joints to be carved—all the dishes were "in a sort of hash form," and he said that "the universal odor and flavor soon destroyed all appetite." He left well before the end of the meal. Outside, a banker, who had left a little earlier, said, "let's go and get something to eat." He wanted "a good square meal." They crossed the street to an American restaurant, and Bowles's appetite was satisfied with mutton chops, squabs, fried potatoes, and a bottle of champagne.[6]

In the early months of 1850, William Kelly found that San Francisco was able to fill most of his needs. There was excellent bread, abundant prime beef, ample venison, and good water. Mrs. Megquier bought soft water from the men who brought it through the streets in barrels. Surprisingly, in view of San Francisco's later food history, fish was "a rarity." Kelly's main complaint about the food was that the mutton was "wretched," fit only for hashes and pies.[7]

The great objective of most who arrived in California in 1849 and 1850, whether by land or sea, was to reach the mines. Although they were referred to as "northern" and "southern" mines, the mining regions were in northern and central California. The "northern" were mainly in the Sacramento and Feather river valleys, and the town of Sacramento became the supply center; the "southern" spread southward into central California down the San Joaquin valley from Stockton. With tens of thousands rushing to the mines, providing necessities for miners was a surer way of making money than mining itself.

5. William Kelly, *A Stroll through the Diggings of California* (1852; repr., Oakland, Calif.: Biobooks, 1950), 149–50.

6. Bowles, *Across the Continent*, 248–54.

7. Kelly, *Stroll*, 161; Megquier, *Apron*, 55.

In August 1849, Franklin Buck left San Francisco for Sacramento to open a store with some partners. They bought flour in San Francisco at eighteen dollars for a two hundred-pound sack; it sold in Sacramento for forty-four dollars. By late October he was able to write home, "I think we are in a fair way to make our pile," commenting that two months in California were equal to a whole year at home. He was about to take a steamer to San Francisco with six thousand dollars' worth of gold dust.

More flour from Chile began to reach Sacramento toward the end of the year, and prices dropped a little, but at the mines flour was two dollars a pound. One miner writing from Sacramento in December complained about the prices but said they were only half of those at the mines. There, he had lived mostly on hard bread and old "rusty" salt pork. Earlier that fall, Joseph Stephens wrote home to Marietta, Ohio, and after listing the prices for food (including onions at a dollar each), said money was nothing in Sacramento—"One hundred dollars is not much more than *ten cents* in Marietta."[8]

In the fall of 1849, when William Kelly arrived in Sacramento he found nowhere to stay. The "boarding-houses" simply provided board not bed. Meals cost twenty-five dollars a week, and he had to sleep on the ground in a blanket. Kelly commented sarcastically that the board was "as good as it could be without fish, milk, butter, or vegetables." In October, a miner found raccoons plentiful along the riverbank and shot three. He ate one, which he said was "delicious, tender juicy & fat," and sold two to the City Hotel. Earlier that fall, when the City Hotel opened, it had a free day and provided joints of beef, mutton, venison, hams, pastry, and champagne for a great crowd of people.

A German, who settled a few miles outside the city, made a good living from raising muskmelons, watermelons, and pumpkins. He hired Indians, who were still scattered throughout the region. They lived in a simple state and had no chance of putting up any real resistance to the newcomers. They hunted game, caught salmon, and made bread by grinding acorns into flour. Most of them did not live to see the total transformation of the lands on which they lived.[9]

Lucy Wilson was twenty-eight when she went to California with her husband and two children in 1849. Much later in life she recalled her first winter in Sacramento. Like many others, she was struck by the fact that although California was overrun with cattle, fresh milk and butter were

8. Buck, *Yankee Trader,* 50–56; letter of J. Q. A. Cunningham, December 20, 1849, and letter of Joseph L. Stephens, Perkins, *Gold Rush Diary,* 167, 160.
9. Kelly, *Stroll,* 29–34, 44–45; Gray, *Off at Sunrise,* 133–46; Perkins, *Gold Rush Diary,* 144–45.

scarce. Cattle were kept for meat not milk. The Wilsons had a cow, and Lucy sold the milk that was left after feeding her children. A town official stopped at her "fire" one morning to say that he wanted "a good substantial breakfast, cooked by a woman." He gave her five dollars for two eggs, a beefsteak, two onions, and a cup of coffee. Mrs. Wilson recalled that in the early days beans and dried fruit from Chile and yams and onions from the Sandwich Islands (Hawaii) were the best items she could put on their table.

At the time Mrs. Wilson was there, Sacramento had numerous tiny "stores" set up along the streets. A small-time entrepreneur could set a board across the head of a barrel to use as a counter and sell his "stock" of a few barrels of flour, a sack or two of yams, a keg of molasses, a barrel of salt pork, a barrel of corned beef, some gulls' eggs, a sack of onions, a few picks and shovels, and a barrel of whiskey.

The Wilsons soon moved to the Coyote Diggings at Nevada City, a mining town west of Donner Pass consisting mostly of canvas tents and a host of saloons and "gambling tables." At first they lived in a temporary brush shack. Mrs. Wilson made money by buying provisions and feeding the miners. She cooked at a fire outside. On the first night, twenty sat down at her table. There were great profits to be made. Within six weeks, the Wilsons paid back seven hundred dollars they owed and gradually strengthened and expanded their home. Mrs. Wilson fed anywhere from seventy-five to two hundred miners at twenty-five dollars a week each. She was able to hire a cook and a waiter and became the manager of the operation.[10]

Many who arrived overland went directly to the mines. Samuel Cross arrived at the Bear River diggings in mid-September with a pound of bacon, a pound of crackers, four pounds of flour left in his pack, and $2.50 in cash. He moved on through Sacramento and camped on the American River. He lived mainly on damaged flour, which was all he could afford to buy. Near his campsite he found a white heron, which apparently had been dead for "a couple of days." He plucked it, cleaned it, broiled it on a bed of coals, and with the "sour dough made as enjoyable a supper as I ever sat down to." Sadly, he was not to have a great many more, for within six months he was dead at the age of twenty-four.[11]

The price of provisions was a constant problem for new arrivals. One group arrived at the Yuba River with the hope that they could buy just

10. Luzana Stanley Wilson, in Christiane Fischer, ed., *Let Them Speak for Themselves: Women in the American West, 1849–1900* (New York: E. P. Dutton, 1978), 151–63.
11. Letter of Samuel E. Cross, in Perkins, *Gold Rush Diary*, 164, 174.

enough provisions to take them on to a larger town where supplies would
be cheaper. At a store set up to sell to miners, the prices were too high
for them. They then decided to work in the mines for a week to earn
money but could find no one to hire them. They tried to pan for gold
themselves. After finding only a little, they used what money they had to
buy spoiled flour, mixed it with water, and baked it into "a heavy unhealthy mess."[12]

In the winter of 1849–1850, the problem of finding food at the northern mines was compounded by incessant rains that turned the tracks into
quagmires and made the already expensive shipment of goods from Sacramento impossible by road and very difficult by water. In mid-January there
was a major flood. Sacramento had five feet of water in the street, and at
Franklin Buck's store the water came over the counter. The partners saved
most of their provisions by putting them in the living quarters upstairs but
lost more than five hundred dollars' worth of rice, and their dried fruit was
also damaged. A great number of the cattle in the surrounding areas were
drowned.[13]

The flood created great problems for those at the mines. Jerome Howard
wrote from Bidwell's Bar on the Feather River that wagons could not get
through, and transportation costs for goods brought from Sacramento increased by 100 or even 200 percent. During this period, some supplies were
sent by boat to within nine miles and were then packed on mules for the
last part of the journey. In listing the exorbitant prices, Howard gives a
good idea of foods shipped to the upcountry—flour, pork, potatoes, onions,
cheese, butter, dried apples, sugar, tea, coffee, saleratus, rice, beans, pickles,
molasses, and vinegar. For a time, flour, which he said came almost entirely
from Chile and Oregon, was unobtainable at any price.

The most common foods eaten in the Bidwell's Bar area were "slap jacks"
with pork or beef. There were also various types of bread. Some depended
on hard sea biscuit; others used fat from their fried pork as shortening to
make a type of shortcake, or some simply baked the flour without the fat,
making what Howard called a "long-cake." Just a few men had "nice light
bread made by their wives." Most of the miners around Bidwell's Bar lived
in tents, and each tent had a fireplace and chimney at one end. A few had
an iron stove. One of the few pleasures resulting from the dreary food was
the delight when something different appeared. Howard invoked "ten
thousand blessings" on the Yankees who had brought in the large sweet

12. Perkins, *Gold Rush Diary,* 134–38.
13. Buck, *Yankee Trader,* 58–60.

potato he baked, and he wrote of the pleasures provided by a pickle or a piece of cheese.[14]

When the rains came, Franklin Buck decided to profit from the situation by leaving Sacramento and moving closer to the mines. He went by steamer up the Feather River to the Yuba River, taking provisions, lumber, and "a canvas house." In Marysville, at the head of steamboat navigation, some eighty miles from Sacramento and only eight miles from the mountains, he bought a vacant lot, put up his portable store, and went into business. He stayed for just over two weeks, then sold his store, held onto the lot, and returned to Sacramento.[15]

Young Sally Hester and her family came to Fremont in October 1849, after crossing the plains and Rockies. The rains had already begun, and they were "worn out," so they decided to stay for the winter. Fortunately, her father had some money and the good sense to go into Sacramento to buy provisions. Even so, Sally found everything "enormously high": eggs and apples were a dollar each, and onions were fifty cents. The rain continued throughout the fall and into winter. Sally said that it was a sad Christmas for her mother, but Sally herself was invited to "a candy pull," and had a good time. For a young girl there were compensations in Fremont. She was invited out all the time because girls were scarce. By the end of February, she happily wrote, "I am beginning to feel quite like a young lady."[16]

William Kelly and his companions, who had moved north of Sacramento to spend the winter prospecting, managed to cook an ample Christmas dinner by combining game with their own stores. They had a loin of grizzly bear, roast venison, boiled bacon, pies made from dried apples, shortbread, sweetbread, a plum pudding, raisins, and six bottles of wine. For a table, they used boards from their wagon, with legs made from sticks of willow.[17]

Kelly and his friends experimented with various dishes. When one of their party shot a deer, he made what he called a trappers' feast of "Coney-cum-quero." He used most of a side of venison, with the skin still attached; paring away enough of the flesh so that the skin could be wrapped around the remaining meat. He flavored it, fastened the skin, and put the whole

---

14. Letters of Jerome B. Howard, February 16, March 17, 1850, in Perkins, *Gold Rush Diary,* 180–82, 185–86.

15. Buck, *Yankee Trader,* 60–64.

16. "Sally Hester's Diary," in Holmes, ed., *Covered Wagon Women,* 1:243–45; "Gray Diary," in Gray, *Off At Sunrise,* 125 and n.

17. Kelly, *Stroll,* 95–96.

package on red-hot fire. The meat was done before the skin burned through. They also took advantage of what was available to make a stew of large frogs and small land turtles combined with "the limbs of a few woodpeckers," and a ground squirrel. They needed anything they could find, because, when the rains came, provisions became very expensive, and sickness was rampant, particularly scurvy, which Kelly ascribed to the absence of vegetables among the salty, greasy provisions.[18]

Their difficulties increased when some men who had separated from the others to mine in a different spot were attacked by Indians. Some of them were wounded, and Kelly and two others set off to get help from their main camp. They were delayed because of very heavy rains and became so hungry that they finally decided to kill Kelly's dog. Kelly commented that their first meal from it was on "raw flesh before the animal heat had cooled out." On the following morning they were able to light a fire and broil what was left. On their way to Sacramento in February 1850, they stopped at a ranch, and Kelly had his first milk since leaving Salt Lake City the previous spring. They bought enough to fill "every canteen bottle, flask, and phial we had."[19]

Sarah Royce and her husband set up business in October 1849 in the mining camp of Weaverville. They put two tents together, living in the back one and using the front one for a store. They also bought a large cookstove and placed it near where the tents met. Her husband entered into a partnership. Their goods had to come from Sacramento, and one of the partners had been in the cattle business, so they were able to buy some cattle and sell beef. Mrs. Royce later wrote that this "drew quite a crowd every morning; for fresh meat had not yet become very plentiful in the mines." Like many others in this wet winter, Sarah Royce came down with a fever. Just after Christmas, her husband put her on a bed in a wagon and set out for Sacramento. When they stopped at a house catering to travelers, she asked the landlady to bake her a sweet potato, "a luxury which had lately been introduced into the mines from 'The Islands.'" It cost seventy-five cents. A few days later, in Sacramento, someone traveling with them paid a dollar for an onion.[20]

The mining region dependent on Sacramento was in a strange state of transition in the winter of 1848–1849. There were miners working frantically at the diggings in the foothills of the Sierras, and small towns were

18. Ibid., 69–70, 75–76, 93–94.
19. Ibid., 99–103, 115–18.
20. Sarah Royce, *A Frontier Lady: Recollections of the Gold Rush and Early California*, ed. Ralph H. Gabriel (1932; repr., Lincoln: University of Nebraska Press, 1977), 79–89.

springing up to serve their needs. But there were still ranches in operation in the same area, and there were still Indians trying to cope with the end of the world as they knew it.

When Charles Gray came overland to the Sacramento valley in October 1849, he experienced some of this variety. Traveling down the valley, he and his companions gathered grapes before they reached a small ranch where there were "poor goods" at "enormous prices." They bought some beef and liver but avoided the "miserable candied *raisins*" and cheese. Cheese was a rare item in these first months of the gold rush. At a ford on the Feather River, Gray saw "Indians entirely naked" and gave an Indian a shirt in exchange for about ten pounds of salmon. Later, on the American River, Gray killed half a dozen quail for his supper.

Gray and his friends constantly had problems both with the availability and price of provisions. Trying to buy beef, molasses, and rice, they could get nothing but poor molasses, and on one day their only provisions were boiled wheat and roasted acorns. At Vernon, they bought a little pork, beef, and cheese "at *ruinous rates*," and on November 10 reached Sacramento, "with its theatre & hells & drinking saloons without number." The provisions there were of a "*miserable character*." From Sacramento, Gray took a steamer to San Francisco and experienced what was available for those who had money. The steamer had a "splendid cabin, brussels carpet, rose wood doors, mahogany chairs & marble pier tables, mirrors, lounges, and ottamans [*sic*]," and they were served by an "army of waiters." When he reached his hotel in San Francisco, Gray sat down to a dinner of "roast beef, roast mutton—beef soup, potatoes, rice, molasses, pickles & pudding, all well cook'd & very good tasting."[21]

Those who had been able to buy sufficient provisions before heading to the mountains were able to survive the rainy season with a certain degree of comfort. A group of young men from Ohio wrote home to say it had rained, with only one break, from the beginning of November to the beginning of February, but they had lived well. Game had been abundant, and by spring they were able to get fresh beef.[22]

Spring, and the end of the rains, brought a transformation to Sacramento. Buildings, including two new ornate gambling saloons, were going up all over the town. These saloons were described by Franklin Buck as equaling anything in New York. Gambling was constant on the mining frontier, and Buck wrote that in Sacramento "everyone drinks—some more

21. "Gray's Diary," in Gray, *Off at Sunrise*, 127–59.
22. Letter of young men of Marietta County, April 9, 1850, in Perkins, *Gold Rush Diary*, 192.

and some less." Buck and his partners had put up a new store. The price of provisions had come down as more were brought in from San Francisco, and more food was now being grown locally. By May, local gardens were producing peas, lettuce, turnips, and other crops.[23]

While most of the arrivals in 1849 made for the northern mines, some went farther south to the mines initially dependent on Stockton. In the spring of that year, William Perkins went to Sonora, east of Stockton in the foothills of the Sierras, and found a town with a character quite distinct from those in the Sacramento area. Although Sonora was increasingly attracting gold seekers from the East, it had already become a center for Mexicans, Chileans, and Peruvians drawn by the discovery of gold. There were also Hawaiians, French, Basques, and other immigrants. Many of the Mexican gold seekers had brought their families so that there were more women than in the northern mines.

Perkins described a town of some five thousand that on Saturday and Sunday evenings in that first summer took on "an almost magic appearance." Lights from "gaily decorated houses" lit up crowded streets that were lined with tables loaded with varieties of "dulces" (sweets), drinks cooled with snow from the Sierras, cakes, dried fruit, meat, and pies. Mexican and Indian women tended portable kitchens, on which they made "the national dish of meat and chile pepper," served in tortillas. There were cries of "agua fresca" from Mission Indians who pushed through the crowds with "pails of iced liquor on their heads." On Sundays, Sonora's main street was blocked by monte tables "piled with gold dust and thronged with bettors."

In the winter of 1849–1850, deer, bear, elk, and quail were still abundant in the vicinity of Sonora, and deer were often killed close to the town. Perkins particularly liked California quail, which he referred to as "a delicious bird." He found bear meat coarse and greasy, except for the paw, but conceded that dried bear meat was "not unpalatable." Elk meat was too coarse and too dry. By the fall of 1851, most game had gone from the immediate area, and it was now usually brought in by hunters who had to go high into the mountains to hunt. By this time, however, there were good supplies of beef and mutton.

Perkins had seen few vegetables in his first two years in Sonora, and, although potatoes had been introduced as a crop, they were still difficult to get. As a substitute for the vegetables he had been used to in the east, Perkins made use of "the large red Chile bean." Also, he particularly

23. Buck, *Yankee Trader*, 64–69.

enjoyed the grapes that were brought from San Francisco. They were grown on the coast south of the city.

On special occasions Perkins ate very well. In July 1851 he gave a ball for fifty people with music provided by a piano, violin, cello, harp, and two guitars. He described the supper as "something really wonderful for the mountains"—cold hams and fowl, pheasant pies, quail pasties, ices, creams, blancmange, and pastry, with an abundance of good wine. In the first excitement of the discovery of gold, more wine was sent to San Francisco from France and the Mediterranean than could be disposed of. Perkins was able to buy "exquisite champagnes, clarets, Burgundies, sherries, even Lachrymachristi" at half the original cost. His guests drank three dozen bottles of champagne, two dozen bottles of claret, and a dozen bottles of burgundy.[24]

After the discovery of gold in the Mariposa River country, the mining areas south of Stockton and Sonora developed rapidly. This area was closer for gold seekers arriving in California by southwestern routes and also attracted miners who had been unsuccessful in the mines farther north. Those who made the trek across the arid southwest and pushed north through California toward the mines must often have thought their problems were over. South of Los Angeles there were large ranches with numerous cattle and other resources, and provisions could be bought in Los Angeles, then a small Mexican town. Even the back country at first appeared to offer no problems. Benjamin Harris arrived in southern California from Texas in September 1849 and described the San Joaquin and Tulare valleys as "a hunter's paradise." There were great herds of antelope and elks, and the skies were noisy with waterfowl.

When Harris reached the mines on Agua Fria Creek along the Mariposa River, he quickly realized that food costs were outlandish. He was able to pan about one ounce of gold a day, but much of it went for food, which consisted mainly of salt pork, hard bread, and coffee. Deer were quite scarce in the immediate vicinity of the mines, but those who could afford it were able to buy game from professional hunters (often ex-trappers). Many, however, were on a Spartan fare, and in the winter of 1849–1850 scurvy was common.[25]

24. Perkins, *Three Years in California*, 99–114, 129, 149, 180, 242–45, 260–62, 269; also, Benjamin B. Harris, *The Gila Trail: The Texas Argonauts and the California Gold Rush*, ed. Richard H. Dillon (Norman: University of Oklahoma Press, 1960), 121.

25. Robert Eccleston, *The Mariposa Indian War, 1850–1851: Diaries of Robert Eccleston: The California Gold Rush, Yosemite, and the High Sierra*, ed. C. Gregory Crampton (Salt Lake City: University of Utah Press, 1957), ii, 4–8; Harris, *Gila Trail*, 106, 113–23.

In the early years of American settlement, although California had extensive stocks of cattle and game, it depended heavily on the importation of other food. Much of the flour that was needed was supplied by Chile, great flocks of sheep were driven across the deserts of the Southwest from New Mexico, and a variety of provisions and fruits were brought in from Oregon. Dependence on imports lessened as Californians realized that with the help of irrigation their own climate would produce much of what they required.[26]

Although conditions in the mining camps continued to be primitive, food soon became more generally available. In the fall of 1852, Mary Ballou, who cooked in a boardinghouse kitchen at a mining camp, wrote of preparing soups, steaks, chicken, pork, and rabbits, quail, squirrels, trout, codfish, and oysters, with potatoes, cabbage, and turnips. For desserts, she made apple, mince, and squash pies, turnovers, doughnuts, minute pudding filled with raisins, plum and blueberry puddings, and Indian bake pudding. This last was usually made with cornmeal and molasses. Her kitchen was simply four posts covered with canvas.[27]

As mining spread throughout the Rockies in the following decades, it became apparent that compared to some of the later mining areas, California had been fortunate. California benefited greatly from its Hispanic heritage of cattle ranches and mission agriculture, abundant game resources, and a long coastline that facilitated the importation of food. In the years after the California gold rush, mines sprang up in some Rocky Mountain areas that had little to offer except the gold and silver in the earth.[28]

From the 1850s into the 1890s, a series of strikes sent miners through the length of the Rocky Mountains: over the border into Canada, to the desert regions along the Gila River, and to Colorado, Nevada, Idaho, and Montana. For the miners themselves, and the families that joined them, it was a hard existence. In the first months, food was often very difficult to obtain. Resources were fewer and prices even higher than they had been on the first California mining frontier. For years, many of the mining regions of the high Rockies depended heavily on food that was brought in by

26. See Bieber and Bender, ed. *Exploring Southwestern Trails,* 53–57; Conlin, *Bacon, Beans, and Galantines,* 92–93.

27. Letter of Mary Ballou, in Cathy Luchetti, *Home on the Range: A Culinary History of the American West* (New York: Villard Books, 1993), 63–64.

28. Franklin Street, *California in 1850* (Cincinnati, 1851), 42; Charles W. Towne and Edward N. Wentworth, *Shepherd's Empire* (Norman: University of Oklahoma Press, 1945), 87–100; Davis, *El Gringo,* 74–75.

wagon or pack mule from Oregon, California, or Utah. Women in these raw areas often had to provide for families under the most difficult circumstances.

In 1858, strikes in the Denver region drew thousands of new gold seekers across the plains, and they were followed by wagons full of provisions to feed them. In the winter of 1858–1859 flour, onions, and beans were brought in from New Mexico, and there was soon a regular trade in provisions not only from New Mexico but also from Utah and across the plains from the Missouri valley. At first, imported supplies were supplemented by local game, and, when that began to diminish, some of the need for meat was supplied by sheep driven up from New Mexico. From the spring of 1859, locally grown vegetables—lettuce, onions, radishes, peas, turnips, and beets—began to appear in the markets. Fresh fruit, except for that which could be gathered wild, was practically unobtainable.[29]

Newspaperman Horace Greeley visited the mines in the vicinity of Denver in June 1859 and found food there restricted to a few staples—pork, bread, beans, and coffee. A butcher's shop was selling meat from oxen that had dragged wagons across the plains. Denver itself, where only a short time ago the usual bread, bacon, and beans had been the basis of every meal, now had a few refinements: milk had just been reduced in price from twenty-five to ten cents a quart; there were some eggs; a man was selling lettuce in the streets; and peas were expected in the following month.[30]

Twenty-one-year-old Mollie Sanford arrived in Denver with her husband in June 1860, when there were still no real houses, and hundreds of families were "living in wagons, tents and shelters made of carpets and bedding." The Sanfords had enough basic provisions for several months but little money to buy anything else. Mollie's sister had come earlier, and Mollie found her camped on Cherry Creek. The dinner that she provided for the newcomers included "a treat" of lettuce, radishes, and young onions. These were some of the first vegetables raised locally.

Early in July, Mollie moved into a ten-by-twenty-foot board shanty built by her husband. They had a few hens and were able to exchange their eggs for meat, vegetables, and milk. Mollie also was able to trade for items by sewing (a rooster cost her five dollars' worth), and she added to their food

29. Walker, *Wagonmasters*, 181–85; Towne and Wentworth, *Shepherd's Empire*, 64–65; Martin, *Standard of Living in 1860*, 69–70.

30. Horace Greeley, *An Overland Journey from New York to San Francisco in the Summer of 1859*, ed. Charles T. Duncan (1860; repr., New York: Knopf, 1964), 104, 137–38.

supplies by walking four miles up Cherry Creek and gathering wild currants and gooseberries.[31]

Late in July, the Sanfords left Denver to go up into the mountains to the booming mining area of Gold Hill, northwest of Boulder. Mollie's husband worked as a blacksmith while she did the cooking for eighteen or twenty men building a mill. The people in Gold Hill, including only five women, lived in about a dozen crude cabins. The Sanfords' log cabin was unfinished. It was uncaulked and had no floor, and they slept on a bunk in the corner. A hole had been cut for what should have been the door or a large window. Most of Mollie's cooking had to be done outside at a fire. It was built in a pile of rocks which became so hot that the reflected heat burned her face. She had a small stove, but it would hold only one loaf at a time. The food was bread, meat, and coffee. The men ate off tin plates at a long table set up in a shed made of pine boughs. Mollie's first week was spent in "monotonous routine"—"Cook, cook, bake, bake!" Her husband decided it was all too much and quit his job.

They now moved a short distance farther up the hill to stay with friends. There were three or four cabins together at a spot where another mill was being built. The cabins had dirt floors, but as they had doors, glass windows, and a large stove, Mollie was able to write that "things look home-like." She became "housekeeper" for men building another mill. Again she had twenty men to cook for, but this time it was manageable. They had milk from two cows and eggs both from their own hens and from some owned by the company. The work was still extremely hard. One day, late in September, after an exhausting day, Mollie wrote that "the item of bread alone is something *awful* to keep up."[32]

In November, the Sanfords visited Denver, which Mollie found "so much improved, I hardly know the place." They returned through four-foot snow drifts, and by November 30 were back in Gold Hill. Provisions were running a little low, but one of the company owners had obtained the luxury of a few bushels of very small potatoes, the first they had seen since they had been there. Mollie used some in soup and on Sunday fried some for breakfast. They had no cellar, but they dug a hole in the floor to store the potatoes that were left. Most of them were carried away by ground squirrels.

31. Mollie Dorsey Sanford, *Mollie: The Journal of Mollie Dorsey Sanford in Nebraska and Colorado Territories, 1857–1866,* ed. Donald F. Danker (Lincoln: University of Nebraska Press, 1959), 131–135.
32. Ibid., 136–43.

The company was doing badly. It had built its mill where there was insufficient water and had to move. There was no money to continue paying Mollie, who, in any case, was finding the work too much to manage. The Sanfords decided to move into a small cabin of their own but stayed with the company until the cabin was finished. Christmas dinner consisted of meat, bread, and dried apple pie.

By January 1, 1861, they were in their new cabin, which had a window with three panes of glass. There was an oiled wagon cover on the floor. One of the men had made them "a fancy top bedstead" out of white pine boards taken from a packing box. Mollie stained it with brick dust and linseed oil to make it look like "light cherry." She also made a rocker out of a barrel, with a cover and cushions, and there was a stove and some stools. With a large fireplace piled with pine logs, Mollie was able to enjoy getting their own meals, and she was "invited out to tea" by a family in a nearby gulch. For her first wedding anniversary on February 14 she made "a nice supper" and served it on her whitest tablecloth.[33]

Mollie was now pregnant, and in March harsher reality returned. In the middle of the month, they left their cabin to go three miles to Left Hand Gulch, where her previous employers were building a new mill. The cabin they moved into had a hole for a doorway but no door. In its place there was a blanket with a rock tied on the end to keep it in place. There was no hole for a window, and when the blanket was over the door the only light came from the spot where the stovepipe went through a hole in the roof. Mollie stayed there for about two months before going into Denver to wait out the last months of her pregnancy. Her baby was born on August 28, but she wrote that "when I first looked on his little face, he was in his little coffin." Mollie had other children and was to survive into the twentieth century. In 1895, she made a copy of her original journal, which had been damaged by water, because "I do not want to be forgotten."[34]

The combination of trans-plains freighting, supplies from New Mexico and Utah, and the expansion of agriculture in the Colorado valleys, gradually provided more food and lower prices. When Ellen Tootle and her husband reached Golden City outside of Denver on July 25, 1862, they were able to get a supper of biscuit, boiled ham, fried potatoes, eggs, a large dish of green peas, peaches, "elegant rich cream," tea, and milk, and they had the whole meal again at breakfast. She was told that the only vegetables that could be raised in the mountains were radishes and turnips but

33. Ibid., 146–52.
34. Ibid., 1, 153–57.

that wagons passed every day from Denver to Central City and over other mountain roads, often carrying fresh meat, vegetables from the valleys, and canned fruit and vegetables. She noticed that canned supplies were used extensively.[35]

In the 1860s, although crops were harmed by the periodic visit of locusts, vegetables became quite abundant. Barley was the most popular grain crop, but by 1866 there was a wheat surplus. In 1864, a visitor to the mining camps wrote, "Bread is considered the staff of life. Whiskey the life itself." There were many sheep in the southern part of Colorado, but stock raising had not yet become important. It was said that this was because it was cheaper to buy and slaughter the oxen that were used to drag wagons across the plains.[36]

The Indian wars of 1864–1865 made travel across the plains precarious and brought a steep rise in Colorado prices. Newspaperman Samuel Bowles who was there in 1865 testified to the high cost of food and noticed that canned goods were now in extensive use. West of the Missouri River, said Bowles, they were on every table at hotels, stage stations, and private homes, but he exaggerated when he wrote that Colorado people lived on canned fruits and vegetables imported from the East. The most common canned foods were corn, tomatoes, beans, pine apples, strawberries, cherries, peaches, oysters, and lobsters. Families bought some of the items in cases of two dozen each.[37]

At the same time that Colorado began to receive its first great rush of miners, many were crossing the Sierras from California to new mines that had opened up in what became the extreme western part of Nevada. In 1859 and 1860 Virginia City, perched precariously on Davidson Mountain, was a tumultuous, largely male preserve of shanties, tents, and crude saloons. Food had to be brought in from California.[38]

Mining spread into other parts of Nevada, and while life there was often described as harsh, some women quickly found a way to live a "normal" life. A fragment of a journal kept by Rachel Haskell in 1867 in the mining town of Aurora has survived to cast a brief light on how the wife of a tollkeeper ran her home. The Haskells lived in a "frame shanty" at a toll

35. "Diary of Ellen Tootle," in Holmes, ed., *Covered Wagon Women*, 8:78–79.

36. Ovando J. Hollister, *The Mines of Colorado* (1867; repr., New York: Promontory Press, 1974), 420–29; "Journal of Harriet Hitchcock," in Holmes, ed., *Covered Wagon Women*, 252.

37. Bowles, *Across the Continent*, 21–23, 64–66.

38. Martin, *Standard of Living in 1860*, 70, 420; Dan De Quille [William Wright], *A History of the Comstock Silver Lode & Mines* (1889; repr., New York: Promontory Press, 1974), 45–50.

gate on a road about a mile from town. A visitor described a welcoming, clean interior with books and magazines on the tables and Mrs. Haskell's watercolors on the walls. Rachel was the daughter of a Pennsylvania teacher and superintendent of schools. She had taught school and studied piano and guitar before coming out west.

Her diary begins on a Sunday early in a snowy March when she rose late, breakfasted at noon, and washed and dressed her boys while her girl, Ella, read *Gulliver's Travels* to them. Later, Rachel lay on the sofa and read a book till supper was ready. Her husband kept the supper going on the stove. After the meal, she washed the dishes, and Ella played the piano while the family sang. Rachel finished her book (Alfred Mondet's *Light*), which she characterized as "pleasant writing but not extra deep." There was no church that Sunday because both ministers were sick.

The food they ate in March 1867 was not elaborate, but there were no important shortages. Main meals were generally plain: on March 9, a boiled dinner of cabbage, potatoes, and carrots (she does not mention any meat); on the eighteenth, liver and onions, with pickles brought by a male neighbor; on the following day, liver for breakfast, and beans boiled with bacon for dinner, "a dish savory enough for Jupiter"; on the twenty-first, she had beans cooking all day, and she made hot rolls to eat with them; on the twenty-second, they had a large ham and a tongue cooking; she gave up on the ham as "too dry to boil into eating state," but they had roasted potatoes, slaw, tomatoes, ham (presumably cooked earlier), and eggs; on the thirtieth, there was boiled cabbage and bacon; on April 1, boiled beef, slaw, potatoes, and biscuits; on the second, bacon, mashed potatoes, eggs, and slaw. The tomatoes they had on the twenty-second must have been from a can, and they had other canned goods. On the twenty-eighth, the oyster stew was "hailed as glorious" by the children.

Rachel baked bread and other items quite regularly: on the tenth "plum pies and cunning little tarts" (a delight to her five children); on the thirteenth, "Cup Cake Ginger bread and currant cake of light dough"; on the fourteenth (when he husband unexpectedly invited two men as guests), plum pies; on the sixteenth, bread and doughnuts; on the 23nd, gingerbread and two pans of custard pie; on the twenty-fourth, milk toast for breakfast and biscuits for supper. For about two weeks she made biscuits instead of bread, but on April 3 (the last diary entry) she mixed and baked more bread, and after supper they had fried doughnuts, with the children "poking in dough of their own cutting." Neighbors also brought in baked goods. One man brought in a cake he had made, and another brought a mince pie.

Mr. Haskell helped with the cooking. On the twenty-second she mentioned him as "working at" the ham before they finally decided it was inedible; on the twenty-fourth, when she made biscuits for supper, her husband made codfish balls, "only he baked them in an entire cake in the oven." On the twenty-sixth, Rachel ate supper without her husband because he came home late. When he came in he brought bacon. He fried some for his own supper, eating beside the stove.

There were not many extras, although on one occasion Mr. Haskell went into town to get peanuts, which they ate with the addition of a few pine nuts. One of the male neighbors also brought them "some nice apples." Mrs. Haskell dealt with them "in old fashioned style," handing them round in a silver basket with a plate of gingerbread. The Haskells were not living in Spartan style. On March eleventh, when a neighbor came with a cake and stayed to supper, Mrs. Haskell noted "how comfortable and cozy" the sitting room looked by twilight: "The shelves laden with books, specimens, minerals, shells. The Piano, the Sewing Machine, comfortable sofa and easy chair, with healthy, happy, prattling chippy, little children. . . . I with Guitar in hand and Mr. Chapin [the visitor] looking at pictures in 'Home Scenes.'" Later she played the piano. Mrs. Haskell was not destined to spend the rest of her life in Aurora. Her husband prospered, became an agent for the Central Pacific Railroad, and later built a big house in San Francisco.[39]

In the late 1860s, as the Central Pacific Railroad pushed eastward across Nevada to link up with the Union Pacific, new opportunities arose in the eastern part of the state. In 1869, Franklin Buck, who had first experienced the mining frontier in California, went by way of the new railhead town of Elko to the White Pine mining area of Nevada. At Elko, where most of the buildings were built of canvas, the stores had "every article you can call for," including fresh salmon and green peas from California. The prices were reasonable, but the town itself was a typical new mining supply center. Buck wrote his diary in a barroom. He said the town had "several families and a great many women that ain't families."

Buck traveled south to Hamilton, the county seat, which was crowded with teams and pack mules, and went up the hill to Treasure City. This was more substantial than Hamilton, with many buildings of stone, good hotels, "magnificent whisky saloons," and stores filled with a variety of goods. It had all been accomplished since the beginning of the year. The

39. "A Literate Woman in the Mines: The Diary of Rachel Haskell," ed. Richard C. Lillard, in *Mississippi Valley Historical Review* 31(1944), 81–98.

mines, with some ten thousand miners in them, were scattered all around. Water and wood were carried into the town by Indians or on mules.[40]

In the following weeks, Buck took a long tour southward through the mines. At the springs in the valleys, there were houses where you could get bacon, bread, tea, and "lightning whiskey," but no sugar. In a little town in Lincoln County, so far east, he said, they used greenbacks instead of gold or silver coins, Buck ate with one of the Mormon families living in the valley and "feasted on potatoes, tomatoes, green corn, water melons, and vegetables generally."[41]

Early in 1870, Buck settled in the region, at what became the mining town of Pioche in Meadow Valley. It was a new town, and there had been a rush to stake out lots. Many houses were being built. In the following year, Buck said that about half the town of Pioche consisted of whiskey shops and brothels. The town was situated close to the Utah border, and southern Utah supplied the Pioche area with large amounts of fruit and vegetables—apples, peaches, grapes, green corn, and new potatoes.

Buck, who knew the mining frontier well, and for twenty years had made his living as a retail merchant, had decided to make money by filling a need for a dairy. There was plenty of grass and timber where they set up their farm, but to get water they had to go seven miles to a spring where it cost them ten cents a gallon. In the year after he settled, Buck went into Utah and bought 158 head of cattle—cows, heifers, and steers. He pastured them on a range about twenty-five miles away and hired a man to look after them. It took him several years to set up his dairy, but by 1874 he had a special, patented churn that could churn forty pounds at a time, and he was able to sell about one hundred pounds of butter a week. In this region there was more money to be made from dairy products than from beef. Beef cattle could be obtained easily and cheaply.[42]

Virginia City continued to be the best known center of mining in early Nevada, and in the early 1870s it was prospering. In 1869, Mary Mathews, a widow from New York State, went to Nevada with her young son to find out about property that had been owned by her dead brother. In the 1870s, she lived in Virginia City. Although she worked hard to survive, she found that for those who succeeded, Virginia City offered rich living. It had many restaurants and fifteen or twenty "of the finest markets to be found in the United States."

Many of the families, children and all, "boarded" (that is arranged to

40. Buck, *Yankee Trader*, 219–23.
41. Ibid., 225–27.
42. Ibid., 230–48.

have all their meals) at restaurants. The family males had breakfast at the restaurant and went to work at 6:00 A.M. or 7:00 A.M. At 10:00 A.M. or 11:00 A.M., the women would come to the restaurant with their children for breakfast, have dinner at 1:00 P.M. or 2:00 P.M., and supper at 7:00 P.M. or 8:00 P.M. Sometimes in bad weather the women would carry a plate of food home for the children. This was also done for those who were sick. Mrs. Mathews said that even those families who cooked their own food went out when they wanted "a square meal," and on Saturdays, Sundays, and holidays nearly everyone went out for at least one meal.

Mrs. Mathews commented caustically about women going to breakfast at 10:00 A.M. or 11:00 A.M., about the amount of food that was eaten at restaurants, and about extravagant tastes. The markets offered "everything that grows which is fit to eat and a thousand and one things which are not fit to eat." "Epicures" or "gormandizers," she said, brought in special foods for "their perverted tastes." They wanted many kinds of rich dishes at any one meal, and the "table groans with food of every kind from every kingdom of the globe"—eight to twelve different vegetables, many kinds of meat, cakes, and all sorts of pastries and puddings. On Sundays and holidays there were always the best kinds of fruit, candies, raisins, nuts and wines. To cater for those who had not struck it rich, several "two-bit" restaurants had been set up. At these you could get only two kinds of meat, two kinds of vegetables, pie or pudding, and tea or coffee.[43]

Along with its abundant food, Virginia City had constant drinking. Saloons and gambling halls competed with the restaurants on the main streets. Some never closed, and those that did simply shut for about three hours in the early morning when the miners had left for their 7:00 o'clock shift, night workers had gone to bed, and all-night carousers had gone home. The only days they were all closed were those of elections and town meetings and on July 4. Mrs. Mathews said that all classes, "high and low," drank. Beer by the keg and wine and spirits by the case were kept in private homes. To counter the drinking, a temperance society was organized, and Mrs. Mathews was asked to join. She did and entered fully into their activities which included petitioning the legislature to limit the sales of alcohol.[44]

Providing sufficient water was a problem. In 1876, a visitor commented that it was scarce, not very safe to drink, and best drunk mixed with California wine. The local water company originally had channeled available

43. Mathews, *Ten Years*, 165–71; Conlin, *Bacon, Beans, and Galantines*, 137–95, discusses extensive eating out in the various the mining areas.
44. Ibid., 115–16, 191–92, 193, 195.

local water into cisterns on the streets, but it was only available in the day. After a large fire in 1875, the company brought water in mains from high above the town. It was expensive. Even small families paid a dollar a week for their water.[45]

Mrs. Mathews reached the conclusion that "every nationality under the sun" had found its way to Virginia City, among them the Chinese, against whom she held the deepest prejudice. "Filthy" was her favorite adjective in describing the Chinese, their customs, and their food. Virginia City's Chinatown, she wrote, was, like all other Chinatowns, "a loathsome, filthy den." Even a brick grocery store there, with abundant supplies, including rice, ham, bacon, and all kinds of foreign nuts, dried fruit, and candy, did not escape her prejudice. The candy was "the most loathsome kind to look at, and in taste too." In writing of the fine restaurants in the town, she commented that many of the best had shifted to whites rather than using "filthy Chinese cooks." Anyone employing them, she wrote, never knew what he was eating. Although she acknowledged that the Chinese could live on rice and tea and were very fond of ham, bacon, chickens, and any kind of poultry or soup, she could not resist saying that she had been told that "rat pie" was a favorite Chinese dish.[46]

In her intense prejudice against Chinese, Mrs. Mathews was at her worst, but she appeared in a more favorable light in the Virginia City depression of 1877 when most of the mines closed and the streets were "filled with starving men, women, and children." With another woman she decided to start a soup kitchen "like they have in Chicago." She asked restaurants for leftover food and grocery shops for wilted vegetables, broken packages of tea, and other items. Butchers donated meat, and others gave milk. They were not given enough bread so they added to what they had by buying day-old loaves. They also received other items, including corned beef, flour, hominy, and molasses, from several restaurants that failed.

From money collected from those who could afford it, the two women bought butter and sugar and hired a man and a girl. They fed four to five hundred people three times a day. For breakfast, there were cold meats, hot potatoes, hash, coffee, bread, and butter; for dinner, soup, vegetables, cold meats, baked beans, pork, bread, and coffee; for supper, the same along with cakes, pies, and puddings. The food was served on seven large tables, provided with pepper, salt, mustard, vinegar, and Worcestershire sauce.

The recipe for Worcestershire sauce, a mixture of vinegar, molasses, shal-

45. Ibid., 183–84; De Quille, *History of Comstock*, 50–51, 56, 63–66.
46. Mathews, *Ten Years*, 171, 249–57.

lots, tamarinds, garlic, and various other ingredients kept secret by its makers, had originated in England, where it had been brought to the English grocers Lea and Perrins by its original maker. The firm had begun to produce it commercially in the 1830s. It became a great success, known as Worcester sauce in England and Worcestershire sauce in the United States.[47]

Mrs. Mathews's anti-Chinese prejudice was modified a little at the soup kitchen. If there was any soup left, it was given to the Indians and Chinese who waited around the door at mealtimes. When the donated money ran out, the two women had to close up. In their last week of operation they gave a "lunch," designed to last three or four days, to each of about one hundred young men who left the city to look for work. The mining regions were particularly vulnerable in times of depression because mining, and the providing of food, drink, and entertainment for miners, was often the sole activity of the isolated towns.[48]

In the 1860s the mining frontier began to expand into Idaho and Montana. In Montana, the most dramatic developments began in the southwestern corner of the state. In late 1862, Granville Stuart went to Bannack with partners to open a butcher shop and grocery. They did well, sold up, and in the following year moved to the new town of Virginia City. By November, they had moved into their new store (a "log house") and were selling flour, bacon, beef, beef tallow, beef sausage, sugar, coffee, salt, keg butter, eggs (when they had them), turnips, potatoes, candy, and raisins. Molasses was a luxury—it was scarce and expensive. Gold dust was used for all transactions.[49]

At the time of the first strikes in Montana in 1862–1863, supplies for Bannock and the Virginia City were brought in from Fort Benton, at the head of steamer navigation on the Missouri River, but, as the population increased, there was an extensive importation of foodstuffs from Salt Lake City, and supplies were shipped on the Columbia River. Utah benefited greatly from the mining strikes in Nevada, Colorado, Montana, and Idaho. Most of the flour used in Montana in the 1860s was brought in from Utah, and wagons carried flour, butter, vegetables, eggs, barley, and oats from Salt Lake to Denver. In 1864, 200,000 pounds of dried peaches were sold by the Mormons to settlers in Montana and Idaho.[50]

47. John Ayto, *The Diner's Dictionary: Food and Drank from A to Z* (Oxford: Oxford University Press, 1993), 382.

48. Mathews, *Ten Years*, 268–79.

49. Stuart, *Prospecting the Gold*, 257–66.

50. Walker, *Wagonmasters*, 171–73, 201–8; Arrington, *Great Basin Kingdom*, 204–5.

There was also a steady stream of wagons bringing supplies from the Columbia River region to Montana and Idaho. One woman on her way to Oregon in 1864 met long lines of pack animals and covered wagons taking provisions to Boise City and other places. She also passed a circus on its way to the mining towns. While California sent most of its supplies to the Nevada mines, a few sheep herds were driven from California to the mines of Idaho and Montana before the end of the Civil War.[51]

Virginia City in the winter of 1863–1864 was a wide-open town, filled with saloons, gambling houses, and dance halls. There was also a hotel and several restaurants, but most of the miners did their own cooking. There were some families in the town, and when there were dances or other socials they brought their children with them. Parents took turns looking after the children, who were put in beds in adjoining rooms. For dances, tickets cost five dollars. This included a "fine supper," usually served at midnight, and dancing went on into the early hours. Miners who were working for larger operators were paid in gold dust on Sundays and came into Virginia City to buy their provisions.[52]

For a time in 1865 there was a great shortage of flour. In the previous fall, early snows had stranded wagon trains from Utah on the south side of the pass leading to Virginia City. All provisions were expensive, but flour was particularly difficult to buy. Many merchants and others hoarded what they had. The price soared, and in April a mob of incensed miners roamed through the town forcing those with flour to put it up for sale at a set price, much lower than the price it had reached. At a meeting, it was decided to ration flour: a single man could buy twelve pounds, a married man, twenty-four. One woman kept her flour from forced sale by emptying a barrel of beans, putting flour in it, and then putting beans on top.[53]

In these first years, Virginia City also suffered from a shortage of vegetables, butter, and eggs. In the spring of 1864 some young girls made money by gathering wild greens—goosefoot and lamb's quarters—and selling them to hotels, boardinghouses, and restaurants. They also sold wildflowers to be put on the tables, "most of which were laid out with red-

51. Harriet A. Laughey, "Travels and Incidents, 1864," in Holmes, ed., *Covered Wagon Women*, 8:153; Towne and Wentworth, *Shepherd's Empire*, 168, 170.

52. Stuart, *Prospecting*, 267–68; John S. Collins, *My Experiences in the West*, ed. Colton Storm (Chicago: Lakeside Press, 1970), 40.

53. Granville Stuart, *Pioneering in Montana: The Making of a State, 1864–1887*, ed. Paul C. Phillips (1925; repr., Lincoln: University of Nebraska Press, 1977), 28–30; Mary Ronan, *Frontier Woman: The Story of Mary Ronan as Told to Margaret Ronan*, ed. H. G. Merriam (Missoula, Mont.: University of Montana, 1973), 28; Collins, *My Experiences*, 47–48; Albert J. Dickson, ed., *Covered Wagon Days: A Journey across the Plains in the Sixties* (1929; repr., Lincoln: University of Nebraska Press, 1989), 206–7.

checked cloths, half-inch thick earthenware or tin cups and plates and cheap, strangely assorted knives, forks, and spoons." The girls were paid in gold dust.[54]

While the supply of provisions was erratic, there was plenty of meat. Beef was quite cheap, and there was a good supply of game. One resident described "a wonderful display" put out by a meat market at Christmas in 1864, with half a dozen each of freshly killed buffalo, buffalo calves, mountain lions, and grizzlies, a dozen each of mountain sheep, elks, deer, and antelope, with many small black bears and sage grouse, along with a large display of beef.[55]

In 1865, supplies began to reach Virginia City with greater regularity. Salt Lake City continued to be a major source of supply, but merchants also shipped in provisions from the east, and individuals brought in foodstuffs as a speculation. When James Miller came from Salt Lake City in June 1865, he arranged for dried apples, peaches, and a large quantity of eggs to be shipped after him. He began work as a bookkeeper at a store in Virginia City and was able to make a profit by selling dried apples and peaches to the owner. His only loss was on some of his peaches, which arrived full of worms.

There were indications that Virginia City was beginning to consist of more than saloons, gambling houses, and dance halls. In December, after a sleigh ride, Miller went to a restaurant for an oyster supper, and later in the month he attended the "Inauguration Ball of the Literary Society." There was a dedication speech by the editor of the *Montana Post*, a "splendid supper" and dancing until 3:00 A.M. This somewhat compensated for his "very poor Christmas dinner" of beef.

For those with gold dust, the mining towns soon had plenty of food to offer. In May 1867, when traveling from Virginia City to Bannock, Miller had a breakfast "fit for an epicure"—tender beefsteaks, fresh eggs, pure coffee, and milk, and when he reached Bannock he had a supper of mountain trout. Canned oysters were readily available. In 1867, in Helena, Miller visited an oyster saloon, and a girl who settled there with her family at this time said that sleighing parties and oyster suppers at a hotel or at someone's home were the "social diversions of the winter season." She also remembered long summer walks to gather gooseberries to add to the still scarce fruits and vegetables.[56]

When new mines opened up, traders quickly followed the miners with

54. Ronan, *Frontier Woman*, 26–27.
55. Collins, *My Experiences*, 50–51.
56. Miller, *The Road to Virginia City*, 74–112; Ronan, *Frontier Woman*, 35–41.

the certainty that if gold was found there would be money to be made. In February 1866, John Collins left Virginia City with a mule team loaded with provisions to go to Silver Bow, near the German Gulch mines. He intended to open a store. He had a few bags of flour, various canned goods (including canned peaches), bacon, sugar, and coffee, as well as pans, picks, and shovels. He found that Silver Bow had only two buildings, one of them a store that had the only cast-iron stove within eighty miles. There were some 250 miners in log cabins within five miles, and on Sunday about 100 of them came into town. Collins stayed there trading until July, occasionally visiting Virginia City to replenish his stock.[57]

From the earliest years of mining, efforts were made to develop food supplies within Montana itself. The first area where this was successful was along the Gallatin River valley some sixty miles from Virginia City. Settlement began there in the early sixties, and by 1863 wagon loads of produce were being sent south to the mines. Young Arthur Dickson, who had come west from Wisconsin, went with the Ridgley family to the Gallatin valley in the fall of 1864. After he and his companions reached Virginia City, they heard of the farming opportunities and decided to continue north to the Gallatin valley. They staked out claims along the West Gallatin and built a cabin. By taking wagons a short distance farther north, they were easily able to kill enough deer and elk to last them for the winter. In the cold Montana winter, they were able to keep the game by hanging it, beyond the reach of predators, outside their cabin.

In the following spring, the Ridgleys, who had a plow made in Virginia City, broke about ten acres and planted potatoes, cabbage, and rutabagas as cash crops, together with a small vegetable plot. Settlers on the east branch of the Gallatin had raised their crops by irrigation in the previous year, and because rainfall was problematical, fourteen settlers on the west Gallatin joined together to cut a five mile ditch from the river to their ranches. In the summer of 1865, at first the Ridgleys' only income came from selling flour. They received gold dust in return. Once the rutabagas and early cabbage were ready, they loaded them into two wagons and decided to go to Helena, about ninety miles away, to make their sale. To do this they had to cross the Missouri. The journey took them five days, but they were able to sell all they brought to a general store in the town.[58]

The gold fever that had brought miners to California by the tens of thousands in 1849 continued to send miners throughout the Rocky Moun-

57. Collins, *My Experiences*, 53–57, 62.
58. Dickson, ed., *Covered Wagon Days*, 174–75, 189–98, 209, 229–44.

tains until the 1890s. The pattern of sudden growth and turmoil was created again and again. When Englishman Charles Trevelyan visited Colorado in 1898 he said of Cripple Creek, where mining had begun in the early 1890s, that "the main street is devoted to gambling halls and brothels open to the air." Yet, Denver now had "asphalt paving, electric cars and light, telephones, buildings 13 stories high, five railroads, the Brown Palace Hotel, and all the comforts of civilization."[59] In 1898, dining in Denver was like dining in New York.

59. Charles Philips Trevelyan, *Letters from North America and the Pacific, 1898* (London: Chatto & Windus, 1969), 83.

Part 5

Army Life

CHAPTER 10

Rank and File

⁓

It is really the poorest beef that can be imagined and not only is there
a lack of fat, but it covered with sores caused by the blows received
from day to day in order to get the poor thing along through the deep
sands.

Henry Standage, Mormon Battalion, 1846

T he basic rations for soldiers in the United States Army had been
established as early as 1775. In November of that year, Congress decreed that the daily allowance for those who served in
the Continental army would be either one pound of beef, or
three-quarters of a pound of pork, or one pound of salt fish, together with a pound of bread or flour, and a pint of milk. There
would also be three pints of beans or peas (or some other vegetable), and
a half pint of rice or a pint of cornmeal per week, and either a quart
of spruce beer or cider each man per day, or nine gallons of molasses for
each one hundred men per week. This was more elaborate than the typical nineteenth-century ration, and, in the Revolution, it existed more on
paper than in reality.[1]

The army was on the cutting edge of the advance of settlers across the
whole American continent. When the advance was still east of the Mississippi, a thin line of army posts was situated near the edge of settlement.
Beyond the Mississippi, army posts gave protection on the overland trails
and provided an army of occupation for the Southwestern areas conquered
in the Mexican War. Ultimately, posts were scattered from Alaska to the
Mexican border.

In the years immediately following the Revolution, the ration settled
into a form that was only slowly modified in the course of the nineteenth

1. Erna Risch, *Quartermaster Support of the Army: A History of the Corps, 1775–1939* (Washington, D.C.: Quartermaster Historical Office, 1962), 9–10.

century. Each day, a soldier was entitled to a pound of beef or three-quarters of a pound of pork, a pound of bread or flour, and a gill of rum a day replaced beer or cider. For every one hundred men, there was a quart of salt and two quarts of vinegar. Vegetables, fish, and milk were no longer part of the ration. In 1798 the beef was increased to one and a quarter pounds, the bread or flour to eighteen ounces, the salt to two quarts, the vinegar to four quarts, and brandy or whiskey were allowed as possible alternatives to rum.[2]

For many years, the army used private contractors to supply the army rations, often opting for cheapness over efficiency or quality. Contracts were given to the lowest bidder. Quite often supplies did not arrive, and contractors were frequently accused of providing inferior or tainted meat. In 1791, on Arthur St. Clair's disastrous expedition against the Indians, the contractor was unable to deliver all the supplies that were contracted for, and the troops had to be placed on reduced rations. The same problem occurred on Anthony Wayne's successful expedition in 1794.[3]

Sometimes the beef in the army ration was fresh, but much of the beef and nearly all the pork was salted. Vinegar was included in the ration because, wrongly, it was believed that it prevented scurvy. Although individuals in the British navy had grasped that there was a relationship between scurvy and a lack of fresh fruit and vegetables as early as the eighteenth century, there was still considerable confusion about ways to prevent it well into the nineteenth century.

From 1775 some in authority had recognized that it would be beneficial to provide vegetables as part of the soldier's ration, but in practice this was not done. A physician who played a leading role in the War of 1812 commented that replacing a part of the meat ration with beans and peas would be conducive to health but concluded that on active service this was impossible. Animal food, he argued, was less bulky and less expensive, and the beef ration could often travel with the troops.[4]

Because of the absence of vegetables from the ration, officers and soldiers at army posts tried to give variety to their diet by planting gardens. The work, and the money needed to maintain them, came from the troops and their officers, not from the War Department. As early as the 1780s,

2. Ibid., 78, 118; Francis P. Prucha, *Broadax and Bayonet: The Role of the United States Army in the Development of the Northwest, 1815–1860* (Madison, Wis.: State Historical Society, 1953), 153.

3. Risch, *Quartermaster Support,* 73–80, 83–108, 117–19.

4. Dr. James Mann, quoted in Fanny J. Anderson, "Medical Practices in Detroit during the War of 1812," *Bulletin of the History of Medicine* 16 (1944): 271; Mary C. Gillet, *The Army Medical Department, 1775–1818* (Washington, D.C.: Center of Military History, United States Army, 1981), 14.

when Indian wars raged along the Ohio River, visitors to Fort Harmar at the mouth of the Muskingum were impressed by the excellent gardens adjoining the fort. On the well-watered lands of the eastern half of the Mississippi valley, good gardens became a regular feature of army posts. In 1834, an inspector reported that the commander's vegetable garden at Fort Howard at Green Bay was perhaps better than any in the country at that latitude, and that there was a separate garden for each company. Every kind of vegetable was "in abundance" in the men's messes, and the inspector thought that they were the best he had ever seen.[5]

In the middle years of the nineteenth century, emigrants on the Oregon Trail were often surprised by what they found at army posts. In 1850, a woman emigrant described Fort Kearny, in what is now Nebraska, as "a pleasant place on the river," where the soldiers cultivated land, "& have fine gardens." In well-watered areas, post gardens often made up for the lack of vegetables in the ration, but in arid areas, at new posts, and on campaign, soldiers often did not have the vegetables necessary to avoid dietary deficiencies and scurvy.[6]

Another source of variety in food was the sutler. It was typical for any post or sizeable unit of troops to have a sutler who sold small "luxury" items to the soldiers. In the early years, sugar and coffee were not part of the ration, and, along with tobacco, these were the main items purchased. In 1849, at Fort Kearny, the sutler's store carried "all sorts of notions, cigars, sardines, & some few extras for officers use." Soldiers often took money out of their pay to create mess or company funds which were used to buy extras. In 1850, at Fort Leavenworth, the mess fund of one enlisted man was used to buy vegetables brought by "Hucksters" from Missouri. Company funds were also created by making savings out of the ration.[7]

In the years after the Civil War, post traders were licensed to operate stores at some posts., and the position of post trader could, at times, be an extremely lucrative one. In the 1870s John S. Collins and his brother were post traders at Fort Laramie, the key post on the central plains. Collins had obtained the position through President Ulysses S. Grant, a friend of his family. It was said that the profits were eight thousand to fifteen thousand dollars a year. The Collins brothers had the great advantage that they

5. Reginald Horsman, "Hunger in a Land of Plenty: Marietta's Lean Years," *Timeline* 19 (2002): 23; "Fort Howard (1824–1832)," in *Green Bay Historical Bulletin,* 4, no. 5 (1928): 25.

6. Holmes, ed., *Covered Wagon Women,* 2:246.

7. Perkins, *Gold Rush Diary,* 29; Percival G. Lowe, *Five Years a Dragoon ('49 to '54) and Other Adventures on the Great Plains,* ed. Don Russell (Norman: University of Oklahoma Press, 1965), 21, 24; Robert W. Frazer, *Forts and Supplies: The Role of the Army in the Economy of the Southwest, 1846–1861* (Albuquerque: University of New Mexico Press, 1983), 195; Prucha, *Broadax and Bayonet,* 170.

did not have to depend on officers and their men for profits. Many emigrants and travelers came through Fort Laramie, and Collins provided lodging and meals for travelers who came to Fort Laramie on their way to the Black Hills. While officers frequently made purchases from post traders, ordinary soldiers had insufficient pay to make any large purchases, particularly as many wanted to use any money they had to buy liquor.[8]

Drunkenness was a constant problem in frontier posts. Until 1831 the daily ration included one gill of rum, whiskey, or brandy, and after 1819 troops employed in building posts or roads, or other construction projects, for more than ten days were allowed an extra gill each day. The main problem, however, was not the regular ration but the availability of cheap liquor in the vicinity of the posts. Forts near towns had particular problems, but liquor dealers set up shanties in the vicinity of even the most isolated posts. In 1804, at Fort Wayne, the commanding officer said he could "no longer overlook the habit of Intoxication: there is scersely a parrade but some of the men appear Drunk." Three years later Christmas celebrations had produced so much drinking that he ordered that in future July 4 would be the only day allowed for celebration at the post. The abolition of the liquor ration in 1830 did little to reduce the problems of drunkenness. At Fort Crawford, in Wisconsin, soldiers working on laundry outside the post brought in blankets soaked in whiskey to wring out when they were inside.[9]

In 1836, at Fort Leavenworth, a sergeant was sent to burn down the log cabin of a whiskey dealer near the fort because soldiers were trading their pistols for liquor. The dealers were not deterred. Thirteen years later there was a place one mile above the fort called Whiskey Point, "where anything could be sold or traded for whisky." Some traded their overcoats there. The trooper who described this also wrote that at any one time in winter 10 percent of his troop were undergoing punishment in the guardhouse, nearly all for offenses arising out of whiskey drinking. At posts on the Oregon Trail, soldiers sometimes obtained whiskey from overland emigrants. In 1850, at Fort Kearny, men on a wagon train who sold liquor to the soldiers were fined and their remaining liquor poured out of the cask.[10]

8. Collins, *My Experiences*, v, vi, xvi, 97–129; Don Rickey Jr., *Forty Miles a Day on Beans and Hay: The Enlisted Soldier Fighting the Indian Wars* (Norman: University of Oklahoma Press, 1963), 201.

9. Bert J. Griswold, ed., *Fort Wayne: Gateway of the West, 1802–1813* (Indianapolis: Historical Bureau of the Indiana Library, 1927), 202, 264; Prucha, *Broadax and Bayonet*, 45–49, 100 n.

10. George Walton, *Sentinel of the Plains: Fort Leavenworth and the American West* (Englewood Cliffs, N. J.: Prentice Hall, 1973), 52; Charles W. Ayars, "Some Notes on the Medical Service of the Army," *Military Surgeon*, 50 (1922): 511–12; George Croghan, *Army Life on the Western Frontier: Selections from the Official Reports Made between 1826 and 1845 by Colonel George Croghan*, ed. Francis P. Prucha (Norman: University of Oklahoma Press, 1958), 111–112, 143; Lowe, *Five Years*, 20 (quotation), 97; "Sarah Davis Diary," in Holmes, ed., *Covered Wagon Women*, 2:177.

Although some officers made efforts to promote temperance among the men, problems caused by excessive drinking continued throughout the century. In June 1867, when James Miller was traveling on a steamboat from Fort Benton down the Missouri, he wrote in his journal that "a soldier, taken with delirium tremens, is howling hideously below the hurricane deck." There were particular problems if temptation was close. Fort Dodge, in Kansas, was just five miles from Dodge City, and in the 1870s Dodge City was a wide-open cattle town. An officer's wife who was there at that time remembered the men going into town, drinking rotgut whiskey, getting crazy drunk, and being thrown into the street after their clothes and everything else they owned had been stolen. She did not mention that in all likelihood they had been in one of Dodge City's many brothels.[11]

Much of the impetus for the improvement of the army diet came from army surgeons. James Lovell, who became surgeon general of the army in 1818, made enthusiastic efforts to improve the health of the army. He objected to the constant dependence on salt pork and whiskey and argued for the benefits of bread and vegetables. His recommendation to Secretary of War John C. Calhoun was that there should be a proper mixture of "animal and vegetable food," and that, when possible, there should be soups as well as fried food. Lovell deplored the effects of excessive drinking, and his efforts were an important factor in bringing about the eventual abolition of the liquor ration. He also did much to encourage gardens at the military posts.[12]

In 1818, Congress changed the way in which the army dealt with private contractors for rations. A commissary general was appointed, and while contracts were still given to private contractors, supplies were inspected before being distributed. In 1821, the ration was altered so that twice a week half the allowance of meat was replaced by peas or beans, and at least twice a week fresh meat replaced salted meat. The War Department also specifically ordered the establishment of gardens at any permanent posts where it was possible to have them.[13]

Yet, in spite of concerns that the army ration was unhealthy, its basic ingredients remained intact. When the Civil War began, the daily ration was one and a quarter pounds of fresh or salt beef or three-quarters of a pound of pork or bacon, and eighteen ounces of soft bread or flour. The

11. Miller, *Road to Virginia City*, 126; Ellen McGowan Biddle, *Reminiscences of a Soldier's Wife* (Philadelphia, 1907), 108–9.

12. Gillett, *Army Medical Department*, 16; Reginald Horsman, *Frontier Doctor: William Beaumont, America's First Great Medical Scientist* (Columbia, Mo.: University of Missouri Press, 1996), 80–81.

13. Risch, *Quartermaster Support*, 181–204.

eighteen ounces of soft bread could be replaced by twelve ounces of hard bread or twenty ounces of cornmeal. Concerns for health and variety were reflected in the bulk amounts to be issued twice a week for every hundred men. These consisted of eight quarts of beans or ten pounds of rice, one hundred and fifty ounces of dried potatoes, one hundred ounces of dried vegetables, ten pounds of coffee or one and a half pounds of tea, fifteen pounds of sugar, and four quarts of vinegar. Minor adjustments were made during the war, but the basic ration remained much the same. Further adjustments were made later in the century, but it was 1890 before vegetables were added to the standard ration.[14]

To those who lived on it for long periods of time, the army ration became remarkably tedious. In the fall of 1851, Percival Lowe, a dragoon on the plains, was sent to a Potawatomi village to guard the agent who was distributing the annuities. Lowe had been on the plains all summer, eating a steady diet of bread, rice, beans, bacon, a little sugar and coffee, occasional game, and no vegetables. In his journal he wrote of his pleasure in having "pumpkin sauce, with salt and pepper, flavored with a little bacon grease, boiled cabbage, mashed potatoes, baked potatoes, potatoes baked in the ashes by the campfire, eaten with salt or a thin slice of bacon broiled on a stick."[15]

When Lowe was sent to escort the taking of pay from Fort Leavenworth to Fort Laramie, he and his fellow dragoons were sent into camp near Fort Laramie. At their location, it was simple to kill deer, there were ample fish in the river, and one of them could make good bread. They ate venison regularly and fried catfish for breakfast. At meal times, they placed the end gate of the wagon on four stakes driven into the soil, used water buckets and boxes for seats, and used flour sacks for a tablecloth and napkins.[16]

During the Mexican War the army temporarily abandoned the system of civilian contractors, sending its own wagon trains along the Santa Fe Trail into the Southwest. The army that was sent into the region under the command of Stephen Watts Kearny was not well provisioned. Even though they took herds of cattle with them, and were able to hunt in the buffalo country they passed through, troops on the march to Santa Fe were often on half rations, and they suffered from a lack of water.[17]

14. Ibid., 447, 505–7.

15. Lowe, *Five Years*, 73–75.

16. Ibid., 46–47.

17. Risch, *Quartermaster Support*, 277–79, 308; Walker, *Wagonmasters*, 228; Frazer, *Forts and Supplies*, 2, 5–6.

The battalion that was enlisted from among the Mormons at first suffered less from lack of food than from a scarcity of water. They left Leavenworth in mid-August, and on their march to Santa Fe were well supplied with game and fish. By mid-September, however, water had become very difficult to obtain. On September 17, one of the marchers wrote: "I drank some water today that the Buffaloes had wallowed in and could not be compared to anything else but Buffalo urine." He said the troops were glad to get it. They reached Santa Fe on October 9, after existing on short rations over the last hundred miles.[18]

On October 19, the Mormons left Santa Fe to march to San Diego. There were about four hundred of them, including five wives. They began their march with sixty days' rations of flour, sugar, coffee, salt, and thirty days rations of salt pork. They also had a small herd of cattle. It was to take them over three months to reach San Diego. It was helpful that their march took them by many small towns and villages where the quartermasters were able to buy sheep and other foodstuffs to add to the rations, but there was constant concern about supplies and in the desert areas always concern about water. They killed some game (including wild goats and numerous wild cattle), caught fish, gathered wild plants, including the pods containing mesquite seeds, and bought corn, beans, dried pumpkins, and watermelons from the Pima and Mariposa Indians.

The amount and quality of the food varied widely. Within two days of leaving Santa Fe, the men were on three-quarter rations, and within two weeks this had become half rations. By the middle of November, meat was so scarce that a decrepit, old white ox was killed. Henry Standage wrote: "it is really the poorest beef that can be imagined," lacking in fat, and "covered with sores caused by the blows it received from day to day in order to get the poor thing along through the deep sands." Two days later, Standage ate "guts" for the first time, and in the last two weeks in November the men continued to eat meat from "worn out Oxen."

In early December, the food improved because of the large numbers of wild cattle that had drifted away from deserted Mexican ranches. The hunters brought in large quantities of beef that was put on scaffolds to dry. In the middle of the month, at Tucson, where the battalion camped outside the town, the residents brought flour, cornmeal, quinces, and tobacco to sell. Many even gave items when they saw the condition of the soldiers. Two thousand bushels of wheat that belonged to the Mexican

18. "Journal of Henry Standage," in Golder, *March of the Mormon Battalion,* 142–71, 165–66 (quotation).

government was confiscated, but this was given to the animals rather than the soldiers. It could not be taken on the rest of the march, because the teams pulling the wagons did not have the strength to pull it.

At the Pima Indian villages, near the Gila River, the soldiers used their own money, as well as trading clothing and other personal items, to obtain corn, beans, dried pumpkins, and watermelons. Standage's comment was that "we have full rations once more, though at our own expense." They soon had eaten what they could afford to buy. By the end of the first week in January, Standage was "quite weak and hungry," and he bought a piece of bread and meat from a soldier who waited on the colonel. The men were detailed to gather seeds from the mesquite trees.[19]

Only by constant efforts to supplement their provisions was the battalion able to survive. On January 18, when they were about to reach the first of the main ranches in southern California, Standage noted that "we are now without Flour, Bread, Coffee or sugar. Nothing but beef and very small rations of it." Their commander commented that "the men are weak for want of food." Since leaving Fort Leavenworth they had marched over two thousand miles in about five months. Their problems were not completely over even after they reached San Diego. There was insufficient food for the large influx of troops, particularly as American naval ships in the port were also short of supplies. There was abundant beef but little else. In mid-February, Standage commented that he had not eaten anything but beef for nearly a month.[20]

The amount of beef consumed was remarkable. On January 22 the beef ration for each man of the Mormon battalion was increased to four pounds a day. Before this, they had been receiving two and a half pounds. Even the four pounds was little compared to that issued to the men of John Frémont's California force. His men received about ten pounds of beef a day.[21]

By mid-March, the food situation was causing considerable unrest among the Mormon troops. They were still depending heavily on meat, although the meat ration had been reduced to between two and three pounds per day. Flour and beans had been issued in the previous month, but the daily ration for each man was only eight to twelve ounces of flour, with half a pint of beans to every nine men. The men complained that beef abounded in the surrounding country, that there were plenty of other

19. Ibid., 179, 182, 184, 189, 190, 195–96, 198–99, 201–2.

20. Ibid., 203, 210; "Cooke's Journal of the March of the Mormon Battalion, 1846–1847," in Bieber and Bender, eds., *Exploring Southwestern Trails*, 65–240, 229 (quotation); Risch, *Quartermaster Support*, 280–81.

21. "Journal of Standage," in Golder, ed., *March*, 209–10.

provisions in San Diego, and that there was no need to reduce the ration. In one company, several men refused to drill and were put in the stocks. Standage commented in mid-June that the men had fared badly and that the colonel had been "very stingy."[22]

During the Mexican War, Santa Fe became the great distribution center for the troops that moved west to California or moved south into Mexico. From 1846, long supply trains of wagons rolled southwest from Fort Leavenworth to meet the needs that could not be met in the region itself. The army had not modified the basic ration to take into account mutton—the most abundant meat in New Mexico. Most troops, like most other Americans, avoided mutton when they could. Supplying bread was made easier by the provision that twenty ounces of cornmeal could be substituted for flour or bread. There was a lack of fresh vegetables because in other parts of the country these had usually come from the post gardens, and it was often difficult, if not impossible, to establish such gardens in the arid Southwest.[23]

The great acquisitions of territory in the Mexican War and the movement of large numbers of emigrants to California and Oregon brought about the establishment of posts throughout a vast new region. California and Oregon had abundant local resources, but the military posts established in New Mexico were at first very difficult to supply. Flour, beans, onions, and salt were available locally, but much of the beef and pork and many other supplies were brought in along the Santa Fe Trail from Fort Leavenworth. New Mexico had the advantage for officers that there was a good supply of fruit. The men, however, often did not want to use what little money they had to buy it.[24]

Fort Leavenworth had been established in 1827 on the west bank of the Missouri, in what is now Kansas. The fort supplied not only the New Mexico posts but also Fort Kearny, in present-day Nebraska, and Fort Laramie, in modern Wyoming. These posts had been established in the late 1840s to protect emigrants traveling west along the Platte to Oregon and California. Food at Fort Laramie reflected its position as a main supply depot. An English visitor in the mid-1830s wrote that it was well supplied with beef and other meat from a farmer who lived immediately opposite, and it had a good supply of locally caught catfish. In the 1850s, the fort had over

22. Ibid., 204–7.

23. Frazer, *Forts and Supplies*, 3–4; Risch, *Quartermaster Support*, 282.

24. Frazer, *Forts and Supplies*, 2, 3–8, 43, 46; Risch, *Quartermaster Support*, 282; Mansfield, *Mansfield on the Condition of the Western Forts*, xx–xxi; George Archibald McCall, *New Mexico in 1850*, ed. Robert W. Frazer (Norman: University of New Mexico Press, 1968), 46, 88, 97.

thirteen hundred acres under cultivation by hired farm hands. They grew a variety of crops, including corn, wheat, oats, barley, buckwheat, pumpkins, turnips, and potatoes.[25]

Officers ate particularly well at Fort Leavenworth. A historian of the fort has written of a Fourth celebrated with a "sumptuous repast," and Christmas dinners of "antelope, buffalo, ham, prairie hen, canned vegetables, preserves, and an assortment of pies and cakes." Enlisted men did not always share in the abundance. For Christmas dinner in 1849, Percival Howe had a slice of boiled pork on a piece of bread, and a tin cup of coffee. He later learned that the shortages stemmed from the actions of a first sergeant responsible for the rations that were distributed in bulk to the company. Soon after this debacle, this same sergeant deserted with the company funds, much of which came from savings on the rations.[26]

Howe's Christmas experience was not typical. At most posts there was an effort to provide the men with special food at Christmas. In 1871, at Fort Lyon in Colorado, the men sat down at three long tables loaded with buffalo meat, antelope, boiled hen, boiled ham, pickles, vegetables, pies, cakes, and coffee. At the center of each table was a large, iced cake made by the officers' wives.[27]

In 1850, an officer appointed to survey the New Mexico posts found that flour was usually being supplied locally, but there were complaints that it was not fine enough and had grit in it. Although there was beef in winter, mutton was the most abundant fresh meat in summer. Much of the salt pork and bacon was brought in from Fort Leavenworth. The presence of American troops, and the creation of new posts, meant that greater efforts were made to provide what was needed in New Mexico. Local entrepreneurs now found it worth their while to invest in flour mills and in livestock. The army was also interested in finding more efficient and cheaper ways of feeding its troops and in the early 1850s ordered that all permanent posts were to have kitchen gardens. Posts west of the Mississippi were also instructed to begin farms for the production of grains for bread and forage for the animals. To get the men interested, any profits were to be divided among them. Many of the gardens were a success, but the farms were generally failures and were soon abandoned.[28]

25. Walker, *Wagonmasters*, 230; Risch, *Quartermaster Support*, 315.

26. Walton, *Sentinel of the Plains*, 43, 88–89; Howe, *Five Years*, 18–19.

27. Frances M. A. Roe, *Army Letters from an Officer's Wife, 1871–1888* (New York: D. Appleton, 1909), 26–27.

28. McCall, *New Mexico in 1850*, 62 and n., 122, 127, 134, 141, 150, 155, 161, 165, 169, 172, 174, 188.

The extent to which efforts to obtain local supplies had succeeded was shown three years later when another tour of inspection was made of the New Mexico posts. Col. Joseph Mansfield found that Mexican settlements had increased their production of grain and beans to supply the Americans, and some posts also obtained food from nearby Indian settlements. At Fort Defiance, about two hundred miles west of Albuquerque, corn was obtained from Indian pueblos.[29]

Most men, Mansfield wrote, complained that the individual allowances of fresh beef and the amounts of coffee, sugar, and salt given for each hundred rations were too small. They missed salt pork, which was generally unavailable in the territory, and there was only a limited quantity of ham and bacon. There had also been complaints about the way in which bacon was being shipped into the territory. It was packed in large quantities in barrels, and, because of the heat, the grease was being forced out of the bottom layers and wasted. This loss was particularly felt in the Southwest where butter and lard were scarce. Soldiers on the march used the bacon grease mixed with flour to make biscuits. Mansfield thought the bacon should be packed in boxes.[30]

In the following year, Mansfield's tour of inspection was extended to the Department of the Pacific. Except for Fort Yuma, at the junction of the Colorado and Gila rivers, the posts in this department had few problems in obtaining food supplies. There were still great herds of cattle in California, and there had been a rapid increase in crop production to meet the demand created by the great influx of miners. To the north, agriculture was flourishing in the Oregon settlements. Much of the flour for the posts had been previously sent from the east, but, as there had been a high degree of spoilage, Mansfield assumed that in future most of the flour would be obtained from the abundant sources in California and Oregon. For the most part, the West Coast posts were clearly better off for food supplies than many of the posts in the interior.[31]

Fort Yuma was an exception. At first, this post had been supplied by land from San Diego but that source of supply was being replaced by steamers coming directly from San Francisco to the mouth of the Colorado. The post was in extremely hot, inhospitable country. An attempt to have a garden at the post had been a failure, although the men obtained some vegetables from the nearby Indians. Mansfield found that the complaints here differed markedly from those at other southwestern posts. In

29. Mansfield, *Mansfield on the Condition of the Western Forts*, xiii, xxvii–xxx, 13–57.
30. Ibid., 61–63.
31. Ibid., 94–97, 140.

much of New Mexico, the men had complained of a lack of salt meat, but here they complained of too much. They also said there were too few vegetables and too little coffee and sugar.[32]

Army inspections gave a general impression of the extent of food supplies at the various posts but missed the many vagaries of daily existence. Reading Mansfield's comments that Fort Yuma had good supplies and good water, it is difficult to imagine just how difficult life had been at such a post. It was established in 1850, abandoned for a time, but by 1854 it had five officers and one hundred and six men. Lt. Thomas Sweeny, who was there in the early 1850s, before there were permanent quarters, noted in his journal on June 19, 1851, that it was 108° in the shade. "I really begin to despair," he wrote, "of getting out of this horrible place." He pointed out that they were two hundred and fifty miles from any settlement, ignoring the Yuma Indians who farmed in the vicinity of the fort on lands inundated in most springs by an overflowing Colorado River.

Sweeny's despair arose not only from isolation and heat but also from the poor food. He was worried that his men might come down with scurvy. On June 24 he had no food to give a destitute traveler because he did not have sufficient rations for his men. Rations had been reduced to salt pork and hard bread. Relief arrived on the following day in a wagon from San Diego. It had taken twenty days for the wagon to cross the desert. In one stretch, water had been so scarce that the drivers had been forced to kill one of the oxen and drink its blood. A few days later more supplies arrived in a wagon train from California. Supposedly, the wagons had enough supplies for five months. Sweeny thought they could only last four and was very disappointed that there were no vegetables, antiscorbutics, or medicines of any kind. To try to avoid scurvy, Sweeny was having his men collect mesquite seeds. The men pounded and steeped them and drank the liquor. Unfortunately, they do not have the vitamin C necessary for avoiding scurvy.

In the following years, Sweeny struggled with the problems of heat, food, and health. In 1852 an attempt to raise vegetables at the post failed, but the men received pumpkins and melons from the Indians, and meat was distributed from cattle that were contracted for and brought in. In the following winter, the food supply improved. In November, eighteen wagons arrived from San Diego with potatoes, onions, and barley, and in the following month the steamer *Uncle Sam* arrived with supplies. These came from a schooner that was anchored at the mouth of the Colorado, about one hundred and twenty miles away. The *Uncle Sam* was the first steamer

32. Ibid., 147–48.

to ply the waters of the Colorado, traveling between the schooner and the post with supplies.

The better food situation was reflected in the dinner that the officers sat down to on Christmas Day 1852. After eggnog in the morning, they sat down to an afternoon meal of beef soup, roast venison, potatoes, onions, squash, apple and pumpkin pies, cheese, gingerbread, and another glass of eggnog. Sweeny still worried about scurvy, and that spring he had the men go out every day to collect "weeds" to use as antiscorbutics. In March, four wagons arrived with potatoes and onions, but many of the onions were rotten. At that time, Sweeny also received his own special box with jars of pears, peaches, pineapple, and other special items.

There was a major setback for the post when the *Uncle Sam* sank at her moorings. Supplies now had to be hauled by wagon from the mouth of the Colorado, and in the summer of 1853 provisions again ran short. For some time they lived on "bad pork, musty flour" and the weeds they collected, but this was temporary. By 1855 the troops at the fort were in permanent quarters, and they even had a pump to bring water out of the river. Usually the water was pumped in the evening, left to sit for the silt to settle, and distributed by carts on the following morning. Fort Yuma could be made more liveable, but it could never become a desirable posting.[33]

In the course of the nineteenth century, food for soldiers on the frontier gradually improved, but for those on the march, particularly in hostile areas, the supply of adequate rations always remained a problem. In 1857, when the United States government sent some 2,500 men to assert United States authority over the Mormons in Utah, the troops met far more resistance than expected. In early October, after the troops had advanced into the Rockies, Mormons attacked and succeeded in destroying a large number of the wagons carrying supplies. As the weather grew worse, the American commander, Col. Albert S. Johnston, decided they would have to go into winter quarters near Fort Bridger, in the southwestern corner of the present state of Wyoming. This old fur traders' fort had been burnt by the Mormons.

After marching for two weeks in heavy snow, the army spent the winter at "Camp Scott." Fortunately, although many supply wagons had been destroyed, there were still enough oxen to provide a meat ration, with a limited amount of flour, rice, and beans. The daily ration was set at two pounds of fresh beef and twelve ounces of flour per man. Rice was issued every other day, beans three times in ten days, bacon once a week, one

33. Thomas W. Sweeny, *Journal of Lt. Thomas Sweeny, 1849–1853*, ed. Arthur Woodward (Los Angeles: Westernlore Press, 1956), 60–222, 256, 264; Mansfield, *Mansfield on the Condition of the Western Forts*, 146–48.

gallon of molasses to each one hundred rations twice in fifteen days, and ten pounds of dried peaches per hundred rations once every fifteen days. Although salt ran out early in December, more was sent out from Fort Laramie. A more unusual feature of the rations was "dessicated vegetables." These had been sent with the supplies for the expedition, and for the first time they were to form part of the ration. At Camp Scott they were issued twice in every ten days.[34]

In the summer of 1858, American troops built the new military post of Fort Bridger. This was a great improvement over "Camp Scott." A soldier who went west to Utah with the dragoons, that September described Fort Bridger as "a perfect little paradise . . . in the midst of a howling wilderness." Mormons in the area brought all kinds of vegetables and fruit to the fort for sale "at pretty fair prices," and a soldier with savings from his basic ration could provide himself with a variety of extras.[35]

The soldier was much less pleased when he reached Camp Floyd, which had been established south of Salt Lake City. He described it "as one of the most miserable, disagreeable and uninteresting places that ever disgraced the earth." The troops were living in tents while adobe barracks were being built, and conditions were harsh. The only water came from "a dirty little stream" that ran near the camp, although milk, butter, eggs, and other items could be obtained from a nearby Mormon village at "reasonable rates." When Horace Greeley came by in the following year, he noticed that the a satellite settlement had developed near the camp. Here the troops could buy "execrable whiskey."[36]

In the years after the Civil War, new army posts in the West became necessary as the Indians of the Great Plains and the Rockies made a last effort to resist the relentless advance of the settlers. Indian life had been totally disrupted by the massive emigration across the continent in the middle decades of the century. The expansion of the mining frontier throughout the Rockies and the advance of cattlemen and homesteaders onto the Great Plains provoked extensive Indian resistance. The Indian Wars of the years from the 1860s to the 1890s necessitated a strong military presence in the West, and, in 1867, when Alaska was purchased, military responsibilities extended even into that distant region.

34. Risch, *Quartermaster Corps*, 325–26; Harold D. Langley, ed., *To Utah with the Dragoons and Glimpses of Life in Arizona and California, 1858–1859* (Salt Lake City: University of Utah Press, 1974), 7–8.

35. Langley, ed., *To Utah*, 69, 72; Risch, *Quartermaster Support*, 325–26.

36. Langley, ed., *To Utah*, 86–87, 101; Greeley, *An Overland Journey*, ed. Charles T. Duncan (1860; repr., New York: Knopf, 1964), 207–10; Arrington, *Great Basin Kingdom*, 196–97.

As troops returned in greater numbers to the West, rations for the ordinary soldiers were still very much what they had been for most of the century. There was still a great dependence on salt pork, bread, and beans, although the expansion of the cattle kingdom meant that there was more fresh beef. Army rations still did not include fresh vegetables, milk, butter, or eggs, although commissaries now often had dried vegetables. They could also supply, at cost, items such as canned fruits, and the post sutlers usually had a wider variety of special items. Military life could also be improved by the policies of individual commanders. In 1865, an officer's wife who went to Fort Bascom in southeastern New Mexico reported that the men were allowed all the hardtack, beans, and beef they wanted and were also given four pounds of coffee and a quarter pound of tea each month.[37]

For vegetables, the rank-and-file soldiers still largely depended on their gardens. These were often difficult to maintain in the arid regions of the plains and Southwest but flourished in fertile, well-watered areas. Some of the gardens became elaborate later in the century. It was said in 1877 that at Camp Harney in Oregon there were vegetables "of the finest kinds," and that cabbages weighing twenty pounds were not rare. The soldiers had "some splendid fields of oats and barley." In the 1870s at Fort Halleck, in the foothills of the Humboldt Mountains in Nevada, the men "had a fine garden and raised all kinds of vegetables." In one year they made twelve hundred dollars from their potatoes for their company fund. They also raised pigs.[38]

Although food was generally better and often more like civilian food than it had been in earlier years, it was still possible to find many echoes of the past. In campaigns against the Indians, soldiers often experienced conditions that had been familiar fifty years earlier. In 1868–1869, when George Custer was engaged in the Washita campaign against the southern Indians, his men had an autumn in which they feasted on vast numbers of wild turkeys, but in the following winter they struggled to find enough food. In February, in a campaign against Indian villages, they went without wagons or tents, ran out of provisions, could find no game, and lived on "parched corn and horse-flesh." The horse meat came from horses that had died of exhaustion.[39]

37. Russell, *Land of Enchantment,* 112–13.

38. Hickey, *Forty Miles a Day,* 79–80, 97–98, 116–18; Wallis Nash, *Oregon: There and Back in 1877,* ed. J. Kenneth Mumford (Corvallis: Oregon State University Press, 1976), 126–27; Biddle, *Reminiscences of a Soldier's Wife,* 99; Martha Summerhayes, *Vanished Arizona: Recollections of the Army Life of a New England Woman* 2nd ed. (1911; repr., Glorieta, N. M.: Rio Grande Press, 1970), 249–50.

39. Elizabeth R. Custer, *Following the Guidon,* intro. Jane R. Stewart (1890; repr., Norman: University of Oklahoma Press, 1966), 12–13, 49–50.

In the field, the experiences of different units, even in the same region of the country, could be vastly different. When Custer led an expedition into the Black Hills in July 1874, there was an "abundance of game . . . in every direction." Antelope were killed regularly, fish were readily available, and the men gathered large quantities of wild raspberries, gooseberries, currants, and cherries.

Two years later, when the Fifth Cavalry was ordered north from Kansas to help in the campaign against the Sioux, food became very scarce after they moved beyond the Yellowstone. They left their wagons behind and traveled with sacks of bacon and hardtack tied onto their mules. They had to go onto half rations. There was no game, and they ate dozens of their horses. Finally, there was some relief when they took an Indian village, capturing some four hundred ponies. These provided "grass-fed, sweet, and succulent" pony rib roasts, a welcome change from "tough and stringy" horse meat. As they left the Bad Lands, wagons finally reached them with rations, and at Deadwood and Crook City the commissary was able to buy bacon, flour, and coffee. The regimental adjutant, Charles King, described two hours in which he ate "flap-jacks" with his colonel, as fast as the cook could make them.[40]

In areas difficult to reach, or where there were Indian hostilities, men in forts could still suffer shortages, and even experience scurvy. Where the Indians were hostile, it was often difficult either to bring in supplies or to hunt. In 1866, Fort Phil Kearny was built on the Powder River in Wyoming to protect the road from Fort Laramie to the mining areas of Montana. This was a particularly dangerous area, and, on the last day of the year, the garrison suffered many deaths in an Indian ambush. The rest of the garrison spent the bitterly cold winter besieged in their new fort, each man receiving only a ration of bacon and hard bread. One third of them came down with scurvy.[41]

Scurvy was also a major problem at Fort Stevenson on the Missouri River in the winter of 1867–1868. The post had been built in the summer of 1867. In the first winter, beef and bread were the principal foods for the men. As it was a new post, the men had not yet planted gardens. The post commander, Philippe Régis de Trobriand, was concerned about the lack of vegetables, and as early as September 11 he noted that some cases

---

40. James Calhoun, *With Custer in '74: James Calhoun's Diary of the Black Hills Expedition,* ed. Lawrence A. Frost (Provo: Brigham Young University Press, 1979), 20–84; Charles King, *Campaigning with Crook, and Stories of Army Life* (New York: Harper and Brothers, 1890), 102–4, 141–142.

41. Risch, *Quartermaster Support,* 481, 483.

of scurvy had occurred. Scurvy reached its peak in March. By the first week in April, there were thirty-two men sick in the hospital, and another thirteen were recovering. In all, including employees of the quartermaster, there were fifty-one cases of scurvy, a quarter of the garrison. During the winter, the men's main food had been salt pork and salt fish. There were no fresh vegetables, and fresh meat was distributed only twice a week. In an attempt to combat scurvy, the men had been given wild onions and a type of tuber tasting "like a parsnip or the most insipid turnip." These tubers were supplied by the Indians in exchange for biscuit.[42]

Even in an age when post gardens were often quite elaborate, and canned vegetables were readily available, the diet of many soldiers still leaned heavily on meat and bread. Their meager pay was often expended on liquor in some nearby town or shanty. Much depended on the location of a post and on the degree of care that officers gave to men under their command. But when soldiers were on the march in campaigns against the Indians, even the best officers often could do little to ensure that food was readily available.

---

42. Philippe Régis de Trobriand, *Military Life in Dakota: The Journal of Philippe Régis de Trobriand,* trans. and ed. Lucille M. Kane (St. Paul, Minn.: Alvord Memorial Commission, 1951), 71, 261–63.

CHAPTER 11

Officers' Wives

⁓

Beef is only issued to us once a week and we can't get much more than
20 to 25 pounds. You know that won't last such meat eaters as Doctor
and me a week.

Emily Fitgerald, Sitka, Alaska, 1874

I n the years from the 1850s to the 1890s, American officers and
their wives developed a distinct way of life in military posts scattered from the Mexican border to Alaska. Apart from the Civil
War, when the whole of America was in arms, this was a small
army, and long-serving officers and their wives came to know
each other as they crisscrossed at their various posts. The wives
and children of officers usually went with them unless they were on actual
campaigns. For many, this meant experiencing life in the arid Southwest—
in Texas and in the posts set up on the lands taken from Mexico in 1848.
But army postings were unpredictable, and a family could leave searing
summer heat and spend its next winter on the frigid central plains. The
food was usually better for officers than for their men, but in lonely out-
posts, where there were few extras to be bought, army rations became the
standard fare.

Because of the concentration of posts in the Southwest, many army wives
had the experience of traveling the Santa Fe Trail, and some husbands took
pains to make the journey as comfortable as possible. This was much easier for a colonel or a major than for a second lieutenant. In May 1850, when
Anna Maria Morris, the wife of an army major, went along the trail from
Fort Leavenworth with her husband, other officers, and one hundred re-
cruits, she had her maid, Louisa, with her. Thirteen miles from the fort,
when they made their first stop, the major and his wife invited other officers for a drink. Mrs. Morris was able to provide ice, which they had brought
with them, and one of the officers brought her a glass of champagne.

On the banks of the Delaware River, while some of the officers fished, an army surgeon shot birds that he thought were golden plover. They may well have been. Golden plovers were found in great numbers in the Mississippi valley in the early nineteenth century. Extensive hunting much reduced their number. Louisa boiled some of the plovers for dinner, and Mrs. Morris said the meal "would have been called good anywhere." On the following day the surgeon brought her fish for dinner.

The Morrises continued to live well for the rest of the trek. There was fresh beef from the herd of cattle that accompanied the column, and venison and buffalo meat were provided by the hunters. The Morrises also had "an abundance of milk and cream." On July 4, they were able to toast the day with eggnog. The surgeon had saved eggs for the occasion. Some foods were less abundant. When the adjutant sent her half a loaf of bread, she commented that "it was quiet a treat." She gives no explanation why they were not baking bread routinely as was often done on the trail. After a journey that had been remarkably free of hardship, they reached Santa Fe, which Mrs. Morris thought was "the most miserable squalid looking place I ever beheld."[1]

In the years immediately following the Mexican War, some of the new southwestern posts had few amenities. Ringgold Barracks (later Fort Ringgold) was established on the Rio Grande in 1848. Teresa Viele went there with her officer husband in the early 1850s and remembered it as a depressing experience. There were rows of long, low, whitewashed buildings around a flat drill ground, with no vegetation, not even grass. As in many officer families, the Vieles had a soldier acting as cook, and there was also an African American man as "chambermaid, waiter, and housekeeper." There were no other officer wives, and Mrs. Viele complained that she never saw a woman except "a Mexican peasant or a camp woman."

The food available to the Vieles varied greatly in quality. Sometimes a Mexican or Indian hunter would bring wild turkeys, deer, prairie hens, or other game. At other times, "if a piece of kid, or rabbit, or a few turnips . . . could be obtained, it was looked upon as almost too good fortune to be real." At one time, the quartermaster's stores were reduced to "mouldy flour and rancid pork." They depended on a monthly steamboat for their supplies, and when it failed to arrive they were in very hard straits; even beans became scarce, and butter, milk, bread, and various other items were lacking for weeks at a time.

1. "Journal of Anna Maria (De Camp) Morris," in Holmes, ed., *Covered Wagon Women*, 2:19–42.

Even at best, the food was often covered with red ants, which were nearly impossible to avoid eating. The water was brought from the Rio Grande, strained, and put in a stone jug that was wrapped in wet flannel and hung in the air in an attempt to cool the water for drinking. They also had a mixture of milk taken from cows and goats. Butter was kept in stone jars under the ground with bricks on top, but it was still unpalatably soft and liquid. Mrs. Viele's only consolation was that her African American servant took care with her table. "No matter how forlorn the fare," she wrote, "the silver, glass, and china glistened in immaculate purity."[2]

In July 1854, when recently married, Mrs. Lydia Lane went to Fort Inge, Texas, with her officer husband, she began an experience in southwestern posts that lasted until after the Civil War. On their first assignment, they went by sea to Corpus Christi and lived for a brief time in a tent. Neither Mrs. Lane nor Mike, the Irishman she had as a servant and cook, had much knowledge of cooking. For a time this hardly mattered as they had little more than soldier's rations—"hard tack, fried salt pork, and coffee without milk." When the detachment left for Fort Inge, the women and children traveled in an army "ambulance."

These "ambulances" were usually sprung wagons with canvas top and sides, and special seats, sometimes leather covered. This one only had space to sit straight up, and six or eight times a day the women had to get under the seats for a lunch box for the children. Problems of crowding eased along the way, as some of the officers assigned to other posts left with their wives. Beyond Fort McIntosh, Mrs. Lane had the ambulance to herself. Officers at the various posts sent the Lanes on their way with food, champagne, and books.

During the trek, Mrs. Lane and Mike began to learn how to cook. As the only available bread was hardtack, they made biscuits in their Dutch oven. A big problem was discovering how hot the oven needed to be in order to work properly. After hopelessly burning one batch of biscuits, they gradually began to produce better ones. They ate them with molasses. Each evening, after supper was over, Mrs. Lane made biscuits for the next day; setting the dough on top of a mess chest and pounding it with a long-necked bottle.[3]

Soldiers were often drafted to do the cooking for officers and their fam-

2. Theresa Griffin Viele, "*Following the Drum*": *A Glimpse of Frontier Life*, intro. James M. Day (1858; repr., Austin, Tex.: Steck-Vaughn Co., 1968), 129–40, 243.

3. Lane, *I Married a Soldier*, 16–28; see also Eveline M. Alexander, *Cavalry Wife: The Diary of Eveline M. Alexander, 1866–1867*, ed. Sandra L Myres (College Station: Texas A. & M Press, 1977), 138.

ilies. When Eveline Alexander crossed the plains with her cavalry-officer husband, her first soldier cook was quickly removed when, supposedly by accident, he put two dead polecats in the lunch box. His excuse was that he thought they were young raccoons.[4]

Fort Inge, which had been established in 1849 near the present Uvalde, Texas, on the route from San Antonio to El Paso, turned out to be "dilapidated." The Lanes moved into a four-room house with a kitchen "in an advanced stage of decay" behind it. They had a cooking stove, good china, glass, house linens, and silver they had brought with them. The commissary had coffee, flour, sugar, rice, ham, and pork, but there was little else to buy; canned goods had not yet reached Fort Inge. The nearest stores were in San Antonio. Butter, eggs, and chickens were sometimes brought to the post from ranches in the area, and there was abundant game—deer, turkeys, partridges, and ducks. The stream in the back of the post had "magnificent black bass," and these were easy to catch. The Lanes grew tired of the game and missed beef. In this small garrison, beef was issued only once or twice a month. For guests, usually officers on their way to other posts, the Lanes were able to serve game or fish, but to go with the main dishes there were few choices—beans, hominy, rice, and sometimes macaroni, which they obtained from San Antonio.[5]

In the spring of 1855 Fort Inge was temporarily abandoned, and Mrs. Lane went with her husband to several other Texas posts in rapid succession. She had her first child, and in the summer of 1856 her husband was transferred from Fort Clark, near Brackettville, Texas, to Cantonment Burgwin, nine miles north of Taos, New Mexico. This meant an arduous trek of nearly one thousand miles, which was eased by the gifts of butter, eggs, milk, and other items from officers and their families stationed at posts along their route, but they badly missed fruit and vegetables.

Near the end of August, after nearly two months on the trail, they reached Fort Bliss at El Paso and were delighted to find "delicious peaches and grapes." In twelve days at Fort Bliss, Mrs. Lane preserved peaches at a camp fire, "in the broiling sun," and they took fruit and chickens with them when they left. The chickens were taken in coops tied to the back of the wagons. It was mid-October when they finally reached Cantonment Burgwin. Later, the Lanes were stationed at Fort Bliss for a time. It was Mrs. Lane's favorite southwestern post. In nearby El Paso there was abundant fresh fruit, and stores where "everything imaginable was bought and sold."

4. Alexander, *Cavalry Wife*, 39.
5. Lane, *I Married a Soldier*, 29–32.

In the next dozen years, the Lanes served in a variety of western posts, interspersed with trips to the East. Mrs. Lane became adept at coping with travel on the Santa Fe Trail. In 1857, when she went to visit her family in the East, she traveled in company with another officer and his family in wagons that were empty after bringing supplies to New Mexico. They had discharged soldiers as an escort.

A spring bottom was made for the floor of the wagon in which Mrs. Lane and her baby lived for nearly a month. The discharged soldiers did the cooking. Supper was usually hot biscuits, fried bacon, and buffalo or other game killed by the Mexican teamsters. Buffalo were still abundant along the route, and the teamsters jerked the meat by hanging it in the sun when they camped. On moving they took it down, put it in gunnysacks, stamped on it to make it less bulky, stored it in the wagons, and at the next stop took it out for more treatment by the sun. Mrs. Lane later wrote, "to me it is horrible."[6]

In 1860, when the Lanes returned from leave in the East, it was midsummer and the heat was intense. Along the trail reveille was usually at 2:00 A.M., and by 3:00 A.M. breakfast was over and they were on their way. Cooking was carried out on a small camp stove of sheet-iron, designed to use very little wood. It had four holes on the top for pots and pans, and behind the fire there was a small oven for baking bread and roasting meat. As they got farther into the plains, water became a problem. Often, they had to take it from a standing pool, "hardly fit for horses or mules." They carried several kegs and a two-gallon canteen to fill up with water when they found a good supply. To try to keep it cool the canteen was covered with wet felt or a piece of blanket and hung in any breeze.[7]

During the Civil War, Colonel Lane was chief mustering officer in Pennsylvania, but when the war ended and the Lanes returned to the Southwest, Mrs. Lane traveled the Santa Fe Trail for the fifth time. Six new army brides in the party began the trek "in dainty costumes far more suitable for 5th Avenue than camp and a hot, dusty ride in the broiling sun day after day." They had trouble getting in and out of the ambulances in the hoops that were then so fashionable. Mrs. Lane was ready for the trek in a calico frock, no hoops, and a sunbonnet. Some of the other wives soon followed her example.

Women dressed in the voluminous outfits of the 1860s and 1870s often found the heat of the plains and the Southwest intolerable. In July 1866,

6. Ibid., 37–59.
7. Ibid., 64–72, 82–90.

when Eveline Alexander was on the march with her cavalry officer husband from Fort Smith, Arkansas, to Fort Union in New Mexico she finally found it too hot to wear her dress. She sat in the "ambulance" in "a white wrapper."[8]

The detachment that Colonel Lane commanded did everything possible to avoid the heat. He began each day's march in the middle of the night to take advantage of marching with no sun. The new brides in the party had trouble eating at that time and made do with a cup of coffee. The Lanes had no such problem. They ate breakfast by candlelight while their cook (a woman they had brought with them) baked pans of biscuits and fried ample bacon and any fresh game they had. This was saved for later in a large tin box, sometimes with a huge pie made with dried apples. They also took a canteen of tea, with the canteen kept wet outside to keep the tea cool. At 7:00 A.M. or 8:00 A.M. they opened the box and had their lunch. Later in the century, when she wrote her memoirs, Mrs. Lane mentioned that she had recently come across "the battered tin box" they had used to carry their lunch on the march.[9]

The experiences of those who established new posts differed widely. In the spring of 1865, Marian Russell went to join her husband at Camp Nicholls, about one hundred and thirty miles east of Fort Union. It was a temporary camp set up to protect pioneers, and there were some three hundred soldiers quartered in tents. Mrs. Russell lived with her husband in a dugout with a dirt floor and an army blanket as a door. A soldier was assigned as their cook. There was no stove, so he cooked their meals outside in a Dutch oven, carrying water from the river.

For the most part, the meals were monotonous—"hard tack, beans, coffee, venison, or beef," but the soldier-cook managed to produce "savory stews." The detachment had brought a beef herd with them, and hunters killed deer and antelope. When freight wagons arrived from Fort Union, Lieutenant Russell bought forty-two dollars' worth of groceries. It did not buy much (a can of peaches was two dollars), and they ate all of it within ten days.[10]

Later in 1865, when the Russells moved to Fort Bascom on the Canadian River in southeastern New Mexico, they found that they could buy supplies from a man operating a store just outside the confines of the fort. They also had milk, as they owned the only cow in the fort. In summer they kept the milk pans cool by placing them in the unused fireplace; the draft

8. Alexander, *Cavalry Wife*, 68.
9. Lane, *I Married a Soldier*, 130–32.
10. Russell, *Land of Enchantment*, 101–5.

passing up the tall chimney made it the coolest place in the house, but putting the pans there created other problems. One day Mrs. Russell heard rustling in the fireplace and found that two large snakes had been attracted by the milk. Potatoes at the fort were often of the dried variety, which looked "a great deal like brown sugar." They made potato cakes by pouring a cup of boiling water over a cup of the dried potatoes and then forming patties from the mixture and frying them. Unsurprisingly, they were "not very good."[11]

Occasionally, even in temporary quarters, good food could be produced for a special occasion. In September 1866, Eveline Alexander went with her husband from Fort Union to the Cuchara River because there were plans to build a post there. These were later abandoned. In the temporary camp, the Alexanders lived in a large hospital tent and entertained a visiting general with an elaborate dinner. It began with beef vegetable soup, followed by saddle of mutton with jelly, green peas, squash, cabbage, and beets, and finished with soft custard, blancmange with cream, sugar, and coffee.[12]

The best known of the army wives who described life on the central and northern plains was Elizabeth Custer, whose husband, George, achieved permanent fame when he was killed at the battle of the Little Big Horn. In *Following the Guidon,* Mrs. Custer wrote about life in Kansas and Indian Territory in the late 1860s. When Custer was not leading a raid against Indian villages, the Custers' food was abundant but somewhat monotonous. Except for the time in the spring and summer of 1869, when they were in buffalo country, their meat was usually beef, which was issued once a day. Often the meat was cooked at breakfast by Eliza, their African American cook, and they ate it for the rest of the day. If guests arrived, and there was not enough left, they usually borrowed from others or, as a last resort, went to the commissary for "inexpressibly salty and dry" ham or bacon. To flavor the beef, Eliza made tomato catsup out of the canned tomatoes that were always available in the commissary. They could not regularly vary the beef with game because there were often hostile Indians in the vicinity. Butter, eggs, and cream were available, but Mrs. Custer explained that they often did not have cakes or pastries because they had become used to living without delicacies.[13]

In the spring and summer of 1869, near Fort Hays in Kansas, there were great herds of buffalo all around them, and they enjoyed constant buffalo meat, particularly tongues and rump steaks, as a change from their usual

---

11. Ibid., 108–13.
12. Alexander, *Cavalry Wife,* 84–96.
13. Custer, *Following the Guidon,* 233–34, 238–39, 241.

fare. If possible, they flavored the game with a jelly made from buf-faloberries. These berries were common in the area. Antelope, elk, and wild turkey were also available, and Eliza kept chickens. George Custer, always willing to take a gamble, tried rattlesnake after a scout told him the meat was "fine, juicy, and white." Custer agreed. He thought the meat was "as white and delicate as that of a young quail." They rarely had small game, except a few ducks that came to the pools formed by heavy rains in the fall. When he was not on the march, George Custer "was almost incon-solable" without soup. It was usually oxtail.[14]

Mrs. Custer also wrote of the Dakotas in the 1870s, in the years before her husband was killed at the Little Big Horn. On the march of the Sev-enth Cavalry from Yankton to Bismarck, a wagon carried their small stove, made of sheet iron, their kitchen utensils, and a mess chest with their dishes. In the evening, when the weather was bad, they put their stove in a kitchen tent, with a pipe to carry the smoke through a hole in the can-vas. They generally rose before 4:00 A.M., had a quick breakfast, and stopped for lunch when they watered the horses. Their usual fare was beef and biscuits, while the men had salt pork. Cattle were driven with them and killed every other day. They were able to vary the beef with numerous plover they saw while on the march. Soldiers brought in sacks of them to be broiled over the hot coals. On a rest day, they fished—soldiers and Gen-eral Custer alike.[15]

At Fort Sully, which had been built in what is now South Dakota in 1863, their life was temporarily more comfortable. The fort was on the Missouri some twenty-five miles above the present city of Pierre, and, when the Custers were there, it was the headquarters of an infantry regi-ment. The men had company gardens and kept cows, pigs, and chickens. There was still ample game in the Dakotas, and the Custers were invited to a lunch in which there were nine varieties on the table: antelope, buf-falo tongues, wild turkey, elk, black-tailed deer, plover, duck, wild goose, and beaver tail. Mrs. Custer thought the beaver tail was "like pork," but so fat she merely tasted it. The duck was served with a jelly made from wild berries. They also had ham, cured at the garrison, "homemade bread," and dessert made with cream, fresh butter, and eggs.[16]

After they reached Fort Rice, on the Missouri River in North Dakota, the Seventh Cavalry was assigned to guard the surveyors for the Northern Pacific Railroad from Bismarck to the Yellowstone River, and Elizabeth

14. Ibid., 116–20, 212–19, 305.
15. Custer, "*Boots and Saddles*," 26–28, 38–39, 55, 63–64.
16. Ibid., 53–55.

Custer had to return home to Michigan. In June, General Custer set out west from Fort Rice. He wrote to his wife that game was abundant and antelope was plentiful in the mess. He reached the Yellowstone in mid-July and spent the rest of the summer in that region, doing a great deal of hunting and eating much game. He shot antelope, deer, buffalo, elks, wolves, a fox, geese, ducks, prairie chickens, and sage hens "without number." In September, when a steamboat arrived, he ate on board and had his first potatoes and cucumbers for many months. The greatest luxury, however, were the raw onions given to him by the captain. He told Elizabeth that he had "supped on RAW ONIONS."[17]

In the fall of 1873, Elizabeth traveled from Michigan to Fort Abraham Lincoln on the Missouri River near Bismarck. This was where her husband was based in the following years. It was to be their last home together. The post was reasonably well fitted out with a sutler's store as well as the commissary. Hopes for vegetables were dashed in their first summer of 1874 when the garden they had planted in the corner of their yard, together with all the company gardens down by the river, were totally ruined by great swarms of grasshoppers. Fortunately, however, canned vegetables were now readily available. Fresh eggs were considered a great luxury, but the Custers were able to make use of "crystallized eggs" put up in airtight cans. These were dried eggs with the yolks and whites mixed together. In winter, their beef was supplemented with game, but in summer this was usually unavailable as, in this time of trouble with the Sioux, it was considered too dangerous to hunt. Within two years, General Custer was dead, and Mrs. Custer's army life was over.[18]

While most of the new forts in the second half of the century were established in the areas conquered from Mexico, or to protect trails to the mines, the American army continued to build and garrison posts along the Missouri. In 1867, Frenchman Philippe Régis de Trobriand, a Civil War Union veteran, was sent to command the new post of Fort Stevenson on the Missouri River in what is now North Dakota. He was also responsible for two other North Dakota posts—Fort Totten and Fort Berthold. In August, when Trobriand arrived, Fort Stevenson was still under construction, and officers and their wives were in temporary dwellings made of planks, referred to as "tents." The officers with wives ate with their families, the other officers all messed together, except for Trobriand, who ate with the major serving as quartermaster for the district.

17. Ibid., 225–58.
18. Ibid., 75–84, 139–41; Calhoun, *With Custer in '74*, 4.

In the first winter, the men at Fort Stevenson, who lived mainly on beef and bread, suffered badly from scurvy, but the food for Trobriand and the officers was significantly better. It had been arranged for Fort Stevenson and Trobriand's other two posts to have their own cattle, and early in October a herd was driven in from Minnesota. There was fresh beef once or twice a week, salt pork, ham, and wild game, kidney beans, tomatoes, "and other canned vegetables," as well as preserves and conserves. Many of the officers' families also had cows and chickens, and they were able to buy vegetables and corn from Arikara and Grosventres Indians.[19]

Early in September, when a boat arrived with supplies from St. Louis, officers from the fort went on board to buy potatoes, onions, and wines. The wine, said Frenchman Trobriand, was of "bad quality." Steamboat navigation on the upper Missouri often ended in early September because of low water, but this year the boats continued to come up the river for the next two months.[20]

One feature of this assignment that delighted Trobriand was the abundance of game birds. Waterfowl crowded the waters near the fort. At first hunting was very easy. There were numerous ducks, and by the middle of September officers were also killing geese. At the end of the month, Trobriand saw more wild geese than he had ever seen before. Without the waterfowl, he said, they would have had a steady diet of nothing but beef and ham.[21]

As the creeks began to freeze, the waterfowl began to leave. In frustration, after one unsuccessful hunt, Trobriand killed over twenty of the small blackbirds—about the size of thrushes or robins—that had come in swarms after the waterfowl left. Trobriand had them roasted. In December and January, the winter became very harsh, and on the day after Christmas, Trobriand was happy to move into his new quarters—a seven-room log cabin with all the rooms on the same floor—but it was not properly caulked.

On January 6, in a raging blizzard, snow came in everywhere. At breakfast the kitchen "resembled a miniature opera setting." Amid whirls of snow and long icicles hanging from the roof, the cook cooked Trobriand a beefsteak for breakfast. Trobriand was kept in the kitchen all day by a bank of snow blocking the door. For dinner, he was given another beefsteak, with coffee and a slice of peach pie. On the following days, fried ham and "codfish" replaced the beefsteak. Codfish was certainly uncommon on

19. Trobriand, *Military Life*, 40–50, 71, 120–21.
20. Ibid., 58–59, 75, 118, 149–51.
21. Ibid., 49, 76, 119–20.

western army posts, but it is likely that the commissariat had bought salt cod from a merchant who had imported it from the East Coast. Salt fish was a basic part of the ration at Fort Stevenson in this first winter. In the bitter cold and snow they had trouble keeping the cattle alive, and the cow that furnished milk for Trobriand was put into the adjutant's old office.[22]

In February, Trobriand described his daily eating routine: breakfast at 9:00 A.M., a ten-minute lunch, and dinner at 6:00 P.M. At dinner he usually had soup, a piece of beef or rabbit, canned vegetables, and a slice of pie. There were no fresh vegetables, fruit, or eggs. Rabbit was possible because there was a great number of white rabbits in the vicinity of the fort. These were white-tailed jackrabbits, which turned white in the winter.

When an Indian chief visited in March, he was given "thick corncakes, three or four slices of bread and molasses." The "corncakes" were probably plain johnnycakes made from a dough of unleavened cornmeal and water, cooked on a griddle.

By late March, Trobriand was eating much better. The first flocks of geese and ducks had returned from the South, and prairie chickens were again becoming abundant. At the end of the month, Trobriand dined on fresh buffalo tongues and a beaver tail flavored with wild onions. He boasted that these were "table delicacies that an Epicurean could not get in Paris even for gold."[23]

In mid-April, a supply of fresh fish was sent from Fort Totten at Devil's Lake, and later in the month the officers were able to buy a few expensive luxuries—butter, eggs, potatoes, and apples—from their first steamboats of the year. The captain of one of the boats also gave Trobriand champagne. In the following months, waterfowl were present in great numbers, and the men planted a post garden in an attempt to solve the problem of scurvy. In July, it was endangered by swarms of grasshoppers, but, fortunately, most of them were swept away in a storm. The chickens gorged on those that landed, and only the onions were seriously damaged.[24]

One of Trobriand's posts—Fort Totten—became a source of concern because of the amount of drinking and a resulting "deplorable lack of discipline." The commandant, Trobriand asserted, was a drunkard, along with two of the other four officers at the post. One night the soldiers broke into the commandant's tent and stole five or six gallons of whiskey. In the morning nearly all the men in the company were drunk. In the summer of

22. Ibid., 207, 217.
23. Ibid., 233, 237, 249, 252, 256, 258.
24. Ibid., 271–315.

1868, after a new commander was sent to the post, several officers at Fort Totten were court-martialed for drunkenness, with Trobriand presiding. The commander of Fort Buford, a lieutenant colonel who went with Trobriand to take part in the trial, also became drunk while there and on the return journey. Trobriand put him under arrest and commented that this type of incident was "too characteristic," especially among regular officers of the old army. Later that year Trobriand heard from Fort Buford that the commander was continually drunk and almost never left his room or his bed.[25]

Excessive drinking was not confined to the old guard. In November 1868, when one of his lieutenants died at the age of twenty-three, Trobriand said that he was "a victim of whiskey." Trobriand had ordered that no officer could buy liquor from the traders without his signed permission but had often given his signature for this lieutenant to obtain a gallon of whiskey. He left a young widow and two children. That year, during the Christmas and New Year celebrations, another "completely drunk" lieutenant threatened one of his superiors with a revolver.[26]

Army personnel had experienced life along the Missouri for much of the century, but the purchase of Alaska from Russia in 1867 opened up a new area for military postings. In 1874, Emily Fitzgerald's husband was sent as post surgeon to Sitka. The pregnant Mrs. Fitzgerald and her husband went from New York to Alaska with their infant daughter and their African American maid. It took from May to August to make the trip. They went by ship from New York to Panama, across the isthmus by rail, by ship to Portland, Oregon, and finally by another ship from Portland to Sitka. On this last leg of the journey they took a cow with them.

Emily's first impression was that while the bay and surroundings at Sitka were beautiful, Sitka was "a dirty little town . . . full of Russians." It was cool when they arrived, but they were pleasantly surprised that the climate was not a problem. In February 1875 Emily referred to "the continuous warm." The post was in the town, and there was a village of Inuits close by. The Inuits came to their back door every day selling venison, birds, fish, and berries. The Fitzgeralds hired an African American cook who had been employed by the previous surgeon. Their quarters had "a sweet little dining room" with silver on the surrounding shelves and a kitchen with a wood-burning stove. Emily sent cakes to be baked by the post baker.[27]

25. Ibid., 67–68, 319, 326–29, 333–34, 349, 352.
26. Ibid., 349, 357.
27. Emily M. Fitzgerald, *An Army Doctor's Wife on the Frontier: Letters from Alaska and the Far West, 1874–1878*, ed. Abe Laufe (Pittsburgh: University of Pittsburgh Press, 1962), 25–52.

There were severe limitations to the food that could be obtained at the Sitka post. For most of its supplies it depended on what was supposed to be a monthly boat from Portland, and they lacked both vegetables and fruit. Meat was not in short supply, but this was an age of great meat eaters. Emily complained that the post only issued beef once a week, and they could not get much more than twenty to twenty-five pounds! That she said would not last "such meat eaters as Doctor and me a week."

The beef ration was supplemented with game bought at the market. There was ample venison—a hind quarter was only fifty cents—but Emily was not fond of game. When they had a roast of venison for dinner, her comment was "I hate venison." They often ate ducks and grouse and bought a snipe from an Indian woman for a bar of soap, but the one item of game praised by Emily was a pheasant. She thought that it was as good as chicken. Fish were abundant for part of the year, but in her first months in Sitka it was not the fish season. By mid-December there was plenty of both fish and game.[28]

Fruit was very difficult to obtain. It had to be brought from Portland on the monthly boat, and in some months the boat did not arrive. Locally, all that was available were salmonberries picked by the Indians. Emily thought they resembled raspberries and blackberries but found them not quite as sweet or good as either.

In their first months in Sitka, Emily's husband made special efforts to obtain fruit for her as she was in her last months of pregnancy. He sent for boxes of apples and a box of pears, and, when the boat arrived, he bought a box of plums from the steward. Emily may also have brought some dried fruit with her as she made fruitcakes, which were among the cakes she sent to the post baker for baking. In October, a friend sent apples, fresh tomatoes, and a box of candy for her daughter. This was just a few days before she gave birth to a son. The birth must have been a difficult one, because in mid-November Doctor Fitzgerald wrote to Emily's mother to say that she had been very ill but was now well on the way to recovery. Her milk for the baby had returned "in abundance."[29]

The boat failed to arrive in November, and by mid-December there had been no potatoes in Sitka for the past two weeks. The commissary tried to keep a six-month store of supplies on hand, but there was no cornmeal and the flour was running low. Fortunately, the steamer arrived just before Christmas and came again in January. The January boat brought the

28. Ibid., 61–62, 73.
29. Ibid., 51, 60–61, 65–66, 148.

Fitzgeralds a cow. The one they had brought with them from Portland had stopped giving milk as soon as it arrived, and they had been obliged to buy "pale blue milk" at twenty cents a quart. They decided to send for another cow. It had cost eighty-five dollars in gold, but there was now plenty of milk and cream.

The household was fond of candy, and Emily regularly made her husband chocolate caramels. Other treats were few and far between, although the officers' families occasionally entertained back and forth. On New Year's morning, Emily had others from the garrison over for fruitcake and eggnog, and in March entertained them one evening with fruitcake, sponge cake, coffee with real cream, and candy. On July Fourth, the Fitzgeralds were invited by another family to play poker and eat ice cream.[30]

One problem with the meals in Sitka stemmed from the difficulty in obtaining help. The cook, who lived out, was always late in arriving to make breakfast. Emily was up at 6:30 A.M. with her children. Breakfast sometimes did not appear until 9:00 A.M. On March 24 when this happened, her husband made her an early-morning brandy punch to tide her over. Early in April, they fired the cook, giving the cooking to their young maid, Mary. She cooked meats "nicely," and in the Fitzgerald family that was one of the main things that mattered. Even their infant daughter would not touch milk or other appropriate infant food. Apparently, she preferred meat and potatoes. Mary's general cooking skills were meager, so Emily was soon complaining again.[31]

In the fall of 1875, Emily felt ill for a month and suffered a miscarriage. At this time her husband bought her a case of "Blood's Stout." Stout was a beer that was looked upon as nourishing and was often recommended for nursing mothers. Emily was still nursing her boy, who had been born a year before, but she stopped a week after the miscarriage. After recovering from the initial shock, Emily admitted to her mother that she was "thankful" she was not having another child, because she thought she was capable of supplying the family with enough babies: "I don't believe there is a safe day in the month for me." She said that she and two other wives had "meetings of horror" on the subject.[32]

The weeks leading up to Christmas 1875 were bleak. From October, two or three feet of snow were on the ground, and by mid-December daylight lasted only from about 10:00 A.M. to 3:00 P.M. This year, special food for the holiday presented a problem as the November boat came in too late

30. Ibid., 71, 73, 85–86, 105, 112, 143–44.
31. Ibid., 42, 111, 114, 118–19, 132.
32. Ibid., 160, 165.

for them to order anything from Portland. Fortunately a friend had sent candy for their daughter, and they had a Christmas tree. Emily lit candles on it on Christmas Eve. They had other members of the garrison over for cake while the children had a tea party under the tree (presumably keeping well away from the candles).[33]

That winter it was discovered that the hospital steward at the post had used up all the hospital's liquor, including brandy and whiskey. He was arrested, but before he could be tried he shot himself. At Sitka the usual army fondness for drink was further encouraged by loneliness, long dark nights, and snow.[34]

In March 1876, Emily tried a dish she had never tasted before—clam chowder. When the tide was out, the locals went to the beach to dig for clams. They could be bought cheaply, but Emily and her family went on their own clam-digging expedition. She found a recipe for clam chowder in a cookbook sent by her mother. Her husband was delighted with it, but Emily said "there was rather too much of a mixture for me."[35]

In the spring of 1876, Emily returned to a more typical army situation when her husband was transferred to Fort Lapwai in Idaho Territory. In April, they sailed for Portland. While in a hotel there, Emily wrote to her mother asking her to send the old blue China that she "fell heir to." She particularly wanted the four or five plates with Chinese figures on them to serve fruit and bread because "army people are great on nice tables. No matter how plainly they furnish their houses, you almost always find their tables stylish and well-provided for."[36]

Fort Lapwai was on the recently created Nez Percé reservation, near to the Clearwater River and modern Lewiston, Idaho. By June 1876, the Fitzgeralds were settled there. Emily found it to be "a pleasant post, as far-away posts go" but quiet and lonely. One of her first reactions was amazement that the three other officers' wives there had no children. In Sitka, she and her intimate friends had spent their time wondering how to prevent any more babies. "Now," she wrote, I am "among these people who would give their heads to have a baby and are just as busily engaged trying all sorts of means so as to have one."[37]

Finding a cook at Fort Lapwai was a major problem because of the attraction of the mines. Mary had been let go, and for a time they tried a sol-

33. Ibid., 168, 170–71.
34. Ibid., 175.
35. Ibid., 178.
36. Ibid., 186–90.
37. Ibid., 198.

dier. He did not suit them as a cook and was soon sent to other duties. For a brief time, Emily did her own cooking. All but one of the officers at the fort had Chinese help, and her husband went into Lewiston and hired a Chinese cook. The cook stayed for four months before he left for the mines, leaving Emily and her maid, Jennie, to cook. In these first months at Fort Lapwai, the Fitzgeralds had some respite from the heavy meat diet of Sitka. They were able to get salmon, which the Chinese cook served baked and stuffed, and vegetables were more readily available. Early in November Emily made pumpkin pies. They also enjoyed wild mushrooms, having them on toast for dinner.

Emily was particularly impressed by the cooking skills of Mrs. Perry, the wife of the colonel at the post, whose kitchen was next to Emily's. Mrs. Perry dressed her food with elaborate sauces—"Oysters, drawn butter, and such things are scattered about in a delicious manner." Her dinners were famous among army people throughout the region. Emily thought Mrs. Perry's example helped her do a better job of stuffing the prairie chickens her husband shot.[38]

Winter at Fort Lapwai was much colder than in Sitka, and the inhabitants tried to liven the winter months by occasional entertaining. The Fitzgeralds ate their Christmas dinner at the Indian agency, having traveled there in a sleigh. At home, they filled the children's Christmas stockings with a trumpet, a little china doll, bells, an apple, a little cake, and two or three pieces of candy ("all their papa would allow them to have").

After Christmas, the Fitzgeralds planned a whist party for the officers and wives of the garrison. The occasion nearly went awry when their maid, Jennie, went on a whiskey spree. This happened from time to time. Her drinking began the night before and went on into the day of the party. Fortunately the food had been prepared the day before, but on the day itself, after Jennie burned three pounds of coffee while roasting it on the stove, Dr. Fitzgerald sent her to bed. This was at 4:00 P.M. Before the guests arrived, Emily, who had been setting out the food prepared on the previous day, also gave up and went to bed. Before she retired, she had laid out "a nice little lunch," with baked ham, cold roast chicken, chicken salad, buttered biscuit, and three kinds of cake. Left to manage alone, the doctor coped ably, making "the best coffee they had ever had."[39]

In the following summer, the usual round of activities at Fort Lapwai changed dramatically. The Nez Percé Indians were suffering from white

38. Ibid., 200–203, 208, 210, 215, 218.
39. Ibid., 228–30, 232.

encroachments on their lands and began to attack white settlers. Colonel Perry took a force of about one hundred against them. Fortunately for Emily, her husband was elsewhere when they marched, for at the end of the engagement about half of the force was either dead or missing. In the following days, as more troops arrived, the post was in turmoil with the parade ground full of horses. Porches were piled high with trunks and blankets. Emily entertained the officers—on one day she had eight for lunch and seven for dinner—but her army life was nearing its end. In November she went with her husband to his new assignment as post surgeon at Fort Boise, but in January 1879, while on leave in the East, he became ill. He died later that year. Emily lived until 1912.[40]

In 1874, the year that young Emily Fitzgerald began her epic journey from New York to Sitka, the newly married Martha Summerhayes left New York with her officer husband to begin her army life at Fort Russell, at Cheyenne in Wyoming Territory. She knew little about cooking. One of her few skills, she wrote, was that like all New England girls of the period, she knew how to make "quince jelley and floating islands." It seemed unlikely that she would have too many opportunities to make these islands of beaten mounds of egg white, poached in milk and floated in a custard sauce.[41]

The stay at Fort Russell was a short one. In June 1874 the regiment was ordered to Arizona. She was to spend much of the next dozen years in army posts in Arizona. She was to find that even in the last decades of the nineteenth century, life in southwestern army posts could still be very difficult. Martha and her husband went by the Union Pacific Railroad to San Francisco and by ship to the mouth of the Colorado River. It was so hot in the cabins that the butter ran like oil. They slept on deck. Ice ran low, and the meat began to turn. Martha was reduced to eating the only things she could keep down—black coffee, bread, and a baked sweet potato. Fortunately, when they anchored off Mazatlán, they were able to buy coconuts, limes, and bananas from boats that came alongside.

After laying at anchor off Port Isabel at the mouth of the Colorado for several days, where they were able to give some variety to their food by catching fish, they went by boat up the Colorado to Fort Yuma. There, one of the lieutenants invited them to breakfast, and, after over three weeks of continuous heat and stale food, Martha delighted in the "oatmeal with fresh milk, the eggs and butter, and delicious tomatoes, which were served to us

40. Ibid., 261–62, 351–52.
41. Summerhayes, *Vanished Arizona*, 20–32; Sharon Tyler Herbst, ed., *The New Food Lover's Companion* 3d. ed. (Hauppauge, N. Y.: Barron's Educational Series, 2001), 239.

in his latticed dining-room." Food at Fort Yuma had obviously improved since its early days; many supplies arrived from San Francisco by steamer.[42]

From Fort Yuma, the Summerhayeses continued up the Colorado by steamer. It was now even hotter, and on one day it reached 122° in the shade. There was neither ice nor fresh provisions, and the dining room was so hot that the knife handles were uncomfortable to touch. The heat did not prevent them from eating salt-boiled beef, canned vegetables, biscuit, and pies made from preserved peaches or plums. At night, the officers and their wives slept on mattresses on the deck.

On September 8, they landed at Camp Mohave and after two days set out for their new post—distant Camp Apache on the White Mountain River. Martha rode in an army "ambulance," which had two seats facing each other, a seat outside for the driver, and canvas sides that could be raised or lowered. The mess chest was packed with provisions bought at the commissary. The troops marched ahead of the wagons.

On the march, the Summerhayeses slept in a tent, and their meals were cooked by a soldier. For breakfast at 4:00 A.M. they had black coffee, thick slices of bacon, and dry bread, and supper was usually bacon, coffee, and biscuits baked in a Dutch oven. As they marched through the lonely country they passed isolated ranches. At one ranch they had "delicious quail" and milk with their supper; at another a peach pie. After one of the lieutenants shot an antelope, their tent was pitched under tall pines, the tent flaps tied back, and they sat at a candlelit table to eat broiled antelope steak with hot biscuits and black coffee. There was ample fresh meat, as deer and wild turkeys were readily available, so they were in good spirits when they finally reached Camp Apache.[43]

Although the officers lived in log cabins, Martha thought Camp Apache was "picturesque and attractive." It had some unusual features. Soon after they arrived, Martha mentioned finding an officer's wife playing tennis, her baby carriage sitting near the court. If Martha had not confused her dates, this must have been one of the first tennis courts in the country. The game had been invented in England in the previous year. The Summerhayeses were given half a log cabin—one room, a small hall, and a detached shed for a kitchen. They had lost their barrel of china when a wagon rolled down the side of a mountain, but Martha was able to buy some china from a woman who was leaving the post. A stove and some other kitchen items were sent over from the quartermaster's stores.

42. Summerhayes, *Vanished Arizona*, 32–47.
43. Ibid., 48–88.

At this camp, the officers bought their meat directly from the contractor. There were cows, and the Summerhayeses received about a pint of milk each night. A soldier continued to cook for them, and he turned out to be quite good. Martha also did some of her own cooking. At one dinner party she used a can of Baltimore oysters to make oyster patties. Served after the soup, it brought gasps of surprise from one cavalry officer. Their food at Camp Apache also included "excellent wild turkeys," and "good Southdown mutton."[44]

In the spring of 1875, Martha's husband accepted an unusual assignment—to be the only officer stationed at Ehrenberg, a tiny Mexican town on the Colorado, about ninety miles upriver from Fort Yuma. It was an important stopping place for the trans-shipment of freight into the interior. They had stopped there on the journey up the Colorado, and Martha had described it as "a row of low thatched hovels" with a store and "some mean-looking huts of adobe." For meat on their trek to Ehrenberg, they took two sheep, and they also killed wild turkeys as they traveled. To celebrate after they passed through a dangerous pass, Mrs. Bailey, the tennis-playing wife from Camp Apache, produced a bottle of champagne that had been kept as cool as possible in a wet blanket. They drank it from mess cups.[45]

They arrived at Ehrenberg in mid-May. There was one street along the river and a few cross streets leading back into the desert. Their home— the government house—was a one-story adobe building that formed two sides of a square. A wall and a government freight house completed the enclosure, and there was a chicken coop in the corner. The floors, like the walls, were adobe. Their kitchen had no windows—merely openings to let in air and light. At night, they put their beds in the courtyard.

Ehrenberg, Martha decided, was "no fit place for a woman." The other women in the town were Mexicans or Indians. Martha described the various Mexican foods—tortillas, *frijoles,* chili verde, and chili colorado— eaten in the town but said that she kept up her table "in American fashion," and ate American food whenever possible. In reality, they often ate Mexican food. Cooking was carried out by a series of soldiers sent from Fort Yuma and by a Mexican woman as well as an Indian man, who also brought water from the river and did other chores.

There was no market in the town, but there were two large stores. Occasionally a Mexican inhabitant killed a steer, and Martha bought enough

44. Ibid., 88–115.
45. Ibid., 53–55, 117–47.

meat for one meal. With intense heat and no ice, there was no way of keeping meat fresh for any length of time. They also bought beef jerky, which their Mexican servant usually pounded and cooked with green or red peppers. In the following winter, their problems with fresh meat were eased when many ducks flew in.

From the quartermaster, who had a small quantity of stores, they obtained flour, canned items, and jam, and they had a few eggs from their own chickens. Often they were without milk. When the river was low, the cows sometimes wandered across the sandbars to graze and could not get back again. In the hottest months there was no butter. Their water—which looked like "melted chocolate"—was brought from the river every morning and put in barrels to settle. On one very hot day they checked the temperature of their drinking water—it was 86°.[46]

From time to time, they were visited by officers and wives on their way to other forts, and on such occasions they tried to serve the best they could provide. A party of staff officers and their wives traveling to Fort Whipple were given a supper of cold ham, chicken, fresh biscuit, wine, milk, preserves from a tin, and coffee, all served on fresh table linen and with good silver.[47]

For a short time the Summerhayeses were able to replace their soldier cook with a young woman from the North. She had traveled to the Southwest because of her persistent cough. Their household was also increased by Martha's sister and her young son, a boy in "delicate" health who was also brought south in the hope of a cure. The young northerner did not stay long, and when she moved on, the Summerhayeses struggled with the cooking until another soldier could be sent from Fort Yuma.[48]

Unable to stand the thought of another summer in Ehrenberg, Martha went back East for eight months. In November 1876, she returned to the Southwest. Her husband had been transferred from Ehrenberg to Camp MacDowell on the Verde River. Martha had once thought of Camp MacDowell as a dismal, isolated post, but after Ehrenberg it had a new attractiveness. There were two companies of soldiers there—one of infantry and one of cavalry—and, unlike Ehrenberg, it had other officers and their wives. The officers' quarters were of adobe, with separate kitchens, and a wire-covered safe hanging outside. During the winter months, fresh meat was readily available—roasts of beef, haunches of venison, and ducks. Martha again depended on soldier-cooks. When intense heat returned in

46. Ibid., 147–60, 163; Biddle, *Reminiscences of a Soldier's Wife*, 150–51.
47. Summerhayes, *Vanished Arizona*, 161–62, 170.
48. Ibid., 172–83, 185–91.

the late spring of 1877, they moved their beds outside but were overrun with ants until they placed the beds' legs in cans of water. That summer much of their food came from cans.[49]

Martha was to spend many more years in army forts, mostly in the Southwest, but never again was life to be so hard, fresh food so scarce, and heat so difficult to avoid as it had been at Ehrenberg. In 1886, when Martha arrived at Tucson by rail, she was served iced cantaloupe at the railroad restaurant. Ice had been unobtainable when they had been there a dozen years before. At Fort Lowell, near Tucson, it was still hot, but there was now ice, various summer drinks, and lemons.[50]

In the last decades of the nineteenth century, conditions at most army posts improved considerably for officers and their families, but occasionally even a colonel's wife had assignments that recalled earlier days. In the early 1870s, Ellen Biddle was stationed with her husband and children at Benham, Texas. The troops were in tents about a mile from the town, and the colonel rented half a house, furnished. At first the Biddles had a maid but no cook. For several days the colonel got up, made the fire, and put on a kettle of water while Ellen fried bacon and boiled eggs. As she was dissatisfied with the bread that was provided, she also began to bake her own. She continued doing this even after they got a cook. She was better off than the rest of the officer's wives. They were living in tents because house rents were so expensive.[51]

In the course of the 1870s, Colonel Biddle was frequently reassigned, and most of Ellen's memories of these years were quite happy ones. At Fort Halleck in Nevada, they had adobe quarters with a separate kitchen and a Chinese cook. They were living in the foothills of the Humboldt Mountains, with ample game nearby and a clear mountain stream alongside their quarters. Her husband was often able to catch trout for their breakfast. He also shot ducks, grouse, quail, prairie chickens, and sage hens for their larder.[52]

In the mid-1870s, Colonel Biddle was transferred to Fort Whipple as inspector general of the department of Arizona. The Biddles traveled from San Francisco by steamer to the mouth of the Colorado, where they were transferred to a smaller vessel. At the mouth of the river, men were spearing huge "jewfish" (large groupers). Some were three hundred pounds each. The Biddles took a large quantity with them, cut up and packed in ice.

49. Ibid., 209–22.
50. Ibid., 250–51.
51. Biddle, *Reminiscences,* 64–65.
52. Ibid., 80–82.

Mrs. Biddle said the fish tasted very much like black bass. They went by way of Fort Yuma to Ehrenberg, the trans-shipment point where Martha Summerhayes was living in isolation with her lieutenant husband. The Biddles received "a very good dinner." This was presumably the dinner of cold ham, chicken, fresh biscuit, milk, preserves from a tin, coffee, and wine, served on fresh table linen with good silver that Martha Summerhayes remembered serving to staff officers on their way to Fort Whipple.

From Ehrenberg, the Biddles went overland for seven days through desert country. Mrs. Biddle was in an army ambulance in "intense" heat, traveling across what she called a "desert," but she also made the strange statement that the "out-door life was delightful." She had a female cook, a "fine mess chest," and a Dutch oven for baking bread and biscuit. Colonel Biddle shot enough game not only for themselves, but also for the escort and the teamsters. The Biddles' cook broiled the meat on "an arrangement made of wire."[53]

When they arrived at Fort Whipple, the officers greeted the colonel and his wife with champagne. Mrs. Biddle described it as "a very gay post," with some kind of entertainment—dinners, dances, play rehearsals—almost every day. The quarters for the ordinary officers were "poor and unattractive," but those for the staff officers were much better. This was just as well as the Biddles were to be there for five and a half years. During that time Mrs. Biddle had one baby who died and a child who lived. Prescott, the territorial capital, was about a mile from the fort. It was a mining town, and this made help and food very expensive. Mrs. Biddle decided to raise chickens and turkeys. They had plenty for their own table, enough to give to friends, and Mrs. Biddle sold over two hundred chickens and fourteen turkeys. They also bought a cow from a herd that had been driven from Texas and later added two more.

Before they had enough milk and eggs, they had to improvise. Mrs. Biddle remembered two recipes that had been handed down from a woman who had been on the frontier at midcentury. "Custard" was made without eggs or milk by using six tablespoons of cornstarch in enough water to thicken it when cooked. It was flavored with essence of lemon and sugar. "Apple pie" was made without apples by using soda crackers that were soaked in water, warmed until soft, and flavored with essence of lemon, sugar, and "a great deal of nutmeg." This mixture was baked in pastry with a crust on top.[54]

53. Ibid., 145–61.
54. Ibid., 162–74.

Early in the fall of 1878, Mrs. Biddle served a special dinner for a visiting general. She asked two lieutenants stationed at Fort Verde on the Verde River, some forty miles away, to provide game and fish, and they sent a cart filled with wild turkeys, ducks, quail, other game, and two big fish. At that time Mrs. Biddle had a Chinese man as a cook, and he served a fine meal. Mrs. Biddle was shocked, however, when he brought in dessert, which appeared to be a large fish. In reality it was a charlotte russe, shaped exactly like a fish. The Chinese cook obviously knew what was proper for a visiting general.

The residents of the fort were fortunate in that delicacies could be bought at the commissary cheaper than they could be bought in the town, because the government absorbed the freight charges. As the wife of the colonel, Mrs. Biddle also received special gifts of food from townspeople and local ranchers. On one occasion, she was given twelve Baltimore oysters. A man coming to the territory from Baltimore had brought half a dozen cans. They had been put on ice and sent by rail as far as the railway had reached—three days from Prescott. They were then brought into the town. Mrs. Biddle gave as well as received. She sent beef tea and wine jelly to the men in the hospital and to women in the town.[55]

The Biddles were in western posts for many more years, and Mrs. Biddle was in an excellent position to see the improvements that became possible with the expansion of the railroad network. At Fort Robinson, Nebraska, in the 1890s, where her husband commanded the Ninth Cavalry, they had excellent quarters with good plumbing. The fort was on a railroad, there was a fine market only twelve hours away, and they "got everything good to eat through the canteen." At table, she said, you could have been in some large city, as "the silver, glass and china were so beautiful." Water still had to be brought in from several miles away, but it ran in ditches all around the fort to water the trees.[56]

Many army wives outlived their husbands. Fortunately, in their later years, some of them felt the urge to write of the time when they had sat in army ambulances on the Santa Fe trail, trekked for seemingly endless scorching days across the deserts of New Mexico, or wondered what to eat at lonely posts scattered throughout the West.

55. Ibid., 176–95.
56. Ibid., 222–28.

View of the dining table at the celebration of a church dedication, 1876 (courtesy Wisconsin Historical Society)

Stagecoach in Montana, c. 1875 (courtesy Minnesota Historical Society)

First settlers in Dakota, c. 1875 (courtesy Minnesota Historical Society)

Summer kitchen of a farmhouse, 1898 (courtesy Wisconsin Historical Society)

Woman carrying pails of milk to the house, c. 1900 (courtesy Minnesota Historical Society)

Christmas dinner for Company C, Third Infantry Regiment, United States Army, 1900
(courtesy Minnesota Historical Society)

Woman churning butter with a dasher churn, c. 1905
(courtesy Library of Congress)

Theodore Roosevelt on a hunting trip, 1905 (courtesy Library of Congress)

Woman with spinning wheel outside a log cabin in rural Washington (?),
1908 (courtesy Library of Congress)

Farm family with copious produce, 1895 (courtesy Wisconsin Historical Society)

Part 6
The Travelers

CHAPTER 12

Food on the Run

⌒

The American bill of fare . . . comprised sundry dainties which might be looked for in vain in railway England. We were offered prairie-chicken, blue-winged teal, and golden plover, oysters cooked in half-a-dozen styles, stewed tomatoes, and a pleasing variety of omelettes.

George Sala, Chicago and Northwestern Railroad, 1880

For much of the century, most of the pioneers who left their farms in the East to move into the West used their own wagons, and took food with them, but some settlers and many visitors and other travelers paid for their western journeys. Immigrants who had enough money to leave the East Coast often took some form of public transportation for at least part of their journey. Early in the nineteenth century, before steamboats, canals, and railroads transformed American transportation, an immigrant group would sometimes hire wagons and teamsters for their trek into the West. In 1819, a group of nine Englishmen who planned to settle in Ohio contracted for two wagons, each with six horses and a driver, to take them and six thousand pounds of luggage over the mountains from Baltimore to Wheeling. It cost the nine men the substantial sum of $350. Much was new for this group of Englishmen. They noticed that even the traffic was different— it kept to the right rather than to the left.

For food, the men hoped to make their own dinners and suppers from provisions they took with them, and they planned to eat their breakfasts at taverns along the way. This plan did not work out. Their provisions ran out within a week, and they had to buy other meals. They received help, however, at several cabins. One woman offered them cherries if they would pick them, and they gathered two or three pounds. They found them palatable but not as good as those they were used to in England. At another cabin they were given milk and apples.

One of the travelers later listed the different foods that they were served at their breakfasts: "chickens, hams, veal-cutlets, beef-steaks, roast pork, and several sorts of fish; various kinds of hot bread viz.:—wheat and corn bread, buck wheat cakes, and waffles, a sort of soft cake, said to be of German origin; butter, honey, jelly, pickles, apple-butter, and the following dried fruits: peaches, cherries, apples &c." One tavern keeper gave them a watermelon, the first these Englishmen had tasted. It was a disappointment because it was not quite ripe. These immigrants ate well, but they were far better off financially than most settlers.[1]

Many travelers who went west tried to go as far as possible by water. If they had enough money, they could take passage on a ship from New York or another eastern port to New Orleans. After 1815, steamboat navigation spread rapidly on inland lakes and rivers, and it was possible to penetrate into the interior of the continent up the Mississippi River from New Orleans. After 1825, it was also possible to go by water from New York into the trans-Allegheny West. In that year the Erie Canal was completed. Many immigrants and others booked passage on steamboats and found their way into the Great Lakes region by way of the Hudson River, the Erie Canal, and Lake Erie.

In the 1850s, Polish traveler Kalikst Wolski went by sea from New York to New Orleans. He ate at the captain's table but liked the captain's wife more than the food. Meals usually began with what Wolski thought was an overpeppered and oversalted soup, and continued with a main course that made use of one of the geese, hens, or turkeys that were normally kept cooped up on deck. This was followed by "a great variety of dainties." The captain's pantry, Wolski wrote, had a great many of the "sweet preserves that American ladies are so fond of." When the ship reached the mouth of the Mississippi, local fishermen came out in small boats to sell all sorts of fresh foods, particularly fish and oysters, and the captain bought a supply for their supper.[2]

From New Orleans, Wolski went north on one of the numerous steamboats that plied the Mississippi. He had no difficulty in finding a "fantastically cheap" passage. At 5:00 P.M. every day, at least fifteen of these "floating palaces" left New Orleans to go up river. For four dollars he sailed for three days and three nights and ate three "elegant meals" a day. He contrasted this with the three dollars a day it had cost him for meals alone in

1. Woods, *Two Years Residence,* 27–49, 30 (quotation).

2. Kalikst Wolski, *American Impressions,* trans. Marion Moor Coleman (Cheshire, Conn.: Cherry Hill Books, 1968), 117–18.

New Orleans. Breakfast at 9:00 A.M. consisted of several dishes along with coffee and tea. At 3:00 P.M. there was "a wonderful dinner with at least twenty dishes to choose from," and they were served excellent Bordeaux or Spanish wine. Supper, at 9:00 P.M., was as generously supplied as dinner. There were two men to a cabin (in upper and lower berths), but each woman had a cabin to herself.[3]

Steamboats could be a very comfortable way of traveling in the West. When Miriam Colt went by steamboat from St. Louis to Kansas City in 1856 she, like Wolski, referred to the steamboats as "floating palaces." At dinner there was a great variety of meats and fish placed smoking hot on the table. There were also cakes, pastries, nuts, candies, tea, and coffee. Much of this was wasted on the Colts, as Mrs. Colt's husband was a vegetarian, and she also favored simple foods. She had "to pick here and there" to get plain food. One of her favorites was a dish of very white hominy. She had heard that "Hogs and hominy" were western fare, and believed she could thrive on the hominy, "let alone the hog."[4]

Steamboats continued to ply western rivers until well after the Civil War. On the Missouri the head of navigation was at Fort Benton, some forty miles from the Great Falls in what is now Montana. Fort Benton had long been a trading center for the American Fur Company, and in 1869 it became a United States Army post. Larger vessels could not navigate the last stretch of the two thousand-mile trip from Omaha, and in low water even small steamboats had difficulty in reaching the fort. These steamboats on the Missouri did not have the opulence of many of those that steamed north from New Orleans, and problems on the Fort Benton run were quite common.

In May 1866, when Arthur Dickson was returning from Montana to Wisconsin, he took passage at Fort Benton on the *Amelia Poe*. At first he was quite pleased with the trip. Buffalo were shot from the boat, men landed and brought the meat from the buffalo cows on board, and Dickson thought it "the best meat" he had ever tasted. The trip began to go wrong when the *Amelia Poe* was requisitioned to take troops up to Fort Benton. Transferred to another boat, the passengers became very unhappy at the scantiness of the food. There were three sittings for meals, and the food grew less at each sitting. Passengers rushed to try to get to the first serving. A committee was formed to protest to the captain, but not until passengers threatened to take over the boat did he finally agree to find more food. They tied up at

3. Ibid., 137–38.
4. Mrs. Miriam (Davis) Colt, *Went to Kansas* (1862; repr., Ann Arbor: University Microfilms, 1966), 33–34.

Niobrara, and scoured the surrounding countryside until midnight for butter, eggs, meat, and anything else they could find. This effort succeeded,
and they reached Sioux City without further complaints.[5]

James Miller, who came south from Fort Benton in 1867, had a mixed
experience on his steamboat. A few days after he left the fort, he wrote
that "our table on the steamer is thus far most excellent. Tender beef, light
bread, and good coffee," and on the same day when he was hungry at 11:00
A.M. he persuaded a steward to give him "some pine apple, cheese, & crackers for lunch." Buffalo and antelope were being shot from the boat, and
the meat was brought on board. But on the following day, as they passed
Fort Union, a decline set in. Miller was too late for the first or second sitting at breakfast, and found that the third was "miserable."[6]

When miners returning from the Montana mines found the steamboats
too expensive, they came down the Missouri on flatboats, known as Mack-
inaw boats. These were rowed, and they carried from six to fifteen men.
These boats, or ones similar to them, were also used when the water was
too low for even the smallest of the steamboats. Passengers brought what
provisions they could, bought more, if they had any money, at posts along
the river, and supplemented the provisions by hunting.

Two small boats that left Fort Benton early in September 1866 had
hunters ahead of them bringing in venison, buffalo, and elk meat. Game
became scarce farther down the river. Reduced to bacon and coffee, the
men on the boats replenished their supplies at a riverside trading store
where dried buffalo tongues were fifty cents a dozen. They cost less if
bought in quantities of a thousand or more. Some men from the boats also
landed to collect wild plums, cherries, and berries. Provisions ran out, but
they met a steamboat coming from Yankton with supplies for the military
posts up the river, and they were able to get bread, crackers, two boiled
hams, some bacon, and coffee.[7]

In 1867, Col. Phillipe Régis de Trobriand came up the Missouri from
Omaha to Fort Stevenson. His steamboat was hardly luxurious. He was
traveling in the middle of August, it was very hot, and as they approached
Fort Rice, in what is now North Dakota, they ran out of fresh meat. The
meals were now fried ham, potatoes, and corn cakes. There was wine for
sale, but Trobriand said it was so bad that it was better to drink "the yellow, dirty, unpurified and tepid water of the Missouri."[8]

5. Dickson, ed., *Covered Wagon Days,* 260–73.
6. Miller, *Road to Virginia City,* 117–27.
7. Collins, *My Experiences,* 65–79; Trobriand, *Military Life,* 129–30.
8. Trobriand, *Military Life,* 36–37.

Steamboats were convenient ways to travel on the major rivers, but for much of the century, even after the coming of the railroads, travelers depended on stagecoaches for an intricate network of connections between the main routes. East of the Mississippi, stagecoach passengers usually ate in inns, but in the 1850s, when stage routes were established across the plains to the Rockies and California, stage companies established way stations to provide the necessary relays of horses, food, and sometimes lodging, for the passengers.

Before stagecoaches traveled regularly across the plains, mail was carried in wagons, and the mail service also took passengers. In 1853 William Davis was sent to Santa Fe as United States attorney. He traveled with the mail along the Santa Fe Trail from Independence. There were three mule-drawn wagons—one for mail, one for baggage, and one to serve as an "ambulance" for the five passengers. They left on November 1, and traveled twenty miles to their first stop, a place where the mail company had an agent. His wife served them "a good supper" in a "rude clapboard cabin," where they stayed the night. As there were still no regular stage stations on the mail routes across the plains, they had to carry provisions with them for the rest of the trip. They took bacon and flour, along with a few "luxuries"—butter, cheese, and molasses. Although they brought coffee, they had no mill to grind it, so they made do with tea. For cooking, they had a frying pan and a stewing pan.

On the first one hundred and fifty miles to Council Grove, there were tribes of friendly Indians and a few cabins with settlers. There were then six hundred miles of the plains to cross before they reached the mountainous stretch leading to Santa Fe. Near the Great Bend of the Arkansas, they began to see great herds of buffalo. Food was no problem—they had soup, fried buffalo meat, and flapjacks—but there was difficulty finding enough water. At one point they went thirty miles without it, and when they finally filled their kegs, they had enough to drink but not enough to use for cooking.

By the time they reached Fort Union, they had used the last of their provisions, but they were now able to buy food at Mexican villages. At Las Vegas, which Davis described as a "a dirty mud town" with a population of about seven hundred, they were able to eat "a sumptuous meal" of fried ham, bread, molasses, eggs, goat's milk, and other items. Near Tecolote, they bought eggs and onions but could not get any milk. There were no cows, and the goats were grazing elsewhere. When they reached the Pecos River, one of the mailmen bought a sheep for them to eat, and they arrived in Santa Fe without going hungry. Food on this very early passenger ride across the plains differed little from traveling in an emigrant wagon train.[9]

Later in the decade, when Horace Greeley traveled in mail coaches across the plains and through the Rockies, the trip was becoming more organized, although the stage stations were still being built. Greeley left Fort Leavenworth for Denver late in May 1859. He ate in Leavenworth before he left and thought the "cold hog and corn dodger" was "the hardest I ever yet paid half a dollar for." Corn dodger was usually a fried cake of corn bread, although sometimes the cake was baked.

One of the first stations they reached consisted of two small tents and a brush arbor. The station keeper had a wife and two young daughters. Greeley, who was developing a good appetite on the road, was given his food in one of the tents because the last time the table had been set in the arbor the wind had blown everything off into the dirt. He thought he had "rarely made a better dinner" than the "bacon and greens, good bread, applesauce and pie" he was served. There were two cows but no butter as the cows "needed rest." The water was too muddy for Greeley to drink.

At the next station, the family who ran it also were living in two small tents while a log cabin was being built, but again Greeley enjoyed his meal. He was given "a capital supper, butter included," although the benches he had previously sat on at meals had now been replaced by bags and boxes. He had begun to miss a few of the usual amenities of city living and reminisced that his last beefsteak had been in Topeka, his last chocolate and morning newspaper in Chicago, and his last potatoes and eggs in Manhattan. At the station at Clear Creek, in buffalo country, there was buffalo meat "hanging or lying all around." Buffalo meat was not to Greeley's taste. He thought the flesh was "tough and not juicy."[10]

After spending some time in Colorado, Greeley traveled north to Fort Laramie and took another mail coach to Salt Lake City. Greeley, who was the only passenger on a stagecoach pulled by mules, said he was "perched on the summit" of seventeen mailbags. He was now on the much-traveled trail to Oregon and California, and mail stations were interspersed with jerry-built stores, and other places to buy provisions. Beyond Fort Bridger, when they reached the Bear River, they stopped for breakfast at a "grocery" that consisted of old boxes covered with tent cloth. They were able to buy sardines and canned lobster, as well as ready-prepared coffee. The owner had no liquor, but they were able to send for some from a similar

9. Davis, *El Gringo*, 3–37.
10. Greeley, *Overland Journey*, 40–92, 154–74.

place less than two miles away. From Salt Lake, Greeley was able to take a mail coach, or what he called a "wagon," to reach California.[11]

There is an excellent account of stage travel on the eve of the Civil War in the writings of the famous British traveler Richard Burton who in August 1860 left St. Joseph, Missouri, for Salt Lake in a "Concord coach." It was not really a coach but a sprung wagon drawn by mules. The mules were changed frequently, and on the first days of the trip the coach drove night and day. Burton took a few extras with him, including tea, sugar, cognac, and some citric acid. The citric acid was for use in his green tea when there was neither milk nor sugar.

Burton was traveling with an American army officer, James Dana, his wife, and their little daughter. The Danas were going to the army garrison in Utah. When the coach made its first one-hour stop to allow the driver to change mules and the travelers to eat dinner, Burton was not impressed. The dinner, which cost fifty cents, "consisted of "doughnuts, green and poisonous with saleratus, suspicious eggs in a massive greasy fritter, and rusty bacon, intolerably fat." He said that only two stations turned out to be worse. They finally halted at 1:00 A.M. for "an hourful of sleep" before resuming the trip in the middle of the night. On the next day they stopped for their noon dinner at a station kept by a native of Alsace, and the food was good. They had ham and eggs, hot rolls, coffee, and an abundance of peaches and cream. That evening, after fording the Big Blue River, they changed mules and drove into Nebraska. Two additional passengers—a woman and a man—got on at Cottonwood Station, and at about 10:00 P.M. they all had "cold scraps of mutton and a kind of bread" at a ranch.[12]

They set out again about midnight. At dawn, at a station in the valley of the Little Blue River, they were served pieces "off half a sheep" which was hanging from the ceiling. The mutton was fried in melted tallow. At midmorning they changed mules and went on to a station that provided them "with the eternal eggs and bacon of these '*mangeurs de lard.*'" That night, their meal was much better. At a station kept by a man from Vermont, they had well-cooked chicken followed by peaches. They then drove all night to reach Kearny station, seven miles from Fort Kearny, at 4:00 A.M. There, they paid seventy-five cents for "vile bread and viler coffee." Dinner, eaten about 1:30 P.M., was at Plum Creek, where they were served buffalo meat. Burton thought it was probably from a bull and found it to be "the worst and driest meat, save elk," he had ever eaten.

11. Ibid., 153–70, 218–23.
12. Burton, *City of the Saints,* 12–35.

That night they reached Midway Station at 8:00 P.M. They were able to change mules, but the woman who cooked would not give the passengers supper because she had not been warned of their arrival. Employees of the line were given bread and buttermilk. At 1:30 A.M., they reached Cotton Wood station. Aching after four days and nights in the wagon, they slept on mattresses in a small room. Breakfast the next morning was "cakes of flour and grease, molasses and dirt" fried in a skillet. The charge was fifty cents. Dinner at Fremont Springs was pigeon, onions, and light bread. Burton, for once, had no complaints about the food, possibly because he found the station keeper's wife to be "a comely young person." Early that evening, at Alkali Lake Station, they were served buffalo meat, as well as ice that had been taken from the Platte. The station keeper had managed to keep it stored since winter. A few days later, Burton was given ice with a drink of whiskey.[13]

Before crossing the Platte, they made a stop for breakfast at 3:15 A.M. Everyone at the station was asleep, but they managed to rouse themselves enough to serve what Burton thought was a miserably cooked breakfast of meat, bread, and coffee. At the upper crossing of the South Fork of the Platte, two passengers destined for Denver were transferred to another coach, while the original coach continued to Salt Lake. Their dinner that day was "juicy, fat, and well-flavoured" antelope meat, which Burton found did not sit well on his stomach. That night, at Mud Spring station, they ate in an open shed. After a breakfast of "tough antelope steak," and "a frugal dinner of biscuits and cheese," they stayed at a station kept by a French-Canadian. He had an Indian wife who prepared their supper and breakfast. Burton described the food as prepared in the usual western style—fried "rusty" bacon swimming in fat, with stewed antelope steak, and bread.

At Fort Laramie, which they reached the next day, Burton dined with the commanding officer. It must have been a reasonable meal, as Burton found nothing to criticize. After the first four or five days of twenty-four-hour driving, they were now stopping to sleep each night at different stations. Lieutenant Dana, with his wife and child, usually slept in the wagon. Burton was very tired of hunks of fat bacon, but in the valley of the Sweetwater at last he found something to praise at a small ranch kept by an English woman. There was even a clean tablecloth. After a large breakfast, they rested there for the day. Their coffee at supper was described by Burton as the best he had since leaving New Orleans, and there was excellent cream and cheese. The freshly killed antelope they ate that night and on the

13. Ibid., 36–61, 156.

following morning was less satisfying; like earlier antelope it upset their stomachs.[14]

As they reached South Pass, standards of cleanliness again declined. Burton described Foot of Ridge Station as "a terrible unclean hole," but they fared somewhat better at their next stop, where they were given the rarity of potatoes. The station on Green River was the home of their driver, and they ate well on freshly caught trout with jelly made from buffalo-berries. As they drove on toward Fort Bridger, the road was crowded with Mormon emigrants on their way to the Great Basin.

Stations now varied from one described as a "disgrace," because of its squalor and filth, to a clean and neat station kept by an American Mormon and his English wife. At Fort Bridger they refilled the whiskey keg they had brought with them, and bought a large supply of "biscuits" for Dana's little daughter. Burton was presumably using "biscuits" in the English sense of sweet cookies, and Dana was probably buying sugar biscuits (which were leavened), not corn bread biscuits or sea biscuits. On August 25, after an arduous journey of eighteen days, they crossed the Wasatch mountains and reached Salt Lake City.[15]

In the following month, Burton wanted to travel on to California but found it difficult to arrange transportation. Finally, he met a man who was about to drive thirty-three horses and mules to California. For $150 each he agreed to take Burton and several others in an "ambulance" that he would provide. As trouble with the Indians was anticipated, he also agreed that there would be sufficient armed men for protection. They took their own provisions—flour, biscuit, eggs, bacon, butter, and "a few potted lux-uries," pans for cooking, china and tin tableware, and "a goodly allowance of whiskey and kornschnapps." They also ate at stations along the road.

Their usual supper consisted of "dough, butter, and coffee, but they were also served salt beef, bacon, antelope, excellent beef steak, *frijoles*, and po-tatoes. One of the few stops that Burton commented on favorably was when "a Venetian" at one station made "good, light bread" out of wheat flour, leavened with hop-water, and also served them corn bread, made with butter and eggs.[16]

When newspaperman Samuel Bowles went west immediately after the Civil War, he was able to travel by rail from Springfield in Massachusetts all the way to Atchison, Kansas. From there he went in a new Concord stage, pulled by horses. In two days, traveling day and night, they reached

14. Ibid., 69–173.
15. Ibid., 174–221.
16. Ibid., 495–551.

Fort Kearny, and in another three days they were in Denver. The whole trip of some six hundred and fifty miles took only five days. Stops had been very brief—half-hour for meals, and five minutes or so to change horses or drivers. Stage stations for changing horses were ten or fifteen miles apart, and at alternate stations there was a place to eat.[17]

Bowles's opinion of the meals was more favorable than Burton's. He wrote at Fort Kearny that so far the meals had been better than those at the hotels and restaurants along the railroad line west of Chicago and later said the meals had been "very good" all the way to Denver. They stopped for three meals a day, and the food, which cost $1 or $1.50, changed little at any of them. Basic items were bacon, eggs, hot biscuits, dried peaches and apples, green tea, and coffee. Occasionally, there was beef. For at least half of the time the fruit and vegetables were from cans. Bowles said that there was a good variety of canned vegetables and fruits everywhere west of the Missouri River. When one man they were traveling with left the stage at Julesberg at the forks of the Platte, they had a parting breakfast of canned chicken and oysters.[18]

There were more problems on the stage ride from Denver to Salt Lake City. Indians had raided the stables over a fifty-mile stretch, and for lack of horses the coach was delayed for two or three days. Bowles, however, continued to be satisfied with the food. Bacon was still a staple, but they also had antelope that Bowles found to be "luscious eating." Canned fruits and vegetables, along with clean tablecloths, disappeared for a while, but he found little to complain about. At Fort Bridger, he had "a sumptuous breakfast."[19]

In 1868, John Collins was able to take a train from Omaha to Cheyenne, but he went by stage to Salt Lake and then on to Helena, Montana. It was February, the snow was deep, and from Cheyenne there was only one other passenger on the stage. They reached Fort Bridger the first night, and at the station there were given a supper of canned tomatoes, half-cooked beans, and unpalatable biscuits called "dobies." These were made of "a tough dark dough with a burned crust around them." Collins explained that the beans were half cooked because at that altitude it was difficult to make them tender without adding soda.

On the following morning they pressed on through the snow to a swing station (a small station where horses were changed). A Mormon had been snowbound there for four days with a wagon loaded with coops of live

17. Bowles, *Across the Continent*, 1–5, 10–12, 18–20.
18. Ibid., 12, 21, 25–26.
19. Ibid., 67, 71, 78.

chickens. There was no food at the station, so they bought some of the chickens, dressed them, and cooked them in a camp kettle. They had to eat them partially cooked because they had not finished by the time the stage was ready to leave to go to a home station about sixteen miles away.

After reaching Salt Lake, Collins rested for a day and then took a Wells Fargo stage to Helena. All the stations were low on provisions, and Collins thought that "nothing could be worse than the meals served along the route."[20] Five years later a woman who went by stage from Corinne, Utah, to Helena, remembered it as "a terrible trip." It was in the winter, and the journey took nine days. They changed horses at regular swing stations, but stations with lodging and eating places for the passengers were forty to fifty miles apart. Some days they could not travel the distance between the larger stations, and at one stop they had to sleep in buffalo robes on the floor. Her only pleasant memory was of stopping at a comfortable house where a woman served them "a delicious breakfast with the unusual item of waffles on the menu."[21]

Few travelers had anything good to say about the food at stage stations. In 1883, a traveler from Pierre to Rapid City, South Dakota, went in the mail coach. He sat in a small space in the middle of cases and other baggage, and the trip was supposed to take thirty-six hours. Friends told him that time had been achieved only once in four years. The passengers were already very hungry before they reached the first coach station, but on the way their hunger was eased by men in a wagon train who shared their dinner of bacon, haricot beans, and coffee.

The stations on this route were "long sheds of rough planks" for fifteen or twenty horses. At one end, separated by a partition, there was an area that served as lodging for drivers or for any travelers "who have the ill-luck to be detained there." At one station, the sole custodian was an Irishman who served them some potatoes "with rancid bacon." Everywhere there was fried bacon and boiled potatoes but nothing alcoholic to drink. They were told that "fermented drinks" were prohibited by the company. It took them four days to cover just over one hundred miles.[22]

Even on roads adjacent to rich agricultural areas, stage travel could be a dismal experience. In 1877, Englishman Wallis Nash went by stage from Redding, California, into Oregon. He had gone by rail to Redding, the

20. Collins, *My Experiences*, 81–84.

21. Ronan, *Frontier Woman*, 74–75.

22. Edmond Baron de Mandat-Grancey, *Cow-Boys and Colonels: Narrative of a Journey across the Prairie and over the Black Hills of Dakota*, trans. William Conn (1887; repr., Lincoln: University of Nebraska Press, 1984), 24–64.

farthest point that the California and Oregon railroad had reached. The coach left at 1:00 A.M. and drove through the night. At breakfast Nash encountered "the first of the fly-filled rooms and dirty tablecloths." To eat "there was fried meat, and heavy hot bread, and unwholesome-looking pies, all of which we were to become so familiar with during the next day or two." The trip was not completely dismal. At Soda Springs there was a large jug of naturally fizzy, cool water on a wall next to the road, and when they reached Oregon, Nash ate "an abundance of cream and wild strawberries" at a roadside inn.[23]

A passenger traveling on a stage line between the Columbia River and Puget Sound in Washington Territory had an unvarying round of "fried meat and clammy pie." The only pleasant experience was at a stopping place run by a Scots family, where boiled meat, a cornstarch pudding, and stewed plums was served. The owner sent to California or Oregon for dried fruit and cornstarch.[24]

In the 1870s, the stations in the Arizona region were usually long adobe structures—a store, a saloon, and a hotel—around a large dusty square. Meals cost about a dollar, and whether at breakfast, dinner, or supper the usual fare was "black coffee, red beans, bacon, and biscuits." Stage stations in this dry region had to be located where there was sufficient water. At Picacho Station, some fifty five miles northwest of Tucson, Arizona, there was a well three hundred feet deep, dug so that it would supply water even in the driest seasons.

The station at Maricopa Wells had two coaches arriving each day—one going east, one going west. It was a comparatively busy station and had its own cook. Travelers who arrived here were more fortunate than at most stations in the region. A herder who kept fifty head of cattle supplied the station with fresh meat in the winter and dried beef in the summer. The beef had to be jerked in the summer because it could not be kept fresh. At one time it had been necessary to haul water to the station from the Gila River, but by 1875 there was a deep well. Coaches going west had to take enough water to last them across the forty-five miles of desert from Maricopa to Gila Bend.[25]

Emerson Stratton, who had been clerk and bookkeeper for the stage

23. Wallis Nash, *Oregon: There and Back in 1877*, ed. J. Kenneth Mumford (1878; repr., Corvallis: Oregon State University Press, 1976), 86–100.

24. Caroline C. Leighton, *Life at Puget Sound, with Sketches of Travel in Washington Territory, British Columbia, Oregon, and California, 1865–1881* (Boston, 1884), 114–116.

25. Emerson Oliver Stratton, *Pioneering in Arizona: The Reminiscences of Emerson Oliver Stratton and Edith Stratton Kitt*, ed. John A. Carroll (Tucson, Ariz.: Arizona Pioneers' Historical Society, 1964), 10–13, 19.

line, store, and restaurant at Maricopa Wells, left there in the summer of 1875. In the following year his wife, Carrie, came from California to join him in Florence, Arizona. She took the stage from Los Angeles by way of Ehrenberg and Phoenix, and was in the coach for six days and six nights with her small daughter in her arms. It was very hot, and the little girl was sick for most of the way, helped only by a little tea when they stopped at the stage stations. Mrs. Stratton decided to stay over for one night in Phoenix to rest. It was so hot that most people were sleeping in cots put out on the sidewalk. Mrs. Stratton tried this with her daughter, but she became so frightened she went back inside and suffered the heat for the rest of the night.[26]

The speed of traveling, and, to some extent, comfort, both to and within the West was transformed by the expansion of railroads. Railroads had been built on the East Coast as early as the 1830s and before the Civil War spread rapidly across the Appalachians into the Mississippi valley. Some settlers began to use the railroads as a quick way to begin their long journey into new western regions, and in the last decades of the century, railroads were used both by travelers to the Far West and by many immigrants.

In the first years of the railroads, the companies did not regard it as part of their obligation to provide food either on the trains or at the stations. Railroad travel was complicated not only by the existence of different companies but also by different track gauges. When Polish traveler Kalikst Wolski went by rail from New York to Buffalo in the 1850s he had to change cars four times. He also had to take food to eat on the journey. Though trains stopped for a few minutes at the stations on the way, only beer or "vodka" was available. By "vodka" Wolski undoubtedly meant some form of hard liquor—probably bourbon or rye. Traveling from New York to Buffalo, he had to go hungry for a day and a half.[27]

Some journeys that had previously taken months could now be accomplished in weeks. In 1867 army wife Lydia Lane left Fort Union, New Mexico, with her husband and children. Her husband was returning east on medical leave. They traveled overland through Colorado into Wyoming to reach the head of the railroad and took the train east by way of Omaha. As yet, there was no regular system of station restaurants, and the Lane family took a box with provisions. At some stations there was food, but the train stopped for only a brief time—sometimes only twenty minutes. The Lanes

26. Ibid., 30–31.
27. Wolski, *Impressions,* 53–54.

found it too difficult and too expensive to get the children off the train for a twenty-minute meal, so Captain Lane left the carriage with a tin coffee pot, ate as much as he could of a dinner, and brought the rest of the food back for his family. They ate by spreading out their food on the carriage seats.[28]

The great breakthrough in travel to the Pacific coast came with the completion of the Union and Central Pacific Railroads in May 1869. The two lines were linked at Promontory Point, near Ogden, Utah. The rail trip across the continent remained complicated. Passengers had to change at Chicago and at Council Bluffs, Iowa. There, they crossed the Missouri to Omaha to board the Union Pacific. At Ogden, Utah, they changed to the Central Pacific, and finally at Oakland, the passengers had to leave the train to take a ferry into San Francisco.

Station restaurants became more common with the completion of the transcontinental line, but the brief time allowed for stops meant that many travelers simply brought back what they did not have time to eat. In 1869, when Mary Mathews traveled west from Chicago, she quickly discovered that the stops for meals were too brief. "Before we could scarcely get to eating," she wrote, "the whistle blew, and we would make all haste to the cars." A man who was in the same carriage showed how to cope. He would lay out a large newspaper, "empty his plate of meat and potatoes, or whatever he had on it, catch up roast beef, boiled ham, cakes, bread, pie, or anything within reach," and carry them onto the train. Other passengers soon followed his example. They piled their plates high, and, when the train bell rang, slid what was left onto papers, and spread them out in the carriages. Some suggested that as all the dining rooms were owned by the company, people were hurried from their meals to save money on food.[29]

In 1869, when Elizabeth Custer traveled east on the Kansas Pacific to Fort Leavenworth, she found that the train did not run at night. They had to stop over in Ellsworth, where there was only one hotel. For eating, there was a large room on the ground floor, with a bar and a billiard table at one end and tables at the other. Four years later, when Mrs. Custer took a train from St. Paul, Minnesota, to Bismarck, North Dakota, arrangements for food had hardly improved. Soon after they left St. Paul "the usual struggle for decent food began." At each dining room one of the children in the party tasted the butter to see how rancid it was. If it was particularly rancid, they put a layer of bread on top to smother the taste.[30]

When army wife Ellen Biddle went by train from New York to Nevada

28. Lane, *I Married a Soldier*, 156–59.
29. Mathews, *Ten Years*, 29–31.
30. Custer, *Following the Guidon*, 168–72; Custer, *"Boots and Saddles,"* 76.

in the early 1870s, she had to worry about keeping her little daughter's milk bottle cool. To provide for this, her own mother had a tinsmith make a small "refrigerator." It was fifteen inches long, ten wide, and eight high, with handles and a double-bottom to catch water from the piece of ice. When they stopped at stations for meals (which they did three times a day) Mrs. Biddle was able to get fresh milk, and the refrigerator kept it cool overnight.[31]

A few years later, Mrs. Biddle and her husband took the Atchison, Topeka, and Santa Fe Railroad for part of their journey from Fort Leavenworth, Kansas, to Fort Lyon, Colorado. At that time, the terminus of the line was at Dodge City, which was at the height of its reputation as the destination of the northern cattle drive from Texas. Mrs. Biddle thought it was "a terrible little frontier town." The hotel that they stayed in overnight was a wooden building with two front doors—one leading into a saloon, the other into a parlor. Her supper, at which she ate her first buffalo meat, was "not bad." From Dodge City, the Biddles made the rest of their trip overland.[32]

In the following decades, the Atchison, Topeka, and Santa Fe Railroad became the dominant line in the Southwest. Railroad food in the region was transformed by the efforts of English-born Fred Harvey, who in 1876 began his operations modestly when he leased the lunch counter in Topeka. His success there quickly led to a whole chain of Harvey dining rooms and lunchrooms along the length of the railroad. Some locations also had Harvey hotels, which became increasingly elaborate toward the end of the century.

The Harvey restaurants became recognized for good food, cleanliness, efficiency, and for their waitresses—the famous Harvey Girls, who were recruited in the Midwest and the East. Customers still had to eat quickly—stopping times were no longer than thirty minutes—but Harvey and the railroad made the stop as simple as possible. Before the train reached the station, the conductor passed through the cars to find out how many would be eating in the dining room or the lunchroom, and the information was telegraphed ahead. The restaurants became so well regarded that the railroad was slow to introduce the new dining cars that were often added to trains in the 1870s and 1880s. It was 1892 before dining cars appeared on the Atchison, Topeka, and Santa Fe west of Kansas City.[33]

31. Biddle, *Reminiscences*, 78–80.

32. Ibid., 107–9.

33. Keith Bryant, *History of the Atchison, Topeka, and Santa Fe Railway* (New York: Macmillan, 1974), 107–121, 327–28; Lesley Poling-Kempes, *The Harvey Girls: Women Who Opened the West*

The Union and Central Pacific lines had more difficulty in providing consistent railroad food. In 1876, when Mrs. Biddle traveled across the continent from the East Coast to California, she thought rail travel "had greatly improved" since her first trip, but her train encountered major difficulties because of snow. This was quite common in these early years. Going from Ogden to California, the train Mrs. Biddle was traveling in was marooned in the Sierras for three days. Snowplows were used to open a road to a little town they had just left, and their meals were brought from there to the train. Mrs. Biddle survived quite well as her mother had sent her with "some tins of pâté de foie gras, chicken and deviled ham, also tea, an alcohol lamp and many other little things." The problem of snow on the line was eased in the course of the '70s by the construction of miles of snow sheds to enclose the track.[34]

For the Union and Central Pacific lines, the ultimate solution to hurried food stops at tiny stations was the provision of dining cars, but these were very slow to come into the region west of Omaha. For food on board, passengers had to depend on what they took with them or on the vendors who passed through the cars to sell food and other items. In the early 1870s, Englishman J. W. Boddam-Whetham traveled west on the Union Pacific from Omaha and found that the only food he could obtain on the train came from a young vendor who passed through the cars selling small items that he kept in chests in the smoking car. He began his rounds as soon as the train left, first coming with new and secondhand books. Then he came back with "decayed pears, pea-nuts, apples, and peaches" and finally with "figs, cigars, and chewing candy."

By this time there was a regular system of dining rooms at the stations along the route, and three times a day there were quick stops for meals. Whetham thought they needed "great improvement." The best were "moderately good," but for the most part the food was "ill-cooked and worse served." In trying to describe what was available, Whetham used language that perhaps better reflected his English origin than the actual breadth of the choices. At every meal, he wrote, there was the same request—"mutton-chop, beefsteak, ham and eggs, sir?" Mutton was very popular in late-nineteenth-century England, but, except in the Southwest, still found little favor in the United States.

The main point Whetham wanted to make was that the food was unin-

(New York: Paragon House, 1989), pp. 13–25, 29–42, 231–33; Barbara Haber, *From Hardtack to Home Fries: An Uncommon History of American Cooks and Meals* (New York: Free Press, 2002), 87–103.

34. Biddle, *Reminiscences,* 142; see also Buck, *Yankee Trader,* 217–18; and Nash, *Oregon,* 33–36.

spiring and ill cooked—"dry chops, gutta-percha steaks" and "ubiquitous pie"—and that it had to be bolted down before the all-too-soon cry of "All aboard." It was easy to tell old from new travelers. Before the train stopped, an experienced traveler was already on the platform "dashing wildly" toward the saloon and his seat, ordering coffee as he arrived. He was out on the platform, "picking his teeth," before the inexperienced traveler had his first drink.

The only station Whetham singled out for praise was Evanston, Wyoming, just before they entered Utah. Here the "table was neatly arranged, the napkins and the tablecloth were white and clean, and the cooking far better than usual." When they pressed on across Utah into the "forbidding" scenery of Nevada, residents began to talk of "square meals," an expression still unfamiliar to most easterners and Englishmen.[35]

In 1873, English travel writer Isabella Bird traveled east from Oakland on a train that had two cars loaded with peaches and grapes. She frequently broke her journey to experience what was available in the various towns. At Truckee in Nevada, which they had reached at 11:00 P.M., she went to a hotel and was told that no supper could be provided at that hour, but a man returned with a cup of tea and a slice of bread. On the train, the only food was provided by vendors. After they changed cars at Ogden, young men passed through the cars selling "newspapers, novels, cacti, lollipops, pop corn, peanuts, and ivory ornaments." Colorado pleased her no more than Nevada. At Greeley, she took a room at "a small, rough, Western tavern" kept by an Englishwoman and helped to make her own supper: "Its chief features were greasiness and black flies." Her bed that night was infested with bugs. Eventually, she got up and dozed in a chair.[36]

While meals on the transcontinental lines improved in the 1870s and 1880s, on smaller routes there was little change. In 1883, Frenchman Edmond Baron de Mandat-Grancey went by rail from Chicago into the Dakotas. The train stopped three times a day while passengers ate "in some house, more or less distant from the station." In a large room, with tables covered with dirty red cloths, a girl loudly announced the choices: "Boiled beef, roast beef, salt beef, bacon, potatoes, cabbage, tea, coffee." These Americans, said Mandat-Grancey, "eat nothing but bacon."[37]

Polish author Henryk Sienkiewicz, who later became famous by writing

35. J. W. Boddam-Whetham, *Western Wanderings: A Record of Travel in the Evening Land* (London, 1874), 50–144.

36. Isabella Bird, *A Lady's Life in the Rocky Mountains,* intro. Daniel J. Boorstin (1881; repr., Norman: University of Oklahoma Press, 1960), 5, 7–9, 24–25, 27, 29–32.

37. Mandat-Grancey, *Cow-Boys & Colonels,* 5, 14.

Quo Vadis, traveled from New York to California in 1876. For the first part of his journey, Sienkiewicz traveled in a sleeper. During the day there were regular seats, but at night an African American porter transformed the seats into upper and lower berths along the length of the carriage. Privacy was somewhat protected by curtains. If you were traveling alone, there might be either a man or a woman in the other berth of your section. Two years earlier, when Martha Summerhayes had traveled west from Chicago, a German who lived in Nebraska was in the berth above her. When Sienkiewicz awoke after his first night, most of the other berths were already made up, and some of the women were sitting drinking coffee or tea at small tables between the remade seats.[38]

The train stopped at Syracuse for a thirty-minute breakfast before they went through Rochester and Niagara to Detroit. In Detroit, after a walk in the city, Sienkiewicz had "an excellent oyster stew" for breakfast at the station. Sienkiewicz, like other European visitors in these years, was surprised that Americans usually did not accept tips. However, on this occasion a tip was accepted by the part-Indian waiter. Another earlier Polish visitor, Kalikst Wolski, had been surprised in the 1850s in New Orleans when an African American had asked him for a tip. He said that Americans in New York, Buffalo, and Chicago had refused tips, saying, "I am American, and I am paid for my work."[39]

From Chicago, Sienkiewicz went through Omaha to California. In Nevada, at tiny Toano, the passengers were told that snow had blocked the line. They were delayed for several days with supplies running low. There were plenty of crackers, sugar, coffee, tea, and California apples, but meat became scarce. Finally, snowplows cleared the line, and they were able to finish the journey.[40]

The addition of "hotel cars" or dining cars to some trains brought a great improvement for those who had money. George M. Pullman, who was the most important figure in the introduction of sleeping cars, also was a key figure in bringing dining cars to the railroads. His first effort, in the late 1860s, was a "hotel car." This was a sleeper with a small kitchen so that those in the car could have their meals on board. These were convenient for passengers in the car, but the train still had to stop for other passengers to eat at station restaurants. Dining cars devoted solely to food were in-

38. Henryk Sienkiewicz, *Portrait of America: The Letters of Henry Sienkiewicz,* trans. and ed. Charles Morley (New York: Columbia University Press, 1959), 31–35; Summerhayes, *Vanished Arizona,* 194–95.

39. Sienkiewicz, *Portrait of America,* 39, 46; Wolski, *American Impressions,* 126.

40. Sienkiewicz, *Portrait of America,* 47–88.

troduced shortly afterward, but both hotel and dining cars were slow to reach the regions west of Kansas City or Omaha.[41]

In 1877, when Wallis Nash traveled west from New York, he was able to eat on the train all the way to Omaha. The meals were excellent and cheap. "All the dishes of the season" were served, and there were clean tablecloths, bright glasses, and silver. In Utah, children at the various stops brought jugs of cider to sell to the passengers. After Ogden, where they changed into the cars of the Central Pacific, the waiters at the station restaurants were Chinese. The passengers were served peach or apricot pie, milk, and iced water, but no wine, beer, or spirits. Those who wanted alcohol had to go into a saloon. Across California many men and boys came onto the train to sell fruit. At every station there were large quantities of figs, strawberries, plums, grapes, and cherries.[42]

In January 1878 and again in January 1879, after ten years in Virginia City, Nevada, Mary Mathews traveled back to the East. On her first return journey, she had little need of station restaurants. Seven of her friends sent her off with "a very nice lunch" of jellies, honey, pickles, cold turkey, baked chickens, corned beef, cheese, bread and butter, sponge jelly, fruitcakes, sardines, oysters, and a variety of other edibles. Her butcher had also given her a present of ten pounds of "dried beef." She must have needed some help to carry her "lunch."

On both trips, Mrs. Mathews noticed vast improvements since she had first traveled on the line. Where there had been wilderness, there were now towns, fields of grain, orchards and fine gardens. Meals at the stations were cheaper. Ten years before she often had to pay $2.50 for a meal. Now a "square meal" was available for fifty cents, and a lunch could be had for twenty-five cents. At almost every stop east of Nevada, women and children came onto the cars at every station to sell provisions. A few years before the vendors had all been men. The presence of many women and girls reflected the increase in settlement along the line. Many of the women sold baked prairie chickens, carrying them through the cars in large pans to sell at fifty or twenty-five cents, or even less.[43]

Owners of the new railroads took an active role in establishing hotels in the towns served by their lines. When the Colorado Central came near to

41. See August Mencken, *The Railroad Passenger Car: An Illustrated History of the First Hundred Years with Accounts by Contemporary Passengers* (Baltimore: John Hopkins Press, 1957), 28–29, 79, 149–50, 154–57; Lucius Beebe, *Mr. Pullman's Elegant Palace Car* (Garden City, N.Y.: Doubleday, 1961), 105, 141–42; *Oxford Encyclopedia of Food and Drink in America*, 1:391; 2:330–31.

42. Nash, *Oregon*, 6–42.

43. Mathews, *Ten Years*, 330, 338–39.

reaching Central City, Henry Teller, the president of the railroad, said he would invest thirty thousand dollars in a hotel there if the community would give twenty-five thousand dollars more. The resulting hotel seated one hundred in its dining room. The eight-course dinner at the opening ball in June 1872 included saddle of antelope with clove sauce, sugar-cured ham, fancy cakes, and champagne. Ten years later, the Denver and Rio Grande built a hotel in Salida, a supply point for the Colorado mines. The hotel, which the line leased to different managers, gained a great reputation for its food. Its Christmas Menu in 1886 included oxtail soup, oysters, salmon, lobster, tongue, roast loin of beef, turkey, elk, duck, chicken, and venison, with peas, corn, Irish potatoes, sweet potatoes, squash, celery, radishes, and pineapple fritters. For dessert there was plum pudding, various pies, charlotte russe, ice cream, macaroons, a variety of fruits, and Edam cheese. To drink there was punch, claret, and cider.[44]

In 1879, English author Robert Louis Stevenson encountered a new feature of western settlement—emigrant trains. Stevenson left from Jersey City on a Monday morning in August. Four immigrant ships had arrived in New York over the weekend, and, as there was no immigrant train on Sunday, many of the passengers from these ships were going west with Stevenson. A "Babel of bewildered men, women, and children" went by ferry from the railroad terminal in New York to Jersey City to board the train. The train cars were locked; there was no waiting room, and Stevenson and the immigrants waited on the platform. Oranges and nuts were the only foods available. Stevenson bought half a dozen oranges from a boy. Only two of them seemed to have any juice, so he threw the rest away under the cars. Adults and children scrambled down onto the tracks to retrieve them.

The railroad could hardly cope with the great crowds that were traveling. To those who had money, vendors sold fruit in the cars, and the train was supposed to make brief stops for meals. The first meal stops were a fiasco, because on the following day, in Pennsylvania, there was an accident on the line, and the train was delayed. This threw off the times of reaching the stations, and so there were no regular meals available, just "a meagre show of rolls and sandwiches" Stevenson found that with all his efforts of elbowing to the counter, the coffee was always gone before he got there. Stevenson was sitting with a Dutch widow and her children who had their own basket of food. Stevenson had made no preparations, and when he ate in Pittsburgh it was his first real meal in thirty hours.

44. Sandra Dallas, *No More Than Five in a Bed: Colorado Hotels in the Old Days* (Norman: University of Oklahoma Press, 1967), 27–29, 55–59.

Stevenson did not let the experience of the delayed train sour him on America or its food. Traveling across Ohio and Indiana, he wrote to a friend that "in America you eat better than anywhere else: fact. The food is heavenly." At Chicago, Stevenson and the other passengers were transferred by "omnibus" to a different railroad at a different station. There he managed to get a meal of ham and eggs, and later, at Burlington, Iowa, he breakfasted on porridge, "sweet milk," hot cakes, and coffee. At Council Bluffs, on the eastern bank of the Missouri, Stevenson and the emigrants left the train to cross the river and transfer to the Union Pacific. Before making the transfer, most stayed that night at an emigrant house ("a kind of caravanserai"), but Stevenson stayed at the Union Pacific Hotel.

On the following day, in front of the emigrant house, officials sorted the passengers. There were separate cars for families, for men traveling alone, and for Chinese. As men traveling alone were the most numerous, some of them had to go with the families and some with the Chinese. The emigrant trains of the Union Pacific were "only remarkable for their extreme plainness." Stevenson rode in a "long, narrow wooden box," with a stove at one end, a toilet at the other, and wooden benches, separated by an aisle, for seats. The benches were reversible, and bed boards and straw-stuffed cushions were sold to stretch between them. Like other foreign travelers, Stevenson stressed the importance of the newsboy on American trains: "He sells books (such books!), papers, fruit, lollipops, and cigars; and on emigrant journeys, soap, towels, tin washing-dishes, tin coffee-pitchers, coffee, tea, sugar, and tinned eatables, mostly hash or beans and bacon." Two or three men often banded together to buy sugar, coffee, bedding, and other items.

West of Council Bluffs the train stopped at stations for breakfast, lunch, and dinner, and some of the passengers bought milk, eggs, coffee, and cakes from locals who came on board for a short time. Stevenson thought the station meals were palatable, and the prices were reduced for those on the emigrant trains. At one station, Stevenson ate his emigrant meal in the same room as express passengers from a train going east. For half the price, he received the same dinner. West of Omaha there were often separate, cheaper emigrant restaurants as well as the usual ones for regular passengers.

At Ogden, the travelers left the Union Pacific and transferred to the Central Pacific. The cars on the new train were nearly twice as high as those they had just left, airier, and freshly varnished. The seats drew out and joined in the center, so there was no need for bed boards, and there were also upper berths that could be opened at night. By this time the only immigrants left with Stevenson were a German family and a group of

Cornish miners, but now there were Americans from all over the nation. The train sped rapidly across Utah, and in Nevada stopped at Toano and Elko for meals. At Toano, the Scotsman who managed the restaurant explained to Stevenson how the original Spanish division of eight "bits" to a dollar still affected what you bought. Technically the bit was worth twelve and a half cents, and prices were often quoted in bits. If you put down a quarter and got a dime in change you had paid a "*long bit,*" but if you could put down a dime you paid a "*short bit,*" and had saved five cents. In another two days, Stevenson arrived in San Francisco.[45]

The Chicago and Northwestern developed a reputation as the best of the three lines from Chicago to Council Bluffs. In February 1880, Englishman George Sala waited for a day so he could travel on one of the newest and best Pullmans on that line. The car lived up to his expectations. The travelers were offered capital "prairie-chicken, blue-winged teal, and golden plover, oysters cooked in half-a-dozen styles, stewed tomatoes, sweet potatoes, and a pleasing variety of omelettes." One couple had an "*omelette au rhum,*" served flambé.

The Pullman cars only traveled as far as Council Bluffs, and before Sala continued his journey on the Union Pacific, across the river in Omaha, he stocked up on food. He had been warned not to depend on the station eating stops, so he bought a "canvas valise" and filled it with tins of boned turkey and boned ham, English biscuits, sardines, anchovies, mustard, pickles, butter, and half a cold roast turkey. He added buffalo tongues when they stopped in Ogden, and a "chunk" of salt from a vendor at one of the stations. For coffee and milk, he bought two stoneware jugs, and for twenty-five cents a pint an African American porter filled them morning and night. The porter also brought bread and hot rolls. Except for Ogden, where he ate in "a capital restaurant kept by a German," he avoided the station eating places. He ate in his drawing room on the train, and for dessert bought apples, oranges, and "chocolate lozenges" from a vendor. Sala's butter lasted as far as Ogden, where he replaced it with margarine. A type of margarine had been developed in France in the 1860s, although it took years to reach its modern form.[46]

By the early 1880s, it was quite usual for English travelers and writers

45. Robert Louis Stevenson, *From Scotland to Silverado,* ed. James D. Hart (Cambridge, Mass.: Belknap Press of Harvard University Press, 1966), 100–104, 107, 110, 112–20, 133, 143–47; Robert Louis Stevenson, *The Letters of Robert Louis Stevenson,* ed. Sydney S. Colvin, 2 vols. (New York, 1899), 1:168; Lady Duffus Hardy, *Through Cities and Prairie Lands: Sketches of an American Tour* (London, 1881), 91.

46. George A. Sala, *America Revisited,* 2 vols. (London, 1882), 2:137–39, 177–83.

to take trains across the American continent, and Lady Duffus Hardy came with the intention of describing the facilities for future visitors. Like Sala, she was extremely impressed by the Chicago and Northwestern Railroad from Chicago to Omaha, and praised the "easy and luxurious" carriages. The train had an excellent hotel car. From an "*embarras de richesses*," Lady Hardy selected mulligatawny soup, broiled oysters, lamb cutlets, and peas, "cooked to perfection."

To obtain knowledge for her book, Lady Hardy went through the narrow passage from the dining car to "a perfect gem" of a kitchen. It was about eight feet square, scrupulously clean, with a range, a pantry with polished silver, glass, and china, a refrigerator with a plentiful supply of ice, a larder, and a beer and wine cellar beneath the car. The cook and the waiters were African American.

At Council Bluffs, she left the Chicago and Northwestern, and crossed the bridge over the Missouri in "a long, comfortless wagon-like car with a host of nondescript folk." Some were carrying babies, bundles, and baskets of fish and vegetables. The Omaha station was crowded with emigrants, and Lady Hardy decided to stay for a day before boarding the Union Pacific. The Grand Pacific Hotel had been destroyed by fire, so she stayed at the Cosmopolitan, "second-rate in style, but also second-rate in price." It had sanded floors. The meals were "excellently cooked, though roughly served."

On the Union Pacific from Omaha to Ogden, Lady Hardy was in a Pullman, but no food was served. They stopped for meals. Like many other travelers, Lady Hardy was unhappy with the station restaurants. Only at Cheyenne was she really pleased. There she had "excellent" hot soup, "broiled trout and a roast of black-tailed deer, the most delicious-flavored tender meat conceivable; fresh vegetables and fruit," and black coffee to drink. Either they had a longer stop than usual, or Lady Hardy was a quick eater. Good meals were also available at Laramie and Humboldt, but usually the eating places were "wretchedly supplied" with tough steak and watery soup. As they were also quite expensive, Lady Hardy recommended a well-filled luncheon basket or braving the crowds at the emigrants' refreshment bar.

At Ogden, where they transferred to the Central Pacific, Lady Hardy had "an excellent, well-cooked meal" and stayed the night. For passengers transferring from the Union to the Central Pacific, there was a long, narrow wooden building, with offices and dining room below and about a dozen rooms upstairs. Lady Hardy was the only guest. She thought that it was "more like a cosy English inn" than a hotel. The Central Pacific took her into California, and, as they pulled into Sacramento, she saw a table running the whole length of the platform, laden with chicken salad, ham and eggs, abundant fruit, tea and coffee. The buffet cost twenty-five cents, and the waiters were Chinese. There was little time to eat, for in twenty minutes they left for Oakland to take the ferry into San Francisco.[47]

Competition increased rapidly in the 1880s, and new transcontinental lines made great efforts to impress the public with their opulence. When the Northern Pacific was completed in 1883 from Lake Superior to Oregon, its president, Henry Villard, invited dignitaries from Great Britain, Germany, and the United States to make a leisurely journey on his new line. Over three hundred eventually made the trip in forty-three private cars pulled by four trains running just thirty minutes apart. For food on the trip, the first train had a refrigerator car attached.

German newspaperman Nicholaus Mohr traveled from Bremen as one of the German party. He described the train accommodations as offering "the same peak of excellence as any New York hotel," and luxurious by German standards. This was not surprising as they were in cars built for the board of directors. For each six or eight men there was a sitting room that converted to a bedroom, a washroom, a dressing room, and a pantry. "What the kitchen and the pantry have to offer," Mohs wrote, "is incredible." Eating, he wrote, followed the American pattern: meat, fish, or eggs with morning coffee or tea, a light lunch at 1:00, and a grand dinner at 7:00. His car had an excellent wine cellar with Bordeaux, Rhine wine, Moselle, and Champagne, as well as "Milwaukee beer" and mineral water.[48]

Railroads all over the country were now taking far greater pains to please their customers, but not all had changed. When Englishman Charles Trevelyan traveled by rail from Colorado Springs to Glenwood Springs, he described a scene in Leadville that would have been typical a quarter of a century before. They all got out at Leadville and rushed to the end of the platform. A man "whacking a cracked gong" stood by a door marked "Eating House." There they "gobbled moodily and silently as in Martin Chuzzlewit for ten minutes."[49]

By the 1890s, if travelers in the West were going to isolated towns they could still expect to use a coach and experience conditions and food that had been typical forty or fifty years earlier, but, if they had the money to travel in style on one of the main railroads, they could dine as well as in the best hotels in the largest cities.

47. Hardy, *Through Cities*, 75–132; Sala, *America Revisited*, 137, 280–81.

48. Nicholaus Mohr, *Excursion through America*, ed. Ray A. Billington (1884; Chicago: Lakeside Press, 1973), 75–76, 233.

49. Charles P. Trevelyan, *Letters from North America and the Pacific, 1898* (London: Chatto & Windus, 1969), 90.

Part 7

Conquering the Plains

CHAPTER 13

Ranch and Chuck Wagon

⌐

[For dinner we had] platters of smoked elk meat, loaves of good bread, jugs and bowls of milk, saddles of venison or broiled antelope steaks, perhaps roast and fried prairie chickens with eggs, butter, wild plums, and tea or coffee.

Theodore Roosevelt, Dakota ranch, 1880s

C attle were not native to the New World. They were introduced to the American continents by Europeans. There was extensive cattle raising east of the Mississippi, but the ranches and cattle drives that have remained in the American memory are those of Texas and the Great Plains. Cattle originally introduced into Texas by the Spanish increased dramatically in the years before the Civil War. In the years immediately following that conflict, it was realized that if these cattle could be driven north to the railroads that were advancing across the plains they could be marketed in the East.

From the late 1860s to the mid-1880s, a succession of small Kansas towns—Abilene, Ellsworth, Dodge City—became famous as the focal point for the northern drives. For many, the phrase *American West* evokes an image of cowboys on the trail from Texas, herding cattle, fending off rustlers and Indians, and sprawling around their campfires eating beans and bacon. Most cowboys had far more trouble from balky cattle than they ever did from Indians or rustlers, but this image of the West as a specific place at a specific time—the cattle frontier in the twenty years after the Civil War—has sunk deep into the American psyche.

Much of the writing on cowboy food has concentrated on the cowboys who took herds north from Texas, but that was only a small part of the cattle industry on the Great Plains. While the northern drives were in their heyday, ranching expanded throughout the plains—as far north as Wyoming, Montana, and the Dakotas, and westward into Arizona. In the early days, ranchers often had to take wagons for long distances to obtain basic supplies, and ranch owners often bought just what were considered absolute necessities—coffee, tobacco, bacon, flour, and perhaps beans. Like settlers in other areas, they often added to their food supplies by hunting. The expansion of railroads made a great difference in providing cheap provisions for ranch owners. By the 1880s, prices for supplies were much reduced and, for most ranches, supplies were far more accessible.[1]

Whether in the 1860s or the 1880s, normal life on a ranch was transformed on the northern drives and at roundup times. The most important of the roundups was in spring, when the new calves were branded and the ranch owner established his ownership, but there were also roundups in the summer to brand late calves and to cull out the steers that were to be sent to market. During these roundup periods, cowboys had to leave their bunkhouse at the ranch and live on the range. A similar situation prevailed for longer periods of time for those who took part in the northern drives from Texas, and in winter for those cowboys who lived out on the range to prevent cattle drifting into areas that were considered undesirable.

At the roundup or on the trail, the cowboy cook had use of a chuck wagon. By the 1870s these were usually four-wheeled wagons drawn by horses or mules. They carried the supplies, the cooking and eating utensils, and a water barrel. The basic food supplies were flour, beans, coffee, salt, pepper, a keg with sourdough, perhaps rice and dried fruit, and cans of tomatoes or fruit. If there was no separate wagon, the chuck wagon also carried the bed rolls, extra saddles, and tools used by the men. Cooking was carried out in the open over a fire in Dutch ovens, skillets, and iron pots.[2]

The roundups were often times for celebration. Edith Kitt said of her life as a young girl in Arizona in the 1880s that "the semi-annual roundups were great events." Stockmen moved from ranch to ranch to find and brand their stock. Big outfits brought their own chuck wagon, and Edith remembered dinner as "a big and jolly meal." There was no drinking during work days, but, when the roundup was over, her father brought out a jug of whiskey to treat all the hands.[3]

1. *Trinidad (Colorado) Weekly News*, October 2, 1883, in Clifford L. Westermeier, ed., *Trailing the Cowboy: His Life and Lore as Told by Frontier Journalists* (1955; repr., Westport, Conn.: Greenwood Press, 1978), 80–81; Ramon F. Adams, *Come an' Get It: The Story of the Old Cowboy Cook* (Norman: University of Oklahoma Press, 1952), 118, 145.

2. Adams, *Come an' Get It*, 5–16.

3. Emerson Oliver Stratton, *Pioneering in Arizona: The Reminiscences of Emerson Oliver Stratton and Edith Stratton Kitt*, ed. John A. Carroll (Tucson, Ariz.: Arizona Pioneers' Historical Society, 1964), 122–23.

Warren Woodson, who spent much of his life with sheep not cattle, wrote of cattle roundups in Montana in the late nineteenth century. There was always plenty of beef, potatoes, baked beans, biscuits or sourdough bread, with dried prunes, apples, and peaches, canned tomatoes and corn. The cook, he wrote, usually butchered a yearling heifer every few days. The best parts had to be eaten quickly because of the heat. It was usual to provide fresh beef for cowboys on the roundups, although, surprisingly, on the northern drive and at many of the ranches, cattle were not regularly slaughtered to provide food. For meat, they often depended on "bacon" or game.[4]

The cowboy cooks worked long hours and were up long before daybreak to have breakfast ready as soon as it was light enough for the men to eat. A rancher commented that "a good-natured cook at a cow-camp was a rare article, as he was liable to cook a meal for one or more strangers at any hour of the day and until he retired for the night. It was not to be marveled at that cow-camp cooks were cross-grained." When they were on the trail north from Texas, the cook had to feed the men in shifts so that the cattle could be tended at all times. Twice a day he hitched up the whole outfit and drove the horses or mules that pulled the chuck wagon. For his varied duties, he was paid considerably more than the regular hands.[5]

Oliver Nelson, who was born in Indiana in 1861, went west, became a cowboy, and in 1880 and 1881 worked as a cowboy cook in southern Kansas and the Cherokee strip in Oklahoma. His first cooking job was out on the range, cooking for cowboys who were herding cattle and returning to the camp at night. He had only a few basic utensils—a frying pan, a Dutch oven, a coffee pot, and knives and forks. At first he made bread with yeast, but baking soda was expensive so he turned to sourdough.

There were variations in making sourdough bread, but the usual method was to keep a container constantly replenished with a sourdough mixture—flour, salt, and water. This was placed in the sun to ferment. To prepare the biscuits, the cook put a portion of his sourdough batter into the middle of a pan of flour with a little soda and lard. Pieces of this mixture were then placed in the Dutch oven in hot fat, put near the fire to rise, and eventually put on the fire itself to bake. The sourdough container was refilled with flour and water, and perhaps a little sugar, and left until more biscuits

4. Warren Woodson, *Pioneering Tales of Montana* (New York: Exposition Press, 1965), 13.

5. Benjamin S. Miller, *Ranch Life in Southern Kansas and Indian Territory* (1896; repr., New York: Arno Press, 1975), 38; *Georgetown (Colorado) Courier,* August 28, 1890, in Westermeier, ed., *Trailing the Cowboy,* 67–68; Adams, *Come an' Get It,* 19–52.

were needed. In camp, Nelson used a jar for the mixture; on the roundup he made use of an empty kerosene can.[6]

In June 1881, Nelson began work at a "through camp" located at the bend of a creek. This was a herd on its way from Texas north. The "camp" was a wagon, from which the cowboys herded about one thousand head of cattle. Under the wagon there was a platform made of boards. This held their store of salt bacon. Nelson said they had "the usual supply of stuff at a through camp"—coffee, flour, cornmeal, bacon, salt, and soda. He thought that they should also have had beans and dried apples. For utensils, he had a frying pan, two ovens, a coffee pot, a bucket, two knives, one fork, and one spoon. Nelson managed to vary the basic fare by killing soft-shelled turtles (fourteen to sixteen inches across) from the creek. He would cut up the meat, soak it in saltwater, and cook the white meat for one meal and the dark meat for the next. Nelson also managed to get some potatoes and vinegar. He sliced the potatoes, soaked them in salt water, and then added vinegar. The cowboys ate them in place of cucumbers.[7]

Nelson took another job with a herd near Caldwell, Kansas, very close to Indian Territory. When he began, he took an inventory of the supplies in the wagon. There were one hundred pounds of sugar, five hundred pounds of salt pork, twenty sacks of flour, two hundred pounds of beans, fifty pounds of dried apples, a box of soda, a sack of salt, and a one hundred and sixty pound sack of green coffee. At the rear of the wagon there was a grub box with a coffee grinder nailed to its side. There was also a cut-off kerosene can for sourdough, and two five-inch-deep ovens. He does not mention a frying pan. He either forgot or perhaps used one of the "ovens" for frying. The first supper he cooked—bread, bacon, flour gravy, coffee, and sugar—was for ten men.[8]

When the cowboys took the herd back to the home ranch in Oklahoma, Nelson went with them. There were about forty men on the ranch, and for a time Nelson worked under a chief cook. The first meal they served after he arrived was "dry salt bacon," coffee, and biscuits covered with sugar. The cowboys "half lived" on coffee. In one year, Nelson used thirteen 160-pound sacks. He had plenty to do. Apart from cooking, there were ten cows to be milked, a hundred chickens and a few turkeys to be taken care of, and a garden. In the evenings, Nelson would grind coffee, slice the bacon, and put it in water to soak out some of the salt. Nelson had to be

6. Oliver Nelson, *The Cowman's Southwest: Being the Reminiscences of Oliver Nelson . . . 1878–1893*, ed. Angie Debo (Glendale, Calif.: A. H. Clark Co., 1953), 56–62; Adams, *Come an' Get It*, 76–81.
    7. Ibid., 55, 73–74, 77–78.
    8. Ibid., 97–100.

up early to wake the cowboys, put on the coffee, fry the bacon, and make flour gravy. It became more complicated when the head cook quit. Nelson had to cope alone.

His tasks went well beyond simple cooking. When they killed a steer, Nelson helped to jerk the beef. He hung strips on ropes stretched between posts, and built a smoky fire to keep the flies away. The jerked beef was then fried in tallow for eating. Nelson commented that some cooks boiled it, then put in flour, salt, and pepper to make a dish called "jowler." He never made this but did learn how to cook another cowboy specialty—bull testicles, known as "prairie oysters" or "mountain oysters." When the first batch was brought to him, he threw them away but later he served them fried.[9]

Nelson never became used to another cowboy favorite—marrow gut. He was introduced to it one day when he was frying "a slab of steak." He went away, and when he came back he found that one of the men had put several pounds of marrow gut on top of the steak. Nelson described marrow gut as "fresh, unwashed entrails," cut into four-inch pieces. Nelson learned to cook it flavored with sage, salt, and pepper. It was popular with the cowboys but not with Nelson. He thought it had "a low-down, cow-lot flavor—sort of a hound-dog relish."[10]

In southern Kansas and Oklahoma, Nelson was working with cowboys and herds that were often on their way north. Granville Stuart, who began to ranch in Montana in 1880, estimated that more than half the cattle on the Montana range cattle had been brought from Texas. The usual herd coming north to Montana consisted of two to three thousand head of cattle, with a trail boss, eight cowpunchers, a horse wrangler, about sixty-five horses for the cowboys, and a four-horse chuck wagon. The standard provisions were cornmeal, sorghum molasses, beans, salt, sugar, and coffee. They ate breakfast at daylight, allowed the herd to graze for a time, and then pulled out. The spare horses and chuck wagon left first.

At about noon the chuck wagon would make camp, and half the cowboys would go in to eat dinner, change horses, and then go back to the herd. The other cowboys would then come in to eat and get new mounts. They would move on again until late afternoon, when they would camp at a spot where there was enough water for the cattle. Again, the cowboys ate in two separate groups. The usual daily drive was ten to fifteen miles. During the night, the cowboys divided into four night watches, although in

9. Ibid., 100–110, 113.
10. Ibid., 161.

stormy weather, with its dangers of stampedes, everyone would be up and working in order to control the herd.

Even though Stuart himself was a cattleman, he, like so many others who wrote about these years, had a somewhat romanticized view of cowboy life. The real cowboys, he wrote, came from the Southwest, usually Texas, and called themselves "cowpunchers." He said they were chivalrous and held women in high esteem. When they came into town, they wore the best clothes they could buy, patronized the best restaurant, and made sure they had fresh oysters and ice cream. Stuart was obviously thinking of the end of a long drive when many cowboys came into town to spend much of the money they had earned.[11]

Stuart's idealized view of the cowboys may have been true of some, but it also reflected what he believed his readers wanted to read. Whatever cowboys thought of women, many of them patronized the prostitutes in the cattle towns, and though, after weeks on the trail, they were eager to try restaurants to give some variety to their food, many were even more eager for saloons to quench the dust of the trail. Generalizing about cowboys was common from an early date. In 1900 an article in a Denver newspaper contrasted cowboys and sheepherders. Cowboys, it said, were Americans, while sheepherders were usually Mexicans, Frenchmen, or Basques; cowboys ate pork, beef, and beans, and drank strong black coffee, while sheep herders lived for months on tea and mutton.[12]

James Harshman, who in the late 1870s worked on a ranch in the Texas Panhandle, much later in his life described a cattle drive from Texas to the railhead at Nickerson, Kansas. A boss, six cowboys, and a cook were responsible for about one thousand head of cattle. The mess wagon, which also held the blankets and tools, was pulled by two ponies. There was a mess box in the back of the wagon for flour and other domestic items. Harshman remembered their provisions as "a sack of Navy beans a sack of dried apples, coffee and a side of bacon." He was writing in the late 1920s and explained that this was not the kind of bacon that was then eaten for breakfast but "a big fat slab of 'sow belly.'" After days in the sun, he wrote, the melted fat from the salt pork seeped through the wagon bed and dripped onto the ground, but the pork was the only meat they had for months. As in so many other cases, driving cattle did not mean that cattle were regularly slaughtered for food. One of Harshman's most

11. Stuart, *Pioneering in Montana*, 181–84, 188–93.
12. *Denver Republican*, December 9, 1900, in Westermeier, ed., *Trailing the Cowboy*, 180.

pleasant memories of food was eating watermelons after they reached Kansas.[13]

In his book on cowboy cooks, Ramon Adams describes the basic cowboy food as meat, biscuits, coffee, and beans, and usually dried fruit. Cowboys liked their meat freshly killed. As there was no refrigeration, killing was often done toward evening, and the meat hung up overnight. In the heat of the day it was covered and put in the chuck wagon. It was usually eaten as fried steaks, but there was also a special cowboy stew made of tenderloin, sweetbreads, liver, marrow, and brains, usually from a freshly killed calf. In 1885 a Cheyenne newspaper reporter described cowboys eating this stew along with milk, tomatoes from a can, and biscuits fresh from the oven.[14]

Although canned goods were available, their weight and cost long limited their use. They became much more common on ranches in the 1880s and 1890s. A newspaper article in the mid-1880s wrote of roundups in which "an abundance of canned fruit" was served, along with fresh meat, bacon, dried fruit, beans, soda biscuits, tea, and coffee. Chuck wagons usually had a coffee grinder attached to the side. Along with meat, biscuits, and coffee, often there were beans, usually flavored with salt pork. In later years, as communications improved, the better outfits had dried fruits—raisins, prunes, and dried apples—which enabled the cook to provide some pies and puddings.[15]

As on all American frontiers, a summary of what was most usual is often a poor reflection of the variety of human experience at different times and in different places. Cowboys who took part in the northern drives usually came from Texas and the Southwest, but many who established ranches came from the East Coast or even from Europe.

In 1878 Benjamin Miller left New York with his cousin to begin ranching in southern Kansas and Indian Territory (later Oklahoma). They first settled near Medicine Lodge, Kansas, a little town of about twenty buildings nearly one hundred miles southwest of Wichita. The region was described by Miller as "lovely country"—great stretches of prairie, with bluffs, canyons, and clear streams fringed with timber. Already, there was "a sprinkling of cattle and horses on all sides."

When they first went from Wichita to scout out the region, the cousins

---

13. J. H. Harshman, *Campfires and Cattletrails: Recollections of the Early West in the Letters of J. H. Harshman*, ed. Neil M. Clark (Caldwell, Idaho: Caxton Printers, 1970), 102–5.

14. Adams, *Come an' Get It*, 67–118; Westermeier, *Trailing the Cowboy*, 73.

15. Adams, *Come an' Get It*, 67–76, 99–107; Westermeier, *Trailing the Cowboy*, 70.

stayed at a log hotel in Medicine Lodge where little was served but pork, "heavy bread," and coffee. This was particularly frustrating, because the area still had a good deal of game. They saw antelope, prairie chickens, and quail, were told that there were also deer and turkey, and heard that there were buffalo not more than twenty-five miles away. Later that summer they found that the buffalo were more a hope than a reality, because, like elks, they were "a thing of the past" in the region.[16]

The cousins eventually decided to buy a ranch about thirty miles from Medicine Lodge and just six miles from Indian Territory. They settled there in the early summer of 1878. The two cousins had a partner, a hand, and a man "almost used up with liquor" as their cook. As they could not take possession of their ranch for a month, they first lived in a tent. While they were waiting, they planted a garden. Their meals, cooked outside, soon became monotonous. Breakfast consisted of fried bacon, fried mush or potatoes, bread (without butter), and black coffee. For dinner, at noon, they ate mush and molasses, and there was milk when the family in the house had some to spare. For supper, there was again bacon, mush, bread, and coffee, "sometimes adding the luxury of canned corn." In order to have regular milk, they bought a milk cow. Their garden produced early vegetables, but the summer sun soon ruined everything except the melons; and they lost these when the cow got in among them.

That summer they took trips both to Wichita and to Dodge City, then at its height as a cow town. In Wichita, they varied their usual fare by buying cheese, crackers, and bologna, which they stopped to eat on the way back. They rode into Dodge City on a Sunday, but Miller said no easterner would have guessed the day. The saloons were "were crowded with revelers," and the whole town "was swarming with cowboys, half-breeds and Mexicans." New to them were the "women roaming around bareheaded, going in and out of saloons, shaking dice for drinks, and mingling with the cowboys in an easy manner very novel to us." They camped outside the town and cooked and ate alongside the Arkansas River. One novelty was condensed milk to put in their coffee. Canned, condensed milk, sweetened to help preservation, had become much more common in the years after the Civil War. On their way home they killed an antelope and fried some of it for supper. In the following weeks, they were able to kill both turkeys and quail.[17]

They moved into their house late in August, and, as they kept chickens,

16. Miller, *Ranch Life*, 10–13, 16–17.
17. Ibid., 21–34.

they were able to vary their diet with eggs. One Sunday they had a custard for dinner. It was made with eighteen eggs, three quarts of milk, "and other ingredients in proportion." They also kept hogs, and finally in mid-September, they set out for Dodge City to buy a small herd of cattle. On the way, they killed a jackrabbit and began to stew it but abandoned it when they heard there were Indians nearby.[18]

In early winter, fresh meat became scarcer. By November, turkeys were proving hard to find, and although they saw more of them when the snow came, and sometimes an antelope, they were too busy to take time to hunt. Their meat now consisted largely of "fat side-meat" bacon. They were able to have butter once a week. The rest of the time they substituted a "gravy" made out of "flour and water stirred into the bacon grease." They also had limited sugar, and their only desserts were stewed wild plums. They were considerably cheered by the arrival of a box sent from the East. It was packed "with all sorts of good things to eat, wear and use."

In late November, three neighbors invited Miller to go into Indian Territory on a ten-day hunt. They rode about twenty-five miles on the first day before sitting down to a supper of bacon, sourdough biscuits, molasses, and coffee. On the following day they killed two antelope, and that night had fried antelope cooked over a buffalo-chip fire. On the next morning, it was snowing and very cold, but they did not have breakfast because they had nothing to burn for a fire. Fortunately, they came upon a cow camp. Three cowboys in a dugout were frying beef tenderloin in its own tallow, and on the next morning they gave Miller and his party twenty or thirty pounds of beef to take with them. The cowboys would not take antelope in exchange, saying they preferred beef. In the course of their hunt Miller and his friends killed seven antelope, twenty-four turkeys, twenty quail, and six prairie chickens. Miller's share of the game provided fresh meat for a few weeks, and when this was nearly gone, they went out in the snow and were able to kill some turkeys.[19]

On his hunting trip, Miller had learned how to make sourdough biscuits, and he taught this to their cook. It was not simply, or even mainly, a matter of taste. The biscuits saved them "a heap of expense" on baking soda, "which was costing us more than half as much as our flour." The flour was running short, and they decided that for Christmas they would ride into Wichita for provisions and for "fun." Their trip went well. Christmas dinner at their hotel included fifteen varieties of game, including bear

18. Ibid., 35–37.
19. Ibid., 51–62.

and buffalo. After Christmas, they hauled some twenty-five hundred pounds of provisions back to their ranch.[20]

With snow on the ground, they continued to kill game, particularly turkeys. They kept the game on a line stretched between two walnut trees in front of their house. By spring, they had eaten so many turkeys that, to add a little variety to a particularly large bird, the cook made a dressing out of dried biscuits and canned oysters. They also killed one of their pigs so that they could enjoy pork and applesauce. Occasionally they had a wild duck, but water was scarce in the area, and ducks were rare.

Miller and his friends did not plan to be large-scale cattle ranchers, and they hoped to make a little extra money from planting. By early March they had plowed some six acres. They wanted planting to be well advanced by the time of the spring roundup, but when this was over they decided that their ranch was not working out quite as they had hoped. They were worried that there would not be enough summer grass for their cattle and decided that three of them (including the cook) would take the cattle south into "a full-fledged cattle country" in Indian Territory. Miller and one other man stayed at the ranch. The planting proved to be a failure; there was too little water and too much sun. Their chickens were also proving to be a problem. They were constantly being picked off by predators, and those that were left were laying only about five eggs a day.

Food had once again become monotonous. Game was scarce, and they were living mainly on fried bacon and fried mush. Their problems were eased when young wild turkeys became large enough to eat. "If there is better eating than a young, wild turkey," Miller wrote, "I have failed to taste it." With their garden a failure, Miller went along the Medicine River to try to buy some vegetables, but he came home with only a few little cabbages. In late August, he reported in a letter home that for "for days and days" their food had consisted of mush and coffee for breakfast, mush and milk for dinner, and fried mush and tea for supper. He was undoubtedly exaggerating; he soon mentioned that he had killed five turkeys.[21]

The men who were with the cattle in Indian Territory wrote that prospects were much better there, and, after Miller rode down to look at the area, the partners decided to abandon their first ranch. In September, they moved their operations to the "Circle Bar Ranch," about thirty miles from Anthony, Kansas, and some forty-five miles from Caldwell. In the

20. Ibid., 62–65.
21. Ibid., 66–84.

following years they grazed their cattle on the "Cherokee Strip," paying the Cherokee Indians a grazing fee.

Soon after they moved to their new ranch, they ran into an Englishman they had met earlier in Wichita. They gave him coffee and bacon, and on the next day he brought them a piece of venison and a soft-shelled turtle. He stayed to dinner, the man he had with him cooked, and they all sat down to a meal of turtle soup, broiled turtle, roast venison, mallard duck, yams, ducks' hearts and livers with raw onions, wheat bread, and coffee. That auspicious start was followed by their going into partnership, but they quickly returned to a diet largely consisting of bacon.

At their new location, they temporarily lived in a stable while they built a twelve-by-fourteen-foot log cabin. They had settled near a stream with a line of ponds near to it, and this was a stopping point for birds flying south. The first that came were small, flavorful teal. They ate a dozen of them stewed in a pot with dumplings. Later they killed "mallards, redheads, pintails, a sort of fantail, two or three kinds of gray ducks, and a few canvasbacks," as well as geese and a few swans. They used a pointer as a retriever, and Miller commented that their home looked more like a hunter's cabin than a cow camp, particularly as they were also able to kill deer and turkeys.[22]

By winter they were settled in their log cabin. There was no room for a fireplace, and the cooking stove provided their heat. Writing to his mother in mid-December, Miller tried to give her some idea of what Christmas would be like on the ranch. He wrote that on Christmas Day the men in the cabin would represent West Virginia, Indiana, New York, Illinois, and England. The food he said would not take long to describe: for breakfast "some rather heavy biscuit, fat side-meat," black coffee and molasses; and for dinner and supper some kind of game and canned goods. Miller tended to exaggerate his difficulties a little in writing to his mother.

In his personal account of this winter of 1879–1880, he recorded that it was "a great winter for game for us." They killed many waterfowl, as well as quail, prairie chickens, and turkey. More unusual was a swan, which Miller thought weighed at least thirty pounds. They skinned it and made a stuffing of dried bread and sage. Miller basted it as he remembered his mother basting fowl. The meat was still dry but was "quite palatable." For this special occasion, they were more lavish than usual with canned goods, and had what Miller called "almost a Thanksgiving dinner."[23]

22. Ibid., 86–103, 142.
23. Ibid., 104–15.

In the summer of 1880, Miller, who had been in the West for two years, went back east for a short visit but soon returned to the ranch. In the following winter, game continued to be abundant, and they could often vary their staple meal of bacon. Early in January, a visitor who had heard of poor food in the cow country was surprised they were eating so well. There was half a deer and a quarter of a two-year-old steer on hand, a box had just arrived from the East, and Miller had learned how to make buckwheat cakes. Both buckwheat and maple syrup had come in the box. They were able to serve the visitor more than "regulation hot biscuits, bacon, coffee, and sorghum [molasses]."

When Miller's mother wrote to say that she was worried that the constant use of baking powder would not be good for them, he was able to write back to tell her that there was no need for her to worry as nearly all their bread was sourdough. They kept their sourdough mixture of flour and water (sometimes with a little vinegar added) in a jar near the fire.

Miller commented that although few cowboys were fat, food became better as the cow camps grew older. Many camps began to use milk, although "the idea was ridiculed at first." It is clear from Miller's account that the standard cowboy meal was bacon, biscuits, molasses, and black coffee, but that there was often variety in the form of other provisions, game, canned goods, and, in the case of this particular ranch, presents from the East.[24]

At about the same time that Benjamin Miller was ranching in southern Kansas and Indian Territory, prominent frontiersman Granville Stuart was establishing himself on a much larger scale in Montana. In April 1880, Stuart left Helena, Montana, to look for a good cattle range in the Yellowstone country. Several of his friends had already settled there. The area was rich in game—particularly buffalo, antelope, and deer. As Stuart rode through the country to Miles City, the grass was "liberally sprinkled with the carcasses of dead buffalo." In many places they were "thick on the ground." The meat was still on them as they had been slaughtered only for their hides. Stuart estimated that some 10,000 had been killed in the area during the winter—"a waste of the finest meat in the world!"

Stuart and his party had taken some provisions with them, and they also had all the game they needed. In spite of complaining about the waste of meat, they took little of the buffalo they killed. On the eastern side of the Rosebud, they killed a buffalo bull, taking out only the tongue, the tenderloin, and the "fries." Stuart preferred his tenderloin fried in a pan with

24. Ibid., 120–41.

strips of bacon. In the weeks after they left Helena, they had a variety of different meals: a dinner of bread, buffalo tongue, and coffee; another dinner of fresh antelope; a supper of freshly caught fish; a meal of "a fine fat goose" roasted on a spit; and a breakfast of boiled beans with Worcestershire sauce.[25]

After returning to Helena, where he talked to his partners in the "cattle venture," Stuart decided to settle on the Little Big Horn in northern Montana. Early in the summer he established his home ranch on Ford's Creek, about three miles from the foot of the Judith Mountains. Fort Maginnis (about twenty miles northeast of Lewistown), which was established that summer, was close enough for supplies. By October, they had built their main buildings and some range cabins, had five thousand head of cattle, and sixty horses. In the following spring they planted forty acres of oats and a potato patch. They also tried to start an apple orchard, but it failed. They had more luck with rhubarb, currants, and gooseberries. The area also had chokecherries, cherries, wild strawberries, and other berries.[26]

According to Stuart, the typical headquarters ranch of one of the big Montana outfits usually consisted of a log bunkhouse, a log cook house, a blacksmith's shop, a corral, and enough hay land fenced off to produce one hundred tons of hay. The foods provided for the cowboys were typically beans, bacon, coffee, molasses, bread, and beef. A can of tomatoes or oysters was regarded as a luxury.[27]

In the mid-1880s, as cattle spread throughout the northern plains, the young Theodore Roosevelt bought a ranch in Dakota Territory, and for three years lived the life of a rancher on the Little Missouri River, not far from Medora. In the 1880s, after it was reached by the railroad, this town became a major shipping point for cattle. In writing of these years, Roosevelt depicted the life of the ranchers at a time when the Dakotas still had a great area of open range. The region north of the Black Hills and Big Horn Mountains, from the Dakota wheat fields to the Rockies, was "one gigantic, unbroken pasture where cowboys and branding-irons take the place of fences." This area had only been developed after 1880.

The ranches in the region were clusters of log buildings, often twenty to thirty miles apart, and in the early years supplies had to be brought a great distance from the nearest towns. Roosevelt prided himself that at his ranch they lived better than at most. "Many ranches," he wrote, "are provided with nothing at all but salt pork, canned goods, and bread," usually

25. Stuart, *Pioneering in Montana*, 99–109, 111, 114, 125.
26. Ibid., 145–49, 165.
27. Ibid., 239.

neither milk nor butter were available. For this situation Roosevelt blamed the owners or managers. At his ranch, he wrote, two or three cows were always kept. These provided plenty of milk, as well as butter when they had time to churn it. They also kept hens to supply them with eggs, and "when our rifles have failed to keep us in game," there was "stewed, roast, or fried chicken." Their garden supplied them with potatoes, "and unless drought, frost, or grasshoppers interfere (which they do about every second year), other vegetables as well." Fresh meat mainly came from their hunting. Like many other ranchers, they did not regularly slaughter cattle for their own use.

At the home ranch, breakfast was early—rarely later than sunrise and often earlier. The midday dinner varied in time, depending on when the men returned from their chores, but it was the main meal of the day. Roosevelt described "a table on the clean cloth of which are spread platters of smoked elk meat, loaves of good bread, jugs and bowls of milk, saddles of venison or broiled antelope steaks, perhaps roast and fried prairie chickens, with eggs, butter, wild plums, and tea or coffee." After the afternoon work they had supper, "and bed-time comes soon afterward."[28]

The Roosevelt ranch had a four-horse wagon with a mess chest in the rear, and it was used to carry both the food and the bedding on the roundups. The cook drove the wagon. A few ranches had a separate wagon for the food and cooking implements. On the roundup, breakfast was usually ready at 3:00 A.M. It was a quick meal in which a cowboy would simply eat a few biscuits that had been baked in the Dutch oven, and perhaps also "a slice of fat pork swimming in the grease of the frying pan," with beans if any were available. The midway meal was taken in shifts, and supper was the last thing at night. Roosevelt said that the "food, if rough, is good: beef, bread, pork, beans, coffee or tea, always canned tomatoes, and often rice, canned corn, or sauce made from dried apples."[29]

The ranch was at its quietest in the winter, when "most of the cattle are left to shift for themselves, undisturbed." The exception was that some cowboys were out in "line camps," established to prevent the cattle drifting in undesirable directions. The ranchers had a row of camps fifteen or twenty miles apart, usually with two cowboys in each one. From a dugout, a small log cabin, or even a tent the cowboys patrolled the line to stop the cattle from drifting farther east.

The cowboys on the line patrol had a harsh existence in the bitter north-

28. Theodore Roosevelt, *Ranch Life and the Hunting-Trail* (1890; repr., Ann Arbor: University Microfilms, 1966), 1, 4–6, 26–27, 31, 35.
29. Ibid., 45–48, 56–71.

ern winter, and their food was basic—salt pork, beans, and bread. There was fresh meat only when they could kill game. One winter, when Roosevelt was out hunting, he stayed at a small dugout in the side of a butte at the edge of the Bad Lands. It was occupied by two cowboys from his ranch. It had two bunks and a fireplace at one end. After a night there, Roosevelt breakfasted on bread, beans, and coffee, sitting at a mess box that was being used as a table.

Except in winter, the ranchers hunted regularly, and sometimes they went out in the winter months if the weather made it possible. Roosevelt made a comment that has an odd ring for an area devoted to the raising and marketing of cattle. He said that the ranchman "save for his prowess as a hunter and his skill as a marksman," would usually "be sadly stinted for fresh meat." Cattle were not around the ranch in winter, and, except at roundup time, they did not serve as a major source of meat.

From April to August, antelope was the main game animal (Roosevelt killed only the bucks), and in those months they killed enough antelope bucks to keep the ranch in fresh meat. This was followed in midsummer and early fall by the hunting of black- and white-tailed deer. Venison was smoked and stored. It usually lasted into the first weeks of spring. Occasionally, in the Bad Lands, they were also able to kill mountain (bighorn) sheep, and even more occasionally, larger game, usually elks. The elks were fast vanishing. There were none around the ranch, though there was a small band about thirty-five miles away. Bears were also increasingly rare. There were a few grizzlies in the neighborhood, but they lived in inaccessible areas.[30]

The 1870s and 1880s saw the climax of the expansion of the cattle industry. In the South, the cattle industry advanced out of Texas into Arizona. While Theodore Roosevelt was braving winters in the Dakotas, Edith Stratton Kitt's father and his family were enduring the heat of Arizona. The Kitts established a ranch in southwestern Arizona, about forty miles north of Tucson. Both Edith Kitt and her father later wrote their memories of the early years. At first they lived in a dugout but soon moved into a cabin made of cedar posts chinked with mud. In their first year at the ranch, Edith's father killed fifty rattlesnakes.

As on so many other ranches, the Kitts at first made extensive use of game for food. Rabbits, squirrels, deer, and antelope were all plentiful, and regularly provided meat. There were also bears and wild hogs, although Edith's mother would not cook the hogs. Edith remembered that on one

30. Ibid., 45, 74, 131–32, 147, 151, 153, 165.

occasion her father brought in one that he had already dressed. Her mother refused to cook it.

Every two or three months her father went into Oracle to buy supplies, and occasionally they would go to Tucson, taking two or three days each way. He would buy three or four one hundred-pound sacks of flour, one or two sacks of potatoes, a sack of onions, a barrel of molasses, cereals, rice, beans, boxes of macaroni, boxes of raisins on the stem, and lump sugar in one hundred-pound sacks. They also gathered wild honey, which her mother put up in jars. Another treat Edith remembered was mescal root baked in the ground by Mexican *vaqueros*. The finished product was very sweet, and tasted a little like smoky molasses. The *vaqueros* used the same technique to cook a cow's head.[31]

In 1888, when Sadie Martin went to southwestern Arizona to join her husband on a ranch ten miles from Agua Caliente, she found in her first year that quail were "so thick" that they had all that they could eat. Otherwise fresh meat was scarce. They were delighted when a neighbor killed "a beef" and following "desert custom" sent word for them to come for a share. That night they cooked "delicious, tender steak."[32]

The classic era of the expansion of ranching came to an end in the 1880s. On the northern plains the turning point was the winter of 1886–1887. The ranges had become overstocked, and, when a summer of prolonged drought was followed by an extremely harsh, snowy winter, tens of thousands of dead cattle dotted the plains in the spring of 1887. Problems caused by the overcrowding of the range were compounded by the advance of homesteaders. The use of the plains for great roaming herds of cattle had become totally impractical, and the open range came to end as barbed wire fencing began to enclose individual ranches. By the time the open range was enclosed, ranches were scattered from Mexico to Canada.[33]

In 1909, Elinor Pruitt went to Burnt Fork, Wyoming, as a housekeeper for rancher Clyde Stewart. She married him within two months. The ranch, which was near the Utah line, had about one hundred head of cattle. Soon after she arrived, Elinor wrote with delight of the location. The ranch was between two trout streams in which she fished, and she had a fine flock of hens, plenty of eggs, and all the cream she wanted. She milked

31. Edith Stratton Kitt and Emerson Stratton, in Stratton, *Pioneering in Arizona*, 55–56, 112–14, 128–30.

32. Sadie Martin memories, in Ruth B. Moynihan et al., eds, *So Much to Be Done: Women Settlers on the Mining and Ranching Frontiers* (Lincoln: University of Nebraska Press, 1990), 289–95.

33. See Stuart, *Pioneering in Montana*, 186–88, 227–37; Roosevelt, *Ranch Life*, 77–78; Edward Everett Dale, *The Range Cattle Industry: Ranching on the Great Plains from 1865 to 1925* (1930; repr., Norman: University of Oklahoma Press, 1960), 77–101.

seven cows a day and used wild gooseberries, currants, raspberries, and cherries to put up thirty pints of jelly, thirty pints of jam, and two gallons of cherry butter.

It was a custom in the area for the women to make up a party in September to travel over a hundred miles to Ashland, Utah, to gather fruit. The outing itself, which took a week, was as eagerly anticipated as the fruit. Mrs. Stewart decided to go on the trip, and she described a little of what she ate. Her first main meal was a jackrabbit which she shot, dressed, and put on a spit over a fire. She had already fried some slices of bacon to get grease for basting and had put potatoes in the embers of the fire. Another main meal was a string of trout caught in a small lake. The uneaten trout were salted and put in an empty can with two squirrels the women had killed.[34]

Late that year, a girl who was staying with the Stewarts was married, and Mrs. Stewart provided a wedding dinner. Every woman for miles around contributed. The food was put on three long tables: one with the meat, pickles, and sauces; a second with vegetables, soup, and coffee; and the third with pie, cakes, ice cream, and other desserts. The tablecloths were of "tolerably good linen, and we ironed them wet so they looked nice."[35]

The Stewarts ate well. They had a variety of food, ranging from dinners of pot roast and baked beans to suppers of grouse and sage chicken. Mrs. Stewart clearly enjoyed cooking. At the end of May 1910 she gave a birthday party at another ranch. This was no cake and ice cream party. She prepared a supper of T-bone steak, mashed potatoes, hominy, hot biscuits, butter, and stewed prunes.

There was a good deal of visiting back and forth between ranches, and Mrs. Stewart, without telling her husband, even visited women in the sheepherding area. The cattle and sheep men, said Mrs. Stewart, cordially hated each other, but one woman in the sheep area, who was a fine cook, demonstrated one of the advantages of sheepherding. She gave Mrs. Stewart an excellent leg of lamb for supper, as well as "delicious" bread and a large amount of carrot jam. A German woman who lived alone in the sheep area, two miles from her nearest neighbors, became a good friend. On Mrs. Stewart's first visit, the German woman was celebrating an anniversary and had cooked goose and various other delicacies.[36]

34. Elinore Pruitt Stewart, *Letters of a Woman Homesteader* (1914; repr., Lincoln: University of Nebraska Press, 1989), 5–28.

35. Ibid., 57.

36. Ibid., 43, 46, 66–68, 93, 123–24.

At Christmas 1909, Mrs. Stewart's German friend decided to cook and take food to the sheepherders. Mrs. Stewart helped her. She saved all the butter she could, because the sheepherders never had any. Mrs. Stewart went to the German woman's house to help her cook. The plan was to visit twelve sheepherder camps (each had two men) on the day before Christmas and afterward to spend the night at the ranch of an Irish widow, Mrs. O'Shaughnessy. They roasted six geese, boiled three hams and three hens, and made several meat loaves and links of sausage. They also took twelve large rye loaves, twelve coffee cakes (which Mrs. Stewart said were more like fruitcakes), a batch of small white, brown, and pink iced cakes with seeds, nuts, and fruit in them, some doughnuts, thirteen pounds of butter, and six pints of gooseberry jelly. They melted the gooseberry jelly and poured it into glasses.

They started out early on Christmas Eve morning with twelve boxes on a sled drawn by four horses. To help them keep warm they had a wagon box filled with straw, hot rocks, and blankets. Not surprisingly, the sheep men were "delighted" at the arrival of the food. They lived, said Mrs. Stewart, "solely on canned corn and tomatoes, beans, salt pork, and coffee." One man did the cooking, and the other herded. In spring they had lamb or mutton, but the meat was not fit to eat in winter. After visiting the sheepherders, the two women spent the night at Mrs. O'Shaughnessy's. For Christmas Eve dinner, she served them "a beautifully roasted chicken" with tea to drink. At her own home on Christmas morning, Mrs. Stewart gave her young daughter two stockings filled with candy and nuts.[37]

Mrs. Stewart also had the chance to experience French (or at least French-Canadian) cooking. At a ranch where the owner had "a Frenchman" looking after the place, Mrs. Stewart was served trout, "most delicious biscuit," a head of lettuce with potato salad in the center, preserves made from canned peaches, and "the firmest yellow butter."[38]

Several years later, at the same ranch, she was given a "Leather-Stocking dinner." She had lent the Frenchman a set of James Fenimore Cooper's Leatherstocking Tales, and he prepared a dinner in which he served as many of the food items mentioned in the Leatherstocking Tales as possible. The Stewarts stayed two days for "one long feast." They ate venison "in half a dozen ways," antelope, porcupine, beaver tail, grouse, sage hen, and trout. They had to break ice to catch the trout. In the cellar, there was a barrel of trout "prepared exactly like mackerel" but tasting better.[39]

37. Ibid., 68–72, 74.
38. Ibid., 108–10.
39. Ibid., 154–55.

Within a few weeks of the Leatherstocking dinner, the Stewarts were served a Mexican meal at the adobe house of Carlota Juanita and her husband. They had been there "for many years," with a few sheep, goats, cows, pigs, chickens, and turkeys, and a small patch of corn. Corn would not mature at the Stewarts', but the Mexican family, who were higher up, had "a sheltered little nook" where it would grow. The house had a dirt floor, the largest fireplace Mrs. Stewart had ever seen, and a very wide, clean hearth where the cooking was done.

Supper was simmering on the hearth when they arrived, and Mrs. Stewart was impressed with the main course. "I can't say I really like Mexican bread," she wrote, "but they certainly know how to cook meat." The main dish was what Mrs. Stewart called a "a most wonderful pot roast with potatoes and corn dumplings." The roast had cuts in it and garlic, bacon, and pepper, and possibly parsley had been inserted. At the end of the cooking, a can of tomatoes had been put in the pot. Dessert was "a queer Mexican pie." It had been made with dried buffaloberries, stewed and sweetened and placed on batter in a deep baking dish with more batter on top, then baked and served with "plenty of hard sauce." Mrs. Stewart's conclusion was that "it was powerful good." The "very peculiar coffee" had been brought from Mexico, and was served with goat's milk. She stayed the night and had a breakfast of tortillas, cheese, rancid butter, and coffee.[40]

Another of Mrs. Stewart's trips was up the valley of Henry's Fork, which was dotted "with prosperous little ranches," to a cow camp with five hundred steers belonging to one of her neighbors. There were about fifteen cowboys there, because the cattle had been bought in different places and were difficult to control. As they reached the chuck wagon, the cook came in with an antelope slung across his saddle and a dozen sage chickens. While he had been hunting, the cook already had food cooking. When he came back, he removed stones from where the fire had been, to reveal a pit in which there were pots and [Dutch] ovens with "the most delicious meat, beans, and potatoes." The meat was beef. They were also served bread and apricot pie from the mess box. The cowboys came in later for supper, sitting around the fire, and eating from their tin plates. Mrs. Stewart stayed the night and at breakfast the next morning had steak, an egg, biscuits, and black coffee.[41]

In the fall of 1913, when Mrs. Stewart summed up how she had fared on her ranch, she made it clear that though this was not the best area for

40. Ibid., 143–53.
41. Ibid., 160–76.

planting a garden, she had provided much of what they needed. She had cultivated and irrigated a vegetable garden almost an acre in size. That fall the cellar was filled with more than two tons of potatoes, half a ton of carrots, bins of beets, turnips, onions, parsnips, and more than one hundred heads of cabbage. By experimenting, Mrs. Stewart had found a type of squash that could be raised on their ranch and from it had made pies and pickles. She had also raised beans and green tomatoes. The tomatoes were made into preserves. As her tomatoes would not ripen, she had found a way of making catchup, "as delicious as that of tomatoes," out of gooseberries. All summer she had been milking ten cows a day and had sold enough butter to buy a year's supply of flour and gasoline for their gasoline lamp. She also kept chickens and turkeys, using the turkeys for all their birthdays and holidays. It was a hardworking life, but Stewart clearly took great pleasure in what she had accomplished.[42]

For cowboys on the trail or at the roundups, food was often monotonous, but for those who ranched in the great stretch of country from Mexico to Canada, there was far more variety. In the early years, ranchers often had to ride long distances to stock up on provisions, but in most areas this was usually offset by the availability of game. In many areas of the plains, because of the blazing sun and lack of rainfall, vegetables were often difficult to grow, but many ranchers, or more usually their wives, managed to plant gardens. For those who failed, canned produce was now readily available. Life on the plains was often harsh, but cattlemen usually had a rough abundance of food.

42. Ibid., 280–81.

CHAPTER 14

Long Horizons

During the three years we had all been in North Dakota none of us had tasted meat and everyone agreed that this would be a fine time to butcher an ox.

Rachel Calof, 1897

U ntil the last decades of the nineteenth century, farmers avoided the Great Plains. It was an obstacle to be crossed rather than an area to settle. The plains were thought of as uninhabitable. The general dividing line between the reasonably familiar and an area requiring a new style of settling and farming was the ninety-eighth meridian. West of that line, rainfall was insufficient to support agriculture in the traditional manner. The plains encompassed most of the Dakotas and vast areas of Nebraska, Kansas, Oklahoma, and Texas.

Farmers first began to move into Kansas and Nebraska in the 1850s, but they confined their settlements to the prairie lands in the eastern parts of those states. When Mollie Dorsey came to Nebraska with her family in 1857, they were able to settle in a region that had familiar features. The Dorseys stayed for a time in Nebraska City before moving about thirty miles to a quarter section of land that Mollie's father had secured in the prairies along the Nemaha River. There was timber there, and her father went in advance, quickly building a twenty-foot-square log cabin. The family joined him early in June. At first they had no vegetables, milk, butter, or eggs, but they planted a garden and bought a cow. In the summer and fall they were able to gather berries and currants, and Molly's father and brothers brought in a good deal of fresh meat in the form of prairie chickens and squirrels. It soon became too hot to cook indoors so, at the end of the cabin, they put up "a brush kitchen" for the stove that they had brought with them.

In the three years that Mollie stayed with her family before marrying and moving, they were able to develop a farm that would have seemed familiar to the generation of settlers that had preceded them. By their second summer they had "loads of fine vegetables," continued to gather and put up wild fruits, to hunt for small game, and to catch fish. Of course, not everything was as they wished. On their first Christmas, there were no presents. For the little children they fixed up what they could. "Poor little tots," wrote Mollie, "they attribute the absence of Santa Claus to not having any chimney. Our stove pipe goes through a hole in the roof."[1]

For a time, Mollie taught in a school north of Nebraska City. When she stayed with a southern family, she quickly learned that not all in eastern Nebraska were as well off for food. The meals were very different from those Mollie was used to. For breakfast, there was corn bread, salt pork, and black coffee; for dinner, wild greens, boiled pork, cold corn bread, and a drink which was a mixture of "vinegar and brown sugar and warm creek water;" for supper, they had hoecake, cold greens, and pork with coffee. Mollie commented that "it just about used me up." Hoecake was another name for the flat, corn johnnycake that was a favorite all the way across America.

In February 1860 Mollie married. Within two months, the new bride and groom had decided to move west to Denver. Her comment about this move was that they were going to travel "about 700 miles over the Great American Desert." This was the way that most thought about the Great Plains from the time that explorer Stephen Long had given the plains that name some forty years earlier.[2]

Even as homesteaders advanced after the Civil War, settlers were still able to find prairie lands without the problems that would have confronted them just short distances to the west. In 1870, a young English immigrant, Percy Ebbett, went to Kansas with his father and several other young men. Emigration came after his father's upholstery business burned down. Only one of the young men was a farmer, but they were going to Kansas with the hope of both farming and raising cattle.

They settled some twenty-five miles from Junction City in northeast Kansas, in an area some sixty or seventy miles east of the ninety-eighth meridian. Trees were few and far between, but it did not have the desolation of areas a little farther west. They were on the prairie, some seven miles outside the small town of Parkersville. Parkersville held a surprise

    1. Mollie Dorsey Sanford, *Mollie: The Journal of Mollie Dorsey Sanford in Nebraska and Colorado Territories, 1857–1866*, ed. Donald F. Danker (Lincoln: University of Nebraska Press, 1959), 1, 11–77.
    2. Ibid., 87, 108–116.

for the immigrants. The temperance movement was growing in Kansas in the 1870s, and there were no saloons in this town. Anyone who wanted a drink went to the drugstore, where it was possible to buy "a little whiskey 'medicinally.'" In the town's general store, "the loafers congregated in good force, sitting around the roaring, red-hot stove, with their heels high up, and chewing tobacco, talking politics, whittling sticks, and eating crackers and cheese."[3]

The four men and two boys moved onto the prairie in February 1871, putting up a shanty made of boxes and boards. It was too low to stand up-right, but they put an iron stove in one corner. They had a good supply of provisions: bacon, flour, rice, biscuits, eggs, cheese, coffee and sugar. Their cook had been a clerk on the railway in England, and his first attempt at baking bread in a large iron pan resulted in bread that needed a hatchet to cut it. For fuel, they had to go a mile to a small creek that had a few trees growing on its banks. They had some money, so they were able to buy horses, oxen to plow with, and some cows, hogs, and ducks. After plowing, they planted corn, spring wheat, oats, barley, potatoes, and sorghum. They also put in seeds to make a small garden. The cows provided plenty of milk and they churned butter. They had good spring water on their land, and they made a "cool house" by "digging out a spring and lining it with flat stones." Water ran over the stones. Over the spring, they made a roof cov-ered with earth.[4]

Other emigrants began to move in nearby, and a large Irish-American family did their washing in return for milk. Small game was plentiful in the area—prairie chickens, quail, snipe, ducks, rabbits, and jackrabbits. In the fall, wild berries and currants were abundant along the creeks. There were raspberries, gooseberries, blackberries, mulberries, cherries, strawberries, and pawpaws. Grapes were particularly abundant, and they dried them in the sun to use them in the winter—stewed or in pies. They also gathered wild plants—artichokes, wild onions, and a plant that tasted like celery. They were pleased with teas they made from the dried leaves of "a wild tea plant," and from the leaves of the raspberry canes. Children in the area had a chewing gum that they obtained from the sap that ran out of rosin-weeds. Rosinweed, a plant that can grow to nine or ten feet tall, is common on the plains. It has yellow sunflowerlike blossoms. The sap comes from the stems.[5]

3. Percy G. Ebbutt, *Emigrant Life in Kansas* (1886; repr., New York: Arno Press, 1975); 15; Joanna Stratton, *Pioneer Women: Voices from the Kansas Frontier* (New York: Simon and Schuster, 1981), 254.
    4. Ebbutt, *Emigrant Life,* 17–44.
    5. Ibid., 47, 50, 68, 70–73.

Their first growing season was a success. Even in sod still filled with roots, their wheat, oats, and rye did quite well, and the sorghum did excellently. Only the corn was disappointing, but it did much better in the following years. The garden produced abundantly, particularly melons, pumpkins, squashes, cucumbers, and tomatoes. Although they had little corn, they were able to feed their pigs on produce from the garden, and from wild plants—pigweed and lamb's quarter—that grew everywhere in the neighborhood. In winter, after they had killed a pig, they kept it hanging, frozen hard, in the corner of the room. They used a hatchet to cut off what they needed to fry. Heat was provided by a stove, but in winter coffee would freeze in a short time if it was put on a table a few feet away.[6]

For their first Christmas dinner, they had roast suckling pig, wild ducks, prairie fowl, and an English Christmas pudding. They made a special trip to town to get the ingredients for the pudding. These presented no problem except for the beef suet. They had none, and there were no butchers in town. Finally, they were able to get some buffalo suet from a hunter returning from farther west.[7]

The severity of the Kansas winter was a surprise to these English immigrants, and, in preparing for it, they had made a number of mistakes, including having their corral facing north. In their first winter they lost about half their cattle. They found it too cold to milk the cows, and only kept one in milk, sometimes not even that. They enjoyed cooking because it warmed them. Nearly all they ate was fried—mainly fried pork and flapjacks, varied from time to time with johnnycake and fried mush. Ebbett's winter diet was so restricted, with its interminable salt pork and lack of vegetables, that he suffered from "a slight attack of scurvy." His teeth began to loosen as his gums receded. The problem went away in the spring, but some of his teeth remained loose.[8]

Ebbett said pork was their basic meat—"fresh or frozen, in winter, and smoked or salted in summer." They rarely had beef because, although they had cattle, they only killed once a year, and Ebbett only tasted mutton twice in six years. Their main relief from the interminable pork was when they killed one of their hens or ate some of the small wild game. They also caught a few fish, and they even caught frogs and ate their legs.[9]

Although they made a success of their farm, they suffered in the 1870s, like so many others in these years, from natural disasters. In one year, a

6. Ibid., 74–75, 79.
7. Ibid., 76–77.
8. Ibid., 80–81, 118.
9. Ibid., 100–101, 122.

prairie fire badly hurt their crops, and in the following winter, as they had little to trade, they were forced to give up the use of various items, including coffee and sugar. As a substitute for coffee, they used roasted rye, and they used sorghum molasses as their sweetener. Ebbett noticed that Americans in the West made great use of molasses. It was on the table at every meal, and the Americans often poured it over their pork and beans.[10]

A disaster Ebbett and his friends shared with the whole plains region was a visitation from grasshoppers. The grasshoppers arrived near Parkersville early in August 1874, having taken about two weeks to travel the thirty-five miles from Junction City. Fortunately, wheat and some of the other grains had already been reaped and made secure, but the corn and garden crops were destroyed. The grasshoppers "alighted on houses, people, animals, fences, crops, covering everything, while the ground was strewn several inches thick." Every day for about a month, Ebbett had to climb down into the well to clear out the grasshoppers. He wrote of a band of grasshoppers twenty miles deep, and at least two hundred and fifty miles wide, extending across Kansas. In the following winter there was great distress in the state. A "Grasshopper Fund" was organized to help those in need, and money and goods were sent from other parts of the United States. The Ebbett farm was not as badly hit as some, but they were given coats, boots, flour, and haricot beans.[11]

Ebbett was fortunate in that they had settled just east of the ninety-eighth meridian on prairie land that though difficult to plow and lacking in ample timber at least had sufficient water. Settlers who moved still farther west entered a region where old methods of living and farming became increasingly difficult. There was often a lack of sufficient water for the farming that had been carried out across the eastern sections of the United States. Settlers tried to offset this by settling near rivers or creeks, by digging deep wells to reach the water table, by plowing and hoeing in ways that would draw up and retain as much moisture as possible, and, ultimately, by irrigation.

The lack of water also meant a lack of trees. The first settlers quickly used up trees along the watercourses, and this created problems for housing, fencing, and heating. Instead of log cabins, Great Plains settlers had to use homes dug out of the side of bluffs or made out of sod. To offset the lack of wood as a fuel, they burnt buffalo chips or corncobs. Special stoves were developed for the settlers who could afford them. The invention of

10. Ibid., 107–8.
11. Ibid., 126–32, 144–45; Stratton, *Pioneer Women*, 102–6.

barbed wire in the mid-1870s ultimately provided a solution to the problem of finding a fencing material. As railroads advanced onto the plains,
they were able to bring building materials. Also, technological advances in
the years after the Civil War provided a variety of machinery that made
farming the Great Plains more practicable. These advances were of little
use, however, to farmers too poor to take advantage of them.

In March 1877, Howard Ruede, a printer from Bethlehem, Pennsylvania, went west to Kansas with a group of friends. The men intended to
settle in north-central Kansas, and they went as near as they could by train,
traveling by way of Kansas City and Russell. From Russell, they went north
with freight wagons to Osborne, some forty miles away. On the way, they
stayed overnight in a frontier cabin. They had fried pork and coffee for
breakfast, but they had run out of bread. For fifty cents the woman who
owned the cabin made them "a lot of biscuit." She must have been very
pleased with the money, for, as they sat outside eating, a girl brought them
eighteen fried eggs.

At Osborne, which consisted of "a little bunch of houses along both
sides of a single short street, with the prairie running right up to the
houses," they stayed at the City Hotel. The dining room reminded them
of "a farmer's home." The roast was set in the middle of the table, and
whoever sat close had to carve. Vegetables and pies were set at intervals
for each man to help himself. The cooking was excellent, and the hotel "as
neat as a pin."[12]

Like Percy Ebbett from England, Ruede was surprised at Kansas atti-
tudes toward alcohol. There was no bar at the hotel, and it did not sell
liquor. At a time when Kansas cattle towns were wide open, and saloons
filled their main streets, many other parts of the state were moving toward
temperance.

Ruede and his friends settled about fifteen miles from Osborne, on a
small creek running into the South Salmon River. They moved there in
late March, and while they built a sod house they stayed with a family of
settlers. The house took less than three weeks to finish. In the meantime,
Ruede ate quite well. He was given "some of the best bread I ever ate,"
and, for Easter, the woman of the family cooked about four dozen eggs.
One evening, Ruede, who came from Moravian stock, felt a little more at
home when he was given "knep und milch" (dumplings and milk). The
settlers in the area shot prairie chickens and jackrabbits to vary their food.[13]

12. Howard Ruede, *Sod-House Days: Letters from a Kansas Homesteader, 1877–78*, ed. John Ise
(New York: Cooper Square Publishers, 1966), 4–12.
    13. Ibid., 27–46.

On April 16, Ruede moved into a dugout with two of his friends. It seems to have been more a sod house than an actual dugout. On the day he moved in, he had to build a fireplace and chimney before he could make dinner, which consisted of a dish of mush. On the following day, he again had mush as well as boiled ham. The ham had to be eaten quickly as meat flies had got at it. In these first days in his sod house, Ruede had endless trouble with flies laying eggs on his ham. The smallest ham he had been able to buy was twenty pounds, and he removed "thousands of eggs" from it.

As he had no stove, Ruede cooked in his fireplace. He had only rudimentary cooking skills and had to write home for a recipe for johnnycake. After two days of his own cooking, he went over to a friend's house for supper and had meat he could not recognize—he was told it was "coon." Many would have recognized it, because raccoon was often eaten by American pioneers.

Ruede was not happy with the cornmeal he obtained locally; unlike that from Pennsylvania, it had hulls mixed in. To get away from the everlasting mush, he mixed the cornmeal with salt and water and "baked" it over the fire. From his description it seems that he was actually frying it. He also treated himself by buying a loaf of the bread he had liked so much and "felt as good as if I had drawn a prize in the lottery." He had a supper of a slice of ham boiled with beans and a slice of the bread, but his pleasure was lessened when wind from the northeast filled his sod house with smoke.

Late in April, after less than two weeks with his friends in his new home, Ruede listed their household goods—two buckets, one crock, one earthen dish, one saucepan, one spider [a frying pan], one tin dish, three pie plates, three pairs of knives and forks, three spoons, three cups and saucers, one cracked china cup for salt, and a tin cup. They were living on ham, beans, cornmeal mush, and corn cakes.[14]

In the summer of 1877, while sporadically tending to his own farm, Ruede worked for others to earn money. Usually he ate much better when he was working for others than he did in his own sod house. In the first part of May, he worked in Osborne for two weeks, and lived at the house of a woman who took in boarders. On his first Sunday there, he ate a breakfast of steak, fried potatoes, five fried eggs, two rounds of bread, cake, and coffee. Much of his work for others was helping in harvesting. This got well under way at the beginning of July, and Ruede relished the food provided for the harvesters. "They set a first rate table." There was turkey, duck, and chicken, "and the gardens are drawn upon for the best they can

14. Ibid., 48–59.

furnish." There was a lot of cooking to be done, but the wife of the family that employed the harvesters had help. Most of the men who came from neighboring farms to work in the harvest brought their families with them.[15]

Back on his own property, Ruede and his friends were eating far more basically. When they could get them, or afford them, they bought bread and pails of milk. One of their few luxuries was real coffee. Green coffee beans usually cost between forty and sixty cents a pound, "and such a price," Ruede wrote, "is beyond the means of the average person." The main source of cash for many of the local sodbusters was the sale of eggs and butter, but prices were usually so low that they could afford little real coffee. Instead they used rye coffee, parching the grain brown or black, depending on the strength they wanted. They flavored it with a product known as "coffee essence," which came in two-ounce tins. This was a hard, black paste that Ruede thought was probably made of bran and molasses. Parched wheat was sometimes used for coffee, but it was never as popular as rye. Once, in the fall, a local woman ran out of both real coffee and dried rye, and she made coffee out of millet. Ruede called it the "queerest tasting coffee any of us had ever put into his mouth."

The lack of a profitable market for eggs or butter was a continuing problem for local sodbusters. At the beginning of April, eggs were only bringing five cents a dozen in Osborne, and it was hardly worthwhile taking them into town. In Bull City, the nearest "market town," which was seven and a half miles away, butter was selling at twelve and a half cents. By the middle of June, it was only bringing seven or eight cents. Some settlers made butter and packed it away until winter, when at times it could be sold for twenty cents a pound. Ruede does not say how they preserved it, but he mentions that in winter the people in the area stored up ice so that they could later make ice cream.[16]

The sod house the men had built quickly became a ruin. In mid-June, they moved into a temporary tent made from a wagon sheet and began to build a better dugout. They were helped by Ruede's father, who had just arrived from Pennsylvania. At the same time, they were also preparing the land for their first planting. Ruede wanted his first crop to be potatoes, but he also intended to plant rye, wheat, and corn. He asked his family to send him peach and plum stones and cherry pits so that he could plant an orchard. A neighbor had peach trees five feet high, raised from seeds planted

15. Ibid., 69–81, 111, 114, 120.
16. Ibid., 34, 99–100, 108, 162.

three years ago. On their first night of preparing the land, the men ate a supper of ham, fried eggs, bread, butter, cheese, and coffee and then slept under the wagon.[17]

From mid-August, after spending a good deal of time working for others, Ruede concentrated on his own farm. While working, he stayed with his father, five other men, and the owner in a nearby house that was a mixture of log and stone. The owner had a cow, a few pigs, and some chickens, and provided them with eggs, milk, and green corn. He also indirectly provided bread by supplying wheat. A neighbor hauled it to a mill for grinding and brought back flour for his wife to bake bread. For this, she received one-third of what she baked. In return for the supplies provided by the owner, the boarders gave him coal oil and plug tobacco. Occasionally, Ruede's group also got butter from the neighbors. They were often short of meat. Bacon cost ten cents a pound, and at times they did not have the ten cents to buy it.

Sometimes, they added to their food by shooting jackrabbits. On one Sunday morning in mid-August, Ruede fried three rabbits. He had no lid for his frying pan (a "spider" with legs to stand in the fire), and the meat was not cooked through. They ate it anyway. Ruede had eaten no meat since the previous Tuesday. They lived mainly "on roasting ears, potatoes and bread, with now and then a mess of fried eggs." Ruede was very hungry for meat, and after eating the Sunday rabbits it was four days before they found another one to shoot. Ruede decided to give up a day's work and go into town to get meat—"meat I must have, or I can't work."[18]

By the end of August, with very hard work, they finished a new sod house, which Ruede usually referred to as a dugout, because on one side they had dug about three feet into the ground, and on the other about twenty inches. Before winter they also built a potato cellar and a henhouse—both of them made of sod and partially dug into the ground.[19]

From the money they had earned from working for others, they had been able to add various items, including a new stove, to their limited possessions. On moving into the new house, Ruede gave an inventory of what they owned. In addition to the new stove they had "a tin wash boiler, 2 iron pots, teakettle, 2 spiders, 3 griddles, 3 bread pans, 2 tin plates, a steamer, coffee pot, coal oil can, gridiron, 4 tincups, wash basin, pepper box, and 2 lb. nails." There were also half a dozen knives and forks, a dozen spoons, a lamp, a bucket, salt, rice, half a dozen china plates, two bowls, two

17. Ibid., 98, 102, 105.
18. Ibid., 126–33.
19. Ibid., 137, 141–42, 159.

storage boxes, sugar, soap, coffee, and coal oil. He intended to buy baking soda and a dishpan when he next went into town.

When one of them went to the mill and bought one hundred pounds of flour, Ruede tried his hand at biscuits (usually they had been buying bread) and served up a supper of steamed potatoes, hot biscuits, roasting ears, and coffee. On the following morning they had bread, butter, and coffee for breakfast but decided it cost too much to eat light bread. Ruede decided that in future he would bake biscuits. His recipe was three cups of flour, "enough water to make a stiff dough, a lump of butter as big as a walnut, and a teaspoonful of salt." He could sometimes get a cup of buttermilk from a neighbor, which he substituted for the water. It made much better biscuits.[20]

Ruede was hopeful that in the second year in Kansas, he would be able to plant a garden. In the first year, they had only managed to plant corn and potatoes. He wrote and asked the people at home to send the seeds of "a first rate pumpkin," and cuttings from the roots of raspberry plants. He already had seeds for watermelons and muskmelons. These were abundant in the neighborhood and could be had for the asking.

In the early fall, Ruede was living in the new sod house with his father. The two of them, and the others who had come from Bethlehem, were still spending days working for others to earn money, and, at times, for food. Ruede's father was given ten bushels of potatoes for one stint of work, and one of the other men worked for a gallon of molasses a day. The money they earned enabled them to buy a few luxuries, including sugar and two-thirds of a box of herrings. Ruede thought sugar was "a very costly luxury," but his father insisted on it. They also occasionally received a box from Bethlehem—one box included smoked beef and coffee.[21]

In the middle of November, Ruede listed all they had bought since moving into their new sod house in August. The food items were rice, flour, butter, eggs, coffee, sugar, apples, herrings, potatoes, crackers, and molasses. Most of the purchases were very small: a total of five cents for apples, twenty-five cents for rice, ten cents for salt. The most frequent items they bought were butter and eggs. They also bought a pig and some chickens.[22]

Ruede and his father passed a Spartan winter, the short days enlivened occasionally by a good meal. It was never fancy. Their Thanksgiving dinner consisted of "a piece of cold boiled beef, beef broth, potatoes, biscuit and coffee." They were only having two meals per day—breakfast at seven

20. Ibid., 137–39, 141.
21. Ibid., 140, 143, 146, 149, 151–52, 154, 156, 158.
22. Ibid., 170–72, 201.

and dinner at four. If they were hungry at noon, they ate biscuits. On a day when Ruede wrote to his mother, their dinner was soup, potatoes, corn, beef, biscuit, molasses, and coffee. His mother's sugar cakes, turkey, and cranberries were constantly in their thoughts. They also missed the barrel of apples that used to sit in the corner at home. From time to time, they had fried or stewed jackrabbit, and on one evening Ruede sifted out the cornmeal so they could have mush.[23]

The big event in December was not Christmas dinner, which Ruede did not even mention, but the butchering of their pig. On the day they killed it, they had fried liver for supper. New Year's Eve brought another treat. Ruede was invited to a neighbor's (the Herzogs) to wait for the New Year to come in and was served a supper of chocolate and special cookies— "liebesmahl kuchen"—with raisins in them. A few weeks later, Ruede's father came home from a neighbor's with a pig's heart and liver. Ruede cooked the heart and half the liver with some potatoes for their dinner. After killing a pig, it was typical in the area first to eat the heart and liver, and then, piece by piece, cut off and fry the rest of the meat. They were now used to eating what Ruede thought of as corn bread but was usually called johnnycake by the locals. They had it "about every other day for breakfast," usually with fried pork, molasses, and coffee. Ruede came to like corn bread better than wheat bread.

Life was hard, but Ruede made the best of it. In his first year—1877— he managed to break five acres and to plant two acres of wheat and three of rye. He had been told that it did not pay to raise rye, but Ruede thought it was more dependable than wheat—"I want something to eat if the wheat don't grow well." He had also planted potatoes, raspberry cuttings, and various other seeds. In 1878 he was able to break another six acres and to plant two acres of corn. He was hoping that in the future he would be able to buy a cow and a horse. He had survived.[24]

In 1884, a few years after Howard Ruede went to Kansas, Charley O'Kieffe, as a young boy, went with his family from eastern Nebraska to the Sandhills region of the northwestern part of the same state. He stayed there until 1898. Charley's mother and brother went out in advance and filed claims on adjacent homesteads. While her son stayed to put up a sod house straddling the two claims, Mrs. O'Kieffe returned to bring Charley, two other brothers, and a sister. The family went in a wagon with a chicken coop attached on the rear and six milk cows alongside, but the chickens were

23. Ibid., 183, 186, 188–90, 192.
24. Ibid., 172, 194–95, 200, 206, 212, 227–28, 230–31, 237, 240.

drowned when the family forded a river. Charley's mother fried them all—twenty-four hens and a rooster—and packed them in lard to preserve them.[25]

The year after they arrived they built a new sod house, thirty-four by twenty-four feet. It had what Charley said was the only wood floor in that section of the county and "a half-high cellar house" extending out twelve feet from the west wall. This was dug five feet into the ground with walls four feet high, so there was plenty of head room. It was used to keep vegetables in the winter, and milk, butter, and eggs in the summer. Other foodstuffs were kept in a small boarded-off area of the main house where there was also a stove and a wood-burning heater. Outside, they built a sod stable for their milk cows and horses. Eventually, they also built a granary of lumber, set on stilts. This was divided into separate compartments. They also had a man dig a well that was over one hundred and thirty feet deep. It gave cool, soft water.[26]

The O'Kieffes managed to establish themselves fairly well from the beginning. Many who later wrote reminiscences of early life on the plains had memories of great hardship and food shortages, but the O'Kieffes seem to have been lucky. Their fields were soon producing wheat, oats, corn, and rye. Much of the corn was given to their livestock as feed, but they took some into Rushville to be ground. Charley remembered mush and milk at night, fried mush with molasses in the morning, and parched corn "as a delicacy." They sold most of their wheat, but sometimes their mother would parch some to mix with their coffee beans. The crop of oats was mainly used as feed for the horses.

The O'Kieffes had a garden that produced potatoes, turnips, squash, pumpkins, and rutabagas. These were eaten in season and kept in the cellar during the winter. When they were no longer fit for people to eat, they were given to the livestock. In some years, the O'Kieffes also raised a patch of sorghum cane. The stalks were cut in the fall and taken to a sorghum mill, where the juice was crushed out and boiled. The resulting molasses was used throughout the year—poured on fried mush or pancakes or mixed with lard to spread on bread. The family also made good use of what could be gathered in the surrounding areas. In summer, Charley remembered, "weeds contributed much to our table." The main plants used were pigweed, purslane, and lamb's quarters. His mother often cooked these with a small piece of salt pork.[27]

25. Charley O'Kieffe, *Western Story: The Recollections of Charley O'Kieffe, 1884–1898*, intro. A. B. Guthrie Jr. (Lincoln: University of Nebraska Press, 1960), viii–ix, 3, 7–22.

26. Ibid., 30–35.

27. Ibid., 36–37, 40–41.

Along the nearby Niobrara River, the O'Kieffes collected a good many wild fruits. Yellow and blue currants, red and blue plums, wild grapes, and chokecherries were abundant. They also picked buffaloberries, serviceberries, and another type of cherry. The cherries were tart except when fully ripe, but they were gathered "by the washtub-full," pitted, and dried. When Charley's mother obtained dried apples from the store in town (in trade for butter and eggs), she put a few of them in a gallon of dried cherries. Serviceberries were a favorite—"just plain perfect whether fresh with cream, stewed into sauce, or baked in a pie." Buffaloberries were not as abundant, and were "very acid" in taste. Those who had sugar made jelly or sauce out of them.[28]

The O'Kieffes kept cows, hogs, and chickens. Much of their meat came from the hogs they slaughtered. They ate the liver, and sometimes the hams, while they were fresh, but the side-meat was salted in a barrel of brine, taken out and dried, and put "under a foot or two of clean, dry oats" in the granary. This helped to keep the air out. Many made sausage after slaughtering, but Charley's family never learned how. Some families had smokehouses in which they smoked pieces of pork. A change from pork was occasionally provided by chickens, which gave them eggs for at least part of the year.[29]

In this part of Nebraska, salt pork could no longer be varied with large amounts of game. Buffalo had gone from Sheridan County by the time that the O'Kieffes arrived, and antelope disappeared soon after. Charley said that he never tasted venison, buffalo, or bear meat. The family fished in a creek some three miles from their house. There was a good deal of smaller game, particularly jackrabbits, and there were geese in the fall and spring. Hunting small game sometimes presented a problem, for "there was plenty of game, but little ammunition and practically no money to buy it."

Another problem, in an age when most food was produced at home, or bought in bulk at the store, was finding containers for the many items that had to be stored in the house and cellar. The O'Kieffes made use of lard tins and large coal oil barrels. The tins were from lard bought when their own lard from butchering ran out. The coal oil barrels had to be paid for, because they were returnable items. Milk from their cows was stored in wide, shallow pans on the floor of the cellar to keep cool. When the cream rose, it was skimmed and churned into butter. This was put in tall earthen

28. Ibid., 45–48.
29. Ibid., 36, 38–40.

jars until there was enough to take into town. There it was sold or traded. Charley O'Kieffe's memories may have been colored by time, but clearly his family did not suffer the extreme hardships of many other Great Plains settlers.[30]

While the vanguard of the movement onto the high plains was in Kansas and Nebraska, settlers soon moved north of that region into the Dakotas. There, the harsh winters made life miserable for many. An additional difficulty was that many who peopled the region came directly from Europe and had little of what they needed to survive and prosper.

Rachel Calof, who was born in Russia in 1876, came to northeast North Dakota in 1894 to marry a man she had never met and to settle there with other Jewish immigrants. This Jewish settlement was in an isolated rural area. The nearest town was Devil's Lake, and that was twenty miles away. When Rachel arrived at her future home, she was shocked to see that some of her husband's relatives had rags around their feet instead of shoes. The welcoming supper consisted of "flat pieces of boiled dough and cheese, with water or milk to drink." For Rachel and her future husband, Abraham, the relatives had put up a twelve-by-fourteen-foot shack with a dirt floor. It was a primitive dwelling, and the roof had recently blown off. Abraham's father and mother and his elder brother and family each had a small shack close by. While their shack was being repaired, and while her future husband worked for a farmer to get money for fuel and food for the winter, Rachel lived with Abraham's parents in their nearby shack.[31]

The couple were married in November 1894. The wedding dinner, cooked in a relative's kitchen, consisted of chicken soup, roast chicken, beans, and rice with raisins. They were ready to move into their own shack which had been repaired and moved to a new location. Fuel and food for the winter was to come from seventy-five dollars that Abraham had earned working for a more successful homesteader. Rachel was again shocked to discover that to save fuel Abraham's father, mother, and younger brother were to move in with them for the winter. The twelve-by-fourteen shack was also home to a calf and twenty-four chickens. The chickens were kept under the two beds, and the calf was tethered in the corner. Two cows were apparently kept outside.

Apart from the chickens, and such eggs as they provided, the Calofs had

30. Ibid., 42–44.
31. Rachel Calof, *Rachel Calof's Story*, ed. J. Sanford Rikoon (Bloomington: Indiana University Press, 1995), 22–30, 105–53. There are examples of the experiences of other Jewish immigrants in the region in Linda Mack Schloff, *"And Prairie Dogs Weren't Kosher": Jewish Women in the Upper Midwest Since 1855* (St. Paul, Minn.: Minnesota Historical Society, 1996).

three one hundred-pound sacks of flour and one sack of barley. Their basic food was "bread and anything else which could be made from flour." There was a problem finding enough water. They had made three attempts to dig a well, going down seventy-five feet each time without much success.

By spring, Rachel was pregnant, and the only food left was a little flour, some barley, some sour milk, and a small amount of butter. Rachel brought water from a hollow where snow had melted. It was full of worms and grass and had to be boiled. As they were out of fuel, Rachel gathered dried grass to boil the water. She also collected what looked like wild garlic and wild mushrooms, kneaded dough, and fried the lot together. It was "simply delicious." As they had no tea or coffee, she ground up some barley and boiled it in water.[32]

That summer, while Rachel waited for her baby to be born, the Calofs tried to improve their hut, as well as find enough to eat. In the hot weather milk soured within a day, and to make use of it they made cheese, which was their main food. The men raised hay and sold it to get money for fuel and food for the next winter. Again they would depend on bread. They bought one hundred pounds of flour, twenty-five pounds of sugar, some yeast, and a little coffee. This was not simply for Abraham and his wife. Rachel wrote that nine people would have to depend on these supplies.

When Rachel gave birth to the baby, she encountered another problem. Her mother-in-law, who had been at the birth, came back shortly after with bread and milk, but said that she could not warm the milk for the baby because it was the Sabbath and she could not light a fire. After dark she did cook noodles ("taiglach") and milk and a piece of chicken, but the chicken smelled bad, and Rachel could not eat it.

Two days after the birth, Rachel's husband left to go to a new job for which he had been hired. The wells had again run dry, and the nearest water was five miles away. Each day the cattle had to be driven ten miles. There was still a little well water in the house, and for the first three days after the baby was born, until Rachel's milk came, the new baby only had sweetened water to drink. The only food left in the house was flour and yeast. Rachel milked the cow and was able to bake bread.[33]

They survived the winter, but Rachel again gave birth. Rachel's mother-in-law was in attendance and, because Rachel was cold, a hot lid from the stove was placed close to her. After the birth, as Rachel was being taken care of, the baby was laid on the table. No one noticed that for some time

32. Calof, *Rachel Calof's Story*, 34, 37–43.
33. Ibid., 44–50.

the baby's arm was in contact with the hot lid, and "a large hole" was burned into her elbow. Abraham soon left for town with a load of hay to exchange for fuel, food, and something for the baby's burn.

The cow was no longer giving milk, but they had not yet even considered slaughtering it, or one of the oxen, because they could not be ritually slaughtered. To survive, Rachel made use of four sacks of grain seed—two of wheat and two of barley—that they had been saving to plant in the spring. So far, their only crop had been hay. Rachel ground wheat seed in their coffee grinder to make bread and made a hot drink by roasting barley. Because of a blizzard, it was four days before her husband could return with two buckets of coal, twenty-five cents' worth of sugar, a pound of coffee, a pound of butter, and what he thought were pickled herring, which were shared among three families. The pickled herring turned out to be pig's feet. This they kept quiet from the others. It would seem from his purchases that Abraham was wilting under the pressure of near-disaster. He did, however, bring ointment for the baby's arm, which gradually healed.[34]

In summer, their situation at last improved. Abraham planted ten acres of wheat, and much of this grew and was harvested, although some was ruined in the field. People in the town said it was probably from gophers feeding on the roots. Rachel worked on a potato patch that provided "quite a lot of potatoes;" the cow calved; and their flock of chickens increased to about fifty. They were now able to have regular milk and butter, and they sold wheat, butter, and eggs in town. With the proceeds of their sales they mainly bought coal and wood and were in a somewhat better situation to provide for the next winter. "The winters," wrote Rachel, "dominated our lives."[35]

Once again, Abraham's parents and younger brother moved in for the winter. This meant there were now seven in the twelve-by-fourteen-foot shack—five adults and Rachel's two little girls—and Rachel again found she was pregnant. This time she had a boy, and, in the spring, they made preparations for the *bris* when the baby boy's circumcision would be celebrated. The dinner was the most elaborate since Rachel had arrived in North Dakota, and plans for it grew as the occasion neared. At first they had decided there would be cheese and butter, then that they would roast two of their chickens. Finally, they decided that one of the two oxen that the three families owned should be slaughtered. "During the three years we

34. Ibid., 65–67.
35. Ibid., 68–70.

had all been in North Dakota," Rachel wrote, "none of us had tasted meat and everyone agreed that this would be a fine time to butcher an ox."

The plan was for the forequarters to be shared by the three families, and the hindquarters, which were not considered kosher, would be sold in town. The happiness created by all these plans soon disappeared when Abraham returned with the *mohel,* who would perform the circumcision, and the *shochet,* who would slaughter the ox. The *shochet* decided that the ox was "*traif* [not kosher]." It would have to be sold, not eaten. But, in a decision that would completely sour Rachel's relations with her mother-in-law, he also decided that Rachel, who was still weak after the birth, should cook and eat some of the meat, saying that he interpreted Jewish law as requiring her to regain her strength both for herself and for her children. He told her to use plenty of salt on the meat before cooking it.

Abraham's older brother also decided to eat some of the meat, but Rachel's mother-in-law was furious. She said she would now not even drink water in their house, and for Rachel there was "a wonderful bonus": her mother-in-law refused to move in with them to save fuel in the next winter. When Rachel next became pregnant (she had another son) her husband, not her mother-in-law, helped with the birth. The worst days were over, although in 1900 a devastating hailstorm destroyed their wheat crop, and two of their horses were killed as they ran into wires in a panic. They were able to build a better house with an attic and a cellar, and Rachel wrote that by 1910 their farm was prosperous.[36]

Another Russian immigrant, Sophie Trupin, who in 1908 came with her mother to join her father in North Dakota, found conditions considerably better. Sophie's mother, however, was just as shocked as Rachel had been when she found out where she had to live. In her case it was "a sod house with a rough, splintered floor." In reality, they were much better off than the Calofs, for Sophie's father had already cleared land, planted fields, and dug an adequate well. Soon after they arrived, the threshing machine that went from farm to farm arrived to harvest the wheat, and Sophie's mother was helped by the neighbors in preparing "enormous platters of food" for the men who would thresh. Sophie's memories of this occasion blended into her memories of later threshing days when she was older and the farm was more established. There were "piles of pancakes, bowls of oatmeal served with heavy sweet cream, dozens of sunnyside eggs fried in butter, heaps of home fried potatoes, loaves of homemade bread, coffeecakes, cheese blintzes, pitchers of milk, and gallons of coffee."

36. Ibid., 71–85.

At midday, when the threshers returned for dinner, they were served "a huge pot roast with potatoes browned in gravy, bean and barley soup or whole yellow pea soup made with beef and mushrooms, pickles, sauerkraut, beets, carrots, more milk and more coffee, and, most important of all, homemade pumpkin pies." They had not known pumpkins at home in Russia, but the neighbors showed her mother how to make the pies. Supper was for the most part a repeat of dinner.[37]

Many of Sophie's memories of food centered on what they kept in the cellar. Although the chickens did not lay from late summer until the following spring, they always had eggs. Her mother placed eggs in layers of salt in a box, making sure that none of them touched and that they were completely covered. The box was placed in the cellar, where the salt hardened, keeping the air out and preserving the eggs. Sophie remembered taking eggs out of the salt for her mother to make a coffee cake that called for eggs, butter, sour cream, sugar, and cinnamon. The cellar also had wooden barrels of sauerkraut (made from their own cabbages), dill pickles, sacks of potatoes, onions, carrots, and pickled watermelons. Sophie's favorites were the watermelons, which her mother pickled whole in large barrels. She wrote, "I had never tasted anything more delicious."[38]

Sophie also had happy memories of Jewish holidays. It was difficult to maintain a kosher home because kosher meat was unavailable, but her father learned to kill chickens in the proper way, using a ritual knife and making a special prayer. For *Purim* her mother would fast while baking "*hamantaschen*, cakes filled with poppy seeds and prunes." On the night before the Sabbath, her mother would prepare dough. The next morning she was up while it was still dark to begin the steps to making *challah*, the oval Sabbath loaf of braided dough, with a beaten egg rubbed over it. Sophie particularly remembered one spring when her father took his two-day trip into town, bringing back not only the usual provisions but also a large wooden crate full of provisions for Passover. Her father had ordered them from Chicago months beforehand.[39]

In this rural Jewish community, weddings were held only in the winter, when there would be enough time for the celebrations. Sophie particularly remembered one double wedding, when two daughters from a nearby farm were married at the same time. Families came from all around, and "every table, every sideboard and chest was covered with a spotless white table-

37. Sophie Trupin, *Dakota Diaspora: Memoirs of a Jewish Homesteader* (Berkeley, Calif.: Alternative Press, 1984), 35–37.
38. Ibid., 59–60.
39. Ibid., 56–57, 89–90.

cloth and laden with every good thing to eat: herrings and homemade relishes; roasted ducks, geese, and chickens . . . huge *challahs* . . . and strudel." The strudel, Sophie wrote, "was a symphony of nuts, raisins and dried fruits, candied orange peel, cinnamon and sugar." There were also "honey cakes and sponge cakes and coffee cakes," as well as schnapps and wine. Most of the wine was homemade.[40]

One fresh food that was greatly missed by the Jewish community was fish, particularly *Gefilte fish,* which in Russia had been prepared every Friday from fresh fish. Some of their neighbors had tried to make something resembling it with chicken breast, but it was nothing like the original. Sophie remembered one December day, years after she arrived, when a peddlar came and sold them a pail of frozen fish. It was a great treat, because their only fish since arriving from Russia had been salmon and sardines packed in cans. That evening, her mother made "a huge potato *kugel*" to go with the fish. It was made from grated potatoes, onions, eggs, and a little flour and was "baked with plenty of goose fat." Sophie's memories of early days on the plains were much happier than those of Rachel Calof.[41]

Many of the families who went out to homestead in the Dakotas in the late nineteenth or early twentieth century had ambitions that went well beyond simply surviving on a small farm. In 1898 Grace Wayne, who had grown up in Wisconsin, went west to Parker in southeastern South Dakota to teach school. She married a widower, Shiloh Fairchild, who had a son as old as she was. Shiloh was no impoverished settler. When he sold his farm and livestock near Parker and paid off his mortgage, he had seventeen hundred dollars left over.

Four years later, the couple had two children of their own, and the family moved beyond the Missouri into Stanley County, some ninety miles west of Pierre, settling on a homestead of one hundred and sixty acres. Grace's husband and her stepson had gone ahead to build a house, and, when Grace and her children came by train to Pierre in April 1902, her husband was supposed to be there to meet them. He had forgotten the date and arrived a week later. Shiloh hoped to "get rich raising horses," but this was to be a vain hope.[42]

The wagon they drove west from Pierre carried supplies and board timber to use in the house Shiloh was building. It took them eight days to reach their claim. There had been heavy rains, the track was very muddy, and their route took them by a depressing mixture of sod houses and log

40. Ibid., 95–98.
41. Ibid., 109–110.
42. Wyman, *Frontier Woman,* v–vii, 1–10.

cabins. Their house, which was going to be a log cabin, was unfinished, and they moved in with a neighbor for a month, "sleeping on the dirt floor."

They had settled in an area that had little timber except along the rivers, but they found trees near a creek some seven miles away from their claim. From these, they were able to build a log cabin of fourteen by twenty-eight feet. Most of the houses around had sod roofs, but Grace persuaded her husband to use wooden shingles so that she would not have to face the problem of dirt dropping onto the table or the risk that the roof would completely collapse in wet weather. As quickly as they could, they added a barn, a henhouse, and a pig sty. In the following year, they also added a room twelve by fourteen feet on the west side of the house, using lumber that they brought from Pedro some thirty miles away.[43]

Grace had a stove, but cooking created problems as the stove pipe running through the roof set the shingles on fire three different times. Shiloh solved the problem by putting in a brick chimney, but Grace was annoyed because he put the chimney in the middle of the house rather than at one end. It created a very awkwardly placed kitchen. From the beginning, however, the Fairchilds lived better than most homesteaders on the plains. They were not impoverished when they came, and this made a huge difference in their way of life. Grace commented that once they had got their farm going "we had plenty to eat—butter, cream, eggs, chickens, meat, and garden vegetables." They had to buy very little from the store—mostly coffee, sugar, salt, and pepper. Like most homesteaders, they sold butter and eggs, and they also raised some extra money by putting up visitors from the East who were looking for South Dakota land.

As they became established, their diversified farm provided them with ample food. They grew grain, had a garden and chickens, and kept cattle, hogs, and horses. Meat was the essential part of their diet. Grace commented that once, when her sister visited her in the spring, they were short of meat, "and on a homestead when you are short of meat you are short of food." They used freshly slaughtered beef from their farm, and vegetables from the garden that Grace had planted. They soon added chickens and a few turkeys. When they were short of fresh meat, they hunted for jackrabbits.

Like all settlers, the Fairchilds ate salt pork, although it was by no means the basic part of their diet. Their first pig was given to them by a neighbor, and they fed it on surplus milk rather than grain. Grace described how, after her husband had tried to corn some beef and it went bad, a hired

43. Ibid., 11–16.

man told them that he could salt meat from a slaughtered hog so that it would not spoil. He used an old whiskey barrel that the Fairchilds had been using as a water barrel, put the meat in between two-inch layers of salt, and covered it with a strong brine solution. It was cured so well "it petrified." Hard as it was to chew, they still ate it.

From a German neighbor, Mrs. Stuffenberg (probably Staufenberg), Grace eventually learned how to preserve meat correctly. She also learned how to preserve vegetables. The first sweet corn she ever saved was in salt brine, and it needed "sugar and plenty of cream to make it go down better." She also canned corn by boiling it for twenty minutes, putting it in quart jars, adding a tablespoon of salt, and sealing it with a rubber seal and a glass-lined metal lid. This method she thought preserved corn so that it was "as sweet and good as any I ever tasted." She also used jars to preserve tomatoes and cucumbers.[44]

Mrs. Stuffenberg also taught Grace how to make blood sausage. After a hog was slaughtered, the intestines were turned inside out, washed, and the lining scraped off. They were then thoroughly washed again in a tub of water on a washboard, and a stuffing machine was used to push "good meat seasoned with various spices" into the intestines. Mrs. Stuffenberg had a smokehouse. She liked to smoke all her meat.[45]

Grace was able to have sauerkraut with her blood sausage because another neighbor taught her how to make it in a whiskey keg. As it had a strong smell, they kept it on the porch with a wooden spoon in it. The children often paused to take out a handful as they passed. In winter the sauerkraut froze, and they had to use an axe to get it out.[46]

Grace continued to assume full responsibility for a large garden, eventually producing enough to supply neighbors as well as her own family. From Mrs. Stuffenberg, she learned ways of planting that had been used by many earlier settlers—taking care to plant beans in the light of the moon and potatoes when the moon was dark. The effort to start an orchard was not a success. When the trees were small, a deep snow practically covered them, and jackrabbits ate what was uncovered. They had more luck with gooseberries and strawberries, and they gathered wild fruits—currants, buffaloberries, and other berries—for use in pies and sauces and for canning. They did not always have to use sugar, as they eventually bought two swarms of bees and had several hives providing honey. Grace Fairchild was more prosperous than most homesteaders, and her disappointments came

44. Ibid., 20–21, 65–66, 74.
45. Ibid., 44.
46. Ibid., 21.

more from her husband than from the harshness of existence on the Great Plains.[47]

For small farmers, life on the Great Plains was never easy. Many of those who survived in the late nineteenth and early twentieth centuries were eventually ruined in the Great Depression and in the droughts of the 1930s. It was not only the shortage of water, the lack of timber, and the harshness of the climate, it was also a lack of future prospects. For these settlers there was no hope that if things turned out badly they could move on to fresh new lands. For those who had failed in Kentucky, there was always Missouri, and for those who failed in Missouri, there was Oregon or California, but for those who failed in the Dakotas, there was only work as a farm laborer or a move to some town or city. Throughout most of the nineteenth century, there were always dreams of new and better lands. For the settlers of the Great Plains that hope had disappeared.

47. Ibid., 44, 108–10.

Conclusion

Discussions of why millions of Europeans came to America in the nineteenth century have often ignored the degree to which simply having enough to eat played a major role. In Europe, the prosperous lived in luxury, but the majority of the poor often went hungry. In America, for much of the nineteenth century, hunger was a rarity. It became more prevalent only with large-scale industrialization, and a dramatic growth in eastern cities.

When American troops arrived in Europe in World War I, they were easily recognized not simply because of their accents or their uniforms but because it seemed that most of them—not just the officers—were taller and fitter looking. They provided a sharp contrast to the industrial workers and miners who filled the British trenches. The Americans had eaten more, they had drunk more milk. They were healthier. This was the legacy of conquering and settling a rich continent, a continent that was able to provide food far beyond the needs of its inhabitants.[1]

Most American pioneers had amounts of food unknown to the great mass of Europeans, and they had many varieties of food. The most striking difference from most Europeans, however, was the amount of meat in the American diet. Most of this meat came from hogs and from game. In Europe, most game was a luxury, reserved largely for the rich and privileged. For most American pioneers, meat was available in quantities that had not been seen in western Europe in hundreds or, in some cases, thousands of years. For much of the century, new settlers in any area could expect ample game. When larger herds became scarcer, Americans could still

---

1. J. C. Drummond and Anne Wilbraham, *The Englishman's Food: A History of Five Centuries of English Diet* (1939; rev. ed., London: Jonathan Cape, 1957), 440; Lyn Macdonald and Shirley Seaton, *1914–1918: Voices and Images of the Great War* (London: Joseph, 1988), 285; Paul F. Brain, *The Test of Battle: The American Expeditionary Force in the Meuse-Argonne Campaign,* 2nd rev. ed. (Shippensberg, Pa.: White Mane Books, 1998), 17.

expect good hunting and good fishing. Game, however, was only the beginning. Throughout North America, the wide ownership of land and livestock meant that meat was usually at hand.

Though some American settlers were unlucky or improvident, a vast majority in the new settlements of nineteenth-century America could live with the knowledge that their children were unlikely to go hungry. This was a privilege unknown to a great many Europeans.

In Europe, most of those who lived on the land were farm laborers who did not own the land they farmed or the stock they tended. In his study of English diet from 1815 to the mid-twentieth century, John Burnett concludes that in nineteenth-century England, especially in the first fifty years, the basic food of both country and urban workers was bread. In 1843, a report by poor law commissioners on the employment of women and children in agriculture reached the conclusion that in many areas of the country the diet was inadequate.

In Wiltshire, "the food of the labourer and his family is wheaten bread, potatoes, a small quantity of beer, but only as a luxury, and a little butter and tea." Sometimes there might also be cheese or bacon, or, in one district, "a portion of the entrails of the pig." East Anglia was very much the same. Bread and potatoes were seen as the basic items of diet. There was some butter, cheese, and bacon but "fresh meat rarely, if ever." Only in Yorkshire and Northumberland did the commissioners find a more varied diet, with pies, bacon, milk, and oatmeal porridge more common than in the south.[2]

Although English laborers saw some improvement in their basic diet in the second half of the nineteenth century, conditions were still bleak. In 1863, a governmental enquiry into the food of "the poorest labouring classes" (including farm laborers), reached the conclusion that bread was the most common food, supplemented by potatoes. Even after improvement, the average meat consumption was sixteen ounces a week, and in some areas less than half that was eaten. Burnett concludes that even in rural England, "underfeeding was still the lot of the majority of English labourers in 1914."[3]

There were good reasons for millions of European immigrants to pour into the United States in the nineteenth century. If you were white and unprivileged this was the place to be. For some, it offered political and re-

2. John Burnett, *Plenty and Want: A Social History of Diet in England from 1815 to the Present Day* (London: Nelson, 1966), 23–26, 50; Drummond and Wilbraham, *Englishman's Food*, 327–31.
3. Burnett, *Plenty and Want*, 121–23, 135.

ligious freedoms unknown at home, but for the great mass of ordinary Europeans, it offered the chance of a standard of living far beyond anything they had known. Many Europeans often went to bed hungry and regularly had to exist on a meager diet. America offered the possibility of a better life. Certainly some pioneers suffered from food shortages, but, for most, temporary shortages were soon succeeded by a rich abundance.

Index

Aarthun Anne, 47

Acapulco (Mexico), 183

Adams, Cecilia, 137–38

Adams, Ramon, 305

African Americans, 30, 34, 190, 193, 253, 290, 294

Aguirre, Mary Barnard, 124

Aguardiente. See Alcoholic drinks

Alcoholic drinks: wine, 1, 2, 10, 30, 108, 113, 117, 120, 124, 155, 164, 179, 182, 183–84, 186, 206, 242, 251, 260, 276, 295, 296; punch, 10, 22; brandy, 20, 60, 91, 114, 117, 119, 155, 158, 186, 255, 279; whiskey, 20–21, 30, 31, 33, 57, 63, 91, 92, 98, 109, 111, 117, 200, 211, 213, 214, 228, 238, 257, 285, 300; tafia, 30; beer, 37, 164, 182, 183–84, 256, 295, 296; drunk-enness (among fur traders), 91–92, 97–98; arak, 109; mescal, 114; *aguar-diente,* 114, 117, 119; Mexican mod-eration, 117; and the Mormons, 155–56, 164, 166; milk julep, 179; temper-ance, 283, 321, 324; drunkenness (in the army), 228–29, 252–53, 256, 257; vodka, 285

Alexander, Eveline, 245, 247, 248

Ambulance, 224, 259, 281

American Cookery (Simmons), 17

American Fur Company, 87, 91, 92, 94, 97, 98, 173, 275

American Indians: help from, 4, 59, 60, 62, 66, 67, 69–70, 72, 73–74, 75, 80, 130–31, 132, 135, 138, 140, 174, 193, 235; food of, 5–6, 16, 59, 59–60, 62, 64, 65, 66, 68–70, 71, 72, 73–74, 75, 85, 87, 89, 96, 110–11, 113–14, 118, 190; resistance of, 23, 25, 203, 211, 238, 239, 240, 257–58

—tribes: Ojibwa, 28; Ottawa, 28; Mandan, 56, 59–60, 94; Missouri, 59; Otoe, 59, 89; Arikari, 59, 251; Shoshone, 60, 65; Nez Percé, 66, 70, 71, 256, 257; Chinook, 69; Clatsop, 69; Blackfeet, 71, 81; Pawnee, 73; Arapaho, 75; Osage, 75; Delaware, 80; Crow, 86, 193; Kansas, 89; Gros Ventre, 95, 251; Navaho, 114; Pueblo, 118, 235; Cayuse, 138; Yakima, 142; Pima, 190, 231, 232; Yuma, 191; Pota-watomi, 230; Mariposa, 231; Inuit, 253; Cherokee, 301, 308

Anderson, William, 92

Antelope (pronghorns), 2, 58, 59, 90, 91, 130, 206, 306, 331; meat of, 74, 87, 113, 134, 173, 234, 240, 247, 249, 259, 276, 280, 281, 282, 299, 307, 313, 331

Appert, Nicolas, 76

Applegate Cutoff, 132

Arizona: cattle in, 313, 314

Army, U.S.: rations of, 225–241 *passim,* 251–52, 254; sutler, 227, 239; com-missariat: 228, 252, 254, 259, 264; Fifth Cavalry, 240; quartermaster,

Acknowledgments

⁓

I would like to thank Sara Davis of the University of Missouri Press for the care and skill with which she edited the manuscript.

Illustrations appear on pages 99–104 and 265–70. Credits are listed below in order of appearance.

Old French Market, New Orleans, Wisconsin Historical Society, image no. 37358

Fort Union on the Missouri, c. 1832, Wisconsin Historical Society, image no. 6742

Herds of bison and elk on the Upper Missouri, c. 1832, Wisconsin Historical Society, image no. 6553

Buffalo bull grazing, 1844, Wisconsin Historical Society, image no. 23620

Men skinning buffalo, Library of Congress, reproduction no. LC-USZ62-55602

Herndan Hotel on the Missouri River, 1858, Wisconsin Historical Society, image no. 28205

Fort Laramie, 1849, Wisconsin Historical Society, image no. 3935

Pacific Railroad dining car, 1869, Library of Congress, reproduction no. LC-USZ62-110531

Pilgrims of the plains, 1871, Wisconsin Historical Society, image no. 44675

Wild turkey shooting, 1871, Library of Congress, reproduction no. LC-USZ62-8296

Montana cowboys loading the chuck wagon, Wisconsin Historical Society, image no. 37347

View of the dining table, church dedication, 1876, Wisconsin Historical Society, image no. 27287

Stagecoach in Montana, c. 1875, Minnesota Historical Society, location no. HE2.5 r38, negative no. 10574

First settlers in Dakota, c. 1875, Minnesota Historical Society, location no. E200 p29, negative no. 62076

Summer kitchen, 1898, Wisconsin Historical Society, image no. 25054

Woman carrying pails of milk, c. 1900, Minnesota Historical Society, location no. SA4.9 r85, negative no. 11146

Christmas dinner, Co. C, 3rd Infantry Regiment, U.S. Army, 1900, William Haas and Company, Minnesota Historical Society, location no. U1.1 p7, negative no. 56413

Woman churning butter, c. 1905, Library of Congress, reproduction no. LC-USZ62-56652

Theodore Roosevelt on hunting trip, 1905, Library of Congress, reproduction no. LC-USZ62-94229

Woman outside log cabin, 1908, Library of Congress, reproduction no. LC-USZ62-90894

Farm family with produce, 1895, Wisconsin Historical Society, image no. 1979